D0857810

ISAIAH 40–55

VOLUME 19A

THE ANCHOR BIBLE is a fresh approach to the world's greatest classic. Its object is to make the Bible accessible to the modern reader; its method is to arrive at the meaning of biblical literature through exact translation and extended exposition, and to reconstruct the ancient setting of the biblical story, as well as the circumstances of its transcription and the characteristics of its transcribers.

THE ANCHOR BIBLE is a project of international and interfaith scope: Protestant, Catholic, and Jewish scholars from many countries contribute individual volumes. The project is not sponsored by any ecclesiastical organization and is not intended to reflect any particular theological doctrine. Prepared under our joint supervision, THE ANCHOR BIBLE is an effort to make available all the significant historical and linguistic knowledge which bears on the interpretation of the biblical record.

THE ANCHOR BIBLE is aimed at the general reader with no special formal training in biblical studies; yet it is written with the most exacting standards of scholarship, reflecting the highest technical accomplishment.

This project marks the beginning of a new era of cooperation among scholars in biblical research, thus forming a common body of knowledge to be shared by all.

William Foxwell Albright
David Noel Freedman
GENERAL EDITORS

THE ANCHOR BIBLE

ISAIAH 40–55

◆

A New Translation
with Introduction and Commentary

JOSEPH BLENKINSOPP

THE ANCHOR BIBLE
Doubleday
New York London Toronto Sydney Auckland

THE ANCHOR BIBLE
PUBLISHED BY DOUBLEDAY
a division of Random House, Inc.
1540 Broadway, New York, New York 10036

Library of Congress Cataloging-in-Publication Data

Bible. O.T. Isaiah I–XXXIX. English. Blenkinsopp. 2000.
Isaiah 1–39: a new translation with introduction and commentary / By Joseph Blenkinsopp.—1st ed.
p. cm. — (The Anchor Bible; vol. 19)
Includes bibliographical references and indexes.
ISBN 0–385–49717–2 (v. 1 : alk. paper)
1. Bible. O.T. Isaiah I–XXXIX—Commentaries. I. Title: Isaiah one-thirty-nine. II. Blenkinsopp, Joseph, 1927– III. Title. IV. Bible. English. Anchor Bible. 1964; v. 19.

BS192.2.A1 1964 .G3
[BS1515.3]
224'. 1077—dc21

00–021326
CIP

Printed in the United States of America
February 2002

First Edition

10 9 8 7 6 5 4 3 2 1

Dedicated to colleagues in the Society for the Study of the Old Testament in the United Kingdom in gratitude for my appointment as President for the millennial year 2000–2001

CONTENTS

◆

Preface

◆

It is a pleasant task to thank, once again, those who have helped me to think through the issues arising out of these chapters. They include my colleagues and doctoral students past and present at the University of Notre Dame, others with whom I have had discussions and arguments at annual meetings of the Society of Biblical Literature, and fellow-members of the British Society for the Study of the Old Testament, to whom this second volume of the commentary is dedicated. To name all of these would take up much space and time, as well as putting me at risk of sinning by omission. I owe a special debt of gratitude to my wife, Jean Porter, with whom I have discussed matters arising from the commentary almost on a daily basis. My thanks go, finally, to the series editor, David Noel Freedman, Mr. Andrew Corbin of Doubleday, and doctoral student Angela Kim for their valuable support and assistance.

LIST OF ABBREVIATIONS

◆

AASOR	*Annual of the American Schools of Oriental Research*
ABD	*Anchor Bible Dictionary*. Edited by D. N. Freedman. 6 vols. New York, 1992
ABR	*Australian Biblical Review*
AcOr	*Acta Orientalia*
Ag. Ap.	*Against Apion*, Josephus
AJSL	*Americal Journal of Semitic Languages and Literature*
Akk.	Akkadian language
AnBib	Analecta Biblica
ANEP	*The Ancient Near East in Pictures Relating to the Old Testament*. Edited by J. B. Pritchard. Princeton, 1954
ANET	*Ancient Near Eastern Texts Relating to the Old Testament*. Edited by J. B. Pritchard. 2d ed. Princeton, 1955
Ant.	*Jewish Antiquities*, Josephus
AP	*Aramaic Papyri of the Fifth Century B.C. Edited by A. Cowley. Oxford, 1923*
Aqu.	Aquila
AR	*Archiv für Religionswissenschaft*
ARAB	*Ancient Records of Assyria and Babylonia*. Edited by D. Luckenbill. 2 vols. Chicago, 1926-1927
Arab.	Arabic version
Aram.	Aramaic language
ASTI	*Annual of the Swedish Theological Institute*
ATA	Alttestamentliche Abhandlungen
ATD	Das Alte Testament Deutsch
AThR	*Anglican Theological Review*
AUSS	*Andrews University Seminary Studies*
b.	Babylonian Talmud
BA	*Biblical Archaeologist*
BAR	*Biblical Archaeology Review*
BASOR	*Bulletin of the American Schools of Oriental Research*
BAT	Die Botschaft des Alten Testaments
B. Bat.	*Baba Batra*
BcO	*Bibbia e Oriente*
BETL	Bibliotheca ephemeridum theologicarum lovaniensium
BHS	*Biblia Hebraica Stuttgartensia*. Edited by K. Ellinger and W. Rudolph. Stuttgart, 1983
Bib	*Biblica*
BibInt	*Biblical Interpretation*
Bijdr	*Bijdragen: Tijdschrift voor filosofie en theologie*
BIOSCS	*Bulletin of the International Organization*

	for Septuagint and Cognate Studies
BJRL	*Bulletin of the John Rylands University Library of Manchester*
BKAT	Biblischer Kommentar: Altes Testament. Edited by M. Noth and H. W. Wolff
BL	*Bibel und Liturgie*
BM	*Beth Mikra*
BN	*Biblische Notizen*
BR	*Biblical Research*
BSac	*Bibliotheca Sacra*
BT	*The Bible Translator*
BTB	*Biblical Theology Bulletin*
BWANT	Beiträge zur Wissenschaft vom Alten und Neuen Testament
BZ	*Biblische Zeitschrift*
BZAW	Beihefte zur Zeitschrift für die alttestamentliche Wissenschaft
CAD	*The Assyrian Dictionary of the Oriental Institute of the University of Chicago*, Edited by I. J. Gelb et al. Chicago, 1956–
CAH	*Cambridge Ancient History*. Edited by I. E. S. Edwards et al.
CANE	*Civilizations of the Ancient Near East*. Edited by J. Sasson. 4 vols. New York, 1995
Cant. Rab.	*Canticles Rabbah*
CB	The Century Bible
CBC	The Cambridge Bible Commentary
CBQ	*Catholic Biblical Quarterly*
CHJ	*The Cambridge History of Judaism*. Edited by W. D. Davies and L. Finkelstein. Cambridge, 1984–
ColT	*Collectanca theologica*
CQR	*Church Quarterly Review*
CTR	*Criswell Theological Review*
DBSup	*Dictionnaire de la Bible: Supplément*. Edited by L. Pirot and A. Robert. Paris, 1928–
Did	*Didaskalia*
DJD	Discoveries in the Judaean Desert
EBib	*Études bibliques*
ʿEd.	*ʿEduyyot* (Testimonies)
En.	*Enoch*
EncJud	*Encyclopedia Jucaica*. 16 vols. Jerusalem, 1972
ErIsr	*Eretz-Israel*
EstBib	*Estudios bíblicos*
Eth.	Ethiopic version
ETL	*Ephemerides Theologicae Lovanienses*
EvQ	*Evangelical Quarterly*
EvT	*Evangelische Theologie*
ExpTim	*Expository Times*
Frg.	Fragment
FRLANT	Forschungen zur Religion und Literatur des Alten und Neuen Testaments
Gen. Rab.	*Genesis Rabbah*
GKC	*Gesenius' Hebrew Grammar*. Edited by E. Kautzsch. Translated by A. E. Cowley. 2d, ed. Oxford, 1910
HALOT	Koehler, L., W. Baumgartner, and J. J. Stamm. *The Hebrew and Aramaic Lexicon of the Old Testament*. Translated and edited under the supervision of M. E. I. Richardson. 5 vols. Leiden, 1994–2000
HAR	*Hebrew Annual Review*

HAT Handbuch zum Alten Testament
HeyJ *Heythrop Journal*
HKAT Handkommentar zum Alten Testament
HSAT *Die Heilige Schrift des Alten Testaments*. Edited by E. Kautzsch and A. Bertholet. 4th ed. Tübingen, 1922–1923
HTR *Harvard Theological Review*
HUCA *Hebrew Union College Annual*
IB *Interpreter's Bible*. Edited by G. A. Butrick et al. 12 vols. New York, 1951-1957
IBS *Irish Biblical Studies*
ICC International Critical Commentary
IDB *Interpreter's Dictionary of the Bible*. Edited by G. A. Buttrick. 4 vols. Nashville, 1962
IDBSup *Interpreter's Dictionary of the Bible: Supplementary Volume*. Edited by K. Crim. Nashville, 1976
IEJ *Israel Exploration Journal*
Int *Interpretation*
JAOS *Journal of the American Oriental Society*
JBL *Journal of Biblical Literature*
JBQ *Jewish Bible Quarterly*
JCS *Journal of Cuneiform Studies*
JETS *Journal of the Evangelical Theological Society*
JJS *Journal of Jewish Studies*
JNES *Journal of Near Eastern Studies*
JNSL *Journal of Northwest Semitic Languages*
JPOS *Journal of the Palestine Oriental Society*
JQR *Jewish Quarterly Review*
JSem *Journal for Semitics*. University of South Africa
JSJ *Journal for the Study of Judaism in the Persian, Hellenistic, and Roman Periods*
JSOT *Journal for the Study of the Old Testament*
JSOTSup Journal for the Study of the Old Testament: Supplement Series
JSP *Journal for the Study of the Pseudepigrapha*
JSPSup Journal for the Study of the Pseudepigrapha: Supplement Series
JSS *Journal of Semitic Studies*
JTS *Journal of Theological Studies*
K Ketib (what is written)
KAT Kommentar zum Alten Testament
KD *Kerygma und Dogma*
Kenn. Kennicott edition of the Hebrew Bible, 1776
KHC Kurzer Hand-Commentar zum Alten Testament
KJV King James Version
KTU *Die keilalphabetischen Texte aus Ugarit*. Edited by M. Dietrich, O. Loretz, and T. Sanmartín, AOAT 24/1. Neukirchen-Vluyn, 1976
LD Lectio Divina
Leš *Lešonénu*
Lev. Rab. *Leviticus Rabbah*
LXX The Septuagint
Meg. *Megillah* (the Esther Scroll)
MH Mishnaic Hebrew

Migr.	Philo, *De migratione Abrahami*
MSS	manuscripts
MT	Masoretic Text
MTZ	*Münchener theologische Zeitschrift*
Mus	*Muséon: Revue d'études orientales*
NAB	New American Bible
NCB	New Century Bible
NEAEHL	*The New Encyclopedia of Archaeological Excavations in the Holy Land.* Edited by E. Stern. 4 vols. Jerusalem, 1993
NEB	New English Bible
NICOT	New International Commentary on the Old Testament
NJPSV	New Jewish Publication Society Version
NKZ	*Neue Kirchliche Zeitschrift*
NRSV	New Revised Standard Version
NRTh	*Nouvelle revue théologique*
NT	New Testament
NTS	*New Testament Studies*
NTT	*Norsk Teologisk Tidsskrift*
OBO	*Orbis Biblicus et Orientalis*
OBT	Overtures to Biblical Theology
OEANE	*Oxford Encyclopedia of Archaeology in the Near East.* Edited by E. M. Meyers. New York, 1997
OG	Old Greek Version
Or	*Orientalia*
OrChr	*Oriens Christianus*
OTE	*Old Testament Essays*
OTG	Old Testament Guides
OTL	*Old Testament Library*
OtSt	*Oudtestamentische Studiën*
OTWSA	*Oudtestamentiese Werkgemeenskap van Suid-Afrika*
P	Priestly writer
Par.	Parallel passages
PEQ	*Palestine Exploration Quarterly*
PG	*Patrologia Gracea.* Edited by J.-P. Minge. 162 vols. Paris, 1857–1886
PIBA	Proceedings of the Irish Biblical Association
PL	Patrologia Latina. Edited by J.-P. Migne. 217 vols. Paris, 1844–1864
POuT	De Prediking van het Oude Testament
Q	Qere
QC	*Qumran Chronicle*
Qere Or	Qere Orientale
RB	*Revue biblique*
RevExp	*Review and Expositor*
RevQ	*Revue de Qumran*
RHPR	*Revue d'histoire et de philosophie religieuses*
RHR	*Revue de l'histoire des religions*
RivB	*Rivista biblica italiana*
RSR	*Recherches de Science Religieuse*
RSV	Revised Standard Version
RTP	*Revue de théologie et de philosophie*
Sanh.	*Sanhedrin* (tractate of Babylonian Talmud)
SB	Sources bibliques
SBLDS	Society of Biblical Literature Dissertation Series
SBLSP	Society of Biblical Literature Seminar Papers
SBS	Stuttgarter Bibelstudien
SBT	Studies in Biblical Theology
Scr	*Scripture*

SEÅ	*Svensk exegetisk årsbok*
Sem	*Semitica*
Sib. Or.	*The Sibylline Oracles*
SJOT	*Scandinavian Journal of the Old Testament*
SJT	*Scottish Journal of Theology*
ST	*Studia Theologica*
Symm.	Symmachus
Syr.	*Vetus Testamentum Syriace* (The Peshiṭta Version)
TB	Theologische Bücherei
TBC	Torch Bible Commentaries
TBT	*The Bible Today*
TDNT	*Theological Dictionary of the New Testament.* Edited by G. Kittel and G. Friedrich. Translated by G. Bromiley. 10 vols. Grand Rapids, 1964–1976
TDOT	*Theological Dictionary of the Old Testament.* Edited by G. J. Botterweck and H. Ringgren. Translated by J. T. Willis, G. W. Bromiley, and D. E. Green. Grand Rapids, 1974–
Tg.	Targum
THAT	*Theologisches Handwörterbuch zum Alten Testament.* Edited by E. Jenni and C. Westermann. 2 vols. Munich, 1971–1976
Theod.	Theodotion
TLZ	*Theologische Literaturzeitung*
TRu	*Theologische Rundschau*
TS	*Theological Studies*
TTZ	*Trierer theologische Zeitschrift*
TynBul	*Tyndale Bulletin*
TZ	*Theologische Zeitschrift*
UF	*Ugarit-Forschungen*
VD	*Verbum Domini*
VH	*Vivens Homo*
VL	*Vetus Latina* version
VT	*Vetus Testamentum*
VTSup	Vetus Testamentum Supplements
Vulg.	*Editio Vulgata*
WBC	Word Biblical Commentary
WC	Westminster Commentaries
WMANT	Wissenschaftliche Monographien zum Alten und Neuen Testament
WTJ	*Westminster Theological Journal*
Yebam.	*Yebamot* (tractate of Babylonian Talmud)
ZAW	*Zeitschrift für die alttestamentliche Wissenschaft*
ZDMG	*Zeitschrift der deutschen morgenländischen Gesellschaft*
ZDPV	*Zeitschrift des deutschen Palästina-Vereins*
ZKT	*Zeitschrift für katholische Theologie*
ZNW	*Zeitschrift für die neutestamentliche Wissenschaft die Kunde der älteren Kirche*
ZTK	*Zeitschrift für Theologie und Kirche*

ISAIAH 40-55: A TRANSLATION

◆

PROLOGUE: THE REVIVAL OF PROPHECY (40:1–8)

i

40 [1]"Comfort, O comfort my people,"
says your God;
[2]"speak tender words to Jerusalem,
proclaim to her
that her servitude is over,
her debt has been paid;
she has received at Yahveh's hand
double for all her sins."

ii

[3]A voice proclaims:
"Clear in the wilderness
a way for Yahveh;
level in the desert
a highway for our God!
[4]Let every ravine be filled in,
every mountain and hill flattened out;
the crooked made straight,
the rough places leveled.
[5]Then the glory of Yahveh will be revealed;
All humanity as one shall see it."
For Yahveh himself has spoken.

iii

[6]A voice says, "Proclaim!"
I replied, "What shall I proclaim?"
"All humanity is grass,
and all its splendor like the wild flower."
[7]Grass withers, flowers fade
when Yahveh's breath blows on them;
[surely the people is but grass!].
[8]Grass withers, flowers fade,
but the word of our God stands firm forever.

GOOD NEWS FOR THE CITIES OF JUDAH (40:9–11)

40 [9]Climb to the top of a mountain,
Zion, herald of good news;
lift up your voice with power,

Jerusalem, herald of good news;
lift it up without fear.
Say to the cities of Judah:
"See, here is your God!"
[10]See, Yahveh is coming with power,
his strong arm affirms his rule;
see, his reward is with him,
his recompense precedes him.
[11]Like a shepherd he tends his flock,
he gathers them together with his arm,
the lambs he lifts into his lap,
the ewes he gently leads on.

A DISPUTATION ABOUT THE POWER OF ISRAEL'S GOD (40:12–26)

i

40 [12]Who has measured out the waters with the hollow of his hand
or marked off the sky by handbreadths
and enclosed the earth's dust in small measure?
Who has weighed the mountains in a balance,
the hills on the scales?
[13]Who has taken the measure of Yahveh's spirit
or advised him as his counselor?
[14]With whom did he consult to be enlightened?
Who taught him the right way to go?
Who imparted knowledge to him
or showed him the way of discernment?
[15]Observe: the nations are but drops from a bucket,
they are reckoned as dust on the scales.
Observe: the islands weigh no more than specks of dust.
[16]Lebanon yields not fuel enough,
its beasts do not suffice for burnt offerings.
[17]All the nations are as nothing in his presence,
they are reckoned as less than nothing,
as void and empty in his sight.

ii

40 [18]To whom, then, will you liken God?
What form compare with him?
[19]An image that a craftsman casts,
that a smith overlays with gold
and forges for it silver welds?

[20]The one placed in charge of the offerings
chooses wood that will not rot,
seeks out a skillful craftsman
to set up an image that won't topple.
41 [6][Each assists his companion,
says to his colleague, "be resolute!"
[7]The craftsman encourages the goldsmith,
the one who levels with the hammer him who pounds the anvil,
he pronounces the soldering satisfactory;
they attach the statue with nails so that it won't move.]

iii

40 [21]Do you not know?
Have you not heard?
Has it not been told you from the beginning?
Have you not grasped how the earth was founded?
[22]He sits enthroned over the circle of the earth,
its inhabitants seem like grasshoppers;
he stretches out the sky like a curtain,
spreading it out like a tent to live in.
[23]He has turned princes into nothing,
he has reduced the earth's rulers to naught.
[24]Scarcely are they planted,
scarcely are they sown,
scarcely has their stem taken root in the ground,
when he blows on them and they wither;
the whirlwind carries them off like chaff.
[25]So, to whom will you liken me?
To whom shall I be compared?
[says the Holy One].

iv

[26]Lift up your eyes to the sky,
consider who has created these;
he leads out their host one by one,
summoning each by name;
because of his great power and overwhelming might
not one of them fails to appear.

v

[27]Why, Jacob, do you say,
why, Israel, proclaim,
"My way is hidden from Yahveh,
my cause is ignored by my God"?
[28]Do you not know? Have you not heard?
Yahveh is God from of old,

Creator of the earth from end to end.
He neither faints nor grows weary,
his understanding cannot be fathomed.
[29]He gives vigor to the dispirited,
power in abundance to those without strength.
[30]Youths may faint from exhaustion,
the young may stumble and fall,
[31]but those who wait for Yahveh will renew their vigor,
they will grow new pinions like eagles,
run and not be worn out,
walk untiringly on their way.

A FIRST MOCK-TRIAL SPEECH (41:1–5)

41 [1]Hear me in silence, you islands!
You peoples, summon up your strength!
Let them approach, then let them speak up,
let us come together for the trial!

[2]Who was it that roused from the east
one victorious at every step?
Yahveh delivers up nations to him,
beats down kings beneath him.
He makes their swords like dust,
their bows like windblown chaff.
[3]He pursues them and continues unscathed,
his feet do not touch the ground.
[4]Who has brought this about, who has done it?
The one who summons the generations from the beginning.
I, Yahveh, am the First,
and I, the One, am with the last.
[5]The islands look on in fear,
the earth trembles from end to end.
They draw near, they are here!

WORDS OF ENCOURAGEMENT TO ISRAEL, THE SERVANT (41:8–16)

41 [8]But you, Israel, my servant,
Jacob whom I have chosen,
offspring of Abraham, my friend,
[9]you whom I took from the ends of the earth

and called from its furthest reaches;
to you I said, "You are my servant,
I chose you, and I have not rejected you."
[10]Don't be afraid, for I am with you,
don't be perplexed, for I am your God.
I strengthen you, I will surely help you,
I sustain you with my victorious right hand.
[11]See, all who rage against you
will be ashamed and disgraced;
those who contend with you
will be as nothing, they will perish.
[12]You will look for them, but you will not find them.
Those who strive against you will be as nothing,
those who wage war against you will be less than nothing.
[13]For I am Yahveh your God,
I clasp you by your right hand;
I say to you: "Don't be afraid,
I am here to help you."
[14]Don't be afraid, you worm Jacob,
you maggot Israel,
I am here to help you,
your Redeemer is the Holy One of Israel.
[15]See, I make of you a threshing board,
sharp, brand new, equipped with spikes;
you shall thresh the mountains into dust,
reduce the hills to chaff;
[16]you shall winnow them, and the wind will carry them off,
the whirlwind will scatter them.
But you will rejoice in Yahveh,
exult in the Holy One of Israel.

ECOLOGICAL TRANSFORMATION OF THE LAND (41:17–20)

41 [17]When the poor [and the needy] look for water
where there is none,
their tongues parched with thirst;
I, Yahveh, will provide for them,
I, the God of Israel, will not forsake them.
[18]I will open up streams on the bare hills,
fountains on the plains;
I will turn the wilderness into pools of water,
the arid land into springs of water.

[19]I will place in the wilderness cedar, acacia,
myrtle, and wild olive;
I will plant in the desert cypress, fir, and box together,
[20]so that they may observe and acknowledge,
once for all consider and comprehend,
that the hand of Yahveh has accomplished this;
the Holy One of Israel has created it.

A SECOND MOCK–TRIAL SPEECH (41:21–29)

i

41 [21]Set forth your case, says Yahveh,
present your strongest arguments, says Jacob's King.
[22]Let them step forward and tell us what will happen,
let them declare events before they happen
that we may take note,
or announce things to come
that we may know how they will end.
[23]Declare what is to happen in advance,
and we will acknowledge that you are gods.
Do anything, be it good or bad,
to fill us with awe and fear.

[24]You see, you are less than nothing,
your works are nonexistent;
those who choose you are execrable!

ii

[25]I have roused one from the north, and he has come;
from the sunrise he is summoned in my name;
he tramples down governors like mud
as the potter treads on the clay.
[26]Who declared this from the start that we may acknowledge it?
Who announced it in advance, that we may say, "He is right!"
No one declared it, no one announced it,
no one heard you say anything.
[27]I, the First, declared it to Zion,
giving to Jerusalem a herald of good news.
[28]But when I looked there was no one,
not one counselor among them
who could answer if I were to inquire.
[29]They are all insignificant,
their works are of no avail,
their images nothing but wind.

THE COMMISSIONING OF YAHVEH'S SERVANT (42:1–9)

i

42 1This is my servant whom I sustain,
my chosen one in whom I take delight;
I have put my spirit upon him.
He will establish a just order for the nations;
2he will not shout, he will not raise his voice
or let it be heard in public places.
A broken reed he will not crush,
a dimly smoldering wick he will not extinguish.
He will truly establish a just order for the nations;
4he will not grow faint or be discouraged
until he has set up a just order on the earth;
the islands wait for his law.

ii

5These are the words of Yahveh God who created the sky and laid it out, who spread out the earth and its issue, who gives breath to the peoples on it, the spirit of life to those who tread upon it:

6"I, Yahveh, have summoned you in righteousness,
I have grasped you by the hand;
I preserve you and present you
as a covenant for the people,
a light for the nations;
7to open eyes that are blind,
release captives from prison,
those sitting in the dark from the dungeon.
8I am Yahveh; that is my name.
I do not surrender my honor to others,
nor the praise due to me to idols.
9The events predicted have come to pass,
new events I now declare;
before they emerge I announce them to you."

NEW EVENTS CALL FOR A NEW SONG (42:10–17)

i

42 10Sing a new song to Yahveh;
sing his praise to the ends of the earth,
you who sail the sea, you creatures in it,
islands and their inhabitants.

[11]Let the wilderness and its settlements raise up their voice,
with the villages that Kedar inhabits.
Let the dwellers in Sela celebrate,
shouting from the mountaintops.
[12]Let them give glory to Yahveh
and proclaim his praise in the islands.

ii

[13]Yahveh goes forth as a hero,
as a warrior he fires up his fury;
raising the battle cry, he shouts aloud;
he prevails over his enemies.
[14]"Too long have I held my peace,
kept silent and held myself back;
but now I cry out like a woman giving birth,
breathlessly panting.
[15]I will scorch the mountains and hills,
searing all of their verdure;
I will turn the rivers into islands,
dry up all the pools.
[16]I will lead the blind along the way,
guide them in paths they have not known,
turning the darkness to light before them,
the rough spots into even ground.
These are the things I will do;
I will not abandon them."
[17][They who put their trust in idols
have turned back and are utterly shamed;
they who say to molten images,
"You are our gods!"]

THE SPIRITUAL IMPERCEPTION OF THE SERVANT (42:18–25)

42 [18]You that are deaf, listen!
You that are blind, look and see!
[19]Who is as blind as my servant?
Who so deaf as the messenger I dispatch?
[Who is as blind as Meshullam?
Who so deaf as Yahveh's servant?]
[20]He has seen much but does not pay heed;
his hearing is sound, but he hears nothing.
[21]Yahveh desired his servant's vindication
to make his law grand and glorious;

[22]but this is a people plundered and despoiled;
they are all trapped in holes,
hidden away in dungeons;
they have been plundered with none to rescue,
despoiled, with none to say, "Give them back!"
[23]Who among you will attend to this?
Who will pay heed from now on?
[24]Who delivered Jacob to the despoiler,
Israel to the plunderers?
Was it not Yahveh, against whom they have sinned?
They were unwilling to follow his guidance
and heed his teaching.
[25]So he poured out upon them his wrath,
his anger in the fury of battle;
it blazed all around them, but they did not comprehend;
it burned them, but they gave no heed.

Divine Reassurance: All Will Be Well (43:1–7)

43 [1]Now, these are words of Yahveh who created you, Jacob,
who formed you, Israel:
"Don't be afraid, for I have redeemed you;
I have called you by name, you are mine.
[2]If you cross over water, I am with you,
or over rivers, they will not overwhelm you.
If you pass through fire, you will not be scorched,
the flames will not burn you.
[3]For I am Yahveh your God,
the Holy One of Israel, your Savior.
I have set aside Egypt as your ransom,
Ethiopia and Seba in your stead,
[4]for you are precious in my sight;
you are honored, and I love you.
So I set aside people in your stead,
nations in exchange for your life.
[5]Don't be afraid, for I am with you;
I shall bring your descendants from the east,
I shall gather you in from the west;
[6]I shall say to the north, 'Give them up,'
to the south, 'Do not restrain them;
bring my sons from afar,
my daughters from the ends of the earth,

[7]all that bear my name,
whom I created, whom I formed,
whom I made for my glory.' "

THE GOD OF ISRAEL AND THE GODS OF THE NATIONS (43:8–13)

43 Bring forth the people who have eyes yet are blind,
who have ears yet are deaf.
[9]All nations have come together,
all peoples have assembled.
Who among them can proclaim this
or announce events to us before they happen?
Let them produce their witnesses to prove them right,
so that people will hear it and say, "It is so."
[10]You are my witnesses, Yahveh declares,
my servant whom I have chosen,
that you may know me and trust me
and understand that I am the One.
Before me no god was formed,
and there will be none after me.
[11]I, I am Yahveh;
there is none that can save but me.
[12]I proclaimed salvation, I announced it;
this is no alien god in your midst.
You are my witnesses, Yahveh declares,
[13]I am God; from the very first I am the One.
There is none can deliver from my hand.
When I act, who can undo it?

SOMETHING NEW: A WAY INTO THE FUTURE (43:14–21)

i

43 [14]These are the words of Yahveh your Redeemer, the
Holy One of Israel:
"For your sake I send to Babylon
to lay low all those who flee;
the triumphant cries of the Chaldeans
will be turned to lamentations.
[15]I, Yahveh, am your Holy God,
the creator of Israel, your king."

ii

[16]This is what Yahveh says,
he who cut a passage through the sea,
a track through the mighty waters,
[17]who led on chariot and horse to destruction,
all that powerful array;
they lay down never to rise,
extinguished, quenched like a wick:
[18]"Call no more to mind these past events
or ponder deeds done long ago;
[19]I am about to do something new,
now it is unfolding; do you not perceive it?
Even in the wilderness I am making a roadway
and paths through the wasteland.
[20]The wild beasts will pay me respect,
the jackals and ostriches,
for I provision the wilderness with water,
the wasteland with streams,
so my chosen people can drink;
[21]this people I formed for myself,
they will proclaim my praises."

THE CASE AGAINST ISRAEL RAISED AND DISMISSED (43:22–44:5)

i

43 [22]But you did not invoke me, Jacob;
you grew weary of me, Israel.
[23]You did not bring me burnt offerings from your flocks,
you did not honor me with your sacrifices.
I did not burden you with cereal offerings
or weary you with frankincense.
[24]You have not bought sweet cane for me with your money
or sated me with the suet of your sacrifices.
But you burdened me with your sins,
you wore me out with your iniquities.

ii

[25]I, I am the One
who for my own sake wipe out your transgressions
and do not call your sins to mind.
[26]Call me to judgment, let us argue the case together.
Set out your case that you may be proved right.

[27]Your first ancestor sinned;
your spokesmen transgressed against me,
[28]so I profaned the princes of the sanctuary;
I delivered Jacob up to ruin,
Israel to reviling.

iii

44 [1]But hear now, Jacob my servant,
Israel whom I chose for myself.
[2]These are the words of Yahveh who made you,
who formed you from the womb, and who will help you:
"Don't be afraid, Jacob my servant,
Jeshurun whom I have chosen.
[3]I will pour out water on the thirsty ground,
streams of water on the parched land;
I will pour out my spirit on your descendants,
my blessing on your offspring.
[4]They will flourish like well-watered grass,
like willows by the runnels of water.
[5]This one will say, 'I belong to Yahveh,'
another will take the name Jacob,
yet another will write Yahveh's name on the hand,
and add the name Israel to his own."

ISRAEL CALLED TO WITNESS TO YAHVEH AS THE ONE GOD (44:6–8, 21–23)

i

44 [6]These are the words of Yahveh, Israel's King,
Yahveh of the heavenly hosts, Israel's Redeemer:
"I am the First and I am the Last;
there is no god but me.
[7]Who is like me? Let him speak up, let him state his case,
let him set it out for me.
Who has announced from time past what is to be?
Let them declare for us the things to come.
[8]Do not be perplexed, do not be afraid.
Did I not announce this to you long ago?
I declared it, and you are my witnesses.
Is there any god but me? Or is there any Rock?
I know of none."
. . . . . .

ii

[21]Remember these things, Jacob,
Israel, for you are my servant.
I formed you, you are my servant;
Israel, you are not forgotten by me.
[22]I have swept away your transgressions like clouds,
your sins like mist.
Turn to me, for I have redeemed you.

iii

[23]Exult, you sky, for it is Yahveh's doing;
shout aloud, you depths of the earth.
Break into song, you mountains,
forests with all your trees;
for Yahveh has redeemed Jacob;
in Israel his glory is manifest.

POLEMIC AGAINST CULT IMAGES (44:9–20)

i

44 [9]Those who make idols are all as nothing,
the objects they cherish serve no purpose;
their devotees are without discernment,
they know nothing and so are put to shame.
[10]Who would make a god or cast an idol
that serves no purpose?
[11]See, all his associates are put to shame,
the craftsmen are but mortal.
Let them all assemble, let them take their stand;
they will be afraid, they will be utterly shamed.

ii

[12]The ironsmith fashions it with an adze, working it over the charcoal, shaping it with hammers, forging it with his strong arm. But he also gets hungry and his strength fails; when he has not drunk water, he is exhausted. [13]Having stretched the line taut, the carpenter outlines the object with a chalk. He planes the wood and picks out the shape with callipers. Then he fashions it in the form of a man, with the beauty of the human form, to reside in a shrine. [14]He chooses a plane tree or an oak and lets it grow strong among the trees of the forest. Or he plants a cedar and the rain makes it grow, so that eventually he will have trees to cut down. [15]Then it can serve someone as fuel. He can take some of it and warm himself. He can light a fire, bake bread, and satisfy his hunger. But he can also make a god of it and worship it; he can make an

idol and prostrate himself before it. [16]Half of it he burns in the fire. On this half he can then roast meat, so that he can eat and satisfy his hunger. He can also warm himself, saying, "All right! I'm getting warm in front of the fire." [17]Then what is left of it he fashions into a god to serve as his idol. He prostrates himself before it and worships it; he prays to it and says, "Save me, since you are my god!"

iii

[18]They have no knowledge or understanding,
for Yahveh has shut their eyes so that they cannot see,
their minds, so that they cannot understand.
[19]No one takes it to heart;
there is neither knowledge nor understanding to think,
"Half of it I burned in the fire.
I also baked bread on its coals.
I roasted meat and ate it,
and what is left I am going to make into an abominable thing;
I am going to prostrate myself before a block of wood!"
[20]Such a one rides herd on ashes,
a deluded mind has led him astray.
He cannot save himself,
he cannot bring himself to say,
"Is not this object in my right hand a sham?"

CYRUS MY ANOINTED (44:24–45:8)

i

44 [24]These are the words of Yahveh your Redeemer,
he who formed you from the womb:
"I am Yahveh, who made all things.
I alone stretched out the sky,
spread out the earth when none was with me."
[25]He frustrates the omens of liars,
and makes fools of diviners;
he turns sages back to front,
reducing their knowledge to folly.
[26]He confirms the word of his servant,
fulfills the counsel of his messengers;
of Jerusalem he says, "She shall be inhabited,"
of the cities of Judah, "They shall be rebuilt;
I shall restore her ruins."
[27]He says to the Deep, "Be dry;
I shall make your streams run dry."

[28]Of Cyrus he says, "He is my shepherd;
he will fulfill all my purpose
[saying about Jerusalem, it shall be rebuilt,
the temple's foundations shall be laid].

ii

45 [1]This is what Yahveh says about his anointed one, about Cyrus:
"I have grasped him by the right hand,
to beat down nations before him;
depriving kings of their strength,
to open doors before him,
no gates will be closed to him."
[2]"I myself will go before you,
leveling all the mountains.
I will shatter the doors of bronze,
cut through the iron bars;
[3]I will hand you treasures concealed in the dark,
treasures hoarded away,
so that you may acknowledge
that I, Yahveh, have called you by name,
I, Israel's God.
[4]For the sake of Jacob my servant,
Israel my chosen one,
I summon you by your name,
I give you a title of honor,
though you have not known me.
[5]I am Yahveh, there is no other;
beside me there are no gods;
I gird you with strength,
though you have not known me,
[6]so that all may acknowledge,
from the rising of the sun to its setting,
there is none apart from me.
I am Yahveh; there is no other.
[7]I form light and create darkness,
I bring about well-being and create woe;
it is I, Yahveh, who do all these things."

iii

[8]Sky, drop down dew from above,
clouds, rain down vindication!
Let the earth open and salvation blossom;
let victory spring forth with it.
I, Yahveh, have created it.

GOD CANNOT BE CALLED TO ACCOUNT FOR CHOOSING CYRUS (45:9–13)

i

45 [9]Should one take issue with one's Maker,
one sherd among others made of earth?
Should the clay say to the one who shapes it,
"What are you doing?"
Or his handiwork say, "He has no skill"?
[10]Should one say to a father,
"What is this you are begetting?"
Or to a woman,
"What are you bringing to birth?"

ii

[11]These are the words of Yahveh, the Holy One of Israel and its Maker:
"Would you question me about my children,
or tell me what I am to make?
[12]It is I who made the earth
and created humanity upon it;
my hands stretched out the sky
and marshaled all its host;
[13]it was I roused him to victory;
I will make his progress smooth.
He will rebuild my city
and let my exiles go,
but not for payment, not for a reward."
[A saying of Yahveh of the heavenly hosts]

THE GOD WHO HIDES HIMSELF (45:14–19)

i

45 [14]These are Yahveh's words:
"The traders of Egypt and the merchants of Ethiopia
and the Sabeans, tall of stature,
will come over to you; they will be yours,
they will walk behind you in chains;
they will do homage to you, they will plead with you.
They will say:
'Surely God is with you, there is no other,
there is no God but he.'"
[15]You are, in truth, the Almighty One who hides himself,

God of Israel, Savior!
[16]Those who fashion idols are shamed and disgraced,
all of them together.
They live out their lives in dishonor,
[17]while Israel is saved by Yahveh
with salvation long-lasting.
You will be neither shamed nor disgraced
forever and ever.

ii

[18]For these are the words of Yahveh, the One who created the sky, the One who is God, who gave the earth form and substance, who firmly established it. He did not create it an empty void but formed it to be inhabited:
"I am Yahveh; there is no other.
[19]I did not speak in secret,
somewhere in a dark realm.
I did not say to Jacob's descendants,
'Seek me in the empty void.'
I, Yahveh, speak what is right;
I declare what is truthful."

SALVATION OFFERED TO THE NATIONS (45:20–25)

i

45 [20]Assemble and come together; draw near,
survivors of the nations!
Those who carry around their wooden idols know nothing;
they make their petitions to a god that cannot save.
[21]State your case and present it; consult together:
Who has announced this from the beginning,
who declared it long ago?
Was it not I, Yahveh?
There is no god apart from me,
a god who overcomes and saves;
there is none but me.

ii

[22]Turn to me and accept salvation,
all the ends of the earth!
For I am God, and there is none other.
[23]I have sworn an oath by my life;
the word that overcomes has gone forth from my mouth,
a word that will not be made void:
"To me every knee will bend,

by me every tongue will swear an oath."
[24]About me it will be said,
"Victory and strength come only from Yahveh."
All who rage against him
will come shamefaced into his presence,
[25]while all of Israel's descendants
will triumph and exult in Yahveh.

THE DEFEATED AND EXILED BABYLONIAN GODS (46:1–7)

i

46 [1]Bel crouches low, Nebo cowers;
their images are loaded on to animals, beasts of burden.
These things you once bore aloft
are a load for weary animals.
[2]They cower, they crouch down low;
they are unable to rescue the load,
but they themselves have gone into captivity.

ii

[3]Listen to me, household of Jacob,
all that remain of the household of Israel,
you who were sustained from birth,
who were carried since leaving the womb:
[4]"Until you grow old I will be the same;
when your hair turns grey I will uphold you;
I sustained you, I will carry you still;
I will uphold and rescue."

iii

[5]To whom will you liken me?
Who will you say is my equal?
With whom compare me on equal terms?
[6]Those who lavish gold from the purse,
who measure out silver on the scales,
hire a goldsmith who makes it into a god,
whom they then bow down to and worship.
[7]They hoist it on their shoulders and carry it;
they set it down in its place; there it stays.
It does not move from its place.
If they cry out to it, it cannot answer;
it cannot deliver them from their distress.

REASSURANCE FOR THE DOUBTERS (46:8–13)

i

46 [8]Remember this and be ashamed;
come to your senses, rebellious people!
[9]Remember deeds done long ago,
for I am God; there is none other;
I am God; there is none like me.
[10]I declare the outcome from the beginning;
from of old, things yet to be.
I say, "My plan will prevail,
I will achieve all that I purpose.
[11]I summon a bird of prey from the east,
from a far land the man to carry out my plan.
Yes, I have spoken, and yes, I will bring it about;
I have conceived it, and yes, I will do it."

ii

[12]Listen to me, you stubborn people,
far removed from deliverance as you are:
[13] "I bring my deliverance near, it is not far off;
my salvation will not be delayed.
I will place salvation in Zion,
for Israel, my splendid possession."

QUEEN BABYLON DETHRONED (47:1–15)

i

47 [1]"Get down, sit in the dust,
maiden Babylon!
Deprived of a throne, sit on the ground,
Chaldean maiden!
No longer will you be called
the tender and delicate one.
[2]Take the handmill, grind the meal,
remove your veil;
take off your skirt, uncover your thighs,
wade through rivers!
[3]Your nakedness will be uncovered,
your shame will be exposed.
I will take vengeance,
and no one will intervene."

[4]A word of our Redeemer;
Lord of the heavenly hosts is his name,
Israel's Holy One.

ii

[5]Sit in silence, go into the darkness,
Chaldean maiden;
nevermore will you be called
Mistress of Kingdoms.
[6]I was angry with my people,
I dishonored my inheritance;
I delivered them into your power,
but you showed them no mercy.
Even on the aged you laid your heavy yoke.
[7]You thought, "I shall forever remain eternal mistress."
But you gave no thought to these things;
you did not bear in mind their outcome.

iii

[8]Now listen to this, you lover of pleasure
dwelling in security,
you who think to yourself,
"I am, and there is none other;
I will never be widowed,
I will never be bereft of my children."
[9]These two things will overtake you,
in a moment, in a single day:
loss of children and widowhood
in full measure will overtake you,
in spite of your many incantations
and the great power of your spells.

iv

[10]You felt safe in your evil ways,
you thought no one could see you,
your wisdom and your science led you astray;
you thought within yourself,
"I am, and there is none other."
[11]Evil will overtake you,
and you will not know how to dispel it;
ruin will fall upon you,
and you will be unable to ward it off;
disaster will overtake you,
suddenly, when you least expect it.

v

[12]So persist with your spells,
your numerous incantations,
in which you have labored from your youth.
Perhaps you can gain some profit,
perhaps you will yet inspire terror.
[13]You are worn out with your many consultations;
let them persist so they can save you—
these scanners of the sky and star-gazers
who predict month by month what will befall you.

vi

[14]See now, they have become like stubble;
the fire is burning them up,
they cannot save themselves from the flames.
These coals are not for warming,
not for sitting beside the fire!
[15]Much good have these magicians done you,
at whose arts you have toiled since your youth;
they have wandered off, each his own way;
none of them is left to save you.

THE ARGUMENT FROM PROPHECY REITERATED (48:1–11)

i

48 [1]Hear this, household of Jacob,
who are called by the name of Israel,
who came forth from Judah's womb,
who swear by Yahveh's name
and invoke the God of Israel—
but not in truth and sincerity.

ii

[2]They bear the name of the holy city;
they rely on the God of Israel,
whose name is Yahveh of the heavenly hosts:
[3]Long ago I declared what would happen;
it came forth from my mouth, I announced it;
then suddenly I acted, and it came about;
[4]for I knew you were stubborn,
that your neck is like an iron sinew,
your forehead as hard as brass,

[5]so I declared it to you long since;
I announced it to you before it happened,
lest you should think, "It was my idol's doing;
my carved and metal images ordained it."
[6]You have heard, now discern all this;
will you not acknowledge it?

iii

From now on I divulge new things to you,
hidden things of which you have no knowledge;
[7]they are created not ages since but now;
before this day you never heard of them;
lest you should think, "I knew it already."
[8]You never heard of it, you never knew it,
and from of old you never gave heed.
I know how unfaithful you are,
how from birth you were called a rebel.

iv

[9]For my name's sake I was slow to anger;
for the sake of my praise I held back,
so as not to destroy you completely.
[10]I refined you but not like silver;
I assayed you in the furnace of affliction.
[11]Only for my own sake I did it,
for how should my name be profaned?
My honor I surrender to no one.

ONCE MORE AND FINALLY: THE MISSION OF CYRUS (48:12–22)

i

48 [12]Listen to me, Jacob,
Israel, whom I have called:
"I am the One, I am the First,
and I am also the Last.
[13]My hand established the earth,
my right hand spread out the sky;
when I summoned them, they at once existed."

ii

[14]Assemble, all of you, and listen:
"Who among them foretold these things?
Yahveh loves him and fulfills his purpose

against Babylon and the Chaldean race.
[15]I, I myself have spoken and have summoned him.
I have brought him thus far; his mission will succeed.
[16]Draw near to me and hear this:
From the beginning I never spoke in secret;
from when it first began, I was present."

[and now the Sovereign Lord Yahveh has sent me, and his spirit . . .]

iii

[17]These are the words of Yahveh, your Redeemer, the Holy One of Israel:
"I am Yahveh your God,
who instructs you for your benefit,
who guides you in the way you are to go.
[18]If only you had heeded my commandments!
Your prosperity would have flowed like a river,
your vindication like the waves of the sea,
[19]your descendants would be as countless as the sand,
your offspring like its grains in number;
their name would never be extinguished
or effaced from my sight."

iv

[20]Get out of Babylon, get away from the Chaldeans!
With a shout of joy declare this out loud,
send forth the message to the ends of the earth;
tell them: "Yahveh has redeemed his servant Jacob!
[21]They suffered no thirst when he led them through the wastelands,
he made water flow from the rock for them,
he split the rock, and the water gushed out."

[22]"There can be no well-being for the wicked," says Yahveh.

THE SERVANT'S ADDRESS TO THE NATIONS (49:1–6)

i

49 [1]Listen to me, you islands;
take heed, you peoples far distant!
Yahveh called me before I was born,
from my mother's womb he pronounced my name.
[2]He made my mouth like a whetted sword
and hid me in the shadow of his hand;

he made me a sharpened arrow,
concealed me in his quiver.
[3]He said to me: " You are my servant,
[Israel,] through whom my glory will be manifest."

[4]But I thought, "In vain have I toiled,
I have spent my strength entirely to no purpose;
yet surely my cause is present to Yahveh,
my reward is with my God.
[5b]I shall gain honor in Yahveh's sight,
my God will be my strength."

ii

[5a]Now this is what Yahveh says,
he who formed me from the womb to be his servant,
to bring Jacob back to him,
that Israel may be gathered to him:
[6]"Is it too light a task
for you to be my servant,
to establish the tribes of Jacob
and restore the survivors of Israel?
I appoint you a light to the nations
that my salvation may reach to the ends of the earth."

TWO COMMENTS ABOUT THE SERVANT (49:7–13)

i

49 [7]These are words of Yahveh, Israel's Redeemer, Israel's Holy One, to one despised, to one abhorred by the nations, enslaved to foreign rulers:
"When they see you, kings will rise to their feet;
princes will pay you homage
on account of Yahveh, who is faithful,
the Holy One of Israel who chose you."

ii

[8]These are words of Yahveh:
"At the time of my good pleasure I answer you;
on the day of salvation I assist you;
I preserve you and present you
as a covenant to the people,
to establish the land,
to apportion the devastated holdings,
[9]to tell those in prison to come out,
those in darkness to emerge.

They will feed by all the waysides,
with pasture on all the bare heights;
[10]they will suffer neither hunger nor thirst;
neither scorching wind nor sun will afflict them.
For the One who pities them will guide them,
lead them to springs of water.
[11]I will make all my mountains into pathways,
my highways will be built up.
[12]Look, these are coming from afar;l
look, these others from the north and the west
and yet others from the land of Syene."

iii

[13]Sky, shout for joy; earth, rejoice!
Mountains break out into joyful song!
For Yahveh has comforted his people;
he has pitied his afflicted ones.

ZION AND HER NEW FAMILY (49:14–23)

i

49 [14]But Zion says, "Yahveh has deserted me;
my lord has forgotten me."

[15]"Can a woman forget her baby
and show no love for the child of her womb?
But even if women should forget,
I will not forget you.
[16]See, I have inscribed you on the palms of my hands;
your walls are present to me always.
[17]Those who build you up work faster
than those who tore you down.
Those who laid you waste have left you alone.
[18]Lift up your eyes, look about you;
they are all assembled, to you they have come.
As I live—a pronouncement of Yahveh—
surely you will wear them all like an ornament;
you will deck yourself with them like a bride.
[19]Surely your ruins, your desolate places,
and your devastated land—
surely your land is too confined for its people,
while those who destroyed you have gone far away.
[20]The children born when you were bereaved
will say once again in your hearing,

'This place is too cramped for us;
make room for us to settle.'
[21]Then you will say to yourself,
'Who has begotten these children for me
when I was bereaved and barren,
exiled, cast aside;
who has brought them up?
I was left all alone;
where then have all these come from?'"

ii

[22]This is a word of Yahveh:
"Observe: I raise my hand to the nations,
I lift up a signal for the peoples;
they will carry your sons in their laps,
your daughters will be borne on their shoulders;
[23]kings will look after your children,
their queens will serve you as nurses;
with their face to the ground, they will pay you homage
and lick the dust of your feet.
Then you will acknowledge that I am Yahveh;
those who wait for me will not be disappointed."

FURTHER REASSURANCE GIVEN AND OBJECTIONS ANSWERED (49:24–50:3)

i

49 [24]Can prey be taken from a warrior?
Or can prisoners of a tyrant be rescued?
[25]This, then, is what Yahveh says:
"Prisoners will be taken from a warrior,
prey will be rescued from a tyrant;
I myself shall contend with your adversary,
I myself shall save your children.
[26]I shall make your oppressors eat their own flesh,
they will get drunk on their blood as on wine;
then all flesh will know that I, Yahveh, am your Savior,
your Redeemer, the Strong One of Jacob."

ii

50 [1]This is what Yahveh says:
"Where is your mother's bill of divorce
by which I put her away?

Or to which of my creditors
have I sold you into slavery?
It was, rather, for your wickedness that you were sold,
for your transgressions that your mother was put away.
[2]Why was no one there when I came?
Why did no one answer when I called?
Is my reach too short to rescue?
Do I lack the strength to deliver?
By my rebuke I dry up the sea.
I turn rivers into barren land;
their fish stink, deprived of water,
and dying on the parched ground.
[3]I clothe the sky with mourning garb;
I make sackcloth its covering.

THE PROPHETIC SERVANT OPPOSED AND ABUSED (50:4–11)

i

50 [4]The Sovereign Lord Yahveh has given me
the tongue of those who are instructed,
to know how to sustain with a word the dispirited.
Morning after morning he sharpens my hearing
to listen as disciples do.
[5]The Sovereign Lord Yahveh has opened my ears,
and I, for my part, was not defiant,
nor did I draw back.
[6]I offered my back to those who beat me,
my cheeks to those who plucked out my beard.
I did not hide my face from insults and spittle.
[7]The Sovereign Lord Yahveh is my helper;
therefore, no insult can touch me,
therefore, I set my face like flint;
I know I will not be disappointed.
[8]The one who will vindicate me is at hand,
who dares to bring an accusation against me?
Let us confront each other.
Who will pass judgment on me?
Let him draw near to me.
[9]Yes, the Sovereign Lord Yahveh is my helper;
who is the one who will condemn me?
They will all wear out like a garment,
the moth will devour them.

ii

[10]Whoever among you reveres Yahveh,
let him heed the voice of his servant;
whoever is walking in the dark
and has no glimmer of light,
let him trust in the name of Yahveh
and rely on his God.
[11]But all you who light your own fire
and set your own firebrands alight,
walk by the light of your fire
and by the firebrands you have kindled.
This is my message for you:
You shall lie down in torment.

THREE WORDS OF COMFORT FOR THE WELL DISPOSED (51:1–8)

i

51 [1]Listen to me, you who pursue what is right,
you who seek after Yahveh:
look to the Rock from which you were hewn,
the quarry from which you were cut;
[2]look to Abraham your father
and to Sarah who gave you birth.
When I called him, he was but one,
but I blessed him and made him many.
[3]Yahveh comforts Zion,
he brings comfort to all her ruins;
he will make her wilderness like Eden,
her deserted places like the garden of Yahveh.
Gladness and joy will be in her,
thanksgiving and the sound of music.

ii

[4]Pay heed to me, my people,
my nation, listen to me!
A law will go out from me,
my justice as a light for the peoples.
[5]In an instant I will bring about my victory;
my deliverance goes forth like light,
my arm will govern the peoples.
The islands wait for me,
they look to my arm for protection.

[6]Raise your eyes to the sky,
look at the earth beneath—
for the sky will be dispersed like smoke,
the earth will wear out like a garment,
its inhabitants will die like gnats;
but my salvation will endure forever,
my triumph will not be eclipsed.

iii

[7]Listen to me, you who know what is right,
you people who have taken my law to heart:
do not fear any human reproach,
do not let their insults dismay you.
[8]Grubs will consume them like a garment,
worms will devour them like wool,
but my triumph will endure forever,
my salvation for ages to come.

AN URGENT PRAYER FOR DIVINE INTERVENTION (51:9–16)

i

51 [9]Rouse yourself, rouse yourself, put on strength,
arm of Yahveh!
Rouse yourself as in days of old,
as in ages long since.
Was it not you that hacked Rahab in pieces,
that ran the Dragon through?
[10]Was it not you that dried up the Sea,
the waters of the Great Deep?
Was it not you that made the depths of the Sea
a route for the redeemed to traverse?
[11]Those ransomed by Yahveh will return,
shouting for joy they will enter Zion
crowned with joy everlasting;
gladness and joy will be theirs,
sorrow and sighing will depart.

ii

[12]I, I myself am the one who comforts you;
why, then, fear mortals doomed to die,
who fare no better than grass?
[13]You have forgotten Yahveh who made you,
Yahveh who stretched out the sky,

who established the earth.
You are in constant fear all day long
of the fury of oppressors set on destruction;
but where now is the fury of these oppressors?
[14]The one who now cowers will soon be released;
he will not go down to death, to the Pit;
he will not lack for food.
[15]But I, Yahveh your God,
who stirs up the sea so that its waves roar
[Yahveh of the hosts is his name],
[16]who stretched out the sky and established the earth,
who says to Zion, "You are my people"
[I put my words in your mouth,
I hide you in the shadow of my hand].

THE CUP OF WRATH (51:17–23)

i

51 [17]Bestir yourself, bestir yourself, rise up, Jerusalem!
You who have drunk from Yahveh's hand
the cup of his wrath;
you have drained to the last drop
the goblet that made you stagger.
[18]Among all the children she had borne,
there was none to lead her;
among all the children she had raised
there was none to take her by the hand.
[19]This twofold disaster has befallen you:
devastating destruction—who will grieve for you?
famine and the sword—who will console you?
[20]Your children have fainted; they are lying
at the corner of every street
like antelopes caught in the net.
They have felt the full force of Yahveh's wrath,
the rebuke of your God.

ii

[21]Hear, then, this, you that are afflicted,
you that are drunk but not with wine:
[22]Thus says Yahveh, your sovereign Lord and your God,
he who pleads the cause of his people:
"See now, I take from your hand
the cup that makes you stagger,

the goblet of my wrath;
you will never have to drink from it again.
[23]I shall put it in the hands of those who afflict you,
those who torment you, saying:
'Lie down, so we can walk over you.'
You made your back like the ground under their feet,
like a road for those who pass by."

THE COMING OF THE KINGDOM (52:1–12)

i

52 [1]Zion, awake! awake! clothe yourself with your strength;
clothe yourself with your splendid robes, Jerusalem, holy city!
For the uncircumcised and the unclean
will enter you no longer.
[2]Arise, shake yourself free of the dust.
Jerusalem, ascend your throne;
loose the bonds from your neck,
captive daughter Zion!

ii

[3]For this is what Yahveh says: "You were sold into slavery for nothing, and you will be redeemed but not with payment." [4]This is what the Sovereign Lord Yahveh says: "In the beginning my people went down to Egypt to settle there, and then the Assyrians oppressed them without cause. [5]So now, what do I find here? [a pronouncement of Yahveh] My people are taken away without payment, and their leaders are boasting about it [a pronouncement of Yahveh] and unceasingly, all day long, my name is reviled. [6]Therefore, on that day my people will acknowledge my name; (they will acknowledge) that I, Yahveh, am the one who is speaking; here I am."

iii

[7]How welcome on the mountains are the footsteps of the herald
announcing well-being, bringing good tidings, announcing victory,
declaring to Zion: "Your God reigns as king!"
[8]Listen! Your watchmen raise their voices,
with one accord they shout out for joy,
for with their own eyes they are witnessing
the return of Yahveh to Zion.
[9]With one accord break out into joyful shouts,
you ruins of Jerusalem,
for Yahveh has comforted his people;
he has redeemed Jerusalem.

[10]Yahveh has bared his holy arm
in the sight of all the nations.
All the ends of the earth shall witness
the victory of our God.

iv

[11]Away! Away! Go thence,
touch nothing unclean;
purify yourselves as you depart,
you who bear the vessels of Yahveh;
[12]for you shall not leave in haste,
nor shall you depart in flight,
for Yahveh goes on before you;
the God of Israel is your rearguard.

THE SERVANT: FROM HUMILIATION TO EXALTATION (52:13–53:12)

i

52 [13]See, my servant will achieve success;
he will be highly honored, raised up, and greatly exalted.
[14a]Just as many were once appalled at him,
[15]so will he astonish many nations.
Because of him kings will observe silence,
for what was never told them they now see,
and what they had never heard they now understand.

ii

53 [1]Who would believe what we have heard?
To whom has Yahveh's power been revealed?
He grew up like a sapling in Yahveh's presence,
rooted in the parched ground.
He had no outward beauty, no distinction,
we saw nothing in his appearance to attract us,
52 [14b]so marred was his appearance beyond human semblance,
his form beyond human likeness.
53 [3]He was despised, shunned by people,
a man who suffered, no stranger to sickness,
like one from whom people turn away their gaze.
He was despised, and we held him of no account.
[4]Yet it was he who bore our affliction,
he who bore the burden of our sufferings.
We reckoned him stricken,
smitten by God and afflicted;

[5]yet he was wounded because of our transgressions,
crushed on account of our iniquities.
On him was laid the chastisement that made us whole;
we found healing because of his wounds.
[6]We had all gone astray like sheep,
all of us going our own way,
but Yahveh laid upon him
the iniquity of us all.
[7]He was abused, yet he was submissive;
he did not open his mouth.
He was led like a lamb to the slaughter,
like a ewe that is dumb before the shearers.
He did not open his mouth.
[8]By oppressive acts of judgment he was led away,
and who gives a thought to his fate?
He was cut off from the land of the living,
stricken to death for his people's sin.
[9]His grave was located with the wicked,
his sepulcher with reprobates,
though he had done no violence,
and no falsehood was on his tongue.
[10]But it was Yahveh's good pleasure to crush him, [he brought sickness upon him].
If his life is laid down as a guilt offering,
he will see posterity, he will prolong his days;
through him Yahveh's purpose will prevail.
[11]After his painful life he will see light and be satisfied.

iii

By his knowledge my servant will vindicate many;
it is he who bears the burden of their iniquities.
[12]Therefore, I allot his portion with the great;
with the powerful he will share the spoil,
since he poured out his life-blood to death
and was numbered among transgressors.
Yet he bore the sin of many,
and interceded for their transgressions.

Apostrophe to Zion (54:1–17)

i

54 [1]Sing out, you barren woman, who has borne no child;
break out in shouts of joy, you who have never been in labor;
for the children of the wife that was abandoned

will outnumber those of the wife with a husband.
[2]Enlarge the space of your abode,
let your tent hangings out to the full,
do not stint.
Lengthen your ropes, drive the tent pegs home,
[3]for you will spread out to the right and the left;
your offspring will dispossess nations
and people cities now abandoned.
[4]Do not fear, you will not be disappointed;
do not cringe, you will not be disgraced;
you will forget the shame of your youth,
no longer recall the reproach of your widowhood.
[5]The One who made you is the One who will espouse you;
Yahveh of the hosts is his name.
your Redeemer is the Holy One of Israel;
he is called the God of all the earth.
[6]Yahveh has summoned you back
like a wife once forsaken and sad at heart,
a wife still young, though once rejected,
says your God.
[7]For a brief space of time I forsook you,
but with love overflowing I will bring you back.
[8]In an outburst of anger I hid my face from you for awhile,
but with love never failing I have pitied you,
says Yahveh, your Redeemer.

ii

[9]This is for me like the lifetime of Noah,
when I swore an oath
that Noah's floodwater would never again
pour over the earth;
so now I swear an oath
no longer to be angry with you or rebuke you.
[10]Mountains may depart,
hills may be shaken,
but my love will not depart from you,
nor my covenant of friendship be shaken,
says Yahveh in his pity for you.

iii

[11]City in distress, battered by storms,
with no one to comfort!
I will lay your stones with the finest mortar,
your foundations with lapis;
[12]I will set up your shields with rubies,
your gates with beryl;

the walls that enclose you will be precious jewels.
[13]When all your children will be taught by Yahveh,
great will be the well-being of your children.
[14]You will be triumphantly established;
you will be far removed from oppression.
You will be free from fear
and from terror, for no terror will come near you.
[15]If anyone attacks you, it will not be my doing,
and whoever attacks you will fall by your side.
[16]See, I have created the smith,
blowing on the charcoal fire,
making weapons, each one for its purpose.
I have also created the Destroyer to wreak havoc;
[17]no weapon designed to be used against you will prevail;
you will silence every tongue of those who contend with you.

iv

This, then, is the lot of Yahveh's servants,
their vindication from me. A word of Yahveh.

A CONCLUDING INVITATION TO FAITH IN THE PROPHETIC WORD (55:1–13)

i

55 [1]All you there who are thirsty, come to the water!
Come even if you have no money;
buy food and eat;
come, buy wine and milk
without money, at no cost.
[2]Why spend your money for what is not food?
Why spend your earnings for what does not satisfy?
Listen closely to me if you want to eat well;
you will be delighted with the richest fare.
[3]Come to me and incline your ear;
listen, and your spirit will revive.
I shall make with you a perpetual covenant,
the tokens of faithful love shown to David.
[4]As I made him a witness to peoples,
a prince who ruled over nations,
[5]so you will summon nations you do not know;
nations that do not know you will come running to you
for the sake of Yahveh your God,
the Holy One of Israel who made you glorious.

ii

[6]Seek Yahveh while he may be found,
invoke him while he is near.
[7]Let the wicked forsake their ways,
the sinful their devices.
Let them turn back to Yahveh
that he may take pity on them,
to our God, ever ready to pardon.
[8]For my thoughts are not your thoughts,
nor are my ways your ways. [A word of Yahveh]
[9]For as high as is the sky above the earth,
so are my ways above your ways,
my thoughts above your thoughts.
[10]For as the rain and the snow fall from the sky,
nor return there without watering the ground,
causing it to bring forth vegetation,
giving seed for the sower
and bread for food,
[11]so is it with my word that issues from my mouth;
it does not return to me empty
but accomplishes what I purpose
and achieves what I send it to do.

iii

[12]You will go out with joy,
you will be led out in peace;
mountains and hills before you will break out in shouts of joy;
all the trees in the countryside will clap their hands.
[13]In place of the thornbush, cypresses will grow;
instead of nettles, myrtles will grow.
All this will be a memorial for Yahveh,
a perpetual sign that shall not be cut off.

INTRODUCTION

◆

INTRODUCTION TO ISAIAH 40–55

◆

1. ISAIAH 40–55 AS PART OF THE BOOK OF ISAIAH

WHAT IS A BIBLICAL BOOK?

The fact that these sixteen chapters form a little more than a quarter of the book of Isaiah and that they carry no title of their own obliges us in the first place to justify giving them separate treatment and in the second place to explain their relation to what precedes and follows them and their function in the book as a whole. Modern readers understand a book to be the production of one or, less commonly, more than one author, protected legally from the intrusion (well-meaning or otherwise) of later interpolators, and, unless it is a *Festschrift* or something similar, exhibiting some degree of inner coherence and uniformity in style and subject matter. Problems inevitably arise, however, when we transfer this understanding of books and book production to biblical books, and the fifteen books of the Latter Prophets in particular. The concept of a *book* in something like the modern understanding of the term arose only in the post-biblical period.

Perhaps the first clear example is the Wisdom of Sirach (Jesus ben Sira), written in the early second century B.C.E. Sirach identifies himself as the author toward the end of the composition (Sir 50:27) and is so identified in the Preface, written by his grandson. Though we have no direct information on the time and circumstances of the compilation of the four scroll-length prophetic books (Isaiah, Jeremiah, Ezekiel, the Twelve), we may safely surmise that they belonged to a stage of literary history somewhat earlier than Sirach, who seems to have been familiar with at least sections of Isa 1–39 and 40–66 as well as the Book of the Twelve (Sir 48:22–25; 49:10). The title of Isaiah provides a useful clue in this respect, since the designation *ḥăzôn yĕšaʿyāhû* ("Isaiah's Vision") corresponds to the title of a composition mentioned by the author of Chronicles, writing in the late Persian or early Hellenistic period (2 Chr 32:32). Furthermore, the expression "Judah and Jerusalem," which appears in the title of the book of Isaiah, has the same order as in Chronicles and Ezra–Nehemiah (e.g. 2 Chr 11:14; 20:17; Ezra 9:9; 10:7) but the reverse of the order in passages deemed to be of an early date (Isa 3:1, 8; 5:3; 22:21).

While some attributed prophetic material would presumably have survived from the time of the kingdoms, it seems that the compiling and arranging of the extant prophetic material and the assigning of authorship allowed for a considerable degree of fluidity and indeterminacy. This is particularly in evidence in the Twelve. Malachi is acknowledged to be a fictitious name, and two anonymous sections (Zech 9–11 and 12–14) have been added on to Zech 1–8 in order to avoid exceeding the symbolically important number twelve. The considerable amount of overlap in language and subject matter between Isaiah on the one hand and some of the other attributed units of the Twelve on the other (Micah, Obadiah, Nahum, perhaps also Habakkuk), an issue still in need of investigation, suggests that the creativity of the compilers was not confined to the end of the Twelve-Prophet collection. The Book of Isaiah, compiled probably at about the same time as the Twelve, exhibits a somewhat similar kind of editorial creativity, since it attributes a fairly wide range of anonymous writings to a named prophetic figure active in the eighth century B.C.E. We should add that, making all due allowance for the fact that prophetic material is not self-referential, attribution to Isaiah of the sayings is weakly attested, being confined to three titles (1:1; 2:1; 13:1), all of them attached at a late date. In sum, the concept of authorship and book production underlying these features, so different from ours as it is, should be borne in mind in evaluating claims advanced on theological grounds for Isaian authorship of the entire book and for the book of Isaiah as a canonical unit.

Literary-critical study of the book of Isaiah, systematically undertaken from the late eighteenth century, has identified distinct sections composed at different times and by different authors. Credit for identifying the distinct origin of chs. 40–66 is generally assigned to Johann Christoph Döderlein writing in the 1770s, though it seems to have been hinted at by medieval Jewish scholars including Ibn Ezra. Döderlein's, proposal was widely accepted following the publication of the three-volume commentary of Wilhelm Gesenius in 1821, though conservative scholars, continued, and still continue, to defend Isaiah's authorship of the entire book. The further step of separating off chs. 56–66, "Third Isaiah," as a distinct, later composition was taken by Bernhard Duhm in his commentary published in 1892. Though Duhm did not argue his case at any length, this distinction has also won general acceptance.

ISAIAH 40–55 IN RELATION TO ISAIAH 35

Assuming for the moment that this critical consensus still holds good, the question of the relation of 40–55 to what precedes and follows requires explanation. While it is possible that section 40–55 or 40–66 was tacked onto 1–39 simply because space was available on the scroll, a close reading of the text suggests better explanations, and in fact few critical commentators have found this account of the matter satisfactory. Lack of evidence also makes it difficult to accept the explanation proposed by Sigmund Mowinckel (1946, 66–71), and taken up more recently by Douglas Jones (1955) and John Eaton (1959; 1982, 58–76), of an uninterrupted succession of Isaian disciples between the eighth and the sixth centuries B.C.E. The book does refer to Isaiah's disciples (*limmudîm* 8:16), and occasional commentary on earlier passages in the second half of the book (e.g. 50:10–11 on 50:4–9), together with allusions to a prophetic plurality (e.g. 59:21), would be consistent with the activity of disciples. However, these indications do not amount to evidence for an uninterrupted prophetic succession covering more than two centuries. Despite valiant attempts to prove otherwise, the language and rhetorical style of chs. 40–55 have little in common with chs. 1–39, which also tells against a relationship of prophetic master and disciple.

This issue will force itself on our attention at several points throughout the commentary, but for the moment one or two observations are in order. Several recent commentators have convinced themselves of close editorial or compositional connections between 1–39 and 40–66 on the basis of the motifs and turns of phrase that appear throughout both major sections, but on the whole the differences are more in evidence than the similarities. With the exception of the Holy One of Israel (*qĕdôš yiśrāʾēl*), not peculiar to Isaiah, the titulary of Yahveh in chs. 40–66 (Creator, Redeemer, Savior, the First and the Last), to be set out in a later section of the Introduction, below, is quite different from the ones used in 1–39. There is polemic against the worship of gods other than Yahveh in both sections, but the approach, again, is quite different in 40–48 from the treatment of this theme in 1–39. The terminology is different, and satire targeting the manufacture of images, obtrusively present in 40–48, is completely absent from 1–39. Even more counterindicative is the prevalence of the servant motif in chs. 40–55 and its absence from chs. 1–39. Since *ʿebed* ("servant") is the standard term for the prophet in Deuteronomic writings, this would suggest influence on Isa 40–66 from that quarter rather than a legacy from the Isaiah of the eighth century. More will be said on this point below.

Since we do not know when, by whom, and under what circumstances the section Isa 40–55 was attached to 1–39, we can only speculate on the basis of internal literary evidence. From the point of view of Israel's relations with the great empires, ch. 40 takes over where ch. 39 leaves off with the disaster of the Babylonian conquest and thus extends the historical horizon beyond Assyria, Babylon, and the eclipse of the Babylonian Empire during the reign of its last ruler, Nabonidus, and into the epoch of Persian domination. Isaiah 1–55, therefore, read as a literary continuum, provides coverage of the three great empires—Assyria, Babylonia, Persia—preceding Alexander from a specifically prophetic point of view.

The last eleven chapters of the book, the so-called Third Isaiah, deal exclusively with situations internal to the Jewish community in the Persian province of Judah. The desire to establish lines of continuity spanning the disaster of 586 B.C.E. could therefore have suggested linking the two prophetic texts together. The opening statement of chs. 40–55, addressed to a prophetic plurality (40:1–2), assures Jerusalem that its iniquity is now pardoned. The iniquity of Jerusalem, representing the population of the city and the kingdom of Judah, is thematic in chs. 1–39 beginning with the opening poem (1:1–26). Concern with the destiny of Jerusalem, which is in evidence throughout chs. 40–55, especially 49–55, helps to explain why these speeches and poems were attached to those of the First Isaiah.

These general conclusions can stand as a working hypothesis, but they must be tested against the evidence for a more complex linkage and overlap between the two main sections of the book. Commentators have long noted the verbal and thematic connections between ch. 35 and 40–55 or 40–66. Charles Cutler Torrey (1928, 53–67, 279–301) proposed that 34–35 plus 40–66 comprised the work of one author, a religious and literary genius of the highest order who wrote in the late fifth century B.C.E. While few have taken up Torrey's radical views about the origin of Second Isaiah, many commentators have been persuaded that at least ch. 35 was once an integral part of 40–55, having been separated from it by the insertion of the account of critical events in Hezekiah's reign involving the prophet Isaiah (e.g. Hans Wildberger 1982, 1330–41; Ronald E. Clements 1980, 271–77).

The most thorough investigation of the issue is that of Odil Hannes Steck (1985a) who argued that ch. 35 was inserted as a redactional bridge between 1–34 and 40–62. He derived this conclusion from the many points of linguistic and thematic contact between ch. 35 and both First and Second Isaiah, especially chs. 32–34 on the one hand and 40:1–11 on the other. Isaiah 35 is, therefore, he maintained, dependent on both First and Second Isaiah, and he went on to suggest that the chapter was composed when these two distinct and already fully formed literary corpora were first linked together.

One complicating factor that makes it difficult to accept Steck's proposal whole and entire is the detailed and apparently deliberate way in which the contrast between Edom in ch. 34 and Judah in chapter 35 is worked out. These two chapters seem to have been composed as contrasting panels in a kind of diptych, representing judgment and salvation respectively. Edom will be subjected to total ecological degradation (34:9–10, 13) while Judah will become miraculously fertile (35:1–2, 6b-7a); Edom will become the haunt of unpleasant and unclean animals presided over by the demon Lilith (34:11, 13b–15), while in Judah dangerous animals will be removed (35:7b, 9); travel will be impossible in Edom (34:10b) while there will be a highway in Judah (35:8–9). Both chapters speak of an imminent and definitive judgment, a day of retribution (34:8 *yôm nāqām* cf. 35:4 *nāqām yābôʾ*).

These are the main points, but a detailed study of the language of ch. 34 suggests the conclusion that the author has drawn on material in both 1–33 and 56–66. There are indications of borrowing from the Babylon poems, especially the scenario of ecological devastation, a return to nature, and the site of the city turned over to wild animals (13:1–22). While the language of ch. 34 has little in common with 40–55, we find the same juxtaposition of salvation for Judah and judgment on Edom in 62:1–63:6 (*yôm nāqām* 63:4; also 61:2). This is one instance of the theme of eschatological reversal that is a prominent feature of the last section of the book (especially 65:13–14). It seems that, by the time of writing, Edom had replaced Babylon as the evil empire *par excellence*, and it is well known that Edom remained a symbol of forces hostile to Israel and the God of Israel down into the Roman period. In fact, the Targum substitutes Rome for Edom in 34:9: "the streams of Rome shall be turned into pitch."

Turning now to ch. 35: It was understandable that several commentators, perhaps the majority, concluded that this chapter is of a piece with 40–55 and that the connection has been broken by the insertion of the narrative about events during Hezekiah's reign taken from the History. The theme of ecological transformation is common to 35 and 40–55, especially the motif of water in the wilderness and in the barren land (41:18–19; 43:19–20; 44:3; 50:2; 51:3; 53:2). Both anticipate the vision of God's glory (*kĕbôd YHVH* 35:2; 40:5, 9) and a time of judgment and recompense (35:4; 40:10), the prospect of which will strengthen the faint-hearted (35:3–4; 40:9, 29–31). The most impressive link, however, is the motif of the highway for the return to Zion at the end of 35 and the beginning of 40–55 (*maslûl vāderek* 35:8; *derek mĕsillâ* 40:3). It seems that the only remaining issue was whether to align 35 alone (e.g. Steck) or 34–35 (e.g. Torrey) with Second Isaiah.

The problem with this alignment is that the historical particularities of 40–55 are completely lacking in ch. 35, which reads like an ahistorical and imaginative projection into the future. As in 57:14 ("build up, build up, prepare the way") and 62:10 ("build up, build up the highway"), the route from Babylon to Judah in 40:3 has been eschatologized in 35:8–10 and is now a metaphor for passage to the new age about to dawn.

A survey of the language of 35:1–10 will confirm the primary and more direct association of ch. 35 with the third rather than the second section of the book. We must be content with a few examples: compared with the first strophe (35:1–2), the twin verbs for rejoicing (*śôś, gîl*) are found together only in chs. 56–66 (61:10; 65:18–19; 66:10), the corresponding substantive (*gîlâ*) only in 65:18, and the phrase "the glory of Lebanon" (*kĕbôd hallĕbānôn*) only in 60:13. The association of vengeance (*nāqām*) and retribution (*gĕmûl*) with a theophany ("See, here is your God," 35:4) is, once again, characteristic of the final section of the book (e.g. 63:4). We can form some idea of the intertextual situation by reading these three passages in sequence:

See, here is your God!
See, Yahveh is coming with power,
his strong arm affirms his rule;
see, his reward is with him,
his recompense precedes him. (40:9b–10)

Say to daughter Zion,
"See, your salvation is coming;
see, his reward is with him,
and his recompense precedes him." (62:11b)

See, here is your God!
Vengeance is at hand,

fearsome retribution;
it is he who comes to save you. (35:4b)

Isaiah 62:11b and 35:4b are both, in all probability, dependent on 40:9b–10 but, in the context of the contrasting destinies of Judah and Edom in 62:10–63:6 and ch. 34–35, both texts develop 40:9b–10 in the direction of an eschatological dualism, symbolically expressed.

In the final strophe of the poem, the miraculous removal of disabilities with respect to sight, hearing, speech, and bodily integrity is combined with an equally miraculous ecological transformation (35:5–10). The same combination appears in 29:17–18, but there is nothing similar in chs. 40–55, where blindness and deafness are metaphors for obtuseness and disorientation (42:18–20; 43:8) or, in one instance, imprisonment (42:7).

The conclusions reached on this issue up to this point may be summarized as follows: (1) Isaiah 34–35 is essentially one text which serves to recapitulate and bring to a point of eschatological definition the Isaian message about judgment and salvation in ch. 1–33. It therefore serves as a fitting conclusion to 1–33. (2) Neither 34–35 nor 35 alone has any *direct* connection with 40–55, but 34–35 does have much in common with 56–66. Like the latter, it represents an exegetical development elaborated on the basis of both 40–55 and material in 1–33. (3) It is possible, nevertheless, that the theme of the joyful return to Zion at the end of ch. 35 was seen by the compiler to form a suitable nexus with chs. 40–55. This seems to make better sense than the proposal that 35 was originally an integral part of 40–55 but was left isolated by the insertion of 36–39 between chs. 35 and 40. It is not clear why an editor would break up a text in this way, placing the insertion within rather than either before or after the text at hand.

ISAIAH 40–55 IN RELATION TO ISAIAH 36–39

This brings us to the problem of the place and function of chs. 36–39 in the book. At first sight, it seems that Isa 36–39 is a simple and straightforward case of a historical appendix taken from the History (2 Kgs 18:13–20:19) with minor adaptations and then positioned after the summary in chs. 34–35. A parallel instance would be Jer 52 (= 2 Kgs 24:18–25:30), appended to the last passage in the book, which predicts the fall of Babylon and concludes with the colophon "thus far the sayings of Jeremiah" (51:59–64). Chapters 36–39 do in fact serve as a historical appendix. They were taken with modifications from the History, though they did not originate there, and they do serve as an appendix to chs. 1–35. That, however, is not all that needs to be said about their function. For, apart from setting up a contrast between the crisis of 701 and the account of a similar crisis during the reign of Ahaz, in which Isaiah was also involved (chs. 7–8), and therefore between Ahaz and Hezekiah to the advantage of the latter, the narrative also serves in a quite objective way as a bridge between the two major sections of the book as we have it. The question then arises and has been much under discussion in recent years: how do these chapters relate to the second major section of the book?

Some scholars, principally Peter R. Ackroyd (1974, 1981, 1982), have suggested that chs. 36–39 or at least 38–39 were edited and arranged, perhaps even composed, precisely to serve as a preface to 40–55 or 40–66. Arguments that the narrative as a whole serving this function (e.g. assigning a symbolic value to the anticipated death of Hezekiah) are speculative, but one point at least is reasonably secure. The order in which the incidents are related is ostensibly chronological but, since Isaiah promises Hezekiah both that he will recover and that the city will be saved (38:5–6), Hezekiah must have taken ill either before or during Sennacherib's punitive campaign, according to the logic of the narrative, if not in historical actuality. Hence, the visit of the Babylonian envoys during the king's convalescence, which concludes with Isaiah's prediction of a future deportation to Babylon (39:1–8), has been deliberately displaced, and most commentators have concluded that the reason must have been to create a nexus with the announcement of the return from exile at the beginning of the following chapter (40:1–5).

There are some thematic similarities that could have led an editor or compiler to attach Isa 40–55 to 1–39, in whatever form both texts then existed. The victory over the Assyrians recorded in 36–37, brought about by miraculous intervention, could have been seen as presaging the defeat of the Babylonians, and the fulfillment of Isaiah's prediction of deportation to Babylon could have furnished proof for the argument from prophecy elaborated in 40–48.

But the arrangement of Isa 36–39 is adopted unchanged from the History and therefore would have been dictated more by the *Tendenz* of the Historian, for whom Hezekiah was a more central figure than Isaiah, than by factors internal to the book of Isaiah. This point will emerge more clearly when we take into account the implausibility of a purely social visit of Babylonians to the Judean king, especially since we know that the rebellion against Assyria of Merodach-baladan II (Marduk-apla-iddina) had been decisively crushed *before* Sennacherib's Palestinian campaign. Ackroyd (1982, 15) made the plausible suggestion that behind the present form of the story there lies an account of overtures between Babylon and Judah for an anti-Assyrian alliance and that Hezekiah's display of his wealth had the purpose of establishing his credibility as a Babylonian ally. Hence, the *overt* intention of the incident as described in 2 Kgs 20:12–19 = Isa 39:1–8 would be to exonerate Hezekiah from responsibility for the catastrophe of 586 and place the blame squarely on Manasseh, an intent that is made abundantly clear in the subsequent history (2 Kgs 21:10–15; 23:26–27; 24:3–4). In this case, the narrative would still serve as an appropriate introduction to 40–55 but without our making the additional supposition that it was composed or even edited expressly as a preface to Second Isaiah or that therefore it must postdate the latter.

LINGUISTIC, STYLISTIC, AND THEMATIC FEATURES

There has been a tendency in recent years, especially in English-language scholarship, to reassert the unity of the book of Isaiah on literary, structural and occasionally theological rather than authorial grounds and to minimize the distinctions and differences among the three major sections of the book. For some scholars (e.g. Ronald E. Clements 1982, 1985) this is a matter of identifying motifs that appear throughout the book (e.g. seeing and not seeing, hearing and not hearing) and finding in chs. 40–66 indications of the development of themes present in 1–39. Rolf Rendtorff (1984, 1996) goes further in asserting that 1–39 and 56–66 were shaped and edited with reference to 40–55. Isaiah 1–39 never existed as a literary unit independent of 40–55, though the editorial and authorial activity of "Second Isaiah" is confined for the most part to chs. 1, 12, and 35. At this point Rendtorff's position is somewhat unclear. He concludes that "the central themes of chapter 40 are all to be found in the first and third parts of the book" (Rendtorff 1996, 155), but at the same time maintains that the treatment of major themes (e.g. Zion, the Holy One of Israel, righteousness) in First Isaiah is quite different from Second Isaiah. In keeping with a trend in English-language scholarship, these conclusions are argued on the basis of a rather scattershot study of the incidence of such key terms as *nḥm* (comfort), *kābôd* (glory), and *ṣĕdāqâ* (righteousness, vindication, victory).

This kind of linguistic and thematic study has its place, but it is generally unsatisfactory when unsupported by other considerations and especially when the occurrence outside of Isaiah of the terms or motifs in question is disregarded. Roy F. Melugin (1976, 176) took the absence of a superscription and call narrative to imply that the section 40–55 was never intended to stand alone but was conceived from the beginning as a continuation of 1–39. Though Melugin claimed that the editor obliterated all historical allusions from the work (a surprising claim in view of the mention of Cyrus, his campaigns, and the anticipated fall of Babylon), he did not consider the probability that an editor who wished it to be understood that section 40–55 was authored by the Isaiah of chs. 1–39 would presumably have eliminated any existing title.

In agreement with Melugin, but from a more explicitly theological perspective, Brevard S. Childs (1979, 325–30) explained the elimination of historical allusion from chs. 40–66 and the absence of a superscription as required by the pattern of prophecy and fulfillment that emerges once 1–39 and 40–66 are read as one canonical text. By this means the message of Second Isaiah is severed from the history of events in the sixth century B.C.E. and becomes fully eschatological. The implication seems to be that Second Isaiah derives its canonical meaning exclusively from its connection with First Isaiah and cannot be grasped theologically apart from it.

While it is certainly possible to read Isaiah 40–55 theologically with reference to Isa 1–39, however we explain the connection, we must question the proposition that these chapters only make sense theologically when read in this way. The author of 40–55 is doing what prophets during the time of the kingdoms were doing—that is, commenting and making judgments on contemporaneous international affairs from a specific theopolitical perspective. The manner is quite different, but the basic concerns—the destiny of the people of Israel, the primacy of faith in God's word communicated through the prophet, and the need for moral regeneration—are the same.

There is also the problem for both Melugin and Childs that they must postulate that 40–55 contained more precise historical data before being attached to 1–39 and that these historical particulars were removed, a completely arbitrary assumption. And, as noted above, they must also minimize or disregard the historical references, either direct or indirect, that these chapters do in fact contain.

On the issue of the connection between chs. 40–55 and 1–39, the maximalist position is occupied by Hugh G. M. Williamson (1994), who argues not only for the pervasive influence of First on Second Isaiah but for the latter's editing and expanding of the former. Both were therefore intended to be read as one text. In some respects Williamson gives the impression of attempting, by a more detailed study of the text, to shore up Childs' proposal—namely, that Second Isaiah announces the fulfillment of the plan announced in First Isaiah, that Second Isaiah cannot be understood theologically without First Isaiah, and that in fact it never circulated independently of First Isaiah.

He leads off with the assertion that the author of Second Isaiah saw himself authorized to open the book sealed by his predecessor (Isa 8:16; 30:8–9) who, he claims, is actually referred to in one of the sayings (44:26). This idea of the unsealing of earlier prophecy is attractive and in itself by no means implausible, though chs. 40–55 unfortunately provide no basis for it and never refer even indirectly to the relevant texts in First Isaiah.

That the First Isaiah is the prophetic servant referred to in 44:26 also seems unlikely, since the servant in question predicts the rebuilding of the ruined cities of Judah and the repopulation of Jerusalem, which cannot be true of the original Isaiah. Most of Williamson's study is taken up with cross-referencing terms and turns of phrase occurring in both parts of the book in an effort to demonstrate the influence of First on Second Isaiah and, in some instances, the authorial activity of the latter in the first part of the book. There is no reason to deny that the author of 40–55 was familiar with Isaiah's pronouncements, but he was familiar with the pronouncements of other early prophetic figures as well.

The uncertain dating of much of the material in chs. 1–39 also causes problems. An example may suffice. On the basis of similar phrasing in 49:22 and 11:12, both of which speak of a standard or rallying point (*nēs*) for the repatriation of dispersed Israelites, Williamson (1994, 125–42) attributes 11:12 (and the entire passage 11:11–16) to Second Isaiah. This is one of several possibilities but not, in my view, the most probable. A text omitted from consideration appears in the third part of the book: "A pronouncement of the sovereign Lord Yahveh, who gathers in the dispersed of Israel: 'I will gather yet more to him

(Israel) in addition to those (already) gathered'" (56:8b). Unlike 49:22, this appears to be a direct reference to and expansion of the scope of 11:12 and, if so, would put the discussion on a rather different basis.

Of particular importance for the linkage between the first and second sections of the book is the alleged parallelism between the vision narrative in 6:1–13 (or, for some commentators, 6:1–11) and 40:1–8. As will be seen at the relevant point in the commentary, the view that 40:1–8 reproduces the heavenly court scenario of 6:1–11 has achieved practically the status of an assured scholarly datum, at least among English-language scholars (e.g. Christopher Seitz 1990, 229–46; Hugh Williamson 1994, 30–56), following on the study of Frank Moore Cross (1953, 274–77); and this in spite of the fact that the heavenly court scenario is actually described and the speakers identified in 6:1–13 but not at all in 40:1–8. It can also be easily overlooked that 40:1–8, in which six imperatives are addressed to a plurality and one (v 6) to an individual, is quite unlike the deliberative sessions in the celestial audience chamber as described in 1 Kgs 22:20–22 and Job 1–2 and also for that matter in Isa 6:8 where the seer preempts further deliberation by volunteering his services. In 40:1–8, however, deliberation and debate are completely absent.

It could also be urged that comforting God's people (40:1–2), preparing the people for a new divine intervention (40:3–5), and proclaiming the impermanence of all human pretensions, political and otherwise (40:6–8), are tasks for prophets, not for members of the divine entourage. Neither 6:1–13 nor 40:1–8 is a call narrative comparable to that of Jeremiah, Ezekiel, or Moses. Both, however, record a commissioning for a specific charge at a critical point in history, with the not unimportant difference that 40:1–8 is addressed to an individual prophet but also to a prophetic plurality. In sum, I agree with Hans-Jürgen Hermisson (1998b, 144) that "the core content of Deutero-Isaiah provides no basis for understanding it as a literary extension (*Fortschreibung*) and interpretation of First Isaiah."

PROPHECY AND FULFILLMENT

Much discussion has been occasioned by references scattered throughout chs. 40–55 to first or former events (*riʾšōnôt*: 41:22; 42:9; 43:9, 18; 46:9; 48:3). Several commentators propose to interpret some or all of these references as allusions to the prophecies of the First Isaiah which, being now fulfilled, would provide grounds for confidence in the Second Isaiah's prediction of a reversal of fortune. This "argument from fulfilled prophecy" could then explain, at least in part, why the author of 40–55 himself, or a disciple closely associated with the author, attached his discourses to the collection of prophecies attributed to Isaiah. This reading of "the former things" with reference to First Isaiah would then form an important connecting link binding the two major sections of the book together.

Before these conclusions can be accepted, however, each case must be decided on its own merits. One instance (43:18) at least can be eliminated from consideration, since the context requires that the term *riʾšōnôt,* parallel with *qadmōniyyôt* ("ancient things/events"), refers to the tradition of God's liberating intervention in the Exodus (Isa 43:14–21). A similar appeal seems to be implied in 46:9, where the prophet's public is called on to remember "the former things," that is, to strengthen their links with the historical traditions. In the first occurrence of the expression, 41:22, the deities of foreign nations are challenged to prove their divinity by predicting the future and then making it happen. They are being challenged, in other words, to demonstrate their ability to control the flow of historical events as only gods can do. The term *hāriʾšōnôt* could therefore refer in a quite general way to earlier events that happened as predicted, and this is how several exegetes have understood it.

But if we take into account the broader context in which the challenge is issued, which involves the conquests of Cyrus (41:25–29), the reference would more naturally be to an earlier phase of Cyrus's career, successfully predicted by the author of these sayings. These predictions may no longer be extant, though the argument as presented here suggests that they may correspond to the good news proclaimed at the beginning of the section that is, 41:26–27 may correspond to (40:9–11).

> Who declared this from the start that we may acknowledge it?
> Who announced it in advance, that we may say, "He is right!"
> No one declared it, no one announced it,
> no one heard you say anything.
> I, the First, declared it to Zion,
> giving to Jerusalem a herald of good news. (41:26–27)

If the one who is spoken about and then addressed in 42:1–9 is Cyrus, as proposed in the commentary, the *riʾšōnôt* of 42:9 would very likely have an identical connotation. The same conclusion is at least possible in 43:9 and 48:3.

We can conclude, then, that the repeated allusion in 40–55 to "former things" can be explained in a satisfactory manner without reference to the prophecies of the First Isaiah, certainly without *exclusive* reference to them. Even if prophecies other than those of the author are in some instances included among "the former things," there would be no need to limit them to Isaiah. The author of 40–55 was familiar with Isaian prophecies but also with sayings attributed to Hosea, Jeremiah, Ezekiel, and possibly others. (For examples, not all clearly borrowings, as claimed, see most recently Benjamin D. Sommer 1998.)

ISAIAH 40–55 AND THE DEUTERONOMISTS

The distance separating Isa 1–39 and 40–55 will be better appreciated by noting the points of contact, stylistic and thematic, between Isa 40–55 and Deuteronomic writings. (To avoid unnecessary confusion, I will make no distinction between "Deuteronomic" and "Deuteronomistic," and I will refer to the Deuteronomistic History simply as "the History" and its author as "the Historian.") Comparison between Isa 40–55 and the Deuteronomic corpus may also suggest, if not an alternative reason for the combination of the two major sections of Isaiah, then at least an alternative way of viewing the relation between them. Following a well-substantiated opinion, "Deuteronomic" will here be understood as the common denominator for certain men in learned circles, perhaps associated in some way with the Levitical class, who were engaged in writing and preaching in the half-century or so following the Babylonian conquest and who had in common a certain style of public discourse, certain major themes, and a theological understanding of Israel's history. (See, for example, Rainer Albertz 1994, 382–87.) They would have been roughly contemporaneous, therefore, with the *floruit* of the author of Isaiah 40–55.

We have already noted one respect in which a major Deuteronomic theme produces a contrast between Isa 1–39 and 40–55: namely, the idea of prophetic servanthood. The term *ʿebed*, which is standard in the Deuteronomic corpus as a designation for individual prophets (1 Kgs 15:29; 2 Kgs 9:36; 10:10; 14:25) and prophets in general (*ʿăbādâv hannĕbîʾîm*: 2 Kgs 9:7; 17:13, 23; 21:10; 24:2; Jer 7:25; 25:6; 26:5; 29:19; 35:15; 44:4), appears in a religiously significant rather than purely sociological sense thirty-two times in Isa 40–66 but is absent from 1–39 ("my servant Isaiah," Isa 20:3, appears in a brief narrative of Deuteronomic origin, and "my servant David," in Isa 37:35 = 2 Kgs 19:34). This datum references not just the four "servant songs" but a fundamental theological theme throughout chs. 40–55, continuing on into 56–66—that of prophetic instrumentality at both the individual and collective level. Some scholars have picked up echoes of the tradition of Moses as prophetic *ʿebed* (who intercedes for and suffers on behalf of his people) in the attribution of servant features to Israel and its prophetic representative in Isa 40–55. On this point more will be said later. Prophecy also plays a pivotal role in the argument from prediction and fulfillment encapsulated in the phrase "the former things" (*hāriʾšōnôt*). The same basic pattern of prophecy and fulfillment, often explicitly noted, determines the course of events in the History, and the warnings issued by prophets are an essential factor in explaining why the disaster happened and where the blame for it lies. It will be apparent that the need to justify the ways of God to men, and to Israel in particular, is a major issue in Isa 40–55 (see, for example, Isa 43:27–28).

Perhaps the most striking feature common to Isaiah 40–55 and the Deuteronomic corpus is the insistence on the incomparability of the God of Israel. The Deuteronomic resonance is unmistakable in the frequently repeated "I am," and "I am Yahveh" formulas (Isa 41:4, 10; 43:10–13; 46:4; 48:12). The characterizations of the God of Israel as king (Isa 41:21; 44:6 cf. Deut 33:5) and as the Rock (*ṣûr*: Isa 44:8 cf. Deut 32:4, 15, 18, 31) are the most explicit indicators of affinity with the Song and Blessing of Moses (Deut 32–33), and the epithet *neʾĕmān* ("faithful") appears with reference to Yahveh only in Isa 49:7 and

Deut 7:9. The rejection of foreign deities is also a shared theme with several strikingly similar features (e.g. Isa 47:13 cf. Deut 4:19), including vocabulary. The term *pesel* or, less commonly, *pěsîl* (idolatrous image) appears frequently in Isa 40–55 (40:19–20; 42:8, 17; 44:9–10, 15, 17; 45:20; 48:5) and Deuteronomy (4:16, 23, 25; 5:8; 7:5, 25; 12:3; 27:15) but not in Isa 1–39, whereas its synonym *ʾĕlîl* is standard in Isa 1–39 (2:8, 18, 20; 10:10–11; 19:1, 3; 31:3) but absent from Isa 40–55 and Deuteronomy.

The prevalence in Isa 40–55 and Deuteronomy of the appeal to tradition, especially the historical traditions of the Exodus from Egypt and the trek through the wilderness, needs no documentation. The call to remember, to activate the community's social memory (verbal stem *zkr*) is, correspondingly, a feature common to both texts (Deut 5:15; 7:18; 8:2; 9:7; 15:15; 16:3, 12; 24:9, 18, 22; 25:17; Isa 43:18; 44:21; 46:8). Perhaps the most explicitly Deuteronomic passage in these chapters is the exhortation to the people to seek Yahveh and to "turn," that is, change the course of their lives (*ʿšûb* 55:6–11 cf. *tĕšûbâ* = repentance). Particular motifs—Israel's being carried through the wilderness (Deut 1:31; Isa 40:11; 46:3) and being borne aloft on eagles' wings (Deut 32:11–12; Isa 40:31)—are also worth noting. Recollection of the historical traditions is also meant to bring home the reality of Israel's election (verbal stem *bḥr*), a theme that is also prominent in Isa 40–55 (41:8–9; 42:1; 43:10, 20; 44:1–2; 49:7) and Deuteronomy (e.g. 4:37; 7:6–7; 10:15; 14:2) and almost completely absent from Isa 1–39. (Isa 14:1 is a late text, perhaps later than Isa 40–55.) The sobriquet Jeshurun for Israel the Chosen, finally, appears only in the Deuteronomic poems (Deut 32:15; 33:5, 26) and in Second Isaiah (Isa 44:2).

Several biblical texts datable to the period following the fall of Jerusalem on into the early years of Persian rule—including parts of Deuteronomy, the Deuteronomic strand in Jeremiah, Ezekiel, the homiletic framework to the visions of Zechariah (Zech 1:1–6; 6:15–8:23), and Isa 40–55—share a similar rhetorical and homiletic style. Noticeable features are peremptory calls for attention ("see," "listen," etc.), dramatic and often hyperbolic language, and frequent recourse to rhetorical questions. Among the most common appeals addressed to the public this way are the appeal to seek Yahveh (verbal stems *drš*, *bqš*: Deut 4:29; Jer 29:13; Isa 51:1; 55:6) and the appeal to get back in touch with the historical traditions (e.g. Deut 3:21; 4:3, 9; 7:19; Isa 42:20), both understandable ways of dealing with the deep sense of discontinuity and disorientation of this post-disaster generation. Unless these authors were simply writing for their own edification, we would be practically obliged to postulate an appropriate social setting—perhaps an inchoate synagogue network of some kind—in which this activity was going on.

The admittedly tentative conclusions to which these considerations point may be stated as follows. (1) Chapters 40–55 did not become part of the book just because there was space for them on the Isaiah scroll—at least not for that reason alone—or because they emanated from a generation of Isaian disciples that had survived the Babylonian conquest. Nor were they attached to Isa 1–39 on account of similarities of style and substance, since the differences between these sections are more in evidence than the similarities. (2) The historical appendix (chs. 36–39), taken from the History, should be read together with a few other brief narratives in the first part of the book (7:1–17; 20:1–6) as resulting from a move to reconstrue the prophet Isaiah as a "man of God" who interceded, worked miracles, healed, and was supportive of the ruler. This was an Isaiah more consonant with the Deuteronomic understanding of prophecy and quite unlike the Isaiah who pronounced a verdict of judgment on the Judean leadership. In this respect the narratives in 1–39 can be compared with the Deuteronomic editorial strand (Mowinckel's C source) in Jeremiah. (3) The same editor or compiler rearranged the incidents in the narrative appendix to bring the prediction of exile in Babylon (39:5–8) into juxtaposition with the good news proclaimed in 40:1–11. (4) Chapters 34–35 have more in common with the third than with the second part of the book and postdate the composition of 40–55. The insertion of 36–39, taken from the History, would then initially have followed directly, and appropriately, after 33:17–22, which foresees the defeat and disappearance from the scene of the hated Assyrians and the security of Jerusalem under the rule of Yahveh as king and his human representative. (5) Isaiah 40–55 is not a Deuteronomic text, needless to say, but its affinities with the Deuteronomic theology and agenda help to explain why it was attached to 1–39.

2. Isaiah 40–55 as Part of the Biblical Canon

ISAIAH 40–55 IS *CANONICALLY* INDEPENDENT OF ISAIAH 1–39

The issue of the canonicity of Isa 40–55 is inseparable from the matter discussed in the previous section—that is, the relationship of chs. 40–55 to chs. 1–39. Critical commentators in the modern period reject a solution based on unity of authorship not, as conservative scholars sometimes claim, because they exclude the possibility of genuine prophetic prediction but because the attribution of chs. 40–55 to an eighth-century B.C.E. prophet leads to logical and theological absurdity. The conquests of Cyrus are not presented as a prediction similar to the prediction of exile in 39:5–7 but as the fulfillment of earlier predictions and a pledge of future well-being. It would moreover be unprecedented for a prophet, actively engaged in politics during the high point of Neo-Assyrian aggression, to console his fellow-Judeans living two centuries later for disasters not yet in view. We might also ask, especially in view of the remarks made earlier about authorship and book production during the biblical period, why anonymous authors should be denied access to divine inspiration.

The tendency of exponents of canonical criticism to focus on the final form of biblical books led to the conclusions about chs. 40–55 referred to earlier. It also leads to irreconcilable tensions between theology and criticism. Once chs. 40–66 are attached to 1–39, "Chapters 40ff are now understood as a prophetic word of promise offered to Israel by the eighth-century prophet Isaiah of Jerusalem" (Childs 1979, 325). This seems to imply that we must affirm theologically what we know not to be the case critically; or, alternatively, that we are invited to pretend that Isaiah of Jerusalem was the author of the entire book after all. Childs, in fact, comes as close as possible to unity of authorship without actually affirming it by suggesting that Second Isaiah probably never circulated independently of First Isaiah as it then existed (Childs 1979, 329).

It seems that none of these rather tortuous conclusions necessarily follows from accepting chs. 40–55 as a canonical text. Whatever we decide about this particular case, a biblical book is not necessarily a well-thought-out, cohesive literary unit, and there is no need to make *the book* the only appropriate object of theological reflection. One might as well conclude that the book of Leviticus is theologically unintelligible detached from its context in the Pentateuch. Recontextualizing a literary unit like Leviticus or Isa 40–55 can add new increments or levels of meaning without depriving the unit of meanings—*canonical* meanings—proper to itself. Dostoyevsky's *Brothers Karamazov* was conceived as the first volume of a two-part work entitled *Memoirs of a Great Sinner*, but few would argue that it cannot be read by itself with profit, pleasure and edification.

It is also a fact that Isa 40–55 never actually functioned canonically in the way postulated by Childs. Early Christian writers made ample use of these chapters, considerably more than 1–39, without feeling obliged to refer their interpretations to 1–39 (for example, the Suffering Servant of 52:13–53:12). Even when the Isaiah whose name is in the superscription (1:1; 2:1) was acknowledged as the author of a passage in chs. 40–55, there is no indication that this made any difference in the way it was read. Likewise in the Jewish exegetical tradition, the relation between the two parts of the book had no influence on the way texts from 40–55 were interpreted or appropriated.

ISAIAH 40–55 IN LATTER PROPHETS

Isaiah is one of four books constituting the Latter Prophets. The conventional order (Isaiah, Jeremiah, Ezekiel, and the Twelve) differs from that of the LXX (The Twelve, Isaiah, Jeremiah, Ezekiel) and from the sequence in *b. B. Bat.* 14b–5a (Jeremiah, Ezekiel, Isaiah, the Twelve). The order does not seem to be significant, though *Baba Batra* serves to recall that in Isaiah's compositional history it is closer to the Twelve than to the other two major prophets. To these four correspond the four books in the Former Prophets (Joshua, Judges, Samuel, and Kings). That both tetrads are categorized as prophecy is a result of the developments and transformations to which prophecy was subject beginning in the biblical period, including the idea of prophetic historiography. Writing in the late first century C.E., Josephus (*Ag. Ap.* 1.38–42) referred to thirteen books composed by prophets, covering the history from the death of Moses to the reign of Artaxerxes. These would be Job, Daniel, Esther, Ezra–Nehemiah, and Chronicles, in addition to the eight just mentioned. Together with the "five fifths of Torah" and the four books containing hymns and precepts, these constituted for Josephus a closed collection, since for him the prophetic succession (*diadochē*) came to an end during the reign of the Persian ruler Artaxerxes. This would have been Artaxerxes I (465–425 B.C.E.), who was for Josephus the Ahasuerus (Asueros) of the book of Esther; and according to his chronological scheme Esther was the last scriptural book (*Ant.* 11.184–296). On this view, then, the canonical period and therefore the prophetic succession is coterminous with the biblical period.

According to Josephus the entire biblical canon is prophetically inspired, and he is quite explicit that prophecy includes laws and history. To the prophets alone, he tells us, was reserved the privilege of writing history since they obtained their knowledge of the past through divine inspiration. In viewing prophecy as confined to the period between Moses and Artaxerxes, and therefore essentially a thing of the past, he anticipates the many rabbinic statements about the end of prophecy (*sôp hannĕbû'â* e.g. *b. B. Bat.* 12a; *b. Yoma* 21b; *b. Sanh.* 11a). Writing in the early second century B.C.E., Sirach (Jesus ben Sira) treats of biblical prophets in a series of brief biographical sketches beginning with Moses and Joshua (Sir 46:1) and ending with the Twelve (49:10). Isaiah is mentioned exclusively in association with Hezekiah, as intercessor, counselor to the king, visionary, healer and miracle worker; in other words, as a typical "man of God." From the point of view of canonicity, the interesting point is that it is this same Isaiah who also predicted the future, even the end of time, and comforted the mourners in Zion (Sir 48:20–25). Since this allusion is clearly to Isa 40:1 ("Comfort, O comfort my people") and 61:3, which refer to those who mourn in Zion, Sirach must have read the book in the form in which it then existed, as one text composed by one prophetic author. At the same time, his comments are confined to the narrative epilogue (36–39) and, at least partially, to 40–66. Isaiah is therefore a holy man comparable to Elijah, Elisha, and others of whom we read in the History, and any allusion to his numerous pronouncements of judgment, assuming they were in the text at his disposal, were passed over in silence.

Sirach would presumably have been acquainted with Chronicles (*dibrê hayyāmîm*) written rather less than two centuries earlier, probably in the final decades of Persian rule. In Chronicles, Isaiah is featured only in connection with Hezekiah and then only in a minor and ancillary role, as involved with the king in intercessory prayer (2 Chr 32:20). Unlike the Isaiah of the History, he is not called upon by the king during the crisis of Sennacherib's campaign, and he does not predict success. The king is healed after offering a prayer himself, he receives a sign but not from Isaiah (32:24), and there is no prediction of exile in Babylon following the visit of the Babylonian envoys, an event that is mentioned only in passing (32:31). On the other hand, and surprisingly, Isaiah emerges in Chronicles as the historian of the reigns of Uzziah (2 Chr 26:22) and Hezekiah in a work entitled "Isaiah's Vision" (*ḥăzôn yĕša ʿyāhû* 32:32).

The author of Chronicles therefore is working with a prophetic profile very different from what is usually associated with the canonical prophets, who preached the absolute need for moral regeneration and condemned, often in the most absolute terms, their contemporaries and the ruling class in particular. The essential features of this profile in Chronicles can be shown to originate in Deuteronomic writings, Deuteronomy itself and the History in particular. Deuteronomy redefines prophecy by bringing it into close association with the person and work of Moses, subjecting its exercise to rigorous criteria, and bringing it within the confines of the state and its agencies (Deut 18:15–22).

In the History the canonical prophets are conspicuous by their absence, a supportive prophet, Jonah ben Amittai, has replaced Amos (2 Kgs 14:25), and an equally supportive Isaiah offers intercessory prayer together with Hezekiah, predicts the survival of Judah and defeat of the Assyrians, heals, works a miracle, and announces exile in Babylon in the more distant future (2 Kgs 19–20). We have seen that this profile came to be juxtaposed with the Isaiah of the pronouncements of judgment in the book of Isaiah, and that a Deuteronomic editor may have been responsible for linking chapters 40–55 with the expanded version of Isaiah's sayings. From the canonical point of view, the effect of both procedures was to recontextualize Isaiah's radical critique of his society and its leaders without eliminating it and therefore to suggest a new reading of the past in the light of a new situation. The message is that judgment is an ever-present reality but it is not the last word.

The Deuteronomic redefinition of prophecy is the point of departure for the transformations to which prophecy was subject in the post-destruction period, the effects of which are registered in Chronicles, Sirach, and Josephus. Prophecy becomes essentially a past phenomenon enshrined in written texts. The prophet (*nābîʾ*) is no longer the one who makes claims of a peremptory nature in the religious and political sphere but a preacher, a counselor, a liturgical practitioner, a historian, or an interpreter of earlier prophecies. Increasingly in this later period the pronouncements of judgment that survived are reinterpreted or recontextualized in keeping with a changed situation. It is at this point of development that prophetic "books" begin to be produced.

WHEN DID ISAIAH BECOME CANONICAL?

The first stage in the interpretation of a biblical book is the recovery from the book itself of expansive or corrective comments and glosses of different kinds. At a certain point, however, this kind of comment was no longer being inserted into the text but necessarily took the form of commentary apart from it. This is the first clear indication that a book had achieved authoritative or canonical status. The earliest extant commentaries on Isaiah are the two or more Qumran *pĕšārîm* recoverable from several fragments from Caves 3 and 4 (4QpIsa^{a-e} and 3QpIsa = 4Q161–65 and 3Q4), but the complete *Isaiah Scroll* from the first cave (1QIsa[a]) shows that the text was already more or less fixed, probably no later than the mid–second century B.C.E. The very paraphrastic Old Greek version may be somewhat earlier. We saw earlier that Sirach was familiar with material from both major sections of the book. He thereby implicitly acknowledges that there was at that time just one book, though it does not follow that it had reached canonical closure by that time.

More significant is Sirach's naming of Isaiah, Jeremiah, Ezekiel, and the Twelve in sequence (48:23–25; 49:6–10), which suggests that the literary construct known as the Latter Prophets was in existence *in some form* at the time of writing—that is, the early second century B.C.E. In his eulogy on Elijah, Sirach speaks of the great prophet's return at the appointed time to bring together the household of Israel and restore the tribes of Jacob (Sir 48:10–11). This is a paraphrase of the final paragraph of Malachi, which is also the finale to the Twelve and to the Latter Prophets as a whole (Mal 3:23–24[4:5–6]).

The implication appears to be that the prophetic compilation as a whole is to be read as testifying to the final and eschatological reintegration of a twelve-tribal Israel. Efforts that had to be made to maintain the number at twelve in the *Dodekapropheton*, including the creation of a fictitious Malachi and the attachment of two anonymous sections to Zechariah (Zech 9–11, 12–14), give the twelve-tribe message concrete symbolic expression. It would then be a short step to reading the 3 + 12 structure of the Latter Prophets as representing the three ancestors and the twelve sons of Jacob-Israel—in other words, as the ingathered Israel of the end time, to which the prophetic books in their final form beckon.

We can therefore conclude that the book of Isaiah was essentially complete and intact by the early second century B.C.E., during the first decades of Seleucid rule. But what is of special interest for the understanding of canon is the presence within this final form of different and sometimes conflicting ideological or theological points of view, including the point of view of the author of chs. 40–55. In this respect Isaiah reproduces on a smaller scale an important feature of the biblical canon as a whole.

The biblical canon represents a resolution of conflicting claims to authority in the religious sphere not by elimination but by juxtaposition, what has been called "neutralizing by addition" (for this term, see Sandmel 1961). Canonicity is generally taken to imply normativity and, as such, to justify mandatory acquiescence in a comprehensive and internally consistent religious orthodoxy. But what we are seeing in Isaiah leads us to conclude that normativity is not at all a straightforward concept and that there are tensions within what counts as normative that cannot be ignored. Accepting and working through these tensions would, one suspects, lead to a richer and fuller theological appreciation of the biblical canons by the faith communities in which they function.

3. THE LITERARY CHARACTER OF ISAIAH 40–55

STRUCTURE

The internal arrangement or structure of any text can provide important clues to meaning. This is especially the case with ancient texts, more closely tied as they are to traditional forms of expression. The identification of structural features is a more complex operation in texts, such as the book of Isaiah, that have been subjected to multiple redactions and therefore, more often than not, multiple restructurings. Uncovering the structures in such texts calls for something similar to the ground plans of archaeological sites that exhibit successive strata by means of superimposed transparencies. It is therefore unlikely that any one theory will account for the way that the material in chs. 40–55 is presented. With this proviso, we may note some of the more obvious surface features of Isa 40–55, deferring more detailed consideration to the commentary.

That 40:1 marks a new beginning, with the announcement of the end of penal servitude (that is, exile), predicted in the passage immediately preceding, can be taken as certain. The conclusion of the section is flagged with the prediction of a new exodus that serves to bracket the section (55:12–13 cf. 40:3–5). More significantly, the central theme of the permanent validity of the word of God communicated through the prophet is reiterated (55:10–11 cf. 40:8):

For as the rain and the snow fall from the sky,
nor return there without watering the ground . . .
so is it with my word that issues from my mouth:
it does not return to me empty
but accomplishes what I purpose
and achieves what I send it to do.

This validation of God's word, more than anything else, is what is at stake throughout this section of the book.

It is also possible that the entire final chapter of the section (55:1–13) was meant as a summary of the message of chs. 40–54. The implication would be that, at a certain stage in the transmission of the material, 54:17b, which speaks of the heritage of the Servants of Yahveh, functioned as the conclusion to 49–54, which opens with an address by the Servant. It could at the same time have functioned as a prelude to 54–66, in which these Servants, understood as the disciples of *the* Servant, play an important role.

Most commentators agree that chs. 40–48, which are bracketed with their own inclusive passage (48:20–22 cf. 40:3–5), form a section that is quite different in theme and tone from 49–55 in which we hear no more about Cyrus and the fall of Babylon, and no more satire is directed against foreign deities and their devotees. In 40–48 the focus is on Jacob/Israel, while in 49–55 Jerusalem/Zion is in the foreground. Less obviously but no less importantly, usage of the key term *ʿebed* (servant) is significantly different in the two sections. With the exception of 42:1–4 (the first of Duhm's *Dichtungen)* use of *ʿebed* in 40–48, whether in the singular or plural, always refers to the people or, at any rate, never to an individual (41:8–9; 42:19; 43:8–10; 44:1–2, 21, 26; 45:4; 48:20), whereas in 49–55 it is generally acknowledged that an individual figure is indicated (49:1–6; 50:4–11; 52:13–53:12). This circumstance will alert us to the possibility that 42:1–4 may call for an interpretation quite different from that of the passages in 49–55 (see the commentary on 42:1–4).

The marked contrast between chs. 40–48 and 49–55 was taken a stage further by some early commentators, who concluded that the two sections must derive from distinct authors. Thomas Kelly Cheyne (1882, 178) concluded that "the original prophecy ended at xlviii.22 and the remainder of the book grew up by degrees under a less persistent flame of inspiration." Among more recent scholars, K. Kiesow (1979) is one of the few who have followed their lead. But most would agree that the texts do not give us confident access to questions of authorship or allow us to make definitive distinctions between prophetic author and disciple, and that, in any case, the differences of theme and mood could very well be explained in terms of stages in one prophetic career (e.g. Carol Stuhlmueller 1980, 1–29). At any rate, we can agree with Hermisson that Jacob and Zion, as male and female personifications, respectively, belong intimately together and that the issue of authorship is not the best point from which to launch our inquiry (Hermisson 1998b, 117–23, 148–49).

The division into two sections, chs. 40–48 and 49–55, is complicated by the parallel to 40:3–5 and 48:20–22 in 52:11–12 ("Away! Away! Go thence . . ."), especially since both 48:20–22 and 52:11–12 are followed by a passage dealing with a prophetic Servant (49:1–6; 52:13–53:12). In 49–55 we note a fairly regular alternation of apostrophes to Jerusalem with passages dealing with this Servant:

servant passage followed by comment (49:1–13)

apostrophe to Zion with comment (49:14–50:3)

servant passage with comment (50:4–51:8)

apostrophe to (the arm of) Yahveh (51:9–11)

remnant of another servant passage (51:12–16)

apostrophe to Jerusalem (51:17–52:10)

summons to depart Babylon (52:11–12)

servant passage containing comment (52:13–53:12)

apostrophe to Jerusalem as woman (54:1–17a)

Cheyne, cited above, thought that the summons in 52:11–12 looked like the original conclusion to the section. The alternation set out above and the situation of the summons in the sequence may suggest that this was in fact the case *at one stage of redaction.* The final passage about the Servant and the following apostrophe to Jerusalem might then appear to have been added subsequently.

Several of the recent commentators have noticed the structural significance of 52:11–12 but have drawn widely differing conclusions from it. Paul-Henri Plamondon (1982, 241–66) reads 40:12–52:12 as a unity presenting four successive stages in the restoration of Israel. Antti Laato (1990, 207–28) finds five subsections in 40:3–52:12, thus allowing for a chiastic arrangement; while Evode Beaucamp (1991), more plausibly, divides 40:11–52:12 into two parts, the first (40:11–49:13) concerned with Jacob/Israel, the second (49:14–52:12) with Jerusalem/Zion, the subordinate sections indicated by the final doxologies (42:10–12; 44:23; 49:13; 52:9–10). For Odil H. Steck (1992a, 149–72), finally, 52:7–10 is the conclusion of the core material in 40–48.

The confusing variety of structures and divisions in the commentaries suggests that a text such as Isa 40–55 can be scanned structurally in several different ways depending on which criteria are considered decisive. The layout in the commentary that follows is dictated by expediency—that is, the need to keep the pericopes to a reasonable length—but it also represents an attempt to weigh the relative importance to be assigned in each instance according to a range of criteria. To repeat, this represents *one* way of reading the text. In general, sense or subject matter trumps purely formal features since, for example, prophetic formulae ("thus says Yahveh" and the like) can appear within a passage, not just at the beginning or end (e.g. 49:22; 50:1; 52:3). Prophetic *incipits* (41:21; 43:1, 14; 44:6; 45:14; 49:7) and *excipits* (45:13) are nevertheless significant as marking off a particular passage, as are calls for attention (41:1; 42:18; 48:1, 12; 49:1; 51:1), hymn finales (42:10; 49:13), and a change either in speaker or the person addressed (40:9; 41:8; 42:1; 43:8, 22; 46:8; 51:9, 17).

RHETORICAL RESOURCES

Rhetoric is the art of persuading by the effective communication of a message in a particular situation. It involves developing an argument that articulates the speaker's intention and does so by deploying strategies for engaging the interest and emotions of the speaker's public and persuading them to accept the message. It may also involve the speaker's attempting, whether consciously or unconsciously, to persuade himself of the truth of the message.

Isaiah 40–55 is certainly argumentative in character, and on the reasonable assumption that it displays some elements of order and continuity, in spite of the vicissitudes of its editorial history, we might begin by attempting to identify the argument developed by the author. In doing so, we will not be surprised to find that it progresses unevenly and is occasionally sidetracked in one direction or another. A further clarification is in order—namely, that, though we are reading about the argument rather than hearing it, and granted the theoretical possibility of a *purely* written production, it at least reproduces the conventions of effective public speech.

The speaker begins by representing himself and his prophetic associates as authorized to address his public, and the source of the authorization is indicated right from the start ("says your God," 40:1). The frequent use of introductory and concluding formulas from the old prophetic tradition (e.g. "This is the word of Yahveh") keeps this ultimate authorization before the audience throughout. Stated at first in general terms, the message is about a new intervention of the God of Israel, one leading to a reversal of fortune for a beaten and dispirited people (40:9–11). In keeping with established rhetorical procedures in using the argument from authority (one of the six or seven standard types of argument in ancient rhetoric), the speaker goes on to establish the credentials of the one authorizing and does so by claiming for Yahveh a preeminent and incomparable status vis-à-vis other deities, in the first place as creator of the world (40:12–26). This first stage of the argument concludes, again in good rhetorical fashion, with a direct appeal to the hearers to accept the truth of what has been said and draw the appropriate consequences (40:27–31).

Once the ground has been prepared in this way, the speaker passes to the core of his message—namely, that the announced reversal of fortune is to be brought about by the instrumentality of a foreign conqueror (41:1–4, 25–29; 42:1–9). This idea is first insinuated without identifying the one who is to be the designated servant or agent of Yahveh (42:1–4). All that the hearers are told is that he is to come from the east (41:2, 25; cf. 46:11), and there are vague hints of far-reaching changes on the international scene, including the conquest of Egypt (43:3, but cf. 45:14).

Since the traditions with which the hearers are deemed to be familiar speak more often than not of foreign conquerors as agents of punishment ("Assyria, rod of my anger," Isa 10:5), the introduction of this idea of agency is prudently accompanied by many words of comfort and reassurance in keeping with the original commissioning (41:8–20; 43:1–7, 14–21; 44:18). The audience is also reminded redundantly of the ineffectiveness or nonexistence of foreign deities (41:21–24; 42:14–17) and are reassured of their own significance in the great scheme of things, in spite of appearances to the contrary (43:8–13).

The make-or-break point in the development of the argument is the introduction of the name of the Iranian Cyrus, designated as Yahveh's shepherd and anointed one, no less. Appropriately, this statement (44:24–45:7) occupies the center of chs. 40–48. We note how carefully it is anticipated. The speaker makes it clear that the designation of Cyrus for this role is not his, the speaker's, doing, but comes directly from the God of Israel. The statement itself is preceded by a list of ten attributes of Yahveh expressed in participial form, in which the emphasis is on his special relationship with Israel and the creation of the world (44:24–28). One of the ten describes Yahveh as the one who corroborates the pronouncements of his prophets and messengers (44:26). From this it follows that the hearers have every reason to believe that, when they finally hear about Cyrus's role, the message carries the greatest possible weight

(44:28). All of this is rounded off with a solemn, oracular statement about Cyrus and his mission (45:1–7).

After this point the situation becomes less clear on account of editorial activity and our ignorance of developments within the Judaic communities addressed by the speaker to which he is responding. Immediately following the Cyrus oracle, we begin to hear words of reproach addressed to an unresponsive public (45:9–13; 46:13; 48:1–11, 17–19), defense of the truthfulness of Yahveh (45:19; 48:16), and reassertion of the speaker's mission and credentials (48:16b). Even if some of these passages have been inserted editorially, we have the impression that the speaker's credibility is increasingly being called into question and that his strategy is not working out well, either because of the skepticism of his public about the idea in general or because of developments on the international scene that make it seem unlikely that Cyrus would live up to expectations. This seems to have led to the shift of direction that occupies the second half of our text (chs. 49–55). The interpretation adopted in this commentary is that the speaker saw the mission assigned to Cyrus as passing to himself by default but that by this time he had lost his audience, with the exception of a small number of disciples.

How does the author of 40–55 go about constructing and presenting his argument? Judged by the canons of rhetoric laid down by Quintilian and practiced in late antiquity the effect is not overwhelming, but it is impressive, nevertheless, and at a level hardly attainable without professional training of some kind. The author follows the method, familiar among rhetoricians, of arguing by analogy with legal proceedings, using a wide range of legal terminology, and presenting the conclusion of the argument in the form of a verdict handed down in a court of law (41:1– 5, 21–29; 43:8–15; 44:6–8; 45:20–23).

There are few themes repeated redundantly throughout the discourse. The author makes generous use of rhetorical questions, sometimes in the aggressive manner characteristic of cross-examination in a legal case (41:2, 4, 26; 43:9; 45:9–10), sometimes to shame his hearers into admitting something that he thinks ought to be obvious to them (40:21, 28), occasionally as a more interactive and didactic kind of communication, especially in appealing to their own experience (40:12–20, 25–26). Interest is heightened by frequent alternation of theme: for example, the Servant with Zion, Israel with foreign peoples and their gods. The well-tested homiletic tactic of alternating reassurance and censure is also in evidence (e.g. 42:18–25; 43:1–7). There are frequent calls for attention (e.g. 41:1; 44:1; 46:3, 12; 47:8; 48:1, 12) and apostrophes (e.g. to Zion, 52:1, and Yahveh's arm, 51:9). Repetition of words, phrases, and key images (for a list, see James Muilenburg 1956, 389) serves to heighten the emotional effect and sustain interest, beginning with the opening call to comfort Yahveh's people (40:1; see also 51:9; 52:1, 11).

Even to list and comment on the tropes and figures appearing throughout 40–55 would exceed the reasonable limits for a commentary of this kind. One could find in these chapters examples of practically all of the numerous types catalogued in books 8 and 9 of Quintilian's classic *Institutio Oratoria*. One or two examples will have to suffice. First, then, the use of striking imagery. Many of the more vivid images are borrowed from older poetic and prophetic texts: the God of Israel as the Rock (51:1), as a potter (45:9), Jerusalem as bride (49:18; 54:5), as a woman in labor (43:14), as a furnace for refining silver (48:9–11), the labor of salvation ending with a banquet of rich fare (55:1–2).

The way through the wilderness and the provision of life-giving water are among the master metaphors in these chapters (40:3–5; 48:20–21; 52:11–12; 55:12–13). They proved to be very persistent (cf. 57:14; 35:8–10; 30:21) and lived on in early Christianity, Qumranic Judaism, and beyond. Appeal to immemorial myth—the god's struggle to overcome the monsters of chaos and disorder (51:9–11)—has the effect of detaching the discourse about salvation and renewal from its historical particularities and giving it a universal scope; to paraphrase Plato, it is a form of theologizing by means of myth.

Examples of the author's skillful exploitation of the resources of the language on a smaller scale—alliteration, assonance, paronomasia, anaphora—will be presented in the commentary as the occasion presents itself.

The rhetorical enterprise of the author of Isa 40–55 raises the problem of the relation between written text and oral performance in an acute form. We must start from the written text because that is what we have, and it is a text that shows signs of redactional activity and contains literary types not easily reconciled with disputatious public speech—hymn stanzas, in particular (42:10–13; 44:23; 45:8; 49:13; 54:1). The conditions did not exist at that time for the large-scale production and dissemination of writing. Like all other biblical authors, the author of Isa 40–55 stood at the oral end of the orality-literacy continuum. (Susan Niditch 1996, 78–79). If therefore the prophetic author communicated in the first place through writing, we would have to assume some means for his pronouncements or sermons to be read at public gatherings.

The analogy of the Pauline letters read to churches around the Mediterranean rim comes to mind, but in antiquity all writing was meant to be heard, to be read out loud, and therefore writers would be drawn to use phenomena characteristic of oral delivery (see further Yehoshua Gitay 1980, 185–97; 1981). What mechanisms were available and which were actually involved in the interplay between oral performance and written text in the sixth-century B.C.E. Near East we unfortunately do not know. We possess none of the data available to Milman Parry and Albert B. Lord in their investigations of Serbo-Croatian epic. But in the absence of such data, it seems that we must postulate some institutional infrastructure, perhaps a kind of proto-synagogal network by means of which the prophet's message was circulated, perhaps in a succession of leaflets or flyers (*Flugblätter*).

We recall in this connection the elders gathering in Ezekiel's house (Ezek 8:1; 14:1; 20:1) and the religious center at Casiphia in southern Mesopotamia (Ezra 8:15–20), apparently a kind of clergy-training center, a small-scale counterpart to the Egyptian "house of life," where religious learning and training went on. It may be prudent to add that this does not decide the question of the original location of the prophet's activity. We know very little about the social situation of Jewish communities in either Babylon or Judah, but we know less about the latter than the former.

THE QUESTION OF LITERARY GENRES

The impetus to apply the study of literary genres, types, or *Gattungen* to biblical texts supplied by Hermann Gunkel (1862–1932) came to dominate critical writing on prophetic books, including Isa 40–55, during the first half of the nineteenth century. For Isa 40–55 the principal types have often been enumerated: oracle and proclamation of salvation, disputation and trial speech, hymn and thanksgiving psalm (see, inter al., Anton Schoors 1973, 1–31; Roy Melugin 1976, 1–7; Norman Whybray 1983, 22–39). In keeping with good form-critical method, the focus was on identifying and classifying the smallest literary units. In chs. 40–55 the count was anywhere from 40 to 70 but on average around 50, and this on the assumption that Second Isaiah is prophetic in much the same way as Amos, Micah, Isa 1–35, and other prophetic material from the time of the kingdoms.

Continuity with the older prophetic tradition was also assumed with respect to the basic types. These included units peculiar to the prophetic literature: threats, rebukes, and pronouncements of judgment (*Mahnworte, Scheltworte, Gerichtsworte*), the announcement of salvation (*Heilsorakel*), much more in evidence here than elsewhere, and messenger sayings (*Botensprüche*). Also listed were genres co-opted by and adapted to prophetic rhetoric—for example, hymns and disputations.

Without denying the real advances in understanding prophetic texts that we owe to these earlier form-critical studies on Isa 40–55, beginning with the work of Hugo Gressmann in 1914, who divided chs. 40–55 into 49 independent units, we can with hindsight detect problems affecting their work that they were unable to solve or of which they seem to have been for the most part unaware. We note, in the first place, an underestimation of the role of the author. In reading the studies of some of these early form critics—Ludwig Köhler (1923), who divided the text into 70 units, Paul Volz (1932) with 50, or even Otto Eissfeldt (*The Old Testament: An Introduction*, 1966), also with 50—we have the impression that the *Gattungen* are like so many unattached and juxtaposed monads. This approach is understandable, since form criticism was introduced as a way of identifying types of verbal communication at the preliterary and subliterary stage—at a stage, in other words, in which the idea of an individual author recedes into the background. For it to be serviceable in the context of literary activity in the Near East at the time of the composition of Isa 40–55, some serious adjustments would be called for.

We also detect a kind of form-critical positivism that tends to assume a direct correspondence between *Gattung* and social setting (*Sitz im Leben*). One of the most influential contributions to the form-critical study of Isa 40–55 was

Joachim Begrich's identification of the priestly salvation oracle (*das priesterliche Heilsorakel*) which, according to Begrich, in its original form was pronounced by a priest during a Temple service in response to a lament uttered by a pious Israelite. Begrich (1934) read the corresponding passages in Isa 40–55 (41:8–13, 14–16; 43:1–4, 5–7; etc.) as literary imitations of the genre, but Hans-Eberhard von Waldow (1953) took them to have been actually delivered in situ by the author of 40–55 in his capacity not as priest but as cultic prophet, a conclusion for which the text provides absolutely no evidence.

This idea of the cult as a creative matrix for prophetic writings, and for these chapters in particular, was popular at one time, especially with Scandinavian scholars. Though rarely without its advocates (e.g. more recently, J. M. Vincent 1977; John Eaton 1979), it never secured a significant following.

It seems that a more nuanced approach to these prophetic genres, or sous-genres, is now called for, one that would take the frequent residual forms, or *Gattungen*, in Isaiah 40–55 as indicative of the constraints of the literary tradition in which the author or authors spoke or wrote. As is the case with all works of literary art, the tradition in which the writer stands dictates the form assumed by the writer's individual genius. The identification of the forms, therefore, assists in highlighting the balance between tradition and originality characteristic of all significant literary works. This broader approach has seldom been adopted, perhaps partly because most Old Testament form critics were not well equipped as literary critics or widely read outside of their own discipline. It is also a fact that the so-called Second Isaiah was not a prophet in the same way that the author of the core of chapters 1–35 was a prophet or that any of the other great prophetic figures from the time of the kingdoms were.

The author's awareness of this prophetic tradition and his links with it are expressed in frequent use of prophetic incipits and excipits (*kōh ʾāmar YHVH*, *nĕʾum YHVH*, etc.), but these are attached to forms of speech that are quite different from the old prophecy. One explanation for the change, apart from the very different political and social situation existing in the second half of the sixth century B.C.E., is the appearance on the scene in the meantime of a new category of public speakers, or preachers, probably correlative with the emergence of the Levitical class. New and more sustained forms of public discourse must have developed to correspond to them. Among the best examples are the discourses or sermons in Deuteronomy and in the sections of Jeremiah that are usually attributed to a Deuteronomic editor. We take it as a positive sign that, while form-criticism has by no means run its course, in the study of chs. 40–55 attention has shifted to a consideration of the work as a piece of sustained rhetoric within which traditional forms of speech are used, often in original and imaginative ways, to move the argument forward.

ISAIAH 40–55: POETRY OR PROSE?

The widespread assumption that the author of chs. 40–55 wrote as a poet is reinforced by the layout of the text in our printed Hebrew Bibles, with only about five percent in prose and the rest in verse. Since this arrangement goes back no further than the early Middle Ages, it clearly does not settle the issue. Though some Qumran texts, or at least 4QPs[b], are written stychographically as verse, the earliest complete manuscript of Isaiah, the scroll from Cave 1 (1QIsa[a]), is written continuously, as are the surviving fragments of other copies of the book discovered at or near Qumran.

Setting aside the more rigid and metronomic systems of Hebrew verse structure of Gustav-Wilhelm Bickell, Karl Budde, Eduard Sievers, and others, no longer in favor (see Eissfeldt 1966, 57–64), scholars have nevertheless generally taken for granted that section 40–55 is poetry. Torrey (1928, 151–204), for example, did a fairly thorough study of the prosody of his Second Isaiah (chs. 34–35, 40–66), emphasizing the dominance of a 3–3 and 3–2 accentual pattern. At the same time, he held up to ridicule the practice of emending the text exclusively on the basis of prosodic irregularity in an amusing "emendation" of Tennyson's poem "Crossing the Bar" (1928, 180–81), though in fact he was himself by no means immune to this temptation. In spite of his salutary emphasis on rhetoric, James Muilenburg (1956, 384–93) also read chs. 40–55 as a sequence of poetic strophes or stanzas. It has also become second nature to refer to Duhm's four servant passages as songs or poems (*Lieder, Dichtungen*), a curious practice, since it should at least be clear that, whatever else they are, they are not songs.

It would perhaps be pedantic to deny the designation *poetry* to Isa 40–55 in the broad sense in which the term is often used for any stylistically elevated or emotionally charged writing or utterance. In his introduction to the Pocket Canon *Book of Isaiah*, the British novelist and biographer Peter Ackroyd makes the same point, observing that "the words of Isaiah are neither prose nor poetry but, rather, a series of incandescent utterances which effortlessly find their true form," and he quotes Coleridge to the effect that, "wherever passion was, the language became a sort of metre."

The distinction in the biblical context between prose and poetry is in truth somewhat arbitrary and can be misleading. It is not just because these literary categories were unnamed and unknown during the biblical period. The most basic characteristic of Hebrew verse is parallelism (the *parallelismus membrorum* of Robert Lowth's *De Sacra Poesi Hebraeorum*, 1753), but the same phenomenon occurs in cadenced prose as in compositions indubitably written in verse—the canonical psalms, for example. Other features usually associated with verse appear regularly in the kind of elevated, declamatory style characteristic of Isa 40–55. Both verse and this heightened kind of prose can be notably rhythmic and accented to different degrees of regularity, frequency, and intensity.

The rhythmic texture of Hebrew verse forms a basic pattern of tricola and bicola in different combinations. If, for example, we analyze the twenty-one lines of verse in Isa 40:1–11 as set out in BHS (omitting *ʾākēn ḥāṣîr hāʿām*, "surely the people is but grass," 7b, as a gloss), we discover that nine are in the 3–2 rhythmic pattern, four in 2–2, and the remainder in different combinations:

3–3, 2–3, 3–4, 3–3–3, 4–4, 4–2. There is therefore a degree of regularity but not to the extent usually expected of verse composition.

At the other end of the continuum, Torrey (1928, 236–37, 344–45) claims that the tirade against the manufacture of idols (44:9–20), set out as verse in BHS but as prose in most modern versions, is metrically no different from the preceding chapters. Take, for example, his translation of 44:12:

> The ironsmith cuts out the metal, / and fashions it over the coals;
> With hammers he gives it shape, / forges it with his mighty arm.
> Yea, he hungers, and is wearied; / he has tasted no water, and is faint.

Whether we agree with Torrey in this instance or not, there is enough prosodic indeterminacy in these chapters to justify speaking of their author as orator rather than poet in the more specific sense of a composer of verse. The orator, trained in an elevated, declamatory style of public speaking, makes use of as wide a range of linguistic resources as the poet. A close reader of these chapters will note a variety of rhetorical strategies involving repetition of a type that allows for subtle differentiation, often in triadic structure.

Take, for example, the three noun clauses in Isa 40:2:

> *kî mālĕʾāh ṣĕbāʾāh*
>
> *kî nirṣāh ʿăvônāh*
>
> *kî lāqĕḥāh miyyad* YHVH
>
> *kiplayim bĕkol-ḥaṭṭōʾtêhā*
>
> (. . . that her servitude is over,/ her debt has been paid;/ she has received at Yahveh's hand/ double for all her sins.)

This triadic structure is a typical communicative resource of oratorical "high utterance." Compare the well-known line from Lincoln's Gettysburg funerary oration: "in a larger sense, we cannot dedicate, we cannot consecrate, we cannot hallow this ground."

Rhetorical questions often have a similar arrangement, with the purpose of achieving a cumulatively persuasive effect on those addressed. Psalm 94:9–10 may serve as an example:

> Can he who planted the ear not hear?
> Can he who fashioned the eye not see?
> Can he who instructs the nations not admonish?

Rhetorically, this is no different from Isa 40:12–14a, with its threefold repetition of the interrogative pronoun, and quite similar to other series of rhetorical questions in these chapters. I conclude that most of 40–55 lies somewhere between what is clearly discursive prose on the one hand (e.g. 52:3–6) and generically identifiable poetic composition on the other (e.g. the hymn stanzas, 42:10–13; 44:23; 45:8; 49:13). The core of 40–55 may then properly be described as a rhetorical composition and its author as an orator or preacher.

4. The Formation of Isaiah 40–55

How the Issue of the Formation of Isaiah 40–55 Arose

As long as the book of Isaiah, in existence more or less as we have it since the second century B.C.E., was taken to be one undivided composition from one author, the issue of its formation, a fortiori the formation of any one part of it, did not and could not arise. Insistence on the authorial unity of the book sprang from a theory of divine inspiration directly affecting *named* individual writers rather than texts. The concept did not therefore allow for the possibility, which to us must seem theologically unexceptionable, that there could be inspired biblical authors who were anonymous. Doubts began to arise only when the reader was confronted with an evident impossibility or absurdity: for example, that Moses, author of the Pentateuch, wrote a circumstantial account of his own death and burial (Deut 34:1–12); or that Samuel, as author of the book that bears his name, wrote the phrase "and Samuel died" (1 Sam 25:1). This last instance is cited by Abraham Ibn Ezra (1092–1167) to make the point that a writer other than Isaiah must have written about Cyrus and the Babylonian exile. In deference to what he calls "the opinion of the orthodox," he makes the point indirectly in his commentary on Isa 40, and he concludes urbanely with the remark that "the reader will adopt the opinion which recommends itself most to his judgment."

In the event, Ibn Ezra's suggestion was not taken up, and it was left to one Johann Christoph Döderlein, Professor at the University of Altdorf, to detach Isa 40–66 from 1–39, initially in a somewhat tentative way in 1781, then more confidently in the third edition of his commentary on Isaiah in 1789, the year of the French Revolution. The third volume of Johann Gottlieb Eichhorn's monumental *Einleitung in das Alte Testament*, which appeared in 1783, also abandoned the idea of one author. Eichhorn defended the order of the Latter Prophets in *b. B. Bat.* 14a, in which Isaiah is located after Jeremiah and Ezekiel and next to the Twelve, and did so on the grounds that both Isaiah and the Twelve are essentially anthologies of prophetic material produced over a period of several centuries. "Isaiah" is therefore one of those *Kollektivnamen*, like Moses, Solomon and David. As a major part of that anthology, chs. 40–52 were composed in the Babylonian exile in the sixth century B.C.E.

Both Döderlein and Eichhorn were probably influenced by the publication of the German translation of Robert Lowth's commentary on Isaiah in 1781, in which the German editor, Johann Koppe, denied several passages to Isaiah. All of this discussion was part of a broader and often acrimonious debate in late-eighteenth- and early-nineteenth-century German universities between critical biblical scholars and conservative dogmatic theologians, whose principal representative in the first half of the nineteenth century was Ernst Wilhelm Hengstenberg (1802–1869). From Eichhorn's point of view, the goal was to free critical inquiry from the agenda and constraints of dogmatic theology. The distinctive profile of Isa 40–66 emerged clearly in the three-volume commentary of Wilhelm Gesenius published in Leipzig in 1821, one volume of which was dedicated to these chapters. For Gesenius, Isa 40–66 was the longest of several pseudepigraphical compositions in the book, the product of one prophetic author, with his own distinctive agenda.

For both the book of Isaiah and the Pentateuch, Eichhorn's *Einleitung* (1780–1783) marked the beginning of a new phase of historical-critical scholarship and dictated the agenda of the study of the Old Testament throughout the nineteenth century. Without a doubt, the most influential of all commentaries on Isaiah is the one by Bernhard Duhm, the first edition of which appeared in 1892. As far as we know, Duhm was the first to assign chs. 56–66 to a separate author, to whom he gave the title Trito-Isaiah. The case is not argued at any length (see §§24, 25, 33 of his introduction), but Duhm read these chapters as the production of one author, active a generation or so before Nehemiah's administrative and religious reforms.

The considerable linguistic and thematic overlap of Isa 56–66 with 40–55 attest not to authorial unity, as some claimed, but to continuity in interpretative activity. In general, Duhm held firm views on individual biblical authors and was prepared to say when and where they lived. Thus, Isa 40–55, with the exception of the *Ebedlieder*, was composed by an author somewhere in Phoenicia, approximately 540 B.C.E.; the *Ebedlieder* (42:1–4, 49:1–6, 50:4–9, 52:13–53:12) were also composed by one author, some time later but before the composition of 56–66; and the author of 56–66 wrote in Jerusalem, shortly before the time of Nehemiah.

Duhm's division of 56–66 from 40–55 seems to have stood the test of time, though there have been occasional dissenters (Charles Cutler Torrey 1928; James D. Smart 1965) and doubters (Christopher R. Seitz 1992, 501–7). The separation was dictated primarily by Duhm's conviction that these chapters reflect a different and later situation: a community is being addressed that is well established, the temple has been rebuilt, people are going about their business sacrificing, fasting, and engaging in other religious practices, and there are clear signs of internecine conflict and division. And, indeed, once we begin reading 56:1–8, we immediately have the impression of a quite different agenda with a different background from that of the preceding section.

The division into Second and Third Isaiah has, then, been generally accepted (e.g. Whybray 1975, 196) and was confirmed by Karl Elliger's demonstration of the distinctive linguistic features of 56–66 in contrast to 40–55 (Elliger 1928). Duhm's dating of this last section of the book has not been generally accepted, however, nor has his insistence on its authorial unity, but these are issues that can be more properly dealt with in the third volume of this commentary.

COHERENCE OR FRAGMENTATION?

The problem that Isa 40–55 presented to these scholars of an earlier age, and still presents to us, is how to reconcile the evidence for coherence and continuity of argument noted in the previous section with the discontinuities and often rather jerky transitions from one type of discourse to another, phenomena that led to the form-critical fragmentation exemplified in the studies of Gressmann, Köhler, Mowinckel, and others. Like most prophetic texts, Isa 40–55 is intransigently non-self-referential and, therefore, in the absence of a transcript of the author's speeches or sermons, the problem with which we are faced is likely to remain unsolved.

By way of comparison and illustration, we might consider Haggai, whose sayings are dated no more than a quarter of a century after Second Isaiah. Features that both texts have in common are the use of conventional prophetic formulas ("thus says Yahveh," "the word of Yahveh came to Haggai," etc.); encouragement and promise tempered with reproach; a degree of interactivity with the audience; and a strong focus on an individual, Zerubbabel, designated the Servant (*ʿebed*) of Yahveh (Hag 2:23; at one stage, Ernst Sellin argued that Zerubbabel *was* the Isaian Servant). If they are in any sense authentic, the words attributed to Haggai, which can be read in a matter of seconds, cannot be actual addresses but must be brief abstracts of what he said or was believed to have said or what someone thought he should have said, possibly the editor who provided the equally brief chronological framework.

This suggests one possible scenario for Isa 40–55: an associate or disciple wrote from memory, some time after delivery and in greatly abbreviated form, what the master had said, adding his own comments and arranging the material in as orderly a fashion as he could. Whether this was done at one time and in one format, or sequentially in separate batches (five according to Rosario P. Merendino 1981) we can only speculate.

The question facing the interpreter, then, is to decide whether the text is coherent and homogeneous enough for him or her to posit a theory of authorial or at least redactional unity of some kind. The issue can be pursued either synchronically, by a consideration of the internal arrangement of the text irrespective of how it came to be the way it is, or diachronically, by attempting to reconstruct the stages by which it reached its present form. Hermisson (1998, 134) suggested that Isaiah is analogous to an ancient church or cathedral: it may appear from the outside to be a harmonious work of art, and can certainly be appreciated as such, but it probably incorporates many additions and restructurings in different styles (Romanesque, Early English, etc.) and from different centuries.

On this issue of the process of formation, the reader will not be surprised to hear that practically every conceivable position has been adopted in the modern period. Since to survey this literature would be excessively lengthy as well as tedious, some examples from the most recent phase of inquiry must suffice. There are commentators who, while admitting the variety of genres, are more impressed by the unity of the composition (e.g. P. E. Bonnard 1972, 28–36; Jan L. Koole 1997, 14–18, 33–36), while others either show little interest in the process of formation (e.g. John L. McKenzie 1968, xxxi–xxxvii) or doubt whether it is possible to say much about it (Roy Melugin 1976, 82). Norman Whybray's position (1975, 26–29) is puzzling due to the fact that he is impressed by Deutero-Isaiah's "massive religious and theological unity" and also claims that the multiplicity of short units put together by an editor did not amount to "a satisfactory structure suggestive of a coherent plan."

At the other end of the spectrum, Merendino's lengthy study of chapters 40–48 (1981), and of several individual passages in 40–55 falls back on the kind of documentary division of passages and individual verses once prevalent in the study of the Pentateuch but no longer in favor. In Isa 50:4–9a, 10 (the third Servant text), for example, the *Urtext*, which is not from Deutero-Isaiah, is said to consist in 4a (without *lĕšôn limmûdîm* and *lā ʿût ʾet-yā ʿēp*), 5aβb, 7aβ, 7bα, 8aαβ, 8b, and 9a, to which are aggregated four later editorial stages (Merendino, 1985b). Merendino traces the Deutero-Isaian core back to five small collections of sayings representing an abstract of the prophet's preaching, to which were added a universalizing strand, represented by ch. 45, a wisdom strand, a polemic against the cult of images, and numerous individual passages. This type of "literary criticism," now largely discredited, is arbitrary in the extreme and does little to advance our understanding of the text.

The Deutero-Isaian nucleus is even further reduced by Jacques Vermeylen (1978, 1989) but without the degree of fragmentation demanded by Merendino. In Vermeylen's view, the core consists in the Cyrus sayings exclusively, to which expansions and *relectures* were added over the course of time. This corpus was then attached to First Isaiah about the time of Nehemiah (mid–fifth century B.C.E.), and the anti-idolatry material and passages dealing with the destiny of the Gentile world, present in all three parts of the book, were added even later.

In numerous studies published over the last quarter of a century, Odil H. Steck has presented a complex and elaborate hypothesis on the formation of the second part of the book. For our present purpose the main lines seem to be the following: The Zion theme in chs. 49–53 developed in three stages as a *Fortschreibung* of the Deutero-Isaian core, recoverable from 40–48 + 52:7–10, inclusive of the *ʿebed* passages. These three redactional stages are spaced out during the period from the fall of Babylon to the time of Haggai and Zechariah, therefore 539 to 520 B.C.E. The Cyrus references appeared only in the early years of the reign of Darius I, from 520 to 515. At a later date, around the mid–fifth century, the *ʿebed* was reinterpreted to refer to the Judeo-Babylonian element. At the time of the final redaction of the book (ca. 270 B.C.E.), the

ʿebed came to stand for the devout minority whose voice is heard in the final section of the book.

Some aspects of this hypothetical reconstruction reappeared in the dissertation of Reinhard Gregor Kratz (1991), a student of Steck, who divided the literary evolution of Isa 40–55 into five stages, beginning with the *Grundschrift*, which was recovered by the same methods and consisted of 40:1–52:10.

ARRANGEMENT IN LARGE UNITS

In spite of the current confused situation on this subject with respect to both method and results, of which some few indications have just been given, a commentator on the text cannot avoid responsibility for stating some conclusions of his own, however tentative. We cannot recover the origin of the process that eventuated in Isa 40–55, and we do not have access to an author, though occasionally throughout these chapters we do hear the authorial first person, beginning with the question, "What shall I proclaim?" (40:6). Near the conclusion of the first major section of chs. 40–55, the voice breaks in again, only to trail off: "and now the sovereign Lord Yahveh has sent me, and his spirit . . ." (48:16b). What is involved in this sense of mission is further revealed in the words of the prophetic Servant (49:1–6; 50:1–9). One indication that his voice is the same as the speaker in 48:16b is the otherwise rarely attested use of the designation "the sovereign Lord Yahveh" (50:4, 5, 7, 9) in the second of the two Servant passages.

In this kind of redactional investigation it seems justified to assume, as I do, that the burden of proof lies with the advocate of editorial intrusion. As we saw in tracing the fairly clear lines of an argument at least through the first half of chs. 40–55, our text exhibits a relatively high level of coherence and continuity compared with earlier prophetic compilations. There are also indications of large-scale artistic arrangements of fairly brief discourses. One feature, noted earlier, is the break between an Israel/Jacob section in 40–48 and a Jerusalem/Zion section in 49–55 which, it was argued, can be explained without a theory of distinct authorship (Cheyne, Kiesow) or distinct locations (Menahem Haran 1963b, chs. 40–48 in Babylon, chs. 49–66 in Judah).

As Hermisson pointed out in arguing for the unity of Deutero-Isaiah's theology (1998b, 117–31), the two *personae*, Jacob and Zion, male and female, belong thematically together; both are essential for the argument. The divisions are marked by the familiar technique of inclusio (40:3–5; 48:20–21; 55:12–13), which also succeeds in encapsulating the fundamental theme of the permanence of God's word communicated through the prophet: "the word of our God stands firm for ever" (40:6–8; 48:16a; 55:10–11).

As will be pointed out in the commentary, the passage immediately preceding the call to leave Babylon that concludes the first section (48:20–21), consisting in a reproach introduced by the conventional prophetic incipit "this is what Yahveh says" (48:17–19), has much in common with the third part of Isaiah: specifically, the particular usage of the terms *ṣĕdāqâ* (vindication) and *šālôm* (prosperity); the phrase *kĕnāhār šālôm* (literally, "like a river of peace" cf. 66:12); the allusion to the Abrahamic blessing (cf. 60:21–22); and, in general, the elegaic and downbeat mood and tone of the passage, which is quite distinctive when compared with the rest of 40–48.

This is one of several indications of a redactional connection between 40–55 and 56–66. Of these, doubtless the most important is the association between the prophetic Servant of 49–55 and the Servants of Yahveh, who feature so prominently in the final chapters of the book. We note, finally, that the sentence concluding chs. 40–48 ("there can be no well-being for the wicked," 48:22) has been borrowed from 57:21, evidently its original location.

It was part of the plan of the editor of the first series of discourses to summarize their essence in the final chapter, Isa 55—the entire chapter, not just its recapitulatory final two verses. The distinctive tone and character of this chapter vis-à-vis those that precede it is noticeable. It is much more generalized, exhortatory, didactic, and reminiscent of certain passages in the Deuteronomic corpus (see the commentary ad loc.). A closer look at the language of ch. 55 also suggests acquaintance with both 40–54 and 56–66. Isaiah 55:5 reproduces 49:7b with slight variation, while 55:13b, the finale of the chapter, is practically identical with 56:8b. If this is so, the intent to emphasize the Servant motif as a theme binding together both section 49–54 and section 56–66 is placed in high relief.

Chapters 49–54 consist in two units, each beginning with discourse by or about a prophetic Servant (49:1–6; 52:13–53:12), and each following immediately after a call to leave Babylon (48:20–21; 52:11–12). The reader will have noted that, in the third of Duhm's *Dichtungen* (50:4–9), the speaker does not identify himself as Yahveh's Servant. The section as a whole also ends by referring to the heritage and vindication of Yahveh's Servants (54:17b), thus creating a link with a major theme in the last part of the book, chs. 56–66 (see especially 65:8–16). These macro-structural features are compatible with a theory of a meaningful arrangement of the prophet's discourses by a disciple, one of the devout who claimed the title "Yahveh's Servants," those who tremble at his word and mourn for Zion, and who have left their mark on the final section (chs. 56–66).

ADDENDA

There has been a tendency in recent years to accept the satire directed against the cult of religious images in Isa 40–48 as an integral part of Second Isaiah's rhetorical strategy. However, issues of this kind are rarely susceptible of one clear solution. Each case must be considered on its merits. In the first place, one must determine whether a particular passage fits the immediate context, and in the second place, whether it is consonant with the text's ideology, style, and linguistic resources. The frequent condemnation of foreign deities and their images and the satirizing of Bel and Nebu (Marduk and Nabū) can be read as integral to the author's argument for the incomparability of Yahveh (41:29; 42:17; 45:16; 48:5). There is, for example, a deliberate contrast between the Babylonian gods who have to be transported on animals and Yahveh who carries Israel (46:1–4). A problem arises only with the satirical shafts directed at the *manufacture* of cult images—in Isaiah, restricted to chs. 40–48. The pious author of the sustained satire in 44:9–20 apparently could not resist answering the question "Is there any god but me?" (44:8b) in a way that disrupts the rhetorical flow. There are other instances in which similar satirical jabs appear more or less clearly to be intrusive (40:19–20; 41:6–7; 45:20b; 46:6–7). It is widely accepted that these additions derive from one and the same source and were inserted at an early date.

A different type of editorial expansion of the *Urtext* has been proposed by Hans-Jürgen Hermisson (1998b, 139–41, 155), in dialogue with Karl Elliger (1933) and Hans Christoph Schmitt (1979). Elliger argued that the anonymous author of Isa 56–66, a disciple of Deutero-Isaiah, arranged and edited the work of the master in addition to composing chs. 47, 54, and 55, together with the fourth of the *Ebedlieder*. Hermisson does not go this far but claims to identify a *qārôb-Schicht* in 40–55—that is, a strand in which the imminence of salvation and the consequent need for repentance are emphasized. With its close affinity with Third Isaiah, this strand represents for Hermisson the third stage in the formation of Deutero-Isaiah, following the core collection, which preceded the fall of Babylon, and its combination with the originally distinct servant passages.

Actually, the only place in 56–66 where *qrb* appears in either adjectival or verbal form ("near," "to be near") in the sense of an imminent divine intervention in the affairs of Israel, is in the opening verse:

> This is what Yahveh says:
> "Maintain justice and do what is right,
> for my salvation is near at hand,
> my deliverance soon to be revealed"
>
> (*qĕrôbâ yĕšûʿātî lābôʾ/vĕṣidqātî lĕhiggālôt*). (56:1)

Hermisson extends the theme to include anxiety over the delay in divine intervention (compare the delay of the *parousia* in early Christianity) and the related idea of a conditional offer of salvation. However, several of the passages in 40–55 that he identifies as belonging to this strand or layer do not seem to meet these minimal criteria (42:18–25; 46:8; 48:12–16; 49:7, 8–12, 24–26; 50:3; 51:12–14), and it is not clear that the ones that do are intrusive in their immediate contexts (e.g. 51:5). In one case (55:6–7), moreover, the passage may be dependent on Third Isaiah rather than edited or composed by a Trito-Isaianic author.

Finally, it may be instructive to look at the one instance that seems to fit the criteria very well:

Listen to me, you stubborn people,
far removed from deliverance as you are:
"I bring my deliverance near, it is not far off;
my salvation will not be delayed.
I will place salvation in Zion,
for Israel, my splendid possession." (46:12–13)

Here we have the paired terms *qrb* and *rḥq* (near, far), with reference to the event of salvation (cf. 59:9, 11, 14), as well as the pair *ṣĕdāqâ* and *yĕšûʿâ* (deliverance, salvation), appearing often with these meanings in chs. 56–66 (56:1; 59:9, 16–17; 61:10–11; 63:1).

Many uncertainties remain, but we should be prepared to accept the probability that, given the division between 40–55 and 56–66 as stated, section 56–66 was added to section 40–55 advisedly, as an interpretative extension containing a similar line of religious thinking. It was a literary, exegetical extension (*Fortschreibung*), occasioned by the changing situation with which both speakers and hearers were obliged to come to terms.

THE FOUR "SERVANT SONGS"

On the subject of Bernhard Duhm's four "Servant songs," it is much easier to formulate questions—over and above the question about the Servant's identity that the Sudanese official in Acts 8:34 posed—than to provide answers. Are they an original and integral part of chs. 40–55? If not, did they exist as one text prior to their insertion into the book? Irrespective of their origin, how do they function in their immediate contexts and in the context of the section as a whole? Saying goodbye to the "Servant songs" (Tryggve N. D. Mettinger 1983; also Hans M. Barstad 1994) is an understandable reaction of frustration in the face of the immense and inconclusive amount of commentary on these passages since Duhm first singled them out. But by now it is clear that they play a critical role in chs. 40–55 and in the book of Isaiah as a whole and that they present the reader with a unique set of problems. They are not going to go away.

In view of the amount of debate that these passages have generated, it is interesting that in the introduction to his commentary, and in the commentary itself, Duhm dedicated only about 1 1/2 pages to a general discussion of his *Ebed-Jahwe-Lieder* (Duhm 1922, 19, 311). His conclusions may be summarized as follows: the "Servant songs" were composed by a member of a Jewish community, but not of the diaspora, during the first half of the fifth century, between the composition of Job and Malachi; the author drew on Jeremiah, Deutero-Isaiah, and Job and in his turn influenced Trito-Isaiah and Malachi; the protagonist of the "songs" was a historical figure, a teacher of the law who suffered abuse, first of all from his own people; the "songs" are distinguished from their Deutero-Isaian context by a more deliberate and sober style, more regular prosody, and especially by the contrast with Deutero-Isaiah's description of Israel as *ʿebed*; they originally formed one composition, together with editorial additions (42:5–7; 50:10–11); they were inserted into Deutero-Isaiah by a later hand wherever there was space on the papyrus copy.

It would be safe to say that none of these conclusions would pass unchallenged today. Since Duhm wrote, discussion has for the most part focused on the identity of the *ʿebed*. But if we accept, as most do, that Isa 40–55 has been subjected to several redactions, we must take seriously the possibility that these passages have in the course of time been assigned to several individuals or groups, with or without changes to the wording. That is to say, the earliest stages in the history of the interpretation of these texts must be recovered from the texts themselves.

Evidence for a cumulative editorial process occasioned by a changing political and social situation is, at any rate, reasonably clear. If, for example, we compare the first of the four passages (42:1–9, including the comment on the passage, vv 5–9) with 51:4–6, the latter reads like a kind of eschatologized version of the former, in the sense that God's business in the world will be carried out no longer by Cyrus but in an unmediated way by God. Both songs speak of *tôrâ* (instruction) and *mišpāṭ* (world order based on justice), which will be a light to the peoples of the world (*ʾôr ʿammîm* 51:4; *ʾôr goyyîm* 42:6) and for which the coastlands and islands anxiously but hopefully wait (51:5; 42:4).

Of particular interest is the word *ṣedeq*, translated "righteousness" in 42:6, but in 51:5 carrying the same meaning of "deliverance," "vindication" that is attested in the last section of the book. Finally, the created order of heaven, earth, and its inhabitants in 42:5 corresponds to the statement in 51:6 about their final destiny.

Duhm (1922, 311) claimed that 42:1–7 breaks the continuity between 41:21–29 and 42:8–9, but even the casual reader can see that this is by no means obvious. Isaiah 41:29, denying power and reality to other deities, sounds like the conclusion to one phase of the argument, and the inclusio created by the mention of "former things" in 41:22 and 42:9 is unaffected by the presence or absence of the Servant passage. And, if the *ʿebed* is identified with Cyrus, as will be argued in the commentary, his solemn commissioning would not only follow the announcement of "the one from the north" (41:25) naturally but would fit the larger context of 40–48 very well. In any case, the language of this first of the four texts, beginning with the introductory particle *hēn* ("look," "behold"), which appears in 40–55 a bit more often than the alternative form *hinnēh*, is not distinctive vis-à-vis the style of chs. 40–55 in general (for more on the language of 42:1–9, see the commentary ad loc.).

One important effect of the break between 40–48 and 49–55 is that it suggests an interpretation of the Servant passages in 49–55 that is quite different from the interpretation we have offered for 42:1–9. This second major section (49:1–13) opens with the same structure as 42:1–13: Servant discourse (49:1–6) followed by comments (49:7, 8–12) and concluding with a hymn stanza

(49:13). Language, literary conventions, and motifs are also familiar from our reading of 40–48: appeal for a hearing, addressed to islands far off to the west (see especially 41:1); the manner in which the Servant is designated, including being called prenatally (41:9; 42:6; 43:1; 44:1; 45:3–4; 48:15); the accumulation of appositional clauses referring to God (49:5 cf. 42:5); and the theme of the glorification of God through Israel (49:3 cf. 44:23).

The repetitions and duplications are deliberately devised to make the point that the prophetic figure who is speaking in 49:1–6 has taken over the task originally assigned to Cyrus, a task that it is now clear Cyrus is not prepared to discharge. Hence the military metaphors for the equipment of this Servant for his mission (49:2); hence also the insistence that he, like Cyrus, is to be a light to the nations and a covenant for the people (49:6, 8 cf. 42:6).

Nothing is simple about these passages, but the least complicated conclusion to draw from these considerations is that this second of Duhm's *Lieder* represents a distinct, later stage in the career of the Second Isaiah. The second song also marks a fundamental change in the understanding of the contemporary political situation and the role that the Servant, as Israel's representative, is being called on to play in it. On this reading, and even allowing for transmission through a disciple, the voice we are hearing would be the same as the one we heard at the beginning asking what he should proclaim (40:6). One must also take into consideration the intriguing allusion in first person to a prophetic mission, immediately following the last reference to Cyrus in the book: "and now the Sovereign Lord Yahveh has sent me, and his spirit . . ." (48:16b, following 48:14–16a). This could be a confirmation (easily overlooked) of the conviction that the mission, originally confided to Cyrus has now passed by default to this Servant of God, who represents the prophetic presence of Israel in the world.

The part played by associates or disciples in the transmission of the material in this part of the book emerges more clearly in the commentary on the third Servant passage. It will be seen that the anonymous speaker is Yahveh's Servant, doubtless none other than the one in the previous chapter, but he is identified only in the comment that follows the saying (i.e. 50:10–11). Opposition to the prophet has now reached the point of physical abuse, and the attached comment, addressed to a community polarized by the prophet's preaching, is correspondingly harsh and uncompromising.

At this point the editorial history of the section is extremely complex. The transition from 50:1–3 to 50:4–11 is abrupt enough to suggest a process of serial compilation that involved the insertion of 50:4–11, which is Duhm's third Servant passage. The hand or arm of Yahveh as the instrument of redemption and deliverance is mentioned before and after this third passage (50:2; 51:5), as is also the apocalyptic scenario of the darkening and disappearance of the sky (50:3; 51:6).

Both 50:1–3 and 51:4–6 (perhaps also 51:1–6) have close, and unmistakable affinity in theme and language with the third part of the book (chs. 56–66). In 50:1–3 the note of rebuke is reminiscent of such passages as 58:1 and 59:2, with identical vocabulary in 59:12b (note the twin terms *ʿăvônôt, pĕšāʿîm,* "iniquities, transgressions"). The point is that the explanation for the nonfulfillment of the people's expectation of divine intervention should be sought in themselves, not in the short reach of Yahveh's power to act (literally, the shortening of his hand, 50:2b; 59:1). Along the same line of thought, the topos of summons and response or the lack of response ("Why, when I called, was there no one to answer?" 50:2a) recurs throughout section 56–66 (58:9; 65:1, 12, 24; 66:4). Furthermore, the great theme of mother Zion, comforted and joyful at last, which attains its fullest expression in the last chapter, is broached in 50:1–3 and taken up again in 51:1–3.

A provisional conclusion is that the core of section 40–55 was within a relatively short space of time expanded by an associate or disciple of the author whose voice is also heard in section 56–66. Either the same person or another member of the prophet's following transmitted the self-predication of the prophetic master in 49:1–6 and 50:4–9, added the comment in 50:10–11 occasioned by the rejection of the message by the majority, and composed 52:13–53:12 as a kind of panegyric or funerary oration soon after the prophet's death. At this point the entire corpus, once the *ʿebed* passages were included, formed (perhaps by design) a kind of inchoate or elementary prophetic biography.

It could be inferred from the context in which the account of the sufferings, death, and postmortem vindication of the *ʿebed* occurs that the last of the four passages (52:13–53:12) marks the beginning of a subunit within 40–55. Alternatively, and more likely, the context suggests that it has been inserted into the book, as Duhm himself and many others concluded. Like the previous *ʿebed* passage, it immediately follows a summons to return from the diaspora (48:20–22; 52:11–12), and the apostrophe to Zion that begins in 52:1–2 continues immediately afterward with a renewed call for rejoicing (54:1 cf. 52:9).

As set out in the commentary, the structure of this fourth Servant passage is straightforward: Yahveh's statement about the Servant at the beginning and end (52:13–15 with the exception of 14b + 53:11b–12) encloses a threnody or panegyric spoken by a disciple who has come to believe in the Servant and his message (53:1–11a). It does not seem necessary to break up this a-b-a pattern by splitting off 52:13–15 as a separate piece (Norman Whybray 1975, 169, following Harry M. Orlinsky and Norman H. Snaith 1967).

A somewhat unrepresentative analysis was proposed recently by Ernst Haag (1996, 1–20), who read 52:13 and 15 together with most of the third section (iii in the commentary) as a redactional layer added at the time of the Maccabee martyrs and the book of Daniel. This Maccabee strand was then filled out with supplements from a later phase in the Hasmonean period (52:14; 53:7e–9b, 10ab, 11ab, 12ef). Chopping up the text in this way does not seem advisable, but Haag has rightly drawn our attention to the close affinity of the final two verses with the book of Daniel. Toward the end of the interpretation of Daniel's fourth vision, we begin to hear of a relationship between teacher and students, prophetic leader and disciples. "Those of the people who are wise shall bring understanding to the many, though they shall fall by sword and flame"—in other words, suffer martyrdom (Dan 11:33). We learn that these *maśkîlîm* are also those who vindicate (literally, make or declare righteous) the many (*maṣdîqê hārabbîm*, 12:3) and live in the hope of resurrection into a state of astral immortality (Dan 12:2). The Servant also will receive posthumous vindication and vindicate the many (*yasdîq hārabbîm* Isa 53:11b). The affinity with Daniel suggests that *hārabbîm* (with the article) has the technical sense of a community of disciples, as in Daniel, as at Qumran (1QS VI–VII), and perhaps as in the New Testament (Mark 14:24 and parallels).

Haag's hypothesis of a Maccabean and Hasidic strand in ch. 53, in preference to the more common alternative view that Isa 53 influenced the book of Daniel, is alluring but probably not sustainable. It does, however, recall the connection between the Servant in 49–53 and the Servants of Yahveh in 65–66, also known as those who tremble at God's word (*ḥărēdîm*) and who form a persecuted and ostracized minority. At the literary level, this connection is established by the sharply divisive tone of the commentary on the third *ʿebed* passage (50:10–11), the panegyric (53:1–11), and the allusion to the heritage of the Servants of Yahveh (54:17b).

At the time of composition of the last chapters of the book of Isaiah, the "Servants" and "Tremblers" had been excommunicated by the authorities on account of their apocalyptic belief in an imminent divine intervention, or at least their exclusive claim to vindication when that happened (Isa 66:5; 65:8–16). The scenario of these last two chapters reveals a sectarian mentality no less developed than that of the *asidaioi* and the *maśkîlîm* of the book of Daniel. The lurid scene with which Isaiah ends, with the reprobate, that is, the internal enemies of the sect, burning in unquenchable fire, could have come straight out of Daniel (cf. Dan 12:2, the only place apart from Isa 66:24 where the word *dērāʾôn*, "an object that inspires horror," appears). Further discussion of these matters must, however, be postponed to the third volume of this commentary.

It is time to draw together the threads and attempt a provisional statement on the formation of Isa 40–55. We have found a relatively high level of coherence and unity in style and substance, more so in the first part (40–48) than in the second (49–55). Chapters 40–48 show indications of the arrangement of relatively brief discourses into longer units, but few signs of editorializing apart from polemic against the manufacture of cult objects. The only other addenda may be 46:12–13 and 48:17–19 (from Hermisson's *qārôb-Schicht*) and 48:16b, in which the speaker refers to his own prophetic mission.

The situation is different in the second section (49–55), where the hand of a Trito-Isaianic editor is in evidence. The three Servant texts have been inserted to alternate with the Zion theme, and comments have been added to the first two of these (49:7, 9–12; 50:10–11). Affinity with chs. 56–66 is especially in evidence in the immediate context of 50:4–11 (that is, 50:1–3 and 51:1–6) and sporadically in chs. 54–55, especially 55:6–11. The literary evidence therefore points to a partial rewriting or overwriting by a scribe associated with the minority group, whose voice is heard in 56–66 (in agreement on this point with Steck 1992, et alibi).

5. CHAPTERS FROM THE HISTORY OF INTERPRETATION

THE EARLIEST STAGES

The first stage in the interpretation of Isa 40–55 or any other biblical text must be recovered from the text itself by dint of identifying explanatory and expansive glosses and insertions of different kinds. If, for example, the identification of the Servant with Israel in 49:3 is determined to be editorial, then this word "Israel" and the OG translator's insertion of "Jacob" and "Israel" in 42:1 would testify to the earliest stage in the collective interpretation of these two passages. The history of interpretation, therefore, merges with the traditional disciplines of textual criticism and redaction history. Eventually, however, the point came when this kind of commenting and glossing could no longer be folded into the text but had to take the form of commentary external to the text. Writings extant from the Second Temple period provide no sure clues about when this happened. The author of Chronicles briefly mentioned Isaiah in association with Hezekiah (2 Chr 32:20) and identified him as the author of a *historical* work entitled *Isaiah's Vision* (*ḥăzôn yĕšaʿyāhû* 2 Chr 32:32) but showed no acquaintance with the second major section of the book of Isaiah.

Writing toward the beginning of the second century B.C.E., Jesus ben Sira (Sirach) praised Isaiah as great and trustworthy in his visions, mentioned his activities during Hezekiah's reign, and added that he comforted the mourners in Zion and revealed hidden things before they happened (48:20–25). The point about comforting mourners shows familiarity with Isa 61:2–3 and perhaps also with 40:1, and the reference to hidden things is strongly reminiscent of 48:6, the revelation by God of things concealed (*nĕṣûrôt*) and previously unknown. This combination suggests that Isa 1–39 and 40–66 had by that time been joined together, in whatever form these two texts then existed. The same conclusion is suggested somewhat later in Sirach by the reference to the bones of the twelve prophets (Sir 49:10), since the allusion to the *dodekapropheton* implies that the compilation of the prophetic material must have been well advanced by that time.

Josephus's statement that Isaiah wrote his prophecies in books (*en biblois*, *Ant* 10.35) does not, in all probability, refer to Isa 1–39 and 40–66 as two distinct compositions but to the entire book of Isaish as he knew it and the historical work mentioned in 2 Chr 32:32. Josephus solved the chronological problem of Isaian authorship on the improbable assumption that Cyrus read Isa 44:28–45:1 and realized, with the help of divine inspiration, that he was the one designated prophetically to release the Jews from captivity and rebuild the temple (*Ant.* 11.5–7).

SEPTUAGINT, TARGUM, AND LATER JEWISH INTERPRETATIONS

The Septuagint (LXX) or Old Greek (OG) version of Isaiah is a translation that functioned in Jewish communities in Egypt in a way comparable to the Aramaic Targums in Palestine and Babylon. It is also paraphrastic enough to warrant comparison with the Targum, though the Targum itself purports to be a translation rather than a midrash. Convinced of the permanent relevance of the sacred text written centuries earlier, the LXX translators aimed, while respecting the text's integrity, to bring out its contemporaneous relevance for Jewish communities in that part of the world at that time (around the middle of the second century B.C.E.).

One or two examples of contemporizing translation may be given. J. Koenig (1982, 173–93) points out the use of *deiknumi*, "show forth," to translate *bārā'* ("create") in Isa 40:26, with reference to the world as a panorama displayed before the gods, in keeping with philosophical ideas in circulation at that time. Likewise, translating *gibbôr* ("warrior," "strong man") with *gigas* ("giant") in 49:25 may have been prompted by interest in myths about giants, such as the ones that appear in the *Enoch* cycle and *Jubilees* (Stanley E. Porter and Brook W. R. Pearson 1997, 540–41). To take a small-scale example: in 43:3 the translator has substituted Syene (Aswan) at the first cataract of the Nile for the more distant and obscure Seba. Contemporizing substitutions of this kind can be found throughout the book.

It is to our purpose to note how the translators treated the Servant theme in chs. 40–55. The addition of names to 42:1, the first of Duhm's Servant passages, is quite unequivocal:

> Jacob is my servant, on him will I take hold,
> Israel is my chosen one, my soul has received him.

In the second *Dichtung*, Isa 49:1–6, identification of the Servant with the people of Israel was already in the Hebrew text (v 3), perhaps a very early insertion as some think, but the fact that the Servant (the people) is charged with a mission to the people creates a well-known problem for the collective interpretation. The LXX translators were aware of this and attempted to meet it by a small but significant modification of 49:5:

> And now, thus says the Lord that formed me from the womb as his bondsman (*doulos*), to gather together Jacob and Israel to him; *I will be gathered* (*sunachthēsomai*) and glorified before the Lord.

Maintaining the collective interpretation of the Servant became more difficult with the detailed allusions to rejection, physical abuse, disfigurement, and eventually death, in 50:4–9 and 52:13–53:12. The translators may have tried to solve this problem by understanding the text in much the same way as we assume the "Servants" did, about whom we read in Isa 56–66. They applied this language of rejection, suffering, and ultimate vindication to the devout and faithful minority to which they themselves belonged.

The situation to which the LXX translators were responding may be illustrated by the account of the persecution and abuse of the righteous, ending in a shameful death at the hands of the ungodly, in *The Wisdom of Solomon* from the same milieu, although about a century later (Wis 2:10–20). We are probably justified in picking up echoes of the last "Servant song" in this account, especially since the righteous sufferer calls himself the Servant of the Lord (*pais kuriou* Wis 2:13 cf. Isa 42:1; 49:6; 50:10; 52:13 LXX). Our lack of information about Jewish communities in Egypt in the second century B.C.E. prevents us from being more specific. The hypothesis of Arie van der Kooij (1997, 383–96), that the Septuagintal "Servant of the Lord" has the same referent as Isa 19:16–25 LXX—namely, the group that settled in Leontopolis with Onias IV about 160 B.C.E. (*Ant.* 13.62–73)—could perhaps be supported by Isa 40:2 LXX, according to which priests are to utter the words of comfort that follow. But, since we do not know that this settlement suffered persecution or entertained ideas about itself compatible with the Isaian Servant passages, the suggestion remains at the level of interesting conjecture.

Several more-or-less subtle changes in Isa 52:13–53:12 LXX may also be noted. Perhaps the most interesting is the avoidance of imputing the Servant's afflictions to divine action (53:4b, 10a). On the other hand, rather than the righteous Servant vindicating the many (MT), it is the Lord who vindicates the righteous Servant who serves the many aright (53:11b LXX).

Targum Jonathan, an Aramaic translation of the Prophets, of Palestinian origin, went through several editions from the Tannaitic period to the official Babylonian redaction sometime in the fourth or fifth century. Several scholars have assumed that the messianic emphasis would have been played down after the second rebellion against Rome (132–135 C.E.) and have therefore postulated a double redaction, a Tannaitic text and an amplified version of that text from the Amoraic period. This may be the case, though spiritual resistance to Roman rule fueled by resentment could also have intensified after the revolts.

Whatever the case, the messianic hope is clearly in evidence. In the first part of the Targum on Isaiah, the Messiah is a descendant of Jesse and David (11:1; 14:29; 16:1, 5; 28:5), but in the only reference to David in 40–55 (55:3), a messianic allusion is muted if it is there at all. On the other hand, the messianic status of the Isaian Servant is quite explicit. The first of the four passages in the Targum reads, "Behold my servant, I bring him near . . . I will place my Holy Spirit upon him" (42:1). The proximity of the messianic age is also the theme of 46:13: "My righteousness is near, it is not far off, and my salvation will not be held back. I will place in Zion a redeemer (*pārîq*) for Israel, my splendid possession." The congregation is associated with the Messiah as witness to God's project for Israel in 43:10: "You are witnesses before me . . . and my servant, the Messiah, in whom I am well pleased."

The same identification (*ʿabdî mĕšîḥāʾ*) is made at the beginning of the fourth Servant passage (52:13), near the end of which the holy remnant is assured that they will see Messiah's kingdom (53:10). The meturgeman, however, firmly rejects any idea of a suffering and dying messiah, and therefore partly reapplies the passages that speak of rejection and suffering to Israel—ostensibly wretched among the nations, but on whose behalf the Messiah will intercede and atone (52:14; 53:4)—but mainly to foreign oppressors (53:7–9, 11–12). Here and throughout these chapters political allusions are understandably muted, though Rome is mentioned once (54:1 cf. 34:9, where the fate of Rome is equated with that of Edom). The messianic age will be an age of obedience to the Law, which the Messiah will teach (40:29; 42:7; 50:4, 10; 53:5). It will witness a return from exile (49:6; 53:8), the freedom of the land of Israel (53:8, 11), the repopulation of Jerusalem (54:1) and rebuilding of the temple (53:5), eternal punishment for the reprobate (53:9), and the resurrection of the dead (42:11; 45:8; 49:8).

For a summary of later Jewish interpretations of Isa 52:13–53:12, the reader may be referred to Harold H. Rowley (1952, 3–57) and Christopher R. North (1956, 9–22). For the texts themselves, the collection of Abraham Neubauer and Samuel Rolles Driver (1876) is still hard to match for convenience of reference. The messianic interpretation of the suffering servant continued to have its advocates among the rabbis (e.g. *b. Sanh.* 98b; *Gen. Rab.* on Gen 31:3) and on into the Middle Ages. Moshe ha-Kohen, for example, described it as the traditional explanation. The collective interpretation nevertheless came to prevail, especially during the frequent periods of persecution. Rashi read Isa 53:4 as proof that Israel's sufferings atoned for the sins of Gentile nations, and David Kimḥi, after refuting the Christian messianic interpretation, took the Servant to stand for Israel in exile. Some Karaite commentators took this further by identifying the Servant with their own sect. After arguing against the Christian view and refuting Saadia Gaon's identification of the Servant with Jeremiah, Abraham Ibn Ezra expounded at length the *opinio communis* as represented by Rashi but then concluded that, since the section of the book beginning with ch. 40 is all of a piece, the Servant here and throughout is the prophetic author.

THE ISAIAN SERVANT IN THE LATER SECOND TEMPLE PERIOD

One would think that the depth and originality with which the religious idea of prophetic instrumentality is worked out in Isa 40–55, most remarkably in the form of substitutionary suffering in 52:13–53:12, could hardly fail to leave its mark on religious thinking in the later Second Temple period. It has nevertheless proved difficult to pin down clear and substantial indications of its influence in the extant literature prior to the common era (see most recently the survey by Martin Hengel 1996, 49–91). This situation provides another occasion for regret at the scarcity of source material for the period and the uncooperative nature of the few sources that we do possess. If, as many but by no means all scholars would argue, Isa 52:13–53:12 (hereafter Isa 53) was composed shortly after the death of the Servant toward the end of the Neo-Babylonian period, we are left with almost four centuries during which we hear no clear and unambiguous reference to it.

The silence is broken only with the description in the book of Daniel of the destiny of the faithful minority in the fourth and final vision (Dan 10–12). The leaders of this group are the *maśkîlîm*, "the wise," who impart wisdom to the *rabbîm*, "the many" (*ûmaśkîlê ʿām yābînû lārabbîm* Dan 11:32–33 cf. *hinnēh yaśkîl ʿabdî* Isa 52:13). This term, "the many," appears to refer to the community or sect from which the book of Daniel derives, comparable to the Qumran term for the full assembly (e.g. 1QS VI—VII) and perhaps also to usage in the New Testament (see Joachim Jeremias, 1968). Some from this group have died a violent death (Dan 11:33–34) but are assured that they will be resurrected to life and light everlasting, and will therefore, like the Servant, see light (cf. Isa 53:11), while the reprobate will encounter only shame and horror (*dērāʾôn* Dan 12:2–3 cf. Isa 66:24, the only other occurrence of this term). Finally, both the Isaian Servant and the *maśkîlîm*, will vindicate the many (*maṣdîqê hārabbîm* Dan 12:3 cf. *yaṣdîq ʿabdî lārabbîm* Isa 53:11b). The parallels are close enough to justify the conclusion that the author of the apocalypse of Daniel is identifying the group to which he belongs with the Isaian Servant as an example of suffering and martyrdom borne heroically in the expectation of ultimate vindication.

It would be a reasonable conjecture that the servants (*ʿăbādîm*), also known as those who tremble at God's word (*ḥărēdîm*), who are mentioned in the last section of Isaiah (65:8–16; 66:1–5), are associated with the person and teaching of the prophetic Servant of Isa 53 and, as such, form a distant nexus with the Danielic sect of the mid–second century B.C.E. Both are described as a persecuted minority, and both await an imminent divine intervention in the affairs of Israel and in the outcome of their own sufferings (Isa 66:5; Dan 12:5–13). Unfortunately, we have no way to extend the history of the one forward and of the other backward to even begin to cover the intervening centuries. Otto Plöger (1968) attempted to bridge the gap by creating a trajectory in the direction of apocalyptic sectarianism of the Danielic and Asidean type (1 Macc 2:42; 7:13; 2 Macc 14:6) with Joel 3, Zech 12–14, and Isa 24–27 as points on a parabola. The attempt was worth the effort, but beset by too many uncertainties. In any case, Plöger did not incorporate Isa 65–66 into his scheme.

The Similitudes of Enoch (*1 En*. 37–71) contain the oldest interpretation of the visions of Daniel. This passage was dated by R. H. Charles to the period 105–64 B.C.E. (Charles 1917, xiv), and by J. T. Milik to the early Christian period (1971, 333–78). The consensus now is that this strange composition, the only part of the *Enoch* cycle not represented at Qumran, originated in the late first century B.C.E. or the early first century C.E. Its presentation of a preexistent Messiah (48:3,10), who is identified with a Son of Man, seated on his glorious throne (48:10; 52:4), certainly owes a debt to the vision of the beasts and the Son of Man in Dan 7. Allusions to the Isaian Servant passages have been identified where the text speaks of this messianic figure as the Chosen One (39:6;

45:3–5 etc. cf. Isa 42:1 etc.), concealed by God (62:6–7 cf. Isa 49:2), a light to the nations (48:4 cf. Isa 42:6; 49:6), and one before whom the kings of the earth will cower in terror (62:1, 3, 9 cf. Isa 52:15). But none of these amounts to more than a faint echo, and all are amenable to other explanations. Furthermore, there is no indication that this messianic figure suffered or that his sufferings benefited others.

Something must now be said about the Qumran *pěšārîm* (4QpIsa[a-e] = 4Q161–65; 3QpIsa = 3Q4), the earliest extant commentaries on Isaiah. Most of the texts commented on in the *pěšārîm* are taken from chs. 1–39, but one *pešer*, 4QpIsa[d] (4Q164), finds in 54:11 a reference to the council (*yaḥad*) of the Qumran community by dint of identifying it with an allusion to the twelve precious stones on the high priest's breastpiece (Exod 28:15–20). The verse is taken to mean that "they will establish the council of the community, the priests and the people, the assembly of his chosen ones, like a sapphire (lapis?) stone in the midst of (precious) stones," and Isa 54:12 "concerns the twelve [leading priests] who give light by means of the Urim and Thummim." The gates, finally, refer to "the leaders of the tribes of Israel in the last days."

This kind of actualization of prophetic texts is characteristic of the Qumran commentaries in general. Apart from the *pěšārîm*, there are few quotations from Isa 40–55 in the Qumran texts. The best known is doubtless 40:3, in 1QS 8:14, which reads, in agreement with the MT: "A voice is proclaiming in the wilderness: clear a way for Yahveh . . . ." The different punctuation in the LXX (*phōnē boōntos en tē erēmō*), reproduced in the Gospels (Mark 1:3 and parallels), locates the voice itself in the wilderness but makes little if any difference to the sense. The implication is that the Qumran community saw itself as the herald of the new age about to dawn, first proclaimed in Isa 40:1–5 and 52:7–10.

Here and there in the *Hôdāyôt* (*Thanksgiving Hymns*, 1QH[a]), we hear language suggestive of the Isaian *ʿebed*, where the author, perhaps the Teacher of Righteousness (or Legitimate Teacher), speaks of being set aside from the womb (1QH[a] 17:29–31), describes his persecution and sufferings (12:8; 16:26–27), and claims to sustain and enlighten the Many (12:1–6, 27). None of these is more than an echo or warrants the claim that the Teacher was presenting himself as the Isaian Servant. The echo is even fainter in the fragmentary text 4Q541, variously known as 4QAaronA or 4QApocryphon of Levi[b]. It speaks about a priest who makes atonement, brings enlightenment, is opposed and calumniated, but who will see and rejoice in eternal light (cf. Isa 53:11 *yirʾeh ʾôr* in 1QIsa[a], 1QIsa[b], 4QIsa[d], and LXX, but not MT). But to the extent that the fragments allow us to understand them, his sufferings are quite different from those of the Isaian Servant, and no atoning value is attributed to them.

Similar claims have been made for the cluster of fragments known as the *Self-Glorification Hymns* (4Q427 fragment 7; 4Q471b; 4Q491 fragments 11 and 12). The speaker discourses on his exalted status among the angels *ʾēlîm* literally "gods"), he resides in the heavens, he is a friend of the King and companion of the Holy Ones, and his teaching is beyond compare. The only possible point of contact with Isa 53 is the speaker's complaint that, in spite of the claims he makes for his exalted status or perhaps because of them, he is despised (nibzeh 4Q471b, line 1) and bears sorrows (4Q471b, line 2: 4Q491 frg. 11, line 9 partially reconstructed).

Israel Knohl (2000) has, nevertheless, claimed to find in these texts reference to a suffering Messiah based on Isaiah 53, whom he goes on to identify with Menahem the Essene.

However, the *Self-Glorification Hymns* provide no grounds at all for believing that the speaker is a messianic figure, and there is no close verbal or thematic link with Isaiah 53. The verbs "despise" (*bzh*) and "bear suffering" (*sbl*) do appear in Isa 53 (vv 3–4), but the essential point, that the Servant bore afflictions and sufferings on behalf of others and that his sufferings had a salvific effect on others, is entirely absent from the *Hymns*. (For the texts and commentary, see E. Eshel 1999.) As the reviewers have pointed out, Knohl's hypothesis appears to have nothing to commend it. We can conclude in agreement with John J. Collins that "the alleged allusions to a suffering messiah in the Scrolls disappear under examination" (Collins, 1995, 126).

Setting aside the fourth Servant passage, we may say that the complete *Isaiah Scroll* (1QIsa[a]) shows occasional divergence from the MT of a kind that suggests a definite interpretative intent. The addition of *bĕraḥămîm*, "with compassion," at the end of 52:8 makes the point more clearly that this is not a divine visitation in judgment. Four verses later, 1QIsa[a] rounds off the poem in 52:7–12 with the statement *ʾĕlohê kol-hāʾāreṣ yiqqārēh* ("he is called the God of all the earth"). Another interesting case is the change from first to third person in 51:5. The verse speaks of salvation as imminent, and the Qumran version has been interpreted, perhaps correctly, in a messianic sense: "*his* arm will judge the peoples, the islands will wait for *him*, and in *his* power (arm) they will place their hope." There is also a possibly significant change in the opposite direction in 52:14b, where 1QIsa[a] has *mšḥty* for MT *mšḥt* (*mišḥat*). This may simply be a scribal error, but it could also be construed as *māšaḥtî* ("I have anointed"), permitting the translation "I have anointed his appearance beyond [that of] a man" instead of "so marred was his appearance beyond human semblance." Other instances will be mentioned in the commentary.

ISAIAH 40–55 IN EARLY CHRISTIANITY

There can be no question of attempting a comprehensive study of the appropriation and use of these chapters in the formative period of Christianity during the apostolic, subapostolic, and patristic periods. What I hope to achieve is the limited goal of demonstrating and illustrating their decisive influence on the self-understanding of the Christian movement during the first generations and on certain basic convictions that sustained it.

With this in mind, we begin with the earliest texts, the letters that circulated among Christian cells around the Mediterranean, beginning in the early 50s of the first century of the era. To a remarkable extent the agenda of Paul in his

Epistle to the Romans, the most programmatic and explicitly theological of the epistles, is dictated by his interpretation of Isa 40–66, especially ch. 53. The theme of the letter from beginning to end, the gospel or good tidings made available through Jesus, is modeled on the good news of salvation announced to Jerusalem in Isa 40:9; 52:7; and 60:6. Likewise, Paul's conviction of being sent on a mission to proclaim the message is modeled on the mission of the prophetic messenger of Isa 42:19, 48:16 and 61:6. In the exordium he presents himself as a bearer of the good tidings *promised through the prophets* (1:1–6), and in the final paragraph he recommends the gospel to the recipients *as disclosed through prophecy* (16:25–27). In the body of the letter his mission to proclaim the gospel is validated with reference to Isa 52:7: "How welcome are the footsteps of the herald . . . bringing good tidings" (Rom 10:15, omitting "on the mountains" because it is too closely tied to its original context).

Isaiah 52:7 links the argument in Romans with the Gospels as a focal text for early Christian self-understanding, since it identifies the gospel as the proclamation of the Kingdom of God, a message encapsulated in the acclamation "your God reigns" in the Isaian text (52:7). Paul aligns himself more closely with this text by going on to speak of a plurality of heralds, of whom he is one (Rom 10:8, 14–15). To this he adds a citation of Isa 53:1, referring to what has already been broadcast and heard (LXX *akoē*; MT *šĕmûʿâ*), but the question "who has believed what has been heard?" (Rom 10:16) is now referred not to the destiny of the Servant but to the refusal of Israel to receive the message. The point is reinforced by citing Isa 65:1–2: "I spread out my hands all day to a rebellious people."

The gospel (*euangelion*) and its proclamation (*euangelizein, euangelisasthai*) form a nucleus around which are clustered associated themes drawn from these chapters of Isaiah. The most prominent of these is the insistence on a mission to Gentiles, anticipated in several passages in Isaiah and assigned to the Isaian Servant in Isa 49:6b (Rom 11:13, 25; Gal 1:16; 2:2, 8–9). Paul finds confirmation of this mission in the LXX version of the fourth Servant passage: "Those who had not been told about him shall see, and those who had never heard (about him) shall understand" (Rom 15:21 cf. Isa 52:15b). Other Isaian themes articulated in a way favorable to Paul's argument are the renewal of creation (Gal 6:15; 2 Cor 5:17 cf. Isa 43:18–19; 65:17; 66:22), Jerusalem as mother (Rom 4:27 cf. Isa 54:1, which he cites in full), and saying *Amen* to the *faithful* God, a play on the Hebrew root *ʾmn* (2 Cor 1:19–20 cf. Isa 65:16).

The statement that Christ died for our sins and was raised (from death) *according to the Scriptures* (1 Cor 15:3–4) brings up the question of the scriptural warranty for the interpretation of the death of Christ as atoning for the sins of others. In this respect the creedal formula of Rom 4:25 is more revealing than 1 Cor 15:3–4: "he was delivered (to death) for our trespasses and raised up for our justification" (*paredothē dia ta paraptōmata hēmōn kai ēgerthē dia tēn dikaiōsin hēmōn*). The language immediately recalls the Servant of Isa 53 who, in the LXX version, "delivered his life over to death on account of their sins" (*paredothē eis thanaton hē psuchē autou dia tas hamartias autōn* 53:12 cf. v 6) and is to be exalted and glorified exceedingly (52:13). The effect of the death and subsequent exaltation (namely, the rendering of others righteous and acceptable to God, *dikaioi*) is more clearly expressed in the Hebrew text, with which we assume Paul to have been familiar. It reads, "my servant will vindicate (or "justify," *yaṣdîq*) many" (53:11b). We find the same association of ideas based on the Servant text in 2 Cor 5:21: "For our sake he made him to be sin (*hamartia*), he who knew no sin, so that through him we might become the righteousness of God (*dikaiosunē tou theou*)".

The sacrificial metaphor of the *ʾāšām*, guilt offering or reparation offering (53:10), is absent from the LXX. Paul does not use the Greek equivalent (*plēmmeleia*), but he speaks of Christ's being put forward as a sacrifice of atonement or, perhaps, as the place where atonement happens (*hilastērion*). This is brought about by means of his blood (that is, his death by violence), and this showing forth of a death is linked with the idea of rendering others righteous and acceptable to God (*dikaioi* Rom 3:25–26). The *hilastērion* (Hebrew *kappōret*) referred originally to the platform located above the ark on which the atoning blood of the sin offering was sprinkled (Lev 16:11–19). The figure is by no means strange or unexpected, since metaphoric language relating to the sacrificial cult of the temple is quite frequent in early Christian attempts to articulate the significance of the death of Jesus and its effects (e.g. Rom 5:2, 9; 12:1; Eph 2:13–14).

The most extensive citation from Isa 53 appears in 1 Peter, in the apparently unpromising context of exhorting slaves to accept their lot with patience and forbearance (1 Pet 2:18–25). However, the thought of Jesus as servant (slave) quickly brings into play the Pauline theology of the atoning death of Jesus (1 Pet 2:24b cf. Rom 6:18). The author quotes from the LXX, probably from memory, since the wording is imprecise and the sequence of verses quoted is 9, 4, 12, 5, 6. One point is of particular interest. 1 Peter 2:24, *tas hamartias hēmōn autos anēnegken en tō sōmati autou epi to chulon* ("he bore our sins in his body on the cross"), combines Isa 53:4a LXX *tas hamartias hēmōn pherei* ("he bears our sins") with 53:12b *hamartias pollōn anēnegken* ("he bore the sins of many"), using the same verb, *anapherō*. The specifically Christian addition about death on the cross corresponds to the continuation of Isa 53:12b: *kai dia tas hamartias autōn paredothē* ("and for our sins he was delivered up"). The corresponding verb (*paradidōmi*) appears three times in Isa 53 with reference to the suffering and death of the Servant (vv 6 and 12). As a shorthand reference to the death of Jesus interpreted in the light of Isa 53, it entered into early Christian catechesis (e.g. Rom 4:24) and liturgy, most conspicuously in the words of eucharistic institution (*en tē nukti hē paredidoto*, "on the night he was delivered over [to death]," 1 Cor 11:23 cf. Matt 26:24 and parallels). That the same verb is used of the betrayal by Judas has obscured its interpretative scope in relating the death of Jesus to that of the Isaian Servant.

Coming now to the Gospels: The term "gospel," "good tidings" (*euangelion*, Hebrew *bĕśōrâ*), appears not at all in Isaiah, and elsewhere in the OG only three times, in connection with the deaths of Saul and Absalom (2 Sam 4:10; 18:22, 25). However, the corresponding verb, *euangelizein*, appears at important junctures in Isa 40–66 (40:9; 52:7; 60:6; 61:1). According to Mark, by most considered the earliest gospel, the Christian good tidings are announced with a citation from Isa 40:3–5 but parsed to allow reference to John the Baptist's preaching in the wilderness of Judea (Mark 1:1–3 and parallels): "the voice of one calling out in the wilderness. . . ." The inauguration of Jesus' mission with his baptism in the Jordan echoes the commissioning of Yahveh's Servant in Isa 42:1 (Mark 1:9–11). The first utterance by the Jesus of this gospel is the announcement of the good news of the kingdom of God (Mark 1:14), following Isa 52:7, which in the LXX reads:

> Like beauty on the mountains, like the feet of the bearer of good tidings (*euangelizomenou*) of news of peace, like the bearer of good tidings (*euangelizomenos*) of good things; for I shall make public your salvation, saying, "Zion, God shall reign over you."

The announcement of the kingdom of God (*basileia tou theou*; *malkûtāʾ dî ʾĕlāhāʾ* in the Targum), meaning the effective implementation of God's will and purpose in the world to be brought about by God's agents or servants, is central to Isa 40–66, as it is to the Christian Gospels, perhaps most prominently in Matthew (Matt 4:23; 9:35; 24:14; 26:3–13). The healings and exorcisms are signs of the kingdom, and at the same time serve to present Jesus as fulfilling the mission of the Servant. This is explicitly noted at Matt 12:17–21, which quotes Isa 42:1–4 in extenso, and at Matt 8:14–17 where Jesus is identified with the one who "bore our affliction and the burden of our suffering" (citing Isa 53:4).

Matthew also stresses the importance of a Gentile mission once the gospel has been proclaimed among the Jewish people (e.g. Matt 28:18–20). It is difficult to avoid the conclusion that this is dictated by the double mission assigned to the Servant in Isa 49:6. It is emphasized that this mission must take place before the return of Christ in glory (Matt 24:14 cf. Isa 56:1, 8; 66:18–19, 21), just as in Isaiah the mission to the Gentile world must precede the final revelation of God in salvation and judgment (66:18–19).

A comparison of the blessings or beatitudes pronounced on the disciples and woes on their opponents (Luke 6:20–26, cf. Matt 5:3–12), on the one hand, with the contrasting fates of the Servants of Yahveh and their opponents in Isa 65:13–14, on the other, confirms the impression that an attentive reading of the latter part of Isaiah played an important and perhaps decisive part in forming the self-understanding and identity of the earliest discipleship of Jesus. Isaiah 65:13–14 reads:

> See, my servants will eat, while you go hungry;
> my servants will drink, while you go thirsty;
> my servants will rejoice, while you are put to shame;

my servants will exult in gladness of heart,
while you cry out with heartache, wailing in anguish of spirit.

This language of eschatological reversal is a familiar response to ostracism, persecution and the disconfirmation of expectations nourished within a particular group or sect, a situation well attested in the Gospels (Matt 10:22; Mark 13:13 cf. Isa 66:5, "for my name's sake"). The "sense of an ending" that pervades the Gospels and much of early Christian literature also draws its imagery from the latter part of Isaiah. For example, the scenario of the final judgment as described in Matt 25:41 and Mark 9:48, featuring inextinguishable fire and undying worms, paraphrases the last verse of Isaiah (66:24). For the early Christian self-designation "the Way" (*hē hodos*) as deriving from a reading of Isaiah, see vol. 1, p. 98.

In recent years the most discussed and disputed aspect of Isaian (more specifically Deutero-Isaian) influence on early Christianity has been the bearing of the fourth Servant passage (52:13–53:12) on the interpretation of the identity of Jesus, especially in the Gospels. In Acts 8:26–35 the Ethiopian official asks Philip the crucial question about the identity of the suffering Servant of the passage in question. This Ethiopian was presumably a proselyte, since he was en route to Jerusalem and reading (out loud, since Philip heard him) from an Isaiah scroll. The text cited is Isa 53:7b–8a, no doubt because it contains the first allusion in the passage to the death of the Servant, and on this basis Philip gave the Ethiopian the good tidings about Jesus (*euēngelisato autō ton Iēsoun* Acts 8:35).

Even in the absence of any continuous exegetical tradition based on Isa 53 about a prophetic-messianic figure whose death atones for sin, it was inevitable that the death of Jesus would require scriptural validation and would therefore be interpreted in the light of this extraordinary passage: "It is written that the Son of Man must suffer and be treated with contempt" (Mark 9:12); "it was preordained to happen in this way" (Matt 26:54). We have seen that the key term encapsulating both the event and its significance—*paredothē* ("he was delivered up")—is present at every level of the developing Christian tradition and points unmistakably to Isa 53 (Matt 9:31; 17:22; 26:2; Mark 14:41; Rom 4:25; 1 Cor 11:23; Gal 2:20 etc.). The description of what happened to the Servant has also, together with Ps 22, helped to shape the details of the narrative of the passion and death of Jesus: his silence (Matt 26:63 cf. Isa 53:7), his being reckoned among transgressors (Luke 22:37 cf. Isa 53:12), his being subjected to blows and spittle (Matt 26:67 cf. Isa 50:5), and the part played by the wealthy Joseph of Arimathea (Matt 27:57 cf. Isa 53:9 LXX).

In Isa 53:4 and 53:12 the OG version deliberately avoids attributing the Servant's suffering and death to an act of God. A related problem for the individual as opposed to the collective interpretation, and therefore for the Christian interpretation of the passage beginning with the New Testament arose from the idea, clearly expressed in the Hebrew text, that the Servant substitutes for others by taking on himself the consequences of their sins. The moral and theological problems associated with this substitutionary view led, in the patristic period, to a shift in emphasis, already noted in 1 Pet 2:18–25, on to the exemplary use of the Servant figure, especially in writers influenced by Stoic ideas and the *Acta Martyrum*.

The patristic period also saw the beginning of argument between Christians and Jews about the identity of the Servant, an early example of which is Justin's *First Apology* (§§50–51). On the problem of substitution or "place-taking" (*Stellvertretung*) more will be said in the section of the Introduction called "Aspects of Theology," and for more on patristic interpretation see Sawyer (1996b 42–64 and passim.

6. Isaiah 40–55 in Its Historical Context

The Career of Cyrus and the Collapse of the Babylonian Empire

In the Schweich lectures delivered in 1940 and published in 1944, Sydney Smith observed that, though Cyrus is named only twice in Isa 40–48 (44:28; 45:1), he is alluded to without being named throughout this section of the book (Sydney Smith 1944, 49). Smith thought it possible to identify references in these chapters to specific events in the career of Cyrus leading to the overthrow of the Babylonian empire in 539 B.C.E. Isaiah 41:1–5, for example, describes the reaction to Cyrus' spectacular conquest of Sardis in 547. While Smith was overly optimistic in making such precise correlations with historical events, it is certainly true that the historic mission of Cyrus is the theme in the central panel of Isa 40–48 (44:24–45:17), in which his name is used twice (44:28; 45:1). He is also the focus of attention elsewhere even when his name does not appear. The author assigns him a decisive providential role, though always with primary reference to the destiny of Judean communities in the Neo-Babylonian Empire. He swoops down like a bird of prey, first from the east, then from the north, trampling kings and governors underfoot (41:2–5, 25; 45:1; 46:11). His historic mission is to put an end to the Babylonian Empire (43:14; 48:14–15), liberate prisoners and deportees, especially the descendants of Judeans who were deported by the Babylonians (42:6–7; 43:5–7; 45:13), restore Jerusalem to its former state, and rebuild its temple and the cities of Judah devastated during the Babylonian conquest (44:26–28; 45:13).

The Cyrus in question is the Persian ruler Kurush (Cyrus II, 559–530), who appears at the beginning of Ezra–Nehemiah as the author of a decree permitting the return of Judeo-Babylonians to Judah. He was also well known to the Greeks: his career is the principal topic of the first book of Herodotus's *Histories*, and he serves as a mirror for princes in Xenophon's *Cyropaedia*. Cyrus began his career as head of the Achaemenid clan of the Pasargadae tribe in southwest Iran. After gaining the leadership of other tribes in the Persian heartland of Fars (Persis to the Greeks), he went on to conquer and take over the empire of the Medes with its principal city Agamtanu (Ecbatana), the Kingdom of Lydia, much of the Greek-speaking Ionian littoral, the entire Neo-Babylonian Empire, and vast territories to the east. He died fighting the Massagetai tribes east of the Caspian Sea in the summer of 530.

The allusions to Cyrus in Isa 40–48 indicate that the last decade of the Neo-Babylonian Empire (ca. 550–539) was when the core of this section of the book was composed. Founded by Nabopolassar (Nabû-apla-uṣur) in 626, at a time when Josiah reigned in Judah, this empire reached its apogee under Nebuchadrezzar II (604–562). During his reign, the city of Babylon, excavated by German archaeologists over a period of several decades, was rebuilt on a scale unprecedented elsewhere, covering an area of about three square miles. The reconstruction of the Ishtar Gate in the Pergamon Museum in Berlin conveys some idea of its richness and splendor. (For further details, see Wiseman 1985, 42–80).

The authors of the abundant anti-Babylonian polemic in the prophetic books were well aware of the theological and cosmological significance attaching to *babili*, "the gateway to the gods," the navel of the earth, the center of the cosmos and the link between earth and heaven. Our principal source for Nebuchadrezzar's reign, the Babylonian Chronicle, which covers only the first decade of the reign down to 594, records military campaigns in Syria-Palestine ("Ḫattu land") for almost every year of that decade. In the first year after Nebuchadrezzar's accession, the Philistine city-state of Ashkelon was taken and destroyed, and in the seventh year (597) Jerusalem was attacked, Jehoiachin its ruler deported, and a vast tribute exacted.

Nebuchadrezzar's difficulties with Egypt, Babylon's only serious rival, led to further disturbances in Jerusalem a few years later. These in turn persuaded the Babylonians to undertake a punitive expedition with the object of obliterating Jerusalem once for all as a center of disaffection and one particularly dangerous on account of its proximity to Egypt. Jerusalem was in due course destroyed and the native dynasty extinguished. The Historian notes that the Babylonian general Nebuzaradan returned to the city after it had been taken in order to destroy the temple and the royal palace and pull down the walls (2 Kgs 25:8–10). The destruction of Jerusalem was therefore a deliberate, ideological act comparable to the destruction of Ashkelon at the beginning of the reign. A section of the Judean population (the more sober biblical figure puts the number at 4,600, Jer 52:28–30) was deported to Babylon and settled in the Nippur region in at least three successive deportations (597, 586, 582). Others may have voluntarily relocated, at least temporarily, either to Egypt or to one or other of the Transjordanian countries. About the same time, a Babylonian army was deployed around the Phoenician city of Tyre with a view to blocking Egyptian maritime activity.

At the conclusion of his narrative, the biblical Historian reports that the Babylonian ruler Evil-Merodach (Amel-Marduk, 561–560), Nebuchadrezzar's son and successor, released the deported Judean king Jehoiachin, detained at the Babylonian court, and showed him special consideration (2 Kgs 25:27–30;

Jer 52:31–32). Jehoiachin (*ia-ku-u-ki-nu*) and his five sons are in fact mentioned together with Phoenicians, Greeks, Egyptians, and other members of ethnic minorities as recipients of rations, on tablets published in 1939 by Ernst F. Weidner (*ANET* 308). Jehoiachin's name also appears on seal impressions of a certain Eliakim from different sites in Judah. Amel-Marduk's action suggests that he was preparing to restore the native Judean dynasty. If so, nothing came of it, for Amel-Marduk was assassinated and Nabonidus (Nabu-naid), who usurped the throne five years later, showed no disposition to favor his Judean subjects. The point was driven home by his campaigns of conquest launched against Edom to the east and Gaza to the west of Judah.

The name Nabonidus, last of the six Neo-Babylonian rulers (555–539), does not appear either in Isaiah or in any other biblical text, though an Aramaic text from Qumran speaks of his encounter with a Jewish soothsayer and his prayer for deliverance from a skin disorder. The reign is comparatively well documented, but historians continue to differ on the subject of Nabonidus's political and religious agenda. The principal issues are his ten-year residence at the oasis of Teima in the Arabian Peninsula and his promotion of the cult of the Aramean deity Sîn at Harran over the cult of Marduk, imperial deity of Babylon.

Nabonidus was allied with Cyrus for a brief period during the latter's revolt against Astyages, the Median king who ruled from Ecbatana (Hamadan) in west-central Iran. But after the capture and sack of Ecbatana by Cyrus in 550, it became evident that Cyrus was the principal threat to Babylonian hegemony. Cyrus followed up his takeover of the Median Empire by defeating Croesus, ruler of the adjacent Lydian kingdom, and capturing Sardis, its capital city (547). The reduction of the Greek cities on the Ionian coast followed, bringing the Persians into hostile contact with the mainland Greek cities for the first time.

The chronological sequence of Cyrus' conquests after this point is unclear and need not concern us. Sometime between 546 and 539, Elam with its capital city Susa fell to him, after which confrontation with Nabonidus was inevitable. In 539 Cyrus defeated the Babylonian army at Opis east of the Tigris, slaughtered the population of the town, no doubt *pour encourager les autres*, and sent his general, Gobryas, to call for the surrender of Babylon. His propagandistic cylinder text describes the capture of the city as an effortless and bloodless operation, followed by his triumphant entry into the city, to the joyful acclamation of the populace, in October 539.

While Nabonidus's intentions are still a matter of debate, his actions suggest that he was pursuing a policy of political and religious decentralization at variance with that of his predecessors Nabopolassar, Nebuchadrezzar, and Neriglissar. This would be consistent with his restoration of the ancient center of Haran in the north together with its Ehulhul sanctuary dedicated to the god Sîn and his ten-year residence in the oasis of Teima in the south.

The substantial corpus of texts that has survived from his reign is suffused with theological considerations no less than the more-or-less contemporaneous chapters of Isaiah. The Istanbul basalt stele attributes the destruction of Babylon by Sennacherib to the anger of Marduk, who abandoned his city for 21 years. Then Marduk remembered his esagila sanctuary and intervened to bring about the assassination of the Assyrian king. The Medes were his chosen instrument in avenging Babylon, but they went beyond their commission in destroying the sanctuaries of the Assyrians and of those allied with them, including the beloved Ehulhul temple at Haran. Nabonidus (in reality a usurper) was then called to replace the unsatisfactory Labashi-Marduk and rule by the will of Marduk. After the allotted time of 54 years came to an end, he undertook the task of restoring the Haran sanctuary (*ANET* 308–11). The affinity of this kind of theological interpretation and legitimation of political action with certain prophetic texts, and Isa 40–55 in particular, will be at once evident.

NEO-BABYLONIAN JUDAH

What was happening in Judah from the first of several deportations (597) to the restoration of the Jerusalem cult under Darius I (515) is not well known. The Historian provides a figure of either 10,000 or 8,000 for the first deportation, but it is unclear whether this reference is to just one group or to all of the deportees (2 Kgs 24:14–17). The Historian also compounds confusion by stating that only the peasantry (*dallat hāʾāreṣ*) was left behind after both this deportation and the one following the sack of Jerusalem eleven years later (2 Kgs 24:14; 25:12).

In assessing these data we need to bear in mind how important the idea of exile is for the Historian. Banishment or exile is the outcome of a curse incurred for violation of the covenant between the national deity and the people. All are guilty; therefore all, or practically all, suffer the consequences (Deut 4:26–28; 28:36, 41, 63–68 cf. 2 Kgs 17:23; 25:21). In this respect the Deuteronomists are borrowing a common topos from Assyrian inscriptions and vassal treaties, in which deportation is one of the standard curses for a vassal ruler's violation of his oath of allegiance. Tiglath-pileser III, for example, claims to have deported *all* the men (*puḫur nišešu*) of the house of Omri—that is, the Kingdom of Samaria (Oded 1979, 22). The author of Chronicles takes this further by speaking of the seventy years during which the land was empty of inhabitants as the sabbath of the land (2 Chr 36:20–21).

With respect to Judah, Jer 52:28–30 supplies what are generally thought to be the more reliable data: 3023 for the first deportation in the seventh year of Nebuchadrezzar (587), 832 for the second in the eighteenth year (586), and 745 for the third in his twenty-third year (582)—therefore, 4,600 in all. Even if this figure includes only adult males, as some suppose, the total would not exceed about 20,000 in all.

A much more difficult task is that of estimating what percentage of the total population the deportees represented, and therefore what kind of social activity could have been sustained in the province. This issue is clearly of major significance for those who argue for a Judean provenance of Isa 40–48 or 40–55 or 40–66. Unfortunately, a demographic study of Neo-Babylonian Judah calls for data that are more often than not unavailable. Estimates of family size vary from 3.5 to 8 individuals and minimum roofed living space per individual from 5.3 to 10 square meters, therefore allowing for a very large margin of error. Archaeologists covering that region and that epoch have published few floor plans suitable for estimating residential space as opposed to space for public buildings, storage, and stabling. Any conclusions reached in the present state of our knowledge must, therefore, be tentative and provisional.

With this disclaimer behind us, we may note the following. Several excavated sites are quite major, between five and eight acres with an estimated population between 500 and 1,000 (Amihai Mazar 1990, 435). On the basis of an exceptionally good ground plan, the population of Tell en-Naṣbeh (Mizpah) stratum III has been calculated at about 1,000 (Zorn 1994). A survey of the Judean hill country by A. Ofer covered 900 square km south of Jerusalem and listed 235 sites of 1,000 square meters or more with an estimated total population of 23,000 in Iron IIC (Ofer 1993, 815–16). This would represent a fair estimate on the basis of data available at the time of writing (November 2000), but the reader will bear in mind that the interpretation of archaeological data is notoriously subject to revision.

However, assuming that Ofer's calculations are not wildly inaccurate and bearing in mind that most of the major sites lie outside the area surveyed, the total population of the province at the beginning of the Neo-Babylonian period would have been at least two and perhaps three times his estimate. Furthermore, we should not underestimate the resilience of a population afflicted in this way to restore a semblance of normality in a relatively brief time, as happened later during the numerous campaigns in Palestine from the Macedonian to the Roman period. We hear of people who had fled from the Babylonian army into the open country, to the Transjordanian kingdoms, and as far away as Egypt, who returned after the appointment of Gedaliah as the Babylonian appointee in the province (2 Kgs 25:23; Jer 40:7, 11–12).

An overall assessment of the archaeological evidence for Neo-Babylonian Judah suggests that destruction inflicted by the Babylonians was heavy but not so heavy as to destroy the social infrastructure or render any kind of cultural activity out of the question. As noted earlier, the punitive campaign of 589–586 targeted Jerusalem as the political and religious center of unrest, "a rebellious city, hurtful to kings and provinces" (Ezra 4:15), a conclusion supported by archaeological evidence (layers of ash, burned houses, Babylonian arrowheads). Nearby Ramat Raḥel (Khirbet Salih) would not have escaped the attention of the besieging army, though the archaeological evidence is less compelling and more difficult to pin down chronologically. No site, apart from Jerusalem, shows clearer indications of destruction at that time than Lachish (Tell ed-Duweir), no doubt because of its strategic importance on the route taken by armies approaching Jerusalem from the southwest. At Lachish the archaeological indications are reinforced by the twenty-two inscribed ostraca found in a gate annex from a time shortly before the arrival of the Babylonian army (David Ussishkin 1992).

Apart from these major targets of the punitive campaign, the assessment of the archaeological evidence for Judah remains somewhat indeterminate. Earlier claims for 586 B.C.E. destruction levels at several sites—Beth-shemesh, Tell Beit Mirsim, Tell el-Ful, Beth-Zur (Khirbet et-Tubeiqah), Beer-sheba, Arad, Tell Abu Hureireh (Tel Haror), the fortress of Khirbet Abu Tuwein—have either been subject to query or rejected outright. A further complication is the role played by Edomite encroachment on southern Judah both before and after the Babylonian conquest. The Arad ostraca attest to hostile Edomite presence in that region at that time, and some of the southern sites thought to have been destroyed by the Babylonians may have fallen prey to the Edomites instead (e.g. Judean Aroer, Tell el-Hesi). The bad old practice of massaging the archaeological data to align them with biblical texts may be illustrated by the case of En-Gedi. The principal excavator reported that stratum V was completely destroyed by fire in 582, but his failure to produce evidence for such a precise dating, which is hardly surprising, justifies the suspicion that the conclusion was reached not on archaeological grounds but on the basis of Jer 52:30, which lists a third deportation in the twenty-third year of Nebuchadrezzar. Terminating stratum V in 582 also has the inconvenience of leaving a gap between 582 and 500, designated as the beginning of stratum IV, the Persian period (Benjamin Mazar 1967, 85–86; 1993).

In this connection we should also take into account the role of Judah's neighbors, who saw in the Babylonian conquest an opportunity to infiltrate and take over territory in the former kingdom of Judah. With respect to Edom, this is one instance in which the biblical texts and archaeological data converge (Ezek 35:1–15; 36:5; Obad 18–19; Amos 1:11–12; Ps 137:7). Ammonites appear to have taken over Gilead (Jer 49:1 cf. 2 Kgs 24:2), and Phoenicians and Philistines profited by the situation to take over territory and capture or purchase Judean slaves (Ezek 26:1–6; Amos 1:6–10; Joel 4:6). The designs of neighboring peoples on Judean territory remained a major issue well into the Persian period. Witness Nehemiah's struggle against the Samarian Sanballat, the Ammonite Tobiah, and the Kedarite Arab Geshem (Neh 2:10, 19).

For the political organization of Judah under Babylonian control we have to depend exclusively on the biblical texts. The fact that the Neo-Babylonian royal inscriptions provide practically no information on the administration of the empire does not justify the conclusion that no provincial system existed in the west (pace David S. Vanderhooft 1999, 99). It seems evident that some kind of administrative system must have been put in place or, since the Babylonians probably took over the existing Assyrian arrangement with appropriate modifications, maintained in place. In fact, a governor (*bēl pīḥāti*) is attested for Kadesh and Arpad in Syria, and client kings were appointed in several regions, including three successively in Judah. These could not have functioned without some administrative apparatus and the determination of their sphere of jurisdiction.

After the punitive campaign of 588–586, Mizpah (Tell en-Naṣbeh), about twelve km north of Jerusalem, replaced Jerusalem as the administrative center and the residence of the Babylonian-appointed native governor (2 Kgs 25:22–26; Jer 40:6–41:18). Mizpah is on the main north–south highway, and it is possible that the governor's jurisdiction covered territories to the north incorporated into Judah by Josiah half a century earlier. Mizpah is also in the erstwhile territory of Benjamin, and it is noteworthy that no destruction level from late Iron II has so far come to light in this region north of Jerusalem. None was discovered at el-Jib, a major center of wine production, Bethel (Beitin) was destroyed sometime after 586, perhaps in the early Persian period, and Badè's excavation at Mizpah (Tell en-Naṣbeh) in the 1920s and 1930s uncovered evidence consistent with a change from border fort to provincial capital.

The territory of Benjamin, therefore, seems to have escaped the punishment visited on Judah, probably on account of either an early surrender to the Babylonians or active support of the appeasement party. We recall that Jeremiah, a Benjaminite, was aligned with the same party and was arrested for treason while attempting to leave the city during the siege (Jer 37:13). Whatever its original purpose, the census list of Ezra 2 = Nehemiah 7 names twelve or thirteen places in Benjamin in which the Babylonian *ʿolim* settled, only two located south of Jerusalem. This situation will help to explain the designation "Judah and Benjamin" for the people of Israel beginning in the Persian period (Ezra 1:5; 4:1; Neh 11:4; often in Chronicles), perhaps representing a kind of retribalization as a reaction to the loss of statehood. The upshot, at any rate, was that after 586 the political and probably also the religious center of gravity shifted from south to north.

It is difficult for us, in retrospect, to imagine that Jerusalem could ever have been eclipsed, but it would not have seemed inevitable at that time, certainly not to the Babylonians. That it was restored was due to a combination of circumstances and contingencies, not least of which was the transition to Iranian rule. The struggle for Jerusalem and, to a lesser extent and indirectly, opposition to its restoration, is reflected in late prophetic texts including Isa 40–66.

The Babylonian appointee resident at Mizpah was Gedaliah, scion of a distinguished Judean family. The biblical sources are reticent about his precise status (the word "governor" is supplied gratuitously in most modern English versions); understandably, since Gedaliah was not of the Davidic line. But in spite of the fact that the Historian does not say he was made king (using the verb *himlîk*), as with Eliakim and Mattaniah (2 Kgs 23:34; 24:17), there is reason to believe that he was set up as a puppet king, This was at any rate the standard procedure during the Neo-Babylonian period. However, Gedaliah was assassinated by a certain Ishmael, who *was* a member of the royal family. Ishmael's attempted coup, which had the backing of the Ammonite king Baalis, probably took place in 582 B.C.E. Another deportation followed, but it seems that Mizpah retained its importance as an administrative center into the early Persian period, since it served as the official residence of the satrap on visits to the province (Neh 3:7).

Since the temple of Jerusalem had been deliberately torched by the Babylonians and the altar desecrated, an alternative cult site, however modest in size, must have existed from the destruction of the Jerusalem temple in 586 to the completion of the rebuilt temple in 515. The most likely location would have been in connection with the central administration of the province at Mizpah, a situation consistent with biblical references to Mizpah as a place of cultic activity (Judg 20:1; 21:5, 8; 1 Sam 7:5–6, 8–10; 10:17; 1 Macc 3:46).

In view of the great importance of this transitional period in the history of the Israelite-Judean people, it is particularly unfortunate that our documentation is so pitifully inadequate. We can conclude that, while the Babylonian conquest clearly brought about a major disruption of the social and economic life of the province, arguments for extensive, long-term depopulation and for economic and cultural devastation lasting into the early Persian period should be treated with suspicion. It was not in Babylonian imperial interests to let the land go back to nature. We read about the property of the deported (no doubt including fairly large estates) being reassigned to peasants and small farmers (*dallat hāʾāreṣ* Jer 39:10; 40:10; Lam 5:2), a situation that promised trouble in the event of a return of the deportees (Ezek 11:15; 33:24).

THE JEWISH DIASPORA

By the end of the Neo-Babylonian period, Jews had settled in several places around the Mediterranean rim and from the Caspian Sea to Nubia. The two major centers were the alluvial plain of southern Mesopotamia around the city of Nippur (Southern Iraq and Kuwait) and Egypt from the Nile Delta to the southern border at the first cataract of the Nile (Jer 44:1; Isa 11:11; 19:18–25; 49:12). About the settlements in Lower Egypt we have little information. Jeremiah 41–44 records an exodus to Egypt after the assassination of Gedaliah led by Johanan ben Kareah and other military leaders. Some of these may have returned when the danger of Babylonian retribution had passed, while others would have settled in one or other of the Jewish enclaves already established in Egypt. Biblical texts mention Tahpanes and Migdol in the Delta (Jer 2:16; 43:7; 44:1; 46:14; Ezek 29:10). The former, also known as Daphne (Tell Defenneh), was a border post on the route through the Sinai to Palestine manned by foreign mercenaries including Jews. Migdol was somewhere in the eastern Delta region but the exact location is unknown (cf. Exod 14:2; Num 33:7). Their function would correspond to that of the Jewish military colony on the island of Elephantine at the first cataract of the Nile, settled there to guard the southern border of Egypt. There was also a Jewish settlement in Memphis, the ancient capital on the west bank of the Nile, about 20 km south of Cairo (Jer 2:16; 44:1; 46:14, 19; Ezek 30:13; Isa 19:13).

In southern Egypt (Pathros) Jews were already settled at Syene (see Isa 49:12 1QIsa[a]) at the first cataract, on the east bank opposite the island of Jeb (Elephantine). The Letter of Aristeas (line 13) tells us that Jewish mercenaries fought in the Egyptian army of Pharaoh Psammeticus (probably Psammeticus I, mid-seventh century). Some of these would have settled in Egypt, in border garrisons in the Delta region and, either then or later, at Elephantine. This Jewish military colony, known in some detail from the Aramaic papyri discovered there more than a century ago, was established before Cambyses conquered Egypt in 525, but how long before, we cannot say for sure. The settlers built their own temple, which was destroyed in a pogrom and rebuilt with the approval of the Judean governor; worshiped Yahveh (Yahu) after their own syncretic fashion; and maintained a generally peaceful if at times precarious, relationship with the natives and the Persian imperial authorities. But, since the papyri postdate Isa 40–55 (the earliest is from 495 B.C.E.), they are not our concern at the present.

Beginning with the first capture of Jerusalem in 597, Judean deportees were resettled in southern Mesopotamia, and some of the names of their settlements are known: Tel-abib (*til-abūbi*, "Mound of the deluge") on the "river Chebar" (*nār kabāri*, identified with the *Shatt en-nil* near Nippur), Tel-melach ("Salt Mound"), Tel-harsha, Cherub, Addan, Immer, Ahava, Casiphia (Ezek 1:1; 3:15; Ezra 2:59 = Neh 7:61; Ezra 8:15–17). The deportees were introduced into a situation of considerable ethnic diversity, including settlements of Lydians, Carians, Elamites, Egyptians, and others.

There had also been deportations from Palestine during the period of Assyrian domination, most recently during the reigns of Sennacherib (701) and Esarhaddon (Ezra 4:2 cf. the gloss in Isa 7:8b). It was fortunate and perhaps providential that, for economic rather than humanitarian reasons, most of the deportees were not reduced to slavery, and the fact that the Babylonians did not continue the Assyrian practice of cross-deportation determined that the possibility of a return to the Judean homeland remained open. The Babylonian authorities seem to have found it more cost-effective to practice a kind of rent capitalism by settling foreign immigrants on the land rather than using their services as slaves. That the names of most of the locations listed above are formed with *tel*, referring to an unoccupied site, further suggests that the deportees were settled in an area due for redevelopment, perhaps in the wake of the fighting between Nabopolassar and the Assyrians in the Nippur region.

From both biblical sources (Jer 29:5; Ezra 2:65) and the Murashu archive from the second half of the fifth century we learn that some Jews who had settled in Babylon were both landowners and slaveowners. It seems that ethnic minorities were permitted, and probably obliged, for sound administrative and fiscal reasons, to maintain their own distinct identities. In the early Persian period some ethnic minority groups—Scythians, Phoenicians, Egyptians—were organized in a self-governing corporation (*ḥatru*) under the supervision of a prefect (*šaknu*), and this may have been the case with Judean expatriates even earlier. The internal affairs of individual communities seem to have been regulated by a council of elders (*zĕqēnîm*) mentioned in biblical texts (Ezek 8:1; 14:1; 20:1, 3; Jer 29:1), with which we can compare the reference to a "council of the elders of the Egyptians" in a text from the early Persian period (*CHJ* 1984, 339). Thousands of cuneiform tablets from locations in southern Mesopotamia—Ur, Sippar, Nippur, Babylon, and Uruk (this last-named was the site of the temple of the goddess Eanna)—provide information on social and economic conditions during the Neo-Babylonian and Achaemenid periods.

Among these, the most interesting from the point of view of Jewish presence in the region are the archives of the commercial house of Murashu (*bit murašu*) discovered more than a century ago at Nippur and dating to the mid- to late-fifth century B.C.E. At least thirty percent of the names in the archive are non-Babylonian, and about eight percent are Jewish, either theophoric names formed with Yahveh or names familiar from the biblical texts (e.g. Hanani, Shabbetai).

The little that we know or can surmise about the life of these small Jewish or Judeo-Babylonian settlements has to be cobbled together out of inadequate source material with the help of a great deal of inference. The organization of ethnic minorities in distinct enclaves at least created a situation favorable to maintaining group identity by providing social reinforcement, sustaining common memories, and allowing for meeting places for prayer and instruction. The frequent gatherings of elders in Ezekiel's house (Ezek 8:1; 14:1; 20:1) give us an idea of what this entailed. Inevitably, many of the deportees and their descendants were assimilated both culturally and religiously, and others settled into the kind of syncretistic compromise observable in the onomastics of the Neo-Babylonian and Achaemenid periods and perhaps also in biblical texts from that time (e.g. Isa 57:3–13; 66:17). The fact remains that the situation of the deportees permitted a degree of cultural and religious continuity and therefore an eventual return of several Judeo-Babylonians to Judah. The impression conveyed by biblical texts, including Isa 40–55, about the Babylonian diaspora as a place of oppression and deprivation, is not supported by the little we know or can reasonably surmise about the condition of ethnic minorities in Neo-Babylonian Mesopotamia.

For the religious life of Jews in Babylon we have nothing comparable to the Elephantine papyri. We hear that Ezra was able to recruit cult personnel from "the place Casiphia" somewhere in the Nippur region (Ezra 8:17), and the suggestion has been made that a Jewish temple had been built there, comparable to the temple at Elephantine built before the Persian conquest of Egypt and destroyed in a pogrom in 411 B.C.E. The proposal is speculative but neither unreasonable nor implausible since it is difficult to envisage what, with licence, we might call a clergy-training center in the Babylonian diaspora unattached to a place of worship. It is also suggested from time to time that the elders consulted with Ezekiel about building a temple, a proposal which we may be sure he would have rejected (Ezek 20:1, 32). But it is evident that religious traditions could have survived only if there existed some kind of institutional infrastructure—if not a temple, then perhaps a kind of rudimentary synagogue network.

Mention of settlements near running water (Ezek 1:3; Ezra 8:15; Ps 137) suggests an emphasis on rites of purification accompanied by penitential prayer (Isa 63:7–64:12; Ezra 9:6–15) and fasting (Zech 7:3–7; 8:18–19; Ezra 8:21, 23). It was at this time that the need to resist assimilation to a multicultural and multiethnic environment under the patronage of powerful imperial deities encouraged an emphasis on rites of avoidance, dietary rules, circumcision, and the observance of sabbath. The practice of praying toward Jerusalem also seems to date to that time and place (1 Kgs 8:30, 35; Dan 6:10). It has been suggested, moreover, that the homiletic and declamatory style of religious speech well represented in Deuteronomy, Jeremiah, and Isa 40–66 could have originated in the social context of these Babylonian Jewish communities.

A final observation: the diaspora-homeland polarity that entered a new phase with the loss of the monarchy, temple cult, and the apparatus of statehood brought about the passage from national identity to confessional community, from ascriptive, ethnic self-definition to a new situation in which one could, in principle, choose to be a member of the Jewish people. The transition can be traced in the semantic expansion of the term *yĕhûdî*, *yĕhûdîm* and the increasing reference to proselytes in biblical and, eventually, nonbiblical texts.

WAS SECOND ISAIAH COMPOSED IN BABYLONIA, JUDAH, OR ELSEWHERE?

The religious bias of the biblical texts, especially Chronicles and Ezra–Nehemiah, favors the Judeo-Babylonian element as the true heirs of the old Israel and regards the population that remained in Judah and their descendants as religiously compromised. This circumstance will help to explain why we have some scraps of information in biblical texts about the religious life of Jews in Babylon but practically nothing about the situation in Judah.

One consequence is that a Babylonian location for the author of Isa 40–55 has been to all intents and purposes the consensus since the late eighteenth century and continues to be the default position in the commentary tradition (see the history of the issue in Hans Barstad 1997). For earlier commentators it did not seem to call for much argument but followed naturally from the prejudice of the biblical historiographical tradition in favor of the Babylonian Jews, the "good figs" of Jer 24. A Babylonian location also had the advantage of reinforcing the distinct authorship of chs. 40–55 vis-à-vis 1–39 from the time when this became a critical issue, and the same consideration came into play when Duhm identified chs. 56–66 as a distinct composition that he took to be of Palestinian provenance. The absence of a title to chs. 40–55 could then be explained by the need for the author to remain anonymous when proclaiming, in Babylon, the downfall of the Babylonian Empire. On this matter, one could appeal to the fate of less-prudent Judeo-Babylonian prophets and preachers, as noted in Jer 29:21–23. The biblical trope of Judah as depopulated after the fall of Jerusalem and deportations was also a relevant factor.

Once this preferential option was established, it only remained to comb through chs. 40–48 in search of confirmation. The author, it is claimed, reveals a close knowledge of Babylonian religious and intellectual traditions and practices, including the names of deities (46:1–2), ceremonies and processions (46:7), omens (44:25), magic (47:1, 12), and astrology (47:13). Perhaps most importantly, the author's message is driven by the enthusiastic expectation of an exodus from Babylon and a return to the homeland after the pattern of the exodus from Egypt (40:3–11; 42:15–16; 48:20–22; 49:9–12; 52:11–12).

Apart from the few scholars who proposed either a Phoenician (Bernhard Duhm) or Egyptian (Heinrich Ewald, Karl Marti) location, both of which views have now been abandoned, there have always been a few who have questioned the majority opinion and argued for the composition and publication of these chapters in Judah on internal textual grounds. The most prominent of these were Charles C. Torrey, Sigmund Mowinckel, Enno Janssen, and Arvid Kapelrud. Geographical references to the islands (*ʾiyyîm*), with reference to the Mediterranean littoral on the west and the Aegean, and to Kedar and Sela, referring to the Arabian Peninsula on the east (41:1, 5; 42:4, 10–11; 49:1; 51:5), seemed to be more compatible with a Palestinian than a Babylonian perspective. The ecology is claimed to be characteristic of the Syro-Palestinian region and not at all of Babylonia. The author speaks, for example, of cedars, myrtles, pines, and oleanders (41:19; 55:13), characteristic of Syria–Palestine, but never mentions the palm tree. Certain turns of phrase also seemed to point in the same direction. Judeans are urged to flee *from* Babylon (48:20) and to go out *from there* (*miššām* 52:11), Yahveh sends his agent *to* Babylon (43:14), and that agent (Cyrus) comes from a far country (46:11).

The trump card for the proponents of a Babylonian location, and the major problem for those who argued for Judah has always been the assumption that, as a result of the Babylonian conquest and successive punitive campaigns in the province, there was neither the population density nor the social and institutional infrastructure required for cultural and literary activity. But we have seen that this is questionable and that, therefore, in the present state of our knowledge, this argument cannot be pressed.

At the same time, the arguments for a Babylonian location are not as firm as some proponents seem to think. The author would not have had to be a Babylonian resident to possess the knowledge about Babylonian religious practices evinced by these chapters. Judah and southern Babylonia were part of the same empire, and the biblical texts indicate frequent contact between them. The same conclusion holds for alleged parallels with Babylonian *Hofstil* and the Cyrus cylinder in particular (see especially Gerhard Kittel 1898, 149–62; Shalom Paul 1968, 180–86). In some passages, often interpreted as promising repatriation for Judeo-Babylonians, the route in question could be interpreted metaphorically or the issue is, rather, ecological transformation of the wilderness in a more general sense (e.g. 41:17–20; 42:15–16; 43:2, 16–21; 44:3–4; 49:9–12).

The author is certainly concerned with repatriation, principally from Babylon the most important diasporic center, but not exclusively from there (41:9; 43:5; 49:12; 51:11; 55:12–13). On the other hand, the arguments for a Judean homeland for the author are no more persuasive. The positive gain here is that closer analysis of the literary and archaeological data at least permits us to contemplate the *possibility* of a location in Neo-Babylonian Judah, not necessarily in Jerusalem.

The result of the long-standing debate is therefore, disappointingly, a standoff: Isa 40–55 is too unspecific and the nonbiblical source material too exiguous to permit a definite answer. While it seems that the Babylonian consensus has been somewhat eroded in recent years, I would conclude, however that, based on a close reading of Isa 40–55, or at least the core of 40–48, together with the information currently available on the social situation of the respective locations, an origin in the Babylonian diaspora is still marginally preferable. The consideration that could tip the balance in this direction is the extent to which the thinking of the biblical author is shaped by the Babylonian ideology of power reflected in the liturgy of Marduk and its corresponding mythic expressions, a subject to which we now turn.

7. Aspects of the Theology of Isaiah 40–55

COPING WITH DISASTER

All of the biblical texts datable to the sixth century B.C.E. reflect in one way or another the void created by the loss of national institutions. All are therefore attempting in one way or another to cope with the experience of disaster. The sense of bitter abandonment following the collapse of the political and religious structures can be felt most directly and poignantly in Lamentations, composed shortly after the sack of Jerusalem and the destruction of its temple. With the exception of the men and their wives in Jeremiah's audience in Egypt who attributed the disaster to abandonment of the cult of Asherah (Jer 44:15–19), it did not occur to anyone to doubt Yahveh's responsibility for the disaster. And there was no Qoheleth around at that time to suggest that some bad things just happen. If disaster befalls a city—Jerusalem, for example—has not Yahveh done it (Amos 3:6)? If it is not he, who then is it (Job 9:24)? In his anger Yahveh has humiliated Zion and thrown Israel down on the ground (Lam 2:1–10).

Inevitably, therefore, questions arose about the power and the ethical character of the God of traditional religion: sometimes posed explicitly and systematically, as in the conversation between Abraham and Yahveh in Gen 18:22–33, the teaching of Ezekiel on individual moral accountability in Ezek 18 and the book of Job, sometimes just below the surface, as in Ps 89 ("Will you hide yourself forever?"). Questions arose spontaneously: maybe Yahveh was not a match for the Babylonian gods who sponsored the punitive campaign against Judah or, if he was, maybe he just didn't care. Ezekiel reported the kinds of things people were saying: parents eat sour grapes and the children's teeth are set on edge (18:2); Yahveh's way of acting is unfair (18:25).

The situation was further exacerbated by the loss of the normal means of mediation between God and the people. Could Yahveh be worshiped outside of the land in which his writ had run for centuries and in the absence of the temple, in which alone sacrifice could be validly offered? Could one still consult prophets who had either lost their prophetic credentials, and in many cases their lives, after predicting well-being (Lam 2:9, 14); or who had actually contributed to the disaster by pronouncing self-fulfilling prophecies of doom (Jer 44:15–19)?

Our experience teaches us that traditional religion is always in danger of being ambushed by the intractable data of experience. The experience of Judeans in the early decades of the sixth century B.C.E. just happened to be a particularly awful example. The author of the core of Isa 40–55 and his disciples or associates were confronted with the same intractable situation and therefore with the task of coming to terms with a failed history, ending in near-terminal disaster. The questions are implicit throughout and sometimes explicitly stated by the hearers. Not confined to Isa 40–55 are explanations in terms of the silence (42:14) or the hiddenness, or the forgetfulness of God. People were saying: My way is hidden from Yahveh, my cause is ignored (40:27); he has cast me off (41:9); he has forgotten me (49:14–15).

This is the situation with which the prophet is confronted. He represents the catastrophe in traditional terms of the deity's anger (42:24–25; 48:9; 51:17–23) and as a process of refining metal in the furnace (48:10), while the exile is described as a term of penal servitude now coming to an end (40:2; 52:1). This kind of language is not, for the most part, original, since these and similar motifs and figures can be found in older prophetic texts and in psalms of lamentation of which the author seems to have made generous use.

What *is* original in Isa 40–55 is the treatment of the crisis of confidence in predictive prophecy. While the expression "the former things" in Isa 40–55 (*hāriʾšōnôt*, 41:22; 42:9; 43:9, 18, 46:9; 48:3) may have more than one reference, as we have seen, at least some of the occurrences refer to earlier predictions of disaster, the fulfillment of which in the recent past guarantees the validity of the very different prophetic word now being uttered. The speaker therefore turns what was a major source of religious malaise into a positive reason for according his own message a sympathetic hearing.

THE GOD OF ISRAEL AND THE BABYLONIAN GODS

The author of the core of Isa 40–55 defies historical plausibility by concentrating on the theme of the God of Israel as victor, creator, and king. This argument inevitably unfolded against the background of overwhelming political power represented by the Babylonian Empire. The ideology sustaining this power was expressed through the cult of the imperial deity Marduk, and its principal literary expression was the creation myth *enuma elish*, recited in the course of the New Year *akitu* festival. This high point of the liturgical year was held in the god's esagila temple complex in Babylon, including the Etemenanki ziggurat, and in the *akitu* house outside the city limits.

During the Neo-Babylonian period, the festival took place during the first twelve days of the month of Nisannu (Nisan) in the spring. In the course of the first three days prayers were offered to Marduk by the sheshgallu priest, and the god's triumphs were celebrated in hymns of praise. The creation myth was recited on the fourth day, perhaps accompanied by a kind of ritual drama. On the fifth day a purification ceremony was performed, a canopy was erected in anticipation of the arrival of the god Nabū, Marduk's son, and the reigning king was ritually humiliated, stripped of his royal regalia, and received back the emblems of kingship from Marduk for the coming year. Nabū, son of Marduk, arrived from Borsippa, his city, on the following day, and subsequently the statues of the two deities were led in procession along the main thoroughfare of the city, passing through the Ishtar gate on their way to the extramural *akitu* house (*bīt akīti*).

The events of the last days of the festival are not well known, but it is probable that a banquet took place in the *akitu* house followed by a ritualized sacred marriage (*hieros gamos*) of the god and his consort, the fixing of destinies for the following year, all culminating in the triumphant reentry of the gods into Babylon, Marduk's city.

The supremacy of Marduk as imperial patron and embodiment of supreme political power comes to expression in the seven columns of the poem *Enuma Elish*, which may be briefly summarized as follows (for a more complete summary, see Alexander Heidel 1963, 3–10). In the beginning there was nothing but the divine pair Apsū and Tiamat. From these primordial deities several generations of gods were begotten, but the repose of Apsū was disturbed by the secondary gods, whom he therefore decided to destroy, a proposal rejected by his consort, Tiamat. The wise god Ea then discovers the plan and takes preemptive action by killing Apsū with the help of magic. The birth of Marduk follows, and his many attributes are described. Meanwhile, Tiamat prepares for battle to avenge the death of her consort and appoints Kingu as head of the divine assembly, leader of her army, and keeper of the tablets of destiny. Since the gods are afraid to take on Tiamat, Marduk, also known as Bēl, agrees to do so with the condition that he is appointed supreme god in the divine assembly. The gods accept with the acclamation "Marduk is king!" (*Enuma Elish* IV 28) and equip him with scepter, royal robe, throne, and magical weapons.

In the contest that follows, Tiamat is defeated and killed, and out of her body are created the sky, the stars, constellations, sun and moon, the earth and the circumfluent waters. The human being, a lowly creature (*lullu*), is created by the god Ea out of the blood of the slaughtered Kingu, mixed with slime. To humanity is assigned the task of relieving the secondary gods of the duty of serving the high gods. In gratitude, the gods erect the esagila sanctuary for Marduk, Enlil, and Ea. A banquet follows, and the destinies are fixed. The poem ends with the recital of a litany of the fifty names of Marduk and the praise of his incomparable greatness: "none among the gods can equal him" (*Enuma Elish* VII 14).

It seems that the central message of Isa 40–55 can be construed as a kind of mirror-image of the ideology expressed in the *akitu* liturgy and the *Enuma Elish* myth. The fact that the only foreign deities named in these chapters are Bēl and Nebo—that is, Marduk and his son Nabū (46:1–2), the divine protagonists in the *akitu* festival—supports this reading of the text. The Isaian passage in question can be construed as a satirical rendering of the most visible act of the *akitu* ceremony and therefore the one most likely to be familiar to non-Babylonians—namely, the procession of the statues of the two gods drawn on ceremonial chariots through the city. The idea might then be that, rather than return in triumph into Babylon from the *akitu* house, they would continue on into exile after the fall of the city.

In accord with the Babylonian imperial myth, Isa 51:9–10 revives the old mythic topos of the deity's conflict with the monster of chaos, which at once brings into play the association between conflict and creation:

> Was it not you that hacked Rahab in pieces,
> that ran the Dragon through?
> Was it not you that dried up the Sea,
> the waters of the Great Deep?

In *Enuma Elish* Tiamat, defeated and killed by Marduk (IV 71–104), represents the chaotic salt waters of the ocean. The omens and incantations involved in the struggle (IV 91) are naturally rejected by the biblical author (Isa 44:25).

The presentation of Yahveh as cosmic creator is one of the most salient features of chs. 40–48 (40:12, 26, 28; 42:5; 43:1, 15; 44:24; 45:7–8, 12, 18; 48:12–13), though present only tangentially in 49–55 (51:13, 16). Titles reflecting the same attribute also appear: "the eternal God" (40:28), "the God of all the earth" (54:5), and "the Sovereign Lord" (51:22). In the first place, the author rejects the theogony which, in *Enuma Elish* (I 9–20) and often in other creation recitals, is the first stage in the creative process:

> Before me no god was formed,
> and there will be none after me. (43:10b)

This may also be the point of the repeated insistence that Yahveh is the first and the last (41:4; 44:6; 48:12). That is, he was not generated within a family of deities.

Among other indications, the absence of any need for a counselor (*yōʿēṣ* = Akkadian *tamlāku*) is strongly reminiscent of the role of Ea, "the all-wise one" (I 60), in the creation of humanity (VI 11–16 cf. Isa 40:13–14; 41:28; see

Norman Whybray 1971, 73–74). For both Babylonians and Israelites the creation of the heavenly bodies and the control of their movements was a matter of quite extraordinary religious significance on account of the religious calendar. Yahveh's control of the rising and setting of constellations and stars could well be directed polemically against the similar claims made on behalf of Marduk as creator god (IV 141–V 22):

> Lift up your eyes to the sky,
> consider who has created these;
> he leads out their host one by one,
> summoning each by name. (40:26)

> My hands stretched out the sky
> and marshaled all its host. (45:12)

In *Enuma Elish* the acclamation of Marduk's universal and supreme kingship ("Marduk is king!" *Marduk-ma šarru* IV 28) is closely associated with his creative role but occurs before the conflict with Tiamat and therefore before the creation of the world and humanity. While the acclamation *YHVH mālak* in the so-called kingship psalms (93:1; 96:10; 97:1; 99:1) carries associations of cosmogonic conflict and of other mythical representations, the Isaian author places his similar exclamation squarely in a historical and political context, that of his aspirations for the future of Jerusalem:

> How welcome on the mountains are the footsteps of the herald
> announcing well-being, bringing good tidings, announcing victory,
> declaring to Zion: "Your God reigns as king!" (52:7)

Closely connected with the idea of universal kingship is that of the incomparability of the deity. The claim pronounced by Babylon in the guise of a queen, "I am, and there is none other" (47:8, 10), reproduces the praise of Marduk in *Enuma Elish* as being without equal among the gods (VII 14, 88). If Second Isaiah is generally given credit for the first clear statement of monotheistic faith, it may be on account of formulations generated by polemic of the kind we are discussing. At any rate, the incomparability of the God of Israel is one of the great leitmotifs of chapters 40–48 (40:18, 25; 43:11; 44:6–8; 45:5–6, 14, 18, 21–22; 46:9), and the formula "I am Yahveh/God, and there is no other" (45:5, 6, 18b, 22; 46:9) is practically identical with the praise of Marduk in the creation poem.

This reading of Isa 40–55 allows us to place it among the various attempts in the extant post-destruction biblical texts to account for the recent disasters. The author is not much concerned with the aspect of the problem dealing with worship—how sacrificial cult or indeed cult of any kind could continue to be offered to Yahveh in the absence of a temple and for devotees living outside of Yahveh's land. The prospect of rebuilding the Jerusalem temple is mentioned only once (44:28b), and tribute is brought to Jerusalem but not to the temple (45:14), in contrast to the emphasis on the temple in the last part of the book (e.g. 60:5–7). The one complaint about failure to sacrifice (43:22–24) seems curiously out of place since animal sacrifice is otherwise unattested in that period. If we are not willing to fall back on the time-honored recourse of an insertion, it could refer to the time when the Jerusalem temple still existed. The occasional echoes of psalms of lament and the hymn stanzas interspersed among the discourses (42:10–13; 44:23; 45:8; 49:13) do not affect this conclusion, nor do they provide adequate support for the hypothesis that the author was associated with the temple musicians or their surviving descendants (Claus Westermann 1969, 8; Rainer Albertz 1994, 415).

In this respect, Isa 40–55 contrasts with the concern for worship in Ezekiel. The deportations confronted the deportees with the question whether worship was possible outside of the territorial jurisdiction of the deity. They were therefore challenged to abandon the idea of Yahveh as a purely locative deity, if they were to continue as Yahveh-worshipers at all. We recall David, who cursed those who had driven him out of Judah to serve other gods (1 Sam 26:19), Naaman the Syrian general who took a load of Israelite earth back to Damascus in order to be able to venerate Yahveh (2 Kgs 5:17), and the question asked in Ps 137, "how can we sing hymns to Yahveh in a foreign land?" At the symbolic level, the solution is presented in Ezekiel's vision of the mobile throne (Ezek 1:1–28; 10:1–17) and the migration of the divine radiance (*kābôd*) by stages from Jerusalem to Babylon where the vision could therefore take place (Ezek 10:18–19; 11:23). The implications of severing the links between deity and territory, one of the subplots in the book of Jonah, were far-reaching but, to repeat, this is one aspect of the crisis that is not a major concern in Isa 40–55.

Rather more surprising is the relative lack of interest in the issue of theodicy, painfully debated in Job and explored in the dialogue of Abraham with God about the destruction of Sodom (Gen 18:22–33). We hear a complaint that the people's just cause goes unnoticed by their God (40:27), to which the answer is that God knows what he is doing, he is all-powerful, you must be patient and wait (vv 28–31); not so different an answer, therefore, from the display of divine power in nature with which Job's complaint is answered. The issue is raised later in a more explicitly disputatious context:

Call me to judgment, let us argue the case together.
Set out your case that you may be proved right.
Your first ancestor sinned;
your spokesmen transgressed against me,
so I profaned the princes of the sanctuary;
I delivered Jacob up to ruin,
Israel to reviling. (43:26–28)

The disaster is therefore explained along classical Deuteronomic lines as the outcome of collective guilt and the failure to heed prophetic admonitions:

> Who delivered Jacob to the despoiler,
> Israel to the plunderers?
> Was it not Yahveh, against whom they have sinned,
> unwilling as they were to follow his guidance
> and heed his teaching? (42:24)

If we assume that the guidance referred to comes through prophetic admonition, this is pure Deuteronomic doctrine. A later text (Isa 48:3–5) will add the typically Deuteronomic accusation of adopting non-Yahvistic cults, the principal reason for the disaster according to the History.

The argument advanced in Isa 40–55 required emphasis on the deity's power and effective action in the political arena rather than on justice. To some extent this appeal to divine power sounds disturbingly close to the Rabshakeh's attempt to get Hezekiah to capitulate by asking whether the Judean deity could hope to succeed where the gods of other lands had failed (2 Kgs 18:33–35); we recall that Assyrian campaigns were sponsored by and carried out in the name of the imperial deity, Ashur. The dangers inherent in this approach are obvious. Political failure can leave such claims sounding hollow but, even when the course of events appears to justify the claims, there is the risk of projecting chauvinistic and xenophobic group interests, aspirations, or resentments onto the deity at the expense of outsiders, the others.

As it happened, the worst of such consequences were avoided by the failure of Cyrus to live up to the expectations placed on him in the name of Israel's God. On the other side of the balance, the introduction and development within these chapters of the linked ideas of servanthood and mission, including a mission to other peoples, the outsiders, a mission that could encompass defeat and suffering, is one of the great innovations in religious thinking in antiquity.

DIVINE TITLES AND ATTRIBUTES

The range of designations and titles assigned to Yahveh, Israel's God, in Isa 40–55 provides a good example of the tensive relationship between tradition and situation that seems to be at the core of theology. These cannot be listed and discussed *in extenso*, but some of the more important deserve mention (for a more complete lexicon, see P.-E. Bonnard 1972, 497–505, 520–46). We have seen how centrally important to the message of these chapters is the proclamation of Yahveh as cosmic creator; the verb *br'* is used sixteen times in chs. 40–55 and only once, in a late passage, in 1–39 (4:5). Equally prominent is "redeemer" (*gō'ēl* 41:14; 43:14; 44:6, 24; 47:4; 48:17; 49:7, 26; 54:5, 8), this one entirely absent from Isa 1–39. The idea of redemption originated in the sphere of customary family law, according to which the nearest of kin assumes the obligation or exercises the right (known as the *gĕ'ullâ*) to free a relative from indentured service or repurchase property sold under duress (e.g. Lev 25:25–26, 47–55; Ruth 2:20; 3:9, 12; 4:1–12). There was also the obligation in the kinship group to act as the avenger of blood (*gōʾēl haddām* e.g. Num 35:9–28; Josh 20:3, 9). The basic idea seems to be that of restoring a disturbed divinely sanctioned order. That Yahveh as redeemer is so prominent in these chapters is related to the author's idea of exile as a form of indentured service and his concern for return to and repossession of the land, the "desolate heritages" (49:8). It also implies that, though frustrated by the unforeseen course of events, the initial impulse was toward political and social restoration.

While the language of redemption inevitably brings to mind the tradition of the Exodus from Egypt and trek through the wilderness to Canaan, the verb itself (*gʾl*) is not prominent in the biblical account of those events. Yahveh promises to redeem his people "with an outstretched arm" (*bizrōaʿ nĕṭûyâ* Exod 6:6, a "canonical" phrase in this connection), and the Song at the Papyrus Sea speaks of God's leading his redeemed people to his holy abode (Exod 15:13). Neither of these texts is ancient or even necessarily earlier than Isaiah 40–55, and the same can be said for the few allusions to redemptive divine action during the Exodus in Psalms (Pss 77:16; 106:10). But the closely related verb, *pdh* ("redeem, ransom, rescue"), which often appears in parallelism with *gʾl* (Isa 35:9–10; 51:10–11; Jer 31:11; Hos 13:14; Ps 69:19), is the standard Deuteronomic term for divine intervention during the Exodus (Deut 7:8; 9:26; 13:6; 15:15; 21:8; 24:18), and it seems that the language of redemption in Isa 40–55 has been mediated through Deuteronomic usage. Perhaps *gʾl* was preferred to *pdh* because of the associations with land and indentured service mentioned earlier. This, again, is a theme entirely absent from the sayings of the First Isaiah.

NARRATIVE TRADITIONS IN ISAIAH 40–55

Isaiah 43:14–21 sets up a typology between the passage through the Papyrus Sea and the destruction of the Egyptian army on the one hand and the defeat of the Babylonians, leading to the journey back to Judah on the other. The latter is a chain of events that is new (*ḥădāšâ*) but patterned on what, in common belief, were events that happened in Israel's beginnings (*riʾšōnôt, qadmōniyyôt*). This anticipated return from Babylon is also described as an exodus in 48:20–21, the connection being indicated by the command itself—*ṣĕʾû mibbābel*, "go out from Babylon," using the standard exodus verb, *yṣʾ*, and the motif of water from the rock (cf. Exod 17:1–7; Num 20:2–13). The same typological superimposition has strong mythological undertones in 51:9–10:

> Was it not you that hacked Rahab in pieces,
> that ran the Dragon through?
> Was it not you that dried up the Sea,
> the waters of the Great Deep?

Was it not you that made the depths of the Sea
a route for the redeemed to traverse?

So, the poet continues, you will enable your ransomed people to return rejoicing to Zion; and this is also the destination of the redeemed in the Song at the Papyrus Sea (Exod 15:17).

Allusion to this Exodus typology is not always as overt as in these passages. The description of Yahveh as *ʾîš milḥāmôt*, "a warrior," in Isa 42:13 is paralleled only in the Song at the Papyrus Sea (Exod 15:3, *ʾîš milḥāmâ*), which also ends with the acclamation of Yahveh as king (Exod 15:18 cf. Isa 52:7). The prediction that the descendants of the deportees will not leave their exile in haste (52:12), following an explicit reference to the Exodus (vv 3–4), echoes Exod 12:11 and Deut 16:3, the command to eat the Passover in haste (*bĕḥippāzôn*, only in these three texts).

In Isa 50:2–3 the drying up of the sea, the turning of rivers into a desert, and the resulting stink of dead fish is a rather more elusive reference to the story of those founding events (Exod 7:18, 21; 8:10; cf. Isa 51:10). The frequent reference in these chapters to Yahveh's arm (40:10; 48:14; 51:5, 9; 52:10; 53:1) and hand (41:10, 20; 48:13; 49:22; 50:2) brings to mind the canonical phrase for divine action in the Exodus, "with a mighty hand and an outstretched arm" (Deut 4:34).

This often quite nuanced interplay of theme should not be placed under the rubric of intertextuality, as if the Exodus texts were already in place, waiting to be reread, reinterpreted, and reappropriated, since it is quite possible that, *in their present form*, they postdate the composition of Isa 40–55. It is more a case of typology, of appealing to traditional narrative themes, certainly very familiar by that time, to articulate and make intelligible new prospects and possibilities.

Other titles and designations for Yahveh are closely associated with redemptive activity (*gōʾēl*, "Redeemer") and often appear in parallelism with it. One of the most frequent is "savior" (*mōšîaʿ*, 43:3, 11; 45:15, 21; 47:15; 49:26), also absent from Isa 1–39. More familiar from Isaiah 1–39, though not limited to those chapters, are the titles the "Holy One of Israel" (*qĕdôš yiśrāʾēl* 41:14; 43:14; 47:4; 48:17; 49:7; 54:5) and "Yahveh of the (heavenly) hosts" (*YHVH ṣĕbāʾôt*, 44:6; 45:13; 47:4; 48:2; 51:15; 54:5). Equally traditional, though less in evidence, are the epithets the "Rock" (*ṣûr* 44:8) often predicated of Yahveh in hymns ancient (Deut 32:4, 15, 18, 30–31; 1 Sam 2:2; 2 Sam 22:3, 32, 47; 23:3) and modern ("Rock of Ages"), and the "Powerful One" (*ʾabîr*, 49:26, artificially distinguished from *ʾabbîr*, "Bull," Gen 49:24; Ps 132:2, 5; Isa 1:24).

The author of Isa 40–55 and his circle had much deeper roots in Israelite narrative traditions than the First Isaiah, no doubt on account of the sense of detachment from the traditions at that time and later ("Abraham does not know us, Israel does not acknowledge us," 63:16) and the need to reestablish lines of continuity with the past.

The most visible indication is the frequent use of the personal name *Jacob* for the community addressed, a practice that became common only in the post-destruction period. (There are, at most, two occurrences in the original core of Isa 1–39: that is, 8:17 and 9:7.) It is hardly coincidental that the career of Jacob as narrated in the fascinating story in Gen 25–35 corresponds structurally to the experience and the aspirations of the communities addressed by the author of Isa 40–55. The story pivots on exile in Mesopotamia and return to the land, and what drives the narrative is the repeated promise of blessing, land, and progeny (28:13–15; 31:3, 13). The problematic relations between Jacob and Esau (representing Edom) and the important role assigned to the Bethel sanctuary might also be noted in this respect. But the relation between Isa 40–55 and the Genesis narrative cannot be explained on the assumption that the narrative as we have it was already available to the Isaian author in the mid–sixth century B.C.E. Apart from Hos 12:4–5, 13, there are no narrative traditions about Jacob in texts from the time of the kingdoms outside of Genesis, and the lack of detail about Jacob in Isa 40–55 might suggest that at the time of writing, the story had not yet attained its final form.

While Abraham is a more shadowy figure than Jacob in compositions from the early post-destruction period, it seems that his story could be appealed to by both diaspora Jews and those who remained behind in Judah. The latter could argue that "Abraham was only one man, yet he got possession of the land; we are many, so the land is surely given for us to possess it" (Ezek 33:24). Among the expatriates, however, Abraham, as the first *ʿoleh* (immigrant), could serve as a model for those who contemplated a return to Judah as the nucleus of a new people on its own land. For the author of Isa 40–55 Abraham, friend of God (41:8 cf. *Ibrahim al khalil*), could be presented along with Sarah as the recipient of blessing and the founder of a people, and therefore as a model and source of inspiration (Isa 51:1–2).

The relevance of Abraham to that generation is also apparent in Isa 29:22, which speaks of the redemption of Abraham. Here his departure from Ur is an anticipation of Israel's departure from Egypt (see vol. 1, pp. 407–10). It would therefore not be surprising if some Abrahamic traits have entered into the profile of Yahveh's Servant (Torrey 1928, 136, 141).

The blessing of Abraham, which was passed on to the generations following, was probably in the writer's mind in another place, although the name *Abraham* was not used:

> I will pour out my spirit on your descendants,
> my blessing on your offspring. (44:3b)

The context in which this declaration is made (44:3–5) suggests that the blessing of Abraham (Gen 12:1–3) is here interpreted as applying to adherents of the Yahveh cult—proselytes, in other words (cf. 60:21–22; 61:8–9. In undertaking a journey of faith out of paganism and idolatry, Abraham was seen by later writers to exhibit the characteristics of the perfect proselyte, one who "passes over" (*peratēs* in Philo: *Migr.* 4:20 cf. Heb 11:9, 13; Origen: *PG* 12:725).

Other allusions to narrative traditions of a more fleeting nature can be identified: the great deluge (54:9–10), not necessarily or even probably dependent on Gen 6–9; Israel being borne along by God in its progress through the wilderness (40:11; 46:3–4); or borne aloft on eagles' wings (40:31 cf. Exod 19:4; Deut 32:11); and provided with water (41:17–18; 43:19–20; 44:3; 48:21; 49:9–10).

Little use is made of legal traditions; Moses is not mentioned, though some have found an allusion to the revelation in the burning thornbush in the divine self-predication *ʾănî hûʾ* ("I am he"? "I am the One"? 43:13, 25; 46:4; 47:8, 10; 48:12; 52:6). As in the first section of the book, the term *tôrâ* can refer to prophetic teaching (51:4, 7). In one instance, assuming the identification of the servant of 42:1–4 with Cyrus, *tôrâ* refers to the Persian idea of law and order (*dāta* 42:4). Where *tôrâ* is used in the more familiar sense (42:21, 24), no specific stipulations of law are mentioned.

JERUSALEM/ZION AS THE GOAL OF THE JOURNEY

In his discussion of the linked themes of Jacob and Zion, Hans-Jürgen Hermisson (1998b,148) argues against the opinion of Klaus Kiesow (1979, 197–201), which is that the Zion texts are not part of the original *Wegtheologie* of Second Isaiah but were added to it as the goal of the journey and therefore represent a later redactional layer of the text. Hermisson makes the reasonable point that the author would not have left the Israelites wandering aimlessly around in the desert and that, therefore, the goal must have been in sight from the beginning; hence, the two sections 40–48 and 49–55, are thematically inseparable. In the first section, Jacob/Israel is center-stage, while Jerusalem/Zion is seldom mentioned, either as representing its Judean population (40:2; 41:27; 48:2) or as destined to be rebuilt and repopulated through the agency of Cyrus (44:26, 28; 45:13). In the second section (49–55), the name *Jacob* occurs only once, in the context of divine titulary (49:26). The change in emphasis is noticeable; it indicates a later stage of development, possibly even a different location, but not necessarily different authorship.

In chs. 49–55, therefore, Zion enters the stage as a participant in the dialogue. The traditional symbolism of city as woman is fully exploited. Her complaint of marital abandonment (49:14) is answered with the assurance that she is not forgotten (49:15), that the separation was only for a short time (*běregaʿ qāṭon* 54:7), that the accusation of divorce does not have the support of documentary evidence (50:1), that she need no longer complain of being a widow (54:4), and that she will have a new family, more children than she can count, and good living quarters (49:14–26; 54:1–17). This is, in essence, the message delivered in the three long apostrophes to Zion—49:14–26; 51:12–52:10 (with some confusion with pronomial suffixes in 51:12–16 and a prose addition in 52:3–6); and 54:1–17—which form the nucleus of Isa 49–55.

It is interesting to compare the Jerusalem of Isa 40–55 with references to the city in chs. 1–39. The first section of the book ends with the miraculous deliverance of Jerusalem, which has been under siege by the Assyrians. This deliverance must have given substance to the idea of the inviolability of the city, which was seen as the place chosen by Yahveh for his residence, the cosmic mountain, and the center of the universe, themes celebrated in the temple liturgy (e.g. Pss 48, 87, 122, 132). Apart from chs. 36–39, deriving from the History and featuring a prophetic figure significantly different from the Isaiah of the sayings, we find a counterpoint between condemnations of the empirical Jerusalem, sometimes in language strong enough to earn Isaiah a rebuke from rabbinic commentators (e.g. Isa 1:10, 21), and visions of an eschatological Jerusalem, a place from which will emanate salutary instruction, the epicenter of a world in which there will be no more war and violence, in which God will wipe away all tears, and death itself will be abolished (2:2–4; 25:6–10; 27:12–13). This Jerusalem of the end time will be inhabited by the holy remnant of the people (4:2–6), the penitents who will be set aside from rebels and sinners destined for eternal reprobation (1:27–31).

The social situation to which sayings of this kind corresponded was one of increasing division within the Judean polity, a situation moving in the direction of open sectarianism. From chs. 56–66 we see that the struggle for control of the city and temple was a crucial factor in bringing this situation about. None of this is as yet apparent in 40–55 in which, in spite of the idealization and personification of Jerusalem, the emphasis is on the empirical city, still lying depopulated and in ruins.

From this time on, well beyond the biblical period and indeed down to the present, Jerusalem was to remain an ambiguous and contentious symbol. For some, including the author of Isa 40–55, it was a focus of political aspirations; for others, a metahistorical reality. The range of perspectives can be gauged by a selective reading of texts from the Neo-Babylonian and early Persian periods (e.g. Jer 31:38–40; Ezek 5:5; 38:12; 40–48; Haggai; Zech 1–8) down into late antiquity (e.g. *4 Ezra* 10:25–54), including early Christianity (e.g. Heb 12:22; Rev 3:12; 21:1–22:5). The contrast between the earthly and heavenly Jerusalem developed in allegorical fashion by Paul (Gal 4:24–26) provided a point of departure for the immensely influential theology of history in Augustine's *City of God*.

IS THE AUTHOR OF ISAIAH 40–55 A SPOKESMAN FOR RELIGIOUS UNIVERSALISM?

That the Second Isaiah was the prophet of universalism who proclaimed for the first time that knowledge of the one true God was to be shared with all peoples of the world is one of the more widespread assumptions in biblical scholarship. Underlying the claim is the basic understanding of the importance of this slippery term *universalism* and its antonym *particularism* in the context of religious discourse. No religious group can be universalist in the sense of abdicating the right to define ultimate religious goals and to control access to membership in it if it is to continue in existence.

With regard to the people addressed in chs. 40–55, the evident Israel-centered and Jerusalem-centered outlook that they are assumed to share with the speaker at once sets a limit on what degree of religious universalism we can expect to find in these chapters. The proclamation of the God of Israel as universal creator and ruler is clearly important in this regard, but its universalist significance must be qualified with the reminder that Yahveh's dominion is primarily for the benefit of his own devotees and is to be inaugurated in Jerusalem. Prophets had always been concerned with international affairs, and the designation of Cyrus as agent of the God of Israel was not an innovation (cf. "Nebuchadrezzar my servant," Jer 25:9).

Moreover, the attitude toward foreign peoples in Isa 40–55 is not particularly benign. They and their rulers are to be subject to Israel (49:7; 54:3), they will perform menial labor for Yahveh's people, be forced to prostrate themselves before the elect, and lick the dust of their feet (49:23). Furthermore, one of the principal tasks laid on foreigners is to see to the repatriation of Jews dispersed throughout the vast Babylonian Empire (49:22).

This is the negative side of religious universalism: the correlation between triumphant monotheistic faith and political domination, limited to the realm of fantasy fueled by resentment in exilic prophecy, translated into harsh and intolerant reality in the course of the history of the three great monotheistic faiths. The positive side emerges from the idea of servanthood, the breakthrough idea of prophet and people in the service of a wider public than Israel. The two tendencies, expansionist and integrationist, would remain in tension throughout the entire period of the Second Temple. The author of Isa 40–55 is therefore a universalist only in a very qualified sense. What we can say is that he and his disciples laid the foundations for later developments by making it possible to think of a role for Israel in the salvation of humanity.

We return to a text quoted earlier in connection with Abraham as the model and patron of the proselyte:

> I will pour out my spirit on your descendants,
> my blessing on your offspring. . . .
> This one will say, "I belong to Yahveh,"
> another will take the name Jacob,
> yet another will write Yahveh's name on the hand
> and add the name Israel to his own. (44:3b, 5)

If we are correct in finding here a reference to the Abrahamic blessing (Gen 12:1–3), we may conclude that this well-known text is being reinterpreted by prophetic authority in the light of a new situation, that of a confessional community rather than a nation state, and therefore community adherence to which can come about by personal decision rather than by ascription. Adherence is sealed by certain external, symbolic acts signifying a change of allegiance—perhaps significantly, not including circumcision.

All of this is couched in the future tense, and we have no hard information on what it corresponds to in terms of social realities in that future time and place. Somewhat later we come upon the passage most often quoted in this connection:

> Turn to me and accept salvation,
> all the ends of the earth!
> For I am God, and there is none other.
> I have sworn an oath by my life;
> the word that overcomes has gone forth from my mouth,
> the word that will not be made void:
> "To me every knee will bend,
> by me every tongue will swear an oath,"
> About me it will be said,
> "Victory and strength come only from Yahveh." (45:22–24)

The summons is addressed to survivors among the nations, certainly Gentiles, and it goes out to the ends of the earth. All are invited to turn to Yahveh and accept salvation, but what does this "turning to Yahveh" as the precondition for salvation imply? One could turn to a deity and offer cult in return for favors without making a break with existing allegiances. To use A. D. Nock's well-known distinction (1933, *Conversion* 7 and passim), adhesion was possible without conversion. In this instance, however, the sequel—bending the knee (*proskynesis*) and a confession of faith—suggests the abandonment of previous cults and a radical religious reorientation.

To the taking of a new name and writing the name of the deity on the hand (44:5) is now added a confession of faith. A more explicit formulation appears earlier in the same chapter: "Surely God is with you, there is no other, there is no God but he" (45:14).

Similar formulations can be found in historical narrative, generally if not invariably of Deuteronomic stamp. Rahab of Jericho recites what sounds like a piece of catechetical instruction and then confesses, "Yahveh your God is the one who is God in heaven above and on earth beneath" (Josh 2:9–11). Other examples begin in formulaic fashion with the words "now I know" (*ʿattâ yādaʿtî*). So Jethro, after being catechized by Moses, exclaims: "Now I know that Yahveh is greater than all the gods" (Exod 18:8–12). On being healed, Naaman the Syrian makes the extraordinary confession: "Now I know that there is no God in all the earth except in Israel" (2 Kgs 5:15). The conclusion seems warranted that these and similar formulations reflect the beginnings of proselytism in the Neo-Babylonian period, to which Isa 40–55 also attests, and that this development is in the last resort the most significant aspect of religious universalism in these chapters.

SERVANTS OF GOD IN ISAIAH 40–55

The frequent use of the title "servant" (*ʿebed*), in the sense of "agent" or "instrument," in Isa 40–55 is one of several features distinguishing this section of the book from what precedes and follows. In one respect, the idea of prophetic agency or instrumentality is one of the key contributions of Isa 40–55 to the religious thought of ancient Israel and emergent Judaism. In Isa 1–39 *ʿebed* occurs only twice in a religiously significant sense, and neither of these cases is Isaian, since "my servant David" (37:35) belongs to the long final section taken from the History (2 Kgs 19:34), while "my servant Isaiah" (20:3) appears in a passage (Isaiah walking through the city naked, as a proleptic sign of defeat and captivity) of transparently Deuteronomic origin (vol. 1, pp. 312–23). In the last section of the book (chs. 56–66) *ʿebed* appears ten times, always plural, and I will argue that these Servants are closely connected with the individual Servant of chs. 49–55.

The position taken in the commentary is that the Servant of 42:1–4 is Cyrus and that the remaining twelve uses of the word in 40–48, all singular, denote Jacob, ancestor and representative of the people of Israel. In 49–55, on the other hand, all eight instances except the last (54:17, which speaks of the heritage of Yahveh's Servants) are located in the three Servant passages identified by Duhm, although 49:7, referring to one who is "the servant (slave?) of rulers," appears in a comment on the passage immediately preceding.

The origin of this usage of "servant" as representative can be traced to the Deuteronomists and is therefore in evidence in Deuteronomy, the History, and related writings, including the rewritten book of Jeremiah. In these writings the term *ʿebed* encapsulates the religious significance of the closely related institutions of the monarchy and prophecy. The Davidic ruler is *ʿebed YHVH*, Yahveh's agent, especially in times of political and military crisis (2 Sam 3:18; 1 Kgs 8:24–26; 2 Kgs 19:34; Jer 33:21–22, 26). Prophets are also *ʿăbādîm*, or "his servants the prophets" (*ʿăbādâv hannĕbîʾîm* 2 Kgs 9:7; 17:13, 23 etc.), and the designation is used of individual prophets in the History: Ahijah, Elijah, Jonah ben Amittai (1 Kgs 15:29; 2 Kgs 9:36; 10:10; 14:25).

According to Deuteronomic theory, Moses the protoprophet is the preeminent Servant of God (Deut 34:5; Josh 1:2; 9:24) and, as such, intercedes, suffers, and offers his life on behalf of his people (Exod 32:11–14, 30–34; 33:12–16). This profile signals a new phase of interest in prophetic biography, and it was with this Deuteronomic portrait of Moses and the closely related figure of a persecuted Jeremiah in mind that von Rad argued for a new concept of the prophetic office coming to expression in the Isaian Servant, presented as a "prophet like Moses" (von Rad 1965, 261).

The main features of this prophetic profile can be abstracted from the three key passages in Isa 49–55 (49:1–6; 50:4–9; 52:13–53:12) providing a kind of rudimentary prophetic martyr biography. The prophet is predestined for a mission before birth (49:1), lives his early life under the providence of God (53:2a), is equipped for a mission involving prophetic speech and instruction away from the public eye (49:2; 50:4a), and receives divinely revealed knowledge and guidance (50:4b). The mission is directed first to Israel (49:5–6a; 50:4a) and then to foreign peoples (49:6b). The sense of inadequacy and discouragement in the face of opposition (49:4a) gives way to the assurance of ultimate vindication (49:4b; 50:7–9). Opposition escalates into open abuse (50:6; 53:3), leading eventually to a violent death (53:7–12).

That suffering and violent death can be the price to pay for a prophetic mission is attested in the biblical record, but that they can have a positive, salvific effect on others, that a prophet can substitute for others by taking on himself the consequences of their wrongdoing (as is claimed for the prophetic Servant in ch. 53) is unprecedented, even if it is not entirely unanticipated. In the first place, intercession had always been an important prophetic function, the implication being that, by interceding, the prophet could influence God not to inflict on the guilty the consequences of their guilt (e.g. Amos 7:1–4).

It was also attested that the prophetic mission can be more than episodic, that it can involve a degree of life-investment, including persecution and suffering. Elijah reached the point of wishing to die (1 Kgs 19:4), while Jeremiah expressed his anguish and frustration, together with a fair amount of *Schadenfreude*, in a series of "confessions" that appear to be modeled on the psalms of individual lamentation (Jer 11:18–20; 12:1–4; 15:10–18; 17:14–18; 18:19–23; 20:7–12, 14–18). Others lost their lives in the pursuit of their prophetic mission: we hear of a certain Zechariah during the reign of Joash (2 Chr 24:20–21); Uriah, a contemporary of Jeremiah (Jer 26:20–23), was put to death by Jehoiakim. Furthermore, some who appear to have survived were later accorded the laurels of martyrdom in popular tradition (e.g. Isaiah, Jeremiah). By the time of early Christianity, at any rate, the theme of the martyred prophet was familiar and could be applied retrospectively to Jesus (Matt 23:30–31; Acts 7:52; Heb 11:36–38).

In biblical tradition Moses was the great intercessor (e.g. Exod 32:30–34; 33:12–16; Num 21:7; 11:2; Deut 9:20, 26), and his intercession could take the form of atoning for the sins of his people (verbal stem *kpr*) and even offering his life to God (Exod 32:30–34). But he does not die, not at that point at any rate, and we are not told that his sufferings had a salvific effect on others.

The possibility that the prophet or the righteous person (*ṣaddîq*) can affect the fate of the unrighteous is, however, entertained in the remarkable passage in which Abraham attempts to persuade Yahveh to revoke the sentence of extermination passed on the Cities of the Plain (Gen 18:22–33). We are unfortunately not told how it was thought that this might come about. All we deduce from the conversation is that in principle it can come about by divine decree or decision, but that in this instance the critical mass necessary (at least ten individuals) was lacking. Rabbinic commentary on the passage (e.g. *Gen. Rab. Vayyera* 49:3, 9; *Gen. Rab. Noah* 35:2) contributed to the topos of the thirty-six *ṣaddîqîm*, the *lamed vavniks*, who maintain the world in existence. However, to the same problem Ezekiel provides a quite different solution. In discussing sin and its consequences, the prophet proposes the example of a land (Judah, for example) visited with various disasters on account of its sins. Even if Noah, Daniel, and Job, those ancient models of piety and virtue, lived in it, they would save only themselves, not even their immediate families, by virtue of their righteousness (*bĕṣidqātām* Ezek 14:12–20).

We see, then, that various elements of the situation described in Isa 53 had already developed: intercession and atonement by prophetic agency, an incipient prophetic martyrdom tradition, and the possibility that the righteous could *in some way* influence the fate of the unrighteous. These cannot, however, either singly or in combination, account for the unique feature of the fourth Servant passage. There is, first, a causal connection between the sins of the people represented by the speaker and the sufferings of the servant: "he was wounded because of our transgressions, crushed on account of our iniquities" (53:5a). The traditional teaching posited a causal link between sin and misfortune, but in this instance the misfortune is redirected from its due target to the Servant, and it is quite explicitly stated that the redirection is brought about by a positive act of God: "Yahveh laid upon him the iniquity of us all" (v 6b); "It was Yahveh's good pleasure to crush him" (10a). This is what is meant by the Servant's carrying our afflictions and bearing (the burden of) our sufferings (4a,12b). We note something of the same in Lam 5:7, which uses identical language but in the form of an implicit reproach or accusation: "our ancestors sinned . . . and we have borne (the consequences of) their iniquities" (*ʾābōtênû ḥāṭĕʾû . . . vaʾănaḥnû ʿăvônōtêhem sābalnû*).

The theological difficulties involved in this situation have often been noted. The most obvious problem is that the text seems to attribute to the God of Israel an arbitrary and unjust way of administering justice. Kant's objection (in *Religion within the Boundaries of Mere Reason)* that sin is not a transmissible liability that can be eliminated in the manner of a financial debt, is often cited in this connection. In Christian theology substitutionary views of redemption through the passion and death of Jesus based on Isa 53, especially under the category of satisfaction expounded by Anselm, have given rise to major problems. These cannot be discussed here (see the essays in Janowski and Stuhlmacher 1996 and Bellinger and Farmer 1998), but one final exegetical point of clarification may be noted. The fact that the death of the Servant is represented as a guilt offering (*ʾāšām*, v 10) may have been the integrative factor in the author's attempt to search, in unexplored territory, for an explanation of what had happened.

The sacrifice of the *ʾāšām*, a ram or a lamb, was a form of atonement for those who had incurred guilt as a result of sinning (Lev 5:14–26). The idea would be that now that the temple is in ruins and sacrifice no longer possible, the Servant serves as a substitute for the sacrificial guilt offering, one that is accepted by God and, in some mysterious way in keeping with God's absolute freedom, rendered beneficial to others. The sacrificial metaphor provided a first insight, an initial clue, to the meaning of the Servant's fate, not a comprehensive theological account of the ways of God with his people and with humanity.

8. The Text of Isaiah 40–55 and the Ancient Versions

The text of the Hebrew Bible in common use today, on which recent translations are based, is *Biblia Hebraica Stuttgartensia* (BHS), which reproduces the medieval Leningrad codex of the Hebrew Bible, written in 1009. *The Book of Isaiah*, the first volume of the Hebrew University Bible Project (Moshe H. Goshen-Gottstein [ed.] 1995), reproduces the Aleppo Codex, written in the early tenth century, together with its *masora parva* and *masora magna* and a rich critical apparatus. It represents a distinct advance over BHS and is in every respect an instrument of great value to the student of the book.

These two codices and other members of the same Masoretic textual family exhibit a high level of uniformity in detail. Even the readings from non-Masoretic medieval manuscripts incorporated into this edition of the Hebrew Bible by Kennicott in 1776 show few variants from the standard Masoretic type, an exception being the omission of "Israel" from Isa 49:3 in Kenn. 96. Written about a millennium earlier, the fragmentary Isaiah scroll from the first Qumran cave (1QIsa[b]), containing the continuous though often fragmentary text of chs. 41–66, is practically identical with the medieval Masoretic Text—a remarkable testimony to the fidelity with which the biblical text was copied and transmitted. It is fortunate that, compared with other prophetic material, Isa 40–55 is relatively free of textual problems.

The discovery of fragments of twenty manuscripts of Isaiah from the Qumran caves, a fragment from nearby Wadi Murabaʿat, and a complete scroll from Cave 1, testifies to the popularity of the book in the Qumran community and in the Judaism of late antiquity. All of the chapters of Isa 40–55, except ch. 50, and more than half of the 332 verses of this section, are represented whole or (more commonly) in part in five of the fragments (4QIsa[b, c, d, g, h]), dated to the early first century B.C.E. (4QIsa[h]), up through the mid–first century C.E. (4QIsa[c, d]).

These fragments derive from copies that belong to the same textual tradition as the one that eventuated in the Masoretic text. The few variants that appear in them will be noted in the course of the commentary. Apart from orthographic details, the only significant variants in 1QIsa[b] appear in the fourth "Servant song." In Isa 53:11, as well as IQIsa[a], 4QIsa[d], and the LXX, the word *ʾôr* ("light") is added ("After his painful life he shall see light"), and in the following verse the same four texts add the third plural masculine suffix to MT *vĕlappōšĕʿîm*, reading "he (the Servant) interceded for their transgressions," a reading adopted in the present translation and commentary.

For the reader's convenience the verses reproduced entirely or in part in the fragmentary Qumran texts are here set out:

1QIsa[b] 40:2–3; 41:3–23; 43:1–13, 23–27; 44:21–28; 45:1–3; 46:3–13; 47:1–14; 48:17–22; 49:1–15; 50:7–11; 51:1–10; 52:2, 7; 53:1–12; 54:1–6; 55:2–13

4QIsa[b]	40:1–4, 22–26; 41:8–11; 42:2–7, 9–12; 43:12–15; 44:19–28; 45:20–25; 46:1–3; 48:6–8; 49:21–23; 51:1–2, 14–16; 52:2, 7; 53:11–12
4QIsa[c]	44:3–7, 23; 45:1–4, 6–8; 46:8–13; 48:10–15, 17–19; 49:22; 51:8–16; 52:10–15; 53:1–3, 6–8; 54:3–5, 7–17; 55:1–7
4QIsa[d]	45:20; 46:10–13; 47:1–6, 8–9; 48:8–22; 49:1– 15; 52:4–7; 53:8–12; 54:1–11
4QIsa[g]	42:14–25; 43:1–4, 16–24
4QIsa[h]	42:4–11

As Christopher North observed (1964, 28–29), the complete *Isaiah Scroll* from Cave 1 (1QIsa[a]) agrees with the medieval text to a degree no one would have imagined possible before its discovery. It has been subject to many corrections by a second scribal hand and, not surprisingly, it shows a good number of orthographic variations and variant spellings (e.g. 41:19; 44:10–17). It is not always easy to determine whether the frequent changes from singular to plural and vice versa, or from third to second person and vice versa, are intentional. Chamberlain (1955, 366–72), for example, argued that the third-person forms in 51:5 refer to the Messiah ("His arm will judge the peoples, the islands will wait for him, and in his arm they will hope"), but if this were so we would expect a more consistent interpretative pattern throughout. The same uncertainty besets other alleged instances of ideological changes: for example, "I form light and create darkness, I make *good* [for MT "peace"] and create evil" (45:7) as a more dualistic formulation; or "thus says the LORD, the one who forms the signs" (45:11) with respect to the astrological interests of the Qumran community.

There are few clearly deliberate pluses (additions) in the *Isaiah Scroll.* In the passage about the announcement of the good news of the kingdom, the readers are assured that Yahveh will return to Zion *with compassion* (52:8), and the following injunction to leave Babylon ends with the assurance that *He is called the God of all the earth* (52:12). There are also few readings superior to the MT. 1QIsaiah[a] *bdʿtk,* "(you trusted in) your knowledge" is clearly superior to MT *brʿtk,* "in your evil" 47:10); 1QIsa[a] *ʿryṣ,*"tyrant," has the support of the LXX against the MT *ṣaddîq*, "righteous person," in 49:24; and we have seen that the 1QIsa[a] reading "he (the Servant) will see light" is supported by 1QIsa[b], 4QIsa[d], and the LXX. In sum, the relevant Qumran material confirms the remarkable fidelity with which the medieval text has been transmitted over roughly a millennium, and none of it diverges significantly from the Masoretic text tradition.

As a result of the labors of several generations of scholars over the last century (Ottley, Ziegler, Seeligmann, Tov, van der Kooij, and others), we now have a clearer picture of the nature and *Tendenz* of the LXX translation of Isaiah, written in good *koinē* Greek about the middle of the second century B.C.E. The LXX of Isaiah has generally had a poor reputation as being paraphrastic and often incorrect. Writing nearly a century ago, Ottley described

Isaiah as one of the worst translated parts of the Septuagint (Ottley 1904, 1:9).. It made an even worse impression on Torrey:

> When the author of the Greek translation of Isaiah knows what his Hebrew means, he is likely to render with some freedom. He does not feel himself bound to the wording of the original text. It is ordinarily much the easiest course to follow it closely, but sometimes he finds it more convenient to cut loose from it entirely. When, as very often happens, he does not know the meaning of his Hebrew, he is likely to render literally, without much regard to sense, whatever words he recognizes. (Torrey 1928, 210)

More recent studies have mitigated this judgment by emphasizing the deliberately contemporizing intent of the translator. Numerous disagreements with the MT now seem to be due more to the translator's paraphrastic tendency than to an imperfect knowledge of Hebrew. We can, at any rate, generally detect a rationale or at least a reason for variants. Some result from simple misreading. For example: 41:1, *egkainizesthe* ("be renewed") for MT *haḥărîšû* ("be silent") resulted from daleth/resh confusion, with a similar instance in 44:28. In 42:19 the translator has confused *mal'āk* ("messenger") with *melek* ("ruler"), and in 48:9 MT "I will defer my anger" becomes LXX "I will show you my anger," reading *'erēk* (> *r'h*) mistakenly for *'a'ărîk*.

Some of the pluses in comparison with the MT are interesting. The people invited to address Jerusalem in 40:2 are identified as priests, a deliberately interpretative addition, and the call to prepare the way of the Lord no longer proceeds from the wilderness, perhaps with the idea of bringing the preparation home to the readers (40:3). In 42:1, the Servant is identified explicitly with Jacob/Israel, that is, with the Jewish community of the translator's own day, and in the second Servant passage a collective interpretation is maintained, in spite of the mission *to* Israel, by the deliberate addition of the phrase "I will be gathered" (49:5).

At several points we detect an intent to clarify obscurities in the Hebrew text or to render what is taken to be the sense of the *Vorlage* more explicit. In 40:6 "all flesh is grass" is more clearly stated as "all human glory" (*pasa doxa anthrōpou*), and Jeshurun (44:2) is rendered "the beloved" (*ho ēgapēmenos*). These attempts at clarification are not always successful. In Isa 41:25, for example, the translator was misled by the one aroused from the north and the sunrise in the MT (i.e. Cyrus) into positing two individuals. At other points, the translator reworded in order to avoid anthropomorphic expressions (e.g. allusion to the mouth and the arm of the Lord, 40:5; 51:9–10) and omitted expressions deemed inappropriate (e.g. Jacob described as a worm, 41:14).

There are, finally, instances of contemporizing, though this is perhaps not as common as some recent scholars have maintained. Rendering "create" (*br'*) and "form" (*yṣr*) by *katedeixen* (cf. Vulg. *ostendit*) in line with a contemporaneous philosophical idiom was noted earlier, and there are one or two allusions to immortality and eternity absent from the Hebrew text (44:7; 48:12). Replacing Seba with the more familiar Syene (43:3) and "the land of Sinim" with "the land of the Persians" (49:12) would be minor instances of the same tendency.

The LXX has few readings in common with the *Isaiah Scroll* (1QIsa[a]) against the MT. The very few instances in which an LXX reading is preferred to the MT will be noted as we work our way through the commentary. In general, the MT is well preserved, almost always intelligible, and in need of relatively little emendation. The other ancient versions rarely play more than a corroborative role where there is room to doubt an MT reading. The Targum is paraphrastic and haggadic and therefore more important for knowledge about how these chapters were read in Jewish communities during the first two centuries of the era than for textual reconstruction. (For a list of variants, see Stenning 1949, xvii–xix.)

The Vulgate, translated by Jerome from a Hebrew original close to the MT, introduces an occasional alteration to bring out the Christological potential of the text, for example, translating *ṣedeq* and *yēšaʿ* with *iustus* and *salvator*, respectively, in 45:8 and 51:5. The few instances in which a Vulgate or Peshiṭta reading elucidates the MT are pointed out in the Notes in each section of the commentary.

9. A PREFATORY WORD ABOUT READING

It is no secret that the historical-critical reading of biblical texts has fallen out of favor in large sections of the biblical studies guild, not least among English-language practitioners. As long ago as 1976, David Clines, in his literary study of the Suffering Servant chapter (*I, He, We, & They*), complained that "Isaiah 53 has become a casualty of historical-critical scholarship. It is not the only biblical text in that plight, but its injuries are more grave than those of many others" (Clines 1976, 25).

Historical-critical readings are indicted on the grounds that they objectify the text, reducing it to a puzzle to be solved or a potential source of information: in the case under consideration, information about the identity of the Servant and the other *dramatis personae* in ch. 53. The historical-critical method is also taken to imply that a text has only one correct interpretation, the one intended by the author, and dictated by the circumstances and contingencies in which the text was produced—in the case of Isa 53, at least two and one-half millennia ago.

According to Clines, the multiplicity of incompatible interpretations of Isa 53 produced under the aegis of historical-critical scholarship (on the identity of the Servant and the other persons mentioned, what happened to the Servant, whether he died or survived etc.) underscores the essentially enigmatic nature of the chapter and points to the need to adopt a different approach. This is so even if the enigma is simply a function of our own ignorance of the situation at that time, a conclusion that Clines is reluctant to accept.

Apropos of this critique, it may be important to recall that the historical-critical method was concerned, no less than any other method, with *meaning*, not just with identifying the historical referents of the text (individuals, events, social situations etc.). The difference is that it operates on the assumption that the circumstances of the production and reception of the text are integral aspects of its total meaning.

The historical-critical method is located somewhere near one end of a spectrum to which corresponds, at the other end, the idea of the text as a kind of Rorschach ink blot that serves to elicit responses, insights, and emotions that differ from one reader to the next. Meanings inscribed in texts are as fluid, indeterminate, and perspectival as the cloud to which Hamlet draws the attention of Polonius:

H: Do you see yonder cloud that's almost in shape of a camel?
P: By th'mass, and 'tis like a camel, indeed.
H: Methinks it is like a weasel.
P: It is backt like a weasel.
H: Or like a whale.
P: Very like a whale. (*Hamlet*, Act III Scene 2)

Biblical texts, like all texts, are open to a multiplicity of interpretations. But to state this raises at once the question whether there are criteria for demonstrating that some interpretations are better than others, or that this or that interpretation is simply wrong. To put it differently, we could ask whether the text imposes any constraints on the interpreter. We can subscribe, with reservations, to the "intentional fallacy"—that is, we can admit that the intention of the author does not foreclose discussion, though it may provide important clues to meaning. With biblical texts, however, the issue does not arise, since the authors are unavailable and, for the most part, unidentifiable. But we can speak in a certain sense of the *intention of the text*, as manifested or betrayed by the adoption of certain literary conventions. This was the point of the study of the literary forms of biblical texts in their historical and social particularity (*Formgeschichte*).

The idea behind form criticism was, and is, that adoption of a specific literary genre, type, or *Gattung* embodies, especially in ancient texts, an intentionality dictated directly or indirectly by the social situation in which the form had its original home. Even when used in an artificial or ironic way, the *Gattung* provides the reader with clues to the range of appropriate readings of the text. One would think that neglect of this aspect of the reader's task would not make for good interpretations.

Clines was, of course, aware of all this, and he himself made a formal distinction between literary works of art and such workaday kinds of texts as legal documents, technical manuals, and business letters (1976, 55). Even if the distinction is not as arbitrary as it seems to be, it leaves the biblical scholar with the task of separating texts that can count as works of art from texts that do not qualify, texts such as the so-called covenant code in Exod 20–23 and the manual about sacrifices in Lev 1–7. There are also questions to be asked about literary works of art. Isaiah 53 is not a poem in the same way that a poem by T. S. Eliot or Charles Baudelaire is a poem. Isaiah 53 is not only an ancient text, it is also part of a larger ancient text with its own conventions, Isaiah 40–55 or the entire book of Isaiah. It is, moreover, a text that has generated its own persistent interpretative traditions within Judaism and Christianity, and these too merit the attention of the exegete.

A good reading is always a matter of delicate and precarious balance between text and reader. As Umberto Eco put it, the text is a *macchina pigra*, a lazy machine, needing the cooperation of the reader for the production of meaning. The encounter between text and reader should be like a successful conversation, in which both partners listen and in which there takes place what Hans-Georg Gadamer calls a fusion or overlapping of horizons. For this to happen, the reader must respect the otherness of the textual interlocutor, which also includes the need for awareness that the text is speaking from a different culture and a different epoch. I would view the historical-critical method, when practiced in a discriminating and imaginative manner, as essential for enabling the text to hold up its end of the conversation and to say what it has to say.

It remains true that the historical-critical method is one of a multiplicity of approaches and perspectives available to the exegete. Some may be surprised to hear that the idea that biblical texts, like all texts, are patient of multiple interpretations is not a discovery of modern or postmodern literary theory. It was already part of the received wisdom during the patristic period and came to classical expression in the four senses of Scripture of the medieval scholastics: literal, allegorical, moral, and anagogical.

It was precisely the tendency of the allegorical method to slip into an arbitrary and self-interested mode of interpretation, however, that led to the promotion of the *sensus litteralis* in Christian exegesis and the *pĕšat* in Jewish exegesis in the Middle Ages. But there are other interpretative options, and Clines's monograph is, in my view, a disciplined and productive application of an alternative rhetorical method, which concludes by focusing on the silence of the Servant, twice noted in the text, homologous with the reticence of the poem confronted with the questions that we put to it. But there is more to be said about this poem, and about the rest of Isa 40–55, which also needs to be heard.

In keeping with the character and aims of the Anchor Bible series, the commentary that follows is in the historical-critical manner, while remaining open to other readings.

A SELECT BIBLIOGRAPHY

◆

ISAIAH 40–55

◆

COMMENTARIES

The constraints imposed by the genre of the modern critical commentary, an essential element of which is the provision of bibliographical information, can give a skewed impression of the history of the interpretation of Isaiah. With the exception of one or two classics (Ibn Ezra, Calvin), none of the works listed here predates Gesenius 1821, and few are earlier than Duhm 1892 (first edition), the two major commentaries of the nineteenth century. It would take a different kind of commentary, and a range of competence broader than most modern commentators can claim, to accommodate within the covers of a critical commentary a serious study of patristic exegesis (Origen, Eusebius, Theodoret, the Syriac fathers), medieval interpretations (Rashi, Ibn Ezra, Kimḥi, Andrew of St. Victor, Nicholas of Lyra), and those of the Reformers (Luther 1528; Zwingli 1529; Calvin 1570). This is an unfortunate but apparently unavoidable situation, but we will bear in mind notwithstanding that past interpretations of these chapters have generated a great deal of discussion and have had an important and sometimes decisive influence on the formation of religious ideas and practice, and on people's lives in general, throughout the history of Judaism and Christianity.

Most of the commentaries listed are in English, including some from the great period of Isaiah interpretation in the late-nineteenth and early-twentieth centuries (Thomas Kelly Cheyne, George Adam Smith, John Skinner, Charles Cutler Torrey). Limitations of space, time, and linguistic competence—the interpreter's and perhaps also the reader's—have resulted in few other languages apart from German and French being represented in the list. I have made as judicious a selection as I could, bearing in mind the aims of the series as a whole and the needs of readers prepared to engage seriously with the text.

Alexander, J. A.
1847 *Commentary on the Prophecies of Isaiah*. Grand Rapids: Eerdmans. [Reprinted, 1953]

Baltzer, K.
1999 *Deutero-Jesaja*. KAT. Gütersloh: Gütersloher Verlagshaus.

Beaucamp, E.
1991 *Le Livre de la Consolation d'Israël: Isaïe XL–LV*. Paris: Cerf.

Bentzen, A.
1944 *Jesaja fortolket, Bind II: Jes. 40–66*. Copenhagen: G. E. C. Gads.

Beuken, W. A. M.
1979-89 *Jesaja II–III*. 4 vols. POut Nijkerk: Callenbach.

Bonnard, P.-E.
1972 *Le Second Isaïe, son disciple et leurs éditeurs*. EBib. Paris: Gabalda.
Box, G. H.
1908 *The Book of Isaiah*. London: Pitman.
Budde, K.
1922 *Das Buch Jesaja, Kap. 40–66*. Volume 1 of *HSAT*. Tübingen: Mohr.
Calvin, J.
1979 *Commentary on the Book of the Prophet Isaiah*. 2 vols. Translated by W. Pringle. Grand Rapids, Mich.: Baker.
Caspari, W.
1934 *Lieder und Gottessprüche der Rüchwanderer (Jes. 40–55)*. BZAW 65. Berlin: de Gruyter.
Cheyne, T. K.
1882 *The Prophecies of Isaiah*. Volume 2. London: Kegan Paul, Trench.
Childs, B. S.
2000 *Isaiah: A Commentary*. Louisville: Westminster-John Knox.
Clifford, R. J.
1984 *Fair Spoken and Persuading: An Interpretation of Second Isaiah*. Theological Inquiries. New York: Paulist.
Croatto, J. Severino
1994 *Isaias: La palabra profetica y su relectura hermeneutica II: 40–55*. Buenos Aires: Lumen.
Delitzsch, F.
1889 *Commentar über das Buch Jesaia*. 4th ed. Leipzig: Dörfling & Franke.
1890 *Biblical Commentary on the Prophecies on Isaiah. Vol. 2*. Edinburgh: T. & T. Clark.
Dillmann, A.
1890 *Der Prophet Jesaia*. 5th ed. Leipzig: S. Hirzel.
Duhm, B.
1922 *Das Buch Jesaja*, 4th ed. HKAT 3/1. Göttingen: Vandenhoeck & Ruprecht.
Elliger, K.
1978 *Deuterojesaja: 40,1–45,7*. BKAT 11/1). Neukirchen-Vluyn:Neukirchener Verlag.
Feldmann, F.
1925 *Das Buch Isaias*. Münster: Aschendorff.
Fischer, J.
1939 *Das Buch Isaias*. Volume 2 of HSAT. Bonn: Hanstein.
Fohrer, G.
1964 *Das Buch Jesaja: 3. Band, Kap. 40–66*. Zürich and Stuttgart: Zwingli.
Freehof, S. B.
1972 *Book of Isaiah*. The Jewish Commentary for Bible Readers. New York: Union of American Hebrew Congregations.
Frey, H.
1967 *Das Buch der Weltpolitik Gottes: Kapitel 40–55 des Buches Jesaja*. 6th ed. Stuttgart: Calwer.
Gesenius, D. W.
1821 *Philologisch-kritischer und historiker Commentar über den Jesaia*. Leipzig: F. C. W. Vogel.

Glahn, L., and L. Köhler
1934 *Der Prophet der Heimkehr*. Giessen: Alfred Töpelmann.
Grimm, W., and K. Dittert
1990 *Deuterojesaja: Deutung-Wirkung-Gegenwart*. Stuttgart: Calwer.
Hanson, P. D.
1995 *Isaiah 40–66*. Interpretation. Louisville: John Knox.
Herbert, A. S.
1975 *Isaiah 40–66*. CBC. Cambridge: Cambridge University Press.
Hermisson, H.-J.
1987 *Deuterojesaia*. BKAT 11/9. Neukirchen-Vluyn: Neukirchener Verlag.
Ibn Ezra, Abraham
1873 *The Commentary of Ibn Ezra on Isaiah, Vol. 1: Translation of the Commentary*. Translated by M. Friedländer. New York: Philipp Feldheim.
1996 *Commentary on Isaiah*. Edited by M. Cohen. In *Mikra'ot Gedolot 'Haketer.'* Ramat Gan: Bar-Ilan University Press.
Kelley, P. H.
1971 *Isaiah*. Broadman Bible Commentary. Nashville: Broadman.
Kissane, E. J.
1943 *The Book of Isaiah*. Vol. 2. Dublin: Browne & Nolan.
Klostermann, A.
1893 *Deuterojesaja*. Munich: Oskar Beck.
Knight, G. A. F.
1965 *Deutero-Isaiah: A Theological Commentary on Isaiah 40–55*. Nashville: Abingdon.
1984 *Isaiah 40–55: Servant Theology*. International Theological Commentary. Grand Rapids, Mich.: Eerdmans.
Köhler, L.
1923 *Deuterojesaja (Jesaja xl–lv) stilkritisch untersucht*. Giessen: Alfred Töpelmann.
König, E.
1926 *Das Buch Jesaja*. Gütersloh: Bertelsmann.
Koole, J. L.
1997 *Isaiah, Part 3, Vol. 1: Isaiah 40–48*. Historical Commentary on the Old Testament. Translated by A. P. Runia. Kampen: Kok Pharos.
1998 *Isaiah, Part 3, Vol. 2: Isaiah 49–55*. Historical Commentary on the Old Testament. Translated by A. P. Runia. Leuven: Peeters.
Kraus, H.-J.
1990 *Das Evangelium der unbekannten Propheten: Jesaja 40–66*. Kleine Biblische Bibliothek. Neukirchen-Vluyn: Neukirchener Verlag.
Levy, R.
1925 *Deutero-Isaiah: A Commentary Together with a Preliminary Essay on Deutero-Isaiah's Influence on Jewish Thought*. London: Oxford University Press.
Marti, K.
1900 *Das Buch Jesaja erklärt*. Tübingen: Mohr.
McKenzie, J. L.
1968 *Second Isaiah: Introduction, Translation and Notes*. AB 20. Garden City, N.Y.: Doubleday.

Miscall, P. D.
1993 *Isaiah*. Readings: A New Biblical Commentary. Sheffield: JSOT Press.
Motyer, J. A.
1993 *The Prophecy of Isaiah: An Introduction and Commentary*. Downers Grove, Ill: InterVarsity.
Muilenburg, J.
1956 Isaiah: Chapters 40–66. Pages 381–773 in vol. 5 of *IB*.
North, C. R.
1952 *Isaiah* 40–55. TBC. London: SCM. [5th ed., 1965]
1964 *The Second Isaiah: Introduction, Translation and Commentary to Chapters XL–LV*. Oxford: Clarendon.
Oesterley, W. O. E.
1916 *Studies in Isaiah XL–LXVI*. London: Robert Scott Roxburgh.
Orelli, C. von.
1889 *The Prophecies of Isaiah*. Edinburgh: T. & T. Clark.
Oswalt, J. N.
1998 *The Book of Isaiah: Chapters 40–66*. NICOT. Grand Rapids, Mich.: Eerdmans.
Penna, A.
1964 *Isaia*. La Sacra Bibbia. Turin: Marietti.
Ridderbos, J.
1985 *Isaiah*. Translated by J. Vriend. Bible Student's Commentary. Grand Rapids, Mich.: Zondervan.
Rignell, L. G.
1956 *A Study of Isaiah Ch. XL–LV*. Lunds universitets årsskrift 52. Lund: C. W. K. Gleerup.
Sawyer, J. F. A.
1986 *Isaiah: Volume* 2. The Daily Study Bible Series. Edinburgh: Saint Andrew.
Schoors, A.
1973 *Jesaja II*. De Boeken van het Oude Testament 9. Roermond: Romen & Zonen.
Scullion, J. J.
1982 *Isaiah 40–66*. Wilmington, Del.: Michael Glazier.
Simon, U. E.
1953 *A Theology of Salvation: A Commentary on Isaiah XL–LV*. London: SPCK.
Skinner, J.
1917 *The Book of the Prophet Isaiah: Chapters XL–LXVI*. Revised ed. CBSC. Cambridge: Cambridge University Press.
Slotki, I. W.
1949 *Isaiah*. Soncino Books of the Bible. London: Soncino.
Smart, J. D.
1965 *History and Theology in Second Isaiah: A Commentary on Isaiah* 35; 40–66. Philadelphia: Westminster. [Reprinted, London: Epworth, 1967]
Smith, G. A.
1927 *The Book of Isaiah, Vol. 2: Isaiah XL–LXVI*. 2d ed. The Expositor's Bible. London: Hodder & Stoughton.

Smith, S.
1944 *Isaiah Chapters XL–LV: Literary Criticism and History*. The Schweich Lectures on Biblical Archaeology, 1940. London: Oxford University Press.
Steinmann, J.
1949–55 *Le Prophète Isaïe*.Paris: Cerf.
Torrey, C. C.
1928 *The Second Isaiah: A New Interpretation*. Edinburgh: T. & T. Clark.
Vermeylen, J.
1978 Du Prophète Isaïe à l'Apocalyptique. Volume 2. Paris: Gabalda.
Volz, P.
1932 *Jesaja II—Zweite Hälfte: 40–66*. Leipzig: Deichert. [Reprinted, Hildesheim: Olms, 1974]
Wade, G. W.
1911 *The Book of the Prophet Isaiah* with Introduction and Notes. WC. London: Methuen. [Revised ed. 1929]
Watts, J. D. W.
1987 *Isaiah 34–66* . WBC 25. Waco, Tex.: Word.
Westermann, C.
1969 *Isaiah 40–66: A Commentary*. Translated by D. M. G. Stalker. OTL. Philadelphia: Westminster. [Translated from *Das Buch Jesaia: Kapital 40–66*. ATD 19. Göttingen: Vandenhoeck & Ruprecht, 1966]
Whitehouse, O. C.
1908 *Isaiah Vol. 2: XL–LXVI*. CB. Edinburgh: T. C. & E. C. Jack.
Whybray, R. N.
1975 *Isaiah 40–66*. NCB. Grand Rapids, Mich.: Eerdmans.
1983 *The Second Isaiah*. OTG. Sheffield: JSOT Press.
Wildberger, H.
1982 *Jesaja 3: Jesaja 28–39*. BKAT. Neukirchen-Vluyn: Neukirchener Verlag.
Wright, G. E.
1964 *Isaiah*. Layman's Bible Commentaries. London: SCM.
Young, E. J.
1972 *The Book of Isaiah*. 3 Vols. NICOT. Grand Rapids, Mich.: Eerdmans.
Youngblood, R. F.
1993 *The Book of Isaiah: An Introductory Commentary*. 2d ed. Grand Rapids, Mich.: Baker.

TEXT AND VERSIONS

Aytoun, R. A.
1921–22 The Servant of the Lord in the Targum. *JTS* 23: 172–80.
Barstad, H. M.
1994 Akkadian "Loanwords" in Isaiah40–55 and the Question of Babylonian Origin of Deutero-Isaiah. Pages 36–48 in *Text and Theology: Studies in Honour of Professor Dr. Theol. Magne Sæbø. Presented on the Occasion of his Sixty-fifth Birthday*. Edited by A.Tångberg. Oslo: Verbum.

Barthélemy, D.
1986 *Critique textuelle de l'Ancien Testament, 2: Isaïe, Jérémie, Lamentations.* Göttingen: Vandenhoeck & Ruprecht.
1987 *Isaiah. Volume 3/1 of Vetus Testamentum Syriace.* Edited by S. P. Brock. Leiden: Brill.

Bauchet, J. M. P.
1949 Note sur les variantes du sens d'Isaïe 42 et 43 dans le manuscrit du désert de Juda. *NRTh* 71:304–5.

Ben-Shammai, H.
1990–91 Saadia Gaon's Introduction to Isaiah: Arabic Text and Hebrew Translation. *Tarbiz* 60:371–404.

Brock, S. P.
1988 Text History and Text Division in Peshitta Isaiah. Pages 49–80 in *The Peshitta: Its Early Text and History.* Edited by P. B. Dirksen and M. J. Mulder. Leiden: Brill.

Brockington, L. H.
1951 The Greek Translator of Isaiah and His Interest in ΔΟΞΑ. *VT* 1:23–32.

Brownlee, W. H.
1964 *The Meaning of the Qumrân Scrolls for the Bible: With Special Attention to the Book of Isaiah.* New York: Oxford University Press.

Bundy, D. D.
1983 The Peshitta of ISAIAH 53:9 and the Syrian Commentators. *OrChr* 67: 32–45.

Burrows, M.
1948–49 Variant Readings in the Isaiah Manuscript. *BASOR* 111:16–24; 113:24–32.

Chamberlain, J. V.
1955 The Functions of God as Messianic Titles in the Complete Qumrân Isaiah Scroll. *VT* 5:366–72.

Chilton, B.
1983 *The Glory of Israel: The Theology and Provenience of the Isaiah Targum.* Sheffield: JSOT Press.
1987 *The Isaiah Targum: Introduction, Translation, Apparatus and Notes.* Wilmington: Michael Glazier.

Dahood, M. J.
1960 Textual Problems in Isaiah. *CBQ* 22:400–409.

Driver, G. R.
1935 Linguistic and Textual Problems: Isaiah xl–lxvi. *JTS* 36:396–406.

Elliger, K.
1971a Textkritisches zu Deuterojesaja. Pages 113–19 in *Near Eastern Studies in Honor of William Foxwell Albright.* Edited by H. Goedicke. Baltimore: Johns Hopkins University Press.

Eshel, E.
1999 Self-Glorification Hymn. Pages 421–35 in *Qumran Cave 4/20: Poetical and Liturgical Texts, Part 2.* DJD 29. Leiden: Brill.

Field, F.
1875 *Origenis Hexaplorum quae supersunt sive veterum interpretum Graecorum in totum Vetus Testamentum fragmenta.* 2 vols. Oxford: Oxford University Press. [Reprinted, Hildesheim: Olms, 1964. Volume 2: Pages 431–567]

Flint, P. W.
1997 The Isaiah Scrolls from the Judean Desert. Pages 481–90 in vol. 2 of *Writing and Reading the Scroll of Isaiah*. 2 vols. Edited by C. C. Broyles & C. A. Evans. Leiden: Brill.

Flint, P. W., E. Ulrich, and M. G. Abegg
1999 *Edition of the Cave One Isaiah Scrolls*. DJD 37. Oxford: Clarendon.

García Martínez, F.
1987 Le Livre d'Isaïe à Qumrân: Les textes. L'influence. *Le Monde de la Bible* 49:43– 45.

Gelston, A.
1997 Was the Peshitta of Isaiah of Christian Origin? Pages 563–82 in vol. 2 of *Writing and Reading the Scroll of Isaiah*. 2 vols. Edited by C. C. Broyles & C. A. Evans. Leiden: Brill.

Giese, R. L.
1988 Further Evidence for the Bisection of 1QIs[a]. *Textus* 14:61–70.

Gonçalves, F. J.
1995 Isaiah Scroll. Pages 470–72 in vol. 3 of *ABD*.

Goshen-Gottstein, M.
1954a Die Jesaja-Rolle im Lichte von Peschitta und Targum. *Bib* 35:51–71.
1954b Die Jesajah-Rolle und das Problem der hebräischen Bibelhandschriften. *Bib* 35:429–42.
1981 Bible Exegesis and Textual Criticism: Isaiah 49, 11—MT and LXX. Pages 91–107 in *Mélanges Dominique Barthélemy*. Edited by P. Casetti et al. Göttingen: Vandenhoeck & Ruprecht.

Goshen-Gottstein, M. (ed.)
1995 *The Book of Isaiah*. The Hebrew University Bible. Jerusalem: Magnes.

Guillaume, A.
1957 Some Readings in the Dead Sea Scroll of Isaiah. *JBL* 76:41–42.

Hegermann, H.
1954 *Jesaja 53 in Hexapla, Targum, und Peschitta*. Gütersloh: Bertelsmann.

James, F. D.
1959 *A Critical Examination of the Text of Isaiah*. Ph.D. dissertation. Boston University.

Koch, K.
1972 Messias und Sündenvergebung in Jesaja 53–Targum: Ein Beitrag zu der Praxis der aramäischen Bibelübersetzung. *JSJ* 3:117–48.

Koenig, J.
1982 *L'herméneutique analogique du Judaïsm antique d'après les témoins textuels d'Isaïe*. Leiden: Brill.
1983 Réouverture du débat sur la première main rédactionelle du rouleau ancien d'Isaïe de Qumrân. *RevQ* 11:219–37.

Komlosh, Y.
1965 The Aramaic Translation of the Book of Isaiah. Pages 39–40 in *Fourth World Congress of Jewish Studies. Abstracts of Papers–Bible Studies*. Jerusalem: World Union of Jewish Studies.

Kooij, A. van der
1981 *Die alten Textzeugen des Jesajabuches: Ein Beitrag zur Textgeschichte des Alten Testaments*. Freiburg: Universitätsverlag / Göttingen: Vandenhoeck & Ruprecht.

1989 The Septuagint of Isaiah: Translation and Interpretation. Pages 127–33 in *The Book of Isaiah / Le Livre d'Isaïe*. Edited by J. Vermeylen. Leuven: Peeters and Leuven University Press.

1992 The Old Greek of Isaiah in Relation to the Qumran Texts of Isaiah: Some General Comments. Pages 195–213 in *Septuagint, Scrolls and Cognate Writings*. Edited by G. J. Brooke and B. Lindars. Atlanta: Scholars Press.

Kutscher, E. Y.

1974 *The Language and Linguistic Background of the Isaiah Scroll (1QIsa[a])*. Leiden: Brill.

Olley, J. W.

1979 *"Righteousness" in the Septuagint of Isaiah: A Contextual Study*. Missoula, Mont.: Scholars Press.

1983 Notes on Isaiah XXXII 1. XLV 19, 23 and LXIII 1. *VT* 33:446–53.

1993 Hear the Word of YHWH: The Structure of the Book of Isaiah in 1QIsa[a]. *VT* 43:19–49.

Ottley, R. R.

1904–6 *The Book of Isaiah According to the Septuagint (Codex Alexandrinus)*. 2 vols. Cambridge: Cambridge University Press.

Parry, D. W., and E. Qimron

1999 *The Great Isaiah Scroll (1QIsa[a]): A New Edition*. Leiden: Brill.

Porter, S. E., and B. W. R. Pearson

1997 Isaiah through Greek Eyes: The Septuagint of Isaiah. Pages 531–46 in vol. 2 of *Writing and Reading the Scroll of Isaiah*. 2 vols. Edited by C. C. Broyles and C. A. Evans. Leiden: Brill.

Praetorius, F.

1913 Zum Text des Tritojesaia. ZAW 33:89–91.

Qimron, E.

1979 *The Language and Linguistic Background of the Isaiah Scroll (1QIs[a]) Indices and Corrections*. Leiden: Brill.

Rowlands, E. R.

1959 The Targum and the Peshitta Version of the Book of Isaiah. *VT* 9:178–91.

Rubinstein, A.

1954 Isaiah LII,14—*mišḥat*—and the DSIa Variant. *Bib* 35:475–79.

1955 The Theological Aspect of Some Variant Readings in the Isaiah Scroll. *JJS* 6:187–200.

Scullion, J. J.

1971 SEDEQ-SEDAQAH in Isaiah cc. 40–66 with Special Reference to the Continuity in Meaning between Second and Third Isaiah. *UF* 3:335–38.

1973 Some Difficult Texts in Isa cc. 56–66 in the Light of Modern Scholarship. *UF* 4:105–28.

Seeligmann, I. L.

1948 *The Septuagint Version of Isaiah: A Discussion of Its Problems*. Leiden: Brill.

Skehan, P. W.

1955 The Text of Isaias at Qumrân. *CBQ* 17:158–63.

1960 Some Textual Problems in Isaiah. *CBQ* 22:47–55.

Stenning, J. F.

1949 *The Targum of Isaiah*. Oxford: Clarendon.

Syrén, R.
1989 Targum Isaiah 52:13–53:12 and Christian Interpretation. *JJS* 40:201–12.
Talmon, S.
1989 Observations on Variant Readings in the Isaiah Scroll (1QIsa[a]). Pages 117–30 in *The World of Qumran from Within: Collected Studies*. Jerusalem: Magnes / Leiden: Brill.
Tov, E.
1997 The Text of Isaiah at Qumran. Pages 491–511 in vol. 2 of *Writing and Readingthe Scroll of Isaiah*. 2 vols. Edited by C. C. Broyles and C. A. Evans. Leiden: Brill.
Ulrich, E. C.
1997 An Index to the Contents of the Isaiah Manuscripts from the Judean Desert. Pages 477–80 in vol. 2 of *Writing and Reading the Scroll of Isaiah*. 2 vols. Edited by C. C. Broyles and C. A. Evans. Leiden: Brill.
Ulrich, E. C., and P. W. Skehan,
1996 An Edition of 4QIsa[e] Including the Former 4QIsa[l]. *RevQ* 17:23–26.
Ulrich, E., et al.
1997 *Qumran Cave 4, X: The Prophets*. DJD 15. Oxford: Clarendon.
Wernberg-Møller, P.
1957 Pronouns and Suffixes in the Scrolls and the Masoretic Text. *JBL* 76:44–49.
Whitley, C. F.
1961 Textual Notes on Deutero-Isaiah. *VT* 11:259–61.
1975 Further Notes on the Text of Deutero-Isaiah. *VT* 25:683–87.
Wieringen, A. L. H. M. van
1996 Parallel Clauses between Third and Second Isaiah: A New Kind of Computer-Concordance. *BN* 82:21–26.
Ziegler, J.
1934 *Untersuchungen zur Septuaginta des Buches Isaias*. ATA 12/3. Münster: Aschendorff.
1939 *Isaias*. Septuaginta 14. Göttingen: Vandenhoeck & Ruprecht.
1959 Die Vorlage der Isaias-Septuaginta (LXX) und die erste Isaias-Rolle von Qumran (1QIsa[a]). *JBL* 78:34–59.
Zijl, J. B. van
1965 Errata in Sperber's Edition of Targum Isaiah. *ASTI* 4:189–91.
1968–69 A Second List of Errata in Sperber's Edition of Targum Isaiah. *ASTI* 7:132–34.
1979 *A Concordance to the Targum of Isaiah*. Missoula, Mont.: Scholars Press.
Zijl, P. J. van
1972 The Root *prq* in Targum Isaiah. *JNSL* 2:60–73.

MONOGRAPHS AND ARTICLES

ISAIAH 40–55 IN GENERAL

Abusch, T.

1999 Marduk. Pages 543–49 in *Dictionary of Deities and Demons in the Bible*. Edited by K. van der Toorn et al. Leiden: Brill.

Ackroyd, P. R.

1963 Hosea and Jacob. *VT* 13:245–59.

1974 An Interpretation of the Babylonian Exile: A Study of II Kings 20, Isaiah 38–39. *SJT* 27:329–52. [Reprinted pp. 152–71 in *Studies in the Religious Tradition of the Old Testament*. London: SCM, 1987]

1981 The Death of Hezekiah: A Pointer to the Future? Pages 219–26 in *De la Tôrah au Messie: Mélanges Henri Cazelles*. Edited by M. Carrez et al. Paris: Desclée. [Reprinted, pp. 172–80 in *Studies in the Religious Tradition of the Old Testament*]

1982 Isaiah 36–39: Structure and Function. Pages 3–21 in *Von Kanaan bis Kerala: Fst. für J. P. M. van der Ploeg OP.* Edited by W. C. Delsman et al. Neukirchen-Vluyn: Neukirchener Verlag. [Reprinted, pp. 105–20 in *Studies in the Religious Tradition of the Old Testament*]

Albertz, R.

1990 Das Deuterojesaja-Buch als Fortschreibung der Jesaja-Prophetie. Pages 241–56 in *Die hebräische Bibel und ihre zweifache Nachgeschichte: Festschrift für Rolf Rendtorff.* Edited by C. Macholz, E. Blum, and E. Stegemann. Neukirchen-Vluyn: Neukirchener Verlag.

1994 *A History of Israelite Religion in the Old Testament Period.* 2 vols. Louisville: Westminster-John Knox.

Allen, L. C.

1971 Isaiah LII 2 Again. *VT* 21:490.

Althann, R.

1987 Isaiah 42:10 and KRT 77–78 (KTU I.14; II.24–25). *JNSL* 13:3–9.

Anderson, B.

1962 Exodus Typology in Second Isaiah. Pages 177–95 in *Israel's Prophetic Heritage: Essays in Honor of James Muilenburg*. Edited by B. W. Anderson and W. Harrelson. New York: Harper & Row.

1976 Exodus and Covenant in Second Isaiah and Prophetic Tradition. Pages 339–60 in *Magnalia Dei—The Mighty Acts of God: Essays on the Bible and Archaeology in Memory of G. Ernest Wright.* Edited by W. E. Lemke, F. M. Cross, and P. D. Miller. Garden City, N.Y.: Doubleday.

Baltzer, D.

1971 *Ezechiel und Deuterojesaja*. BZAW 121. Berlin: de Gruyter.

1987 Jes 40,13–14: Ein Schlüssel zur Einheit Deutero-Jesajas? *BN* 37:7–10.

1992 Stadt Tyche oder Zion Jerusalem? Die Auseinandersetzung mit den Göttern der Zeit bei Deuterojesaja. Pages 114–19 in *Festschrift für Horst Dietrich Preuss zum 65. Geburtstag.* Edited by J. Hausmann and H.-J. Zobel. Stuttgart: Kohlhammer.

1994 The Polemic against the Gods and Its Relevance for Second Isaiah's Conception of the New Jerusalem. Pages 52–59 in *Second Temple*

Studies 2: Temple and Community in the Persian Period. Edited by T. C. Eskenazi and K. H. Richards. JSOTSup 175. Sheffield: Sheffield Academic Press.

Banwell, B. O.
1964–65 A Suggested Analysis of Isaiah xl–lxvi. *ExpTim* 76:166.

Barstad, H. M.
1982 Lebte Deuterojesaja in Judäa? *NTT* 83: 77–87.
1987 On the So-Called Babylonian Influence in Second Isaiah. *SJOT* 2:90–110.
1989 *A Way in the Wilderness*. Manchester: Manchester University Press.
1994a The Future of the "Servant Songs": Some Reflections on the Relationship of Biblical Scholarship to its OwnTradition. Pages 261–70 in *Language, Theology and the Bible: Essays in Honour of James Barr*. Edited by S. E. Balentine and J. Barton. Oxford: Clarendon.
1994b Akkadian "Loanwords" in Isaiah 40–55 and the Question of the Babylonian Origin of Deutero-Isaiah. Pages 36–48 in *Text and Theology: Studies in Honour of Prof. Dr. Theol. Magne Sæbø*. Oslo: Verbum.
1997 *The Babylonian Captivity of the Book of Isaiah: "Exilic" Judah and the Provenance of Isaiah 40–55*. Oslo: Novus.

Barton, J.
1986 *Oracles of God: Perception of Ancient Prophecy in Israel After the Exile*. London: Darton, Longman & Todd.

Beaucamp, E.
1982 "Chant nouveau du retour" (Is 42,10–17): Un monstre de l'exégèse moderne. *RSR* 56:145–58.
1988 Le IIe Isaïe (Is 40,1–49,13): Problème de l'unité du livre. *RSR* 62:218–26.

Beaulieu, P. A.
1989 *The Reign of Nabonidus King of Babylon*. New Haven: Yale University Press.

Becker, U.
1997 *Jesaja: Von der Botschaft zum Buch*. Göttingen: Vandenhoeck & Ruprecht.

Beentjes, P.
1989 *A Way in the Wilderness: The "Second Exodus" in the Message of Second Isaiah*. JSS Monograph 12. Manchester: University of Manchester Press.

Begg, C. T.
1989 Babylon in the Book of Isaiah. Pages 121–25 in *The Book of Isaiah/Le Livre d'Isaïe*. Edited by J. Vermeylen. Leuven: Pieters and Leuven University Press.

Begrich, J.
1934 Das priesterliche Heilsorakel. *ZAW* 52:81–92.
1963 *Studien zu Deuterojesaja*. TB 20. Munich: Chr. Kaiser. [Reprint of BWANT 77. Stuttgart: Kohlhammer, 1938]

Behr, J. W.
1937 *The Writings of Deutero-Isaiah and the Neo-Babylonian Royal Inscriptions*. Pretoria: Rubinstein.

Bentzen, A.
1948–49 On the Ideas of "the Old" and "the New" in Deutero-Isaiah. *ST* 1:183–87.

Berges, U.
1998 *Das Buch Jesaja: Komposition und Endgestalt*. Freiburg: Herder.

Berlin, A.
1979 Isaiah 40:4: Etymological and Poetic Considerations. *HAR* 3:1–6.

Beuken, W. A. M.
1974a The Confession of God's Exclusivity by All Mankind: A Reappraisal of Is 45,18–25. *Bijdr* 35:335–56.
1974b Isaiah 54: The Multiple Identity of the Person Addressed. *OtSt* 19:29–70.
1974c Isa. 55:3–5: The Reinterpretation of David. *Bijdr* 35:49–64.

Biddle, M. E.
1996 Lady Zion's Alter Egos: Isaiah 47.1–15 and 57.6–13 as Structural Counterparts. Pages 125–39 in *New Visions of Isaiah*. Edited by R. F. Melugin and M. A. Sweeney. Sheffield: Sheffield Academic Press.

Blank, S.
1940 Studies in Deutero-Isaiah. *HUCA* 15:1–46.
1956 Traces of Prophetic Agony in Isaiah. *HUCA* 27:81–92.
1958 *Prophetic Faith in Isaiah*. New York: Harper & Row.

Blau, J.
1957 HÔBᵉRÊ ŠĀMĀJIM (Jes XLVII 13) = Himmelsanbeter? *VT* 7:183–4.
1995 A Misunderstood Medieval Translation of *śered* (Isaiah 44:13) and Its Impact on Modern Scholarship. Pages 689–95 in *Pomegranates and Golden Bells: Studies in Biblical, Jewish, and Near Eastern Ritual, Law, and Literature in Honor of Jacob Milgrom*. Edited by D. P. Wright, D. N. Freedman, and A. Hurvitz. Winona Lake, Ind.: Eisenbrauns.

Blenkinsopp, J.
1962 The Unknown Prophet of the Exile. *Scr* 14:81–90, 109–18.
1990 A Jewish Sect of the Persian Period. *CBQ* 52:5–20.
1996 Second Isaiah: Prophet of Universalism? Pages 186–206 in *The Prophets: A Sheffield Reader*. Edited by P. R. Davies. The Biblical Seminar 42. Sheffield: Sheffield Academic Press. [Reprint of *JSOT* 41 (1988) 83–103]

Blythin, I.
1966a Notes on Isaiah 49:16–17. *VT* 16:229–30.

Boadt, L.
1973 Isaiah 41:8–13: Notes on Poetic Structure and Style. *CBQ* 35:20–34.
1983 Intentional Alliteration in Second Isaiah. *CBQ* 45:353–63.

Boer, P. A. H. de
1956 *Second-Isaiah's Message*. *OtSt* 11. Leiden: Brill.

Boer, R.
1998 Deutero-Isaiah: Historical Materialism and Biblical Theology. *BibInt* 6:181–204.

Booij, T.
1982 Negation in Isaiah 43:22–24. *ZAW* 92:390–400.

Brettler, Marc
1989 *God Is King: Understanding an Israelite Metaphor*. JSOTSup 76. Sheffield: Sheffield Academic Press.
1998 Incompatible Metaphors for YHWH in Isaiah 40–66. *JSOT* 78:97–120.

Bright, J.
1951 Faith and Destiny: The Meaning of History in Deutero-Isaiah. *Int* 5:3–26.

Bronner, L. L.
1983–84 Gynomorphic Imagery in Exilic Isaiah (40–66). *Dor le Dor* 12:71–83.
Brooke, G. T.
1994 Isaiah 40:3 and the Wilderness Community. Pages 118–32 in *New Qumran Texts and Studies*. Edited by G. J. Brooke. Leiden: Brill.
Broyles, C. C.
1997 The Citations of Yahweh in Isaiah 44:26–28. Pages 339–421 in vol. 1 of *Writing and Reading the Scroll of Isaiah: Studies of an Interpretive Tradition*. 2 vols. Edited by C. C. Broyles and C. A. Evans. Leiden: Brill.
Bruggemann, W.
1968 Is 55 and Deuteronomic Theology. *ZAW* 80:191–203.
1984 Unity and Dynamic in the Isaiah Tradition. *JSOT* 29:89–107.
1988 Second Isaiah: An Evangelical Rereading of Communal Experience. Pages 71–90 in *Reading and Preaching the Book of Isaiah*. Edited by C. R. Seitz. Philadelphia: Fortress.
1995 Five Strong Rereadings of the Book of Isaiah. Pages 87–104 in *The Bible in Human Society: Essays in Honour of John Rogerson*. Edited by R. Carroll et al. JSOTSup 200. Sheffield: Sheffield Academic Press.
Caquot, A.
1965 Les "grâces de David": À propos d'Isaïe 55,3b. *Sem* 15:45–59.

Carmignac, J.
1960 Les citations de l'Ancien Testament, et spécialement des Poèmes du Servifeur dans les Hymes de Qumran. *RQ* 2:383–94.
Carr, D.
1993 Reaching for Unity in Isaiah. *JSOT* 57:61–81. [Reprinted, pp. 164–83 in *The Prophets: A Sheffield Reader*. Edited by P. R. Davies. *BibSem* 42. Sheffield: Sheffield Academic Press, 1996]
1995 Isaiah 40:1–11 in the Context of the Macrostructure of Second Isaiah. Pages 51–73 in *Discourse Analysis of Biblical Literature*. Edited by W. Bodine. Atlanta: Scholars Press.
Carroll, R.
1978 Second Isaiah and the Failure of Prophecy. *ST* 32:119–31.
Cassuto, M. D.
1973 On the Formal and Stylistic Relationship between Deutero-Isaiah and Other Biblical Writers. Pages 141–77 in vol. 1 of *Biblical and Oriental Studies*. 2 vols. Translated by I. Abrahams. Jerusalem: Magnes.
Charles, R. H.
1917 *The Book of Enoch*. London: SPCK.

Charlesworth, J. H.
1997 Intertextuality: Isaiah 40:3 and the Serek ha-Yahad. Pages 197–224 in *The Quest for Meaning: Studies in Biblical Intertextuality in Honor of James A. Sanders*. Edited by C. A. Evans and S. Talmon. Leiden: Brill.
Chary, T.
1979 La création chez le Second Isaïe. *Le Monde de la Bible* 9:10–12.
Childs, B. S.
1979 *Introduction to the Old Testament as Scripture*. Philadelphia: Fortress.

Christ, F.
1994 *Gottes Wort im Umbruch: Das Evangelium des namenlosen Propheten Jeaja 40–55*. Basel and Berlin: Reinhardt.

Clements, R. E.
1980 The Prophecies of Isaiah and the Fall of Jerusalem in 587 BCE. *VT* 30: 421–36.
1982 The Unity of the Book of Isaiah. *Int* 36:117–29.
1985 Beyond Tradition History: Deutero-Isaianic Development of First Isaiah's Themes. *JSOT* 31:95–113.
1986 Isaiah 45:20–25. *Int* 40:392–97.
1996 A Light to the Nations: A Central Theme of the Book of Isaiah. Pages 57–69 in *Forming Prophetic Literature: Essays on Isaiah and the Twelve in Honor of John D. W. Watts*. Edited by J. W. Watts and P. R. House. JSOTSup 235. Sheffield: JSOT Press.
1997 Zion as Symbol and Political Reality: A Central Isaianic Quest. Pages 3–17 in *Studies in the Book of Isaiah: Festschrift Willem A. M. Beuken*. Edited by J. van Ruiten and M. Vervenne. BETL 132. Leuven: Leuven University Press / Peeters.

Clifford, R. J.
1980 The Function of Idol Passages in Second Isaiah. *CBQ* 42:450–64.
1983 Isaiah 55: Invitation to a Feast. Pages 27– 35 in *The Word of the Lord Shall Go Forth: Essays in Honor of David Noel Freedman in Celebration of His Sixtieth Birthday*. Edited by C. L. Meyers and M. O'Connor. Winona Lake, Ind.: Eisenbrauns.
1993 The Unity of the Book of Isaiah and Its Cosmogonic Language. *CBQ* 55: 1–17.

Coggins, R. J.
1996 New Ways with Old Texts: How Does One Write a Commentary on Isaiah? *ExpTim* 107:362–67.
1998 Do We Still Need Deutero-Isaiah? *JSOT* 81:77–92.

Collins, J. J.
1995 *The Scepter and the Star*. New York: Doubleday.

Condamin, A.
1910 Les prédictions nouvelles du chapitre XLVIII d'Isaïe. *RB* 19:200–216.

Conrad, E. W.
1981 Second Isaiah and the Priestly Oracle of Salvation. *ZAW* 93:234–46.
1984 The "Fear Not" Oracles in Second Isaiah. *VT* 44:133–43.
1985 The Community as King in Second Isaiah. Pages 99–111 in *Understanding the Word*. Edited by J. T. Butler et al. Sheffield: JSOT Press.
1991 *Reading Isaiah*. OBT 27. Minneapolis: Fortress.
1996 Prophet, Redactor and Audience: Reforming the Notion of Isaiah's Formation. Pages 306–26 in *New Visions of Isaiah*. Edited by R. F. Melugin and M. A. Sweeney. JSOTSup 214. Sheffield: Sheffield Academic Press.
1997 Reading Isaiah and the Twelve as Prophetic Books. Pages 3–17 in vol. 1 of *Writing and Reading the Scroll of Isaiah*. 2 vols. Edited by C. C. Broyles and C. A. Evans. Leiden: Brill.

Corney, R. W.
1976 Isaiah L,10. *VT* 26:497–98.

Couroyer, B.
1966 Isaïe xl,12. *RB* 73:186–96.
1981a "Avoir la nuque raide": Ne pas incliner l'oreille. *RB* 88:216–25.
1981b Note sur II Sam. 1,22 et Isa. LV, 10–11. *RB* 88:505–14.

Cowley, A.
1923 *Aramaic Papyri of the Fifth Century* B.C. Oxford: Clarendon.

Croatto, J. Severino
1994 *Isaías: La palabra profética y su relectura hermenéutica: Vol. II 40–55.* Buenos Aires: Lumen.

Cross, F. M.
1953 The Council of YHWH in Second Isaiah. *JNES* 12:274–77.
1973 *Canaanite Myth and Hebrew Epic.* Cambridge: Harvard University Press.

Crüsemann, F.
1969 *Studien zur Formgeschichte von Hymnus und Danklied in Israel.* Neukirchen-Vluyn: Neukirchener Verlag.

Curtis, E. M.
1994 Idol, Idolatry. Pages 376–81 in vol. 3 of *ABD.*

Darr, K. P.
1987 Like Warrior, like Woman: Destruction and Deliverance in Isaiah 42:10–17. *CBQ* 49:560–71.
1994 *Isaiah's Vision and the Family of God.* Louisville: Westminster-John Knox.

Daube, D.
1964 *The Sudden in Scripture.* Leiden: Brill.

Davidson, R.
1963 Universalism in Second Isaiah. *SJT* 16:166–85.
1997 The Imagery of Isaiah 40:6–8 in Tradition and Interpretation. Pages 37–55 in *The Quest for Meaning: Studies in Biblical Intertextuality in Honor of James A. Sanders.* Edited by C. A. Evans and S. Talmon. Leiden: Brill.

Davies, P. R.
1995 God of Cyrus, God of Israel: Some Religio-historical Reflections on Isaiah 40–55. Pages 207–25 in *Words Remembered, Texts Renewed: Essays in Honour of John F. A. Sawyer.* Edited by J. Davies, G. Harvey, and W. G. E. Watson. JSOTSup 195. Sheffield: Sheffield Academic Press.

Day, J.
1985 *God's Conflict with the Dragon and the Sea.* Cambridge: Cambridge University Press.

Deist, F. E.
1985 Reflections on Reinterpretation in and of Isaiah 53. *OTE* 3:1–11.

Dell'Acqua, A. P.
1993 "Come una tarma": Immagini di fragilità e/o di distruzione nell'Antico Testamento. *RivB* 41:393–428.

Dempsey, D. A.
1991 A Note on Isaiah 43:9 *VT* 41:212–15.
1997 *Weneda'ah* and *weno'mar* in Isa 41:26; *we'ere'* in Isa 41:28. *BN* 86:18–23.

Derby, J.
1996 Isaiah and Cyrus. *JBQ* 24:173–77.

DeRoche, M.

1992 Isaiah xlv 7 and the Creation of Chaos. *VT* 42:11–21.

Dick, M. B.

1999 Prophetic Parodies of Making the Cult Image. Pages 1–53 in *Born in Heaven, Made on Earth: The Making of the Cult Image in the Ancient Near East*. Edited by Michael B. Dick. Winona Lake, Ind.: Eisenbrauns.

Dijkstra, M.

1977 Zur Deutung von Jesaja 45:15ff. *ZAW* 89:215–22.

1997 Lawsuit, Debate and Wisdom Discourse in Second Isaiah. Pages 251–71 in *Studies in the Book of Isaiah: Festschrift Willem A. M. Beuken*. Edited by J. van Ruiten and M. Vervenne. BETL 132. Leuven: Leuven University Press / Peeters.

Dion, H. M.

1967 Le genre littéraire sumérien de l'"Hymmne à soi-même' et quelques passages du Deutéro-Isaïe. *RB* 74:215–34.

Dion, P. E.

1970 L'universalisme religieux dans les différentes couches rédactionelles d'Isaïe 40–55. *Bib* 51:161–82.

1991 The Structure of Isaiah 42.10–17 as Approached through Versification and Distribution of Poetic Devices. *JSOT* 49:113–24.

Driver, G. R.

1933 Studies in the Vocabulary of the Old Testament: V. *JTS* 34:33–44.

Eakins, J.

1970 Anthropomorphisms in Isaiah 40–55. *Hebrew Studies* 20:47–50.

Eaton, J. H.

1959 The Origin of the Book of Isaiah. *VT* 9:138–57.

1979 *Festal Drama in Deutero-Isaiah*. London: SPCK.

1982 The Isaiah Tradition. Pages 58–76 in *Israel's Prophetic Heritage: Essays in Honour of Peter Ackroyd*. Edited by R. J. Coggins et. al. Cambridge: Cambridge University Press.

Eichrodt, W.

1970 Prophet and Covenant: Observations on the Exegesis of Isaiah. Pages 167–88 in *Proclamation and Presence: Essays in Honor of G. Henton Davies*. Edited by J. I. Durham. London: SCM.

Eissfeldt, O.

1962 The Promises of Grace to David in Isaiah 55,1–5. Pages 196–207 in *Israel's Prophetic Heritage*. Edited by B. W. Anderson and W. Harrelson. New York: Harper & Row.

1966 *The Old Testament: An Introduction*. Oxford: Blackwell.

Elliger, K.

1928 *Die Einheit des Tritojesaja*. Stuttgart: Kohlhammer.

1933 *Deuterojesaja in seinem Verhältnis zu Tritojesaja*. BWANT 63. Stuttgart: Kohlhammer.

1966 Der Begriff "Geschichte" bei Deuterojesaja. Pages 199–211 in *Kleine Schriften zum Alten Testament*. Tbü 32. Munich: Kaiser.

1971b Der Sinn des hebräischen Wortes שפי. *ZAW* 83:317–29.

Ephʿal, Israel.

1986–89 On the Linguistic and Cultural Background of Deutero-Isaiah. *Shnaton* 10:31–35.

Evans, C. A.
1988 On the Unity and Parallel Structure of Isaiah. *VT* 38:129–47.
Falk, Z. W.
1967 Hebrew Legal Terms: II. *JSS* 12:242–43.
Farber, W.
1995 Witchcraft, Magic and Divination in Ancient Mesopotamia. Pages 1895–1909 in vol. 3 of *CANE*.
Farfan Navarro, E.
1992 *El Desierto Transformado: Una Imagen deuteroisiana de regeneracion*. Rome: Pontifical Biblical Institute.
Feuerstein, R.
1998 Warum gibt es einen "Deuterojesaja"? Pages 93–134 in *Ich bewerke das Heil und erschaffe das Unheil (Jesaja 45,7): Studien zur Botschaft der Propheten—Fst. für Lothar Ruppert zum 65. Geburtstag*. Edited by F. Diedrich and B. Willmes. Würzburg: Echter.
Fichtner, J.
1951 Jahves Plan in der Botschaft des Jesaja. *ZAW* 64:16–33.
1961 Jesaja 52,7–10 in der christlichen Verkündigung. Pages 51–66 in *Verbannung und Heimkehr. Fst. W. Rudolph*. Edited by A. Kuschke. Tübingen: Mohr.
Finley, T. J.
1991 Dimensions of the Hebrew Word for "Create" (*br'*). *BSac* 148:409–23.
Fischer, G.
1984 Die Redewendung *dbr ʿl-lb* im Alten Testament: Ein Beitrag zum Verständnis von Jes 40,2. *Bib* 65:244–50.
Fischer, I.
1995 *Tora für Israel—Tora für die Völker: Das Konzept des Jesajabuches*. Stuttgart: Katholisches Bibelwerk.
Fitzgerald, A.
1972 The Mythological Background for the Presentation of Jerusalem as a Queen and False Worship as Adultery in the Old Testament. *CBQ* 34:403–16.
1975 BTWLT and BT as Titles for Capital Cities. *CBQ* 37:170–80.
1989 The Technology of Isaiah 40:19–20 + 41:6–7. *CBQ* 51:426–46.
Fohrer, G.
1955 Zum Text von Jes. xli 8–13. *VT* 5:239–49.
Fokkelman, J. P.
1981 Stylistic Analysis of Isaiah 40:1–11. *OtSt* 21:68–90.
1997 The Cyrus Oracle (Isaiah 44,25–45,7) from the Perspectives of Syntax, Versification and Structure. Pages 303–23 in *Studies in the Book of Isaiah: Fst. Willem A. M. Beuken*. Edited by J. van Ruiten and M. Vervenne. Leuven: Leuven University Press.
Forster, B.
1993 The Biblical *'Omen* and Evidence for the Nurturance (sic) of Children by Hebrew Males. *Judaism* 42:321–31.
Franke, C. A.
1991 The Function of the Satiric Lament over Babylon in Second Isaiah (xlvii). *VT* 41:408–18.

1994 *Isaiah 46, 47, and 48: A New Literary—Critical Reading.* Biblical and Judaic Studies 3. Winona Lake, Ind.: Eisenbrauns.

1996 Reversals of Fortune in the Ancient Near East: A Study of the Babylon Oracles in the Book of Isaiah. Pages 104–23 in *New Visions of Isaiah.* Edited by R. F. Melugin and M. A. Sweeney. JSOTSup 214. Sheffield: Sheffield Academic Press.

Franzmann, M.

1995 The City as Woman: The Case of Babylon in Isaiah 47. *ABR* 43:1–19.

Freedman, D. N.

1968 Isaiah 42,13. *CBQ* 30:225–26.

1970 Mistress Forever: A Note on Isaiah 47:7. *Bib* 51:538.

1987 The Structure of Isaiah 40:1–11. Pages 167–93 in *Perspectives on Language and Text. Essays and Poems in Honor of Francis I. Andersen's Sixtieth Birthday, July 28, 1985.* Edited by E. W. Conrad and E. G. Newing. Winona Lake, Ind.: Eisenbrauns.

Fröhlich, I.

1996 *"Time and Time and Half a Time": Historical Consciousness in the Jewish Literature of the Persian and Hellenistic Eras.* JSPSup 19. Sheffield: Sheffield Academic Press.

Garbini, G.

1984 Universalismo iranico e Israele. *Henoch* 6:293–312.

Garofalo, S.

1958 Preparare la strada al Signore. *RivB* 6:131–34.

Garr, W. R.

1983 The Qinah: A Study of Poetic Meter, Syntax and Style. *ZAW* 95:54–75.

Geller, S. A.

1984 A Poetic Analysis of Isaiah 40:1–2. *HTR* 77:413–24.

Gelston, A.

1965 The Missionary Method of Second Isaiah. *SJT* 18:308–18.

1971 Some Notes on Second Isaiah .*VT* 21:521–22.

1992 Universalism in Second Isaiah. *JTS* 43:377–98.

1993a "Behold the Speaker": A Note on Isaiah xli 27. *VT* 43:405–8.

Giblin, C. H.

1959 A Note on the Composition of Isaiah 49,1–6(9a). *CBQ* 21:207–12.

Ginsberg, H. L.

1958 The Arm of YHWH in Is. 51–63. *JBL* 77:152–56.

Gitay, Y.

1980 Deutero-Isaiah: Oral or Written? *JBL* 99:185–97.

1981 *Prophecy and Persuasion: A Study of Isaiah 40–48.* Forum Theologiae Linguisticae 14. Bonn: Linguistica Biblica.

Goldingay, J.

1979 The Arrangement of Isaiah xli–xlv. *VT* 29:289–99.

1984 *God's Prophet, God's Servant: A Study in Jeremiah and Isaiah 40–55.* Exeter: Paternoster.

1994 "You are Abraham's Offspring, my friend": Abraham in Isaiah 41. Pages 29–54 in *He Swore an Oath: Biblical Themes from Genesis 12–50.* Edited by R. S. Hess. Grand Rapids. Mich.: Baker.

1995 Isaiah 42.18–25. *JSOT* 67:43–65.

1997 Isaiah 40–55 in the 1990s: Among Other Things, Deconstructing, Mystifying, Intertextual, Socio-critical, and Hearer-involving. *BibInt* 5:225–46.
1998 Isaiah 43,22–28. ZAW 110:173–91.

Golebiewski, M.
1983 Is 51,17–52,2 nella struttura generale dei cc. 51–52 e il suo significato teologico. *ColT* special edition: 147–60.

Görg, M.
1996 Der "schlagende" Gott in der "alteren" Bibel. *Bibel and Kirche* 51:94–100.

Gosse, B.
1993 La création en Proverbes 8,12–31 et Isaïe 40,12–24. *NRTh* 115:186–93.

Gottwald, N. K.
1992 Social Class and Ideology in Isaiah 40–55: An Eagletonian Reading. *Semeia* 59 (Ideological Criticism of Biblical Texts): 43–58.

Gressmann, H.
1914 Die literarische Analyse Deuterojesajas. ZAW 34:263–97.

Gruber, M.
1981–82 Can a Woman Forget Her Infant? *Tarbiz* 51:491–92. [Hebrew]
1985 Feminine Similes Applied to the LORD in Second Isaiah. *Beer Sheva* 2: 75–84.

Gunn D. M.
1975 Deutero-Isaiah and the Flood. *JBL* 94:498–508.

Haag, E.
1977a Bund für das Volk und Licht für die Heiden. *Did* 7:3–14.
1996 Stellvertretung und Sühne nach Jesaja 53. *TTZ* 105:1–20.

Haag, H.
1972 Ich mache Heil und schaffe Unheil (Jes 45:7). Pages 179–85 in vol. 2 of *Wort, Lied und Gottesspruch: Fst. Joseph Ziegler.* Edited by J. Schreiner. 2 vols. Stuttgart: Katholisches Bibelwerk.

Haller, M.
1923 Die Kyros-Lieder Deuterojesajas. Pages 261–77 in *Eucharisterion: Studien zur Religion und Literatur des Alten und Neuen Testaments—Fst. Hermann Gunkel.* Edited by H. Schmidt. Göttingen: Vandenhoeck & Ruprecht.

Hallo, W. W.
1983 Cult Statue and Divine Image: A Preliminary Study. Pages 11–14 in *Scripture in Context II: More Essays on Comparative Method.* Edited by W. W. Hallo, J. C. Moyer, and L. G. Perdue. Winona Lake, Ind.: Eisenbrauns.

Hamlin, E. J.
1954 The Meaning of "Mountains and Hills" in Isa. 41:14–16. *JNES* 13:185–90.

Hanson, P.
1979 Isaiah 52:7–10. *Int* 33:389–94.

Haran, M.
1963a *Between RI'SHONOT (Former* Prophecies) and ḤADASHOT (New Prophecies): A Literary-Historical Study of Prophecies *in Isaiah XL–XLVIII.* Jerusalem: Magnes. [Hebrew]

1963b The Literary Structure and Chronological Framework of the Prophecies of Is. XL–LXVIII. Pages 127–55 in *Congress Volume: Bonn, 1962.* VTSup 9. Leiden: Brill.

Hardmeier, C.
1989 Geschwiegen habe ich seit langsam . . . wie die Gebärende schreie ich jetzt. *Wort und Dienst* 20:155–79.

Harner, P. B.
1988 *Grace and Law in Second Isaiah: "I am the Lord."* Ancient Near Eastern Texts and Studies 2. Lewiston, N.Y.: Mellen.

Hayutin, M.
1991–92 Isaiah 44:13 in Light of the Egyptian Sculpture Technique. *BM* 37:44–49. [Hebrew]

Heidel, A.
1963 *The Babylonia Genesis.* Chicago: University of Chicago Press.

Heintz, J. G.
1979 De l'absence de la statue divine au "Dieu qui se cache" (Esaïe 45,15). *RHPR* 59:427–37.

Hermisson, H.-J.
1971 Discussionsworte bei Deuterojesaja. *EvT* 31:665–80.
1973 Zukunftserwartung und Gegenwartskritik in der Verkündigung Jesajas. *EvT* 33:54–77.
1989 Einheit und Komplexität Deuterojesajas: Probleme der Redaktionsgeschichte von Jes 40–55. Pages 132–57 in *Studien zu Prophetie und Weisheit.* [= Pages 287–312 in *The Book of Isaiah / Le Livre d'Isaïe.* Edited by J. Vermeylen. Leuven: Peeters and Leuven University Press, 1989.
1998a Der verborgenen Gott im Buch Jesaja. Pages 105–16 in *Studien zur Prophetie und Weisheit.* Tübingen: Mohr Siebeck.
1998b *Studien zur Prophetie und Weisheit.* Tübingen: Mohr Siebeck.

Hessler, E.
1965 Die Struktur der Bilder bei Deuterojesaja. *EvT* 25:349–69.

Heyns, D.
1995 God and History in Deutero-Isaiah: Considering Theology and Time. *OTE* 8:340–55.

Hillers, D. R.
1978 *Berit ʿam*: "Emancipation of the People." *JBL* 97:175–82.

Hoffman, Y.
1982 The Root QRB as a Legal Term. *JNSL* 10:67–73.

Holladay, W. L.
1997 Was Trito-Isaiah Deutero-Isaiah after All? Pages 193–217 in vol. 1 of *Writing and Reading the Scroll of Isaiah.* 2 vols. Edited by C. C. Broyles and C. A. Evans. Leiden: Brill.

Hollenberg, D. E.
1969 Nationalism and "the Nations" in Isaiah xl-lv. *VT* 19: 23–36.

Holmgren, F.
1969 Chiastic Structure in Isa li 1–11. *VT* 19:196–201.
1973 *With Wings as Eagles—Isaiah 40–55: An Interpretation.* New York: Scholars Press.

Holter, K.
1992 Die Parallelismen in Jes 50,11aba—im Hebräischen und Syrischen Text. *BN* 63:35–36.
1993 The Wordplay on ʾEL ('God') in Isaiah 45,20–21. *SJOT* 7:88–98.
1995 *Second Isaiah's Idol-Fabrication Passages*. Frankfurt am Main: Peter Lang.
1996 Zur Funktion der Städte Judas in Jesaja XL,9. *VT* 46:119–21.
Hoppe, L. J.
1985 The School of Isaiah. *TBT* 23:85–89.
Hutter, M.
1992 "Asche" und "Trug": Eine antizoroastrische Polemik in Jes 44,20. *BN* 64:10–13.
Jackson, R. S.
1962 The Prophetic Vision: The Nature of the Utterance in Isaiah 40–55. *Int* 16:65–75.
Jacobson, H.
1995 A Note on Isaiah 51:6. *JBL* 114:291.
Janzen, J. G.
1983 Another Look at *yaḥălîpû kōaḥ* in Isaiah xli 1. *VT* 33:428–34.
1986 Rivers in the Desert of Abraham and Sarah and Zion. *HAR* 10:139–55.
1994 Isaiah 41:27: Reading HNH HNVMH in 1QIsa[a] and HNH HNM in the Masoretic Text. *JBL* 113:597–607.
Jenni, E.
1954 Die Rolle des Kyros bei Deuterojesaja. *TZ* 10:241–56.
Jensen, J.
1986 Yahweh's Plan in Isaiah and in the Rest of the Old Testament. *CBQ* 48:443–55.
Jeppesen, K.
1984 The Cornerstone (Isa. 28:16) in Deutero-Isaianic Rereading of the Message of Isaiah. *ST* 38:93–99.
1993 Mother Zion, Father Servant: A Reading of Isaiah 49–55. Pages 109–25 in *Of Prophets' Visions and the Wisdom of Sages: Essays in Honour of R. Norman Whybray on His Seventieth Birthday*. Edited by H. A. McKay and D. J. A. Clines. JSOTSup 163. Sheffield: JSOT Press.
Jeremias, J.
1968 *Polloi*. Pages 536–45 in vol. 6 of *TDNT*.
1972 *Mišpāṭ* im ersten Gottesknechtslied (Jes. 42:1–4). *VT* 22:31–42.

Jerger, G.
1986 *"Evangelium des Alten Testaments": Die Grundbotschaft des Propheten Deuterojesaja in ihrer Bedeutung für Religionsunterricht*. Stuttgart: Katholisches Bibelwerk.
Johnston, A.
1994 A Prophetic Vision of an Alternative Community: A Reading of Isaiah 40–55. Pages 31–40 in *Uncovering Ancient Stones: Essays in Memory of H. Neil Richardson*. Edited by L. M. Hopfe. Winona Lake, Ind.: Eisenbrauns.
Jones, D.
1955 The Traditio of the Oracles of Isaiah. *ZAW* 67:226–46.

Jones, G. H.
1972 Abraham and Cyrus: Type and Antitype? *VT* 22:304–19.

Joüon, P.
1906 Le sens du mot hébreu שפי. *Journal Asiatique* 10/7:137–42.

Kahmann, J.
1951 Die Heilszukunft in ihrer Beziehung zur Heilsgeschichte nach Isaias 40–55. *Bib* 32:141–72.

Kaiser, W. C.
1989 The Unfailing Kindnesses Promised to David: Isaiah 55,3. *JSOT* 45:91–98.

Kapelrud, A.
1982 The Main Concern of Second Isaiah. *VT* 32:50–58.

Kaufmann, Y.
1970 *The Babylonian Captivity and Deutero-Isaiah*. Translated by C. W. Efroymson. New York: Union of American Hebrew Congregations.

Kent, R. G.
1953 *Old Persian: Grammar, Texts, Lexicon*. New Haven: American Oriental Society.

Kessler, W.
1956–57 Studien zur religiösen Situation im ersten nachexilischen Jahrhundert und sur Auslegung von Jes 56–66. Wissenschaftliche Zeitschrift 6:41–74.

Kida, Kenichi
1990 The Prophet, the Servant and Cyrus in the Prophecies of Second Isaiah. *Annual of the Japanese Biblical Institute* 16:3–29.

Kiesow, K.
1979 *Exodustexte im Jesajabuch: Literarkritische und motivgeschichtliche Analysen*. OBO 24. Fribourg: Editions Universitaires / Göttingen: Vandenhoeck & Ruprecht.
1990a Deuterojesajas Prozeß gegen die Götter- der Durchbruch zum Ein-Got-Glauben. *Bibel und Liturgie* 63:96–99.
1990b Deuterojesaja: Der unbekannte Prophet. *BL* 63:219–21.

Kittel, R.
1898 Cyrus und Deuterojesaja ZAW 18:149–62.

Klein, H.
1985 Der Beweis der Einzigkeit Jahwes bei Deuterojesaja *VT* 35:267–73.

Klengel-Brandt, E.
1997 Babylon. Pages 251–56 in vol. 1 of *OEANE*.

Knibb, M. A.
1996 Isaianic Traditions in the Book of Enoch. Pages 217–29 in *After the Exile: Essays in Honour of Rex Mason*. Edited by J. Barton and C. J. Reimer. Macon, Ga.: Mercer University Press.

Koch, K.
1972 Die Stellung des Kyros im Geschichtsbild Deuterojesajas und ihre überlieferungsgeschichtliche Verankerung. ZAW 84:352–56.

Köhler, L.
1923 *Deuterojesaja (Jes 40–55) stilkritisch untersucht*. BZAW 37. Giessen: Alfred Töpelmann.

Koole, J. L.
1982 Zu Jesaja 40:3. Pages 137–42 in *Von Kanaan bis Kerala: Fst. für Prof. Mag. J. M. P. van der Ploeg, O.P.* Edited by W. C. Deisman et al. Kevelaer: Butzon & Bercker.
Korpel, M. C. A.
1991 Soldering in Isaiah 40:19–20 and 1 Kgs 6:21. *UF* 23:219–22.
1996a The Female Servant of the LORD in Isaiah 54. Pages 153–67 in *On Reading Prophetic Texts: Gender Specific and Related Studies in Memory of Fokkelien van Kijk-Hemmes.* Edited by B. Becking and M. Kijkstra. Biblical Interpretation Series 18. Leiden: Brill.
1996b Metaphors in Isaiah lv. *VT* 46:43–55.
1999 Second Isaiah's Coping with the Religious Crisis: Reading Isaiah 40 and 55. Pages 90–105 in *The Crisis of Israelite Religion: Transformation of Religious Tradition in Exilic and Post-exilic Times.* Edited by B. Becking and M. Korpel. Leiden: Brill.
Kratz, R. G.
1991 *Kyros im Deuterojesaja-Buch: Redaktionsgeschichtliche Untersuchungen zu Entstehung und Theologie von Jes 40–55.* Tübingen: Mohr (Siebeck).
1993 Der Anfang des Zweiten Jesaja in Jes 40,1f und seine literarischen Horizonte. *ZAW* 105:400–419.
Kraus, H.-J.
1990 *Das Evangelium der unbekannten Propheten: Jesaja 40–66.* Kleine Bibliothek. Neukirchen Vluyn: Neukirchener Verlag.
Krinetski, L.
1972 Zur Stilistik von Jes 40:1–8. *BZ* 16:54–69.
Kuntz, J. K.
1982 The Contribution of Rhetorical Criticism to Understanding Isaiah 51:1–16. Pages 140–71 in *Art and Meaning: Rhetoric in Biblical Literature.* Edited by D. J. A. Clines et al. Sheffield: JSOT Press.
1997 The Form, Location, and Function of Rhetorical Questions in Deutero-Isaiah. Pages 121–41 in vol. 1 of *Writing and Reading the Scroll of Isaiah.* 2 vols. Edited by C. C. Broyles and C. A. Evans. Leiden: Brill.
Kuyper, L. J.
1963 The Meaning of HSDV Isa XL 6. *VT* 13:489–92.
Laato, A.
1990 The Composition of Isaiah 40– 55. *JBL* 109:207–28.
Labahn, A.
1999 *Wort Gottes und Schuld Israels: Untersuchungen zu Motiven deuteronomistischer Theologie im Deuterojesajabuch mit einem Ausblick auf das Verhältnis von Jes 40–55 zum Deuteronomismus.* Stuttgart: Kohlhammer.
Labuschagne, C. J.
1966 *The Incomparability of Yahweh in the Old Testament.* Leiden: Brill.
LaRocca-Pitts, B.
1997 Isaiah and the Future of Israel. *TBT* 35:204–9.
Lauha, A.
1977 "Der Bund des Volkes": Ein Aspekt der deuterojesajanischen Missionstheologie. Pages 257–61 in *Beiträge zur alttestamentlichen Theologie: Festschrift für Walther Zimmerli zum 70. Geburtstag.* Göttingen: Vandenhoeck & Ruprecht.

Leene, H.
1974 Universalism or Nationalism? Isaiah XLV 9–13 and Its Context. *Bijdr* 35:309–34.
1984 Isaiah 46.8: Summons to Be Human? *JSOT* 30:111–21.
1987 *De Vroegere en de Nieuwe Dingen bij Deuterojesaja*. Amsterdam: Free University Press.
1996 Auf der Suche nach einem redaktionskritischen Modell für Jesaja 40–55. *TLZ* 121: 803–18.
1997 History and Eschatology in Deutero-Isaiah. Pages 223–47 in *Studies in the Book of Isaiah*. Beuken Fst. Leuven: Peeters.

Leeuwen, K. van
1997 An Old Crux: Hammesukkan in Isaiah 40,20. Pages 273–87 in *Studies in the Book of Isaiah: Beuken Fst.* Leuven: Peeters.

Leske, A. M.
1995 The Influence of Isaiah on Christology in Matthew and Luke. Pages 241–69 in *Crisis in Christology: Essays in Quest of Resolution*. Edited by W. R. Farmer. Livonia: Dove.

Liebreich, L.
1956–57 The Composition of the Book of Isaiah. *JQR* 46:259–78; 47:114–38.

Limburg, J.
1975 An Exposition of Isaiah 40:1–11. *Int* 29:406–8.

Lind, M. C.
1984 Monotheism, Power, and Justice: A Study in Isaiah 40–55. *CBQ* 46: 432–46.

Lindars, B.
1986 Good Tidings to Zion: Interpreting Deutero-Isaiah Today. *BJRL* 68:473–97.

Lipiński E.
1973 The Comparison in Isaiah LV 10. *VT* 23:246–47.

Lohfink, N.
1972 "Israel" in Jes 49,3. Pages 217–29 in *Wort, Lied und Gottesspruch: Fst. J. Ziegler*. Stuttgart: Katholisches Bibelwerk.

Loretz, O.
1984a Die Gattung des Prologs zum Buch Deuterojesaja (Jes 40 1– 11). *ZAW* 96:210–20.
1984b Mesopotamische und ugaritisch-kanaanäische Elemente im Prolog des Buches Deuterojesaja (Jes 40,1–11). *Or* 53:284–96.

Ludwig, T. M.
1973 The Traditions of the Establishing of the Earth in Deutero-Isaiah. *JBL* 92:345–57.

Maalstad, K.
1966 Einige Erwägungen zu Jes 43:4. *VT* 16:512–14.

Marcus, J.
1995 Mark and Isaiah. Pages 449–66 in *Fortunate the Eyes That See: Essays in Honor of David Noel Freedman in Celebration of His Seventieth Birthday*. Edited A. B. Beck et al. Grand Rapids, Mich.: Eerdmans.

Martin-Achard, R.
1959 *Israël et les nations: La perspective missionaire de l'Ancient Testament*. Neuchatel: Delachaux & Niestlé.

1980 Esaïe 47 et la tradition prophetique sur Babylone. Pages 83–105 in *Prophecy: Essays Presented to Georg Fohrer on His Sixty-Fifth Birthday, 6 September 1980*. Edited by J. A. Emerton. Berlin: de Gruyter.

1981 Esaïe LIV et la nouvelle Jérusalem. Pages 238–62 in *Congress Volume: Vienna, 1980*. VTSup 32. Leiden: Brill.

Matheus, F.

1987 Jesaja xliv 9–20: Das Spottgedict gegen die Götzen und seine Stellung im Kontext. *VT* 37:312–26.

1990 *Singt dem Herrn ein neues Lied: Die Hymnen Deuterojesajas*. Stuttgart: Katholisches Bibelwerk.

Mayer, G.

1995 *kōs*. Pages 101–4 in vol. 7 of *TDOT*.

Mazar, A.

1990 *Archaeology of the Land of the Bible 10,000–586* B.C.E. New York: Doubleday.

Mazar, B.

1967 En-Gedi. *RB* 74:85–86.

1993 En Gedi: Pages 399–405 in vol. 2 of *NEAEHL*.

McConville, J. G.

1986 Statement of Assurance in Psalms of Lament. *IBS* 8:64–75.

McEleney, N. J.

1957 The Translation of Isaiah 41:27. *CBQ* 19:441–43.

McEvenue, S.

1997 Who Was Second Isaiah? Pages 213–22 in *Studies in the Book of Isaiah: Festschrift Willem A. M. Beuken*. Edited by J. von Ruiten and M. Vervenne. BETL 132. Leuven: Peeters.

Melugin, R. F.

1971 Deutero-Isaiah and Form Criticism. *VT* 21: 326–37.

1972 The Typical versus the Unique among the Hebrew Prophets. Pages 331–42 in vol. 2 of *Society of Biblical Literature 1972 Seminar Papers*. Edited by L. C. McGaughy. SBLSP 11. 2 vols. Missoula, Mont.: Scholars Press.

1976 *The Formation of Isaiah 40–55*. BZAW 141. Berlin: de Gruyter.

1982 Isaiah 52:7–10. *Int* 36:176–81.

1997 Israel and the Nations in Isaiah 40–55. Pages 246–64 in *Problems in Biblical Theology: Essays in Honor of Rolf Knierim*. Edited by H. T. C. Sun et al. Grand Rapids, Mich.: Eerdmans.

Merendino, R. P.

1972 Literarkritisches, Gattungskritisches und Exegetisches zu Jes. 41,8–16. *Bib* 53:1–42.

1981 *Der Erste und der Letzte: Eine Untersuchung von Jes 40–48*. VTSup 31. Leiden: Brill.

1982a Jes 49,7–13: Jahwes Bekenntnis zu Israels Land. *Henoch* 4:295–342.

1982b Jes 49,14–26: Jahwes Bekenntnis zu Sion und die neue Heilszeit. *RB* 89:321–69.

1985a Jes. 50,1–3 (9b,11): Jahwes immerwahrende Huld zum erprobten Volk. *BZ* 29:221–44.

1985b Allein und einzig Gottes prophetisches Wort: Israels Erbe und Auftrag für alle Zukunft (Jesaja 50,4–9a.10). *ZAW* 97:344–66.

1989 Is 40,1–2: Un'analisi del materiale documentario. *RivB* 37:1–64.

1997 Is 40,3–5: Osservazioni sul testo. *RivB* 45:3–30.

Merrill, E. H.

1987a Isaiah 40–55 as Anti-Babylonian Polemic. *Grace Theological Journal* 8:3–18.

1987b The Literary Character of Isaiah 40–55, Part 1: Survey of a Century of Studies on Isaiah 40–55. *BS* 144:24–43.

1987c The Literary Character of Isaiah 40–55, Part 2: Literary Genres in Isaiah 40–55. *BS* 144:144–56.

Mettinger, T. N. D.

1986–87 In Search of the Hidden Structure: Yhwh as King in Isaiah 40–55. SEÅ 51–52:148–57.

Mihelic, J. L.

1966 The Concept of God in Deutero-Isaiah. *BR* 11:29–41.

Milik, J. T.

1971 Problèmes de la Littérature Hénochique à la Lumière des Fragments Araméens de Qumran. *HTR* 64:333–78.

Millard, A. R.

1999 Nabû. Pages 607–10 in *Dictionary of Deities and Demons in the Bible*. Edited by K. van der Toorn et al. Leiden: Brill.

Miscall, P. D.

1992 Isaiah: New Heavens, New Earth, New Book. Pages in 41–56 in *Literary Currents in Biblical Interpretation*. Edited by D. N. Fewell. Louisville: Westminster-John Knox.

Morgenstern, J.

1958–59 The Message of Deutero-Isaiah in Its Sequential Unfolding. *HUCA* 29: 1–67; 30:1–102.

1962 "The Oppressor" of Is 51,13: Who Was He? *JBL* 81:25–34.

1965 Isaiah 49–55. *HUCA* 36:1–35.

Mowinckel, S.

1931 Die Komposition des deuterojesajanischen Buches. *ZAW* 49:87–112, 242–60.

1938 Neuere Forschung zu Deuterojesaja, Tritojesaja und dem Aebäd-Jahwe-Problem. *AcOr* 16:1–4.

1946 *Prophecy and Tradition*. Oslo: Dybwad.

1954 *He That Cometh*. Nashville: Abingdon.

Mulzer, M.

1993 Döderlein und Deuterojesaja. *BN* 66:15–22.

Murphy, R. T.

1947 Second Isaiah: The Literary Problem. *CBQ* 9:170–78.

Murtonen, A.

1980–81 Third Isaiah: Yes or No? *Abr-Nahrain* 19:20–42.

Naidoff, B. D.

1980 *Israel and the Nations in Deutero-Isaiah: The Political Terminology in Form-Critical Perspective*. Ph.D. dissertation. Vanderbilt University.

1981a The Rhetoric of Encouragement in Isaiah 40 12–31: A Form-Critical Study. *ZAW* 93:62–76.

1981b The Two-Fold Structure of Isaiah xlv 9–13. *VT* 31:180–85.

Navarro, E. F.
1992 *El Desierto Transformado: Una imagen deuteroisaiana de regeneración*. Rome: Pontifical Biblical Institute.

Newsom, C. A.
1992 Response to Norman K. Gottwald "Social Class and Ideology in Isaiah 40–55." *Semeia* 59 (*Ideological Criticism of Biblical Texts*): 73–78.

Neyrey, J. H.
1982 The Thematic Use of Isaiah 42:1–4 in Matthew 12. *Bib* 63:457–73.

Niditch, S.
1996 *Oral World and Written Word: Ancient Israelite Literature*. Lousiville: Westminster-John Knox.

Nielsen, E.
1970 Deuterojesaja: Erwägungen zur Formkritik, Traditions- und Redaktionsgeschichte. *VT* 20:190–205.

North, C. R.
1950 The "Former Things" and the "New Things" in Deutero-Isaiah. Pages 111–26 in *Studies in Old Testament Prophecy Presented to Professor Theodore H. Robinson*. Edited by H.H. Rowley. New York: Scribner's.
1956 *The Suffering Sevant in Deutero-Isaiah*. 2d ed. Oxford: Oxford University Press.
1958 The Essence of Idolatry. Pages 151–60 in *Von Ugarit nach Qumran: Fst. Otto Eissfeldt*. Edited by J. Hempel. Berlin: de Gruyter.

Oded, B.
1979 *Mass Deportations and Deportees in the Neo-Assyrian Empire*. Wiesbaden: Reichert.

Odendaal, D.
1970 The Eschatological Expectation *of Isaiah 40–66 with Special Reference to Israel and the Nations*. Philadelphia: Presbyterian and Reformed.
1971 The "Former" and the "New Things" in Isaiah 40–48. *OTWSA* 1967: 64–75.

Ofer, A.
1993 Judean Hills Survey. Pages 815–16 in vol. 3 of *NEAEHL*.

Ogden, G. S.
1978 Moses and Cyrus: Literary Affinities between the Priestly Presentation of Moses in Exodus vi–viii and the Cyrus Song in Isaiah xliv 24–xlv 13. *VT* 28:195–203.

Olley, J. W.
1983 Notes on Isaiah XXXII 1, XLV 19, 23 and LXIII 1. *VT* 33:446–53.
1999 "No Peace" in a Book of Consolation. A Framework for the Book of Isaiah? *VT* 49:351–70.

Oppenheim, A. L.
1977 *Ancient Mesopotamia: Portrait of a Dead Civilization*. 2d ed. Chicago: University of Chicago Press.

Orlinsky, H. M., and N. H. Snaith
1967 *Studies in the Second Part of the Book of Isaiah*. VTSup 14. Leiden: Brill. [Reprinted, with corrections, 1977]

Oswalt, J. N.
1991 God's Determination to Save. *RevExp* 88:153–65.

1997 Righteousness in Isaiah: A Study of the Function of Chapters 56–66 in the Present Structure of the Book. Pages 177–91 in vol. 1 of *Writing and Reading the Scroll of Isaiah*. 2 vols. Edited by C. C. Broyles and C. A. Evans. Leiden: Brill.

Patrick, D. A.

1984 Epiphanic Imagery in Second Isaiah's Portrayal of a New Exodus. *HAR* 8:125–41.

Paul, S.

1968 Deutero-Isaiah and Cuneiform Royal Inscriptions. *JAOS* 88. (*Essays in Memory of E. A. Speiser*):180–86.

1969 Literary and Ideological Echoes of Jeremiah in Deutero-Isaiah. Pages 102–20 in *Proceedings of the Fifth World Congress of Jewish Studies*, vol. 1: *Ancient Near East, Bible, Archaeology, First Temple Period*. Jerusalem: World Union of Jewish Studies.

Pauritsch, K.

1971 *Die neue Gemeinde: Golt sammelt Ausgestossene und Arme (Jesaja 56–66)*. Rome: Pontifical Biblical Institute.

Payne, D. F.

1967 Characteristic Word-Play in "Second Isaiah": A Reappraisal. *JSS* 12: 207–29.

Payne, J. B.

1967–68 Eighth Century Background of Isaiah 40–66. *WTJ* 29:179–90; 30:50–58, 185–203.

Perlitt, L.

1971 Die Verborgenheit Gottes. Pages 367–82 in *Probleme biblischer Theologie: Fst. Gerhard von Rad z. 70. Geburtstag*. Edited by H.-W. Wolff. Munich: Chr. Kaiser.

Phillips, A.

1982 Double for All Her Sins. ZAW 94:130–32.

Phillips, M. L.

1971 Divine Self-Predication in Deutero-Isaiah. *BR* 16:32–51.

Plamondon, P.-H.

1982 Sur le chemin du salut avec le IIe Isaïe. *NRTh* 104:241–66.

Plöger, O.

1968 *Theocracy and Eschatology*. Richmond: John Knox.

Pope, M. H.

1952 Isaiah 34 in Relation to Isaiah 35, 40–66. *JBL* 71:235–44.

Porteous, N. W.

1961 Jerusalem-Zion: The Growth of a Symbol. Pages 235–52 in *Verbannung und Heimkehr: Festschrift für Wilhelm Rudolph*. Edited by A. Kuschke. Tübingen: Mohr (Siebeck). [Reprinted, pp. 93–111 in *Living the Mystery*. Edited by N. W. Porteous. Oxford: Blackwell, 1967]

Preuss, H. D.

1976 *Deuterojesaja: Einführung in seine Botschaft*. Neukirchen-Vluyn: Neukirchener Verlag.

Prinsloo, W. S.

1997 Isaiah 42,10–12: "Sing to the Lord a New Song." Pages 289–301 in *Studies in the Book of Isaiah: Fst. Willem A. M. Beuken*. Edited by J. van Ruiten and M. Vervenne. Leuven: Leuven University Press and Peeters.

Rabinowitz, J.
1954 A Note on Isa. 46:4. *JBL* 73:237.
Rad, G. von.
1965 *Old Testament Theology*. Volume 2. New York: Harper.
1967 KPLYM in Jes 40:2 = Äquivalent? ZAW 79:80–82.
1972 *Wisdom in Israel*. Nashville: Abingdon.
Ravenna, A.
1964 Isaia 43 14. *RivB* 12:293–96.
Rehm, M.
1968 *Der königliche Messias im Lichte der Immanuel-Weissagung des Buches Jesaja*. Eichstädter Studien 1. Kevelaer: Butzon.
Reider, J.
1935 Contribution to the Hebrew Lexicon. ZAW 53:270–71.
Reiterer, F. V.
1976 *Gerechtigheit als Heil: צדק bei Deuterojesaja*. Graz: Akademischer Druck.
Rendsburg, G. A.
1983 Hebrew *rhm* = 'rain'. *VT* 33:357–61.
Rendtorff, R.
1975 *Die theologische Stellung des Schöpfungsglaubens bei Deuterojesaja*. Munich: Chr. Kaiser.
1984 Zur Komposition des Buches Jesaja. *VT* 34:295–320. [Translated as The Composition of the Book of Isaiah. Pages 146–69 in *Canon and Theology*. Edited by R. Rendtorff. Minneapolis: Fortress, 1993]
1996 The Book of Isaiah: A Complex Unity—Synchronic and Diachronic Reading. Pages 8–20 in *Society of Biblical Literature 1991 Seminar Papers*. Edited by E. H. Lovering, Jr. SBLSP 30. Atlanta: Scholars, 1991. Reprinted, pp. 32–49 in *New Visions of Isaiah*. Edited by R. F. Melugin and M. A. Sweeney. JSOTSup 214. Sheffield: Sheffield Academic Press.
Rignell, L. G.
1956 *A Study of Isaiah Ch. 40–55*. Lund: C. W. K. Gleerup.
Ringgren, H.
1971 Die Funktion des Schöpfungsmythos in Jes. 51. Pages 38–40 in *Schalom A. Jepsen*. Edited by K. Bernhardt. Stuttgart: Calwer.
1977a Zur Komposition von Jesaja 49–55. Pages 371–76 in *Beiträge zur alttestamentlichen Theologie: Festschrift für Walther Zimmerli zum 70. Geburtstag*. Göttingen: Vandenhoeck & Ruprecht.
1977b גאל. Pages 350–55 in vol. 2 of *TDOT*.
Roberts, B. J.
1959 The Second Isaiah Scroll from Qumrân (1QIs[b]). *BJRL* 42.1:132–44.
Robinson, H. W.
1944 The Council of Yahweh. *JTS* 45:151–57.
Rofé, A.
1988 How Is the Word Fulfilled?: Isaiah 55.6–11 within the Theological Debate of Its Time. Pages 246–61 in *Canon, Theology and Old Testament: Essays in Honor of Brevard S. Childs*. Edited by G. M. Tucker et al. Philadelphia: Fortress.

Rooker, M. F.
1996 Dating Isaiah 40–66: What Does the Linguistic Evidence Say? *WTJ* 58: 303–12.

Ropes, J. H.
1929 The Influence of Second Isaiah on the Epistles. *JBL* 48:37–39.

Rosenbaum, M.
1997 *Word-Order Variation in Isaiah 40–55: A Functional Perspective.* Studia Semitica Neerlandica 35. Assen: Van Gorcum.

Rowley, H. H.
1952 *The Servant of the Lord and Other Essays on the Old Testament.* London: Lutterworth.

Ruppert, L.
1991 Die Disputationsworte bei Deuterojesaja in neuem religionsgeschichtlichen Licht. Pages 317–25 in *Prophetie und geschichtliche Wirklichkeit im alten Israel: Fst. für Siegfried Hermann zum 65. Geburtstag.* Edited by R. Liwak and S. Wagner. Stuttgart: Kohlhammer.
1994 Das Heil der Völker (Heilsuniversalismus) in Deutero- und "Trito"–Jesaja. *MTZ* 45:137–59.
1996 Der Kritik an die Göttern im Jesajabuch. *BN* 82:76–96.

Rüterswörden, U.
1989 Erwägungen zur Metaphorik des Wassers in Jes 40ff. *SJOT* 2:1–22.

Sæbø, M.
1989 Vom Individuellen zum Kollektiven: Zur Frage einiger innerbiblischer Interpretationen. Pages 116–25 in *Schöpfung und Befreiung: Für Klaus Westermann zum 80. Geburtstag.* Edited by R. Albertz et al. Stuttgart: Calwer.

Saggs, H. W. F.
1959 A Lexical Consideration for the Date of Deutero-Isaiah. *JTS* 10:84–87.
1988 *The Babylonians.* 2d ed. London: Macmillan.

Salvini, G.
1996 La citta fondata sulla giustizia: Reflessioni sul valore del tema della giustizia nel Deuteroisaia. *VH* 7:191–218.

Sanders, J. A.
1978 Isaiah 55:1–9. *Int* 32:291–95.
1982 Isaiah in Luke. *Int* 36:144–55.

Sandmel, S.
1961 The Haggada within Scripture. *JBL* 80:105–22.

Sawyer, J. F. A.
1989a Christian Interpretations of Isaiah 45:8. Pages 319–23 in *The Book of Isaiah / Le Livre d'Isaïe.* Edited by J. Vermeylen. Leuven: Leuven University Press and Peeters.
1996 *The Fifth Gospel: Isaiah in the History of Christianity.* Cambridge: Cambridge University Press.

Saydon, P. P.
1959 The Use of Tenses in Deutero-Isaiah. *Bib* 40: 290–301.

Schmitt, H.-C.
1979 Prophetie und Schultheologie im Deutero-jesajabuch: Beobachtungen zur Redaktionsgeschichte von Jes 40–55. *ZAW* 91:43–61.

1992 Erlösung und Gericht: Jes 43,1–7 und sein literarischer und theologischer Kontext. Pages 120–31 in *Alttestamentlicher Glaube und biblische Theologie: Fst. Horst Dietrich Preuss zum 65. Geburtstag.* Edited by J. Hausmann et al. Stuttgart: Kohlhammer.

Schmitt, J.
1985 The Motherhood of God and Zion as Mother. *RB* 92:557–69.

Schoors, A.
1964 Les choses antérieures et les choses nouvelles dans les oracles deutéro-isaïens. *ETL* 40:19–47.
1973 *I Am God Your Saviour: A Form-Critical Study of the Main Genres in Isa XL–LV.* VTSup 24. Leiden: Brill.

Schreiber, A.
1972 Der Zeitpunkt des Auftretens von Deuterojesaja. *ZAW* 84:242–43.

Schreiner, J.
1967 Das Buch jesajanischer Schule. Pages 143–62 in *Wort und Botschaft.* Edited by J. Schreiner. Würzburg: Echter Verlag.

Schüpphaus, J.
1971 Stellung und Funktion der sogenannten Heilsankündigung bei Deuterojesaja. *TZ* 27:161–81.

Schwarz, G.
1971 Keine Waffe (54:17a). *BZ* 15:254–55.

Scott, R. B. Y.
1935 The Relation of Isaiah, Chapter 35, to Deutero-Isaiah. *AJSL* 52:178–91.
1950 The Literary Structure of Isaiah's Oracles. Pages 175–86 in *Studies in Old Testament Prophecy: T. H. Robinson Festschrift.* Edited by H. H. Rowley. Edinburgh: T. & T. Clark.

Scullion, J. J.
1971 *Sedeq-Sedaqah* in Isaiah cc. 40–66 with Special Reference to the Continuity in Meaning between Second and Third Isaiah. *UF* 3:335–48.

Seidel, M.
1955–56 Parallels between the Book of Isaiah and the Book of Psalms. *Sinai* 38: 149–72, 229–42, 272–80. [Hebrew]

Seidl, T.
1983 Jahwe der Krieger—Jahwe der Tröster: Kritik und Neuinterpretation der Schöpfungsvorstellungen in Jesaja 51,9–16. *BN* 21:116–34.
1992 Offene Stellen in Jesaja 40,1–8: Ein methodenkritischer Vergleich. Pages 49–56 in *Goldene Äpfel in silbernen Schalen: Collected Communications to the XIIIth Congress of the International Organization for the Study of the Old Testament.* Edited by K.-D. Schunck and M. Augustin. Frankfurt am Main: Land.

Seitz, C. R.
1988a Isaiah 1–66: Making Sense of the Whole. Pages 105–26 in *Reading and Preaching the Book of Isaiah.* Edited by C. Seitz. Philadelphia: Fortress.
1990 The Divine Council: Temporal Transition and New Prophecy in the Book of Isaiah. *JBL* 109:229–47.
1992 Isaiah, Book of (First Isaiah, Third Isaiah). Pages 472–88 and 501–7 in vol. 3 of *ABD.*
1996 How Is the Prophet Isaiah Present in the Latter Half of the Book?: The Logic of Chapters 40–66 within the Book of Isaiah. *JBL* 115:219–40.

Seybold, K.
1972 *Das davidische Königtum im Zeugnis der Propheten*. Göttingen: Vandenhoeck & Ruprecht.
1997 Theological Usage: Yahweh as King—Yahweh *mlk*. Pages 364–74 in vol. 8 of *TDOT*.

Sheppard, G. T.
1992 The Book of Isaiah: Competing Structures According to a Late Modern Description of Its Shape and Scope. Pages 549–82 in *Society of Biblical Literature 1992 Seminar Papers*. Edited by E. H. Lovering, Jr. SBLSP 31. Atlanta: Scholars Press.

Simcox, C. R.
1937 The Role of Cyrus in Deutero-Isaiah. *JAOS* 57:158–71.

Simian-Yofre, H.
1980 Exodo en Deuteroisaias. *Bib* 61:530–53.
1981 La teología del Deuteroisaias. *Bib* 62:55–72.

Smith, B. L.
1982 The Significance of Catchwords in Isaiah 43:22–28. *Colloquium* 15:21–30.

Smith, M.
1963 Second Isaiah and the Persians. *JAOS* 83/4:415–21.

Smith, M. S.
1981 *Berit ʿam / Berit ʿolam:* A New Proposal for the Crux of Isa 42:6. *JBL* 100:241–43.

Smith, S.
1944 *Isaiah Chapters XL–LV: Literary Criticism and History*. London: Oxford University Press.

Smith-Christopher, D. L.
1996 Between Ezra and Isaiah: Exclusion, Transformation, and Inclusion of the "Foreigner" in Post-exilic Biblical Theology. Pages in 117–42 in *Ethnicity and the Bible*. Edited by M. Brett. Leiden: Brill.

Snaith, N. H.
1940–41 The Exegesis of Isaiah XL 5.6. *ExpTim* 52:394–96.
1967 "Israel" in Isa. xlix, 3: A Problem in the Methodology of Textual Criticism. *ErIsr* 8 (Sukenik Volume):42–45.
1977 Isaiah 40–66: A Study of the Teaching of the Second Isaiah and Its Consequences. Pages 139–46 in *Studies on the Second Part of the Book of Isaiah*. Edited by H. Orlinsky and N. H. Snaith. VTSup 14. Leiden: Brill.

Snaith, N. H., and H. M. Orlinsky
1977 *Studies on the Second Part of the Book of Isaiah*. VTSup 14: 8. Leiden: Brill.

Soares-Prabhu, G. M.
1995 Laughing at Idols: The Dark Side of Biblical Monotheism (An Indian Reading of Isaiah 44:9–20). Pages 109–31 in *Reading from This Place. Vol. 2: Social Location and Biblical Interpretation in Global Perspective*. Minneapolis: Fortress.

Sommer, B. D.
1996 Allusions and Illusions: The Unity of the Book of Isaiah in Light of Deutero-Isaiah's Use of Prophetic Tradition. Pages 156–86 in *New Visions*

of Isaiah. Edited by R. F. Melugin and M. A. Sweeney. JSOTSup 214. Sheffield: Sheffield Academic Press.

1998 A *Prophet Reads Scripture: Allusion in Isaiah* 40–66. Stanford: Stanford University Press.

Songer, Y. H.

1968 Isaiah and the New Testament. *RevExp* 65:459–70.

Southwood, C. H.

1975 The Problematic *hadûrîm* of Isaiah XLV 2. *VT* 25:801–2.

Spreafico, A.

1995 Jesaja xliv 26α: *ʿabdô* oder *ʿabādāyw*? Ein Prophet oder ein Politiker? *VT* 45:561–65.

Spykerboer, H. C.

1976 *The Structure and Composition of Deutero-Isaiah, with Special Reference to the Polemic against Idolatry*. Franeker: Groningen University Press.

Starkova, K. B.

1992 The Ideas of Second and Third Isaiah as Reflected in the Qumran Literature. *QC* 2:51–62.

Stassen, S. L.

1992 Die rol van Egipte, Kus en Seba in Jesaja 43:3 en 45:14. *JSem* 4:160–80.

1997 The Plot in Isaiah 40–55. *Acta Theologica* 17:128–142.

Steck, O. H.

1967 *Israel und das gewaltsame Geschick der Propheten*. WMANT 23. Neukirchen-Vluyn: Neukirchener Verlag.

1969 Deuterojesaja als theologischer Denker. *KD* 15:280–93.

1985a *Bereitete Heimkehr: Jesaja 35 als redaktionelle Brücke zwischen dem Ersten und dem Zweiten Jesaja*. SBS 121. Stuttgart: Katholisches Bibelwerk.

1986 Heimkehr auf der Schulter oder/und auf der Hufte: Jes 49,22b/60,4b. ZAW 98:275–77.

1988 Zur literarische Schichtung in Jes. 51. *BN* 44:74–86.

1989a Sion als Gelände und Gestalt: Überlegungen zur Wahrnehmung Jerusalems als Stadt und Fraus im Alten Testament. *ZTK* 86:261–81.

1989b Beobachtungen zu den Zion-Texten in Jesaja 51–54: Ein redaktionsgeschichtlicher Versuch. *BN* 46:58–90.

1989c Beobachtungen zur Anlage Jes 54,1–8. *ZAW* 101:282–85.

1990 Beobachtungen zu Jesaja 49,14–26. *BN* 55:36–46.

1992a *Gottesknecht und Zion*: Gesammelte Aufsätze zu *Deuterojesaja*. Tübingen: Mohr (Siebeck).

1992c Israel und Zion: Zum Problem konzeptioneller Einheit und literarischer Schichtung in Deuterojesaja. Pages 173–207 in *Gottesknect und Zion: Gesammelte Aufsätze zu Deuterojesaja*. Edited by O. H. Steck. Tübingen: Mohr (Siebeck).

1993[b] Prophetische Prophetenauslegung. Pages 198–244 in *Wahrheit der Schrift–Wahrheit der Auslegung: Eine Zürcher Vorlesungsreihe zu Gerhard Ebelings 80. Geburtstag am 6. Juli 1992*. Edited by H. F. Geißer et al. Zürich: Theologischer Verlag.

Stegemann, U.

1969 Der Restgedanks bei Isaias. *BZ* 13:161–86.

Steinmann, J.
1960 *Le livre de la consolation d'Israël et les prophètes du retour de l'exil*. LD 28. Paris: Cerf.
Stern, P.
1994 The "Blind Servant" Imagery of Deutero-Isaiah and Its Implications. *Bib* 75:224–32.
Stinespring, W. F.
1965 No Daughter of Zion. *Encounter* 26:133–41.
Stoebe, H. J.
1984 Uberlegungen zu Jesaja 40,1–11: Zugleich der Versuch eines Beitrages zur Gottesknechtfrage. *TZ* 40:104–13.
Stone, B. W.
1996 Second Isaiah: Prophet to Patriarchy. Pages 219–32 in *The Prophets: A Sheffield Reader*. Edited by P. R. Davies. The Biblical Seminar 42. Sheffield: Sheffield Academic Press.
Stuhlmueller, C.
1959 The Theology of Creation in Second Isaiah. *CBQ* 21:429–67.
1967 "First and Last" and "Yahweh-Creator" in Deutero-Isaiah. *CBQ* 29:495–511.
1970a *Creative Redemption in Deutero-Isaiah*. AnBib 43. Rome: Pontifical Biblical Institute.
1970b Yahweh-King and Deutero-Isaiah. *BR* 15:32–45.
1980 Deutero-Isaiah (Chaps. 40–55): Major Transitions in the Prophet's Theology and in Contemporary Scholarship. *CBQ* 42:1–29.
Stummer, F.
1926 Einige keilschriftliche Parallelen zu Jes. 40–66. *JBL* 45:171–89.
Sweeney, M.
1988 *Isaiah 1–4 and the Post-Exilic Understanding of the Isaianic Tradition*. BZAW 171. Berlin: de Gruyter.
1997 The Reconceptualization of the Davidic Covenant in Isaiah. Pages 41–61 in *Studies in the Book of Isaiah: Fst. Willem A. M. Beuken*. Edited by J. van Ruiten and M. Vervenne. Leuven: Peeters and Leuven University Press.
Terrien, S.
1966 Quelques remarques sur les affinités de Job avec Deutéro-Isaïe. Pages 295–310 in *Volume du Congrès: Genève, 1965*. VTSup 15. Leiden: Brill.
Texier, R.
1989 Le Dieu caché de Pascal et du Second Isaïe. *NRTh* 111:3–23.
Thomas, D. W.
1968a A Note on *derakim* in Isaiah 49:9b. *JTS* 19:2–4.
1971 Isaiah XLIV.9–20: A Translation and Commentary. Pages 319–30 in *Hommages à André Dupont-Sommer*. Edited by A. Caquot and M. Philonenko. Paris: Adrien-Maisonneuve.
Toloni, G.
1995 Il significato di JESURUN nei profeti e negli agiografi: TM e versioni greche. *BeO* 37:65–93.
Torrey, C. C.
1929 The Influence of Second Isaiah in the Gospels and Acts. *JBL* 48:24–36.

1938 Some Important Editorial Operations in the Book of Isaiah. *JBL* 57: 109–39.

Troadec, H.-G.
1955 La parole vivante et efficace. *Bible et Vie Chrétienne* 11:57–67.

Trudinger, P.
1967 "To Whom Then Will You Liken God?" (A Note on the Interpretation of Isaiah xl 18–20). *VT* 17:220–25.

Tsumura, D. T.
1988 *Tohu* in Isaiah xlv 19. *VT* 38:361–63.

Turner, E. A.
1996 The Foreign Idols of Deutero-Isaiah. *OTE* 9:111–28.

Uchelen, N. A. van
1968 Abraham als Felsen (Jes 51,1). *ZAW* 80:183–91.

Uffenheimer, B.
1981 Aspects of the Spiritual Image of Deutero-Isaiah. *Immanuel* 12:9–20.

Unterman, J.
1995 The Social-Legal Origin for the Image of God as Redeemer גואל of Israel. Pages 399–405 in *Pomegranates and Golden Bells: Studies in Biblical, Jewish, and Near Eastern Ritual, Law, and Literature in Honor of Jacob Milgrom*. Edited by D. P. Wright, D. N. Freedman, and A. Hurvitz. Winona Lake, Ind.: Eisenbrauns.

Ussishkin, D.
1992 Lachish. Pages 114–26 in vol. 4 of *ABD*.

Vanderhooft, D. S.
1999 *The Neo-Babylonian Empire and* Babylon in the Latter *Prophets*. Atlanta: Scholars Press.

Van Seters, A.
1981 Isaiah 40:1–11. *Int* 35:401–4.

Van Winkle, D. W.
1985 The Relationship of the Nations to Yahweh and to Israel in Isaiah xl–lv. *VT* 35: 446–58.
1997 Proselytes in Isaiah xl–lv? A Study of Isaiah xliv 1–5. *VT* 47:341–59.

Vermeylen, J.
1989 L'unité du livre d'Isaïe. In *The Book of Isaiah / Le Livre d'Isaïe: Les oracles et leurs relectures. Unité et complexité de l'ouvrage. Colloquium biblicum lovaniense XXXVII, août 87. Hommage à C. H. W. Brekelmans.* Edited by Vermeylen. Leuven: Peeters and Leuven University Press.

Vieweger, D., and A. Böchler
1996 "Ich gebe Ägypten als Lösegeld für dich": Mk 10,45 und die jüdische Tradition zu Jes 43,3b,4. *ZAW* 108:594–607.

Vincent, J. M.
1953 *Anlass und Hintergrund der Verkündigung Deuterojesajas.* Ph.D. dissertation. Bonn.
1977 *Studien zur literarischen Eigenart und zur geistigen Heimat von Jesaja, Kap. 40–55.* Frankfurt am Main: Peter Lang.

Waldow, H. E. von
1968 The Message of Deutero-Isaiah. *Int* 22:259–87.

Walsh, J. T.
1993 Summons to Judgment: A Close Reading of Isaiah XLI 1–20. *VT* 43:351–71.

Watts, J. W., and P. House
1996 *Forming Prophetic Literature: Essays on Isaiah and the Twelve in Honor of John D. W. Watts*. JSOTSup 235. Sheffield: Sheffield Academic Press.

Watts, R. E.
1990 Consolation or Confrontation?: Isaiah 40–55 and the Delay of the New Exodus. *TynBul* 41:31–59.

Webb, B. G.
1990 Zion in Transformation. A Literary Approach to Isaiah. Pages 65–84 in *The Bible in Three Dimensions: Essays in Celebration of Forty Years of Biblical Studies in the University of Sheffield*. Edited by D. J. A. Clines et al. JSOTSup 87. Sheffield: JSOT Press.

Weinfeld, M.
1967–68 God the Creator in Genesis 1 and in the Prophecy of Second Isaiah. *Tarbiz* 37:105–32.[Hebrew]

Weippert, M.
1989 Die "Konfessionen" Deuterojesaja. Pages 104–15 in *Schöpfung und Befreiung: Für Claus Westermann zum 80. Geburtstag*. Stuttgart: Calwer.

Werner, W.
1988 *Studien zur alttestamentlichen Vorstellung vom Plan Jahwes*. BZAW 173. Berlin: de Gruyter.

Westermann, C.
1960 *Grundformen prophetischer Rede*. Munich: Chr. Kaiser. [Reprinted, *Basic Forms of Prophetic Speech*. Cambridge: Lutterworth / Louisville: Westminster-John Knox, 1991]
1964a Das Heilsworte bei Deuterojesaja. *EvT* 24:355–73.
1964b Sprache und Struktur der Prophetie Deuterojesajas. *Forschung am Alten Testament*. Munich: Chr. Kaiser. [Reprinted, *Sprache und Struktur der Prophetie Deuterojesajas*. Stuttgart: Calwer, 1981]
1966 Jesaja 48 und die "Bezeugung gegen Israel." Pages 356–66 in *Studia Biblica et Semitica Theodoro Christiano Vriezen Dedicata*. Edited by W. C. van Unnik and A. S. van der Woude. Wageningen: Veenman & Zonen.

Whedbee, J. W.
1971 *Isaiah and Wisdom*. Nashville: Abingdon.

Whitley, C. E.
1957 A Note on Isa. xli 27. *JSS* 2:327–28.

Whitley, C. F.
1972 Deutero-Isaiah's Interpretation of *ṣedeq*. *VT* 22:469–75.

Whybray, R. N.
1971 *The Heavenly Counsellor in Isaiah xl 13–14: A Study of the Sources of the Theology of Deutero-Isaiah*. Cambridge: Cambridge University Press.
1986 Two Recent Studies on Second Isaiah. *JSOT* 34:109–117.

Wieringen, A. van
1989 Jesaja 40,1–11: Eine drama-linguistische Lesung von Jesaja 6 her. *BN* 49:82–93.

Willey, P. T.
1997 *Remember the Former Things: The Recollection of Previous Texts in Second Isaiah.* SBLDS 161. Atlanta: Scholars Press.

Williamson, H. G. M.
1978a "The Sure Mercies of David": Subjective or Objective Genitive? *JSS* 23:31–49.
1979 Word Order in Isaiah XLIII,12. *JTS* 30:499–502.
1986 Isaiah 40,20: A Case of Not Seeing the Wood for the Trees. *Bib* 67:1–20.
1993 First and Last in Isaiah. Pages 95–108 in *Of Prophets' Visions and the Wisdom of Sages: Essays in Honour of R. Norman Whybray on His Seventieth Birthday.* Edited by H. A. McKay and D. J. A. Clines. JSOTSup 163. Sheffield: JSOT Press.
1994 *The Book Called Isaiah: Deutero-Isaiah's Role in Composition and Redaction.* Oxford: Clarendon.
1995a Isaiah and the Wise. Pages 133–41 in Wisdom in Ancient Israel: Essays in Honour of J. A. *Emerton.* Edited by J. Day. Cambridge: Cambridge University Press.
1995b Synchronic and Diachronic in Isaian Perspective. Pages 211–26 in *Synchronic or Diachronic?: A Debate on Method in Old Testament Exegesis.* Edited by J. C. de Moor. *OtSt* 34. Leiden: Brill.

Willmes, B.
1990 Gott erlöst sein Volk: Gedanken zum Gottesbild Deuterojesajas nach Jes 43:1–7. *BN* 51:61–93.

Wischnowsky, M.
1993 Das Buch Deuterojesaja: Komposition und Wachstum in Jes 40–55. *BN* 69:87–96.

Wiseman, D. J.
1985 *Nebuchadrezzar and Babylon.* Oxford: Oxford University Press.

Yalon, H.
1966 LDʿT LʿVT ʾT YʿP DBR (Isa 50:4). *Leš* 30:248–49.

Yee, G.
1988 The Anatomy of a Biblical Parody: The Dirge Form in 2 Samuel 1 and Isaiah 14. *CBQ* 50:565–86.

Young, E. J.
1954 *Studies in Isaiah.* Grand Rapids, Mich.: Eerdmans.

Young, F. W.
1955 A Study of the Relation of Isaiah to the Fourth Gospel. ZNW 46:215–33.

Zenger, E.
1983 "Hört auf dass ihr lebt" (Isa 55:3): Alttestamentliche Hinweise zu einer Theologie des Gotteswortes. Pages 133–44 *Freude am Gottesdienst: Fst. J. G. Plöger.* Edited by J. Schreiner. Stuttgart: Katholische Bibelwerk.

Ziegler, J.
1933 Zum literarischen Aufbau im Buch des Propheten Isaias. *BZ* 21:131–49.

Zimmerli, W.
1982a Jahwes Wort bei Deuterojesaja. *VT* 32:104–24.
1982b *I Am Yahweh.* Atlanta: John Knox.

Zorn, J. R.
1994 Estimating the Population Size of Ancient Settlements: Methods, Problems, Solutions, and a Case Study. *BASOR* 295:31–48.

THE SERVANT IN ISAIAH 40–55

Entries marked with an asterisk deal with the history of interpretation of the Servant passages.

Ådna, J.*

1996 Der Gottesknecht als triumphierender und interzessorischer Messias: Die Rezeption von Jes 53 im Targum Jonathan untersucht mit besonderer Berüchsichtigung des Messiasbildes. Pages 129–58 in *Der leidende Gottesknecht: Jesaja 53 und seine Wirkungsgeschichte*. Edited by B. Janowski and P. Stuhlmacher. Tübingen: Mohr (Siebeck).

Ahlström, G. W.

1969 Isaiah 53.8f. *BZ* 13:95–98.

Albright, W. F.

1957 The High Place in Ancient Palestine. Pages 242–58 in Volume du Congrès: Strasbourg, 1956. *VTSup* 4. Leiden: Brill.

Allen, L. C.

1971 Isaiah LIII 2 again. *VT* 21:490.

Alobaidi, J.*

1998 *The Messiah in Isaiah 53: The Commentaries of Saadia Gaon, Salomon ben Yeruham and Yefet ben Eli on Is 52:13–53:12*. Bern: Peter Lang.

Aytoun, R.*

1922 The Servant of the Lord in the Targum. *JTS* 23:172–80.

Bachl, G.*

1982 *Zur Auslegung der Ebedweissagung (Is. 52:13–53:12) in der Literatur des späten Judentums und im Neuen Testament*. Rome: Pontifical Gregorian University.

Bailey, D. P.

1998 Concepts of *Stellvertretung* in the Interpretation of Isaiah 53. Pages 223–50 in *Jesus and the Suffering Servant*. Edited by W. H. Bellinger and W. R. Farmer. Harrisburg: Trinity.

Baltzer, K.

1971 Zur Formgeschichtliche Bestimmung der Texte vom Gottesknecht im Deuterojesaja-Buch. Pages 27–43 in *Probleme biblischer Theologie: Gerhard von Rad zum 70. Geburtstag*. Edited by H. W. Wolff. Münster: Chr. Kaiser.

Barnes, W. E.

1931 Cyrus the Servant of Jehovah. *JTS* 32:32–39.

Bastiaens, J. C.

1997 The Language of Suffering in Job 16–19 and in the Suffering Servant Passages of Deutero-Isaiah. Pages 421–32 in *Studies in the Book of Isaiah: Festschrift Willem A. M. Beuken*. Edited by J. van Ruiten and M. Vervenne. BETL 132. Leuven: Leuven University Press / Peeters.

Battenfield, J.

1982 Isaiah LIII 10: Taking an "if" out of the Sacrifice of the Servant. *VT* 32:485.

Begg, C. T.

1986 Zedekiah and the Servant. *ETL* 62:393–98.

Bellinger, W. H., and W. R. Farmer (eds.)*
1998 *Jesus and the Suffering Servant*. Harrisburg: Trinity Press.
Beuken, W. A. M.
1972 *Mišpat*. The First Servant Song and Its Context. *VT* 22:1–30.
1973 Jes 50,10–11: Eine kultische Paränese zur dritten Ebedprophetie. *ZAW* 85:168–82.
Blenkinsopp, J.
1997 The Servant and the Servants in Isaiah and the Formation of the Book. Pages 155–75 in vol. 1 of *Writing and Reading the Scroll of Isaiah*. 2 vols., Edited by C. C. Broyles and C. A. Evans. Leiden: Brill.
Blythin, I.
1966b A Consideration of Difficulties in the Hebrew Text of Is 53:11. *BT* 17:27–31.
Brownlee, W.
1953 *Mšḥty* (Is. 52:14 1QIs[a]). *BASOR* 132:8–15.
Bundy, D. D.*
1982 Interpretation of Isaiah 53 in East and West. Pages 17–34 in *Typus, Symbol, Allegorie bei den östlichen Vätern und ihren Parallelen im Mittelalter*. Edited by M. Schmidt. Regensburg: Pustet.
1983* The Peshitta of Isaiah 53:9 and the Syrian Commentators. *OrChr* 67:32–45.
Cazelles, H.
1955 Les poèmes du Serviteur: Leur place, leur structure, leur théologie. *RSR* 43:5–55.
Ceresko, A. R.
1994 The Rhetorical Strategy of the Fourth Servant Song (Isaiah 52:13–53:12). *CBQ* 56:42–55.
Chavasse, C.
1964 The Suffering Servant and Moses. *CQR* 165:152–63.
Clements, R. E.
1998 Isaiah 53 and the Restoration of Israel. Pages 39–54 in *Jesus and the Suffering Servant*. Edited by W. H. Bellinger and W. R. Farmer. Harrisburg: Trinity.
Clines, D. J. A.
1976 *I, He, We and They: A Literary Approach to Isaiah 53*. JSOTSup 1. Sheffield: JSOT Press.
Collins, J. J.
1980 The Suffering Servant: Scapegoat or Example? PIBA 4:59–67.
Coppens, J.
1963 La finale du quatrième chant du Serviteur (Is LIII 10–12). *ETL* 39:114–21.
1972 La mission du Serviteur de Yahvé et son statut eschatologique. *ETL* 48: 342–71.
Dahood, M.
1960 Textual Problems in Isaiah *CBQ* 22:400–409.
1971 Phoenician Elements in Isaiah 52:13–53:12. Pages 63–73 in *Near Eastern Studies in Honor of William Foxwell Albright*. Edited by H. Goedicke. Baltimore: Johns Hopkins Press.
1982 Isaiah 53,8–12 and Massoretic Misconstructions. *Bib* 63:566–70.

Day, J.
1980 *Da'at* 'Humiliation' in Isaiah LIII 11 in the Light of Isaiah LIII 3 and Daniel XII 4 and the Oldest Known Interpretation of the Suffering Servant. *VT* 30:97–103.

Driver, G. R.
1935 Linguistic and Textual Problems: Isaiah xl–lxvi. *JTS* 36:396–406.
1958 Notes on Isaiah. Pages 42–48 in *Von Ugarit nach Qumran: Fst. Otto Eissfeldt*. Edited by J. Hempel. BZAW 77. Berlin: Alfred Töpelmann.
1968 Isaiah 52:13–53:12: The Servant of the Lord. Pages 90–105 in *In Memoriam Paul Kahle*. Edited by M. Black and G. Fohrer. Berlin: Alfred Töpelmann.

Driver, S. R., and A. Neubauer*
1876–77 *The Fifty-Third Chapter of Isaiah according to the Jewish Commentators*. 2 vols. Oxford: Parker. [Reprinted, New York: Ktav, 1969]

Eissfeldt, O.
1933 *Der Gottesknecht bei Deuterojesaja*. Halle: Max Niemeyer.

Ekblad, E. R.*
1999 *Isaiah's Servant Poems according to the Septuagint*. Leuven: Peeters.

Elliger, K.
1971a Textkritisches zu Deuterojesaja. Pages 113–19 in *Near Eastern Studies in Honor of William Foxwell Albright*. Edited by H. Goedicke. Baltimore: Johns Hopkins University Press.
1972 Nochmals Textkritisches zu Jes 53. Pages 137–44 in *Wort, Lied und Gottesspruch: Fst. J. Ziegler*. Edited by J. Schreiner. Würzburg: Echter Verlag.

Emerton, J. A.
1970 A Consideration of some Alleged Meanings of *yd'* in Hebrew. *JSS* 15:145–80.

Engnell, I.
1948 The *'Ebed* Yahweh Songs and the Suffering Messiah in "Deutero-Isaiah." *BJRL* 31:54–73.

Euler, K. F.*
1934 *Der Verkündigung vom leidenden Gottesknecht aus Jes. liii in der griechischen Bibel*. Stuttgart: Kohlhammer.

Fascher, E.*
1958 *Jesaja 53 in christlicher und jüdischer Sicht*. Berlin: Evangelische Verlagsanstalt.

Feldmann, F.
1907 *Der Knecht Gottes in Isaias Kap. 40–55*. Freiburg-im Bresgan: Herder.

Fischer, M.*
1963 Vom leidenden Gottesknecht nach Jes. 53. Pages 116–28 in *Abraham unser Vater: Juden und Christen im Gespräch über die Bibel*. Edited by O. Betz. Leiden: Brill.

Fohrer, G.
1981 Stellvertreter und Schuldopfer in Jes 52:13–53:12. Pages 24–43 in *Studien zu alttestamentlichen Texten und Themen (1966–1972)*. Berlin: de Gruyter.

Gelston, A.
1990 Isaiah 52:13–53:12: An Eclectic Text and a Supplementary Note on the Hebrew Manuscript Kennicot 96. *JSS* 35:187–211.
1993b Knowledge, Humiliation or Suffering: A Lexical, Textual and Exegetical Problem in Isaiah 53. Pages 126–41 in *Of Prophets' Visions and the Wisdom of Sages: Essays in Honour of R. Norman Whybray on His Seventieth Birthday*. Edited by H. A. McKay and D. J. A. Clines. Sheffield: JSOT Press.
Gerleman, G.
1980 Der Gottesknecht bei Deuterojesaja. Pages 38–60 in *Studien zur alttestamentliche Theologie*. Heidelberg: Schneider.
Ginsberg, H. L.*
1953 Oldest Interpretation of the Suffering Servant. *VT* 3:400–404.
Gordon, R. P.
1970 Isaiah LIII 2. *VT* 21:491–92.
Grelot, P.
1981 *Les Poèmes du Serviteur: De la lecture critique à l'herméneutique*. Paris: Cerf.
Haag, E.
1977b Das Opfer des Gottesknechts. *TTZ* 86:81–98.
1983 Die Botschaft vom Gottesknecht: Ein Weg zur Überwindung der Gewalt. Pages 159–213 in *Gewalt und Gewaltlosigkeit im Alten Testament*. Edited by N. Lohfink. Freiburg: Herder.
1984* Der Gottesknecht bei Deuterojesaja im Verständnis der alten Kirche. *Freibürger Zeitschrift für Philosophie und Theologie* 31:343–77.
1996* Stellvertretung und Sühne nach Jesaja 53. *TTZ* 105:1–20.
Haag, H.
1985 *Der Gottesknecht bei Deuterojesaja*. Darmstadt: Wissenschaftliche.
Hegermann, H.
1954 *Jesaja 53 in Hexapla, Targum und Peschitta*. Gütersloh: Bertelsmann.
Hengel, M.*
1996 Zur Wirkungsgeschichte von Jes 53 in vorchristlicher Zeit. Pages 49–91 in *Der leidende Gottesknecht: Jesaja 53 und seine Wirkungsgeschichte*. Edited by B. Janowski and P. Stuhlmacher. Tübingen: Mohr (Siebeck).
Henning-Hess, H.
1997 Bemerkungen zum ASCHAM-Begriff in Jes 53,10. *ZAW* 109:618–26.
Hermisson, H.-J.
1981 Der Lohn des Knechts. Pages 269–87 in *Die Botschaft und die Boten. H. W. Wolff Festschrift*. Edited by J. Jeremias and L. Perlitt. Neukirchen-Vluyn: Neukirchener Verlag.
1982 Israel und der Gottesknech bei Dtjes. *ZTK* 79:1–24.
1984 Voreiliger Abschied von den Gottesknechtsliedern. *TRu* 49:209–22.
1996a Gottesknecht und Gottes Knechte: Zur ältesten Deutung eines deuterojesajanischen Themas. Pages 43–68 in vol. 1 of *Geschichte—Tradition—Reflexion: Festschrift für Martin Hengel zum 70. Geburtstag*. 3 vols. Edited by H. Cancik et al. Tübingen: Mohr (Siebeck).
1996b Das vierte Gottesknechtslied im deuterojesajanischen Kontext. Pages 1–25 in *Der leidende Gottesknecht: Jesaia 53 und seine Wirkungsgeschichte*. Tübingen: Mohr (Siebeck).

1998b *Studien zu Prophetie und Weisheit*. Tübingen: Mohr (Siebeck).

Hillyer, N.

1969 The Servant of God. *EvQ* 41:143–60.

Hofius, O.*

1996 Das vierte Gottesknechtslied in den Briefen des Neuen Testamentes. Pages 107–27 in *Der leidende Gottesknecht: Jesaja 53 und seine Wirkungsgeschichte*. Edited by B. Janowski and P. Stuhlmacher. Tübingen: Mohr (Siebeck).

Hooker, M.*

1959 *Jesus and the Servant*. London: SPCK.

Irsigler, H.

1998 *Ein Weg aus der Gewalt?: Gottesknecht kontra Kyros im Deuterojesajabuch*. Beiträge zur Friedensethik 28. Stuttgart: Kohlhammer.

Janowski, B., and P. Stuhlmacher*

1996 *Der leidende Gottesknecht: Jesaja 53 und seine Wirkungsgeschichte*. Tübingen: Mohr (Siebeck).

Kaiser, O.

1959 *Der königliche Knecht*. Göttingen: Vandenhoeck & Ruprecht.

Kapelrud, A. S.

1971 The Identity of the Suffering Servant. Pages 307–14 in *Near Eastern Studies in Honor of William Foxwell Albright*. Edited by H. Goedicke. Baltimore: The Johns Hopkins Press.

1979 Second Isaiah and the Suffering Servant. Pages 123–29 in *God and His Friends in the Old Testament*. Oslo: Universitetsvorlaget.

Knohl, I.

2000 *The Messiah before Jesus: The Suffering Servant of the Dead Sea Scrolls*. Berkeley: University of California Press.

Koch, K.*

1972 Messias und Sündenvergebung in Jesaja 53–Targum. *JSJ* 3:117–48.

Koenig, J.

1968 L'allusion inexpliqué au roseau et à la mèche (Isaïe xlii 3). *VT* 18:159–72.

Komlosh, J.

1974–75 The Countenance of the Servant of the Lord: Was It Marred? *JQR* 65:217–20.

Kooij, A. van der*

1997 "The Servant of the Lord": A Particular Group of Jews in Egypt according to the Old Greek of Isaiah—Some Comments on LXX Isa 49,1–6 and Related Passages. Pages 383–96 in *Studies in the Book of Isaiah. Fst. Willem A. M. Beuken*. Edited by J. van Ruien and M. Vervenne. Leuven: Leuven University Press and Peeters.

Kruse, C. C.*

1978 The Servant Songs: Interpretive Trends since C. R. North. *Studia Biblica et Theologica* 8:3–27.

Laato, A.

1992 *The Servant of YHWH and Cyrus: A Reinterpretation of the Exilic Messianic Programme in Isaiah 40–55*. Stockholm: Almqvist & Wiksell.

Landy, F.
1993 The Construction of the Subject and the Symbolic Order: A Reading of the Last Three Suffering Servant Songs. Pages 60–71 in *Among the Prophets: Language, Image and Structure in the Prophetic Writings.* Edited by P. R. Davies and D. J. A. Clines. JSOTSup 144. Sheffield: JSOT Press.

Lindars, B.
1961 *New Testament Apologetic*. Philadelphia: Westminster.

Lindblad, U.
1993 A Note on the Nameless Servant in Isaiah xlii 1–4. *VT* 43:115–19.

Lindblom, J.
1951 *The Servant Songs in Deutero-Isaiah: A New Attempt to Solve an Old Problem*. Lund: C. W. K. Gleerup.

Lindsey, F. D.
1982a Isaiah's Songs of the Servant, Part 2: The Commission of the Servant in Isa 49:1–13. *BSac* 139:129–45.
1982b Isaiah's Songs of the Servant, Part 3: The Commitment of the Servant in Isaiah 50:4–11. *BSac* 139:216–29.

Litwak, K. D.*
1983 The Use of Qotations from Isaiah 52:13–53:12 in the New Testament. *JETS* 26:385–94.

Marcus, R.
1937 The "Plain Meaning" of Isaiah 42:1–4. *HTR* 30:249–59.

Martin-Achard, R.
1982 Trois études sur Esaïe 53. *RTP* 114:159–70.

Melugin, R. F.
1991 The Servant, God's Call, and the Structure of Isaiah 40–48. Pages 21–30 in *Society of Biblical Literature 1991 Seminar Papers*. Edited by F. H. Lovering. SBLSP 30. Atlanta: Scholars Press.
1998* On Reading Isaiah 53 as Christian Scripture. Pages 55–69 in *Jesus and the Suffering Servant*. Edited by W. H. Bellinger and W. R. Farmer. Harrisburg: Trinity.

Merendino, R. P.
1980 Jes 49,1–6: Ein Gottesknechtslied? *ZAW* 92:236–48.
1985 Allein und einzig Gottesprophetisches Wort: Israels Erbe und Auftrage für alle Zukunft (Jesaja 50,4–9a.10). *ZAW* 97:344–66.

Mettinger, T. N. D.
1977–78 Die Ebed-Jahwe-Lieder. Ein fragwürdiges Axiom. *ASTI* 9:68–76.
1983 *A Farewell to the Servant Songs: A Critical Examination of an Exegetical Axiom*. Scripta Minora, Regiae Societatis Humaniarum Litterarum Lundensis. Lund: C. W. K. Gleerup.

Millard, A.
1969 Isaiah 53:2. *TynBul* 20:127.

Morgenstern, J.
1961 The Suffering Servant: A New Solution. *VT* 9:292–320, 406–31.

Mowinckel, S.
1921 *Der Knecht Jahwäs*. Giessen: Alfred Töpelmann.

Müller, H.-P.
1969 Ein Vorschlag zu Jes 53,10f. *ZAW* 81:377–80.

Nicholls, B. J.*
1996 The Servant Songs of Isaiah in Dialogue with Muslims. *Evangelical Review of Theology* 20:168–77.

North, C. R.*
1956 *The Suffering Servant in Deutero-Isaiah: An Historical and Critical Study*. 2d ed. Oxford: Oxford University Press.
1965 *Isaiah 40–55: The Suffering Servant of God*. 5th ed. London: SCM.

Olley, J. W.
1987 "The Many": How Is Isa 53,12a to Be Understood? *Bib* 68:330–56.

Orlinsky, H. M.
1967 *Studies on the Second Part of the Book of Isaiah: The So-Called "Servant of the Lord" and "Suffering Servant" in Second Isaiah*. VTSup 14. Leiden: Brill.

Page, S.*
1985 The Suffering Servant between the Testaments. *NTS* 31:481–97.

Payne, D. F.
1971 The Servant of the Lord: Language and Interpretation. *EvQ* 103:77–81.
1979 Recent Trends in the Study of Isaiah 53. *IBS* 1:3–18.

Phillips, A.
1979 The Servant: Symbol of Divine Powerlessness. *ExpTim* 90:370–74.

Raabe, P. R.
1984 The Effect of Repetition in the Suffering Servant Song. *JBL* 103:77–81.

Ratzhabi, Y.*
1988 R. Saadia Gaon's Commentary on the Servant of the Lord Passage (Isa 52:3–53:12). *Tarbiz* 57:327–47. [Hebrew]

Reicke, B.
1967 The Knowledge of the Suffering Servant. Pages 186–92 in *Das Ferne und Nahe Wort. Fst. L. Rost*. Edited by F. Maass. Berlin: Alfred Töpelmann.

Rembaum, J. E.*
1982 The Development of a Jewish Exegetical Tradition regarding Isaiah 53. *HTR* 75:239–311.

Renaud, B.
1990 La mission du Serviteur en Is 42:1–4. *RSR* 64:101–13.

Rignell, L. G.
1953 Isaiah LII:13–LIII:12. *VT* 3:87–92.

Robinson, T. H.
1959 Note on the Text and Interpretation of Isaiah 53:3,11. *ExpTim* 72:383.

Rowley, H. H.*
1965 *The Servant of the Lord and Other Essays on the Old Testament*. London: Lutterworth.

Ruppert, L.
1996 "Mein Knecht, der Gerechte, macht die Vielen gerecht, und ihre Verschuldungen—er trägt sie" (Jes 53,11): Universales Heil durch das stellvertretende Strafleidendes Gottesknechts? *BZ* 40:1–17.

Sawyer, J. F. A.
1989b Daughter of Zion and Servant of the Lord in Isaiah. *JSOT* 44:89–107.

Scharbert, J.
1995 *Deuterojesaja: Der "Knecht Jahwas"?* Hamburg: Verlag Dr. Kovač.

Schwarz, G.
1973 Jesaja 50,4–5a: Eine Emendation. *ZAW* 85:356–57.

Sekine, S.
1996 Identity and Authorship in the Fourth Song of the Servant: A Redactional Attempt at the Second Isaianic Theology of Redemption, Part 2. *Annual of the Japanese Biblical Institute* 22:3–30.

Sellin, E.
1930 Tritojesaja, Deuterojesaja und das Gottesknechtsproblem. *NKZ* 41:73–93, 145–73.
1937 Die Lösung des deuterojesajanischen Gottesknechtsrätsels. *ZAW* 55:332–39.

Snaith, N. H.
1950 The Servant of the Lord in Deutero-Isaiah. Pages in 187–200 in *Studies in Old Testament Prophecy: T. H. Robinson Festschrift*. Edited by H. H. Rowley. Edinburgh: T. & T. Clark.

Soggin, J. A.
1975 Tod und Auferstehung des leidenden Gottesknechtes: Jes 53,8–10. *ZAW* 87:346–55.

Sonne, I.
1959 Isaiah 53:10–12. *JBL* 78:335–42.

Steck, O. H.
1984 Aspekte des Gottesknechts in Deuterojesajas: "Ebed-Jahwe-Liedern." *ZAW* 96:372–90.
1985b Aspekte des Gottesknechs: in Jesaja 52,13–53:12. *ZAW* 97:36–57.
1992b Die Gottesknechts: Texte und ihre redaktionelle Rezeption im Zweiten Jesaja. Pages 149–72 in *Gottesknecht und Zion: Gesammelte Aufsätze zu Deuterojesaja*. Edited by O. H. Steck. Tübingen: Mohr (Siebeck).
1993a Der Gottesknecht als "Bund" un "Licht": Beobachtungen im Zweiten Jesaja. *ZTK* 90:117–34.

Stern, P.
1994 The "Blind Servant" Imagery of Deutero-Isaiah and Its Implications. *Bib* 75:224–32.

Stuhlmacher, P.*
1996 Jes 53 in den Evangelien und in der Apostelgeschichte. Pages 93–105 in *Der leidende Gottesknecht: Jesaja 53 und seine Wirkungsgeschichte*. Edited by B. Janowski and P. Stuhlmacher. Tübingen: Mohr (Siebeck).

Syrén, R.*
1989 Targum Isaiah 52:13–53:12 and Christian Interpretation. *JJS* 40:201–12.

Thomas, D. W.
1968b A Consideration of Isaiah LIII in the Light of Recent Textual and Philological Study. *ETL* 44:79–86.

Tidwell, N.
1974 My Servant Jacob: Is XLII 1—A Suggestion. Pages 84–91 in *Studies on Prophecy. A Collection of Twelve Papers*. Leiden: Brill.

Vermeylen, J.
1994 Isaïe et le ralliement d'Ephraim. Pages 343–54 in *"Wer ist wie du, Herr, unter den Göttern?": Studien zur Theologie und Religionsgeschichte für Otto Kaiser zum 70. Geburtstag*. Edited by I. Kottsieper et al. Göttingen: Vandenhoeck & Ruprecht.

Volgger, D.
1998 Das "Schuldopfer" Ascham in Jes 53,10 und die Interpretation des sogennannten vierten Gottesknechtliedes. *Bib* 79:473–98.

Ward, J. M.
1969 The Servant Songs in Isaiah. *RevExp* 65:433–46.

Werlitz, J.
1997 Vom Knecht der Lieder zum Knecht des Buches: Ein Versuch über die Ergänzungen zu den Gottesknechtstexten des Deuterojesajabuches. ZAW 109:30–43.

White, R. E.
1990 The Meaning of ʿĀLĀW YIQPƎṢÛ MƎLĀKÎM PÎHEM in Isaiah LII 15. *VT* 40:327–35.

Whybray, R. N.
1978 *Thanksgiving for a Liberated Prophet: An Interpretation of Isaiah Chapter* 53. Sheffield: JSOT Press.

Wilcox, P., and D. Paton-Williams
1988 The Servant Songs in Deutero-Isaiah. *JSOT* 42:79–102.

Williamson, H. G. M.
1978b *Daʿat* in Isaiah LIII 11. *VT* 28:118–22.

Wilshire, L. E.
1975 The Servant City: A New Interpretation of the Servant of the Lord in the Servant Songs of Deutero-Isaiah. *JBL* 94: 356–67.

Wolff, H. W.
1962 Wer ist der Gottesknecht in Jes. 53? *EvT* 22:338–42.
1984* *Jesaja 53 im Urchristentum.* Giessen: Brunnen.

Zimmerli, W.
1974 Zur Vorgeschichte von Jes 53. Pages 213–21 in *Studien zur alttestamentliche Theologie und Prophetie*. Munich: Chr. Kaiser.

TRANSLATION, NOTES, AND COMMENTS

◆

ISAIAH 40–55

◆

PROLOGUE: THE REVIVAL OF PROPHECY (40:1–8)

(Barstad 1989, 8–13; Berlin 1979; Brooke 1994; Charlesworth 1997; Cross 1953; 1973, 186–90; Davidson 1997; G. Fischer 1984; Fokkelman 1981; Freedman 1987; Garofalo 1958; Geller 1984; Koole 1982; Kratz 1993; Krinetski 1972; Kuyper 1963; Limburg 1975; Loretz 1984a; Melugin 1976, 82-86; Merendino 1989; 1997; A. Phillips 1982; von Rad 1967; Robinson 1944; Seidl 1992; Seitz 1990; Snaith 1940–1941; Stoebe 1984; van Wieringen 1989)

TRANSLATION

i

40 [1]"Comfort, O comfort my people,"
says your God;
[2]"speak tender words to Jerusalem,
proclaim to her
that her servitude is over,[a]
her debt has been paid;
she has received at Yahveh's hand
double for all her sins."

ii

[3]A voice proclaims:[b]
"Clear in the wilderness
a way for Yahveh;
level in the desert
a highway for our God!
[4]Let every ravine[c] be filled in,
every mountain and hill flattened out;
the crooked made straight,
the rough places leveled.
[5]Then the glory of Yahveh will be revealed;
All humanity as one[d] shall see it."
For Yahveh himself has spoken.[e]

iii

[6]A voice says,[f] "Proclaim!"
I replied,[g] "What shall I proclaim?"
"All humanity is grass,
and all its splendor[h] like the wild flower."

[7]Grass withers, flowers fade
when Yahveh's breath blows on them;[i]
[surely the people is but grass!].[j]
[8]Grass withers, flowers fade,
but the word of our God stands firm forever.

NOTES

1QIsaiah[a] leaves about eight spaces blank after 39:8; 4QIsa[b], containing part of 40:1–4, leaves about two-thirds of a line blank. [a] 1QIsaiah[a] reads *ml'*; since *ṣābā'* is usually masc., it is unnecessary to emend to *millĕ'āh*, transitive; [b] LXX divides differently: *phōnē boōntos en tē erēmō* cf. Matt 3:3 and par.; 1QS 8:14 agrees with MT, which has the disjunctive accent Zaqeph Qaton attached to *qōrēh*, allowing for a clear parallelism in the remainder of v 3; [c] read *qay'* absolute for *gey'* construct; the word can refer to a narrow gorge, defile, or ravine rather than a broad valley; "filled in," literally, "raised up"; [d] 1QIsa[a] *yḥdyv* for MT *yaḥdâv*; LXX fills out the sense theologically: *kai opsetai pasa sarx to sōtērion tou theou* ("all flesh will see the salvation of God"), perhaps influenced by 52:10; more recent attempts to provide *vĕrā'û* with an object are unnecessary, since *r'h* occurs elsewhere without an object (41:5, 21; 49:7, 18); [e] literally, "for the mouth of Yahveh has spoken"; [f] or, possibly, "Listen! One is saying . . . ," interjectional use of *qôl* (GKC 146b); [g] with 1QIsa[a], LXX (*kai eipa*), and Vulg. (*et dixi*) for MT *vĕ' āmar*, "and he said"; [h] MT *ḥasdô* (1QIsa[a] *ḥsdyv/ḥasdayv*), "its loyalty," does not make good sense, and extending the range to mean "durability" (Snaith cf. Tg. *tvqghvn*, "its strength") or "grace," "graciousness" (Torrey 306) is not well supported; perhaps *hădārô* cf. LXX, which is followed by 1 Pet 1:24 *doxa* and Vulg.: *omnis gloria eius quasi flos agri;* [i] LXX omits v 7 by haplography; the 1QIsa[a] scribe omitted vv 7b and 8a, later added in superscript and in the margin; Yahveh's breath is a metaphor for wind cf. Ps 147:18; [j] some commentators (e.g. Elliger 4) read this statement as part of the original text, but it looks like a typical gloss, perhaps referring *ḥāṣîr*, "grass," in a sectarian sense, to the rest of the people, as the Targum suggests; cf. 2:9b, 22.

COMMENTS

In the context of literary conventions characteristic of prophetic writings, we are struck at once by the failure to identify the people addressed at the beginning of this major section of the book. The problem was noticed from early times on, since the Targum identified them as prophets and the LXX as priests. If we could follow Torrey's inclusion of chs. 34–35 in Second Isaiah's book, a simple explanation would be at hand: 40:1 is not where the book begins. Isaiah 34:1 is addressed to a specific audience, the nations and peoples, but the message that follows, far from offering comfort, is all about anger, slaughter, and judgment. This makes it difficult to accept Freedman's argument that the same people are being addressed in 40:1, or even that chs. 34 and 40 belong together in the same book. Torrey himself noted the problem but simply remarked that, if the writer had been pressed to identify those addressed, he would have answered in the words of 66:10, "All those who love Zion" (Torrey 1928, 304). An alternative explanation, proposed in the Introduction, is that the compiler who attached 40–55 to 1–39 would have either omitted the superscription or reworded the introductory verses to fit their new context.

That this introductory passage is concerned with prophetic communication is clear from the identification of the first two statements (vv 1–2 and 3–5) as speech of Yahveh (i.e., prophetic speech) and from the final statement (8b) affirming the permanent validity of that speech, an affirmation repeated at the end of the section, no doubt deliberately (55:10–11). This is the view of the Targumist, who identified those addressed as prophets and substituted "prophesy" for "proclaim," but not of the Greek translator, who identified them as priests. That prophets are being addressed is also the view of most of the medieval commentators.

This introductory apostrophe amounts to an *apologia* for the message that is to follow in chs. 40–48 and therefore makes a fitting prologue to these chapters. The author, an anonymous seer (conventionally known as Deutero-Isaiah), reports a communication from Yahveh (vv 1–2) in which those addressed are given a commission involving three commands: comfort the people, speak consoling words to Jerusalem (meaning, again, the people), and proclaim good news. This theme of comfort is a leitmotif throughout these chapters (cf. 49:13 and 52:9 *nḥm* Piel with *ʿammô*, "his people"), and it makes for good news indeed after all the dire threats and comminations of chs. 1–39. The good news message is also tripartite: the end of indentured service; the liquidation of debts incurred, understood metaphorically; and the bestowing of benefits that will outweigh the punishment inflicted for sins committed.

The hypothesis that this "hall of voices" (Watts 1987, 75) presupposes the scenario of the divine council and that therefore those addressed are members of Yahveh's heavenly court has achieved practically canonical status in recent English-language scholarship but is not well founded. According to Cross (1953; 1973, 187–88), it can be deduced from the imperatives characteristically addressed by YHVH to members of his entourage. But this overlooks the *deliberative* nature of the council, as described in the relevant biblical texts. Wherever such a scenario is clearly presented, Yahveh engages in discussion and solicits opinions but does not give orders (Isa 6:8; 1 Kgs 22:20–22; Job 1– 2). Cross also assumes that *qôl qōrēʾ* (40:3) and *qôl ʾōmēr* (40:6) refer to angelic heralds, presumably on the strength of similar expressions in the vision report of ch. 6 (6:4, 8). At first sight this appears to be a reasonable conjecture, but it ignores the contextually more natural reference of Isa 6:4 to the liturgical call of the seraphim in the previous verse. Since, in addition, Isa 6:8 explicitly identifies the voice as the voice of Yahveh and not the voice of one of his courtiers, the way the vision-call narrative is set up is significantly different from 40:1–8.

It also seems rather too literalistic to assume that only supernatural beings can level hills and raise valleys.

The case for a divine council scenario in dependence on Isa 6 is taken further by Melugin (1976, 82–84), Seitz (1990, 229–47), and Williamson (1994, 37–38). Melugin argues from the plural imperatives in 40:1–2, but it is difficult to see why injunctions in the plural must be addressed to divine beings rather than to a plurality of prophets. In fact, a prophetic plurality is referred to quite often in Isa 40–66 and in other texts from the post-destruction period (Isa 52:8 cf. Jer 6:17; Ezek 3:17; Isa 56:10–11; 59:21; 62:6–7; Jer 29:8). On the basis of Isa 40:6–8, both Melugin and Williamson assume that the prophet is responding to the commission with discouragement or despair, comparable therefore to the reaction of Isaiah in the vision (6:5). But in view of the metaphoric language of grass and flowers occurring elsewhere (Isa 28:1; 37:27; 51:12; Ps 37:2; 90:5; 103:15; 129:6; the last with reference to the enemies of Zion), it seems more natural to assume, either that 40:6b is the reply to the seer's question followed by a prophetic comment in vv 7–8, or that the entire passage, 6c–8b, is the proclamation.

In either case, the intent is to contrast the power and permanence of the prophetic word with the impermanence of political power and human pretensions in general, we would assume with specific reference to Babylon. All of this is quite apart from the fact that there is actually no mention of a heavenly setting in Isa 40:1–8 comparable to Isa 6:1–3, 1 Kgs 22:19–23, and Job 1–2, where that scenario is explicit.

Since the authorial voice is seldom heard in chs. 40–55, it is noteworthy that first-person prophetic speech is found at the beginning of the two main parts of this section of the book—namely, 40:6a and 49:1–6.

The prologue begins, then, with a summons to prophets in general, or to a specific prophetic group, to proclaim a message of comfort and hope to Yahveh's people (*ʿammî* being the object of the transitive verb *nḥm* Piel cf. 49:13; 52:9; and not the vocative, as in Vulg. *popule meus*). The position taken here is that the shifting between plural and singular in vv 1–8 with respect to those addressing and those being addressed is best explained in terms of a prophetic plurality in association with a prophetic individual—namely, the anonymous author. Isaiah 52:7–8 provides an instructive parallel: a *human* herald of good news (*mĕbaśśēr*)is associated with a prophetic plurality (*ṣōpîm*, "sentinels," a synonym for prophets cf. Ezek 3:17; 33:2, 6–7; Jer 6:17; and perhaps Isa 56:10).

It is not stated, here at the beginning, that the message is an assurance of a proximate return to the homeland addressed to Judeo-Babylonians. Juxtaposition with the prediction of exile in Babylon immediately preceding (39:5–8) might suggest this, as also the summons to leave Babylon with which this section ends (48:20–22). But for the moment all we are told is that Jerusalem, representing the people, has served its time of indentured service (*ṣābāʾ*, understood in this sense rather than the military draft, or doing time in prison for nonpayment of debts). She has satisfied her obligations and paid off her debts.

If taken literally, the statement that Israel has paid double (*kiplayim*) for all its sins could raise serious questions about the evenhanded and equitable administration of justice by God. Commentators have therefore preferred to understand it as a technical legal or economic term, either in the sense that Jerusalem has paid the due amount together with interest accruing (cf. Exod 22:3[4] *šnayim*, "twofold"), or the equivalent amount, as in Deut 15:18 (von Rad) or, in a more general sense, superabundantly (cf. Job 11:6). Ibn Ezra took a more direct approach, understanding it to mean that Israel had been called on to suffer twice as much as the nations. Torrey (p. 305), on the other hand, finds support in the Quʾran (e.g. Sura 7:36) for his view that "paying double" is simply a case of rhetorical hyperbole. To these proposals we may add one more, suggested by Isa 51:19: Jerusalem is here being addressed by a seer and told that two bad things have happened to her, the allusion being, in all probability, to famine and military defeat, but that her sufferings are now coming to an end.

If these metaphors sound too legalistic for our taste, we can balance them with the emotional weight attaching to the repetition right at the beginning of this "book of consolation" (*naḥămû, naḥămû*). Repetition of this kind is a recurring feature in these chapters (51:9, 17; 52:1, 11; 57:14; 62:10) and helps to set the upbeat mood. There is also the command: comfort *my* people, speak to the heart of Jerusalem, meaning, speak words of encouragement and reassurance (cf. Gen 34:3; 50:21; Judg 19:3; 2 Sam 19:8[7]; Hos 2:16[14]; Ruth 2:13), since she can look forward to a better future.

As the closing statement of the next stanza shows, vv 3–5 constitute a prophetic proclamation rather than the utterance of a disembodied voice or a summons from a heavenly herald. The purpose is to state what must be done before the comforting words can be translated into reality. There is no mention here of preparing a route for return from exile in Babylon. It is, rather, that a processional way is to be prepared for the return of Yahveh to his people. Given what we imagine to be the state of roads at that time, this would have been normal procedure in preparation for the visit, the *parousia*, of a dignitary.

As we proceed, we shall bear in mind the possibility, suggested by Rabbi Moses Hakkohen and reported by Ibn Ezra, that these early stanzas include an allusion to the eventual rebuilding of the Jerusalem temple. Isaiah 62:10–12 makes the same point, using the same language and even quoting 40:3–5 verbatim: a highway (*mĕsillâ*) is to be built up and cleared of stones to prepare for Yahveh's *parousia* and the salvation that comes with it. A similar passage, Isa 35:8–10, closely associated with chs. 40–48 as we have seen, does speak of a return to Zion by those ransomed by Yahveh along a highway (*maslûl* hapax) known as the Holy Way but does so as part of a larger scenario. Subsequent chapters will speak of a return from other quarters by land and sea (43:2, 16; 49:11–12), even from as far away as the first cataract of the Nile (49:12).

Both 35:8–10 and 62:10–12 seem to be further removed from historical particularities than 40:1–8, to which they are closely related, and we will note as we work through these chapters how the way (*derek*) to be laid down through the wilderness is metaphorized or spiritualized even further (e.g. 57:14 cf. 30:21) and is linked with the traditions of Israel's uneven progress through the wilderness after leaving Egypt (see especially Barstad 1989). Viewed within the context of the book of Isaiah as a whole, the figure of the way or the journey indicates a broader development from historical particularities to an eschatological and, eventually, apocalyptic perspective.

What are those addressed by the seer being called on to do? A route, a highway has to be cleared (*pnh* Piel cf. 57:14; 62:10) and graded, leveling out the uneven ground (*ʿāqob*, the only appearance with this meaning) and the rough places (*rĕkāsîm* hapax). The location is described as wilderness (*midbār*) and desert (*ʿărābâ*), more or less synonymous terms that can have a broad spectrum of meaning, by no means confined to such regions as the Sahara Desert, the great Arabian Desert, or the Arava south and east of the Dead Sea. This "way through the wilderness" is more often than not identified with the route that the Judeo-Babylonian immigrants are presumed to have followed in returning to Judah. As the crow flies, this would have taken them through the central Arabian desert, but a moment's reflection will show how unlikely, not to say suicidal, such an itinerary would have been. The probability is that immigrants from southern Mesopotamia would have taken the well-traveled northerly route along the course of the Euphrates into Syria, then south to Damascus, then either along the coastal route or the central ridge to Jerusalem.

More to the point, the emphasis in these chapters is not just on constructing a highway but also, and more prominently, on the theme of ecological transformation, rendering the land devastated by the Babylonian conquest once again not only habitable but superabundantly fertile. So, for example, 35:1:

> Let the *midbār* and parched land be glad,
> the *ʿărabâ* rejoice and blossom.

Similar predictions can be found throughout chapters 40–66 (41:17–20; 43:19–21; 49:8–13; 57:14; 62:10–12) in which a major motif is the provision of water (35:6; 41:18–19; 43:19; 44:3; 48:20–21; 49:9). Isaiah 51:3 speaks of Zion's *midbār* and *ʿărābâ* being comforted, the comfort consisting in their transformation into a Garden of Eden. This creates a significant though not insuperable problem for the many commentators who assume, generally without argument, a diasporic, Babylonian background for these chapters.

The point of all of this activity is to prepare for the revelation of the glory or radiance of Yahveh to be witnessed by all humanity (v 5). This theologoumenon (Hebrew *kābôd*, Greek *doxa*), used throughout the book of Isaiah, embodies an attempt to combine transcendence and immanence, to give symbolic expression to the real presence of the invisible God.

What is important for the present context is that it is essentially associated with the sanctuary, the place where the deity resides and where the deity's presence can be experienced. When the ark was captured by the Philistines the wife of the priest Phinehas lamented that "the glory has departed from Israel" (*gālâ kābôd miyyiśrāʾēl* 1 Sam 4:21–22) and called her child Ichabod (perhaps "where is the *kābôd?*"). After the recovery of the ark and its installation in the newly-built Jerusalem temple, we are told that the glory of Yahveh filled the building (1 Kgs 8:11). Exploiting the idea of mobility, Ezekiel represented the departure of the *kābôd* by stages from the doomed city and temple (Ezek 9:3; 10:4, 18–19; 11:22–23), its eventual appearance in the Babylonian diaspora (1:28; 3:23), and its anticipated return (43:1–5; 44:4 cf. Hag 2:7; Zech 2:9[5]). In doing so, he made a decisive break with the idea of a territorial and locative deity. The God of Israel can now appear and be experienced outside the land in which his own writ runs.

Closely related to these representations is the mobile sanctuary that served Israel in the wilderness and with which, according to the Priestly writer (P), the *kābôd* was closely associated (Exod 40:34–38 etc.). That all humanity, indeed all living creatures (literally, "all flesh"), will witness and acknowledge the triumphant return of Yahveh to his defeated and dispersed people is the first of many indications in these chapters of the prophetic defiance of political realities (cf. 49:26; 66:16, 23–24).

The following stanza (vv 6–8) is linked with the preceding one by the catchword *kol-bāśār*, literally, "all flesh," meaning all humanity or all living things, depending on the context. This expression is of frequent occurrence in the P source, conspicuously in the account of the great deluge (Gen 6:13, 19; 7:15–16; 8:17). The identity of both the speaker and the one addressed has long been discussed, with many modern interpreters opting for a conversation between heavenly beings, as in Micaiah's vision (1 Kgs 22:19–23) and the opening scene in Job. But if this were so, we would expect both the speakers and the scenario to be more clearly indicated; and, if the speaking voice in the previous stanza is Yahveh's, we would expect the same to be the case here. That Yahveh is referred to in the third person in both stanzas is no obstacle to this solution, since this is common in prophetic *oratio recta* and a normal form of prophetic self-dramatization. But it is also possible that in vv 7–8 we have a commentary on the oracular statement in v 6b, a not uncommon feature of prophetic discourse.

In this second instance the seer is told to proclaim or preach (the term preferred by Smart 50, following Luther) the message that, expressed in many different ways, is at the heart of biblical prophecy: the transforming power of the prophetic word ("the word of our God") contrasted with, or pitted against, the political powers and principalities, which appear to be indestructible but are in reality impermanent. In this sense, at least, the seer can be considered the heir of Isaiah of Jerusalem.

But the message is not a vague, moralizing statement about human frailty, as the combination "grass" and "flower" might suggest (cf. Ps 37:2; 90:5–6; 103:15), and even less is it a lament for the helpless situation of the Babylonian diaspora from which the seer is speaking. It takes aim at the Neo-Babylonian

Empire, then under terminal threat from the victorious progress of Cyrus II. It therefore prepares for the (literally) central theme of chs. 40–48—namely, a new impulse delivered to the stalled historical process with the commissioning of Cyrus as the instrument of Yahveh's designs for his people.

GOOD NEWS FOR THE CITIES OF JUDAH (40:9–11)

(Holter 1996; Stoebe 1984)

TRANSLATION

40 [9]Climb to the top of a mountain,
Zion, herald of good news;[a]
lift up your voice with power,
Jerusalem, herald of good news;[a]
lift it up without fear.
Say to the cities of Judah:
"See, here is your God!"
[10]See, Yahveh[b] is coming with power,[c]
his strong arm affirms his rule;
see, his reward is with him,
his recompense[d] precedes him.
[11]Like a shepherd he tends his flock,
he gathers them together with his arm,
the lambs he lifts into his lap,[e]
the ewes he gently leads on.

NOTES

[a] *Měbaśśeret* is in apposition to *ṣiyyôn/yĕrûšālāyim* as e.g. Isa 41:14 *tôlaʿat yaʿăqob*; Amos 5:2 *bĕtûlat yiśrāʾēl*; and not fem. sing. construct (GKC 122s), on which see the commentary; [b] omitting *ʾădonāy* metri causa, since the line is otherwise overloaded, and in spite of *ʾădonāy YHVH* elsewhere in these chapters (48:16; 50:4, 5, 7, 9); [c] MT *bĕḥāzāq* = *beth essentiae* (GKC 119i), "as/in the guise of a powerful man," but the reading of 1QIsa[a] *bḥvzq* (*bĕḥozeq*) and the versions (LXX *meta ischuos*), "with strength," is more probable; [d] 1QIsa[a] has pl. *vpʿltyv* cf. Tg. "all those whose deeds are disclosed before him"; [e] most commentators find the meter problematic, resulting in rearrangements, omissions, or the assumption that a phrase with two accents is missing (Elliger 32); the simplest solution is to omit the conjunction attached to *bĕḥêqô* (11b), with Aquila and Symmachus, leaving two 3:2 lines, as in the preceding two verses.

COMMENTS

Several commentators have found the image of Zion, also known as Mount Zion, being ordered up a high mountain to proclaim good news singularly inept or even, according to Duhm (1922, 290), "ein groteskes Bild." Whether grotesque or not, this is what the text says. The alternative, familiar from Handel's *Messiah*, "Oh thou that tellest glad tidings to Zion," though perhaps permissible as a feminine-singular collective, is ruled out by the five feminine imperatives following. Furthermore, postulating a female herald would be without parallel in the book. But Torrey is right in taking Duhm to task at this point, since there is nothing inappropriate in supposing that "Zion personified is commanded to assume the office of a herald, and proclaim to her sister cities the joyful news" (Torrey 1928, 306–7).

Beginning in the Neo-Babylonian period, we detect an increasing emphasis on Jerusalem as an entity distinct from Judah. This is not as much in evidence in chs. 40–48, where the people is referred to more often than not as Jacob or Israel. But Jerusalem also serves as a designation for Judeans or Jews in general; in fact, it is explicitly stated that they are to be named for the city (48:2). In the next major section—chs. 49–54(55)—Jerusalem, as it were, emerges from the shadows and speaks and is spoken to in her own name (49:14–26; 51:16–23; 52:1–2, 7–10; 54:1–17), and Israelites are now said to be her children (54:13 cf. 66:8).

In the final section—chs. 55(56)–66—control of Jerusalem and of the temple ("my holy mountain," 56:7; 57:13; 64:9 cf. 11:9) is of central significance. The distinction between Jerusalem and the other "cities" (in reality, settlements, farms, and villages) of Judah is present from the beginning (44:26, 28) but comes increasingly into view and is encapsulated in the designation "Judah and Jerusalem," standard in texts from the late Persian and early Hellenistic periods (2 Chr 11:14; 20:17; 24:6, 8; Ezra 9:9; 10:7; Isa 1:1; 2:1). It is therefore unsurprising and unexceptional if Jerusalem is called on to proclaim good news to the cities of Judah.

The present stanza, 40:9–11, is loosely connected with 1–8, though we detect the usual casual linkage by sound and sense: the voice calling out (vv 6, 9), perhaps also *habbāśār* v 6 ("flesh") and *mĕbaśśeret* v 9 ("herald"; Koole 1997, 70). There is no more justification for postulating an emissary of the heavenly council here than in the preceding passage.

Zion/Jerusalem does not stand for the people here, as in 40:2, and is not to be thought of as a sentinel posted on a hill to look out for Babylonian diaspora Jews on the last leg of their journey back to the homeland. She is on the hilltop so that her voice may be heard far and wide, proclaiming the good tidings that God and the salvation of God are near at hand. This is the core of the message of these chapters which this stanza shares with the preceding one (40:5). Melugin (1976, 84–86) also makes a clear distinction between 1–8 and 9–11 and adds the interesting suggestion that the juxtaposition of these two introductory passages reflects the structure of chs. 40–55: vv 1–8 encapsulate chs. 41–48;

and vv 9–11, chs. 49–55. It would be tempting to think of a conflation of two originally independent introductions, but Melugin does not go this far.

Throughout chs. 40–54(55) the good news is always the same, though expressed in different ways: the revelation of God's glory or radiance (40:5), the coming of Israel's God (40:9–11), Yahveh coming to redeem his people (48:20), the establishing of God's rule (52:7), and the coming of Yahveh to Zion (52:8). The OG rendering *euangelizomenos* for MT *mĕbaśśeret* also helps to explain both the adoption of the Gospel form in early Christianity and the essential content of the gospel—namely, the advent of the kingdom or rule of God through the agency of Jesus, as expressed in the first statement attributed to Jesus in Mark's Gospel (1:15).

What is behind this language is the ancient connection between kingship and salvation, the figure of the savior king. The basic image here, therefore, is that of a royal *parousia*. Yahveh is a royal figure (41:21; 43:15; 44:6; 52:7) ready to impose his will, by force if necessary. The metaphor of the arm that wields the sword or the scepter (51:9; 53:1; 59:16; 62:8), the arm bared for combat (52:10), connotes struggle against political forces opposed to God's purposes, and also echoes traditional liturgical language hymning Yahveh as king in the so-called Enthronement Psalms (Pss 47, 93, 95–99).

The arm imagery also recalls the liberation from Egyptian bondage—"with a mighty hand and outstretched arm" (e.g. Deut 4:34). It is therefore understandable, if textually questionable, that Ibn Ezra emends to *bĕyād ḥăzāqâ*, "with a strong hand," in 40:10a. We will see in due course how the language of royal power and warfare in evidence throughout chs. 40–54(55) coalesces around the presentation of Yahveh's royal and creative attributes as a mirror image of the Neo-Babylonian ideology of power expressed in the *akitu* or New Year Festival.

The reward and recompense that Yahveh brings with him are sometimes understood as Yahveh's own reward, recompense, or booty won in battle, consisting in Israelites ransomed from captivity, who now accompany him on the return journey (e.g. North 1964, 79; O. Kaiser 1959, 45). The terms used here, *śākār* and *pĕʿullâ*, do in fact connote wages and work done for wages, respectively, but both can also be used in the more generally metaphorical sense of recompense or reward (Gen 15:1; Ps 109:20; 127:3; Isa 61:8; Jer 31:16), and *pĕʿullâ* can denote vindication of the righteous by God (Isa 49:4).

While, therefore, the idea of the reassembly of Israelites dispersed in Babylon and elsewhere may be alluded to in the gathering together of the sheep in the following verse, the more natural sense of v 10 is that Yahveh's *parousia* will make up for past sufferings and reward those who have persevered. The repetition of this statement in 62:11 and the similar statement in 35:3–4 point unmistakably in the same direction.

The metaphorical shift from the imperial *parousia* to the shepherd caring for his flock is less sudden than might appear to the modern reader, since the topos of king as shepherd of his people was entirely familiar at that time and in that place. David shepherded his people (2 Sam 5:2), and it is anticipated that

Cyrus will do the same, with special reference to Judeans (Isa 44:28). The representation of Yahveh as shepherd, familiar to many from Ps 23 but also appearing frequently elsewhere (Gen 49:24; Ps 78:52; 80:2; Ezek 34:1–31) is a slippery metaphor that, given the association of sheep with passivity and fecklessness in general, carries potentially unflattering implications for the shepherd's charges. The original intent of the metaphor, however, was to temper the image of absolute royal power with a concern for justice and care for society's losers and outcasts, and in this sense the figure of the good shepherd was taken up in the Gospels (Luke 15:3–7; John 10:1–18).

A DISPUTATION ABOUT THE POWER OF ISRAEL'S GOD (40:12–31 + 41:6–7)

(D. Baltzer 1987; Couroyer 1966; Fitzgerald 1989; Gosse 1993; Korpel 1991; Kuntz 1997; Labuschagne 1966; van Leeuwen 1997; Melugin 1976, 31–36; Naidoff 1981a; Ruppert 1991; Trudinger 1967; Westermann 1964b, 127–32; Whybray 1971 passim; Williamson 1986)

TRANSLATION

i

40 [12]Who has measured out the waters[a] with the hollow of his hand
or marked off the sky by handbreadths[b]
and enclosed the earth's dust in small measure?[c]
Who has weighed the mountains in a balance,
the hills on the scales?
[13]Who has taken the measure of Yahveh's spirit
or advised him as his counselor?[d]
[14]With whom did he consult to be enlightened?
Who taught him the right way to go?
Who imparted knowledge to him[e]
or showed him the way of discernment?
[15]Observe: the nations are but drops from a bucket,
they are reckoned as dust on the scales.
Observe: the islands weigh[f] no more than specks of dust.
[16]Lebanon yields not fuel enough,
its beasts do not suffice for burnt offerings.
[17]All the nations are as nothing in his presence,
they are reckoned as less than nothing,[g]
as void and empty in his sight.[h]

ii

[18]To whom, then, will you liken God?
What form compare with him?
[19]An image that a craftsman casts,

that a smith overlays with gold[i]
and forges for it silver welds?[j]
[20]The one placed in charge of the offerings[k]
chooses wood that will not rot,
seeks out a skillful craftsman
to set up an image that won't topple.

41 [6][Each assists his companion,[l]
says to his colleague, "Be resolute!"
[7]The craftsman encourages the goldsmith,
the one who levels with the hammer[m] him who pounds the anvil,
he pronounces the soldering satisfactory;[n]
they attach the statue[o] with nails so that it won't move.]

iii

40 [21]Do you not know?
Have you not heard?
Has it not been told you from the beginning?
Have you not grasped how the earth was founded?[p]
[22]He sits enthroned over the circle of the earth,
its inhabitants seem like grasshoppers;
he stretches out the sky like a curtain,
spreading it out like a tent to live in.
[23]He has turned princes into nothing,
he has reduced the earth's rulers to naught.
[24]Scarcely are they planted,
scarcely are they sown,
scarcely has their stem taken root in the ground,
when he blows on them and they wither;
the whirlwind carries them off like chaff.
[25]So, to whom will you liken me?
To whom shall I be compared?[q]
[says the Holy One].

iv

[26]Lift up your eyes to the sky,
consider who has created these;
he leads out their host one by one,
summoning each by name;
because of his great power and overwhelming might[r]
not one of them fails to appear.

v

[27]Why, Jacob, do you say,
why, Israel, proclaim,[s]
"My way is hidden from Yahveh,
my cause is ignored by my God"?

28Do you not know? Have you not heard?
Yahveh is God from of old,
Creator of the earth from end to end.
He neither faints nor grows weary,
his understanding cannot be fathomed.
29He gives vigor to the dispirited,
power in abundance to those without strength.
30Youths may faint from exhaustion,
the young may stumble and fall,
31but those who wait for Yahveh will renew their vigor,
they will grow new pinions like eagles,[t]
run and not be worn out,
walk untiringly on their way.

NOTES

4QIsaiah[b] has part of 41:22–26 but with no significant variant from MT. [a] 1QIsaiah[a]: *my ym*, "the waters of the sea"; [b] *zeret* sing., a subdivision of a cubit (length of the forearm); see Exod 28:16; 39:9; Ezek 43:13; 1 Sam 17:4 (Goliath's height); 1QIsa[a] has *bĕzartô*, "with his handbreadth"; [c] *ʿāpār*, "dust" or "earth," is missing from LXX, Aqu., Symm., Theod.; "in small measure" renders the general sense of *šālîš*, literally, "a third," perhaps a seah, which is one-third of an ephah; [d] LXX *kai tis autou sumboulos egeneto*, "who has been his counselor" cf. Vulg. *quis consiliarius eius fuit?*; [e] this line is missing from LXX by haplography; [f] reading pl. *yiṭṭolû* with LXX and versions; [g] retaining MT *mēʾepes*, privative sense (GKC 119x-y), in preference to 1QIsa[a] *kĕʾepes*, "like nothing"; [h] a verse added to express *tōhû* in addition to *mēʾepes;* [i] *rqʿ* Piel (as here) has the meaning of hammering out precious metal (Exod 39:3; Num 17:4[16:39]; Jer 10:9) cf. *rāqîaʿ*, "the (hammered out) firmament" (Gen 1:6); [j] *rĕtuqôt*, the meaning assigned to this difficult word is based on the verb *rtq*, "bind" (Nah 3:10; 1QH[a] 8:35), and Arab. cognate *rtq*, "solder" (Korpel 1991); Vulg. has *laminis argenteis*, "with silver plates"; Tg. "silver chains"; NEB "silver studs"; LXX omits; see further *HALOT* 3:1300; Elliger 76–77; [k] *hamĕsukkān tĕrûmâ*, a famously difficult expression, perhaps wisely omitted in LXX, Syr., and Vulg.; this attempt at translation understands *mĕsukkān* as Pual participle > *skn*, "be familiar with, deal with, administer" cf. Hiphil in Num 22:30; Ps 139:3; Job 22:21, as well as *sōkēn* Isa 22:15; *tĕrûmâ* is read as collective for "cult offerings," which can include gold (Num 31:50–54); others read *hammĕsakkēn tĕmûnâ*, "the one who sets up an image," but *skn*, "set up, erect," is attested in Ugaritic but not in Biblical Hebrew; reading *mĕsukkān* as "impoverished" ("the one too impoverished to make a gift") cf. *miskēn*, "poor, miserable" (Qoh 4:13; 9:15–16), is syntactically impossible, and an impoverished person would not hire a skilled craftsman, a point missed by Torrey (pp. 307–8); taking *mĕsukkan* to be a kind of hardwood, perhaps mulberry (cf. Akk. *musukkānu*), as in Jerome, followed by NEB and

NRSV (see also Williamson 1986), does not fit any better syntactically; these and other options are thoroughly discussed by van Leeuwen 1997; [l] relocated here from 41:6–7; see commentary; [m] 1QIsa[a] has *plṭyš*, perhaps a variant pronunciation; [n] literally, "saying of the soldering, 'It is good'"; [o] "the statue" supplied; [p] retaining MT supported by LXX, Vulg., Syr., and Tg., rather than *mîsudat* or *mîsudôt* (Westermann 1969, 47; et al.); *môsād*, *môsĕdôt* are not used in a temporal sense, and how could the hearers be expected to understand it from the beginnings of the world?; [q] literally, "that I may resemble . . ."; [r] reading *vĕʾomeṣ* with 1QIsa[a] for MT *vĕʾammîṣ*; [s] with LXX *kai ti elalēsas*, but the sense is not affected; [t] *ʿālāh* Hiphil, "cause to rise up" i.e. "grow" (cf. Jer 30:17; 33:6; Ezek 37:6) cf. Ps 103:5, the eagle "renews itself" (*hitḥāddēš*) i.e. moults and gets new feathers; more consistent with the parallel verb *yaḥălîpû*, "exchange something old for something new, renew."

COMMENTS

As the final strophe states quite clearly, this disputation is addressed to Judeans with the purpose of persuading them that, appearances to the contrary notwithstanding, their God had the power and the will to bring about in the political arena what he promised in the initial prophetic proclamation (vv 1–11). The disputation can therefore be read as a reply to the complaints voiced by Jacob/ Israel (v 27b). The target audience is not confined to Judeo-Babylonians or even to diaspora Jews in general, and therefore the positive prognosis for the future should not be limited to an exodus from Babylon.

The idea is to lead those addressed to put aside their doubts and give their assent to faith in Yahveh as the all-powerful creator. The strategy is to lead by means of a series of rhetorical questions, starting out from what is assumed to be common ground. Rhetorical questions, usually in series, can serve a variety of purposes. They are used by didacts as a highly interactive way of holding the attention of the student, imparting information, and eliciting appropriate responses—that is, responses deemed to be appropriate by the instructor. Rhetorical questions can also be hostile in the manner of a cross-examination in a forensic context, or they can aim at reducing the opposition to silence. This last seems to be the point of the long sequence in Job 38–39. The present series is neither didactic nor forensic but aims to *persuade*, and, apart from a rather gentle *ad hominem* in v 21, is not at all hostile.

The discourse or sermon opens (v 12) with five rhetorical questions focusing on the creation of the world (in the usual order: the waters, the sky, the earth), perhaps represented as a microcosm in contrast to the immensity of the creator. Detailed correspondences with vv 15–17 reveal the political point and purpose of this hyperbolic language: the measured-out water of the world and dust of the earth are contrasted with the nations as drops from an empty bucket and dust left on the scales, and the weighing of mountains and hills links with the failure of Mount Lebanon to provide enough wood and livestock for adequate sacrifice.

The six questions following affirm the incomparability of Yahveh in implicit contrast with the Babylonian imperial deity Marduk who, in creating the world, needed the advice of the wise god Ea. In Achaemenid royal inscriptions we find the same connection between Ahuramazda as cosmic creator and the power behind the political activity of the rulers. A Naqš-i-Rustam inscription begins, "A great god is Ahuramazda who created this earth, who created yonder sky, who created man, who created happiness for man, who made Darius king, one king of many, one lord of many" (Kent 1953:138).

The language and the metaphors of the Isaian text draw overwhelmingly on the didactic-sapiential tradition and have little in common with the Priestly version of creation in Gen 1:1–2:4a. The imagery is predominantly architectural: Yahveh is a surveyer (*mōdēd*) who takes measurements and sets up the sky on columns (cf. Ps 75:4). The passage is reminiscent of Job 38:4–7, which represents creation as the building of a temple and which also makes the point by threading together rhetorical questions:

Where were you when I laid the foundations of the earth?
Tell me, if you are so clever!
Who fixed its measurements—surely you know!
Who stretched the measuring line upon it?
On what were its foundations placed,
or who laid its cornerstone
when the morning stars sang together,
and all the sons of God shouted for joy?

Throughout our entire passage the author draws heavily on themes in the didactic tradition and its lexicon (e.g. *ydʿ*, "know"; *bînâ*, "understanding"; *daʿat*, "knowledge," etc.).

The parallelism with Prov 8:22–31 is particularly instructive: there Wisdom (*ḥokmâ*) speaks of the confining of the waters of chaos, the creation of the mountains, hills, the earth and its soil, the setting up of the sky on columns, the circle (*ḥûg*, also Isa 40:22) drawn with calipers on the surface of the deep, and the foundations of the earth (cf. Isa 40:21). The rhetorical affirmation of the inscrutability and incomparability of Yahveh that follows (vv 13–14) is likewise reminiscent of the Joban poem on inaccessible wisdom (Job 28:1–28), one of the finest in the Hebrew Bible. In both texts, attestation of impenetrable divine wisdom is made in the context of the creation of the world. It is hardly coincidental that the same verb (*tikkēn*) is employed for measuring out the waters (v 12) and taking the measure of Yahveh's spirit (v 13).

The following verses (15–17) enclose an affirmation of the insignificance of the nations—that is, of international politics—when set in contrast to the power of God revealed in creation. The metaphor of scales and balances borrowed from the previous verses implies that in the scheme of the created order these nations are lightweights, and in comparison with the God of Israel they can be said (to paraphrase Augustine) more truly not to exist than to exist. Use of the term *ʾên* as a substantive meaning "nothingness," "nonbeing," usually linked, as here, with *ʾepes*, "zero," is practically limited to Isa 40–48 (40:17, 23; 41:11–12, 24). The implications of this usage will be seen more clearly when we note the connection between negativity and idol-worship in these chapters (e.g. 41:12, 29). The formula expressing the uniqueness of Yahveh (typically *ʾănî YHVH (ʾēl) vĕʾên ʿôd*, "I am Yahveh [God] and there is no other," 45:6, 22; 46:9 cf. 45:14) implies that other deities are unreal and the political power of those who worship them illusory and ephemeral. No doubt the preacher really believed this, but it was not an argument calculated to convince non-Israelites, certainly not the Babylonian ruling class, which was making the same claim on behalf of Marduk, their imperial deity (47:8, 10 cf. Zeph 2:15).

Several commentators (Westermann, Elliger, Beuken) have found the allusion to idol manufacture at the beginning of the next stanza (vv 19–20) digressive and intrusive and have therefore simply elided it. Such questions are always difficult to settle decisively. It is true that this kind of laboriously detailed idol polemic is not quite what we would expect at this juncture, though it could have been suggested by the mention of a form or image (*dĕmût*) in the previous verse. The more prudent course is to leave the text as it is, but since 41:6–7 fits well with 40:19–20 and is more evidently out of place in the context of the trial scene, we insert it tentatively at this point.

The anti-idolatry polemic in evidence throughout chs. 40–48 (40:19–20; 41:6–7; 44:9–20; 46:1–2, 6–7) relies heavily on satirizing the manufacture of images. In the ancient Near East, three-dimensional representations of deities were made of either stone or a wooden core (cf. Deut 28:36, 64) and then either painted or, in the case of statues made of wood, covered with silver or gold leaf, adorned with other precious or semiprecious metals (e.g. lapis lazuli), and set on pedestals. The present text is burdened with well-known obscurities, but some specialists engaged in the manufacture of these cult objects are mentioned: a craftsman (*ḥārāš*), a metalsmith (*ṣōrēp*), and perhaps a kind of overseer (*mĕsukkān*), though the word is notoriously obscure (see Notes). Idol-worship will be discussed at greater length in connection with the long diatribe in 44:9–20.

The theme of vv 12–17 is repeated in a different key in 21–25, and the argument is stated in the form of a rhetorical question at the beginning and end of the passage (vv 18, 25). The four questions addressed to the hearers (v 21) imply that they should be familiar with and have already accepted belief in Yahveh as a creator deity, though the preacher is perhaps exaggerating, as preachers are wont to do, in assuming that this "creation theology" was known "from the beginning." It was known, but we do not often hear of Yahveh as a creator deity in texts deemed to be from the time of the kingdoms.

As the speaker warms to his theme, we hear echoes of liturgical psalms of praise with which the audience could be expected to be familiar. Psalm 104, for example, speaks of the foundations of the earth (v 5), God's lofty abode (Ps 104:13 cf. Isa 57:15; 66:1; Amos 9:6), and the heavens stretched out like a tent (104:2). This last contrasts with the creation recital of Gen 1:1–2:4a, in which the earth is covered with a hammered-out bronze bell called the firmament (*rāqîaʿ* 1:6). Our text speaks of a tent and a curtain or other covering made of thin material, something like gauze (*dōq* 22c hapax). The extremely common idea that God lives in the sky is a natural reflex of spatial symbolism (up is good, down is bad) but is also associated with ancient ideas of heavenly temples and liturgies. Most people would not find it flattering to be compared with grasshoppers, but it seems to have been a common way of expressing disparity in size, to judge by the reaction of the Israelite spies to the much taller native inhabitants of Canaan (Num 13:33).

As in 40:15–17, the argument returns to the international scene of princes, potentates, and empires and to the vegetation imagery to express, as in vv 6–8 (grass, flowers), the political leaders' impermanence. The stanza then ends as it began, affirming the incomparability of the God of Israel and identifying the affirmation as that of the Holy One (but without the definite article cf. Job 6:1 and Hab 3:3), one of the few titles of Yahveh found in any part of the book of Isaiah.

The statement about Yahveh's creation and control of the celestial bodies serves to wrap up the polemic against idolatry, appropriately in view of the importance of astral worship and astronomy in the intellectual and religious life of Babylon. The subtext to the invitation to consider these objects visible in the sky by day and night, but especially by night, is the scrutiny of the heavens by Babylonian sages, their naming of the constellations and stars, and the calculations based on their movements that were thought to control human destiny (cf. 47:13). The prophet's audience is urged to look up at these objects in order to acknowledge Yahveh as its creator and not to worship them (cf. Deut 4:19, using the same language). The creative power of Yahveh (verbal stem *br'*) is a major theme in these chapters. Yahveh created the heavens (42:5; 45:18), the sun, moon, stars and constellations (40:26), light and darkness (45:7), and the earth (40:28; 45:18) together with humanity on it (45:12). He is also at work creatively and transformationally in history, chiefly within the people he has set aside for himself (41:20; 43:1, 7, 15; 45:8; 48:7).

Yahveh's leading the host of heaven out from their place and summoning them by name recalls the title *YHVH ṣĕbā'ôt*, "Yahveh of the (celestial) hosts," and therefore suggests the image of a military review. But the verb translated "lead," *yṣ'* (Hiphil), is used in a technical sense for the rising of the sun (Gen 19:23), stars (Neh 4:15[21]), and constellations (Job 38:32), based on the idea that there was a place to which the sun withdrew at night and the stars during the daytime. It also seems unlikely that the author was thinking of the hosts as being summoned to a military parade. The Hebrew phrase translated "summon by name" (*liqro' bĕšēm*) can mean either to summon by calling out the name (e.g. Exod 31:2; 35:30) or to confer a name (e.g. Num 32:38;

Josh 21:9; Isa 45:3–4), generally with a sense of ownership (e.g. Isa 43:1). Probably both senses are implied here. Interestingly, both here and in the Priestly creation recital, explicit naming of the sun and moon is avoided.

The final passage (vv 27–31) brings out the point and purpose of the disputation as originating in the complaint of Judeans that contact and communication with the God of traditional belief has broken down. The complaint is couched in language borrowed from liturgical hymns of communal lamentation. Not uncommonly these question why God has hidden his face (Pss 13:2; 44:25; 88:15) and why the way (*derek*) or righteous cause (*mišpāṭ*) of the plaintiffs is being disregarded (Pss 35:23; 37:5–6; 140:13; 146:7). Both the complaint and the reply suggest that the basic problem, as is not uncommon in times of crisis and transition, is a sense of discontinuity and severance from the past.

It is noteworthy how often those addressed in chs. 40–48 are named after the ancestor who spent twenty years in exile in Mesopotamia, raised a family there, and returned to the ancestral land (Jacob/Israel 41:8, 14; 42:24; 43:1, 22, 28; 44:1, 5, 21; 45:4; 46:3; 48:1, 12; Jacob alone 41:21; 44:2; 45:19; 48:20). The same alienation from the past is expressed in somewhat different terms in a later lament (63:7–64:12: "Abraham does not know us, Israel does not acknowledge us" (63:16)—a lament that receives, not an answer, but an explanation why there is no answer (65:1–7).

The point is reinforced by the response, which repeats the rhetorical questions in v 21a. What they should know is that Yahveh's presence extends over time past, present, and future and over the whole world from one end to the other. The temporal aspect is expressed in the phrase *ʾĕlohê ʿôlām*, rendered "eternal God" by both the LXX translator (*theos aiōnios*) and Jerome (*deus sempiternus*) but serving here the more modest function of registering continuity with the past (cf. "O God our help in ages past"). There may also be an echo of the old divine title, *ʾel ʿôlām*, associated with Yahveh in stories about the ancestors, presumably in circulation at the time of this writing (Gen 21:33).

The speaker concludes his peroration by emphasizing once again that Yahveh is willing and able to dispel the cloud of uncertainty, weakness, and disorientation hanging over his people. This assurance will in due course be restated in terms of an interpretation of current events, specifically the conquests of Cyrus and the imminent demise of the Babylonian Empire. In the meantime, what is called for is a positive attitude of waiting with hope (31a). The theme of "waiting for God" is heard more than once in the first part of the book of Isaiah (8:17; 25:9; 26:8; 30:18; 33:2). Biblical Hebrew differentiates between waiting as a neutral activity, something to be endured (stem *ḥkh* Qal and Piel), and waiting with hope and the anticipation of a positive outcome (*qvh*), which is what is meant here by waiting for Yahveh.

A FIRST MOCK-TRIAL SPEECH (41:1–5)

(Begrich 1963, 26–48; Hoffman 1982; Janzen 1983; Klein 1985; Melugin 1976, 45–63; Merendino 1981, 123–90; Ruppert 1991; Walsh 1993, 351–71; Westermann 1964b, 134–44)

TRANSLATION

41 [1]Hear me in silence, you islands!
You peoples, summon up your strength![a]
Let them approach, then let them speak up,
let us come together for the trial!

[2]Who was it that roused from the east
one victorious at every step?[b]
Yahveh delivers up nations to him,
beats down[c] kings beneath him.
He makes their swords[d] like dust,
their bows[d] like windblown chaff;
[3]he pursues them and continues unscathed,
his feet do not touch the ground.[e]
[4]Who has brought this about, who has done it?
The one who summons the generations from the beginning.
I, Yahveh, am the First,
and I, the One, am with the last.
[5]The islands look on in fear,
the earth trembles[f] from end to end.
They draw near, they are here![g]

NOTES

[a] MT *yaḥălîpû koaḥ* often taken to be dittography cf. 40:31a and to have been exchanged for the last phrase of v 5 (*qarĕbû vayye᾿ ĕtāyûn*) which, however, would have to be converted to Imperfect or Jussive ("let them draw near and come") and would be repetitive; another option (proposed by D. N. Freedman) is *qirbû vĕye᾿ĕtāyûn*, "Draw near and let them advance"; more speculative options are *yaḥălû nikhî*, "wait in my presence" (BHS), or *yaḥălû lĕtôkaḥtî*, "wait for my admonition" (*Beweis*, Elliger 1978, 105); MT has the support of 1QIsa[a], LXX, Vulg., and Tg.; [b] literally, "righteousness (*ṣedeq*) encounters him at his foot," or with 1QIsa[a], probably correctly, "at his feet" (*lrglyv*) i.e. as he progresses; for *ṣedeq* = "victory" see commentary; [c] MT *yard* often emended to *yārod* or interpreted as Hiphil Imperfect > *rdd*, "trample, beat down" cf. 45:1 (said of Cyrus); LXX *ekotēsei* presupposes *yaḥărîd*, "causes to tremble"; I follow 1QIsa[a] *yôrîd*, "brings down, humbles"; [d] *ḥarbô*, *qaštô*

used collectively; as subject, *ḥarbô*, "his sword," would require the verb *yittēn* to have a pronominal suffix; [e] literally, "he does not come [to] the path with his feet"; somewhat similar are Tg. ("a forced march does not tire his feet") and Vulg. (*semita in pedibus eius non apparebit*, literally, "the path will not appear in [under] his feet"), both of which express the tirelessness of his progress; 1QIsa[a] has *ybynv*, "they will comprehend," for MT *yābôʾ*; [f] 1QIsa[a] has *yḥdv*, "together," for MT *yeḥĕrādû*, "tremble"; [g] this last phrase, *qārĕbû vayyeʾĕtāyûn*, is commonly either omitted or transposed to v 1a, but it has solid textual support and makes a fitting conclusion to the strophe; the Aramaicizing verb *ʾātāh* appears quite often in these chapters (41:23, 25; 44:7; 45:11); vv 6–7 have been relocated after 40:20.

COMMENTS

The same kind of disputatious rhetoric is now directed at foreign peoples and their gods. Peoples in the vast Babylonian Empire are invited to witness the contest of Yahveh with foreign deities, specifically Babylonian deities, who are challenged to refute Yahveh's claim to sponsor the successful campaigns of Cyrus II. Isaiah 41:1–5, representing the summons addressed to the nations as witnesses and to the deities as defendants to appear in court, is linked with vv 21–29, which repeat the claim and more definitively exclude the possibility of counterclaims. There has been much discussion about the type of disputation or trial scene that keeps on appearing in these chapters (41:1–5, 21–29; 43:8–15; 44:6–8; 45:20–23). While much remains uncertain, it is at least clear that it does not correspond in a simple, straightforward way to a specific social or institutional situation—for example, a covenant lawsuit in the context of worship or legal proceedings at the city gate. Borrowings from the forensic sphere are obvious—the summons to attend, calling witnesses (cf. 44:8), the presentation of the case (*rîb* v 21), but other echoes can be heard, including themes and phrases from liturgical hymns of praise.

It therefore seems likely that these passages represent creative literary adaptations of language originating in specific social settings. As such, however, they must have had their own setting. On the assumption that they were composed during the time period to which they refer, namely, the final phase of the existence of the Neo-Babylonian Empire under Nabonidus, its last ruler, we might consider the possibility that they were either composed for delivery in a kind of protosynagogal setting or were written and circulated to be read in that kind of setting, in a way somewhat similar to the circulation of letters among early Christian churches.

That they were, at any rate, composed for internal Jewish consumption follows from the unverifiable nature of the claim advanced by Yahveh and the unrealistic judicial setting, which allows for no rebuttal, no judge or independent jury, and has witnesses who are not permitted to speak.

The trial or contest opens with a summons to foreign peoples, meaning in the historical context provinces in the Babylonian Empire, to serve as silent witnesses. Neither here nor elsewhere in these chapters is a definite location mentioned. Most commentators have simply assumed without argument that Second Isaiah is of diasporic Babylonian provenance, though a Judean origin has always had some support, most recently in a series of publications by Hans M. Barstad. Reference in the present passage to "islands" would certainly not decide the issue but would, if anything, favor the minority position. The Hebrew *ʾiyyîm*, well defined by George Adam Smith as "land either washed or surrounded by the sea" (1927, 109), can designate the Philistine or Phoenician Mediterranean littoral (Isa 20:6; 23:2, 6), the Aegean, inclusive of Crete and Cyprus (Jer 2:10; 47:4; Ezek 27:6, 7), or the vast regions west of the Mediterranean in general (Isa 42:15; 59:18).

If the geographical situation is uncertain, the historical circumstances referred to are rather less so. The traditional view in Judaism (stated in the Targum and expounded by Rashi) identified the one roused from the east with Abraham. Though already rejected by Ibn Ezra, it has found defenders in the modern period, conspicuously Torrey (1928, 310–16) who, in this respect as in others, *cantat extra chorum*. Starting out from the word *ṣedeq* (v 2a), and with a further allusion to the messianic code-name *anatolē* = *oriens*, the Vulgate's *iustus ab oriente* ("a righteous one from the east") reflects an overall christological interpretation, and this eschatological reading has also found a modern proponent, in this instance James D. Smart (1965, 68–69).

While I do not exclude the possibility of multiple rereadings and reinterpretations, I conclude the historical allusion must be to the speed and apparent ease with which Cyrus II conquered the kingdoms of the Medes, the former territory of the Assyrian Empire, and the Lydians in the decade preceding the capture of the city of Babylon in 539 B.C.E.

The legal session comes to a head with the question "Who has brought this about, who has done it?" and Yahveh himself answers, usurping, as it were, the function of judge or arbiter. As the creator of the world, Yahveh has been present since the beginning and continues to be present and active throughout history from the start to the finish. "Generation" (*dôr*) is not an abstract term but signifies the people alive in a particular period. Yahveh claims to give the people of each successive age, especially those in a position to have a decisive impact on the course of history, their allotted task. At one time it was Nebuchadrezzar II; now it is the hour for Cyrus II to answer the summons. That Yahveh was (is) the first (also 44:6; 48:12) and will be with those alive in the last generation means that Yahveh controls the course of history.

The second half of v 4b ("I, the One, am with the last") resists exact translation since, in addition to affirming Yahveh's active presence throughout time, it encapsulates the idea of uniqueness and immutability in the formula *ʾănî hûʾ*, which can be translated only inadequately as "I am he" or "I am the One." The recurrence of this formulaic affirmation about deity is one of the most frequently recurring motifs in these chapters (43:10, 13, 25; 46:4; 48:12). As a self-designation of deity it expresses much in small compass: permanence, permanent presence and availability, dependability, and unchangeability.

Inevitably, this language of the First and the Last, and the One and Only, would find its place in the vocabulary of early Christianity (e.g. John 8:28; Rev 1:17; 2:8; 21:6; 22:13).

WORDS OF ENCOURAGEMENT TO ISRAEL, THE SERVANT (41:8–16)

(Begrich 1934; Boadt 1973; Conrad 1984; G. R. Driver 1935; Fohrer 1955; Goldingay 1994; Hamlin 1954; Merendino 1972; Ringgren, H. 1977b; Walsh 1993; Westermann 1964a)

TRANSLATION

41 [8]But you, Israel, my servant,
Jacob whom I have chosen,
offspring of Abraham, my friend,[a]
[9]you whom I took from the ends of the earth
and called from its furthest reaches,
to you I said,[b] "You are my servant,
I chose you, and I have not rejected you."
[10]Don't be afraid, for I am with you,
don't be perplexed,[c] for I am your God.
I strengthen you, I will surely help you,
I sustain you with my victorious right hand.
[11]See, all who rage[d] against you
will be ashamed and disgraced;
those who contend with you
will be as nothing, they will perish.[e]
[12]You will look for them, but you will not find them.[f]
Those who strive against you will be as nothing,
those who wage war against you will be less than nothing.[g]
[13]For I am Yahveh your God,
I clasp you by your right hand;
I say to you: "Don't be afraid,
I am here to help you."
[14]Don't be afraid, you worm Jacob,
you maggot[h] Israel,
I am here to help you,
your Redeemer is the Holy One of Israel.
[15]See, I make of you a threshing board,
sharp, brand new, equipped with spikes;[i]
you shall thresh the mountains into dust,
reduce the hills to chaff;

[16]you shall winnow them, and the wind will carry them off,
the whirlwind will scatter them.
But you will rejoice in Yahveh,[j]
exult in the Holy One of Israel.

NOTES

[a] BHS proposal *ʾăhubî*, Qal passive participle is unnecessary cf. Aqu. *agapētou mou*, "my beloved"; Vulg. *amici mei*, LXX *hon ēgapēsa*, "whom I have loved"; [b] 1QIsa[a] has *vʾvmrh* cohortative; [c] MT *tištāʿ* > *štʿ*, "be afraid, anxious," rather than > *šʿh*, "look around," cf. 41:23; [d] MT *hanneḥĕrîm* Niphal participle > *ḥrh*, "burn with anger" (cf. 45:24) rather than > *nḥr*, "snort" (with anger, presumably), with G. R. Driver 1935, 398; the substantive *naḥar* (Job 39:20) is attested but not the verb; [e] *yihyû kĕʾayin*, "they will be as nothing," is absent from 1QIsa[a], which reads "they will all perish," as does LXX; 1QIsa[b] has *vybšv*, "they will be (are) ashamed"; [f] this line is missing from 1QIsa[a], which leaves one and three-quarter lines between vv 11 and 12; [g] since the two verbs have pronominal suffixes, "those who strive against you" (*ʾanšê maṣṣutekâ*), goes with *yihyû kĕʾayin*, reading therefore as follows:

ʾanšê maṣṣutekâ yihyû kĕʾayin
ûkĕʾepes ʾanšê milḥamtekâ;

[h] MT *mĕtê yiśrāʾēl* may be translated "men of Israel," but this does not make for a good parallel with *tôlaʿat yaʿăqōb*, "worm Jacob," and the same can be said for 1QIsa[a] *vmyty*, "the dead," cf. Theod. *nekroi* and Vulg. *qui mortui estis*; BHS follows G. R. Driver (1935, 399), reading *mōt* ("louse"), but the Akk. cognate (*mutu*) has not held up; the option least open to objection is to emend to *rimmat* ("maggot"), assuming omission of *resh* on account of beth immediately preceding and repetition of yod by dittography (see further Elliger 1978, 146–47); *tôlēʿâ* and *rimmâ* appear together in Isa 14:11 and Job 25:6; [i] the line seems overloaded; perhaps *ḥārûs*, read as a substantive (as in Isa 28:27; Amos 1:3; Job 41:22), is a gloss on *môrag*, "threshing board"; [j] LXX reads, "but as for you, you will rejoice among the holy things of Israel."

COMMENTS

The alternation between address to foreign nations and their gods and address to the Israelite community continues here. Several commentators divide this passage into two addresses (41:8–13, 14–16), but the entire chapter can be read as one articulated whole within a larger unity: the theme of the nations as non-entities creates a link with 40:12–26 (40:17; 41:11–12); the forensic scenario, followed by an allusion to Cyrus, appears in vv 1–5 and 21–27; and the theme of the impotence of foreign deities is repeated (vv 21–24, 28–29). Repetition of significant phrases and expressions serves to bind the whole together: my servant (8a, 9b), chosen (8a, 9b), don't be afraid (10a, 14a), I am your God (10a,

13a), I will help you (10b, 13b, 14b), with my right hand (10b, 13a), and the Holy One of Israel (14b,16b). This type of rhetoric has drawn on the much-discussed oracle of salvation (Begrich); that is, a word of reassurance uttered by a priest or cultic prophet to someone in need during the course of a liturgy (e.g. Pss 20:6–8; 28:6–9; 54:4–7; 60:6–12).

Oracular utterances like these also appear in prophetic discourse in all times throughout the Near East. In the eighth century B.C.E., for example, King Zakir (or Zakkur) of Hamath is reassured of success by the local Baal by means of seers and diviners during a siege: "Don't be afraid, for I made you king and I shall stand by you and deliver you" (ANET 501). The main point is to dispel fear; hence the key phrase "don't be afraid" (*ʾal-tîrāʾ*), the frequent appearance of which in these chapters (40:9; 41:10, 13, 14; 43:1, 5; 44:2, 8; 51:7; 54:4) provides a valuable clue to their character. Significantly, the phrase does not appear in the last section of the book (chs. 56–66).

Addressing the dispersed communities of Jews as Israel/Jacob (see on 40:27) and offspring of Abraham emphasizes the importance for the preacher or writer of reestablishing lines of continuity with the past, of creating a strong sense of the importance of living within a tradition after the profound discontinuity attendant on the destruction of the nation state (cf. the lament, "Abraham does not know us, Israel does not acknowledge us," 63:16). The language of servanthood is intended to give the hearers some assurance of historical significance, in the sense that, just as Abraham was called to a mission in his day, so they are now chosen at this crucial juncture of history to play a role; hence, the close connection between servanthood and election in these chapters (41:8, 9; 42:1, 19; 43:10; 44:1, 2; 45:4).

The term *ʾebed* ("servant"), with the meaning of a special relationship to the deity, is a Deuteronomic creation. In the Deuteronomic oeuvre it refers both to the royal dynasty (2 Sam 3:18; 1 Kgs 8:24–26; 2 Kgs 19:34 cf. Jer 33:21–22, 26) and to prophecy, including the prophetic succession as a whole (*ʿăbādâv hannĕbîʾîm*: 2 Kgs 9:7; 17:13, 23; 21:10; 24:2; cf. Jer 7:25; 25:6; 26:5; 29:19; 35:15; 44:4; Amos 3:7). In the Deuteronomic scheme of things, Moses is the prophetic servant *par excellence* (Deut 34:5; Josh 1:2; 9:24), the protoprophet, and the exemplar of prophecy. But Abraham is also a servant of Yahveh (Gen 26:24; Deut 9:27; Ps 105:42), having been called to a uniquely important mission. While some narrative traditions about Jacob/Israel appear to have been in circulation during the time of the kingdoms (Hos 12:3–4, 12), and the genealogical succession of the three great ancestors was familiar to the Deuteronomists, Abraham as a distinct figure emerges only in texts composed after the deportations of the early sixth century B.C.E. (Ezek 33:23–24; Jer 33:26; Mic 7:20; Isa 29:22–24; 41:8; 51:2; 63:16; Ps 105:6).

The narrative cycle of Gen 12–25 appears to have been put together at a time not far distant from the time of composition of Isa 40–54(55). Whatever the date of composition, it reflects the concerns and aspirations of the people addressed in these chapters as perceived and articulated by the writer; chief among these were the summons to leave his (Abraham's) residence in southern Mesopotamia and go to the promised land, the great nation theme, separation from the native population, and avoidance of intermarriage. To these we may add certain subsidiary topics recurring in the stories about the ancestors and in writings from the early Second Temple period: for example, relations with Arab (Edomite) peoples and disputes about real estate. Abraham's special relationship with Yahveh is expressed in the designation "friend of God," a title that was to become standard in Judaism (2 Chr 20:7; James 2:23) and Islam (*al halil, halil ullahi*, Qur'an Sura 4:124).

The concern to forge links with the past makes it difficult to be sure whether mention of election, being taken from the ends of the earth and so on, refers to the past or the present. Perhaps we do not have to choose: Abraham was summoned from Ur, later from Harran, and Israel from Egypt and, in the meantime, the word of reassurance goes out to Jews dispersed over a wide area of the Near East. Here too, incidentally, the language does not point necessarily or exclusively to a Babylonian location.

Another nexus with traditional religious language and themes is the assurance "I am with you," "I am (Yahveh) your God," reminiscent of words addressed to Moses at the burning thornbush (Exod 3:12) and the self-predication of Yahveh in the decalogue (Exod 20:2; Deut 5:6). However, as often happens in prophetic books, we come next to a sharp reminder that we are reading an ancient text with ideas about appropriate images and metaphors very different from those ideas current today. Israel as a worm and maggot is no more complimentary than the nations as grasshoppers (40:22)—in fact less so. We can well understand why the Targum would paraphrase, "tribe of the house of Israel" and the LXX, "families of the house of Israel." The combination of the two words suggests death and decay (Isa 14:11), and "worm" by itself connotes helplessness and insignificance (Ps 22:7[6]; Job 25:6). The latter is probably the dominant idea, since the worm is to undergo a remarkable transformation into a powerful implement of destruction that will level the mountains and hills, presumably meaning the hostile peoples referred to earlier (vv 11–12).

These metaphors for military violence occur appear from time to time in the History and prophetic books (2 Kgs 13:7; Isa 25:10; Amos 1:3; Hab 3:12). Yahveh, the speaker, identifies himself as "the Holy One of Israel" (*qĕdôš yiśrā'ēl*), the most common designation, appearing with great frequency throughout the book of Isaiah but rarely elsewhere (Jer 50:29; 51:5; Pss 71:12; 78:41; 89:19), and as "redeemer" (*gō'ēl*). This last term originated in the context of the tribal system, in which each person was obligated to assist a fellow clan member in need, principally by buying him or possibly her back from indentured service for nonpayment of debt (Lev 25:47–49; Num 35:19; Ruth 3:11–13). It is in this context that our passage speaks of Yahveh as helper (41:13–14). Since the title *gō'ēl* also appears frequently in chs. 40–66, rarely elsewhere (Jer 50:34; Pss 19:15[14]; 78:35), and not at all in Isa 1–39, it may well have been created by this author.

Ecological Transformation of the Land (41:17–20)

(Elliger 1971; Farfan Navarro 1992; Finley 1991; Joüon 1906)

TRANSLATION

41 [17]When the poor [and the needy][a] look for water
where there is none,
their tongues parched with thirst;
I, Yahveh, will provide for them,[b]
I, the God of Israel, will not forsake them.
[18]I will open up streams on the bare hills,
fountains on the plains;
I will turn the wilderness into pools of water,[c]
the arid land into springs of water.
[19]I will place in the wilderness cedar, acacia, myrtle, and wild olive;
I will plant in the desert cypress, fir, and box together,
[20]so that they may observe and acknowledge,
once for all consider and comprehend,[d]
that the hand of Yahveh has accomplished this;
the Holy One of Israel has created it.

NOTES

[a] *Vĕhā'ebyônîm*, absent in Eth. and Arab. versions, as a secondary result of haplography, overloads the line and has probably been added, understandably, since *'ānî* and *'ebyôn* are often paired; [b] literally, "answer them"; [c] MT has sing. *la'ăgam-mayim*, but the pl. seems to be required, as in LXX (*eis helē*); [d] 1QIsa[a] adds *vybynv* after *vyd'v* followed by *vyśymu* above the line.

COMMENTS

Throughout these opening chapters the challenge directed at foreign powers and their patron deities (40:12–26; 41:1–7, 21–29) alternates with words of reassurance addressed to the Judean community (40:27–31; 41:8–20; 42:1–9), a rhetorical strategy designed to convince the audience that new possibilities are opening up on the international scene. It is therefore intended to prepare for the explicit endorsement of Cyrus, as yet referred to only indirectly (40:6–8; 41:2–5, 25–29).

Westermann (1969, 78–81) suggests that the passage may be understood as the divine response to a communal liturgical lament—for example, during a drought (cf. Jer 14:2–6). The theme of ecological transformation (the "back-to-nature" theme) or degradation appears more frequently in Isa 1–35 than in other prophetic compilations (5:17; 6:11; 13:19–22; 14:22–23; 17:2, 9; 27:10–11; 30:23–25; 32:13–20; 34:8–11, 13–15) and is developed in different directions in the second half of the book (42:11, 15; 43:18–21; 44:3; 48:20–22; 49:9–13, 19; 51:3). In this instance we hear that the land will be rendered fertile once again and will be reforested with trees, providing shade for the land and its inhabitants. Most of the commentators assume that these benevolent acts are to facilitate the anticipated return from the Babylonian diaspora, but the passage says nothing of this. The transformation is to take place on the hills and the plains, the desert (*midbār*), the wilderness (*ʿărābâ*), and the arid land (*ṣiyyâ*); compare 42:15, in which Yahveh brings about a state of ecological degradation expressed in much the same language.

Moreover, the planting of seven species of large trees (only the first four mentioned can be securely identified) along the route from Babylon is a less likely scenario than the reforestation of Judah after the inevitable devastation of native flora and fauna by an army of occupation, especially since the species mentioned are native to Syria–Palestine but not to Mesopotamia. (Note that the palm tree is not even mentioned.) The provision of water in the wilderness is certainly used in the context of a return from the diaspora in Babylon and elsewhere (43:18–21; 48:20–22; 49:9–13), but the motif is not confined to that situation. The terms *midbār* and *ʿărābâ* could apply very well to Judah in the post-destruction period. Zion also has its deserts and wildernesses which, the seer promises, will be turned into a Garden of Eden (51:3).

A SECOND MOCK-TRIAL SPEECH (41:21–29)

(Beaulieu 1989, passim; Dempsey 1997; Gelston 1993a; Gressmann 1914; Janzen 1994; Leene 1987; McEleney 1957; Merendino 1981, 191–273; North 1950; Saggs 1959; Schoors 1964; C. E. Whitley 1957)

TRANSLATION

i

41 [21]Set forth your case, says Yahveh,
present your strongest arguments,[a] says Jacob's King.
[22]Let them step forward[b] and tell us what will happen,
let them declare events before they happen
that we may take note,
or announce things to come
that we may know how they will end.[c]
[23]Declare what is to happen[d] in advance,[e]
and we will acknowledge that you are gods.
Do anything, be it good or bad,
to fill us with awe[f] and fear.[g]
[24]You see, you are less than nothing,[h]

your works are nonexistent;[i]
those who choose you are execrable![j]

ii

[25]I have roused one from the north, and he has come;
from the sunrise he is summoned in my name;[k]
he tramples down[l] governors like mud
as the potter treads on the clay.
[26]Who declared this from the start that we may acknowledge it?
Who announced it in advance, that we may say, "He is right!"
No one declared it, no one announced it,
no one heard you say anything.
[27]I, the First, declared it to Zion,[m]
giving to Jerusalem a herald of good news.
[28]But when I looked[n] there was no one,
not one counselor among them
who could answer if I were to inquire.
[29]They are all insignificant,[o]
their works are of no avail,
their images nothing but wind.[p]

NOTES

[a] *ʿĂṣumôt* hapax but cf. *ʿăṣûm*, "strong," and Arab. *haṣama*, "contend"; Ibn Ezra refers to Prov 18:18 *ʿaṣûmîm*, understood to mean "quarrels"; [b] reading *yiggĕšû* Qal, with LXX (*engisatōsan*), Vulg. (*accedant*), and Tg. (*yitqarĕbûn*) for MT *yaggîšû* Hiphil; [c] reversing the order of the two half-lines of MT 22c; [d] *hāʾōtiyyôt* only here and 44:7; participle > *ʾth*; [e] *lĕʾaḥôr* only here and 42:23; Ibn Ezra notes that it is the opposite of *lĕpānîm*, but in this context the idea seems to be about a declaration made behind, i.e., in advance of, future events; [f] *ništāʾāh* cohortative > *štʿ*; 1QIsa[a] has *vnšmʿ*, "that we may hear"; [g] read K *vĕnirāʾ* cohortative > *yrʾ*, "fear"; [h] the prefixed preposition in *mēʾayin* and *mēʾāpaʿ* is generally explained as the result of dittography and removed, but it may be used in a privative sense, "less than . . ."; [i] read *mēʾāpes* (Pause) for *mēʾāpaʿ*; 1QIsa[a] omits; [j] literally, "an abomination" (*tôʿēbâ*); no need to emend (see GKC §155n) as, for example, Torrey 319 (*tôʿeh habbōḥer bākem*, "the one who chooses you strays"); [k] *qrʾ* + *bĕšēm* can mean (1) invoke (Isa 12:4; 64:6; Jer 10:25); (2) summon (40:26); (3) confer a name (44:5); read *yiqqārēʾ bišmî* cf. LXX and 1QIsa[a] which, however, reads *bišmô*; MT *yiqrāʾ bišmî*, "he will invoke my name", is contradicted by 45:5 ("you do not know me"); [l] for MT *vĕyābôʾ*, "and he will come," read *vĕyābûs*; [m] MT "the first to Zion, behold, behold them" does not make good sense; that the text was corrupted early is apparent from LXX: "I will give rule to Zion and will comfort Jerusalem in the way" and Tg.: "The words of consolation which the prophets prophesied from the first to

Zion, behold they come [to pass]" (Chilton 1987, 81), both seem to have read a form of the verbal stem *nḥm*, "console," for *hinnām*; closer is Vulg.: *primus ad Sion dicet: ecce adsunt*, "the first to Sion will say: behold, they are present"; 1QIsa[a] has *hnvmh* for MT *hinnām*, perhaps with a meaning parallel with *mĕbaśśēr*, "herald," but this does not make a good fit with the context; parallelism seems to require *higgadĕtî* or a verb with similar meaning; see further Elliger 1978,174–5; [n] for MT *vĕʾēreʾ* read *vāʾēreʾ*; [o] for MT *ʾāven* read with 1QIsa[a] *ʾāyin*; [p] *rûaḥ vĕtōhû*, literally, "wind and emptiness/chaos."

COMMENTS

This second mock-trial speech is couched in much the same language as the first (41:1–5) but is addressed directly to the patron deities of foreign nations rather than the nations themselves. They are invited to provide convincing proof of effective divinity by demonstrating control of historical events, past and future. For practical purposes the discourse in these chapters must be considered section by section, and in fact several caesuras are marked in the Hebrew text (e.g. in MT and 1QIsa[a] before v 21 and after v 29).

Beginning with Gressmann in 1914, modern commentators have divided up the chapter in many different ways (on which see the sensible comments of Sydney Smith 1944, 6–11, 93–95), often overlooking the fact that there is a basic continuity in 40:1–42:13, observable in language (especially forensic vocabulary) and rhetorical style. Already noted is the alternation in this first major section between address to the nations and their gods on the one hand and the Judean community on the other, rounded off in 42:10–13 with a psalm. But of course the entire discourse is addressed to the Judean community, so the author is in no danger of having to argue against real opponents—the priests of the Marduk cult, for example.

The forensic setup is clear: the opponents are invited to state their case (vv 21–23); after they fail to respond, the appropriate conclusion is drawn (v 24); then Yahveh proves his claim to be the only deity capable of both predicting and bringing about events in the political sphere with reference to the military successes of Cyrus (vv 25–28), after which the counterclaimants are once again dismissed as totally ineffective (v 29).

The title "Jacob's king" or "Israel's king" (44:6) anticipates the complex of themes involving kingship, victorious combat, and creation developed as a mirror image of Babylonian imperial ideology expressed in the cult of Marduk and specifically in the *akitu* festival and the creation myth *Enuma Elish*. To counter this ideology of power the author expounds an argument from prophecy. The gods (they will be named only later, 46:1) are challenged to predict future events (literally, "what will happen," 22a). The point is made redundantly in what follows: they are invited to announce future events before they happen and to do so in a way that will be verifiable (v 22b); they are to announce things to come in such a way that the outcome of things happening now may be known (v 22c); they are to declare things to come in advance (*lĕʾāḥôr;* see textual Note) so that their divine nature may be acknowledged. Once their inability to meet these criteria is established, the author waxes sarcastic: well, do anything, work a miracle, fill us with awe and fear! But of course he knows that this too is beyond their reach.

The foreign deities are challenged to "declare events before they happen" or, in the more familiar translation, "the former things" (*hāriʾšōnôt*). This much-discussed term is used several times in these chapters. In some contexts it seems to refer to early as opposed to contemporaneous events, perhaps with reference to familiar narrative traditions (43:18, parallel with *qadmoniyyôt,* "early events"; 46:9). More commonly it stands for events as prophesied (41:22b; 42:9; 43:9; 48:3), with reference either to earlier predictions made by the prophet or to earlier prophecies of disaster, including Isaian prophecies, now only too clearly fulfilled.

At this point we are close to the basic idea of prophecy and fulfillment that drives the History and, in effect, creates the continuity that makes the History possible. We note in this brief passage the proliferation of terms for the future: "things that will happen" (*ʾēt ʾăšer tiqrênâ,* 22a), "things to come" (*habbāʾôt,* 22c), and "what is to happen" (*hāʾōtiyyôt,* 23a). The same perspective on the power to predict and control the flow of historical events may also explain why Yahveh is referred to with equal frequency as the First and the Last (*riʾšôn, ʾaḥărôn* 41:4, 27; 44:6; 48:12). These terms can be unpacked to display a sense of historical continuity very similar to the continuity created by the prediction-fulfillment pattern in the History; in other words, as the first stage toward a theology of history.

After the gods are reduced to silence, Yahveh stakes his claim, as in the first mock-trial scene and in similar terms (vv 2–5). Cyrus is not yet named, but he is the one roused, set in motion, by Yahveh. The north would have had a special resonance as the direction from which danger could be expected (cf. Jer 1:13–14), but the allusion here is to Cyrus's successful campaign against the Medes in the northern Iranian plateau culminating in the capture and sack of Ecbatana in 550; perhaps it is also to the conquest of Lydia and the Ionian littoral in 547, though a somewhat later date (e.g. 544–543 proposed by Sydney Smith 1944, 51) cannot be excluded.

The sunrise, indicating a more general eastern direction, would be consonant with either a Babylonian or Judean point of reference. "Rousing" (*ʿûr* Hiphil) seems to have been considered an especially appropriate way of referring to the conquests of Cyrus as set in motion by Yahveh (cf. 41:2a; 45:13). It is adopted by the Chronicler for the "return to Zion" (Ezra 1:1, 5 = 2 Chr 36:22) and elsewhere applied to the Medes as participants in the capture of Babylon (Isa 13:17; Jer 50:9; 51:1, 11).

The claim is made that Yahveh not only set in motion the conquests of Cyrus but predicted them to the Judean community. As at other great turning points in the history of the Near East, there seems to have been a flurry of prophetic activity during the declining years of the Neo-Babylonian Empire;

compare the prophecies addressed to Zimri-lim of the kingdom of Mari on the eve of its conquest by Hammurapi in the early seventeenth century B.C.E, more than a millennium earlier. A cylinder in the Abu Happa collection in the British Museum, dated no earlier than 546 B.C.E., records a dream in which Marduk appeared to Nabunaid, last king of Babylon, and predicted the defeat of the Medes by Cyrus:

> "The Mede whom you mentioned, he, his country and the kings who march at his side will cease to exist." (And indeed) when the third year arrived, he (Marduk) aroused Cyrus, king of Anšan, his young servant, who scattered the large (armies) of the Mede with his small army, and (who) captured Astyages, king of the Medes, and took him to his country as captive. (Beaulieu 1989,108)

In his own propagandistic cylinder, Cyrus himself claims to have been commissioned directly by Marduk:

> He (Marduk) scanned and looked (through) all the countries, searching for a righteous ruler willing to lead him (in the annual procession). (Then) he pronounced the name of Cyrus king of Anshan. (*ANET* 315)

The most likely explanation of vv 26–27, therefore, is that the speaker is referring to earlier, no-longer extant, prophecies concerning Cyrus, rather than to anti-Babylonian predictions elsewhere in the prophetic corpus (Isa 13; Jer 50–51).

Read in the context of international events, Isa 40–48 emerges as the Judean version of current anti-Babylonian and pro-Persian propaganda. Marduk's pretensions as both predicting and bringing about the conquests of Cyrus are rejected. Marduk, famed for wisdom and counselor of the god Ea (*Enuma Elish* VII 97, 104, 107), is even denied the role of consultant to Yahveh in these decisive interventions (40:28 cf. 40:13–14). The passage ends with an accumulation of negatives: the gods are nothingness (*ʾāyin*), nonexistence (*ʾepes*), wind (*rûaḥ*), and empty chaos (*tōhû*).

THE COMMISSIONING OF YAHVEH'S SERVANT (42:1–9)

(Barnes 1931; Begrich 1963, 161–66; Beuken 1972; E. Haag 1977a; Hermisson 1982 (= 1998b, 197–220); Hillers 1978; Jeremias 1972, 31–42; Koenig 1968; Lauha 1977; Lindblad 1993; R. Marcus 1937; Melugin 1976, 64–69; Neyrey 1982; Renaud 1990; Schoors 1964; M. S. Smith 1981; S. Smith 1944, 54–63, 107–11; Steck 1984, 1993a; Tidwell 1974; Werlitz 1997)

TRANSLATION

i

42 [1]This is my servant[a] whom I sustain,
my chosen one[b] in whom I take delight;
I have put my spirit upon him.
He will establish a just order[c] for the nations;
[2]he will not shout, he will not raise his voice
or let it be heard in public places.
[3]A broken reed he will not crush,
a dimly smoldering wick he will not extinguish;[d]
he will truly[e] establish a just order[f] for the nations;
[4]he will not grow faint[g] or be discouraged[h]
until he has set up a just order on the earth;
the islands wait for his law.

ii

[5]These are the words of Yahveh God[i] who created the sky and laid it out, who spread out the earth and its issue, who gives breath to the peoples on it, the spirit of life to those who tread upon it:

[6]"I, Yahveh, have summoned you in righteousness,
I have grasped you[j] by the hand;
I preserve you[k] and present you
as a covenant for the people,[l]
a light for the nations;
[7]to open eyes that are blind,[m]
release captives from prison,
those sitting in the dark from the dungeon.
[8]I am Yahveh; that is my name,[n]
I do not surrender my honor to others,
nor the praise due to me to idols.
[9]The events predicted have come to pass,
new events I now declare;
before they emerge I announce them to you."

NOTES

The entire passage is missing from 1QIsa[b]; some 20 words are preserved in 4QIsa[b] and part of vv 4–11 in 4QIsa[h]; both 1QIsa[a] and 4QIsa[h] leave an empty space between vv 4 and 5. [a] 1QIsaiah[a] has *hinnēh* for MT *hēn*; LXX adds "Jacob"; Matt 12:18 is identical with MT; [b] LXX adds "Israel"; [c] 1QIsa[a] has *vmšpṭv*, "his just order"; [d] 1QIsa[a] has *ykbh* without suffix, probably correctly; [e] the form *lĕʾemet* appears only here but should not be emended to *lāʾummôt*, "to the peoples," since this form is not used in Isaiah; cf. LXX *eis alētheian* and Vulg. *in veritate*; [f] *mišpaṭ* cf. Tg. *dynh*, Vulg. *iudicium*; for the meaning, see Comments; [g] 1QIsa[a] adds the conjunction, but 4QIsa[b] supports MT; cf. LXX *analampsei*, "he will shine forth"; [h] MT *yārûṣ* could be retained as intransitive "he will (not) be broken" > *rṣṣ* or (speculatively) *rvṣ* II cf. LXX *thausthēsetai*, but *yērôṣ* Niphal is preferable; [i] 1QIsa[a] has *h'l h'lhym*, but MT is supported by LXX (*kurios ho theos*), Syr., Tg., and Vulg.; [j] read *vā'aḥzēq* perfect tense; [k] MT *vĕ'eṣṣārĕkâ* is taken to derive from verbal stem *nṣr* (cf. Vulg. *servavi te*), "guard," rather than *yṣr*, "form, shape" (e.g. Elliger 1978, 223); the *Vorlage* of LXX *enischusō se*, "I will strengthen you," is unknown, perhaps > *'zr*, "gird"?; [l] 4QIsa[h] has *librît ʿôlām*, "as a perpetual covenant," independently proposed as an emendation by some modern exegetes, but without adequate textual basis, though the phonetic resemblance may be intentional; 4QIsa[d] has *librît ʿam* in 49:8; [m] Tg. reads, "to open the eyes of the house of Israel who are as blind to the law"; [n] 1QIsa[a] has *ûšĕmî*, "and my name," apparently a slip.

COMMENTS

A servant of Yahveh, that is, one who acts on his behalf and does his bidding, is now presented to the readers or hearers in a manner reminiscent of acts of commissioning or installation in office. The two statements (vv 1–4, 5–9), the second with its own superscription, belong together even if the second was added later, an opinion often expressed but impossible to prove. In the context of these early chapters the language and themes of the passage as a whole are not particularly distinctive, certainly not enough to justify attribution to a different author. We have already heard of a servant chosen and sustained by Yahveh (41:8–10), of the creation of the heavens and the earth (40:12, 22b, 26, 28; 41:20), of Yahveh's holding the hand of his agent (41:13 cf. 45:1; 51:18), the rejection of idols (*pĕsîlîm*, 40:19), and events predicted and new events announced (*ri'šonôt, ḥădāšôt* 41:22). It is possible for an interpolator to have imitated vocabulary and turns of phrase characteristic of the interpolated text, but the burden of proof lies with the scholar who posits an interpolation, not the one who accepts the text as it is.

Isaiah 42:1–4 is the first of Bernhard Duhm's *ebed-Jahwe Dichtungen* (followed by 49:1–6; 50:4–11; 52:13–53:12)—to be translated "poems" in this work rather than "songs" since, whatever else they may be, they are not songs. Duhm (1922, 311) admitted that they are close both in language and thought to Second Isaiah but argued that they were composed in Judah sometime between the composition of Job and Malachi by a disciple of Second Isaiah and teacher of the law. According to him, they were inserted into Second Isaiah in a somewhat haphazard fashion, wherever there was space in the manuscript. He justified the interpolation theory on the grounds of regularity of meter, a calmer and more low-key style of writing in contrast to Second Isaiah, and a completely different profile from the *ʿebed*, identified with Israel elsewhere in Second Isaiah. With respect to this first of the four passages, he identified vv 1–4 and 5–7 as distinct but connected sayings and he made the further point that they break the continuity between 41:25–29 and 42:8–9 and therefore must have been inserted at that point.

It is generally difficult and often impossible to *prove* that a particular passage has been interpolated, and the existence of an interpolation is not established by the mere fact that, when the passage in question is removed, the remaining text does not bleed. Another problem with Duhm's theory is the assumption that the four *Dichtungen* originated as one composition ("ein besonderes Buch," 1922, 311) and refer to one and the same individual throughout. This cannot be taken for granted, and the notable differences in subject matter, mood, and to some extent language between chs. 40–48 and 49–54 (55) must also be taken into account—especially the fact that the career of Cyrus and the end of the Babylonian Empire are the central themes in the former and are absent from the latter.

We must also take into account that fact that, particularly in Isaiah, there has been an ongoing process of incremental and cumulative interpretation of the existing material. The first stage in the long history of the interpretation of Duhm's four passages must be extracted from the text itself. Interpretation can be seen in the addition of "Israel" to 49:3 and similar glossing in 42:1 LXX. Other examples are 51:4–6, which can be read as an eschatologizing commentary on 42:1–9, and 49:1–13, which reapplies the language and themes of 42:1–9 to a different situation. Some of the problems of these "servant" texts, which have defied the ingenuity of exegetes for centuries, may be the result of the reapplication and rewriting of passages such as 42:1–9 in the light of changed historical circumstances or new insights. And 42:1–9 is unspecific and ambiguous enough in its allusions to have been applied to more than one situation without any significant rewriting.

The subject matter of chs. 40–48 in general, the immediate context (41:25–29), and the language in which the commissioning is described create a strong prima facie case that the original identification of the servant was Cyrus. In the first place, the nature of the commission strongly suggests a ruler. The Hebrew term *mišpāṭ* appears three times in vv 1–4. As used in these chapters, it can connote a judicial decision (41:1; 53:8; 54:17), particularly one that vindicates an innocent party (40:27; 49:4; 50:8). But the term here has a broader reference and refers to a social order based on justice that originates in the will and character of the deity (cf. 40:14; 51:4). So understood, *mišpāṭ* is linked with the role of law (*tôrâ* v 4, not to be translated "instruction") as imposed and administered justly and evenhandedly, and this is more obviously the task of a ruler than of a prophet.

The language fits what we know of the early Persian period. That the early Achaemenids did not have their own law code did not prevent them from referring to "the law of the king" (*data ša šarri* cf. *dātaʾ dî malkāʾ*, Ezra 7:26 and *dāt vādîn*, "law and just order," Esth 1:13–14). In his Behistun Inscription (§8), Darius I refers to subject lands "walking" according to his law. According to the propagandistic Cylinder of Cyrus, the god Marduk called him by name, was well pleased with him, chose him to restore Babylon and its inhabitants, which he did (so he says) peacefully and without violence while setting people free (cf. *ANET* 315–16 and Isa 45:1, referring explicitly to Cyrus).

Another inscription, from the Abu-Habba collection in the British Museum, records a dream of Nabonidus that actually refers to Marduk's rousing Cyrus, his servant (Beaulieu 1989, 108), while the grasping of the ruler's hand by the deity is part of official court language in the ancient Near East (cf. Isa 45:1, with explicit reference to Cyrus). The manner in which he is to discharge the task assigned to him seems at first sight to contrast with the violence of his conquests indicated in 41:2–3, 25, but we have just noted Cyrus's claim to have treated the Babylonians nonviolently. Alternatively (with S. Smith 1944, 55), the author could be referring to the way Cyrus was expected to treat the broken, defeated, and battered Judeans.

No one with even a superficial knowledge of the history of the interpretation of these passages will harbor the illusion of having got it completely right, even supposing that any one solution can account for all the features of the passage. Much of what is said in these verses could also be said of Israel either projecting an ideal Israel or an Israel in the guise of one of the great figures from its past, one "who is what Israel is to become" (McKenzie 1968, lv) or an individual who undertakes to speak and act for Israel. That we should leave open the possibility of such an innerbiblical *relecture* (as proposed by Bonnard 1972, 123–28) is suggested by the language of servanthood elsewhere in these chapters. Also suggestive is the self-presentation of an Israelite "servant," with which the next major section begins (49:1–6), together with the two sayings attached to it (49:7–13). These sayings take up some of the language and motifs of 42:1–9—a light for the nations, a covenant for the people, the freeing of prisoners, and the theme of discouragement—but rework them in the light of a changed situation.

The two conjoined passages—in the first of which (vv 1–4) the servant is referred to in first person, and in the second (5–9) is addressed directly—form a *literary* unit that does not correspond directly to any particular institutional form, for example, a liturgy in which the heir apparent to the throne is presented to the heavenly court. The speaker is Yahveh, identified as "the God Yahveh" (*hāʾēl YHVH*) at the beginning of the second saying, no doubt because of the further identification as creator. The attributes of Yahveh follow in three relative clauses: creating the sky and setting out the heavenly bodies (its "inhabitants") in it, laying out the earth like a landscape gardener and filling it with people (*ṣeʾĕṣaʾîm*, not "produce," cf. 22:24; 44:3; 48:19; 61:9; 65:23), and imparting to them breath (*nĕšāmâ*) and the spirit of life (*rûaḥ*). The order is the same as in the creation recital in Gen 1. The discourse is addressed neither to celestial beings nor to foreigners but to the congregation, to whom the designated person is represented as if present to them. The special relationship to God enjoyed by this person is encapsulated in the term *ʿebed* and reinforced by his being chosen, the object of God's good pleasure, and endowed with divine charism ("spirit"), as were so many judges, rulers, and prophets before him. That he is sustained by Yahveh (verbal stem *tmk* cf. 41:10) hints at troubles ahead and insinuates at least a tenuous connection with Duhm's second poem (49:4).

The second oration addresses the servant directly, inviting the readers or hearers to imagine being present at an actual ceremony of installation in office. The profile of the servant as designated world ruler is filled out with the metaphor of holding the hand and the charge to release captives, ascribed explicitly to Cyrus later on (45:1). That he is to be a "covenant for the people" and "a light for the nations" is less clear and has been interpreted in a wide variety of ways: for example, that the servant must restore Israel as a covenant people and be the instrument of universal salvation or that the mission is to emancipate captive peoples (Hillers 1978).

It seems more likely, however, that the primary responsibility of establishing law and just order is here being restated more obliquely. Isaiah 51:4 associates God's *mišpāṭ* and *tôrâ* directly with *ʾôr ʿammîm* ("a light of the peoples"), and it is well known that *bĕrît* ("covenant") has the basic meaning of obligation rather than mutual relationship. The "people" (*ʿam*) on whom the obligation of law and order is to be imposed should be understood in a general and universal sense, as in the previous verse, but the language would prove easily reapplicable to the people of Israel (as in 49:6, 8), as would the allusion to opening the eyes of the blind (42:16, 18–19; 43:8–9; cf. 35:5). The passage concludes with another assurance, based on previous successful predictions, that what is enacted at the literary level in the installation in office will become historical reality (cf. 41:22–23, 26–27).

NEW EVENTS CALL FOR A NEW SONG (42:10–17)

(Althann 1987; Beaucamp 1982; Darr 1987; Dion 1991; Freedman 1968; Hardmeier 1989; Mowinckel 1931, 87–112; Prinsloo 1997; Westermann 1964b, 157–63)

TRANSLATION

i

42 [10]Sing a new song to Yahveh;
sing his praise[a] to the ends of the earth,
you who sail the sea, you creatures in it,[b]
islands and their inhabitants.
[11]Let the wilderness and its settlements raise up their voice,[c]
with the villages that Kedar inhabits.
Let the dwellers in Sela[d] celebrate,
shouting[e] from the mountaintops.
[12]Let them give glory to Yahveh
and proclaim his praise in the islands.

ii

[13]Yahveh goes forth as a hero,
as a warrior he fires up his fury;
raising the battle cry, he shouts aloud;[f]
he prevails over his enemies.
[14]"Too long have I held my peace,[g]
kept silent and held myself back;
but now I cry out like a woman giving birth,
breathlessly panting.[h]
[15]I will scorch the mountains and hills,
searing all of their verdure;
I will turn the rivers into islands,[i]
dry up all the pools.
[16]I will lead the blind along the way,[j]
guide them in paths they have not known,
turning the darkness to light before them,
the rough spots into even ground.
These are the things I will do;
I will not abandon them."
[17][They who put their trust in idols
have turned back and are utterly shamed;
they who say to molten images,
"You are our gods!"]

NOTES

The passage is not in 1QIsa[b]; 4QIsa[b] and 4QIsa[h] have about a dozen complete or partial words but with no variant readings. [a] 1QIsaiah[a] adds the conjunction *vthltv*, "and his praise"; LXX *hē archē autou*, "his dominion/beginning," presupposes *tĕhillatô* for MT *tĕḥillatô*; [b] on the basis of Pss 96:11 and 98:7 it has been common since Lowth to emend MT *yōrĕdē hayyām ûmĕlo'ô*, literally, "those who go down to the sea and what fills it," to *yirʿam hayyām ûmĕlo'ô*, "let the sea roar and what fills it"; the emendation fits the pattern of repeated jussives, but it does not make conspicuously better sense, and MT is supported by 1QIsa[a], LXX, Vulg., and Tg.; [c] LXX *euphranthēti*, "rejoice," perhaps implying *yāśûś* for MT *yiśśā* elliptical for *yiśśā' qôl*, "raise [the voice]," cf. 42:2; [d] LXX and Vulg. translate *Petra*, the "rose-red city half as old as time" in Edom, no doubt correctly; Tg. surprisingly has "let the dead sing for joy when they come forth from their tombs" (Chilton 1987, 82); [e] 1QIsa[a] has *yṣryhv* > verbal stem *ṣrh* (cf. v 13), but MT *yiṣvāhû* > *ṣvh*, hapax, should stay; [f] 1QIsa[a] *yôdîaʿ*, "he makes known," for MT *yārîaʿ* must have *qin'â* 13a as object; since 13a is metrically overloaded, the following arrangement is recommended:

YHVH kaggibbôr yēṣēʾ
kĕʾîš milḥāmôt yāʿîr
qinʾâ yārîaʿ ʾap-yaṣrîaḥ
ʿal-ʾoyĕbâv yitgabbār

[g] LXX, "I have been silent; shall I be silent even forever and hold my peace?" may have been suggested by the initial letter of *heḥĕšêtî* understood as *he* interrogative; Tg. goes off in another direction: "For a long time I have given them respite, that if they repented to the law . . . but they did not repent!" (Chilton 1987, 82); [h] a difficult verse; the verb *pʿh* (here "I groan") is hapax, translated *ekarterēsa* ("I endured") in LXX, which seems to associate 14b ("I will amaze [or devastate] and dry up altogether") with 15, but *ʾešʾap*, "I pant," suggests assigning a similar meaning to the preceding verb, perhaps from an unattested *nšm*; [i] no need to emend *lāʾiyyîm* to *lĕṣiyyîm* or a similar form; [j] *lōʾ yādāʿû*, "they have not known," is elided as metrically obtrusive and repeating the same phrase in the following semistich.

COMMENTS

The psalm-like invocation in 42:10–12, inviting all and sundry to celebrate Israel's God in song, is followed by discourse by Yahveh (vv 14–16), introduced as a warrior god (v 13). After a long period of silence and inactivity, represented vividly in terms of gestation leading to childbirth (14), Yahveh is about to act both in judgment, expressed in the traditional Isaian form of ecological degradation (15), and in salvation, expressed in the equally traditional Isaian motif of "blindsight" (v 16 cf. 40:9; 45:13). The final verse deprecating idolatry gives the appearance of having been appended to the saying for the sake of completeness. We may consider the discourse a response to the preceding celebration, while also acknowledging the links of the passage as a whole with the one preceding (42:1–9). The links are abundantly in evidence: the glory and praise of Yahveh (42:8, 10), the motif of blindness and darkness (7, 16), the islands and coastlands (4, 10, 12), the abjuration of idols (8, 17), and especially the "new events" (*ḥădāšôt* 9), which call for a new song (*šîr ḥādāš* 10). We are therefore not obliged to choose between linking 10–12 with 13–17 or 1–9 (pace Prinsloo 1997; and others).

The invitation to celebrate Yahveh in song is one of several passages in chs. 40–55 (with 44:23; 49:13; 54:1) that are modeled on the liturgical hymns of praise. It is addressed to the ocean, coastlands, and islands—that is, the west—and the territory of the Kedarite Arabs across the Jordan—that is, the east—a perspective that, incidentally, is conformable more to a Judean than a Babylonian location. The song to be sung is qualitatively new, in keeping with the prospect of the new situation held out time and again in Isa 40–48.

Some of the associations can be garnered from hymns containing the same injunction (Pss 33; 96; 98; 149): the response of the sea and the wilderness, the glory of God, and the proclamation of Yahveh's kingship following victory over chaos and disorder. Isaiah 42:10–12 is not an eschatological psalm (pace Westermann 1969, 102), and it is not a psalm composed for a ritual in which Yahveh was ritually enthroned, for which the evidence is lacking (pace Mowinckel 1931, 96). It is a literary composition that uses material from psalms extolling Yahveh as king and creator. We may compare Isa 24:14–16a:

They lift up their voices,
singing joyfully of Yahveh's majesty;
they exult more loudly than the sea!
Therefore give glory to Yahveh in the east,
in the western isles to Yahveh's name,
Yahveh, Israel's God!
From the ends of the earth we hear the refrain,
"Glory to the Conquering One!"

The hymnic associations carry over into the following passage, recalling acclamations of Yahveh as warrior god, going forth from Seir-Edom (Deut 33:2; Judg 5:4) or Sinai (Deut 33:2; Ps 68:9, 18) or Paran (Deut 33:2), his appearance surrounded by cosmic reverberations and natural upheavals (Exod 15:8, 12; Judg 5:4–5; Ps 18:7– 15; 68:8–10).

The catastrophic effects of this violent intervention in nature—mountains, hills, rivers, and lakes—is reminiscent of the anti-Babylonian poem in ch. 13 (vv 9–13) and points to the same historical referent. The period of silence and inactivity (14a), of the hiding of God's face, corresponds to the epoch of the Babylonian conquest. The silence of God, of which we hear frequent complaints in the hymns (e.g. Ps 89:47[46]), was the time of Israel's abandonment by God, the end of which is now proclaimed (cf. 54:7, where the duration of the silence and abandonment is estimated more optimistically as "a brief moment," *regaʿ qāṭon*).

To judgment, expressed in terms of ecological degradation (cf. ecological restoration in 41:18), corresponds salvation, expressed in the familiar Isaian metaphor of restored sight (cf. 6:9–10; 9:1; 42:7, 18–20; 43:8; 59:10). The figure of guiding the blind, dispelling the darkness that surrounds them, and removing obstacles from their path, is a return to the theme at the beginning of the section (40:3–4). It would be natural to refer this figurative language to an anticipated return from the diaspora, which according to Ibn Ezra some were suggesting in his day. But the reference may also be taken in a less metaphorical sense and, as such, would later be understood of a literal disability, to be removed in the end time (35:5 cf. 29:18).

THE SPIRITUAL IMPERCEPTION OF THE SERVANT (42:18–25)

(I. Fischer 1995; Goldingay 1995; Melugin 1976, 41–43, 103–4; North 1955, 89–90)

TRANSLATION

42 [18]You that are deaf, listen!
You that are blind, look and see!
[19]Who is as blind as my servant?[a]
Who so deaf as the messenger I dispatch?
[Who is as blind as Meshullam?[b]
Who so deaf[c] as Yahveh's servant?][d]
[20]He has seen much,[e] but does not pay heed;
his hearing is sound,[f] but he hears nothing.
[21]Yahveh desired his servant's[g] vindication
to make his law grand and glorious;[h]
[22]but this is a people plundered and despoiled;
they are all trapped[i] in holes,
hidden away in dungeons;
they have been plundered with none to rescue,
despoiled, with none to say, "Give them back!"
[23]Who among you will attend to this?
Who will pay heed from now on?
[24]Who delivered Jacob to the despoiler,[j]
Israel to the plunderers?
Was it not Yahveh, against whom they have sinned?[k]
They were unwilling to follow his guidance
and heed his teaching.[l]
[25]So he poured out upon them his wrath,[m]
his anger in the fury of battle;
it blazed all around them, but they did not comprehend;
it burned them, but they gave no heed.

NOTES

1QIsaiah[a] has a gap of one-third of a line after v 17; none of the Cave 4 fragments include this passage. [a] Targum and LXX have the pl.; LXX reads, "who is blind but my servants (*paides mou*) and deaf but they that rule over them; and the slaves of God (*hoi douloi tou theou*) have been made blind"; [b] MT *mĕšullām* should not be emended either to *mĕšullāḥî* ("the one sent by me") or, with LXX, to *mōšĕlêhem* (*mōšĕlâv*) ("their rulers," Elliger 1978, 270–1); for the range of interpretations, see the commentary; [c] though supported only by 2 MSS and Symm., *ḥērēš* ("deaf") is preferred if 19b is a gloss on 19a; [d] the threefold repetition of "blind" in this one verse practically obliges us to regard 19b as a gloss; [e] there is some confusion of verbal forms in this passage; K *r'yt* 2d-person sing. is supported by 1QIsa[a], but Q has Infinitive Absolute (cf. *pāqôaḥ* in the same line), and the context favors 3d-person address; [f] 1QIsa[a] has *ptḥv*, "they have opened . . . ," but MT is correct; [g] "his servant's" supplied to clarify the referent of the masc. pronominal suffix in *ṣidqô*, "his vindication"; [h] 1QIsa[a] has *vy'drhh*, "he will make it (i.e. *tôrâ*) glorious"; [i] MT has *hāpēah*, Infinitive Absolute > *pḥḥ* hapax, denominative verb from *paḥ*, "trap," = "being trapped," which is awkward; read perhaps *hūpaḥû*, "they are trapped"; [j] read *mĕšôseh*, Poel participle > *šsh* for Q and 1QIsa[a] *mĕšissāh* ("plunder"); [k] MT has *ḥāṭā'nû*, "we have sinned," influenced by 1st-person pl. liturgical form, but the context favors 3d person; [l] 1QIsa[a] has pl. *btvrtyv*; [m] 1QIsa[a] has *ḥamat* construct form for MT *ḥēmâ*, "heat," "hot anger," but MT is correct; read: *vayyišpok ʿālâyv ḥēmâ / 'appô veʿĕzûz milḥāmâ*.

COMMENTS

Surprising at first sight is the shift from assurance to censure, but then we note that this kind of alternation is a feature of the entire section, for we hear words of reproach at regular intervals (40:27; 43:22–24; 46:12–13; 48:1–2, 6–8). In other respects the passage is well integrated into its context. The servant has already been identified (41:8–10), and this account of the present condition of the servant Israel contrasts with the profile of a future servant and his mission in 42:1–9, however the latter is identified. Also frequently attested is the theme of incomprehension, the failure to grasp the significance of events as interpreted by the seer, together with the common Isaian motif of guiding the blind (40:21, 28; 42:7, 16; 43:8).

We see how important and at the same time how difficult it was to provide a satisfactory explanation of the disaster of the Babylonian conquest. This period has already been described as a time of penal servitude (40:2), of imprisonment (42:7), of the silence, inactivity, and inaccessibility of God (40:27; 42:14), and of God-forsakenness (42:16) following the murder and mayhem of battle (42:13). The preacher presents the same line of argument as the Historian, that Yahveh willed to preserve and vindicate Israel (42:21a) but was prevented from doing so by sin, including the sin of past generations (cf. 43:27)—specifically, failure to observe the laws (42:24b). In order to counter the widespread impression that Yahveh was powerless to prevent these events from happening or that they happened randomly, the preacher had to make the dangerous claim that Yahveh himself had brought them about (42:24–25). Though in fact none of these claims will seem to us inevitably and obviously true, the hearers are taken to task because they would have gotten the message if they had used their faculties (sight and hearing) and consulted experience—their own and the knowledge mediated to them through their traditions ("he has seen much," 20a).

The passage has been described form-critically as a reproach (*Scheltwort*, Gressmann), a dispute saying (*Streitgespräch*, Köhler), or a disputation in response to a liturgical lament (Westermann, Melugin). The argumentative or disputatious note is certainly in evidence here, as it is elsewhere in these chapters, consistent with other rhetorical features already noted: the call for a hearing (41:1; 44:1; 46:3, 12; 47:8; 48:1, 12), rhetorical questions often in fairly long sequences (40:12–14, 25–26; 41:2, 4, 26; 43:9, 13 etc.), challenges to the opposition to state their case (41:1–5, 21–24; 43:8–9), appeals to experience and tradition (40:21, 28; 42:20; 44:21; 46:8–9), and satire directed against foreign deities and their devotees (e.g. 44:9–20).

These features are consistent with a breakdown in the course of time of the mostly brief types of sayings in earlier prophetic books and the emergence of longer homiletic discourses in evidence in Isa 40–55 and Deuteronomy. Regarding the social setting for this kind of discourse, we can only speculate. The suggestion of a quasi- or proto-synagogue setting, made earlier, seems plausible and would not be inconsistent with the dissemination of brief tracts; but we lack information.

The passage begins, paradoxically, with a call for attention addressed to the deaf and the blind (v 18). Where deafness and sightlessness are understood literally, the context is generally that of the removal of such disabilities in the end time (29:18; 35:5). Elsewhere, these particular disabilities stand for a condition of enslavement (42:7, 16), but here the allusion is to a lack of spiritual discernment on the part of Jewish communities. With the series of rhetorical questions that ensue, the thread becomes difficult to follow. Both the Old Greek version and the Targum consider the servant and messenger of v 19a to be the people as a whole, but the latter term (*mal'āk*) appears elsewhere as a synonym for prophet (*nābî'*; Hag 1:13; Mal 3:1) and appears to have this connotation in Isa 44:26. So far we have not heard of a mission assigned to the Judean people as a whole unless it was in 42:1–9. It is also typically the prophet who is dispatched on a mission (as 48:16 and 61:1). The chiastic arrangement (deaf-blind-blind-deaf) precludes our removing the first half-verse (19a), but we may expect to find a residue of superimposed readings wherever the *'ebed*, "servant," is mentioned.

The second half of the verse (19b) is, however, more often than not elided, if only on account of the inelegant threefold repetition of the word "blind" (*'ivvēr*) in the same verse. Some take it as a gloss that applies the preceding to an individual servant of Yahveh. But then it is unclear why this individual would be charged with a lack of spiritual discernment, unless the servant in question is Cyrus, who did eventually disappoint the expectations laid on him. Much depends on one's understanding of the word *měšullām*. As a Pual participle it has been translated, generally with disregard for the context, as "perfected," "fully paid," "covenant partner," or "submissive one," the last by analogy with Arabic *muslim*.

The suggestion of the Dutch scholar J. L. Palache more than half a century ago that the writer is referring to Meshullam, son of Zerubbabel (1 Chr 3:19), did not win adherents because we know nothing of this individual apart from his father's name (North 1955, 89–90). If 19b is a gloss on 19a, it is just possible that the glossator intended to identify the *ʿebed* as a specific *individual* servant of Yahveh; however, this individual is characterized as blind—that is, imperceptive or misguided. It therefore seems more likely that *məšullām* is a sobriquet for Israel, not unlike Jeshurun (44:2), though in this case its meaning remains obscure. The matter simply cannot be decided.

The note of censure continues in the explanation offered for the spiritual obtuseness of Israel called to Yahveh's service. What follows is essentially a restatement of basic Deuteronomic tenets. Deuteronomic parenesis appeals routinely to experience—ostensibly direct experience, since Moses is presented as addressing the wilderness generation, but in fact experience mediated through historical traditions—what your eyes have seen, what your ears have heard (e.g. Deut 3:21; 4:3, 9; 7:19; 10:21; 11:7). "You have seen everything Yahveh did in your sight (before your eyes) to Pharaoh, all his servants and all his land . . . but to this day Yahveh has not given you a mind to recognize, eyes to see, and ears to hear" (Deut 29:1, 3[2, 4]).

Equally at home in Deuteronomy is the theme of the greatness of the law and the frustration of God's will to vindicate and save by Israel's failure to observe the law. A crucial point in the argument, also shared with the Deuteronomists, is the affirmation that the disaster of the Babylonian conquest was brought about by the national deity as punishment for nonobservance of the law. The fury of the Babylonian onslaught was ignited and fueled by the anger of Yahveh against his own people, a prophetic insight that until the exile they had failed to grasp.

DIVINE REASSURANCE: ALL WILL BE WELL (43:1–7)

(Conrad 1984; Maalstad 1966; Ringgren 1977b; H.C. Schmitt 1992; Stassen 1992; Vieweger and Böchler 1996; Willmes 1990)

TRANSLATION

43 [1]Now, these are words of Yahveh who created you, Jacob,
who formed you, Israel:
"Don't be afraid, for I have redeemed you;
I have called you[a] by name,[b] you are mine.
[2]If you cross over water, I am with you,
or over rivers, they will not overwhelm you;
if you pass through fire, you will not be scorched,
the flames will not burn you.
[3]For I am Yahveh your God,
the Holy One of Israel, your Savior.
I have set aside Egypt as your ransom;
Ethiopia and Seba in your stead,

[4]For[c] you are precious in my sight,
you are honored, and I love you.
So I set aside people[d] in your stead,
nations in exchange for your life.
[5]Don't be afraid, for I am with you;
I shall bring your descendants from the east,
I shall gather you in from the west;
[6]I shall say to the north, "Give them up,"
to the south, "Do not restrain them;
bring my sons from afar,
my daughters from the ends of the earth,
[7]all that bear my name,
whom I created, whom I formed,
whom I made for my glory.' "[e]

NOTES

[a] Supplying 2d-person sing. suffix to *qārāʾtî* with LXX (*ekalesa se to onoma sou*) and Vulg. (*vocavi te nomine tuo*); [b] emending *bĕšimkâ* to *bišĕmî* (as in BHS) because of v 7 is unwarranted; on the different meanings of *qrʾ* + *bĕšēm*, see Note on 41:25; [c] *mēʾăšer* with this meaning is unusual, but the comparative, as in Qoh 3:22, does not fit the context any more than comparison with Assyria (reading *mēʾaššur*, "than Assyria"); [d] rather than MT *ʾādām* (1QIsa[a] *hāʾādām*), "people" (cf. LXX *anthrōpous pollous*, "many men"), we would expect a political term e.g. *ʾiyyîm*, "islands" (cf. 41:1; 49:1), or perhaps a gentilic (*ʾărām* or *ʾĕdōm*), but MT is acceptable, and emending to *ʾădāmôt* ("lands"; BHS) is not an improvement; [e] omitting the conjunction before *likbôdî*, "for my glory."

COMMENTS

While the circumstances under which chs. 40–48 were composed are obscure and will no doubt remain so, the language evidences enough common features from beginning to end to permit reading them as a single text. To be sure, the unity of our text should not be pressed beyond reasonable limits, but it has at least as much homogeneity and internal consistency and is about the same length as the average sermon. Convenience of exposition requires breaking it into small units but must not lead us to overlook the thread of linguistic and thematic continuity as the author attempts to render contemporaneous events intelligible to the audience within a religious frame of reference. The frequent use of prophetic *incipits* and *excipits* (e.g. 43:1, 14, 16) maintains some residual semblance of commonality with an older prophetic tradition, though the type of discourse is quite different.

The linguistic and thematic continuity may be illustrated with reference to the small interconnected subunits within the longer passage, 43:1–44:8. The first of these (43:1–7) begins and ends with the theme of naming and calling and repeats motifs already familiar: Yahveh as Creator God (40:26,28; 41:20; 42:5), redeemer of Israel (41:14), the Holy One of Israel (41:14), the one who guides his people (42:16) and bids them put aside fear (40:9; 41:10, 13–14). The passage following (43:8–13) returns to the forensic mode and rhetorical questions of 41:1–4, 21–24 and again introduces the metaphor of blindness and deafness (42:7, 16, 18). Since 43:14–21 opens with the traditional formula "This is what Yahveh says" (*koh-ʾāmar YHVH*) and concludes in virtually the same way as 43:1–7, it forms a distinctive link in this rhetorical chain. Here, too, we find familiar motifs and expressions: Yahveh as redeemer, the Holy One, the creator of Israel, Israel's king (cf. 41:21), former events and new events (cf.41:22–23; 42:9), and the transformation of the wilderness (cf. 40:3; 41:18–19; 42:16).

We noted earlier that the speaker alternates reproach (as in 43:22– 28) with encouragement, a not unfamiliar homiletic strategy, and offers once again the standard Deuteronomistic explanation for the destruction of Jerusalem and its temple (27–28). The reassuring words that follow (44:1–5) conclude by returning to the naming theme indicative of a close, proprietary and one might say familial relationship between those addressed and their God. Finally, 44:6–8, with its own superscript, summarizes, recapitulates, and rounds off the passage as a whole, resulting in a well-designed and rhetorically effective discourse.

There has been a tendency in recent commentary to break 43:1–7 down into two distinct oracles of salvation, either 1–4 and 5–7 (Westermann 1969, 114–19; Conrad 1984) or 1–3a and 5–7 (Melugin 1976, 104–5). This tendency is based on a fairly rigid idea of structure, especially the repetition of the assurance "don't be afraid" (*ʾal-tîrāʾ*) in 1b and 5a. However, it is doubtful whether any writer or orator at that time felt obliged to respect these form-critical canons and much more likely that forms of speech consecrated by long usage, in the cult for example, entered into public discourse in a much less deliberate and conscious fashion. Leading off with *vĕʿattâ* ("and now") signals a contrast with the preceding address (42:18–25).

The language in which the reassurance is expressed draws on historical traditions presumed to be known, even though no tradition is referred to explicitly. Accordingly, the creation and formation of Israel/Jacob draws on to the Egyptian captivity and the exodus; the assurance "I am (will be) with you" recalls the vision at the burning thornbush (Exod 3:12); and the calling by name evokes the new name given to Jacob on his return from exile (Gen 32:28).

The idea of redemption and of Yahveh as Israel's redeemer (*gōʾēl*) derives from the obligation in ancient customary law to buy back the freedom of a kinsman in indentured service, usually as a result of unpaid debts. This practice provided a ready analogy for the belief that Yahveh had, so to speak, bailed Israel out of Egypt, though the party to whom the payment was made remains unclear. (The problem persisted in the Christian appropriation of this language in the doctrine of redemption by satisfaction: paying a price, but to whom?). At any rate, the language of redemption appears frequently in these chapters.

Though the rescue from Egypt is only rarely on the surface (48:20–21; 51:10; 52:3–4), the historical tradition is always there in the background. Here we find the curious idea that Israel will be redeemed once again not by monetary payment (cf. 52:3) but by handing over, presumably to Cyrus, Egypt, Ethiopia (Sudan), and Seba (probably in the Horn of Africa), though there is also the fantasy that these same peoples will come as captives to Jerusalem (45:14). In the event, it was not Cyrus but his successor Cambyses who conquered Egypt (525 B.C.E.).

The expectation that dispersed Judeans will return from all points of the compass (43:5–6) suggests that the common assumption of a Babylonian provenance for these chapters and an exclusive concentration on repatriation from Babylon should be treated with caution. Lower Mesopotamia (the Nippur region) no doubt represented the largest and most influential of the diaspora communities, and it is therefore unsurprising that Judeo-Babylonians who had settled there should be urged to return to Judah (48:20–21; 52:11–12). But there was also a significant Judean presence in northern Mesopotamia, Egypt as far as Syene (Assuan, Isa 49:12), Ethiopia, Asia Minor, and no doubt other locations unknown to us (see e.g. Obad 20; Zeph 3:10). Most of the references to exiles in these chapters are unspecific (41:9; 43:5–6; 45:3; 49:12; 51:10), and none of the allusions to either topography or cultural matters points unmistakably to a Babylonian provenance.

THE GOD OF ISRAEL AND THE GODS OF THE NATIONS (43:8–13)

(Dempsey 1991; Klein 1985; Merendino 1981, 315–30; Seeligmann 1948; Williamson 1979)

TRANSLATION

43 [8]Bring forth[a] the people who have eyes yet are blind,
who have ears yet are deaf.
[9]All nations have come together,
all peoples have assembled.[b]
Who among them can proclaim this
or announce events to us before they happen?
Let them produce their witnesses to prove them right,[c]
so that people will hear it and say, "it is so."
[10]You are my witnesses, Yahveh declares,
my servant[d] whom I have chosen,
that you may know me and trust me
and understand that I am the One.
Before me no god was formed,
and there will be none after me.
[11]I, I am Yahveh;

there is none that can save but me.
[12]I proclaimed salvation, I announced it;
this is no alien god in your midst.
You are my witnesses, Yahveh declares,[e]
[13]I am God; from the very first I am the One.
There is none can deliver from my hand.
When I act, who can undo it?

NOTES

[a] MT *hôṣî'* is Imperative sing. rather than 3d-person Perfect (cf. Jer 17:18 *hābî'*, "bring"), though the more usual form is *hôṣê'* cf. Vulg. *educ*, "lead out"; 1QIsa[a] has pl. Imperative *hvṣy'v* and 1QIsa[b] *'vṣy'*, 1st-person sing. Imperfect cf. LXX *exēgagon laon tuphlon*, "I led forth a blind people"; [b] since the tense is perfect not jussive, read *vayē'āsĕpû* vav consecutive for MT *vĕyē'āsĕpû;* [c] *vĕyaṣdîqû* Hiphil for MT *vĕyiṣdāqû;* [d] *'abdî* sing. is often emended to *'ăbāday* pl., parallel with *'ēday*, "my witnesses," but *'ebed* is always sing. in chs. 40–48 and stands parallel with *mal'ākâv*, "his messengers," in 44:26; [e] the accents Silluq and Soph Pasuq should be at this point; MT arranges the lines differently.

COMMENTS

The preacher presents to his hearers the same setting here (43:8–13) as previously (41:1–5, 21–29). The nations are already assembled to witness the contest of deities and approve the outcome, rather like the contest between Elijah and the Baalist prophets on Mount Carmel (1 Kgs 18:17–40). Then the summons is given, as if to a court usher, to lead in the Judean people who, though already denounced as spiritually obtuse (42:7, 16, 18), at least have the essentials for witnessing: eyes to observe and ears to listen. The challenge is addressed to the gods of the nations to sustain their claim to divine status by predicting and then bringing about events, and here too the reference is to the conquests of Cyrus. They are invited to produce their devotees as witnesses to their power so that they can be publicly acknowledged.

To this challenge there is, of course, no response. The interesting and unique element here can easily be missed; it is stated well by Westermann:

> "What here decides a religion's title and claim is neither its spiritual or ethical or religious value, nor its enlightenment or high cultural level; instead, it is continuity in history and this alone, the power of a faith to throw a bridge over a chasm torn open by the downfall of a nation." (Westermann 1969, 122).

In putting so much weight on this claim, the author of chs. 40–48 is playing for high stakes, for history has a habit of disappointing expectations and falsifying predictions. But there persists always, even in the face of disappointment, this tremendous need to render events intelligible within a religious context of meaning.

Those addressed by the preacher are called to witness to and affirm the wager. The appearance of "servant" (*ʿebed*) in the singular at this point (43:10a) exemplifies the ambivalence or polyvalence affecting the interpretation of this key term. We saw earlier that in chs. 40–48 it appears invariably in the singular (41:8, 9; 42:1, 19; 44:1, 2, 21, 26; 45:4; 48:20), even when linked with a substantive in the plural (44:26). In this respect the use of *ʿebed* in chs. 49–55 is quite different. While in several instances the designation is explicitly predicated of the Judean people (Israel, Jacob) as a whole (41:8–9; 44:1–2, 21; 45:4; 48:20), enough ambiguity remains to allow for identification with individual figures contemporaneous or future. Hence Ibn Ezra's identification of the servant with the prophetic author; hence also the messianic reading of the Targumist: "you are witnesses before me, says the Lord, and my servant the Messiah with whom I am pleased."

A messianic (according to Seeligmann [1948, 28–29], possibly Christian) allusion may also underlie the LXX: "Become witnesses to me, and I am witness, says the Lord God, and the servant (*pais*) whom I have chosen, that you may know and believe me and understand that I am (*ego eimi*)." Readers of the New Testament will recognize linguistic and thematic links with the scene of the baptism of Jesus (Matt 3:17 and parallels), the *ego eimi* uttered by the Jesus of the Fourth Gospel (e.g. John 18:5, 8) and the faithful witness of Rev 1:5.

This third trial scene (43:8–13), following 41:1–5 and 41:21–29, concludes with a strong affirmation of the uniqueness and incomparability of the God of Israel. The self-predication by Yahveh is encapsulated in the practically untranslatable formula *ʾănî hûʾ* ("I am He"? "It is I"? "I am the One"?), reminiscent, and perhaps deliberately so, of the equally enigmatic *ʾehyeh* ("I am"? "I will be"?) heard by Moses from the burning thornbush (Exod 3:14 cf. Hos 1:9). The formula *ʾănî hûʾ*, which Ibn Ezra described as the most sublime expression of the unity of God, appears at regular intervals throughout chs. 40–48 (41:4; 43:10, 13; 46:4; 48:12). But, just as the answer to Moses' request for a name encapsulates the active and helpful presence of the deity (cf. *ʾehyeh ʿimmāk*, "I will be with you," Exod 3:12), so the "I am" formula in these chapters is associated with Yahveh's helping presence for Israel (46:4) and Yahveh's activity within history (41:4; 48:12).

The similar but more explicit self-designations "I am Yahveh," "I am Godhead" (vv 11, 13) are both accompanied by a rejection of rival claims to demonstrate effective reality by saving or delivering from danger (vv 11, 12). For the preacher, the proof of divinity is stated clearly in this passage: "I proclaimed salvation, I announced it" (12a). A literal translation would make the point more clearly: "I proclaimed, I saved, I announced." Here and elsewhere the author states in a quite positivistic way that the ability and willingness to save (*hôšîaʿ*) is the test of divine status (cf. 45:20; 46:7; 47:13, 15). But the identity of the saving deity only emerges clearly when the saving event is proclaimed in advance by a prophet speaking in the deity's name and then subsequently confirmed; hence the importance of the "proof from prophecy" in Isa 40–48. The communities addressed are called on to attest to this, since the deity in whose name they are being addressed is no alien (*zār*, v 12) but familiar from their traditions. The address to the witnesses ends with a strong affirmation of the ineluctability and irreversibility of events set in motion by the God of Israel.

The practice of linking a self-identification of the deity with a rejection of rival claims—"there is none that can save but me . . . there is none can deliver from my hand" (see also 44:6, 8; 45:6, 21)—resembles a similar formulation attributed to Babylon personified and therefore in all probability spoken in the name of the Babylonian imperial deity, Marduk: "I am, and there is none other" (47:8, 10). We take this to be one of several tokens of the author's familiarity with the religious ideology of empire and the imperial cult, the principal expressions of which are to be found in the creation epic *Enuma Elish* and the New Year *akitu* festival during which it was recited. Unlike Marduk, son of Ea, who was preceded by gods created in pairs (Lahmu and Lahamu, Ashar and Kishar) and succeeded by others, Yahveh does not have a genealogy and is not part of a theogony (v 10b). This is one of several indications in Isaiah 40–55 of a kind of mirror-imaging of the Marduk cult, by means of which the author sought to counter the ideology of power articulated through these liturgies.

SOMETHING NEW: A WAY INTO THE FUTURE (43:14–21)

(Barstad 1989, 83–89; Bentzen 1948; G. R. Driver 1933; North 1950; Odendaal 1971; Patrick 1984; Ravenna 1964; Schoors 1964)

TRANSLATION

i

43 [14]These are the words of Yahveh your Redeemer, the
Holy One of Israel:
"For your sake I send to Babylon[a]
to lay low all those who flee;[b]
the triumphant cries of the Chaldeans
will be turned to lamentations.[c]
[15]I, Yahveh, am your Holy God,
the creator of Israel, your king."

ii

[16]This is what Yahveh says,
he who cut a passage through the sea,
a track through the mighty waters,
[17]who led on chariot and horse to destruction,[d]

all that powerful array;
they lay down, never to rise,
extinguished, quenched like a wick:
[18]"Call no more to mind these past events
or ponder deeds done long ago;
[19]I am about to do something new,
now it is unfolding; do you not perceive it?
Even in the wilderness I am making a roadway
and paths[e] through the wasteland.
[20]The wild beasts will pay me respect,
the jackals and ostriches,
for I provision the wilderness with water,
the wasteland with streams,
so my chosen people can drink;
[21]this people I formed for myself,
they will proclaim my praises."

NOTES

[a] 1QIsaiah[a] *bbbl*, "against Babylon"; 4QIsa[b] *bbl* for MT *bābelāh*; [b] the main problem is the similarity between *bārîaḥ* ("one who flees," "a fugitive"), a rare formation > *brḥ* (Isa 27:1; Job 26:13) and *bĕrîaḥ*, "bar" (cf. Vulg. *vectes*); hence, the proposal "I will bring down all the bars" or "the bars of your prison" (*bĕrîḥê kilʾăkem*) cf. 45:2b; LXX has *kai epegerō pantas pheugontas*, "I will rouse up all the fugitives," perhaps reading *vĕhă ʿîrotî* > *ʿûr* cf. 41:25; the translation offered above is close to MT; other emendations keeping the same general sense—*bōrĕḥîm*, "those fleeing" (Westermann 1969, 120); *baḥûrîm*, "young men" (Kissane 1960, 53, 56), *bĕrîḥîm*, "nobles" (G. R. Driver 1933, 39)—are unnecessary; [c] MT *vĕkaśdîm bāʾoniyyôt rinnātām*, "and the Chaldeans, their cry of joy is in the ships," is unsatisfactory cf. LXX *kai chaldaioi en ploiois deēthēsontai*, "and the Chaldeans will be bound on ships"; Tg. goes overboard: "For your sins' sake you were exiled in Babylon, and I have brought down all of them with rudders, even the Chaldeans in the ships of their praise"; the problem is the close similarity between *ʾoniyyôt*, "ships," and *ʾăniyyôt*, "lamentations"; the translation offered assumes the latter, but the line is still defective and the result speculative; [d] literally, "drew out" (*hôṣîʾ*), with the sense of leading on; [e] reading *nĕtîbôt* with 1QIsa[a] for MT *nĕhārôt*, "streams"; the scribe's eye probably wandered to 20b.

COMMENTS

The conventional prophetic superscripts formally identify two sayings of unequal length (43:14–15, 16–21). The first may have preserved only its beginning and ending either through the vicissitudes of textual transmission or by deliberate omission. If the saying included predictions about the fate of Babylon incompatible with what came to be known about the fall of the city, deliberate suppression would be understandable. Whether in fact one follows the translation of v 14 offered above (cf. NEB) or the alternative, implying a violent irruption into the city (cf. RSV and NJPSV), the result would be inconsistent with the account of a nonviolent occupation in Cyrus's propagandistic Cylinder inscription. The point, in any case, is the author's affirming that Cyrus has a historic mission to conquer Babylon (stated more directly in 45:1–3 and 48:14) and that the fall of the city is the opening act in the drama of Israel's redemption.

This truly historic event, the fall of the city and the consequent collapse of the Babylonian Empire, is to take place for the benefit of the Jewish people (*lĕma ʿankem*)! It would be natural to read such a statement as a dangerous delusion, a typical "fantasy of the oppressed," which in fact it turned out to be. Yet, on reflection, a subjugated people can be forgiven for not taking a detached and objective view of events that are likely to affect them in very basic ways. The faith context of the affirmation is expressed in the self-identification of Yahveh as Redeemer, Israel's Holy One, Israel's Creator and King. The first two of these predicates are often linked (41:14; 43:14; 47:4; 48:17; 54:5; see comments on 41:14 above). They may be taken to refer, respectively, to the activity and nature of Israel's God though, contrary to what is often asserted, the idea of redemption in these chapter is only once (48:20–22) referring explicitly to the Exodus tradition. The accent on Yahveh as sovereign (cf. 44:6) and as the cosmic deity and creator (40:26, 28; 42:5; 45:7, 12, 18)—creation here including transformations brought about in the physical environment and in history, especially the history of Israel (41:20; 45:7–8; 54:16, a particular instance of *creatio ex nihilo* (43:1, 7, 15)—is consonant with and in fact required by the preacher's interpretation of contemporary events.

The second saying (vv 16–21) provides a theological context for the first (referring to the anticipated fall of Babylon to Cyrus) by setting it against the tradition of the epic victory at the Red Sea (or Papyrus Sea) brought about by divine intervention. Since this tradition could be assumed to be known, it is conjured up by the use of familiar phrases: a way through the mighty waters (cf. Exod 15:10), horses and chariots (Exod 15:1, 4, 19, 21), and the stillness of death after the horses and drivers were drowned (cf. Exod 15:10b).

In Isa 40–48 the phrase usually translated "the former things" (*hāriʾšonôt*) appears for the most part in the context of the author's argument from prophecy and fulfillment, whether the reference is understood to be to the prophecies of doom in the first section of the book, now spectacularly fulfilled, or to earlier victories of Cyrus, successfully predicted by the author (41:22; 42:9; 43:9; 46:9; 48:3). But in this instance (v 18) the word *riʾšonôt*, also described as *qadmoniyyôt* ("deeds done long ago"), refers to the events commemorated in the tradition alluded to telegrammatically in the previous two verses. The argument here draws on analogy rather than prophecy. What God did in guiding his people en route to Canaan and providing them with life-giving water (Exod 15:22–27; 17:1–7; Num 20:2–13) is paradigmatic of what God does whenever he acts to save or redeem his people. The point is made with a fine subtlety by the use of present participles in vv 16–17a (*nôtēn, môṣîʾ*); the deed done long ago is superimposed on the drama of redemption, in which the fall of Babylon is to be the first act.

The promise of a way through the wilderness corresponding to the Exodus way through the sea has led most commentators to explain the "new thing" (*ḥădāšâ*) now beginning to unfold as the anticipated return of the Babylonian diaspora to the homeland. While this theme is certainly in view in chs. 40–48, especially in the final exhortation to leave Babylon, with its fairly overt allusion to the Exodus (48:20–22), it neither exhausts the scope of the author's expectations nor obliges us to domicile the author among the Jewish ethnic minority in Babylon. The prophet anticipates a return from the ends of the earth and from all points of the compass, not just from Mesopotamia (41:9; 43:5; 49:12 cf. 51:11; 55:12–13).

Furthermore, while talk of a way through the wilderness and paths through the wasteland evokes the idea of repatriation (but not exclusively from Babylon), the theme of ecological transformation is equally present, as it is elsewhere in these chapters (see Comments on 35:5–7 and 41:17–20); hence the inclusion of jackals and ostriches, an Isaian topos associated with ecological degradation and the collapse of urban life (cf. Isa 13:22; 34:13). Duhm (1922, 327) excised vv 20b–21 on aesthetic grounds, since they repeat v 19b, and set up a bizarre parallel between jackals and ostriches on the one hand and Israelites on the other. But the point seems to be that the journey will be expedited by removing or rendering wild animals innocuous and providing water. The appropriate response of the chosen people to this anticipated redemptive intervention in their affairs is liturgical praise (*tĕhillâ* cf.42:8, 10, 12; 48:9), their failure to render which is the subject of the following passage.

THE CASE AGAINST ISRAEL RAISED AND DISMISSED (43:22–44:5)

(Ackroyd 1963; Booij 1982; B. L. Smith 1982; Toloni 1995; Van Winkle 1997)

TRANSLATION

i

43 [22]But[a] you did not invoke me, Jacob,[b]
you grew weary of me, Israel.
[23]You did not bring me burnt offerings from your flocks,[c]
you did not honor me with your sacrifices.[d]
I did not burden you with cereal offerings
or weary you with frankincense.

[24]You have not bought sweet cane for me with your money
or sated me with the suet of your sacrifices.
But you burdened me with your sins,
you wore me out with your iniquities.

ii

[25]I, I am the One
who for my own sake[e] wipe out your transgressions
and do not call your sins to mind.
[26]Call me to judgment, let us argue the case together,
set out your case that you may be proved right.
[27]Your first ancestor sinned;
your spokesmen transgressed against me,
[28]so I profaned the princes of the sanctuary;[f]
I delivered Jacob up to ruin,
Israel to reviling.

iii

44 [1]But hear now, Jacob my servant,
Israel whom I chose for myself.
[2]These are the words of Yahveh who made you,
who formed you from the womb, and who will help you:
Don't be afraid, Jacob my servant,
Jeshurun whom I have chosen.
[3]I will pour out water on the thirsty ground,[g]
streams of water on the parched land;
I will pour out my spirit on your descendants,
my blessing on your offspring.
[4]They will flourish like well-watered grass,[h]
like willows by the runnels of water.
[5]This one will say, 'I belong to Yahveh,'
another will take the name Jacob,[i]
yet another will write Yahveh's name on the hand,[j]
and add the name Israel to his own."[k]

NOTES

[a] MT *vĕlo'* creates a nexus with the preceding passage and the conjunction should not be omitted (following Syr. and Vulg.); [b] LXX reads *ou nun ekalesa se . . . ou kopiasai se epoiēsa*, "I have not now called you . . . I did not make you weary," but MT is to be preferred; [c] literally, "the sheep of your offerings"; [d] add preposition with 1QIsa[a] *vbzbḥykh*, "with/by means of your sacrifices"; [e] *lĕma'ănî*, "for my own sake," is absent from LXX and *VL* but MT is correct; [f] LXX *kai emianan hoi archontes (sou) ta hagia mou*, "and the rulers defiled my holy things," presupposes *vayĕḥallĕlû* for MT *va'ăḥallēl*. But MT is supported by Vulg. (*et contaminavi principes sanctos*), makes sense, and

should be retained; [g] reading *ṣāmā'* with Syr., Tg. for MT *ṣāmē'*, "thirsty one"; [h] MT *bĕbên ḥāṣîr,* "in among the grass," is unusual; 1QIsa[a], Tg., and LXX presuppose *kĕbên,* "as among," cf. Vulg. *germinabunt inter herbas*; my translation follows LXX *hōsei chortos ana meson hudatos,* "like grass in the midst of water"; an attractive alternative suggested by an Arabic and Akkadian cognate is to take *bēn* as a species of tree, perhaps the green poplar cf. Gen 49:22 *bēn porāt,* but this requires a further emendation, *ḥāṣîr* to *ḥāṣôr,* and inventing a new species, the Hazor poplar; [i] read *yiqqārē'* Niphal for MT *yiqrā'*; [j] read *bĕyādô* with LXX[B] for MT *yādô;* [k] read *yĕkunneh* Pual with Syr., Tg., Vulg. for MT *yĕkanneh.*

COMMENTS

In Isa 43:22–28 again it is important not to isolate the passage from its context. The transition from the reassurances of vv 14–21 to the reproaches of vv 22–28 appears to be abrupt, but abrupt transitions and alternation between reassurance and commination are not out of character with the author's style. The link with the preceding is that Israel's charge, to proclaim the praise of Yahveh liturgically (21b), has in fact not been carried out. The 1QIsa[a] scribe correctly marked the link between 43:22–28 and 44:1–5 by leaving a much longer empty space after 45:5 than after 43:28. And, in fact, Isa 44:1–5 takes up again the motifs and language of the preceding discourses (43:1–21). The passage returns to the theme of Jacob the servant (43:10), the chosen one (43:10, 20) who is formed by Yahveh (43:21), who is told to put aside fear (43:1, 5), and is given a name full of meaning (43:7). Furthermore, the theme of ecological transformation in 43:14–21 is taken up again in 45:1–5.

As an effective means of raising the issue of theodicy in connection with the need to explain the disasters of the not-so-distant past, the author returns once again to the forensic metaphor (41:1–5, 21–29; 43:8–13) with the difference that now the issue is fought out not with foreign deities and their devotees but with the Judean community (as 50:1–3; cf. Hos 4:1–6; Mic 6:1–5). Though the summons to a hearing (v 26) does not appear at the beginning of the passage, the legal scenario is maintained throughout, together with the appropriate terminology: citing or summoning to trial (*zkr* Hiphil), litigating or arguing the case (*špṭ* Niphal), presenting the evidence (*spr* Piel), and giving a positive verdict (*ṣdq* Qal). The situation seems to be that the Judean community has presented its gravamen to Yahveh, the sense of which can be recovered from the final sentence and stated as follows: "You (Yahveh) polluted, that is, rendered ritually impure, the princes of the sanctuary, you delivered Jacob up to ruin and Israel to reviling—and you did this even though the sacrifices we offered to you were designed precisely to prevent it." This is the case they present in response to the invitation (v 26) and to which 22–28 forms the rebuttal.

The problem is to know what precisely is the nature of the counterargument and against whom it is directed. Those to whom it is addressed, or whom those addressed represent, are told that they have not engaged in liturgical prayer, have neglected the *ʿôlâ* ("burnt offering") and *zebaḥ* ("peace or communion offering") with the suet or fat (*ḥēleb*), and have not purchased the aromatic cane used in the production of sanctuary oil (*qāneh*, Exod 30:23; Jer 6:20). On the other hand, 23b seems to make an exception for the cereal offering (*minḥâ*), which involved the use of oil and frankincense (*lĕbônâ*; Lev 2:1). The gravamen seems to be that the audience has either neglected the sacrificial system *tout court* or has skimped by confining itself to the cheapest type of sacrifice, the *minḥâ*, served with a sprinkling of incense.

The alternative understanding, that they have sacrificed but to other deities and not to Yahveh, is amply supported in the historical and prophetic books up to the time of writing and beyond (Isa 57:6–7; 65:3–4; perhaps 66:3). In every instance, however, the non-Yahvistic nature of the act is explicitly noted, whereas here there is no suggestion that sacrifice has been offered to any deity other than Yahveh. The only remaining possibility seems to be that they did indeed sacrifice but their sacrifices were rendered ineffectual through their sins (e.g. Whybray 1975:91, Westermann 1969, 130–31). Adding plausibility to this option is the play on the verb *ʿbd* (Hiphil) in 23b and 24b: "I did not burden you (also: make you serve liturgically) with the cereal offering"; "you burdened me (also: offered service to me—suffix as indirect object) with your sins"; in other words: you served me up your sins instead of sacrifice; your sins got through to me, but your sacrifices did not. This theme of inauthentic sacrifice is also well attested in prophetic writings (e.g. Isa 1:10–17), shading off at times into a questioning of the practice as such (e.g. Jer 7:21–26; Amos 5:25).

The solution of this difficult crux requires us to ask to whom the reproach is addressed. Those who accept the received wisdom and locate the writer in Babylonia rule out a possible reference to contemporaneous practice there, since there was no temple and therefore no sacrificing. This is more than we know, since we cannot exclude the possibility that, like the Jewish settlers at Elephantine, the Jewish ethnic minority in Babylon built a sanctuary, of however modest proportions, perhaps at "the place Casiphia," where Ezra was able to recruit a significant number of cult personnel (Ezra 8:15–20). The suggestion is certainly plausible since it is difficult to imagine a clergy-training center in Babylonia at that time, unattached to a temple of some kind.

Similar reservations apply to the situation in Judah after the destruction of the Jerusalem temple, since we cannot exclude the possibility of an alternative cult site, perhaps in connection with the administrative center at Mizpah or at nearby Bethel. But the entire drift of the accusation, especially the reference to the ancestors, points to religious practice in the pre-destruction period along the lines of a well-established prophetic critique of the sacrificial system (e.g. 1 Sam 15:22; Hos 6:6; Amos 5:21–24; Mic 6:6–8; Isa 1:10–17; Jer 7:21–26), with special reference to the last decades of Judah's independent existence.

The train of thought connecting 43:22–24, 25 and 26–28 is somewhat confusing, especially the introduction of the challenge to the Judean community to present its case at this point (v 26). The repetition at the beginning of v 25 (*ʾānokî, ʾānokî*) discourages the dismissal of the verse as an ameliorating gloss.

The point is important for the author and has been made more than once (42:8, 12, 21; 43:7). Everything is done for the glory and praise of God; this is the premise and the purpose of Israel's existence (43:21). Since it is so, a way will be found to circumvent Israel's sinful history and attain the goal. This history is traced back to the first of the ancestors. Jacob is *the* ancestor for the author of Isa 40–48, the one whose name the community addressed carries. But we know of no sin committed by Jacob and, contrary to an opinion often expressed, none is mentioned in the fragmentary tradition about Jacob preserved in Hos 12:3–4, 12; it seems, in fact, as if the Hosean author is *contrasting* the reprehensible conduct of his contemporaries with that of Jacob (as argued by Ackroyd).

Elsewhere in Isa 40–55 Abraham is *the* ancestor, and Sarah *the* ancestress (51:2), and the community designated Jacob and Israel is his offspring (41:8). At the time of writing, the Abraham traditions were in the early stages of development and elaboration, Ezek 33:24 being the first reference to Abraham in prophetic texts. It is possible that traditions were already in circulation of the kind familiar from the pseudepigraphal *Apocalypse of Abraham* dealing with Abraham's life before his call to abandon the idolatrous city of Ur. The reference to the redemption of Abraham in Isa 29:22–24 may belong in the same context. However, it is very unlikely that Abraham, "friend of God" (Isa 41:8), would be regarded as the primal sinner. In view of the interesting parallels between this discourse and the one following (44:6–8) on the one hand, and the Song of Moses in Deut 32:1–43 on the other (see below), the author may have had in mind the denunciation of Jacob-Jeshurun who, according to the Song of Moses, "abandoned the God who made him and scoffed at the Rock of his salvation" (Deut 32:15–18).

The transgressive "mediators" (*mĕlîṣîm*) are no easier to identify. The term is used in parallelism with "envoys" (2 Chr 32:31) and "messengers" (Job 33:23), and in one instance the *mālîṣ* is a translator (Gen 42:23). The office therefore involves speaking on behalf of the community (Elliger [1978, 360, 382–84], translates *Wortführer*). This could apply to Moses and Aaron, as argued by J. Fischer (1939, 67), especially since their sin is explicitly mentioned (Num 20:12), or it could refer to prophets in general (Duhm 1922, 329–30) or to kings, judges, or other community leaders (Torrey 1928, 343). The denunciation of Jeshurun-Jacob at Deut 32:15 mentioned a moment ago would, however, draw our attention to the connection between Jeshurun and tribal leaders ("the heads of the people") in the Blessings of Moses following (Deut 33:5). The unusual expression translated "princes of the sanctuary" appears in 1 Chr 24:5 with reference to the leading priests in the Jerusalem temple. This may be the reference here, but the context suggests a broader scope: namely, civic and religious leaders (cf. Lam 2:2, "He profaned the kingdom and its princes").

The discourse continues with the change of focus from the past to the present indicated by the anacrusis *vĕʿattâ* ("and now"): that was then, this is now. Still being addressed is Jacob-Israel, the servant, the chosen one (41:8–9; 42:1, 19; 43:10, 20), Yahveh's creation (cf. 43:7). The claim that Jacob-Israel was formed by Yahveh from the womb does not imply any particular interest on the part of the author in the point at which human life begins (cf. Jer 1:5; Job 10:8–11; 31:15; Ps 139:13–16). Since the train of thought pivots on ancestors and descendants, we should not exclude an allusion to the legend about the prenatal adventures of Jacob and his entry into the world in a manner unique in the history of obstetrics (Gen 25:22–23).

The name "Jeshurun" appears in the Song and Blessings of Moses (Deut 32:15; 33:5, 26) and elsewhere only in some manuscripts of Sir 37:25. It is a formation like "Zebulun," and there is no evidence that it is a diminutive. A connection with the lexeme *yšr* (cf. Num 23:10, where Israelites are said to be *yĕšārîm*, "upright ones") is probable; a connection with the name "Israel" less so. The LXX paraphrase *ho ēgapēmenos*, "beloved," points to a hypocorism, perhaps similar to "Meshullam" (see the Note on 42:19).

As is so often the case in chs. 40–55 (40:9; 41:10, 13, 14; 43:1, 5; 44:2; 51:7; 54:4), the reassurance is encapsulated in the injunction to put aside fear (*ʾal-tîrāʾ*, "don't be afraid"). At this point what is feared is national extinction, and the fear is allayed by the assurance of descendants expressed in the metaphoric language of the fertility of the soil. The water image—water poured out, running water, living water (not rain and showers as in NEB 44:3)—aligns with the spirit (*rûah*) as the source of physical and psychic life (cf. 42:5) and serves as a powerful and polyvalent symbol throughout the book of Isaiah. That it is paired with blessing (*bĕrākâ*) inevitably brings to mind the demographic blessing pronounced over Abraham and repeated with Isaac and Jacob (Gen 12:1–3 etc.).

The Abrahamic blessing runs like a strong undercurrent throughout this entire second part of the book. If Israel had obeyed, their descendants would have been like the sand of the seashore (48:18–19 cf. Gen 22:17; 32:17); Abraham and Sarah were blessed and made many (51:2); the people will be all righteous, like Abraham, and will inherit the land as a mighty nation (60:21–22 cf. Gen 12:2; 15:6); their descendants will be known among the nations as a people blessed by Yahveh (61:9). The theme, to which the actual demographic situation in the Jewish ethnos from the Neo-Babylonian into the Achaemenid period corresponds, does not imply that the narrative traditions about Abraham were already in place. All things considered, it seems more likely that the stories in Gen 12–25 were constructed as paradigms illustrative of situations, fears, and hopes for the future, of the kind to which these chapters attest.

The four types illustrative of the future people of Israel with which the passage concludes can only be understood as proselytes, elsewhere *gērîm* ("aliens," Isa 14:1) or *bĕnê-hannēkār* ("foreigners," Isa 56:3, 6) who have "joined themselves" to Yahveh (Isa 56:3, 6; Jer 50:5; Zech 2:15[11]). The Targum identifies the first category, those who affirm their allegiance to Israel's God, explicitly as God-fearers. The second and fourth categories take the name "Jacob" or add the name "Israel" as an adoptive name and a title of honor displaying their religious allegiance. (This I take to be the meaning of the verbal stem *knh* cf. 45:4, often anachronistically translated "to surname.")

Belonging to the third category are those who inscribe "property of Yahveh" on their hands. The reference is to a tattoo or brand of some kind on the hand or forehead (Ezek 9:4; cf. Rev 7:3; 13:16), indicating ownership in the case of slaves, or group identity (cf. the much-discussed stamp impressions on jar handles: *lammelek*, "property of the king"). In the present instance usage may be metaphorical rather than realistic. The enormous demographic expansion of the Jewish people between the Neo-Babylonian and Roman periods can be explained only by a substantial influx of proselytes beginning at the time when these chapters went into circulation. This transition from ascribed to voluntary association that begins to register in writings from the post-destruction period is an issue of incalculable significance for the future. As we work our way through the remainder of the book, we shall see how it also becomes a focus of dispute and division, as in fact it has remained down to the present.

ISRAEL CALLED TO WITNESS TO YAHVEH AS THE ONE GOD (44:6–8, 21–23)

(G. R. Driver 1958; Merendino 1981, 372–80, 390–94; Ringgren 1977b; Ruppert 1991; Schoors 1964; Seybold 1997)

TRANSLATION

i

44 [6]These are the words of Yahveh, Israel's King, Yahveh of the heavenly hosts,[a] Israel's Redeemer:
"I am the First and I am the Last;
there is no god but me.
[7]Who is like me? Let him speak up,[b] let him state his case,
let him set it out for me.[c]
Who has announced from time past what is to be?[d]
Let them declare for us[e] the things to come.[f]
[8]Do not be perplexed, do not be afraid.[g]
Did I not announce this to you long ago?
I declared it, and you are my witnesses.
Is there any god but me? Or is there any Rock?[h]
I know of none."
. . . . . .

ii

[21]Remember these things, Jacob,
Israel, for you are my servant.
I formed you, you are my servant;
Israel, you are not forgotten by me.[i]
[22]I have swept away your transgressions like clouds,

your sins like mist.
Turn to me, for I have redeemed you."

iii

[23]Exult, you sky, for it is Yahveh's doing;
shout aloud, you depths of the earth.
Break into song, you mountains,
forests with all your trees,
for Yahveh has redeemed Jacob;
in Israel his glory is manifest.

NOTES

[a] 1QIsaiah[a] adds *šĕmô*, "Yahveh of the heavenly hosts is his name," cf. 47:4; 48:2; 51:15; 54:5; [b] LXX *stētō, kalesatō kai hetoimasatō moi*, "Let him take his stand, let him call out and make ready for me," cf. Syr. *nqvm*, presupposing *yaʿămod vĕyiqrāʾ*, but MT need not be altered; [c] 1QIsa[a] has *lōʾ*, "for himself"; [d] MT *miśśûmî ʿam-ʿôlām vĕʾotiyyôt* can be taken to read, "Since I established an ancient people and future events" cf. the philosophical line taken by LXX *aph'ou epoiēsa anthrōpon eis ton aiōna*, "since I made humanity for eternity," and Vulg. *ex quo constitui populum antiquum*, "from which I established an ancient people"; similarly Tg. and KJV ("since I appointed the ancient people"); but MT is almost certainly corrupt, and the translation offered assumes a different word division: *mî hišmîaʿ mēʿôlām ʾotiyyôt*, as in BHS and see Elliger 1978, 396–97; [e] read *lānû* for MT *lāmô*, with Tg.; [f] 1QIsa[a] reads *yvʾmr ʾšr tbvʾynh*, "let him say what is to come," for MT and 4QIsa[c] *vaʾăšer tāboʾnāh;* [g] read *tîraʾû* with 1QIsa[a]; since the verbal stem *rhh* is unattested, MT appears to be a misspelling; [h] read either *vĕʾim* or, less likely, *vĕʾîn*, Aram. interrogative particle (G. R. Driver 1958, 47); [i] MT *tinnāšēnî* (> verbal stem *nšh*) is an exceptional but not impossible Niphal (passive) with attached accusative suffix (cf. Ps 109:3 and GKC §57); it should be preferred, as the more difficult reading, to the active "do not forget me" of 1QIsa[a] (*tšʾny*) and LXX (*mē epilanthanou mou*).

COMMENTS

Isaiah 44:6–8 together with 44:21–23 forms a distinct and brief discourse with its own superscription in conventional prophetic form, a regular usage throughout chs. 40–55 (42:5; 43:1, 14, 16; 44:2, 6, 24; 45:1, 11, 14, 18; 48:17; 49:7, 8, 22; 50:1; 51:22; 52:3), less so in the following chapters (56:1, 4, 8; 65:8, 13; 66:1, 12). The point of the superscription is to locate these discourses within the old prophetic tradition even though they are of a quite different nature. The interpolated polemic against idolatry (vv 9–20) has cut off the conclusion of the discourse, an opinion generally accepted since Duhm (e.g. Westermann, Whybray). The call to remember (21) connects not with the polemic but with the things announced to Israel long ago (8), whereas the interpolation could easily have been suggested by the preceding declaration of Yahveh's unique divine status. Furthermore, the brief hymn that calls on creation to rejoice on account of the anticipated redemption of Jacob/Israel (23) forms an inclusio with the beginning of the passage (6). The passage itself is thematically and structurally well integrated into the context, since its conclusion echoes the apostrophe with which the preceding discourse opens (44:1).

The superscription (v 6a) announces the speaker, Yahveh, in the threefold role of king, redeemer and lord of the heavenly hosts. Yahveh has already been presented as king of Jacob (41:21) and creator and king of Israel (43:15), and the proclamation of his rule as king will be made in solemn fashion at a later point (52:7). This theologoumenon of divine kingship, common in the ancient Near East and problematic for many in the modern world, also appears in chs. 1–39, conspicuously in the throne vision report (6:5; also 24:23; 33:22). The common opinion that it draws on the old Jerusalemite liturgy is supported by its frequent use in psalms, especially the psalms that speak explicitly of divine kingship (Pss 29, 47, 95, 98, 99). A closer study of these and other psalmic compositions than is possible here would bring out the degree to which the author of these chapters has drawn on themes richly developed in the temple liturgy. We might mention the affirmation of Yahveh's incomparability ("Who is like thee among the gods?" Exod 15:11) and the association of kingship with the divine glory or effulgence (*melek hakkābôd*, "The King of Glory," Ps 24:8, 10 cf. Isa 40:5; 42:8, 12; 43:7; 48:11).

These traditional themes are given a new relevance in chs. 40–55 as a result of the need to counter the powerful attraction and prestige of the Marduk divine kingship cult. We shall see how the author creates a mirror image of the cult in which the god's defeat of the forces of Chaos is celebrated, following the proclamation of his eternal kingship ("Marduk is king!" *Enuma Elish* IV 28; *ANET* 66).

Neither the identification of Yahveh as redeemer (*gō'ēl*) nor his redemptive activity are concerns in Isa 1–39, but both appears frequently in chs. 40–55 (the substantive ten times, the verb eight times). The sociological root idea involving obligations arising out of kinship relations (e.g. Lev 25:47–54) is carried over into the theological sphere. As close kin, therefore, Yahveh buys back his people out of indentured service. While the language of redemption had acquired a broader and more general scope by the time of writing, the redemption from Egypt (Exod 6:6; 15:13; Ps 74:2) was still the paradigm instance of what God does when he acts on behalf of his people (e.g. Isa 51:10), and it achieved a new relevance with the theme of return from exile (Isa 48:20; 51:10; 52:3).

By virtue of its association with the ark and the temple, the third designation, Yahveh of the (heavenly) hosts (44:6; 45:13; 47:4; 48:2; 51:15; 54:5), is also rooted in the Jerusalemite liturgy and, as the story of the Philistine wars makes clear, is associated with old ideas of divine kingship and of Yahveh as warrior god.

The address is cast in the by-now-familiar form of a disputation or legal contest, though of the rather one-sided kind that we have already observed. The point at issue has also been broached more than once (41:1–5, 21–29; 43:8–13). That the God of Israel is the first and the last (cf. 41:4; 48:12) implies universal jurisdiction and control of history over the entire course of time, beginning with creation (see especially 48:12) and on into the distant future. This control is expressed and put into effect through prophetic utterances over a long period of time that bind together past and future in terms of prediction and fulfillment. Precisely as in the History, prophecy is the way in which the continuum of history acquires meaning. Prophecy *creates* the future (here the terms are *ʾôtiyyôt*, *ʾăšer tābōnāh*) and therefore is, for the author, the wellspring of hope; hence, the numbing effect of unfulfilled prophecy to be experienced by Jewish communities in the generation following the fall of Babylon.

What might be called Yahveh's legal brief includes an affirmation of monotheism similar to, and perhaps in response to, the "I am, and there is no one but me" spoken by a personified Babylon, no doubt representing the imperial deity, Marduk (47:10). The devotees of other gods are challenged to satisfy the criterion laid down here—that is, successful prediction of the outcome of current events. Successful prediction of the future indicates control of historical events and therefore the reality and power of the god in whose name the prophet speaks. Indicative of this is the frequency in this short passage of terms denoting declarative speech: *qārāʾ* ("speak up"), *higgîd* ("declare," three times), *ʿārak* ("state one's case"), *hišmîaʿ* ("announce," twice).

The Judean community is invited once again (cf. 43:10, 12) to serve—that is, to fulfill the servant role (v 21) as witnesses to the veracity of Yahveh's claim. That their witnessing is not confined to present situations and events may be deduced from the admonition to "remember these things" (21), referring to things told to them in former times (v 8 cf. 40:21; 41:4, 26). We take this to be a call to reestablish lively contact with their own traditions in this post-disaster situation, including the historical traditions, constructed as they are on the prophetic pattern of prediction and fulfillment.

Following the brief, the preacher uses again the language of the prophetic salvation oracles. The call to put aside fear, heard often in these chapters (40:9; 41:10, 13, 14; 43:1, 5; 44:2), entails trusting in the efficacy of the word they are hearing or reading. The sobriquet Rock (*ṣûr*), or "Rock of ages" of the old hymn (cf. Isa 26:4), possibly a quite ancient usage (cf. Deut 32:4), appears often in psalms in which trust in God is called for in unpromising circumstances (e.g. Pss 18:3[2], 47[46]; 19:15[14]; 28:1; 31:1; and 73:26, where Yahveh is "the rock of my heart," unemended text). With this comes the assurance that the people are not forgotten (God's forgetfulness is a frequent complaint in the psalms of lamentation) and the pledge of the forgiveness of sins with which the preaching of the prophet opened (44:22 cf. 40:2).

Concluding an address to the Judean community with an invocation addressed to the sky, the underearth, mountains and forests, representing the entire three-decker cosmos, is a characteristic feature of this section of the book

(42:10–13; 45:8; 49:13; 52:9–10). It has been taken to indicate later liturgical adaptation of the discourses, but these hymn-like fragments are well integrated into their contexts and are therefore better understood as a rhetorical device drawing on familiar hymnology.

POLEMIC AGAINST CULT IMAGES (44:9–20)

(Blau 1995; Curtis 1994; Dick 1999; Gelston 1971; Hayutin 1991–1992; Hutter 1992; Matheus 1987; North 1958; von Rad 1972; Soares-Prabhu 1995; Thomas 1971)

TRANSLATION

i

44 [9]Those who make[a] idols are all as nothing,[b]
the objects they cherish serve no purpose;
their devotees are without discernment,[c]
they know nothing and so are put to shame.
[10]Who would make a god or cast an idol
that serves no purpose?
[11]See, all his associates[d] are put to shame,
the craftsmen are but mortal.
Let them all assemble, let them take their stand;
they will be afraid,[e] they will be utterly shamed.

ii

[12]The ironsmith fashions it with an adze,[f] working it over the charcoal, shaping it with hammers, forging it with his strong arm. But he also gets hungry and his strength fails; when he has not drunk water,[g] he is exhausted. [13]Having stretched the line taut, the carpenter outlines the object with a chalk.[h] He planes the wood[i] and picks out the shape with callipers.[j] Then he fashions it in the form of a man, with the beauty of the human form, to reside in a shrine. [14]He chooses a plane tree or an oak and lets it grow strong among the trees of the forest. Or he plants a cedar and the rain makes it grow, so that eventually he will have trees to cut down.[k] [15]Then it can serve someone as fuel. He can take some of it and warm himself. He can light a fire, bake bread, and satisfy his hunger. But he can also make a god of it and worship it; he can make an idol and prostrate himself before it. [16]Half of it he burns in the fire. On this half he can then roast meat, so that he can eat and satisfy his hunger.[l] He can also warm himself, saying, "All right! I'm getting warm in front of the fire."[m] [17]Then what is left of it he fashions into a god[n] to serve as his idol. He prostrates himself before it and worships it; he prays to it and says, "Save me, since you are my god!"

iii

[18]They have no knowledge or understanding,
for Yahveh[o] has shut their eyes so that they cannot see,

their minds, so that they cannot understand.
[19]No one takes it to heart;
there is neither knowledge nor understanding to think,
"Half of it I burned in the fire.
I also baked bread on its coals.
I roasted meat and ate it,[o]
and what is left[p] I am going to make into an abominable thing;
I am going to prostrate myself before a block[q] of wood!"
[20]Such a one rides herd on ashes,
a deluded mind has led him astray;
he cannot save himself,[r]
he cannot bring himself to say,
"Is not this object in my right hand a sham?"[s]

NOTES

[a] 1QIsaiah[a] has sing.; [b] MT *tōhû* can refer to people cf. 40:23; [c] MT reads "and their witnesses, they do not see"; BHS proposes *ʿādêhem* for MT *ʿēdêhem* on the basis of Arab. *ʿāda*, "to frequent," while others emend to *ʿabdêhem*, "their worshipers"; but foreign deities no less than Yahveh can have their witnesses (cf.43:10, 12; 44:8); [d] MT *ḥăbērâv*, "his associates," referring to the one who would make a god or cast an idol; Duhm's version, "all his incantations will be shamed and the spells are of human origin" (1922, 333) is ingenious but does not make a good fit with the context; [e] 1QIsa[a] adds the conjunction, "then they will be afraid"; [f] MT reads, literally, "the ironsmith an adze"; LXX *hoti ōchsunen tektōn sidēron*, "for the craftsman sharpens iron," has suggested emending *ḥāraš* to *yāḥēd*, "he sharpens," but unfortunately the nature of the tool, *maʿaṣād*, only here and in Jer 10:3 in a similar context, is unclear, as are the details of the technology in general; [g] 1QIsa[a] has *švth*, present participle for MT *lo'-šātāh*, "he did not drink"; [h] *śered* is hapax and the precise meaning uncertain; [i] literally, "he does it with planes," but *maqṣûʿâ* is hapax and the meaning "a plane" uncertain; [j] *mĕḥûgâ* is also hapax; LXX reads quite differently; [k] The translation offered is an attempt to make sense of a very obscure verse; MT reads "to cut down cedars for himself; and he takes a plane tree (? *tirzâ* hapax) and an oak, and he lets it grow strong for himself/itself among the trees of the forest; he plants a fir tree (*'orez*, 1QIsa[a] has *'rn*), and the rain makes it grow"; [l] guided in part by LXX and Syr.; MT reads "on its half he eats meat, roasts a roast and satisfies his hunger"; 1QIsa[a] adds "by its coals he sits and warms himself"; [m] reading *neged*, "in front of"; MT reads *hammôtî rā'ītî 'ûr*, "I'm getting warm, I see (the) fire"; [n] after "he fashions into a god," 1QIsa[a] adds "to blocks of wood he prostrates himself," misspelling "blocks" (*blvy*) here and in v 19, perhaps deliberately, to suggest "Baals"; [o] "Yahveh" supplied; this meaning is strongly suggested by the verb in the sing. (*ṭaḥ* hapax) following verbs in the pl.; [p] 4QIsa[b] is without

the conjunction; [q] 1QIsa[a] has pl., as in v 17; [r] preferable to "it cannot save him" (*napšô*, literally, "his life") in view of the following phrase; 1QIsa[a] "it cannot his life" is missing a word; 4QIsa[b], which has preserved most of v 20, is identical with MT; [s] 1QIsa[a] omits the interrogative *hălô'*, but 4QIsa[b] is identical with MT.

COMMENTS

Polemic against the cultic use of images is characteristic of Isa 40–48 and not at all of other sections of the book. It is not prominent in chs. 1–39, and most of the occurrences are acknowledged to belong to late editorial strata. The vocabulary is also significantly different. Practically all of the terms used for cult images are pejorative (with the exception of chs. 36–39, where both the Rabshakeh and Hezekiah speak of *'elohîm*, "gods": 36:18–20; 37:12, 18–19). The standard term in chs. 1–35 is *'ĕlîl*, connoting weakness and futility (2:8, 18, 20; 10:10–11; 19:1, 3; 31:7), which is displaced in 40–48 by *pesel* (40:19–20; 42:17; 44:9, 10, 15, 17; 45:20; 48:5) or *pĕsîl* (42:8), from a verbal stem meaning "to carve" (e.g. Exod 34:1, 4); less commonly *'āṣāb* (or *'ōṣeb*) cf. the verb *'ṣb*, "to form," but allowing for a *double entendre* with a verbal stem meaning "to cause pain or grievance" (46:1; 48:5). The satirical concentration on the manufacture of cult images, as in the present passage, is also confined to this section of the book.

There seems to be broad but not universal agreement that this passage and some but not all of the others on the same subject in this part of the book (40:19–20; 41:6–7; 42:17; 45:16–17, 20; 46:1–7; 48:5) have been interpolated and perhaps derive from one and the same source. Certainly the addition of vv 9–11 could have been suggested by the denial of the existence of gods other than Yahveh immediately preceding (8b), and we have seen that vv 21–22 form the natural sequel to 6–8. The passage also differs from other disputations about the nature of deity in these chapters in that Yahveh is not mentioned, and claims are not made on his behalf. Other arguments for a later hand, deriving from inadequacies of style and substance, may be justified, but not all agree that the writing is clumsy and unsubtle. Torrey, for example, thought that it was spirited and picturesque and as metrically regular as any other passage in Second Isaiah (Torrey 1928, 345).

In any case, differences of style do not necessarily imply different authors. But the passage is almost certainly interpolated, notwithstanding. The core, vv 12–17, clearly in prose, is sandwiched between what could be interpreted as two parts of one poem, though prosodically not entirely regular. Both parts speak of lack of knowledge and discernment on the part of the devotees of cult images. While this hardly justifies deriving this kind of discourse from a "wisdom source" (as proposed by von Rad), it suggests that the prose satire has been spliced into the poem, in effect an interpolation within an interpolation. In that case, the satire could be read as expanding on the words attributed to the image-worshiper in v 19.

The verse section begins by denouncing those who make images and offer cult to them. They are *tōhû*, the word for the primordial chaos in Gen 1:2, somewhere between nonexistence and existence; they are ignorant and stupid. This was the familiar approach in polemic against the cult of images and remained so into the Greco-Roman period (e.g. Wisdom of Solomon 13, perhaps drawing on this passage in Isaiah) and no doubt beyond. We find the same kind of language elsewhere in the prophetic books: worshipers of images are involved in something false (*šeqer* Jer 51:17; Hab 2:18), futile (*hebel* Jer 10:3; 51:18) and lifeless (*ʾên rûaḥ bô* Jer 51:17; Hab 2:19).

It should be said at once that this reads like a willful misunderstanding of the function of the image in cults throughout the ancient and, for that matter, the modern world. The dictionary definition of idolatry as "the worship of a physical object as a god" very clearly implies that the term is prejudicial and that it entails a subjective and, more often than not, false judgment on certain religious expressions. An image can focus the energy and concentrate the attention of a group engaged in common worship. It can give concrete expression to the sense of the real presence of the divinity. That the sense of divine presence fills a powerful and understandable human need can be seen in the incident of the Golden Calf (Exod 32–34). Like any other expression of religious sentiment or conviction, an image is subject to abuse and can degenerate into superstition, but a religion that claims to dispense with such assurances of divine presence expressed by physical symbols can also end up being heartless, cruel, and monomaniacally fanatical. Throughout Christian history, at any rate, the prohibition of images—as in eighth- and ninth-century Byzantium—has had very limited success. Taken individually and out of context, such acts (familiar in the Neo-Babylonian homeland) as making an image, clothing and feeding it, and giving it life by the ceremony of "washing the mouth," seem pointless and futile. To those involved, however, they make sense in a ritual context that gives expression to and draws the worshiper into a world of symbolic meanings.

Whatever its origins and intent, the prohibition of making and offering cult to images is a key feature of what we may call Deuteronomic orthodoxy and orthopraxy and, as such, is enshrined in the Decalogue (Exod 20:4–6 = Deut 5:8–10; also Exod 34:17; Deut 4:15– 18; 27:15; Lev 19:4; 26:1). The prohibition of the use of the divine name in certain circumstances (Exod 20:7 = Deut 5:11) provides an instructive analogy, since to invoke the name of a deity is to constrain the deity to be present, an idea still residually present when we use the phrase "speak of the devil and he will appear." The intent of the legislation was to resist the idea that the God of Israel could be constrained to be present and available whenever and wherever his image was set up or his name invoked.

Viewed from a more concretely political angle, however, the prohibition fits the intent of Deuteronomy, understood as at least theoretically a state document, of promoting the state religion and combating the religious practices that underpinned and validated the kinship network. Needless to say, attempts to impose orthodox ideas and practices are not invariably successful. Cult images were not so easily disposed of, and in spite of successive attempts to get rid of them continued to feature even in the official cult, prominent among which was a three-dimensional representation of the Canaanite-Hebrew goddess Asherah (1 Kgs 15:13; 2 Kgs 21:7; 23:4; Ezek 8:3).

The first verse section (44:9–11) has something of the disputatious character noted in previous passages, including a rhetorical question (v 10) and the call to assemble (11b). The first verse of the second part (18) is often demoted to a gloss on account of the plural verbs followed in the next verse by the singular, but if it is the continuation of vv 9–11 this conclusion would not necessarily follow. The denunciation of the manufacturer and worshiper of the image as ignorant and intellectually obtuse continues. The idea, often stated in this kind of polemic, is that the worshipers become like the lifeless images. They have mouths but do not speak, eyes but do not see, ears but do not hear, noses but do not smell, hands but do not feel, feet but do not walk, and no sound comes from their throats. Then (the point of all these negatives) those who make them are like them (Ps 115:5–8). In a word, the image-worshiper is caught up in a world of unreality and delusion, aptly expressed in the metaphor of herding ashes, comparable to "herding the wind" (Hos 12:2[1]).

The prose passage (vv 12–17) takes off from the words in the poem put into the mouth of the manufacturer and worshiper of the image (19). The description of the making of a wooden image allowed for a more protracted satire than the metal image. We are, so to speak, taken on a guided tour of an idol factory. The satirist could dwell on the entire process, starting with the planting of a tree, ignoring the time that must pass before it could be harvested, and ending with the wood serving as fuel for heating and cooking and, finally, making a god. The last, as Christopher North put it (1964, 139), was "a casual sequel to the drudgery of house-warming and cooking."

The brief account of the manufacturing process, containing four hapax legomena and four other terms used only once or twice elsewhere, leaves many details obscure. The principal technicians are the ironsmith (*ḥārāš barzel*) and the carpenter (*ḥārāš ʿēṣîm*); we have already met the goldsmith (*ṣōrēp* 40:19; 41:7) who overlays (*rqʿ*) the image with gold plate (40:19). In the present passage the carpenter is involved in making an anthropomorphic image. The addition of the phrase "with the beauty of the human form" is strange enough to justify the view reported (but not accepted) by Ibn Ezra that the reference is to a female figure, of the kind abundantly exemplified in the archaeological record.

There is a note of possibly unconscious pathos in the way that the whole laborious process ends with a genuine prayer but one that will not be answered: "Save me, since you are my god!" Saving is what a god is supposed to do, as the Rabshakeh reminded the besieged Jerusalemites in a brief speech in which the verb "to save" (*haṣṣîl*) appears eight times and which ends by asking how Yahveh can save Jerusalem from the Assyrian army (Isa 36:14–20).

CYRUS MY ANOINTED (44:24–45:8)

(Broyles 1997; DeRoche 1992; Dion 1967; Fokkelman 1997; H. Haag 1972; Haller 1923; Jenni 1954; Kittel 1898; Koch 1972; Ogden 1978; Sawyer 1989a; Simcox 1937; M. Smith 1963; S. Smith 1944, 72–73, 161–64; Southwood 1975)

TRANSLATION

i

44 [24]These are the words of Yahveh your Redeemer,
he who formed you from the womb:
"I am Yahveh, who made all things.
I alone stretched out the sky,
spread out the earth when none was with me."[a]
[25]He frustrates the omens of liars,[b]
and makes fools of diviners;
he turns sages back to front,
reducing their knowledge to folly.[c]
[26]He confirms the word of his servant,[d]
fulfills the counsel of his messengers;
of Jerusalem he says, "She will be inhabited,"[e]
of the cities of Judah, "They will be rebuilt;
I shall restore her ruins."
[27]He says to the Deep,[f] "Be dry:
I shall make your streams run dry."
[28]Of Cyrus he says, "He is my shepherd;[g]
he will fulfill all my purpose
[saying about Jerusalem, it will be rebuilt,
the temple's foundations will be laid].[h]

ii

45 [1]This is what Yahveh says about his anointed one,[i] about Cyrus:
"I have grasped him by his right hand,
to beat down[j] nations before him,
depriving kings of their strength,
to open doors[k] before him;
no gates will be closed to him."
[2]"I myself will go before you,
leveling[l] all the mountains;[m]
I will shatter the doors of bronze,
cut through the iron bars;
[3]I will hand you treasures concealed in the dark,
treasures hoarded away,
so that you may acknowledge

that I, Yahveh, have called you by name,
I, Israel's God.
4For the sake of Jacob my servant,
Israel my chosen one,
I summon you by your name,
I give you a title of honor,[n]
though you have not known me.
5I am Yahveh, there is no other;
beside me there are no gods;
I gird you with strength,
though you have not known me,
6so that all may acknowledge,
from the rising of the sun to its setting,[o]
there is none apart from me.
I am Yahveh; there is no other.
7I form light and create darkness,
I bring about well-being[p] and create woe;
it is I, Yahveh, who do all these things."

iii

8Sky, drop down dew[q] from above,
clouds, rain down vindication![r]
Let the earth open[s] and salvation blossom;[t]
let victory[r] spring forth[u] with it.
I, Yahveh, have created it.

NOTES

[a] With Q *mēʾittî*; K, 1QIsa[a], and LXX read it as interrogative: *mî ʾittî*, "who was with me?"; LXX runs the interrogative on into the following verse: *tis heteros . . .* ; [b] *baddîm* cf. Aram. and Syr. verb *bdʾ*, "lie, boast," here and elsewhere alluding pejoratively to some form of divination cf. Jer 50:36 also in a Babylonian context; Duhm's emendation (1922, 338) to *bārîm* cf. Akk. *bārû* = *Mantiker*, "ecstatics," is unnecessary; [c] 1QIsa[a] has *yskl* for MT *yśkl;* [d] MT *ʿabdô*, supported by 1QIsa[a] and 1QIsa[b], should not be emended to pl. with Tg. and LXX (*paidōn*) for the sake of parallelism with "messengers"; the context, referring to the servant formed from the womb (cf. 44:2; 49:5), favors the sing.; [e] MT *tûšāb* Hophal is unusual; with BHS read *tivvāšēb* Niphal (passive); 1QIsa[a] reads *tēšēb* Qal, therefore, "saying *to* Jerusalem, 'you shall dwell . . .' "; [f] *ṣûlâ* is hapax but cf. *mĕṣûlâ/mĕṣôlâ* with the same meaning; Tg. reads "Babylon"; [g] MT and 1QIsa[a] could be read as *rēʿî*, "my friend," but "shepherd" as a metaphor for ruler is well known and supported by Vulg. (*pastor meus es*); LXX has *ho legōn kurō phronein*, "who tells Cyrus to be wise"; Tg. goes even further afield; [h] the initial *vĕlēʾmor* is difficult and variously

rendered in the ancient versions, but MT is supported by 1QIsa[a] and 1QIsa[b]; both LXX and Vulg. change to 2d person: "you will be built"; in 1QIsa[a] a scribe has added a superscript *yod* to change the verb *tvsd* ("will be laid") from fem. to masc. since the noun governed, *hêkāl,* is elsewhere masc.; however, v 28b is probably an addition, repeating 26b in order to include a prediction of the rebuilding of the temple; [i] this opening line has undergone much unnecessary invasive surgery from the commentators, including *limšîḥô* ("his anointed") to *limšîḥî* ("my anointed") cf. LXX *tō christō mou*, Vulg. *christo meo*, and the omission of Cyrus on theological (Smart 1965, 120) or prosodic grounds (Torrey 1928, 357); if MT is preserved, the divine *oratio recta* begins, "I have grasped him by the right hand," with the relative pronoun *ʾăšer* either serving as punctuation (colon) or, in view of metrical regularity, elided; [j] for MT *lĕrad* read *lārod* Infinitive Construct > *rdd*, only here and Ps 144:2; [k] 1QIsa[a] has pl. *dltvt* for MT dual; [l] read K *ʾăyaššēr* as at 45:13 for Q *ʾăvaššēr;* [m] read 1QIsa[a] *hrrym*, "mountains" (cf. 1QIsa[b] *hrvrym*) for MT *hădûrîm* hapax, perhaps daleth-resh confusion; [n] for this meaning of *knh* Piel, see 44:5; [o] reading *ûmimmaʿărābāh* with mappiq, fem. suffix agreeing with *šemeš*, "sun"; [p] *šālôm;* 1QIsa[a] has *ṭôb*, "good"; [q] MT *harʿîpû* > *rʿp* Hiphil = "trickle, drip," is taken to imply dew cf. Prov 3:20 and Vulg. *rorate coeli desuper;* 1QIsa[a] has *hryʿv*, "shout aloud"; [r] for these meanings of *ṣedeq* and *ṣĕdāqâ* see, respectively, 41:10; 42:21 and 1:27; 59:16; [s] since the verb *ptḥ*, "open," is transitive, read *tippātaḥ* Niphal for MT *tiptaḥ* Qal; [t] MT *vĕyipĕrû* pl. with a sing. substantive is impossible; the translation given follows 1QIsa[a] *vyprḥ* > *prḥ*, "blossom"; [u] reading *tiṣmaḥ* Qal for MT *taṣmîaḥ* Hiphil.

COMMENTS

We have now arrived at the central discourse of chps. 40–48. It is made up of two distinct but connected sayings, the first (44:24–28) addressed internally to a Judean audience; the second (45:1–7), after an appropriate introduction, directly to Cyrus imagined as being present; and both rounded off, as is customary in these chapters, with a brief hymn (cf. 44:23). The two parts are linked by the repetition of the name "Cyrus." The link will be especially close if, as suggested, 44:28b is a scribal addition. The two parts are, finally, clamped together by the inclusion of 44:24 and 45:7: Yahveh who made all things, Yahveh who has done all these things.

But continuity is important here as elsewhere. So, for example, this section begins as the previous one ends with an allusion to Yahveh as Israel's redeemer (vindicator) and Yahveh's redemptive activity, a theme that binds the entire section, chs. 40–55, together and often features in the superscriptions or lead-ins to discourses (43:14; 44:6; 48:17; 49:7; 54:8). Other indications of unity of conception, theme and style, appear in the opening statement. One of these is the concern to give world-creator attributes to the national deity, as the one who laid out the sky and the earth (cf. 40:12, 22; 42:5; 45:12, 18), which is meant to provide a sure basis for accepting a powerful redemptive role in history.

Another indication of an integrative concept behind chs. 40–48 is the way that the audience is addressed. The addressee, real or implied, is formed by Yahveh (verbal stem *yṣr* cf. 43:1, 7, 21; 44:21; 45:11), even formed from the womb. As Jeremiah's call narrative shows (Jer 1:5), this is the language of prophetic designation. In fact, where this language occurs elsewhere in these chapters, it refers to the servant (*ʿebed* 44:2; 49:5), and whatever else is obscure about this language of servanthood, it quite certainly denotes the prophetic office.

The first discourse, then, opens, in characteristic fashion for the author (cf. 42:5), with the self-presentation of Yahveh as redeemer (i.e. vindicator) of Israel and cosmic deity (44:24). This type of self-praise attributed to a deity, odd as it may seem to us, was common in antiquity and reached mature development in the aretalogies of the Greco-Roman period—for example, the aretalogy declaimed by the goddess Isis, which some scholars find reflected in the self-praise of wisdom (*ḥokmâ/sophia*) in Sir 24:1–22.

This first section consists essentially in a contrast between standard Babylonian means of mediation and native Israelite prophecy. The insistence that divination and "secular" wisdom differentiate Israel from other nations is a Deuteronomic topos (Deut 18:9–22), one that ignores the fact that specialists in divination (*qōsĕmîm*) and similar techniques were closely associated with prophets in Israel as elsewhere (Jer 14:14; 27:9; 29:8; Mic 3:6–7). Furthermore, far from being exclusively foreign, they served on the Judean palace staff (Isa 3:2; Mic 3:11).

Consulting omens was a basic feature of Babylonian religious life at all times, and it was inevitable that the author would polemicize against such practices (see also 47:8–13). A broad range of techniques is attested in the considerable corpus of surviving texts, including interpretating dreams (oneiromancy), consulting the livers or viscera of sacrificial animals (hepatoscopy, extispicy), and observing patterns made by oil poured on water (lecanomancy). Since the issue for the author is the ability to tell the future, astrology (highly developed by Babylonian savants) would have had special importance (cf. 47:13b), and it will be recalled that Shamash, the sun god, was the patron of these practitioners. The point is that the predicted failure of Babylon to survive the current political crisis and the failure of its religious specialists to predict the course of events revealed the basic impotence of its religious and intellectual traditions.

The polemical issue is laid out clearly. On the one hand Yahveh renders inoperative (*mēpēr*) the Babylonian mechanisms for predicting and therefore controlling the course of events, and on the other he validates (*mēqîm*) the utterances of Judean prophets. We have seen that this is the major *leitmotif* throughout these chapters (41:1–5, 21–29; 42:9; 43:8–13; 44:6–8). The wording, *mēqîm dĕbar ʿabdô* ("he confirms the word of his servant"), leaves no doubt that the reference is to prophetic speech and, since there is no justification for emending *ʿabdô* to *ʿăbādâyv* (plural), the utterance is that of an individual prophet set alongside a plurality of messengers and envoys, just as in 43:10 the *ʿebed* is juxtaposed with witnesses (*ʿēdîm*).

The term used to designate these prophetic messengers (*malʾāk*) appears elsewhere as a synonym for *nābîʾ*, "prophet" (Hag 1:13; Zech 2:2; Mal 3:1). While the ambivalence in the use of the term *ʿebed* is much in evidence in these chapters, I believe it is possible to trace a gradual resolution in the direction of a purely prophetic profile, with the result that the voice of this prophetic servant, whom Ibn Ezra identified not unreasonably with the author of these chapters, will be heard more frequently and insistently in the next major section of the book (chs. 49–55). At the same time, the presence of prophetic associates or disciples will come more clearly into view.

The word of his servant and the counsel of his messengers—that is, Yahveh's counsel (*ʿēṣâ*) communicated by his messengers—is expressed telegrammatically in four prophetic statements that encapsulate the essence of the author's message.

1. *Jerusalem Will Be Repopulated*

It is worth noting that the destiny of Jerusalem, rather than a return from the Babylonian diaspora, is the primary concern at this point. The restoration of the temple will be of major concern only at a later stage (cf. 63:18; 64:11), from which time the scribal addition (v 28b) probably derives. While the author of chs. 40–48 does not seem to have much interest in the restoration of the Jerusalem temple and its cult, the expectation that the city devastated by the Babylonians will be restored by Cyrus is frequently expressed (45:13; 49:14–18; 51:3). At a later point we will hear of sentinels (*šōmĕrîm*) on the walls of Jerusalem, whose task is described as activating God's memory (*mazkîrîm ʾet-YHVH*)—in other words, round-the-clock intercessory prayer for the restoration of Jerusalem (Isa 62:6–7). It seems that this prophecy was fulfilled not by Cyrus but Nehemiah, after he carried out his *synoikismos*, a probably not entirely voluntary transfer of population to the city (Neh 11).

2. *The Cities of Judah Will Be Rebuilt*

This prediction is also repeated (49:19), though we have the impression that either the reconstruction took longer than anticipated or that some of the cities destroyed by Babylonians and Edomites were simply abandoned (58:12 and 61:4 refer to ancient ruins and the passage of several generations). The expectation also finds expression in liturgical hymns:

> Yahveh will save Zion,
> he will rebuild the cities of Judah;
> they will dwell there and possess it,
> the descendants of his servants will inherit it,
> those who love his name will dwell in it. (Ps 69:35–37)

3. *I Will Make Your Streams Run Dry*

This third prediction seems to be out of character with the other three, which deal with concrete historical realia. It is addressed to the Deep (*ṣûlâ* cf. *mĕṣûlâ*), the primordial chaos overcome by the god at the beginning of time (cf. Ps 74:12–17). But such transpositions into the idiom of myth are by no means unusual or unknown to the author, and the Targumist is surely correct in paraphrasing the Deep as Babylon. The practice is well attested. Another Isaian author identifies Egypt as Rahab (30:7), and Yahveh will be reminded of his victory over Rahab and Tannin (51:9–10), here as elsewhere accompanied by a subtext on the victory at the Papyrus Sea (Exod 15:1–18; Isa 43:16–17), drained to allow Israel to pass through dry-shod (Ps 106:9 cf. Isa 50:2b; 51:10). There is therefore no need to give the prediction concrete expression by referring to the draining of the Euphrates canal leading to the capture of Babylon. This was how, according to Herodotus (1:188–91), Cyrus took the city, but whether this actually took place under Cyrus or Darius I or at all is another matter.

4. *He (Cyrus) Will Fulfill All My Purpose*

This statement recapitulates the three preceding ones and serves to introduce the Cyrus oracle that follows. It is prefaced by the identification of Cyrus as Yahveh's shepherd, a familiar figure of speech for a ruler. Yahveh's purpose or desire (*ḥēpeṣ*) is expressed more fully but with the same language elsewhere: I will fulfil all my purpose by summoning a bird of prey from the east, a man from a far country to carry out my plan (46:10–11); he (Cyrus) will fulfill his (Yahveh's) purpose against Babylon (48:14).

There is no doubt that the entire section consisting in chs. 40–48, and only this section, is about Cyrus, his campaigns, and their predicted impact on the fortunes of Jewish communities throughout the Near East and in the province of Judah in particular. The basic premise is that Yahveh set in motion this entire process—he *incited* Cyrus to world conquest—to put an end to the Babylonian Empire and restore Judah to its former state (*ʿûr* Hiphil, "incite," "stir up": 41:2, 25; 45:13 cf. 2 Chr 36:22; Ezra 1:1, 5). What we have already heard about the lightning progress of his conquests (41:2–5, 25–29; 43:14, 19; 44:7–8) reaches a point of definition in the second part of the passage under consideration (45:1–7).

The wording of the first verse of this Cyrus oracle has left it uncertain where the direct address of Yahveh begins. Since there is no second-person suffix in the first verse, the reading given above assumes a brief introduction (v 1) followed by *oratio recta* (vv 2–7). Cyrus is introduced at once and surprisingly, even shockingly, as Yahveh's anointed one (*māšîaḥ* cf. LXX *tō christō mou*, Vulgate *christo meo*). The word is not to be translated "messiah," since it never has this specialized sense in the Hebrew Scriptures and occurs only infrequently with this meaning in postbiblical texts. We hear of the high priest as being anointed (Lev 4:3, 5, 16 etc.) and occasionally of the anointing of prophets (1 Kgs 19:16; Isa 61:1; Ps 105:15 = 1 Chr 16:22), but anointing as a ceremony of induction into office is above all a royal ritual (1 Sam 2:10, 35; 2 Sam 22:51; 23:1; Ps 2:2 etc). What this implies in concrete historical terms is that Cyrus has taken the place of the Davidic royal house, at least for the time being, an affirmation that we suspect not all of the prophet's audience would have agreed with.

The installation symbolism also includes taking the ruler designate by the hand (v 1), pronouncing his name, and conferring on him a throne name (v 4). Since these symbolic gestures are attributed to Marduk in relation to Cyrus in the latter's propagandistic Cylinder text, several commentators have drawn the conclusion either that the author must have been familiar with this text, and therefore must have written *after* the fall of Babylon in 539 (S. Smith 72); or that he only needed to be familiar with the section of the text in which Cyrus is spoken of in the third person (M. Smith 1963); or, finally, that the similarities can be explained by shared familiarity with Babylonian *Hofstil*, the protocol and ceremonial of the Babylonian court (Kittel 1898). It is, of course, possible that the author did have this knowledge, whether resident in Babylon or elsewhere, but close parallels with the Cyrus Cylinder are not extensive and can be explained on the supposition that both the biblical text and the Cylinder reflect pro-Persian propaganda circulating in the Near East, including the various ethnic groups settled in Babylonia and in the city of Babylon itself during the decade before the fall of the city.

The breaking down of bronze doors and gates and the cutting through of iron bars and bolts (vv 1–2 cf. 43:14) are equally unspecific and need not refer to any of the one hundred bronze gates of Babylon mentioned by Herodotus (1:179). Nor need it presuppose the fall of Babylon even if, contrary to the Cylinder's account of Cyrus's troops strolling into the city like tourists, a siege did take place (Herodotus 1:190). The same can be said of the promise of a rich haul of booty (45:3). It would be hazardous to assume that it refers to specific occasions—for example, the confiscation by Cyrus of the legendary wealth of Croesus, ruler of Sardis; or Herodotus's account of Darius rifling through the tomb of Nitocris; or Xerxes' entering the shrine of the god Bel (Herodotus 1:183, 187).

It seems unlikely that the author anticipated the conversion of Cyrus to the Jewish faith. The expectation or aspiration that he would come to acknowledge what Yahveh had done on his behalf (v 3b) is reminiscent of Marduk's choice of Cyrus to set things aright in Babylon and could simply imply the anticipation that he would give preferential treatment to the people of Yahveh.

The passage ends as it began with the self-predication of Yahveh. The conclusion (45:5–7) is set out elegantly as follows:

I am Yahveh; there is no other;
beside me there are no gods;
I gird you with strength . . . setting,
there is none apart from me.

I am Yahveh; there is no other.
I form light and create darkness,
I bring about well-being and create woe;
It is I, Yahveh, who do all these things.

The military power evident in the conquests of Cyrus is placed in the context of the denial of the reality of other deities, with special reference to Marduk, Yahveh's principal rival (cf. 41:4; 43:10–11, 13; 44:6, 8). It is tempting to interpret the two participial clauses preceding the final inclusio (cf. 44:24) as polemic directed against Zoroastrian dualism. The possibility cannot be entirely ruled out, but there is no evidence that the religion of Zoroaster was at that time a force to be reckoned with. If Cyrus himself was a Zoroastrian, for which there is no evidence, it would have made no sense for the author to polemicize against his religion. But in fact the traditional belief that Yahveh is the source of everything that happens, whether good or ill, was still widely, though not universally, accepted as unproblematic (see, for example, Amos 3:6; 5:18–20; Isa 41:23).

The concluding hymn fragment (45:8) corresponds to the one immediately preceding the Cyrus oracle (44:23), thus emphasizing the centrality of this announcement and the cosmic dimensions of Yahveh's involvement in the great events then taking place. The anticipated vindication, victory, and salvation in 45:8 therefore correspond to the celebration of Yahveh's redemptive acts in 44:23. Comparison with Ps 85:11–12[10–11] suggests that this apostrophe to the sky and the earth was modeled, either by the author or a later editor, on cult-prophetic oracles of assurance preserved in liturgical hymns. This is one of several texts in Isaiah that was seen to have a strong Christian resonance, featuring prominently in the Advent liturgy (Sawyer). Here as elsewhere the impetus came from Jerome's *editio vulgata*, in this instance with the help of a slight modification of the Hebrew text: *aperiatur terra et germinet salvatorem*, "Let the earth open and bring forth a Savior."

YAHVEH CANNOT BE CALLED TO ACCOUNT FOR CHOOSING CYRUS (45:9–13)

(G. R. Driver 1933; Leene 1974; Naidoff 1981b; Schoors 1973, 267–73; C. F. Whitley 1972)

TRANSLATION

i

45 [9]Should one take issue with one's Maker,[a]
one sherd among others made of earth?[b]
Should the clay say[c] to the one who shapes it,
"What are you doing?"

Or his handiwork say, "He has no skill"?[d]
[10]Should one say[e] to a father,
"What is this you are begetting?"
Or to a woman,
"What are you bringing to birth?"

ii

[11]These are the words of Yahveh, the Holy One of
Israel and its Maker:
"Would you question me about my children,[f]
or tell me what I am to make?[g]
[12]It is I who made the earth
and created humanity upon it;
my hands stretched out the sky
and marshaled all its host;
[13]it was I roused him to victory;[h]
I will make his progress smooth.[i]
He will rebuild my city
and let my exiles go,
but not for payment, not for a reward."
[A saying of Yahveh of the heavenly hosts]

NOTES

[a] Reading *hăyārîb > rîb* for MT *hôy rāb*, "woe to the one who contends," requiring a slight change in word division and the elision of one letter; the woe form is foreign to Isa 40–66; [b] the term *ḥereś* refers either to the material, i.e. clay (e.g. Lev 6:21; Num 5:17; Jer 32:14), or to a fragment of pottery, i.e. a sherd (Isa 30:14; Ezek 23:34; Ps 22:16[15]; Job 2:8); the unusual *ʾet* with the meaning "among" rather than "with" seems to be required by the context; 1QIsa[a] has the pl. *ḥvrśy hʾdmh*, "the potters of the earth" (?) agreeing with the pl. *yvṣryv*, "one's makers"; [c] 1QIsa[a] *hvy hʾvmr*, "woe to the one who says," making this the second of three woes, but MT is acceptable as it is; [d] 1QIsa[a] *vpvʿlkh ʾyn ʾdm ydym lv*, "and your workman is not a human being who has hands," which seems to imply that the metaphoric language of God as potter is inappropriate, is an attempt to make sense of a difficult sentence. Compare LXX *hoti ouk ergazē oude echeis cheiras*, "for you do not work neither do you have hands"; since there is no evidence that *yādayim* can mean "handles" (pace RSV), MT may be an idiomatic way of saying that a person is clumsy—as we say that someone is "all thumbs"; [e] reading *hayoʾmar* for MT *hôy ʾōmēr* (1QIsa[a] *hôy hāʾōmēr*), as in v 9a; [f] reading *haʾotî tišālûnî*, "will you question me?" for MT *hāʾotiyyôt šĕʾālûnî*, "ask of me future things"; the emendation requires a redivisioning of words (G. R. Driver 1933, 39); 1QIsa[a] divides the lines differently from MT to render another divine attribute, *yōṣēr ʾôtôt*, "creator of signs"; [g] literally, "or command me concerning the work of my hands";

[h] for this meaning of *ṣedeq*, see the Note on 45:8; [i] literally, "I will make straight all his ways."

COMMENTS

We have seen that the disputation, including a series of aggressive rhetorical questions, employed as a strategy for persuading the hearers or readers of the truth of an argument, is much in evidence in chs. 40–48. The present disputation responds to objections raised, or that the speaker anticipates will be raised, against the remarkable idea that Yahveh will choose the Persians as the instrument of Israel's salvation; and the Persian king, who knows nothing of Israel and its deity (45:5), will take the place of the native dynasty, as Yahveh's anointed one—no less. This brief argumentative address is therefore a codicil to the Cyrus oracle immediately preceding. It is also one of several intimations of opposition and the reluctance of the prophet's public to go along with his euphoria, following earlier remarks that accused those addressed of spiritual obtuseness (42:18–25; 43:8, 22–28). This uneasy, negative feeling rose to a groundswell in the early Persian period.

As is usually the case in these chapters, the address is more carefully constructed than it might appear at first reading. It consists in a reproach in the form of five rhetorical questions, addressed to the hearers in the words of the speaker himself (vv 9–10). There is then a reply to the implied objections in the form of an oracle in which Yahveh speaks in his own name, one introduced in the conventional prophetic manner (11–13). The transition is in the form of another rhetorical question, which is, interestingly, linked with the prophetic preamble by means of the figure of Yahveh as father and mother (10–11). "My children" does not, however, refer to Israelites but to what God chooses to bring about on the scene of world events; note how *bānay* ("my children") is parallel with *poʿal yāday* ("the work of my hands"). The reply to real or anticipated objections comes in vv 12–13. The creature cannot question the Creator of heaven and earth about Cyrus or anything else. We may note that here, as in the Cyrus saying (44:24), the role assigned to the Persian ruler is so extraordinary that it requires a repeated emphasis that the one assigning the role is a cosmic rather than a merely national, ethnic, or locative deity.

The metaphor of the potter and the pot and the parable of the pot answering back to the potter may have drawn on earlier Isaian usage with reference to a different situation:

You have things the wrong way round!
As if the potter were no different from the clay,
or as if what is made were to say of its maker,
"He did not make me,"
or the product made of clay of the one who fashioned it,
"He has no skill." (Isa 29:16)

The same point is made in the incident of Jeremiah's visit to the potter's workshop (Jer 18:1–6), and Paul uses the figure of the potter to express the absolute freedom of God to choose whom he will: the thing formed cannot question the artisan concerning why it was made in one way rather than another; the potter can make a vessel suitable for noble or ignoble use (Rom 9:20–21).

The image in our passage is reinforced by a variation on the Yahvist account of the making of the first human being from the dust of the earth (Gen 2:7). The wording is different (*ḥereś ʾet-ḥarśê ʾădāmâ*, "one sherd among others made of earth," cf. *ʿāpār min-hāʾădāmâ*, "dust from the earth"), but the meaning is the same since sherds are made out of clay. Humanity has no right to question and no right of appeal against the omnipotent God imaged as a superpotentate, the dominant image of deity in the ancient Near East and one that is still with us. But, as Duhm points out (1922, 343–44), Job, though acknowledging that he is made of clay and destined to return to dust (10:9), does address the questions to God that are ruled out here: why God acts as he does or refrains from acting; why a world deemed to be under divine governance is the way it is.

The severe textual problems of v 9 appear to have arisen at an early date, to judge by the ancient versions. The Targum goes its own way:

> Woe to him who thinks to arise against the words of his Maker and trusts that the potter's images, which are made from the earthen dust, will do him good. Is it possible that the clay will say to him who makes it, "You did not make me," or, "Your work has no hands"? (Chilton 1987, 90)

Either the *Vorlage* of LXX was very different from MT, or the translator had even less success in dealing with a recalcitrant text than the modern commentators:

> What better thing have I set up as clay of the potter? Shall the plowman plow the ground? [reading *hrš* for *hrś*] Shall the clay say to the potter, "What are you doing, since you neither work nor have hands?"

Passing from making an artifact to bringing a child into the world aroused Duhm's suspicion (1922, 344) that v 10 must be a *Randzitat* (marginal note), especially since a newborn child can protest by crying but hardly by cross-examining its parents. This is perhaps too literalistic, and in any case the questions are addressed to *a* father and *a* woman and not necessarily by a child.

In the answer to the objections implicit in the first part, Yahveh presents himself as the Holy One of Israel and Israel's Maker—or, more literally, former or shaper. The basic idea of holiness is segregation from the sphere of the profane, the ordinary—whether permanently as, for example, the priest (Lev 21:7–8) or temporarily, as the Nazirite (Num 6:8). It is used primarily of designated places, especially the sanctuary (Exod 29:31; Lev 6:9; Ezek 42:13) and anything connected with it. But, by a process of theological elaboration, the holiness of the sanctuary and the priesthood is extended to include the Israelite people as set apart from other ethnic groups, a development in evidence in Deuteronomy (7:6; 14:2, 21; 26:19; 28:9) and the so-called Holiness Code (Lev 19:2; 20:7, 26).

The representation of Yahveh as the supreme embodiment of holiness so understood, combined with his exclusive relationship to Israel, expressed in the designation "the Holy One of Israel," is, with few exceptions (Jer 50:29; 51:5; Ps 71:22; 78:41; 89:19), restricted to the book of Isaiah and is one of the relatively few clear indications that chs. 40–55 have drawn on earlier Isaian material, in whatever form it existed at that time. Rather than originating with Isaiah, however, the concept of holiness seems to have been taken over from the Jerusalem cult and, further back, from the traditions about the holy ark prior to its installation in the temple (1 Sam 6:20).

Yahveh also presents himself as Israel's Maker (*yōṣēr*), which recalls the point made at the beginning of the first section—the more so, since *yōṣēr* also means "potter" (e.g. 41:25). This designation is used frequently in chs. 40–48 (43:1; 44:2, 24 cf. 43:7, 21; 44:21, where the finite verb is used). The association between forming a figure out of clay and bringing a child into the world recalls, and no doubt was meant to recall, the mythic account of human origins (in whatever form the author was familiar with it) as it is narrated in Gen 2:7. The same association of motifs appears in the last section of the book:

> You, Yahveh, are our father;
> we are the clay and you are our maker (*yōṣĕrēnû*)
> we are all the work of your hand. (64:7)

A remarkable feature of this short passage (45:9–13) is its use of seven different verbs to express divine intervention in human affairs: *yṣr* = "form" (9a, 9b, 11a), *pʿl* = "work" (9b, 11b), *yld* = "beget" (10a), *ḥyl* = "give birth," (10b) *ʿśh* = "make," (12a), *brʾ* = "create" (12a); *ʿîr* = "arouse, incite" (13a).

The point of the rhetorical questions and the reaffirmation of the power manifest in creation is revealed in the final verse, alluding once more to Cyrus (following 41:2–4, 25–29; 42:5–9; 43:14–15; 44:24–45:7), whom Yahveh has incited against Babylon (cf. 41:2, 25; Ezra 1:1, 5; 2 Chr 36:22) and whose conquests he has made possible by removing obstacles to his progress—a summary of 45:1–3. We may be sure that Cyrus would have been surprised to hear that the whole point and purpose of his conquest of the Medes, Lydians, Ionians, and Babylonians was to make possible the rebuilding of Jerusalem and return of deported Judeans. Our sources for the early Achaemenid period, as few and often obscure as they are, suggest that the rebuilding and repopulation of Jerusalem were postponed long after the reign of Cyrus, and in fact allusions to the restoration of the city in later sections of Isaiah no longer assign a role to Cyrus (49:17; 51:3; 52:1–2,7–10).

Regarding the return of deportees and their descendants to the province, a specific reference to the Babylonian diaspora in these chapters is limited to

48:20–21 and possibly 52:11–12, which speaks about the return of the sacred vessels (cf. Ezra 1:7–11; 8:28). Elsewhere, expatriates are to return from the ends of the earth (41:8–9), the four corners of the earth (43:5–6), including from as far away as distant Syene (Aswan) in Upper Egypt (49:12). In the later list of Isa 11:11–12, Shinar (Babylon) is one of eight locations, also including Upper Egypt, from which exiled Judeans are to return. The final rather laconic statement is that, in pursuing these goals on behalf of Judah, Cyrus will offer his services gratis; he will not be looking for payment (*mĕḥîr*) and will not need the standard inducement of a bribe (*šōḥad* cf. 1 Kgs 15:19; 2 Kgs 16:8). It has often been pointed out that this contradicts 43:3–4, which seems to be saying that Yahveh will hand over Egypt, Ethiopia, and Seba to Cyrus as payment for his actions on behalf of Yahveh's people. This may be so, but it would be hypercritical to conclude that every inconsistency we encounter in the biblical text, however minor, requires emendation or relegation to the status of a scribal addition.

THE GOD WHO HIDES HIMSELF (45:14–19)

(Beuken 1974a; Dijkstra 1977; Heintz 1979; Hermisson 1998a; Ludwig 1973; Perlitt 1971; Sommer 1998; Texier 1989; Tsumura 1988; Weinfeld 1967–1968)

TRANSLATION

i

45 [14]These are Yahveh's words:
"The traders[a] of Egypt and the merchants[b] of Ethiopia
and the Sabeans, tall of stature,[c]
will come over to you; they will be yours,
they will walk behind you in chains;[d]
they will do homage to you, they will plead with you.
They will say:[e]
'Surely the Almighty is with you, there is no other,
there is no God but he.'"
[15]You are,[f] in truth, the Almighty One who hides himself,
God of Israel, Savior!
[16]Those who fashion idols are shamed and disgraced,
all of them together.
They live out their lives in dishonor,
[17]while Israel is saved by Yahveh
with salvation long-lasting.
You will be neither shamed nor disgraced
forever and ever.

ii

[18]For these are the words of Yahveh, the One who created the sky, the One who is God, who gave the earth form and substance,[g] who firmly established it. He did not create it an empty void but formed it to be inhabited:

"I am Yahveh; there is no other.
[19]I did not speak in secret,
somewhere in a dark realm.
I did not say to Jacob's descendants,
'Seek me in the empty void.'
I, Yahveh, speak what is right;
I declare what is truthful."

NOTES

[a] BHS proposes reading *yōgĕ ʿê miṣrayim*, "toilers (traders?) of Egypt," instead of MT *yĕgîaʿ*, meaning "toil" or the result of toil, i.e. "produce"; BHS is probably correct, since the verbs in 14c–d can only refer to people, and another verb would be required in 14b for produce; LXX has "Egypt is weary" (*ekopiasen*). [b] here, too, BHS proposes people—*sōḥărê-kûš*, "merchants of Ethiopia"—instead of MT *sĕḥar-kûš*, "goods of Ethiopia," the latter supported by LXX *emporia* but not Syr. and Tg.; elsewhere Jerusalem will have at its disposal both foreign goods and foreign slaves (14:1–2; 60:1–18), whereas here the bringing of tribute is implied in naming the bearers (traders, merchants); [c] 1QIsa[a] has *mdvt* pl. cf. Num 13:32, *anšê middôt*; [d] MT repeats *yaʿăborû*, "will come into your power" (literally, "will pass over to you"), but this overloads the verse and is absent from LXX, Syr., and Vulg.; [e] added for the sense, but in fact included in the meaning of the verb *yitpallālû*, "plead"; [f] *ʾattâ*, "you (masc.)," is often emended to *ʾittāk*, "with you (fem.)," which would be feasible only if this were the continuation of the previous citation, on which see the Comments; [g] literally, "who formed the earth and made it."

COMMENTS

After the Cyrus pronouncement and its sequel (44:24–45:13), it becomes difficult to follow a thread of consecutive meaning, to identify distinct discourses of significant length, or to recognize beginnings and endings. At one end of the spectrum, North (1964, 155–62) finds continuity of theme in 45:14–25, the theme being the passage from heathenism to the Israelite religion and the God of Israel. At the other end, Westermann (1969, 168–76) finds only a series of fragments in the balance of this chapter (14, 15, 16–17, 18–19, 20–25), for the most part out of place, and Merendino (1981, 425–61) arrives at a somewhat similar conclusion. Several others attach vv 18–19 to what follows rather than to what precedes (e.g. Melugin 1976, 126–35). The view defended here is that we have two prophetic-oracular sayings (14–17, 18–19) identified by the conventional prophetic *incipit*, which are thematically linked whether they belong at this point or not and whatever their origin.

The first consists in an address of Yahveh to Jerusalem/Zion (v 14), a comment by the prophetic author (15), and a statement contrasting the destiny of idol-worshipers with the destiny of Israel (16–17). That Jerusalem is being addressed and not Cyrus (as Jerome and Ibn Ezra thought) is established by the feminine suffixes, admittedly ambiguous in the Masoretic consonantal text but quite clear in 1QIsa[a] and confirmed by close parallels in Isa 60. Apart from the opening passage of chs. 40–48 (40:2, 9), this is the only place where Jerusalem/Zion is addressed in these chapters, whereas in the following chapters, apostrophe to Jerusalem is extremely common. Hence, Westermann's suggestion of an original association of 45:14 with Isa 60 may be correct (1969, 169–70). Since *ʾattâ* ("you," 2d-person masc. sing.) in the following verse should not be emended to "with you (fem.)" (see Note), the statement about the hidden or self-hiding God cannot be attributed to the Sabeans and the other peoples. In any case, v 15 is incongruous after the confession of faith immediately preceding.

While commentators can always be counted on to find connections of some kind between one passage and another, still, I must say that a denunciation of cult images and their devotees would not be expected at this point (vv 16–17). The denunciation may therefore belong to a later editorial strand together with 44:9–20. To add to the confusion, the suffixes in the final couplet (17b) are second-person plural.

The future Jerusalem is envisaged by apocalyptically-minded seers as the religious center of the world and the goal of pilgrimage for the nations (Isa 2:2–4; 66:18–23; Zech 14:16). It will be enriched with the tribute of subject peoples (e.g. Isa 60:5–7, 11, 13, 16–17; Hag 2:7–8), who will also provide slaves and *Gastarbeiter* to perform tasks for the inhabitants of the city, including care of livestock and building projects (Isa 14:1–2; 60:10–14). Since Second Isaiah is often read as the prophet of universalism, it is important to clarify what the term *universalism* implies. Neither Judaism nor Christianity has ever held out the offer of *unconditional* universal salvation, without some form of confession of faith and adherence in some way to norms defined and accepted by the faith in question. Some of the relevant statements often quoted from prophetic books suggest that foreigners are, so to speak, being made an offer they cannot refuse. The foreigners referred to in 45:14 come in chains, and even if the chains are borne willingly, as some suggest, those who wear them become the property of Israelites.

This situation, which hardly qualifies as religious universalism, reaches a higher level with the profession of faith that follows in the same verse: that the true God is the God of Israel, the God who is in Jerusalem/Zion, the city representing the people of Israel, and that there is no true manifestation of divinity apart from this. We are not told that these foreigners become proselytes (*gērîm*, cf. 14:1–2), much less that they were incorporated into the Jewish people. We do not hear of obligations placed on them by virtue of their confession of faith, either observance of Shabbat (cf. 56:1–8) or laws about what is clean and unclean (Ezra 6:21) or circumcision, of which in any case we hear very little in post-destruction historical and prophetic texts. (The Egyptians and Nubians or Ethiopians bringing tribute would probably be circumcised anyway).

The fact that in the confessional formula Yahveh is confessed to be the only god suggests that v 14 is describing conversion, even if forced conversion, rather than just adhesion, to use A. D. Nock's well-known distinction. A similar confession is attributed to Naaman the Syrian: "Now I know that there is no god in all the earth except in Israel" (2 Kgs 5:15). Less clearly definitive is the confession of Jethro, father-in-law of Moses. After being "catechized" by Moses, he proclaims: "Now I know that Yahveh is greater than all the gods" (Exod 18:11). Rahab, the Jericho prostitute, recites what appears to be a similar piece of catechetical instruction and then makes a similar confession: "Yahveh your God is the one who is God in the heaven above and on the earth beneath" (Josh 2:9–11). It would be interesting to know how these formulations originated and to what actual praxis, if any, they corresponded.

However, as stated earlier, v 15 is not the continuation of the v 14 confession of faith but a comment either by the author of chs. 40–48 or by a later scribe—what Westermann (1969, 171) called an "Amen gloss." The fact that God as Savior (*môšîaʿ*) is a common designation in chs. 40–48 (43:7, 11; 45:21; 47:15) suggests that it was added by the author of chs. 40–48, but the matter cannot be decided. The natural assumption would be that it was intended as a comment on the previous statement, perhaps also enlarging on the confession of faith, rather than as a misplaced comment on the Cyrus poem (Westermann 1969, 170–71). Since the God who hides himself is also the God of Israel and the Savior, we would assume that *ʾēl mistattēr* ("the Almighty One who hides himself") carries a positive connotation, though clearly it could be understood otherwise. Perhaps it was, as we shall see.

At any rate, the Greek translator avoided it, substituting *su gar ei theos kai ouk ēdeimen* ("for you are God, and we did not know it"), placing the responsibility for the hiddenness of God on the devotees. The Targumist went his own way, as was his wont: "In truth you are God who made your Shekhinah dwell in the strength of the height" (Chilton 1987, 90). The Vulgate's *vere tu es Deus absconditus* ("truly you are a hidden God") provided the point of departure for a great deal of mystical speculation and apophatic theologizing. Christians filled out the clause with reference what the New Testament has to say about the inscrutable and incomprehensible nature of God (e.g. Rom 11:33; 1 Tim 6:16), while in recent Jewish religious thought it served as a way of coming to terms theologically with the Holocaust.

The antecedents of this way of speaking about God have not been easy to identify. It may, however, be tentatively suggested that this is one of the relatively few occasions in which the author draws on an older Isaian topos—that of the strange and uncanny ways in which the God of Israel intervenes in human affairs, especially touching on the destiny of his people (Isa 28:21, *zār maʿăśēhû . . . nokriyyâ ʿăbôdātô*, "strange is his deed! . . . uncanny is his work!").

The contrast between Israel and those who make cult images (vv 16–17) is somewhat unexpected but not out of character with the language and themes of this section of the book. All of the terms used here are found elsewhere in these chapters with the exception of *ṣîrîm*, meaning "idols," which is hapax. Shame (> *bôš*) characterizes the opponents of Israel (41:11; 45:24; 49:23; 50:7; 54:4), especially the devotees of cult images (42:17; 44:9, 11). "Shame" becomes a key term in describing the contrasting final destinies of the God-fearers in the community and their opponents, usually in the form of eschatological reversal, familiar also to readers of the New Testament (Isa 65:13; 66:5; cf. Matt 5:3–12).

The second saying (vv 18b–19) with its relatively long introduction (v 18a) is related to the first (vv 14–17), and not just by the repetition of the incomparability formula: "there is no other." The declaration that Yahveh has not spoken in secret (*bassēter*, cf. *ʾēl mistattēr*), echoed later on by a prophetic author (48:16), suggests disquietude with the idea of a God who conceals himself, a frequent subject of complaint to God in Psalms and elsewhere (Pss 10:11; 13:2; 27:9; 30:8; 44:25; 69:18; 88:15; 102:3; 143:7; Isa 8:17; 54:8; 64:6[7]). It also seems to imply a need or desire to clarify a possible misunderstanding latent in the epithet. The saying affirms that Yahveh has always communicated in an open, straightforward and truthful way to his people. There is here an implied contrast between the clear and unambiguous pronouncements of Yahveh's prophets, including of course the one communicating the saying itself (cf. again, 48:16), and what are taken to be essentially foreign forms of mediation: the obscure muttering and whispering that go on during a necromantic séance (Isa 8:19–22; 29:4) or the celebrated ambiguities of the Greek oracles, the kind that misled Croesus of Lydia to do battle with Cyrus (Herodotus 1:53).

The speaker is introduced as the Creator of the heavens, and therefore as the one divinity, and (literally) the one who formed, made, and established the earth, using language familiar from liturgical hymns (Ps 8:4; 24:2; 119:90). It is tempting to read the following statement, that Yahveh did not create the earth as a *tōhû* ("empty void"), as polemic against the Priestly account of creation in Gen 1:1–2:4 (with Sommer 1998, 142–43, following Weinfeld 1967–1968, 123–24). However, all that 18c is saying is that Yahveh did not destine the earth to be an empty void but rather to be inhabited, which is completely in keeping with what the Genesis account says. Once again, therefore, we are reminded that the truth of these prophetic pronouncements is sustained by the power that brought the world into existence at the beginning.

SALVATION OFFERED TO THE NATIONS (45:20–25)

(Beuken 1974a; Blenkinsopp 1996; P. A. H. de Boer 1956, 80–101; Clements 1986; Davidson 1963; Dion 1970; Gelston 1965; Hollenberg 1969; Martin-Achard 1959; Snaith 1950; Snaith and Orlinsky 1977)

TRANSLATION

i

45 [20]Assemble and come together; draw near,[a]
survivors of the nations!
Those who carry around their wooden idols know nothing;
they make their petitions to a god that cannot save.
[21]State your case and present it; consult together:[b]
Who has announced this from the beginning,
who declared it long ago?
Was it not I, Yahveh?
There is no god apart from me,
a god who overcomes and saves;
there is none but me.[c]

ii

[22]Turn to me and accept salvation,
all the ends of the earth!
For I am God, and there is none other.
[23]I have sworn an oath by my life;[d]
the word that overcomes has gone forth from my mouth,
a word that will not be made void:[e]
"To me every knee will bend,
by me every tongue will swear an oath."
[24]About me it will be said,[f]
"Victory and strength come only from Yahveh."
All who rage[g] against him
will come shamefaced into his presence,
[25]while all of Israel's descendants
will triumph and exult in Yahveh.

NOTES

[a] 1QIsaiah[a] has *v'tyv* > Aramaicizing verb *'th*, "come," for MT *yaḥdayv*, but *yaḥdayv* appears frequently in Isa 40–48 and need not be emended; [b] reading *hivvāʿăṣû* imperative for MT *yivvāʿăṣû* Jussive with Syr. and Tg.; LXX *ei anangellousin engisatōsan, hina gnōsin (gnōmen) hama* ("if they declare [it], let them draw near that they may learn together") seems to presuppose the verb

*yd*ʿ ("know") rather than *y*ʿ*ṣ* ("advise, take counsel") in the *Vorlage*; [c] 1QIsa[a] adds a conjunction before *ʾên*, "and there is none but me"; 1QIsa[a] is very free with the conjunction; [d] literally, "by myself," *bî*; [e] *yāšûb*, literally, "return," cf. Amos 1:3 etc.; [f] it is not unusual for the speaker to be introduced within the citation, e.g. 48:22, but the lack of a subject for MT *ʾāmar*, "he (one) said," counsels Niphal *yēʾāmēr* cf. 1QIsa[a] *yʾmr*; LXX *legōn* presupposes infinitive *lēʾmor*; [g] on *hanneḥĕrîm*, see 41:11, Note d.

COMMENTS

The initial three imperatives distinguish this passage from the preceding two with their own superscriptions, the second of which, as argued above, comments on the *ʾēl mistattēr* ("the Almighty One who hides himself") of the first, and to that extent is detached from 20–25. The form is the familiar one of a summons to an assize, a forensic encounter (as 41:1–5, 21–29; 43:8–15; 44:6–8), using the same language as in previous examples (e.g. *haggîdû*, *haggîšû*, stating and presenting the case). The theme is likewise the familiar one of successful prediction as a decisive criterion for divine status. Yahveh addresses the "survivors of the nations" in vv 20–21 and "the ends of the earth" in 22–24a, and this direct address is rounded off with a comment by the author in 24b–25.

On the whole, then, there is nothing new in the first part of the address. Those summoned to come together, confer, and state their case are described as "survivors of the nations" (*pĕlîṭê haggôyîm*). The semantic field in which this and similar expressions (*pĕlêṭîm*, *pĕlêṭâ*) appear is military defeat and its aftermath. The genitival phrase can signify either a part of a larger group (e.g. the survivors of Ephraim, Judg 12:5) or something from which one escapes alive—for example, survivors of the sword (*pĕlîṭê ḥereb* Jer 44:28; Ezek 6:8). The allusion is therefore not to diaspora Jews scattered around the world (pace Martin-Achard 1959, 20–21) or to ethnic minorities settled in and around Babylon or to assimilated Jews who had given up their national and religious identity (pace Hollenberg 1969) but to the much larger mass of people affected by the campaigns of Cyrus, not necessarily or even probably following on the fall of Babylon, as suggested by Ibn Ezra.

The condemnation of processions in honor of and prayers addressed to foreign deities (v 20b) is generally taken to be a gloss, perhaps misplaced, perhaps on 46:1–2 (Westermann 1969, 175). It certainly breaks the sequence of thought, but even if added by a later hand it is not entirely foreign to the context, and in fact underlines the contrast between the many foreign gods that cannot save and the one God of Israel who can. Here, as elsewhere (41:22–23, 26–27; 43:12; 44:7; 46:10–11), what was announced in advance was the successful military career of Cyrus culminating in the conquest of Babylon. Here, too, the temporal phrases used (*miqqedem*, *mēʾāz*, translated, respectively, "from the beginning," "in advance") leave us uncertain whether the author has in mind the distant or the recent past. It therefore cannot be decided whether the allusion is to earlier, no-longer-extant prophecies known to or composed by the author, or to the anti-Babylonian materials in the first part of the book (13:1–22; 14:3–21; 21:1–10)—which, however, seem to presuppose the fall of the city—or to earlier Isaian or even non-Isaian sayings reinterpreted in the light of current events.

The second part of the passage (vv 22–25) has been interpreted by many to refer to an offer of universal salvation and is therefore one of the crucial texts in the long-standing universalism-particularism debate touched on in the Comments to the previous section. Much depends on how the term "the ends of the earth" is understood and what is implied in the *command* to turn to Yahveh (plural imperative) and accept salvation (Tolerative Niphal, GKC §51c).

The "ends of the earth" (*ʾapsê-ʾereṣ* cf. *qĕṣôt hāʾāreṣ*, 40:28; 41:5, 9) can refer to the physical confines of the earth (Prov 30:4) but generally alludes to their inhabitants. Liturgical compositions speak of the realm or kingdom under the jurisdiction of the God of Israel that extends to the ends of the earth or "from sea to sea and from the river to the ends of the earth" (1 Sam 2:10; Ps 72:8; Zech 9:10). The idea of a worldwide empire ruled by Yahveh may have developed out of an older politico-religious fantasy of a Davidic empire on which the sun never set (e.g. Ps 2:8), a fantasy nourished by resentment at subjection to the great powers. But coerced submission to the rule of Yahveh enforced by sanctions falls somewhat short of salvation as we would tend to understand it today. In the only other appearance of the term *ʾapsê-ʾereṣ* in Isaiah (52:10), the role of the inhabitants is limited to *observing* the salvation that Yahveh has wrought for his people and for Jerusalem.

The universalism in question is therefore the claim of universal jurisdiction and dominion advanced on behalf of Yahveh and based on his creation of the world and direction of the course of history. This claim is by no means confined to these chapters in Isaiah:

To you (Yahveh) the nations will come
from the ends of the earth and say,
"Our ancestors inherited only a lie,
a futile, profitless thing;
can people make gods for themselves?
Such are no gods!" (Jer 16:19)

All the ends of the earth
will remember and return to Yahveh;
all the families of nations
will do homage before you,
for sovereignty belongs to Yahveh;
it is he who rules over the nations. (Ps 22:28)

Gentiles are invited to submit willingly—to turn to Yahveh and away from their own gods—and accept the salvation held out to them. But, whether willingly or unwillingly, they *will* submit: every knee will bend, every tongue swear an oath of allegiance (v 23b). Kings and queens will prostrate themselves and lick the dust at the feet of Yahveh's vicegerents (49:23). Those who resist or demur will be called to account and shamed (45:24b). The final verse, contrasting the jubilation of Israelites with the fate of the obdurate, removes any suspicion that the perspective transcends the destiny of Israel as the designated representative on earth of Yahveh's sovereignty.

It should be neither surprising nor disedifying that the religious language in this important passage, expressive of what we call monotheism and universalism, is still closely linked with and dependent on contemporary political circumstances and events and the emotions to which they gave rise. With the passing of time the author and his audience had to come to terms with different situations that, in their turn, precipitated different religious emotions and perceptions. Isaiah 45:20–25 is not the final word. We must also take account of the language of servanthood in these chapters, the mission to establish justice and the rule of law (42:4), the servant as a covenant to the peoples of the world and a light to the nations (42:6–7; 49:6, 8–9; 51:4). Furthermore, since the author of these chapters is only one voice among many, we should also take into account texts that speak of, among other things, Gentiles being attracted to Judaism as a way of life (Isa 2:2–4 = Mic 4:1–4) and of Yahveh's blessing on Egypt, his people, and on Assyria, the work of his hands (Isa 19:24–25).

THE DEFEATED AND EXILED BABYLONIAN GODS (46:1–7)

(Abusch 1999; Boadt 1983; Clifford 1980; G. R. Driver 1935; Franke 1994, 26–50, 82–91; Hallo 1983; Millard 1999; Rabinowitz 1954)

TRANSLATION

i

46 [1]Bel crouches low, Nebo cowers;[a]
their images are loaded on to animals, beasts of burden.[b]
these things you once bore aloft
are a load for weary animals.[c]
[2]They cower, they crouch down low;
they are unable to rescue the load,
but they themselves have gone[d] into captivity.

ii

[3]Listen[e] to me, household of Jacob,
all that remain of the household of Israel,
you who were sustained from birth,
who were carried since leaving the womb:[f]

[4]"Until you grow old I will be the same;[g]
when your hair turns grey I will uphold you;
I sustained you,[h] I will carry you still;
I will uphold and rescue."

iii

[5]To whom will you liken me?
Who will you say is my equal?
With whom compare me on equal terms?
[6]Those who lavish gold from the purse,
who measure out silver on the scales,
hire a goldsmith who makes it into a god,
whom they then bow down to and worship.
[7]They hoist it on their shoulders and carry it;
they set it down in its place;[i] there it stays.
It does not move from its place.
If they cry out to it, it cannot answer;
it cannot deliver them from their distress.[j]

NOTES

[a] Reading perfect *qāras* for MT participle *qōrēs* with BHS, following G. R. Driver 1935, 399 and most commentators, with the exception of Torrey (who also reads *kōrēʿ* for MT *kāraʿ*; 1928, 365) and Hermisson (1998b, 86); [b] 1QIsa[a] omits the conjunction before *bĕhēmâ*, putting it in apposition with *ḥayyâ*, perhaps correctly; [c] an attempt to make sense of a difficult half-verse and verse, which have suffered damage in transmission, as the ancient versions suggest; 1QIsa[a] reads: "Bel bows down, Nebo stoops; their images are on animals, on beasts of burden. Your loads are more burdensome than their reports [*mšmyʿhmh* for MT *maśśāʾ laʿăyēpâ*, "a burden for a tired one," supported by 4QIsa[b]]. They stoop, they bow down together . . ."; cf. LXX "Bel has fallen, Dagon is completely crushed; their graven images [*ta glupta*] were (destined) for wild beasts and livestock. Lift them up, tied up like a load for one who is tired, hungry, and enfeebled, and one without strength also . . ."; cf. Tg: "Bel kneels, Nebo is hewn down; their images are a likeness of beasts and cattle [*hvv ṣlmnyhvn dmvt ḥyvn vbʿyr*]; the burdens of their idols weigh upon those who carry them, and they are weary. They are cut off and hewn down together . . ."; [d] 1QIsa[a] has pl. *hlkv* for MT sing. *halĕkāh*; [e] 1QIsa[a] has sing. imperative *šmʿ* for MT pl., but the latter is in order since *bêt yaʿăqob*, a collective, can take the pl. cf. 48:1; [f] 1QIsa[a] reads *mmny*, "from/by me," for MT *minnî*, "from," and the verbs as active participles rather than passive, as in MT (*ʿvmsym, vnvśʾym*), with what meaning is not clear; [g] *ʾănî hûʾ*, literally, "I am He" or "I am the One" (see Comments); [h] accepting, with some hesitation, an emendation to *ʿāmaśtî*

(*ʿāmastî*) with BHS following Klostermann, which makes a kind of inclusio with v 3b and removes the awkward *ʿāśîtî*; [i] *taḥtâv*; for the idiom, see 2 Sam 2:23; Isa 25:10; [j] in MT the verb *yiṣʿaq* and the suffixes are masc. sing. but without an antecedent.

COMMENTS

This section appears to fall naturally into three units, held together loosely by subject matter and vocabulary. A word of assurance addressed to the Judean hearers (vv 3–4) is bracketed by more polemic against cult images, but now for the first time with specific reference to the principal Babylonian imperial deities, Bel (Marduk) and Nebo (Nabû; vv 1–2, 5–7). The juxtaposition of the first and second of the three allows for the contrast between the Babylonian deities, who, in the act of being carried to safety after defeat, have demonstrated their impotence; and Yahveh, who has carried his people from the beginning and will continue to do so. The implied argument at first seems facile and specious, but we may suppose that the author, in setting it up this way, wishes to convey a sense of the self-authenticating character of his own religion (on which, one might read the chapter entitled "Bearing or Borne" in George Adam Smith's commentary written more than a century ago, 1927, 177–88).

The point is made with linguistic immediacy in both of these units by the use of the same vocabulary with the general sense of carrying and sustaining: *nś'*, *ʿms* (*ʿmś*) (1b, 3b, 4b). The last unit, dealing with the now-familiar theme of the manufacture and installation of cult images (cf. 40:19–20; 41:6–7; 44:9–20), looks like an interpolation to many, perhaps most, commentators, one that has drawn here and elsewhere on an idolatry strand (*Bilderschicht*; e.g. Duhm 1922, 352–53; Hermisson 1998b, 90–91, 102; Whybray 1975, 115 maybe). These determinations are almost impossible to make with any assurance.

On the one hand, v 7 forms an inclusio with vv 1–2, touching as it does on the motif of the god that is carried and cannot save and replicating the key terms of 1–4 (*nś'*, *sbl*). While vv 5–7 are similar to other "idol passages" in both theme and form (rhetorical questions followed by an account of the manufacture of gods), they also have stylistic features in common with the preceding four verses, especially the use of alliteration. The following examples may be noted:

1 *kāraʿ—qāras* (*qōrēs*), *laḥayyâ—labbĕhēmâ*, *ʿămûsôt—maśśā'*

2 *qārĕsû—kārĕʿû*, *mallēṭ—maśśā'*, *napšām—haššĕbî*

3 *minnî-beṭen—minnî-reḥem*

6 *hazzālîm—zāhāb*, *mikkîs—kesep*, *yišqōlû—yiśkĕrû*

7 *yiśśā'uhû—yisbĕluhû*

While it is always possible for an interpolator to imitate the style and lexicon of the original, the weight of probability in this instance does not favor interpolation.

The broader implications of identifying passages as brief as these as distinct units call for attention at this point. Since none of them takes more than a few seconds to read, it makes no sense to describe them *tout court* as discrete *oral* units. If one insists on an oral origin or substratum for the material in these chapters, the individual "bytes" must be part of a larger unit corresponding to a longer oral performance or several such performances. But in that case we must suppose that these performances were recorded stenographically or committed to memory either at the time of delivery or shortly afterwards, and that what we have in front of us is the record of this activity. The first part of this supposition is perhaps possible; the second improbable, to say the least.

The literary indications, as noted above for 46:1–7, lead more readily to the conclusion that these chapters represent an editorial compilation and construction, drawing selectively and probably also in an abbreviated form on diverse *written* materials. They would have had enough consistency of viewpoint, theme, and language to manifest a single original impulse, whether oral or written or both. Not being subject to anything like copyright, this compilation then remained for a long time open to expansive comment and rewriting in the light of changing circumstances. There are instances in which these editorial procedures are fairly easy to detect, but for the most part our reconstructions of the editorial history of these chapters will be hypothetical and speculative.

An important aspect of this work of editorial construction is that of linkage between successive units. Isaiah 46:1–7 continues the polemic against cult images in the preceding passages, with special reference to carrying the images in procession (45:20b cf. 46:1–2, 7), their inability to save (45:20–22 cf. 46:2, 7), and the inefficacy of prayer addressed to them (45:20 cf. 46:7b). There is also linkage by catchword (the verb *krʿ*, "bend the knee, crouch," 45:23b; 46:1, 2a). It seems, moreover, to have been important to allow for an alternation of assurance with reproach and commination (45:9–13; 46:8–13). A further possibility is that revealing the names of the gods who are the principal targets of the polemic only at this point may be a deliberate move, preparing for the full-scale attack on Babylon, its religion, and its intellectual tradition in 47:1–15. Though Cyrus is not named, reference to his anticipated capture of Babylon brackets the anti-Babylonian chapter and at the same time brings the entire 40–48 section to an appropriate conclusion (46:10–11; 48:14–16).

That the wording and word order of vv 1–2 have made it difficult to visualize the scene described is evident both from the ancient versions (see Notes on the text) and the variety of interpretations available in the commentaries. Some of the efforts of commentators to improve the text (e.g. Clifford 455, Westermann 1969, 177) would be quite successful if the task of the interpreter were to improve the text rather than comment on what is there. The situation seems to be that, either in reality or in imagination, the Babylonians have been defeated and Babylon either taken or about to be taken. The Babylonians are loading the statues of their gods on pack animals with a view to taking them to safety, an attempt that, unlike the rescue of Babylonian gods by Merodach-baladan from Sennacherib's army, will not be successful.

This seems to fit the context better than an image of the victors' carrying off the statues as trophies of war, a well-attested practice (see, for example, the Philistines' capture of the ark, 1 Sam 5:1–2, and Mesha of Moab's seizing of a Yahveh cult object from the Israelite city of Nebo, *ANET* 320; also a Nineveh panel representing troops of Tiglath-pileser III carrying off the statues of four gods from a conquered city, *ANEP* #538). The Babylonian gods of 46:1–2, once borne in triumph in the *akitu* festive procession, have demonstrated their inability to save their own people and their city and have not even rescued their own statues.

The gods in question are named for the first time. Bel (*bēlu*, cf. *baʿal*) is an honorific title ("lord") attached to the god Marduk (biblical version: Merodach cf. Jer 50:2) rather than a personal name. Marduk's ascent from the status of a minor deity to the supreme position in the pantheon is correlative with the establishment of the Neo-Babylonian Empire and Babylon itself as its political and religious center. The Marduk cult, especially its principal liturgical expression in the twelve-day *akitu* festival in the spring, served to legitimate and reinforce Babylonian imperialism. The myth of Marduk's cosmogonic victory over Tiamat and subsequent creation of the world (*Enuma Elish*) and humanity was recited on the fourth day of the festival, the high point of which was the procession from Marduk's Esagila sanctuary through the great Ishtar gate to the *akitu-* house beyond the city limits.

In this procession Marduk was accompanied by his son Nabû (Nebo), resident deity of Borsippa, some miles south of Babylon, and patron of scribes, whose task was to fill out and preserve the Tablets of Destiny. Nabû appears to have had a special relationship to the Neo-Babylonian dynasty, to judge by the theophoric names of its most important rulers: Nabopolassar, Nebuchadrezzar, and Nabonidus. The Greek translator replaced Nabû's name with Dagon, perhaps because of the fate of the Philistine deity of that name, whose statue was found smashed in front of the Israelite ark (1 Sam 5:1–7).

The cameo presented in these opening verses is vivid enough to have suggested to some commentators an actual event and therefore a date after the fall of Babylon to Cyrus in 539 B.C.E. (e.g. Sydney Smith 1944, 190). Several others reject this view based on the quite different version of the fall of the city in the Cyrus Cylinder (*ANET* 206–8) in which Cyrus, beloved of Bel and Nabû, accuses Nabonidus of irreverence toward the Babylonian gods and returns the statues of the gods to their rightful sites after his troops have entered the city unopposed. This is, perhaps, to put too much confidence in what is a flagrantly propagandistic document.

Herodotus, often unreliable for different reasons, has another version. Rather than strolling into the city with their weapons tucked away, as in the Cylinder, Cyrus's army ends a frustrating siege by draining the channel of the

Euphrates that ran through the city (Herodotus 1:188–91). But, by the same token, the allusion in vv 1–2 could be to the situation following the twenty-month-long siege under Darius, also described by Herodotus (3:150–60). This siege would have coincided with the defeat of the Babylonian pretenders Nidintu-bel and Arakha by Darius at the end of 520 or the beginning of 519, events that are mentioned on the Behistun Inscription (Akkadian version, lines 18–20).

One might even consider the possibility of an allusion to Xerxes' savage suppression of the Babylonian uprisings of Bel-shimanni and Shamash-eriba thirty-six years later. This last option would gain in attraction if we could be sure that the *daiva* inscriptions from Xerxes' reign allude to the destruction of the principal Babylonian sanctuaries after the suppression of the revolts (the Esagila and adjacent Etemenanki ziggurat) and if we could believe Herodotus that Xerxes removed the gold statue of *Bēlos* (Bel) from its place (1:181, 183).

Certainty in such issues is rarely attainable, but we can at least say that there is nothing in 46:1–2, or indeed in 47:1–15 either, specific enough to *oblige* us to postulate a date after the fall of Babylon. No local features and no individuals are mentioned, and there is nothing that calls for more than an active imagination nourished with a minimum of general cultural information. The author would not even have had to be resident in the Babylonian diaspora to have composed this lively cameo.

The discourse continues with a direct address to the household of Jacob and the remnant of the household of Israel. The call for attention links up with 46:12 and, in this form—*šimʿû ʾēlay*, "listen to me"—appears also in 46:12, 49:1, 51:1, and (in the singular) 48:12 but not in chs. 1–39 or 56–66. The term "remnant" (*šĕʾērît*), on the other hand, here translated "all that remain," signals one of the key concepts in the first part of the book but is used in chs. 40–66 with reference to Israel/Jacob only here. The closest parallels to this usage occur in the context of the post-destruction period—and often enough to suggest that this expression came to be a standard way of referring to those who survived the Babylonian conquest, whether in Palestine, Egypt, Mesopotamia, or elsewhere (Jer 40:15; 41:10, 16; 42:2, 15, 19; 44:7, 12, 14, 28; Hag 1:12, 14; 2:2; Zech 8:6, 11–12; Ezra 9:14; Neh 7:71). It does not, therefore, indicate the remnant of the Kingdom of Samaria, a topic in which the author of chs, 40–55 manifests no great interest.

The message of this direct appeal to the Judean audience is that, unlike the aforementioned Babylonian gods, their God is dependable. He sustains them rather than their being continually obliged to sustain the cult of Yahveh—to keep him going, as it were. The message is therefore registered in the form of a contrast and its impact reinforced by use of the same verbs for carrying, bearing, sustaining (*ʿms, nśʾ*) as in vv 1–2 (the verb *mlṭ*, "rescue," is also repeated). The language about Yahveh carrying Israel is particularly in evidence in Deuteronomistic contexts, perhaps therefore another example of contact between these chapters and the later Deuteronomists. Yahveh can carry Israel as a shepherd can carry a sheep or lamb (Isa 40:11; Ps 28:9) or as an eagle carries its young on its wings or, more likely, in its claws (Exod 19:4; Deut 32:11) or as a father carries his child (Deut 1:31; Hos 11:3).

It is a striking and satisfying image, but we must suspect here another example of the author's penchant for the *double entendre*: Yahveh bears Israel, but Israel continues to be a burden. It is difficult otherwise to explain the choice of the verb *ʿms*, here translated "sustain" but in 46:1 meaning to put a load on an animal, or the verb *sbl* (twice), here translated "uphold" but more often with the sense of putting up with something difficult or unpleasant (e.g. Isa 53:4, 11 and cf. Modern Hebrew *sablānût*, "patience"). On the use of *ʾănî hûʾ*, the self-designation of Yahveh, here translated "I will be the same," see the Comments on 41:4.

The final section of the passage (vv 5–7) introduces the now-familiar theme of Yahveh's incomparability. The form is also familiar: rhetorical questions requiring a negative answer (three here, as in 40:12–14) followed by an account of the manufacture and installation of the cult image. The questions are framed with three verbs connoting comparison: *dmh* (Qal and Piel; also in 40:18, 25 in the same context), *mšl*, and *švh* (both Hiphil). In brief compass the process of making a god is laid out, involving financing, manufacture, and installation, followed by cultic veneration and prayer. Since the verb translated "lavish" (*zallîm* > *zûl* ?) is hapax, it is not entirely clear whether the funds are to pay for the material or the labor, and in addition the verb may include a sense of wasting or squandering money. The work is done by a *ṣōrēp* ("goldsmith," literally, "smelter"), as in 40:18–20, and is therefore for a more elevated socioeconomic clientele than gods made of baser metals or wood, as in 44:9–20.

None of the arguments for vv 5–7 (or, for some scholars, vv 6–7) as an interpolation are conclusive but some are interesting nonetheless. For scholars who see a close connection with the following passage (46:8–13), the people who indulge in the futile activity described here would be not foreigners but Judeans (Duhm 1922, 352–53). While non-Yahvistic cults are attested for the post-destruction period, the fact that the prophet's audience was either engaging in such cults or liable to do so is mentioned only once in chs. 40–55 (48:5). In spite of the author's practice of juxtaposing condemnations of image-worship with direct addresses to his Judean hearers or readers (e.g. 40:18–23; 41:6–10; 44:9–22; 46:1–4), none of the passages similar to 46:5–7 can be read as referring to Judeans rather than foreigners.

Hermisson's point (1998b, 120–21) that the redactor of vv 6–7 emphasizes the immobility of the god rather than the fact that it has to be carried overlooks the mention of a procession in both vv 1–2 and 6–7, using the same verb (*nśʾ*). Duhm's observation about the concept of religion implicit in these verses, a concept that is radically different from that of Second Isaiah, is hardly an adequate reason for excising the passage and is moreover as interesting for what it says about the commentator as for its bearing on the text itself:

"For this author [of vv 5–7], the main purpose of religion is to be of use to people, helping them in the struggles of their daily life. This is a conception at a level to which the private religious practice of the philistine easily sinks, but it is not the conception of Deutero- Isaiah or of the prophets in general." (Duhm 1922, 353)

REASSURANCE FOR THE DOUBTERS (46:8–13)

(Fichtner 1951; Hermisson 1989; Jensen 1986; Leene 1984; North 1950; Scullion 1971; Stuhlmueller 1967; Werner 1988; Zimmerli 1982b)

TRANSLATION

i

46 [8]Remember this and be ashamed;[a]
come to your senses, rebellious people!
[9]remember deeds done long ago,[b]
for I am[c] God; there is none other;
I am God; there is none like me.
[10]I declare the outcome[d] from the beginning;
from of old, things yet to be.
I say, "My plan will prevail,
I will achieve all that I purpose.[e]
[11]I summon a bird of prey from the east,
from a far land the man to carry out my plan.[f]
Yes, I have spoken, and yes, I will bring it about;
I have conceived it,[g] and yes, I will do it."

ii

[12]Listen to me, you stubborn[h] people,
far removed from deliverance as you are:
[13]"I bring my deliverance near, it is not far off;
my salvation will not be delayed.
I will place[i] salvation in Zion,
for Israel, my splendid possession."[j]

NOTES

[a] MT *hit'ošāšû* Hithpolel > *'šš* hapax has been translated in many widely different ways: "abandon hope" (NEB), "consider" (RSV), "stand firm" (NJPSV); the last has some support from Tg. (*tqp*, verbal stem meaning "be strong"), assumed to be based on an Aram. loanword *'šš*, "establish, found" (as Torrey 1928, 366) cf. *Pesiqta baḤodesh* p. 101b, *Cant. Rab.* 2:5 and the expression *hălākôt mĕ'ûššāšôt*, "well-founded teachings"; this may be the best-supported option but unfortunately does not make sense in the present context; LXX has *stenaxate*, "mourn" cf. Akk. *ašašu* III with the same meaning; the translation

offered, *yitbošāšû* > *bôš* (cf. Gen 2:25), implies a change of one consonant cf. Vulg., *confundamini;* [b] the first half-verse should not be elided, as proposed by BHS, but the repeated call to remember (*zikrû*) and the somewhat confused sense sequence suggest some textual disorder; [c] MT and 1QIsa[b] have *ʾānokî*, the long form of the personal pronoun, while 1QIsa[a] and 4QIsa[c] have *ʾănî*, the short form; [d] 4QIsa[c] has *ʾḥrvnvt* fem. pl., "last things," for MT *ʾaḥărît* cf. LXX *anangellōn proteron ta eschata prin auta genesthai*, "declaring the last things before they come about"; 1QIsa[a] has *ʾḥrvt;* [e] 1QIsa[a] *yʿśh* 3rd person attributes the fulfillment of Yahveh's purpose to Cyrus; 1QIsa[b] and 4QIsa[c] as MT; [f] K, with 1QIsa[a], 1QIsa[b], and 4QIsa[d], has 3rd-person suffix, "his plan"; but Q *ʾăṣātî* is required by the context; [g] the object of the verb, implicit in MT and 1QIsa[b], is made explicit with fem. suffix in 1QIsa[a]; as is often the case, LXX is paraphrastic: "I spoke and led him, I created and made, I led him and made his way straight"; [h] LXX *hoi apolōlekotes tēn kardian* translates *ʾōbĕdê lēb*, "discouraged," cf. Jer 4:9, which is accepted by Duhm (1922, 354), McKenzie (1968, 86), and others, but MT is acceptable and fits the context cf. Ps 76:6 and Tg *tqypy lbʾ*, Symm. *sklērokardioi*, Vulg. *duro corde;* [i] MT and 1QIsa[b] have the conjunction, *vĕnātatî;* 1QIsa[a] *ntty* omits it; [j] *lĕyiśrāʾēl tipʾartî* could be read "(I have given) to Israel my splendor," but this is doubtful both because *ntn* would have to be assigned two meanings for two indirect objects and because God never gives his splendor to Israel or anyone else; the alternative is apposition with *lamed* of advantage—i.e. "for Israel my splendor" or, more idiomatically, "my splendid one."

COMMENTS

Several commentators (e.g. Westermann 1969, 182–83) read v 8 as the conclusion to 46:1–7, while others delete it altogether. Neither conclusion is required by the repetition of the injunction to remember in v 9, which is in keeping with a familiar rhetorical device, and it may be noted that a call to remember also follows immediately after the longest of the "idol passages" (44:21). What the people are called on to remember, and to remember ruefully, in v 8 (*zoʾt*, "this") will be spelled out beginning with v 9. The call for attention in v 12 signals a distinct saying that, while certainly not foreign to the one preceding, and while connected to it by the catchword *rḥq* ("far removed," "far off" cf. "a far land"), introduces a new element of the *imminence* of the promised salvation. This will call for comment in due course.

The first of the two stanzas continues the disputatious type of discourse by now thoroughly familiar. The call to remember is, in effect, an appeal to the Judean audience to draw on their historical traditions as a basis for faith in the God of Israel whose incomparability is once again emphasized (cf. most recently 46:5), and faith in the interpretation of current events now offered to them. "The deeds done long ago," more often referred to as "the former things" (41:22; 42:9; 43:9 and especially 43:18, where the hearers are told *not* to remember former things), should be understood to refer to such traditions as then existed about Yahveh's dealings with Israel throughout its history. The call to faith, therefore, "means bringing the nation's experience with God in history to bear upon the present" (Westermann 1969, 185). It is in this sense that the author refers to his Judean hearers as *witnesses* (43:10; 44:8). This rudimentary theology of history is encapsulated in the three verbs in vv 10–11: Yahveh declares in advance by means of prophetic utterance (*maggîd*), he states his purpose in the present (*ʾōmēr*), and he implements it by issuing a summons to a particular person or persons for a mission calculated to change the course of history (*qōrēʾ*).

None of this is unfamiliar, but the reader may begin at this point to pick up a stronger note of asseveration, accompanied by a growing sense of exasperation, from the prophetic author. Those addressed had previously been described as deaf and blind (42:18–25), had been accused of neglecting the cult of Yahveh (43:22–24), and had been raising questions about the role assigned to Cyrus (45:9–13). Now, however, they are described as a rebellious people, a term (*pōšĕʿîm*) previously restricted to their ancestors (43:27; 48:8 cf. 1:2, 28; 66:24).

This prompts the conclusion, unsurprising but not often commented on, that interaction between speaker and public must have been a constituent element in the production of this material. It can be most clearly observed in the occasional quotation attributed to the hearers followed by the speaker's response (40:27–31; 49:14–18) or when the speaker anticipates the reaction of the hearers (48:5,7), but it can also be picked up in the tone of the speaker, as in the passage under discussion. It is theoretically possible that the author is addressing an *implicit* public, but there is a sense of immediacy here that is difficult to reconcile with a work produced at a much later time, as a kind of literary exercise, when the events of the late Neo-Babylonian period were of purely historical interest. What drives the interactivity is the need to persuade, together with the not unimportant fact that the credibility of the author, speaking in the guise of a prophetic figure, is also at stake.

The point that the victories of Cyrus, his conquest of Babylon, and subsequent actions on behalf of the prophet's fellow-Judeans are the outcome of a divine plan (*ʿēṣâ*) communicated by the prophet has already been made:

> He confirms the word of his servant,
> fulfills the counsel (*ʿēṣâ*) of his messengers. (44:26)

Cyrus is "the man of his counsel" (*ʾîš ʿăṣātô*), not in the sense that he advises Yahveh (as the expression is used in 40:13) but in the sense of one designated to implement the plan in the arena of international affairs.

This way of interpreting Israel's relations with the great powers may have originated with Isaiah two centuries earlier during the critical period of Neo-Assyrian domination. At that time the plan or agenda focused on Assyria

(Isa 5:19; 14:26) and Egypt (19:11) but with worldwide implications (14:26). Then, too, it was greeted with skepticism (5:19; 29:15; 30:1). While there is no evidence that here or elsewhere the author of chs. 40–55 is applying these old Isaian ideas to the contemporary situation in anything like a systematic way, it is entirely possible that he was familiar with them and to some extent influenced by them.

That Cyrus is not named in vv 8–11 has left open the option of identifying the one from the east as Abraham, an opinion held by several commentators in the Middle Ages (e.g. Rashi) and by Torrey more recently (1928, 366–67). By associating Abraham with his descendants, the Targum could find a reference to the deportees: "[God] promised to gather the exiles from the east, to bring openly, like a swift bird from a far land, the sons of Abraham" (Chilton 1987, 91–92). But this summoning is one of several allusions in this section to Cyrus's advance either from the east (41:2, 25) or the north (41:25) and his mission to dismantle the Babylonian Empire (41:2–5, 25–29; 43:14; 48:14), to rebuild Jerusalem together with its temple (44:26, 28; 45:13) and the ruined cities of Judah (44:26), and to allow the repatriation of exiled Judeans (45:13).

What species the author had in mind in comparing Cyrus to a bird of prey (*ʿayiṭ*) is not known. As a royal bird, and the emblem of Cyrus according to Xenophon, the eagle would be appropriate (cf. Jer 49:22; Ezek 17:3; 39:4); the vulture, as a scavenger, less so (cf. Gen 15:11; Isa 18:6; Jer 12:9). Since the emphasis is on the speed of Cyrus's conquests rather than their predatory nature, the falcon (*ʾayyâ*, parallel with *ʿayiṭ* Job 28:7) would also fit. We simply do not know.

It is noteworthy that in chs. 40–48 the call for attention with which the second brief passage opens ("listen to me") often has a more-or-less covert note of hostility (41:1; 42:18; 48:1). That this is so in this instance is clear from the way the speaker goes on to characterize the reluctant listeners. The disjunction between this characterization and the assurance that follows looks problematic to many commentators but is in fact the key to understanding the passage. The point is that for the first time in these chapters moral conduct, especially attitudes vis-à-vis prophetic preaching, is related to the present unsatisfactory situation in which the hearers find themselves. The consequences are not spelled out, as they will be in later prophetic utterances. What follows is merely an assurance that Yahveh's saving power is at hand (*qērabtî ṣidqātî*, "I bring my salvation near"); it is not, as they think, far off. God's saving intervention will not be delayed, *not as far as God is concerned*.

The obstacle lies in the stubborn refusal to accept the assurance and act on it. What God has ready to offer is stated somewhat ambiguously in what might be called the anticipatory prophetic perfect (13b). Some understand it to be saying that salvation will be established in Zion and splendor will be given to Israel. This would imply that the verb (*ntn*) is doing double duty ("placing," "giving"), which is possible but very unusual. More significantly, nowhere do we hear of God giving his splendor to Israel or to anyone else. It therefore seems better to take *tip'artî* as being in apposition to *yiśrā'ēl*, an expression that is attested (cf. 60:19; 62:3) in the sense that it is in and through Israel that the divine splendor becomes manifest (44:23; 49:3 and cf. 55:5, God communicates his splendor to Israel).

This brief passage represents something of a turning point in the book, since it is the first attempt at explaining the failure of Cyrus to live up to the expectations placed on him by the prophet's public. The message is that God was always prepared to fulfill the predictions, and the salvation that God has to offer is still there and available. The obstacle does not lie on the side of the power or the compassion of God but on the public's side. Sin is the obstacle, especially an obdurate persistence in doubting the prophetic word. This interpretation permits a reading of vv 12–13 as a comment on the plan concerning Cyrus in 8–11 but a comment addressed to a later generation, probably the same generation targeted by the similar abjurations and assurances in chs. 56–66.

Hermisson's *qārôb-Schicht* (a strand that speaks of salvation's being near or far away) takes a similar view of the passage, though not all or even most of the passages that he assigns to this editorial layer speak of salvation as being far off, and even fewer attribute this situation to sin. But it is only at the later stage corresponding to the last section of the book (chs. 56–66) that we find the combination of a delay in the advent of salvation (which therefore remains far off) with the conviction that the delay is caused by the unsatisfactory moral conduct of those addressed. That vv 12–13 have been added as an explanatory comment a generation or two later than the bulk of chs. 40–48 and later than the passage immediately preceding, on which they comment, is also apparent on the linguistic level. With one exception (51:4–6), the terms for nearness and distance (*qrb*, *rḥq*) with reference to salvation appear only here and in the last section of the book (59:9, 11, 14).

In addition, the terms *mišpaṭ* and *ṣĕdāqâ*, usually translated "justice and righteousness," appear in the latest strands of the Isaian material (either singly or in combination as hendiadys) with the meanings judgment or vindication rather than justice; and triumph, victory, or deliverance rather than righteousness. The shift toward a future-oriented perspective is particularly clear in contexts in which *ṣĕdāqâ* appears by itself with the second meaning (in addition to our passage, 1:27; 51:6, 8; 56:1; 59:9, 16–17; 61:10–11; 63:1). The message, then, is that Yahveh has the power and willingness to intervene, but sin is an obstacle, and it is for this reason that "vindication remains far removed from us, and deliverance does not reach us" (59:9).

QUEEN BABYLON DETHRONED (47:1–15)

(Begg 1989; Biddle 1996; Blau 1957; G. R. Driver 1935; Farber 1995; Fitzgerald 1972, 1975; Franke 1991, 1994, 100–62; 1996; Franzmann 1995; Freedman 1970; Garr 1983; Haran 1963b; Klengel-Brandt 1997; Martin-Achard 1980; Oppenheim 1977; Yee 1988)

TRANSLATION

i

47 [1]"Get down, sit in the dust,
maiden Babylon![a]
Deprived of a throne,[b] sit on the ground,
Chaldean maiden![c]
No longer will you be called
the tender and delicate one.
[2]Take the handmill, grind the meal,
remove your veil;[d]
take off your skirt,[e] uncover your thighs,[f]
wade through rivers!
[3]Your nakedness will be uncovered,
your shame will be exposed.
I will take vengeance,[g]
and no one will intervene."[h]
[4]A word of our Redeemer;[i]
Lord of the heavenly hosts is his name,
Israel's Holy One.

ii

[5]"Sit in silence,[j] go into the darkness,
Chaldean maiden;
nevermore will you be called
Mistress of Kingdoms.
[6]I was angry with my people,
I dishonored[k] my inheritance;
I delivered them into your power,
but you showed them no mercy.
Even on the aged you laid your heavy yoke.
[7]You thought, "I shall forever remain eternal mistress."[l]
But you gave no thought to these things;
you did not bear in mind their outcome.[m]

iii

[8]Now listen to this, you lover of pleasure
dwelling in security,
you who think to yourself,[n]
"I am, and there is none other;
I will never be widowed,
I will never be bereft of my children."
[9]These two things will overtake you,
in a moment, in a single day:
loss of children and widowhood

in full measure[o] will overtake[p] you,
in spite of your many incantations
and the great power of your spells.

iv

[10]You felt safe in your evil ways,[q]
you thought no one could see you,
your wisdom and your science led you astray;
you thought within yourself,
"I am, and there is none other."
[11]Evil will overtake you,[r]
and you will not know how to dispel it;[s]
ruin will fall upon you,
and you will be unable to ward it off;[t]
disaster will overtake you,
suddenly, when you least expect it.

iv

[12]So persist with your spells,
your numerous incantations,
in which you have labored from your youth.[u]
Perhaps you can gain some profit,
perhaps you will yet inspire terror.
[13]You are worn out with your many consultations;[v]
let them persist so they can save you—
these scanners[w] of the sky and star-gazers
who predict month by month what[x] will befall you.[y]

vi

[14]See now, they have become like stubble;
the fire is burning them up,
they cannot save themselves from the flames.
These coals are not for warming,[z]
not for sitting beside the fire!
[15]Much good have these magicians[aa] done you,
at whose arts[bb] you have toiled since your youth;
they have wandered off, each his own way;
none of them is left to save you.

NOTES

1QIsaiah[b] is preserved with gaps; fragments of vv 1–9 are preserved in 4QIsa[d]. [a] MT *bětûlat bat-bābel*, literally, "virgin daughter Babylon," both nouns in apposition to Babylon; [b] MT (with 1QIsa[a] and 4QIsa[d]) *ʾên kissēʾ*, literally, "there is no throne," omitted by LXX, which adds "go into the darkness" from v 5; [c] MT *bat-kaśdîm*, literally, "daughter of the Chaldeans"; [d] this is the probable meaning of *ṣammâ*, which occurs only here and in Cant 4:1, 3; 6:7 and is supported by LXX *katakalumma* and, in Canticles, *siōpēsis*; rather than "hair," as in Ibn Ezra and others; [e] *šōbel* hapax created problems for the early translators: LXX *anakalupsai tas polias*, "uncover the grey hair," cf. Syr. *gvzy hvrtky*, Vulg. *discooperi umerum*, "uncover the shoulder"; 1QIsa[a] has *švlyk*, using the more familiar *šûl* = a long, flowing skirt rather than a "train"; cf. Exod 28:33–34; 39:25–26 = a priest's vestment; cf. also Isa 6:1 and the similar situation in Jer 13:22,26 and Nah 3:5; [f] better than "leg" cf. Deut 28:35, where *šôq* is distinguished from the knees; [g] LXX adds *ek sou*, "on you"; [h] MT *vělo' 'epga' 'ādām*: BHS proposes *yipga'* 3rd person, supported by Symm. *antistēsetai* and Vulg. *non resistet mihi homo*, "no one will resist me," explained by Jerome in his commentary with reference to counterintercession; 4QIsa[d] *'pgy'* Hiphil is possible cf. Isa 59:16 *vayyar' kî-'ên 'îš vayyištômēm kî 'ên mapgîa'* ("he saw that there was no man and was outraged that there was no one to intervene") in a context dealing with Yahveh's vengeance (*nāqām* v 17); Duhm (1922, 355) reads *'eppāga'* Niphal and emends *'ādām* to *'āmar* as the first word of the next verse; [i] insert *'āmar* with LXX, *VL*, Syro-hexapla, Arab., and Eth. versions; [j] 1QIsa[a] has *dmmh* (*dĕmāmâ* cf. 1 Kgs 19:12) for MT *dûmām*); [k] LXX has 2nd-person fem. sing. suffix *emianas tēn klēronomian mou*, attributing the dishonoring to Babylon; [l] D. N. Freedman (1970, 538) and BHS correctly propose to repoint as a genitival phrase cf. *'ăbî-'ad* (Isa 9:5), *'ădê-'ad* (26:4; 65:18), though *'ad* is omitted by LXX, Syr., and Vulg.; 1QIsa[a] reads *'ôd*, "yet"; [m] the fem. suffix in *'aḥărîtāh* is problematic after *'ēlleh*, "these things," leading to emendation (*'aḥărîtēk* 2nd-person fem. sing., suffix) or omission (as in LXX *ta eschata*, "the last things"); 1QIsa[a] has *'ḥrvnh*; the fem. suffix can, however, refer in general to actions or situations immediately preceding; such as *'aḥărîtāh* in Prov 5:4; 25:8; Jer 5:31; and Lam 1:9 ("her [Jerusalem's] uncleanness was in her skirts; she did not bear in mind its outcome"); [n] omit mappiq, ה, with many MSS, thus eliminating 3rd-person fem. sing. suffix; [o] LXX has *exephnēs*, "suddenly" (= *pit'om*), but MT *kĕtummām*, "in full measure," is in order; [p] LXX (*hēxei*) and Tg. (*yytyn*) read future (*yābō'û*), which would be expected after *vĕtābō'nāh*, but MT is supported by 1QIsa[a] and Vulg., and use of tenses in these chapters is somewhat elastic; [q] for MT *bĕrā'ātēk*, "in your evil ways," 1QIsa[a] has *bĕda'ātēk*, "in your knowledge," a result of dalet/resh confusion; [r] 1QIsa[a] has, more correctly, *ûbā'āh* fem. for MT *ûbā'*; [s] MT punctuates *šaḥrāh*, "its dawning" (cf. Syr. *bšpr'* and Vulg. *ortum eius*), but read verbal form *šāḥărāh* with fem. suffix; in the context the meaning "conjure away by means of magic" (*šḥr* III; see *HALOT* 4:1466) cf. Arab. *saḥara*, "enchant"; and Akk. *saḥāru*, with much the same meaning, is superior to the meaning "search," "beseech" adopted by Tg.; [t] MT *kappĕrāh* > *kippēr*, with a broader connotation than "cover," "atone," cf. Prov 16:14; [u] IQIsa[a] adds *vĕ 'ad hayyôm* and omits the rest of the verse and the first word of v 13; the scribe may have been contemporizing or may have been unhappy with the repeated "perhaps" (*'ûlay*), which may have seemed to leave Babylon some hope for the future; [v] MT *'ăṣātāyik* is to be read as pl. cf. LXX *en tais boulais sou*, Vulg.: *in multitudine consiliorum tuorum*, rather than sing. as in 1QIsa[a] and Tg.; emendation to *yōʿăṣāyik*, "your counselors," is not required by the context (pace Duhm 1922, 358–59); [w] K = *hbrv* verbal form, but Q participial form (also 1QIsa[a]) is correct; the verb *hbr* is hapax but often explained as a cognate of Arab. *habara*, "to cut or section," with reference to the division of the heavens into "houses," to which the signs of the zodiac correspond; cf. LXX *hoi astrologoi tou ouranou*, Vulg. *augures coeli*; [x] for MT *mēʾăšer* read *ʾăšer* with LXX, Syr., Tg.; a case of simple dittography; [y] read sing. *yābôʾ* with 1QIsa[a], LXX, Syr., Tg. for MT pl. *yābōʾû*; [z] MT *laḥmām* could refer to a fire for baking bread (*leḥem*) cf. 44:15, 19, but if, as seems more likely, the meaning is "to heat them" we would expect *lāḥummām* or simply *lāḥom*, "for heat," cf. 1QIsa[a] *lḥvmm*; [aa] *sōḥărăyik*, "your traders," i.e. those you trade with, but there is probably a double entendre with another meaning i.e. "magician" cf. the verb *šḥr* v 11a and the Akk. cognate *saḫāru* and see G. R. Driver 1935, 401; [bb] read *baʾăšer* with Syr., Vulg., Tg. for MT *ʾăšer* cf. v 12b.

COMMENTS

Verse 1 begins a poem in which the city of Babylon is represented as a splendid and proud queen, adept in the magical arts, now reduced to shameful slavery. It is cast in the "limping" measure, or *qînâ* (3–2), with 2–2 and 3–2 variations, not all the result of textual corruption. It is not, however, a true lament, like the lament over Saul and Jonathan (2 Sam 1:19–27), since the subject is not dead. It is not even a lament that dramatically and ironically anticipates the death of the subject, like the *qînâ* of Amos over the maiden Israel (Amos 5:2), since the subject's imminent death is not contemplated. The remarkable poem about the descent of a Babylonian king to the underworld and his reception by its denizens (Isa 14:3–23) is formally a *qînâ*, though of the ironic kind, but is introduced as a *māšāl*, an oracular poem.

Isaiah 47 falls into the category of the taunting of the conquered by the victors, the stylization and dramatization of which do not succeed in making such poems pleasant reading. Ritualized verbal humiliation of a defeated enemy is one of several forms adopted in oracles against a political enemy, a genre well represented in the prophetic books (especially Isa 13–23; Jer 46–51; Ezek 25–32). This type of poem seems to have developed out of brief oracular sayings or imprecations uttered by a seer before a campaign (e.g. Balaam in Num 22–24) accompanied by homeopathic ritual acts—such as, for example, the smashing of a pot (cf. the so-called Execration Texts from the Egyptian Middle Kingdom, ANET 328–29).

In its present form, this particular example is couched in *oratio recta* by Yahveh, though the attribution to Yahveh occurs only in the textually insecure beginning of v 4 (see Notes on the text) and v 6, which is often, and perhaps correctly, read as a later interpolation. Division into strophes seems to be indicated by imperatives: get down, sit (1), sit in silence (5), now listen (8), persist

(12), with the principal break at v 8 (*vĕʿattâ šimʿî-zoʾt*, "now listen to this"). Others divide differently: BHS agrees with Duhm (1922, 354) and Westermann (1969, 187–88) in finding five strophes; Muilenburg (1956, 544), Whybray (1975, 119), Watts (1987, 170) and Koole (1997, 522–53) prefer six. It is not a decision on which the overall interpretation of the chapter stands or falls.

Though the language of the poem has several peculiar literary features and a high percentage of rare vocabulary words, it is well enough integrated into chs. 40–55 (pace Merendino 1981, 489, 495, who regards it as an interpolation): the fall of Babylon may have been hinted at right at the beginning of Second Isaiah, in the allusion to human impermanence (40:6–8 cf. 51:12); the capture of the city has been described as part of the mission confided to Cyrus (43:14; 45:2–3; 46:11); and the omens and divination characteristic of Babylonian religion and the cult of Bel and Nebo (Marduk and Nabû) have been dismissed as futile (44:25; 46:1–2, 5–7). More significantly, the female *persona* of Jerusalem-Zion is presented as a mirror image of the dishonored queen of Babylon: whereas the latter sits in the dust, the woman Zion is told to get up off the ground (52:2); and whereas the Babylonian is forced to expose herself, Zion is told to put on beautiful clothes (52:1). The one is widowed and bereaved of children, the other will no longer be bereaved and will have numerous children (49:20–21; 54:1). The one is shamed, the other will no longer experience shame (54:4).

How exactly this mirror imaging or echoing came about we can only speculate. To describe ch. 47 as the pivot of Second Isaiah, the point at which Jerusalem changes places with Babylon (Franke 1996, 121), is exaggerated, since Babylon continues to be of concern in the following chapter (48:14, 20–22). Most of the parallels are confined to the apostrophes to Zion in 52:1–2, 7–12 and 54:1–17 and, to a lesser extent, the address to Jerusalem in 49:14–26. Besides, a much clearer division occurs between chs. 40–48 and 49–54(55). The contrast between the two cities is not worked out systematically, especially since much of what is said about Babylon *qua* woman is made up of familiar and traditional tropes, but it is interesting and structurally significant nevertheless.

Though the "Verse Account of Nabonidus" and the Cyrus Cylinder (*ANET* 312–16) are hostile witnesses, both deriving from the Marduk priesthood, they suggest the likelihood that similar anti-Nabonidus and pro-Persian writings circulated during the last decade of the reign. The twenty or so fragments of such opposition literature in Jer 50–51 seem to have provided the raw material for the more elaborate kind of polemic in Isa 13:1–22; 14:3–23; 21:1–10; and 47: 1–15. The *maśśāʾ* ("oracle") in 13:1–22, while quite different in important respects from Isa 47, has several points of contact with the Jeremiah material: the participation of many nations, including the Medes in the attack on Babylon (13:17; Jer 50:41–42; 51:11, 28), who serve as instruments of Yahveh's anger (*kĕlê zaʿămô* 13:5; Jer 50:25) and are dedicated to his service (13:3; Jer 51:27–28); they rally around a standard (*nēs* 13:2; Jer 50:2; 51:12, 17), and their attack inspires terror in the enemy and puts them to flight (13:14; Jer 50:16); Babylon, conquered and destroyed, will go back to nature (13:20–22; Jer 50:39; 51:37).

Similar overlap, both linguistic and thematic may be observed between Jer 50–51 and Isa 47. The identification of Yahveh as Redeemer and Lord of the heavenly hosts in 47:4 reproduces Jer 50:34 practically verbatim, and the destruction of Babylon is the effect of Yahveh's vengeance (47:3 cf. Jer 51:6 *nĕqāmâ*). Babylon itself is personified in the same way in both texts (*bat-bābel* Isa 47:1; Jer 50:42; 51:33).

The issue of chronological order and dependence is complicated by the tendency of this kind of diatribe to use stereotypical phrases and adopt the same traditional language of abuse and denigration. This type of saying can very easily also be "recycled" in accordance with the changing international scene. Nahum, for example, is directed against the Assyrian capital Nineveh described as a lascivious woman (*zônâ*) addicted to divination (*baʿălat kĕšāpîm* 3:4), whose fate is to be stripped and displayed in public (3:5–6)—not very different, therefore, from the woman Babylon of Isaiah 47. But the name of the city, which occurs only twice in Nahum (2:8; 3:7), could easily have been removed and the polemic redirected, practically unchanged, against Babylon.

Feminine personification was traditional for cities (Babylon, Jerusalem, Nineveh; Sidon in Isa 23:12) and peoples (Egypt, Jer 46:11; Judah, Lam 1:15; Israel, Amos 5:2; Jer 18:13; 31:14, 21). In the case of hostile cities such as Babylon, an unfortunate corollary was the unleashing of violent and at times pornographic imagery focusing on the female body. That several of the commands addressed to the woman Babylon in the first strophe (1–4) are mutually incompatible (sitting on the ground, undressing, grinding corn, wading through rivers) suggests that the author of the poem simply assembled a congeries of images to create an impression of degradation and shame.

Sitting on the ground is not in this instance the posture of mourning, and the standard word pair *ʿāpār, ʾereṣ* ("dust," "ground") does not in this instance imply descent to the underworld. Sitting on the ground connotes the passage from enthroned queen to slave woman and, indirectly, the razing of the city to the ground (cf. 25:12; 26:5). Grinding grain with the handmill is a gender-specific activity (Exod 11:5; Num 11:8); the grinding with which Samson was charged being an example of the practice of humiliating and feminizing male prisoners-of-war (Judg 16:21).

In this instance the author has allowed himself a dreadful double entendre since the verb *ṭḥn*, "grind," is also a euphemism for coercive sexual activity ("let my wife grind for another, and let others crouch down upon her," Job 31:10). The removal of the veil and skirt and the language of "uncovering nakedness" (i.e. the pudenda) make it clear that the shaming of the woman involves rape (cf. the same phrase in the rules about sexual relations in Lev 18). Similar unpleasant allusions appear throughout the prophetic writings (e.g. Jer 13:22, 36; Hos 2:12[10]; Nah 3:5–6; Ezek 16:36–37; 23:10, 18). The wading through rivers has been taken to refer to the journey into captivity, but it was probably suggested quite randomly by the need for women to hitch up their skirts in fording a river. The strophe closes with Yahveh's proposal to avenge his people on Babylon and, in doing so, to brook no intervention, presumably by intercessory prayer addressed to him. (For this meaning of the verb *pgʿ*, see Isa 59:16.)

The second strophe (vv 5–7) the injunction to be silent adds to the command to sit on the ground. As elsewhere in these chapters, darkness is not the darkness of death but of captivity (42:7; 49:9), a miserable condition that is the antithesis of the splendor and glory of Babylon, encapsulated in the title "Mistress of Kingdoms" (the designation *gĕbîrâ* can refer either to a queen [1 Kgs 11:19] or a queen mother, 1 Kgs 15:13; 2 Kgs 10:13; Jer 13:18; 29:2).

The title "Chaldean maiden" (*bat-kaśdîm*) includes not just the city but the people in the personification. The Chaldeans (the form comes to us through the Greek *chaldaioi*, a form that is familiar from the story of Abraham, Gen 11:28, 31; 15:7) are first mentioned in Assyrian annals of the ninth century B.C.E. as a cluster of West-Semitic tribes settled in the marshy southern end of Mesopotamia (southern Iraq and Kuwait) known as the Sealand. The suitability of their territory for conducting guerrilla operations enabled them to give the Assyrians a great deal of trouble, especially under Merodach-baladan II (see 2 Kgs 20:12–19 = Isa 39:1–8).

With the decline of Assyrian power, the Chaldeans under Nabopolassar gained control of Babylon and founded the dynasty that lasted until the fall of Babylon to Cyrus. The title "Mistress of Kingdoms," once appropriate in view of the extent of the Neo-Babylonian empire, will no longer be used (v 5), and the claim of immortality ("eternal mistress," v 7) is ill advised and ill considered. We may suppose that it was natural enough for the ruling class in the city to think that the empire would last forever, but in fact it lasted rather less than a century (626–539 B.C.E.).

The suspicion entertained by Duhm (1922, 356) and Torrey (1928, 370) that v 6 has been spliced into this strophe arose from what they took to be the introduction of a theme out of character with the poem. The idea that the Babylonians were acting as punitive agents on behalf of Yahveh but that they overdid it echoes earlier prophetic statements about the Assyrians (Isa 10:5–19). This idea does not appear earlier in chs. 40–55, but we have noted at several points a concern to explain the disaster of 586 as the effect not of superior hostile power or of chance but of the anger of Yahveh (42:24–25; 43:27–28 cf. 54:8). In itself, therefore, theme is hardly an adequate reason for demoting v 6 to the status of a scribal interpolation. Irregularity of meter, alleged by Torrey, is not more persuasive, since the pattern 2+2/2+3/2+2 is no more irregular than patterns in other verses in the poem. Introduction of *oratio recta* of Yahveh at this point is admittedly somewhat unexpected but by no means unprecedented. Perhaps the only valid consideration is that v 6 breaks the force of the contrast between the claim staked by the woman (v 7) and the reality (v 5). The continuity between the two verses is demonstrated by the titles *gĕberet ʿad* ("eternal mistress") and *gĕberet mamlākôt* ("Mistress of Kingdoms"). But whether this is a conclusive consideration for the interpolation of v 6 we may leave undecided.

The third strophe (8–11) opens in the usual form of a verdict following an indictment (*vĕʿattâ*, "now then," . . .), though the woman has already been reduced to slavery, and the indictment continues. One indication of the use of stereotypical language is the description of Nineveh in Zeph 2:15a in precisely the same language: a city dwelling in security that thinks to itself (literally, in its heart) "I am, and there is none other" (*ʾănî vĕʾapsî ʿôd*). This claim, repeated near the end of the strophe, is borrowed by the prophet as one of several similar expressions about the incomparability and uniqueness of Yahveh (45:5–6, 18, 22; 46:9).

At a more mundane level, the good estate of the woman consisted in pleasure, security, and having a husband and children (v 8). "Pleasure" (*ʿēden*) is associated with wearing fine clothes (2 Sam 1:24), sexual activity (Gen 18:12), and food (Jer 51:34). Given the social conditions at that time and in that place, security for most women would have consisted precisely in having a husband and children. All of this, the woman is told, is about to be taken away (v 9). The city will be widowed (for this metaphor, see Lam 1:1), that is, left without the protection of its (male) deity; and its "children," that is, the Babylonian people, will lose their lives, or at least their independence. With this language the contrast with Jerusalem/Zion comes into clearer focus. Hosea (1:2–9) introduced the figure of Israelites as issuing from the marital union between Yahveh and the land of Israel (*ʾereṣ* fem.). After the disaster of 586, the metaphor of a childless widow could have been transferred to Jerusalem, deprived of her children. That situation is countered by prophetic assurances that Jerusalem is now no longer bereaved, barren, or widowed (49:20–23; 54:1–8); she has not been left unprotected (50:1) but is securely married (*bĕʿûlâ* 62:4).

The author goes on to decry the futile attempt to maintain the good life (as described—security and pleasure, in particular) by recourse to incantations (*kĕšāpîm*) and spells (*ḥăbārîm*). Both of these techniques were forbidden in Israel (Deut 18:10–11), although being forbidden did not prevent them from being practiced there, as indeed they were in all neighboring countries (Jer 27:9). The accusation of magic comes naturally in the context, since in Israel magical practices seem to have been particularly associated with women: the woman Nineveh is such a practitioner (*baʿălat kĕšāpîm* Nah 3:4); a female magician or witch is subject to the death penalty (Exod 22:17[18]); and Jezebel is also used to illustrate the close association between magic and sexual deviance (2 Kgs 9:22). The wisdom and knowledge that the poet goes on to denounce as equally ineffective (Isa 47:10) are also *magical* in nature (cf. Exod 7:11; Dan 2:2, 12) and deemed to be characteristic of Babylonian culture.

It will not escape the reader that the poet is viewing the religious aspects of Babylonian culture unsympathetically from the outside. All religions claim to provide assistance in confronting the vicissitudes, uncertainties, and aporias of human existence in one way or another. The Babylonian view of nature led Babylonians to see connections, or to see the possibility of creating connections, between apparently unconnected events and circumstances, as a way of reducing the sense of insecurity and randomness endemic to human life and particularly in evidence in that culture. Out of this view grew a vast science of omens or signs of good or bad portent drawn from casual events (e.g. dreams, freak births, the flight of birds) or celestial phenomena, or obtained through specific techniques for soliciting omens (e.g. extispicy, hepatoscopy: the inspection of animal entrails or livers). Associated with the science of omens were the many prophylactic or apotropaic rituals for important matters such as promoting fertility or getting rid of disease. It is these that the author has in mind when he assures the woman that she will not succeed in dispelling or warding off disaster.

The last verse of the strophe (v 11) gives a definitive verdict in the form of a threefold prediction of impending evil (*rāʿâ*), ruin (*hôvâ*), and disaster (*šôʾâ*)—the last being the now-familiar (but actually incorrect) Hebrew term for the Holocaust. The awkwardness of this verse—*vĕtābōʾ ʿālayik pitʾom šôʾâ loʾ tēdāʿî* (literally, "disaster will come suddenly on you, you will not know")—has often been noted; it may be due to borrowing from Ps 35:8: *tĕbôʾēhû šôʾâ loʾ-yēdāʿ*, "may disaster come upon him unawares," one of several imprecations in that psalm that would have seemed appropriate for the poet's purpose.

In the final strophe (vv 12–15) the poet rejects astrology as well as apotropaic formulas and rites as means to predict and possibly avoid imminent disastrous events. The woman is encouraged sarcastically to persist in her spells and incantations (reverse order of v 9b), as well as consultations with authors and interpreters of astronomical omens. Since the verb *hbr* is hapax, the translation "scanners of the sky" (*hōbĕrê šāmayim*) is uncertain (see Notes on the text). The term seems to refer to the creators of the so-called astrolabes, diagrams of the night sky divided into thirty-six divisions or "houses" for calculating the position of celestial bodies, a first step toward the zodiac, which emerged in the Achaemenid period.

Astronomical knowledge, for which the Chaldeans were famous, was essential for fixing the calendar and inserting the intercalatory days in it. It did not serve to make horoscopes, since the celestial omens concerned matters of state rather than the destiny of individuals, and the celestial phenomenon was not thought of as causing a predicted event but as indicating certainty that it would happen. Babylonian astronomy, in evidence down into the Common Era (the last cuneiform tablet, an astronomical text, dates to 75 C.E.), was advanced to the point that, by the fourth century B.C.E., lunar eclipses could be predicted a year in advance.

The author of this poem remains unimpressed by all of this, however. He predicts that Babylon will end up not beside a cozy little fire such as the one made by the maker of a cult image (44:15–16) but on a real bonfire, by which time all the magi and their arts will have disappeared. If this prediction was not fulfilled literally—if the city was not destroyed by fire, and the science of astronomy together with the pseudo-science of astrology went from strength to strength—Babylon did lose its independence, and its name continued long after ancient times as a byword for profligacy and oppression (e.g. 1 Pet 5:13; Rev 14:8; 2 Esd 3:1–2; *Sib. Or.* 5:143).

THE ARGUMENT FROM PROPHECY REITERATED (48:1–11)

(Condamin 1910; Couroyer 1981a; Daube 1964; Haran 1963b; North 1950; H.-C. Schmitt 1979; Spykerboer 1976, 156–58; Westermann 1966)

TRANSLATION

i

48 [1]Hear this, household of Jacob,
who are called by the name of Israel,
who came forth from Judah's womb,[a]
who swear by Yahveh's name
and invoke the God of Israel—
but not in truth and sincerity.

ii

[2]They bear the name of the holy city;
they rely on the God of Israel,
whose name is Yahveh of the heavenly hosts:
[3]Long ago I declared what would happen;[b]
it came forth[c] from my mouth, I announced it;[d]
then suddenly I acted, and it came about;
[4]for I knew[e] you were stubborn,
that your neck is like an iron sinew,
your forehead as hard as brass,
[5]so I declared it to you long since;
I announced it to you before it happened,
lest you should think,"It was my idol's doing;
my carved and metal images ordained it."
[6]You have heard, now discern all this;[f]
will you not acknowledge it?[g]

iii

From now on I divulge new things to you,
hidden things of which you have no knowledge;[h]
[7]they are created not ages since but now;
before this day[i] you never heard of them,
lest you should think, "I knew it already."
[8]You never heard of it,[j] you never knew it,

and from of old you never gave heed.[k]
I know how unfaithful you are,
how from birth you were called[l] a rebel.

iv

[9]For my name's sake I was slow to anger;
for the sake of my praise I held back,[m]
so as not to destroy you completely.
[10]I refined you but not like silver;[n]
I assayed you[o] in the furnace of affliction.
[11]Only for my own sake I did it,
for how should my name be profaned?[p]
My honor I surrender to no one.

NOTES

[a] Read *ûmimmĕʿê* for MT *ûmimmê*, "from the waters (of Judah)," cf. LXX *aph'hudatos* and Vulg. *de aquis*, the latter on the understanding of water as a euphemism for sperm (cf. Ibn Ezra, who refers to Deut 33:28, "the fountains of Jacob"); *mēʿîm*, as the source of life in the body of the parent, is used of both male (Isa 48:19; Gen 15:4; 2 Sam 7:12; 16:11) and female (Gen 25:23; 49:1; Ps 71:6; Ruth 1:11), and Judah is here fem.; [b] *hāriʾšonôt*, usually translated "former things" (41:22; 42:9; 43:9, 18; 46:9); [c] MT *yaṣĕʾû* pl. is correct as against 1QIsa[a] sing.; the translation has sing. in vv 3–5, agreeing with "what would happen"; [d] though not grammatically necessary (see GKC 107b), we should probably read vav consecutive *vāʾašmîʿēm*, as in the following verse; [e] MT *middaʿătî*, literally, "from/of my knowledge," cf. 1QIsa[a] *mʾšr ydʿty*, "since I knew," with dots above and below the letters *š*, *r*, and *y* to indicate an uncertain reading; 1QIsa[a] may be correct and MT the result of omitting four letters: *m[ʾšry]dʿty*; [f] many attempts have been made to emend MT *šāmaʿtâ ḥăzēh kullāh*, which is literally, "you have heard, see it all"; the least objectionable emendation is *ḥāzîtâ* for *ḥăzēh* (e.g. Duhm 1922, 362; Whybray 1975, 128), but MT is acceptable as it stands; LXX simply omits; [g] the change to pl. address in the second half of the verse, while not without precedent, is sudden and unusual and increases the suspicion that the entire verse has been transmitted in a garbled state (for proposed emendations, see Hermisson 1998b, 204); *taggîdû* is taken to mean "proclaim" in the sense of an open admission; [h] 1QIsa[a] *lʾ ydtn*, absence of conjunction with fem. suffix, is correct rather than MT; [i] the absence of the article before *yôm* in MT *vĕlipnê-yôm* has led to several proposed emendations, but cf. 43:13, where there is also no article; [j] the addition of the conjunction (*vĕgam*) is not unusual in 1QIsa[a]; 4QIsa[b] supports MT; [k] MT, literally, "your ear did not open" (*pittĕḥâ*) or, repointed as Pual (*puttĕḥâ*) or Qal passive (*putĕḥâ*), "your ear was not opened," as Syr. and Vulg.; cf. 1QIsa[a] *ptḥt*, "you did not open . . . ," and LXX *oute ēnoichsa*, "nor did I

open"; [l] for MT *qorāʾ* Pual 1QIsa[a] has *yqrʾv* Qal, "they will/would call you," but 4QIsa[d] is identical with MT; Vulg. *vocavi te* recognizes that Yahveh is the implicit subject; [m] MT *ûtĕhillātî ʾeḥĕṭām-lāk*, literally, "and (for the sake of) my praise I restrained myself (?) for you" (sing.); the verb *ḥṭm* is hapax; 1QIsa[a] *tḥlty*, "my beginning" or "my profanation" is probably a simple scribal error; 4QIsa[d] is identical with MT; [n] read *kĕkesep*, "like silver," for MT *bĕkesep*, "with silver"; [o] reading with 1QIsa[a] *bĕḥantîkâ* for MT *bĕḥantîkâ* > *bḥr*, "choose," cf. Zech 13:9, where the same verbs (*ṣrp*, *bḥn*) are twinned; [p] MT *kî ʾêk yēḥāl* is defective both in sense and in meter; 1QIsa[a], 4QIsa[c,d] read *ʾyḥl*, 1st-person Niphal ("how could I be profaned?"); the Masoretes omitted *šĕmî* to avoid juxtaposing the Name of God with the verb *ḥll*, "profane."

COMMENTS

This last chapter of section 40–48 is beset by more problems and subject to more diverse interpretations than any of the eight that precede it. A structural analysis should in the first place be based on indications in the text rather than on the commentator's prior decision about what is original and what is not. The divisions of BHS correspond to those of the Qumran *Isaiah Scroll* (1QIsa[a]) with respect to the second half of the chapter (i.e., vv 12–16, 17–19, 20–22) but differ in the first half, with BHS dividing into 1–8 and 9–11 as against 1QIsa[a], into 1–2, 3–9, and 10–11. There seems to be general agreement that a major break occurs after v 11, where the *Isaiah Scroll* has a half-line gap, and I will argue that vv 20–22 serve as the conclusion to section 40–48 as a whole.

Apart from this, I note as structurally significant the initial imperatives: hear this (v 1), listen to me (12), assemble (14), get out of Babylon (20); and the repetitions indicating closure: hear this . . . you have heard (vv 1, 6a), for my name's sake . . . only for my own sake (9a, 11a). In addition, the familiar prophetic *incipit* in v 17 ("This is what Yahveh says") clearly delineates 17–19 as a distinct subunit.

A more intractable problem arises from what are perceived to be sudden shifts of mood corresponding to the alternation of reassurance with denunciation, and denunciation of a severity encountered nowhere else in chs. 40–55. More specifically, by-now familiar themes—former things and new things, Yahveh as the one God and Creator of the world, the divinely mandated mission of Cyrus—alternate in an apparently quite sporadic way with denunciations of disingenuous worship (v 1), recalcitrance (4), addiction to idolatry (5), treachery and rebelliousness (8), and failure to observe the commandments (18–19). But this is by no means the first time that the hearers have been reproached by the author. We have heard about their weak faith in need of constant reinforcement (40:27–31), their history of infidelity leading to political disaster (42:18–25; 43:25–28), and a skeptical attitude toward the prophet's message about Cyrus (45:9–13). They have already been denounced as rebels (*pōšĕʿîm* 46:8) though not yet as idolaters. (This accusation will be taken up with exceptional acrimony in ch. 57.)

Since what is at stake in the first instance is the prophet's credibility and reputation, which rest on his ability to convince his public, it is possible to detect a gradually increasing alienation between prophet and public and to conclude that we are close to the point where skepticism and opposition will eventuate in open rejection. It is clear that in backing Cyrus the author of chs. 40–48 was playing for high stakes in an extremely volatile and unpredictable international situation. In this sense, ch. 48 fits into a trajectory reflected, if only uncertainly and fitfully, in the entire second part of the book, one in which disappointed expectations lead to religious and social polarization within Jewish communities during the early Persian period.

The conclusion to be drawn from this is that shifts of mood and a sudden switch from reassurance to denunciation are not *in themselves* sufficient reason for postulating multiple authorship. I take the first unit (vv 1–6a) to be delimited by the call for attention at the beginning ("hear this," v 1) and the statement "you have heard" at the end (6a). The message itself (3–5), therefore, has an introduction (1–2) and a conclusion (6a). Since the initial imperative is plural and the conclusion is singular, it should be pointed out that changes in number (singular to plural, plural to singular) do not necessarily indicate different sources either. Such changes occur throughout these chapters and are usually occasioned by something in the context. If the audience is addressed as Jacob/Israel, or as servant, we expect the singular, and this is what we find (40:27–28; 41:8–16; 43:1–7, 22–28; 44:1–5, 21–22). If they are addressed as the household of Jacob (e.g. 46:3) or as Yahveh's witnesses (43:10; 44:8), the plural is appropriate. Here too, however, such changes could, in conjunction with other features (e.g. a change from second to third person together with a sudden change of theme), suggest multiple authorship.

In the introduction to the first unit the household of Jacob is described in a sequence of qualifiers. They are those who lay claim to the name "Israel" which, in the historical context, means a claim to continuity with the old Israel destroyed by the Babylonians. How important this claim was in the struggle to set up a viable polity in the early days of Persian rule can be seen in the census list in Ezra 2:1–67 (= Neh 7:6–68) and the need for documentary proof of membership (Ezra 2:59) in the form of a genealogical record of some kind (*sēper hayyaḥas* Neh 7:5).

Since the inhabitants of the Northern Kingdom had all but completely disappeared in the slipstream of history, claiming the name "Israel(ite)" meant in effect claiming family origin in Judah. The fact that the term "Judean" or "Jew" (*yĕhûdî*) appears not at all and "Judah" only infrequently in these chapters (40:9; 44:26; 48:1) is readily explained by the drive to reconnect with the past and the level of generality in which the sayings are cast. At that time, the designation "Judean" or "Jew" applied either to inhabitants of the erstwhile Kingdom of Judah (2 Kgs 25:25 = Jer 41:3; Neh 1:2 etc.) or to those who had left the province voluntarily or otherwise and had settled elsewhere (Jer 40:11–12; 43:9; 44:1; 52:28, 30; Zech 8:23; Neh 4:6[12]; 5:8). As Josephus observed (*Ant.* 11.173), the name came into common use only after the deportations.

Eventually, as it acquired a broader ethnic-religious connotation, it would be borne by those whose families had never been in Judah, as was the case with the Jews of Susa in Esther, and those of the military colony on the island of Elephantine at the first cataract of the Nile (*AP* 6:3–10; 8:2; 10:3 etc.).

Adherence to the cult of Yahveh was also manifested in the invocation of his name in depositions made under oath, a common feature of social activity exemplified in the Elephantine papyri. The name of Israel's God was also invoked in liturgical praise and thanksgiving. (For the verb *zkr* Hiphil used with this meaning see, for example, Exod 20:24; 23:13; Ps 20:8.) Jerusalem is called "the holy city" (*ʿîr haqqodeš* cf. the common Arabic designation *al quds*) only here and in 52:1. While there is no evidence that the term "Jerusalemite" was in use at that time, the name of the city could represent its inhabitants and, by extension, all Judeans (e.g. 40:9), and of course it was common practice to personify cities (e.g. 51:17; 52:1–2, 9).

The last of the qualifiers ("they rely on the God of Israel") is the one that makes it practically certain that the reservation about the disingenuous invoking of Yahveh's name ("but not in truth and sincerity") has been inserted by a disillusioned scribe reflecting a later and less-promising situation. What has been said so far is in itself neither positive nor negative, but disingenuous religious practice is incompatible with reliance on the God of Israel (verbal stem *smk* Niphal), which implies trust and commitment. Compare Ps 71:6, in which the same verb occurs:

ʿālêkâ nismaktî mibbeṭen
mimmĕʿê ʾimmî ʾattâ gôzî
bĕkâ tĕhillātî tāmîd

On you I have relied from birth;
you are the one who took me from my mother's womb.
My praise is continually of you.

The fact that much of the language in this prayer of the devout Israelite also appears in our passage suggests further that the interpolated denunciations are meant to describe an attitude contrary to that of the psalmist. Rather than being associated with Yahveh from birth (depending on the meaning of the hapax verbal form *gôzî*), contemporary Israel is a rebel from birth; rather than receiving the tribute of praise, Yahveh must now secure it for himself (v 9).

Interpolation is also responsible for the repetition of the message in vv 3–5, using the same key words, in keeping with a commonly attested resumptive technique: "long ago I declared what would happen, it came forth from my mouth, I announced it, then suddenly I acted, and it came about" (3); "so I declared it to you long since, I announced it to you before it happened" (5a). This is the by-now familiar argument from the past record of prophecy in Yahveh's name (cf. 41:22; 43:18; 46:9), perhaps including earlier predictions about Cyrus (cf. 46:11) but not confined to the immediate past. That the fulfillment is said to come about *suddenly* (*pitʾōm*) puts the emphasis on the unpredictability of divine intervention in human affairs and therefore the impossibility of calculating the odds of success or failure on the basis of the actual situation.

In this sense, another prophetic saying from about this time predicts the *sudden* fall of Babylon (Jer 51:8). It is unclear to which prophecies made long ago the author is referring. In view of the occasional allusion to the History in these chapters, the reference could be to the prophetic forewarnings about the fall of the Kingdom of Judah and the destruction of Jerusalem that punctuate the History, especially since, in biblical terms, what happens suddenly is almost always bad news. If it is referring to the destruction, the interpolator of v 5b understood it differently. (Compare Jer 44:15–19, in which Jews settled in Lower Egypt attribute the fall of Jerusalem to the abandonment of the cult of the "Queen of heaven," the goddess Asherah, in favor of the exclusive cult of Yahveh.)

The interpolation (vv 4,5b) adds for the first time the observation that prophecy was necessitated by the obduracy of Israel throughout her history. The point is made with considerable force with the help of terms of disparagement familiar from homiletic passages in Deuteronomy (Israel as stubborn, "stiff-necked," Deut 9:6, 13; 31:27) and Ezekiel (Israel has a "hard forehead" and a "stubborn heart," Ezek 3:7–8). The argument from prophecy has often served in previous chapters to undermine the prestige of deities venerated by foreign nations; now, for the first time, it serves to refute the claims made on behalf of deities other than Yahveh *within* Israel. The use of three terms for a cult image is perhaps intended to suggest the extent of this abuse. The first, *ʿōṣeb*, is hapax but probably a dysphemistic alteration of *ʿāṣāb* (e.g. 46:1) to suggest *bōšet*, "shame," and also, for good measure, the homonym *ʿōṣeb*, "pain, grief." The second term, *pesel*, "a carved, wooden image," is of frequent occurrence in these chapters (40:19–20; 42:17; 44:9, 10, 15, 17; 45:20), while the third, *nesek* (also 41:29), refers to a three-dimensional image made by pouring molten metal into a mold.

The next section of the poem (vv 6b–8) moves from the past to the present, specifically from a history of prophecies uttered, fulfilled, but unheeded, to a new and unparalleled situation. These new events (*ḥădāšôt* cf. 42:9 and 43:19), previously undisclosed (*nĕṣūrôt*), are now unfolding on the world scene by virtue of the creative activity of the God of Israel. (The key verb is *brʾ*, "create," cf. 40:26, 28; 41:20; 42:5; 43:7, 15; 45:7–8, 12, 18). The allusion to the conquests of Cyrus and the anticipated fall of Babylon will be made clear in the next section (vv 14–16). Here, too, we suspect the hand of the same interpolator in 7b–8 as in 4, 5b, using the same expression ("lest you should think . . . ," 5b, 7b). As in the past, so now, predictions are being made to preempt counter claims advanced by an unsympathetic public. This public is characterized in a way quite out of line with the language of the author of chs. 40–48, even when this author has occasion to reproach them and speak of sins past and present. They are unfaithful (verbal stem *bgd*), a term of disparagement that may owe something to Jeremiah (3:8, 11, 20; 5:11; 9:1[2]), and rebellious (verbal stem *pšʿ*) from the very beginning of their history, a radical rereading of the religious history of Israel, reminiscent of the magisterial survey of that history in Ezek 20.

The main point of the final strophe (vv 9–11) is that now, as in the past, Israel deserves to be destroyed totally, but Yahveh refrains from obliterating them not out of concern for Israel but for his own honor and reputation. This idea is difficult if not impossible to reconcile with the outlook, the tone, and even the religious vocabulary of the "prophet of consolation." The language of total destruction or *karet* (verbal stem *krt* Hiphil) goes back to the old prophetic tradition (Amos 1:5, 8; 2:3; Mic 5:10–12; Isa 9:13) and was favored by Ezekiel (14:13, 17, 19, 21; 21:8–9 [3–4]), perhaps on account of its use in priestly formulae of excommunication (Lev 17:10; 20:3, 5 etc.).

Indeed, it is only in Ezekiel that we find the complex of ideas that come together in this extraordinary strophe: the restraining of divine anger, Israel as deserving total destruction, Yahveh's concern to avoid the profanation of his holy name:

> I was concerned for my holy name, which the household of Israel profaned among the nations to which they had gone. Therefore, say to the household of Israel: "This is the word of the Sovereign Lord Yahveh: 'It is not for your sake that I am about to act but, rather, for the sake of my holy name, which you have profaned among the nations to which you went.'" (Ezek 36:21–22 cf. 20:8–9)

Dependence on Ezekiel is confirmed by the metaphor of refining and assaying in the furnace. The allusion is not to the sojourn in Egypt, referred to in Deuteronomistic writings as "the iron furnace" (*kûr barzel* Deut 4:20; 1 Kgs 8:51; Jer 11:4), but to Jerusalem besieged and destroyed by the Babylonians. The figure derives from Ezekiel. Israel will be in Jerusalem as silver and baser metals are put in the smelting furnace; the furnace will be heated, and Israel will be melted. "As silver is melted in a furnace, so you shall be melted in Jerusalem" (Ezek 22:17–22). It seems as though our author is taking this further by even ruling out the comparison with silver (48:10). In so doing he has moved far beyond earlier allusions to and explanations of the disaster of 586 in terms of the hiddenness and silence of God (40:27; 42:14) or sins past and present (42:24–25; 43:27–28). This is a different voice speaking out of a different situation.

ONCE MORE AND FINALLY: THE MISSION OF CYRUS (48:12–22)

(Anderson 1976; Crüsemann 1969, 55–65; Merendino 1981, 515–39)

TRANSLATION

i

48 [12]Listen to me,[a] Jacob,
Israel, whom I have called:
"I am the One, I am the First,
and I am also[b] the Last.
[13]My hand established the earth,
my right hand spread out the sky;
when I summoned them, they at once existed."

ii

[14]Assemble, all of you, and listen:[c]
"Who among them[d] foretold these things?
Yahveh loves him[e] and fulfills his purpose
against Babylon and the Chaldean race.[f]
[15]I, I myself have spoken and have summoned him.
I have brought him thus far; his mission will succeed.[g]
[16]Draw near to me and hear this:
From the beginning I never spoke in secret;
from when it first began, I was present."
[and now the Sovereign Lord Yahveh has sent me, and his spirit . . .][h]

iii

[17]These are the words of Yahveh, your Redeemer, the Holy One of Israel:
"I am Yahveh your God,
who instructs you for your benefit,
who guides you in the way you are to go.[i]
[18]If only you had heeded my commandments!
Your prosperity would have flowed like a river,
your vindication like the waves of the sea,
[19]your descendants would be as countless as the sand,
your offspring like its grains in number;
their name[j] would never be extinguished
or effaced from my sight."

iv

[20]Get out of Babylon, get away from the Chaldeans!
With a shout of joy declare this out loud,
send forth the message to the ends of the earth;
tell them: "Yahveh has redeemed his servant Jacob!
[21]They suffered no thirst when he led them through the wastelands,
he made water flow from the rock for them,
he split the rock, and the water gushed out."

[22]"There can be no well-being for the wicked," says Yahveh.

NOTES

[a] 1QIsaiah[a] *šmʿv ʾlh*, "listen to these things"; 4QIsa[d] = MT; [b] 4QIsa[d] has *gam*, "also"; 1QIsa[a] = MT; [c] 1QIsa[a] *yqbṣv kvlm vyšmʿv*, "let them all assemble and listen"; 4QIsa[d] and Vulg. = MT; [d] Syr. "who among you," but MT *bāhem* is supported by 1QIsa[a] and 4QIsa[d]; [e] MT *ʾăhēbô* is unusual but grammatically correct cf. 4QIsa[d] *ʾhbv* and Vulg. *Dominus dilexit eum* ("The Lord loved him"); some emend to participial form *ʾōhăbô* cf. 1QIsa[a] *ʾvhby*, "loving *me*," continuing in 1st person, and LXX *agapōn se*, "loving *you*" (sing.); retain MT; [f] reading *vĕzeraʿ* or *ûvĕzeraʿ* for MT *ûzĕrōʿô*, "and his arm," i.e. "strength," the option taken by Vulg. (*bracchium suum*); cf. LXX "to destroy the seed (*to sperma*) of the Chaldeans"; 1QIsa[a] = MT, 4QIsa[d] caret; [g] for MT *vĕhiṣlîaḥ darkô*, "his way will prosper/succeed," or "he will make his way successful," 1QIsa[a] has fem. *vhṣlyḥh* agreeing with *derek*; LXX *kai euodōsa*, "I made his way prosperous"; 4QIsa[d] = MT; [h] this statement is not textually dubious; it is supported by 1QIsa[a] and, partially, by 4QIsa[d] *vʿth ʾd]ny yhv[h*; it is missing from 4QIsa[c]; LXX and Vulg. = MT; [i] 1QIsa[a] has the fuller form *bdrk ʾšr tlk bh*, "in the way by which you are to go"; 4QIsa[c] and 4QIsa[d] = MT; [j] LXX *to onoma sou*, "your name," sing.

COMMENTS

We have the same problem here as in previous sections, the problem of discerning elements of structure and deciding to what extent these chapters can be said to constitute a unity of some kind, thematically or structurally. The initial imperatives lead into two sections, the first in the singular form of address (vv 12–13), the second in the plural (vv 14–16a), while the standard prophetic incipit marks off 17–19 as a distinct saying. This leaves 16b, in which a different voice intrudes, and it remains to be seen whether this brief interposed statement belongs in its context or is an interpolation and whether we are hearing the authorial voice or something quite different. As noted earlier, vv 20–21 round off the entire section, chs. 40–48, to which a brief observation has been appended (22).

This passage continues the theme of the one preceding, but the tone is quite different, the mild reproach of vv 18–19 notwithstanding. For the most part it restates the major themes of chs. 40–48. Not for the first time, the initial call for attention (vv 12–13) is directed to Jacob/Israel (44:1; 46:3; 48:1). Israel is addressed as the one called by Yahveh (41:9; 43:1); in this instance there is no balancing epithet for Jacob, leading several commentators rather gratuitously to provide one (e.g. *ʿabdî*, "my servant").

The divine self-predication *ʾănî hûʾ*, here as previously translated "I am the One," also appears at frequent intervals (41:4; 43:10, 11, 13, 25; 46:4; see Comments on 41:4 and 43:10, 13). It goes beyond the equally frequent asseveration "I am Yahveh" (43:11, 15; 44:24; 45:5, 6, 18) in affirming not only the distinct identity but the uniqueness, incomparability, and noncontingency of the God of Israel. We may also be justified in hearing an echo of the mysterious "*ʾehyeh* has sent you," uttered from the burning thornbush at Sinai (Exod 3:14) and the related assurance "I will be with you" (*ʾehyeh ʿimmāk* Exod 3:12 cf. Isa 43:5 "I am/will be with you"). The linking of these formulations with Yahveh as the First and the Last (cf. 41:4; 44:6) points us in the same direction. In more mundane terms, it denies that the God of Israel is part of a divine genealogy or theogony with forebears and descendants, of a kind familiar from *Enuma Elish* and a host of other mythological texts from the ancient Near East and Levant.

The point has already been clearly made:

> . . . that you may know me and trust me
> and understand that I am the One.
> Before me no god was formed,
> and there will be none after me. (43:10)
>
> I am the First, and I am the Last;
> there is no god but me. (44:6)

The idea of a cosmic Creator correlative with these self-predications is one of the most frequently recurring themes in chs. 40–48. The emphasis is on the creation of the sky rather than the earth, not only because it seems to call for greater creative power, exercised through Yahveh's *right* hand, but because it is directed polemically against the prestige and fascination of Babylonian astronomical lore. It was therefore the God of Israel who spread out the sky in the first place (40:22; 42:5; 44:24; 45:12; 51:13, 16) according to exact measurements, as in Job 38:4–5 (the verb *ṭpḥ* used here is related to *ṭepaḥ*, meaning "handbreadth," cf. *zeret* 40:12, another hand measurement). The summoning into existence, the control of the location, and the movements of the stars and constellations have also been mentioned (40:26; 45:12), a matter of some importance in view of Babylonian astronomical omens based on the observation and calculation of the movements of celestial bodies (44:25; 47:13).

The call to assemble (vv 14–16a) suggests another variation on the theme of the trial or public disputation, but the real or implied addressees are Judeans, not foreigners. For some time now the main concern of the speaker has been to break down opposition to the proposal that Cyrus is the one chosen to rescue and restore Israel and at the same time to overcome reluctance to move out of the security of faith in a national and locative deity. Those who proved unable to predict what was happening on the international scene are the gods, as previously, and we have reached the point where all that remained for Cyrus to do was to defeat the Chaldeans and capture their city (cf. earlier phases of Cyrus's career alluded to in 41:2–5, 25; 46:10–11).

The statement about Yahveh loving Cyrus is not surprising after we have heard that Yahveh is, so to speak, on a first-name basis with him (45:4) and has taken him by the hand (42:6), nominating him as his shepherd and anointed

(44:28; 45:1). In this instance the verb "love" (*ʾhb*) is, at any rate, more political than emotive, reminiscent of the "love" that imperial overlords professed toward their underlings in the vassal treaties. The author concludes by asserting that Yahveh's love for Cyrus should not prove to be a stumbling block, since the successful outcome of Cyrus's career has been proclaimed openly from the beginning.

The sudden change to first person in 48:16b ("and now the Sovereign Lord Yahveh has sent me, and his spirit . . .") has been read as the continuation of the prophet's comment in 16a. But since (pace Bonnard 1972, 207; Motyer 1993, 304–5) 16a is spoken by Yahveh (cf. the identical phrase *loʾ bassēter dibbartî*, "I never spoke in secret," in what is certainly discourse of Yahveh in Isa 45:19), this understanding of the statement would have to be due to a rereading of the entire passage by a glossator, perhaps from the circle of "Third Isaiah." This hypothesis, defended by Torrey (1928, 378), would not explain why v 16b is either a fragment of a longer statement or syntactically awkward to the point of unintelligibility. None of the many emendations proposed (see BHS) has helped to clarify the situation, and it is hardly likely that we are hearing the imagined response of Cyrus to the mission Yahveh has, once again, assigned him (McKenzie 1968, 99).

It is generally agreed that *rûḥô*, "his spirit," is not a second subject (i.e. "the Sovereign Lord Yahveh and his spirit have sent me"), since the spirit of God is sent but never sends (e.g. Judg 9:23; Ps 104:30), and we can be sure that it is not a second object either ("the Sovereign Lord Yahveh has sent me together with his spirit"). The only alternative seems to be to read *vĕrûḥô*, "and his spirit," as the beginning of a sentence, or several sentences, the remainder of which has been lost. The statement is no less significant for that, since it raises the important issue of authorship.

The authorial voice is first heard, appropriately, at the beginning of chs. 40–48 and is, significantly, accompanied by other prophetic voices (40:6; see commentary on 40:1–8). We hear it again at the beginning of the second major section 49–54(55)—that is, 49:1–6, in which a prophetic servant of Yahveh speaks of his mission. It is understandable that several exegetes have concluded that the 48:16b fragment belongs with 49:1–6 (e.g. Westermann 1969, 203). A prophet (whether the same as the speaker in 49:1–6 or not remains to be discussed) also speaks of himself in 50:4–9, followed by the comment of a disciple (see Comments on 50:10–11). It is noteworthy that this is one of the few passages apart from 48:16b where the title *ʾădōnay YHVH* appears in these chapters (40:10; 48:16b; 50:4, 5, 7, 9; 52:4).

Though it is discourse of Yahveh, Isa 59:21 deserves mention in this connection since it is addressed to a spirit-endowed prophetic figure who is assured that he will have descendants—meaning, in the context, disciples. The individual prophetic voice is then heard for the last time in 61:1–4, a passage that combines spirit-endowment with being sent on a mission and is therefore closely related to 48:16b. While these clues to authorship are too few and too uncertain to allow for definitive conclusions, they attest to continuities throughout section 40–66 and suggest further that these continuities may be explained with reference to a prophetic *diadochē* descending from the inspired figure conventionally referred to as Second Isaiah.

The potential for a striking statement of this kind to generate new readings corresponding to new situations is demonstrated by the way early Christian writers applied it to the doctrine of the Trinity. In his treatise against Celsus, Origen asks the critical question in his own way: "Who is it that says in Isaiah, 'and now the Lord has sent me and his Spirit?' Since the expression is ambiguous, is it the Father and the Holy Spirit who have sent Jesus, or the Father who has sent both Christ and the Holy Spirit? The latter is the true interpretation" (*Contra Celsum* book 1).

That vv 17–19 form a distinct section is clear from the prophetic incipit combined with the titles Redeemer and Holy One of Israel attributed to Yahveh, both of frequent occurrence in section 40–48 (cf. 43:14; 44:6, 24; 45:11; 49:7). But the saying that follows has nothing in common with the passage immediately preceding or indeed with the preceding chapters. The elegiac note of regret and sadness is also quite uncharacteristic of 40–48. A closer look at the vocabulary confirms the initial impression that the passage has more in common with the third than with the second major section of the book. Judah's still absent prosperity is compared to a river (*kĕnāhār šālôm*) only here and in 66:12. *Ṣĕdāqâ*, paired with *šālôm*, and with the meaning of vindication or victory rather than righteousness, appears often in the last section of the book (56:1; 59:9, 16, 17; 61:10–11; 63:1).

The reproachful homiletic note is also heard in the later chapters, especially in the communal lament in 63:7–64:12, as it is in Ps 81:13–16[14–17], a point noted by Westermann (1969, 355–73). The subtext of the description of what would have happened if Israel had kept the commandments is the Abrahamic promise of descendants as numerous as the sand on the seashore together with a great name (Gen 12:1–3; 22:17; 32:12). This, too, joined with the expectation of a land to live on, is heard more insistently in the later chapters (especially 60:21–22). The situation generating this kind of language is no longer that of the high expectations and euphoria preceding the fall of Babylon but the struggle for survival in Judah of the early Achaemenid period. Of this we will hear a great deal in the last section of the book.

The final injunction to leave Babylon and the Chaldeans behind while inviting the whole world to join in the celebration of the redemptive intervention of God on their behalf (vv 20–21) serves to round off chs. 40–48. It does this by referring back to the motif of the trek through the wilderness at the beginning of this section (40:3–4). Both 48:20–21 and the similar 52:11–12 recall the Exodus traditions. The first of the six imperatives in 48:20 (*ṣeʾû*, "go out" > *yṣʾ*) is the key word in the Exodus narratives (Exod 11:8; 12:41; 13:3–4; 16:1 etc.) and their liturgical celebration (e.g. Ps 114:1). The second verb, *brḥ*, usually "take to flight" but also used for rapid departure (cf. Cant 8:14), corresponds to *bĕḥippāzôn*, "in haste," in Isa 52:11–12. Both the verb and the adverbial phrase feature in the Exodus story (Exod 12:11; Deut 16:3; 14:5).

The Exodus also came to be seen as the paradigmatic redemptive act of God; what God does when he acts is redeem, set free (e.g. Exod 15:3). Prominent in these narrative traditions is also the provision of water in the wilderness. The allusion to this tradition in 48:21 assumes the conflation of the two versions in Exod 17:1–7 and Num 20:2–13 and their rendering in liturgical hymns (Pss 78:15–16; 105:41; 114:8). Isaiah 52:11–12 adds the motif of the God of Israel acting as rearguard for the Israelites in their trek through the wilderness, presumably in the guise of fire and a cloud (Num 10:25; Josh 6:9, 13). This cluster of themes will generate new narrative and many new levels of meaning, most obviously in the *Passover Haggadah*, but in an ongoing midrashic development in both Judaism and Christianity (e.g. 1 Cor 10:4; Rev 18:4).

Both 48:20–21 and 52:11–12 may have served as structural markers at one stage of the editorial process. Both immediately precede solemn statements by or about a servant of Yahveh, and there is a noticeable similarity of theme running through the material between them (49:1–52:10). But the complexity of these structural issues comes to the fore with the final motto (48:22), repeated in practically identical form in 57:21: "there is no well-being for the wicked, says Yahveh/says my God." That the 57:21 version is in its original context is clear from what immediately precedes it, where those who mourn are contrasted with the restless wicked within the household of Israel. That the statement was placed at the end of 40–48 as a structural marker is indeed possible but is not by itself an adequate explanation. In its new context it could be understood as adding a word of warning: the anticipated redemption that Israel is commanded to proclaim to the ends of the earth will not be shared by the reprobate within Israel. As such, it reflects the situation described in the final chapters of the book (corresponding with the final stages in the book's formation), in which the former distinction between Israel and the nations has been replaced by the distinction between the righteous (Yahveh's servants, those who tremble at his word, the repentant) and the reprobate (the sinners, those who rejoice in the present age) *within Israel*. This invisible line drawn within the community will one day become visible; there will be a day of redemption but also a settling of accounts.

The need to make these distinctions, which we recognize as a feature of sectarian thinking, has left its mark throughout the book. We recognize it in the injunction addressed to Yahveh not to forgive and not to show favor to the reprobate (2:9b; 26:10), and it is particularly in evidence in the final, dark scenario, in which the bodies of the reprobate are burned like rubbish outside Jerusalem (66:24). Section 40–48 ends with a similar if more prosaic statement of the same conviction.

THE SERVANT'S ADDRESS TO THE NATIONS (49:1–6)

(Begg 1986; Giblin 1959; E. Haag 1983; H. Haag 1985; Hermisson 1996a; O. Kaiser 1959, 53–65; van der Kooij 1997; Landy 1993; Lindsey 1982a; Lohfink 1972; Merendino 1980; Sæbø, M. 1989; Snaith 1967; Steck 1984; Wilcox and Paton-Williams 1988)

TRANSLATION

i

49 [1]Listen to me, you islands;
take heed, you peoples far distant!
Yahveh called me before I was born,
from my mother's womb he pronounced my name.
[2]He made my mouth like a whetted sword
and hid me in the shadow of his hand;[a]
he made me a sharpened[b] arrow,
concealed me in his quiver.
[3]He said to me: "You are my servant,
[Israel,][c] through whom my glory will be manifest."
[4]But I thought, "In vain have I toiled,
I have spent my strength entirely to no purpose;[d]
yet surely my cause is present to Yahveh,
my reward is with my God.
[5b]I shall gain honor in Yahveh's sight,
my God will be my strength."[e]

ii

[5a]Now this is what Yahveh says,
he who formed me from the womb to be his servant,
to bring Jacob back to him,
that Israel may be gathered to him:[f]
[6]"Is it too light a task[g]
for you to be my servant,
to establish the tribes of Jacob
and restore the survivors[h] of Israel?
I appoint you a light to the nations
that my salvation may reach to the ends of the earth."

NOTES

[a] 1QIsaiah[a] has pl. "hands"; [b] rather than *bārûr,* "polished," cf. Jer 51:11; LXX *eklekton* perhaps reading *bāḥûr;* [c] one of the most celebrated *cruces* in

the book; *yiśrāʾēl* is present in all Hebrew MSS except Kenn. 96; also in 1QIsa[a] (missing from 4QIsa[d]), Tg., and LXX; yet, unless it is the name of an individual, which is exceedingly improbable, it is inconsistent with the mission to Israel as described in vv 5–6 and therefore must be an early gloss, perhaps based on 44:21 cf. 42:1 LXX; the glossator would therefore have understood it to be appositional rather than a vocative; [d] translating *lĕtōhû vĕhebel*, literally, "for chaos and nothingness"; [e] 1QIsa[a] *ʿzry*, "my help," as in Tg., for MT *ʿuzzî*, supported by LXX; v 5b is transposed to follow 4; [f] reading *lô* for MT, 4QIsa[d], and LXX *lōʾ*, which gives a less probable translation of the verb *ʾsp* cf. 57:1: "that Israel not be 'gathered'" i.e. annihilated; [g] omitting "he says" at the beginning of the line, probably added after the transposition of 5b; [h] K and 1QIsa[a] *nĕṣîrê*, Q *nĕṣûrê* but with no difference in meaning; it is unnecessary to emend to *niṣĕrê*, "offshoots," "descendants," pace Whybray 1975, 139.

COMMENTS

The inclusio of 48:20–21 (cf. 40:1–5) rounds off 40–48 as a section distinct from the one following. The concluding statement denying well-being to the reprobate (48:22)—in other words, excluding them from enjoyment of the providential benefits mentioned in the previous verse—seems to have been taken from 57:21, apparently its original situation, to judge by the immediate context (57:20). It may be compared with 66:24, the final statement in the book, which has the purpose of maintaining a firm distinction between the righteous and the reprobate in the final judgment.

Isaiah 49:1–6, therefore, marks a new departure. It has no apparent nexus with the preceding apostrophe, unless one represents the servant as a new Moses who will lead the exodus from the diaspora as the old Moses did from Egypt (J. Fischer 1939, 101). We hear no more about Cyrus and the anticipated fall of Babylon, and there is no more polemic against the cult of images. That chs. 49–54 were conceived *at some point in the history of the book* as a distinct unit is suggested by the address of the *ʿebed* ("servant") at the beginning (49:1–6) and the reference to the *ʿăbādîm* ("servants") at the end (54:17). On that reading, ch. 55 would be transitional between 49–54 and 56–66 but closer to what follows than to what precedes (see "the everlasting sign/name that shall not be cut off," 55:13 and 56:5).

A different kind of structural marker is the repetition of the Exodus theme in 52:11–12 and 55:12–13, another variation on the inclusio of 40:3–5–48:20–22. That these passages may be taken as demarcating two subunits of 40–55 is also suggested by the fact that both open with statements by or about an anonymous servant:

49:1–6 ———————— 52:11–12

52:13–53:12 ——————55:12–13

Moreover, both sections combine the themes of servanthood and return with apostrophe to Jerusalem (49:14–50:3 and 51:17–52:10; 54:1–17), the Jerusalem theme alternating throughout with the servant passages.

As we read on through these chapters, we get the impression of successive stages in the composition of chs. 40–66, with very definite elements of continuity, yet corresponding to a changing political and social situation, and a situation generally not changing for the better. Since structural data of the kind just mentioned encode meanings, our interpretation of the new section beginning with 49:1–6 will be guided by them.

Isaiah 49:1–6 is the address of an unnamed individual to foreign nations, describing his special relationship to Yahveh, his designation for a particular mission, and his equipment for discharging the task laid on him (vv 1–3). He reacts to his commission with discouragement and a sense of failure (4, 5b), at which point he is given a new mission to be the means for bringing salvation to the nations of the world (5a, 6). The passage cannot be aligned with any particular literary or rhetorical genre, whether a thanksgiving psalm, a lament psalm, or a report of commissioning (Melugin 1976, 69–71, 142–47). Some features may be borrowed from psalms, as is often the case in chs. 40–66; expressions of discouragement and fear followed by a reassuring message, for example Ps 31:23[22], and some readers have also picked up faint echoes of Jeremiah's laments (e.g. Jer 12:1–6). But by the time these discourses came to be written down, the literary genres identified by standard form-critical procedures in prophetic books had to a considerable extent disintegrated.

While the situation to which the servant's speech corresponds is new, the language of the passage and its rhetorical features have much in common with section 40–48. The call for attention addressed to foreign nations, including coastlands and islands to the west (*'iyyîm* 40:15; 41:1, 5; 42:4, 10, 12, 15), replicates 41:1. Yahveh has often been heard summoning Israel and designated individuals to discharge specific tasks (41:9; 42:6; 43:1; 45:3–4; 48:15). We have heard of Yahveh's forming Israel in the womb (43:1; 44:1), of his glory or splendor manifested through Israel (verb *p'r* Hithpael, 44:23), and of salvation on offer from one end of the earth to the other (42:10; 43:6; 45:22; 48:20). The accumulation of appositional clauses introducing *oratio recta* of Yahveh (v 5a) is also a feature peculiar to the discourses in 40–48 (42:5; 43:1; 44:1–2, 6; 45:1, 18).

Much of this characteristic language in 40–48 refers to the mission confided to Cyrus by Yahveh. It is Cyrus who is summoned (45:3–4; 48:15), whose name is pronounced (45:3–4), who is to be a light for the nations (42:6), and one of whose honorific titles is Servant of Yahveh (42:1–4). This designation "servant" (*'ebed*) indicates an agent chosen for specific tasks. It may be predicated of any human agent chosen by God for a mission, whether an individual or a collectivity. In 40–48, as we have seen, in all instances save one the *'ebed* is Israel presented under the name of the eponym Israel/Jacob (41:8–9; 42:19; 43:10; 44:1, 2, 21, 26; 45:4; 48:20).

In 42:1–4, however, I argued that the description of the mission and the context of chs. 40–48 as a whole strongly favor an identification with Cyrus. Since after 40–48 the focus shifts decisively away from Cyrus, we conclude that we have entered a phase in which it has become evident that the Iranian has not lived up to expectations, that he was not about to discharge the tasks assigned to him—namely, to set prisoners free (42:7; 45:13) and rebuild Jerusalem with its temple and the Judean towns destroyed by the Babylonians (44:26, 28; 45:13). At the same time, it seems that internal opposition to the prophet's religiopolitical ideas had reached a critical point. The seer whose voice we are hearing in 49:1–6 reacts to this situation by taking on himself the burden of being Yahveh's *ʿebed*. That this is the same voice heard at the beginning of 40–48 (40:5) is possible, even probable, though hardly provable. But in view of the situation as described, it is interesting that the last occasion on which the voice of an individual seer was heard—"and now the Sovereign Lord Yahveh has sent me, and his spirit . . ." (48:16)—was a fragmentary sentence appended to the last allusion in these chapters to Cyrus.

The seer's call for attention addressed to foreign nations does not introduce another mock-trial scene, as in 41:1, but is in anticipation of the new mission of taking over from Cyrus the task of enlightening the nations—that is, being an instrument of salvation among them. For this mission the seer was designated prenatally. Originally an element in the type-scene of prophetic commissioning (Jer 1:5, quoted by Paul in Gal 1:15), designation from the womb was applied metaphorically to the prehistory of Israel (44:1–2). The pronouncing of the name (*hizkîr šĕmî* cf. Akkadian *šuma zakāru*) is a solemn act of invocation or conferring a special identity.

The military nature of the seer's equipment is interesting. Representing the mouth, the organ of speech, as a sharp sword plays on the Hebrew idiom of the edge of the sword (*pî-ḥereb*, e.g. Deut 13:16), literally, the "mouth of the sword," a mouth that also devours (Deut 32:42; 2 Sam 11:25). Similar to "the rod of his mouth," the idiom used of the once and future ruler (Isa 11:4), the expression connotes the power of incisive speech, the power to persuade and incite to action, to make a decisive difference in the political sphere. It therefore draws our attention to the *political* role of prophecy, a role illustrated by the prophets Zedekiah and Ahab, who were executed by the Babylonians (Jer 29:22), and by politically-involved prophets in the early Achaemenid period, including Haggai and Zechariah. The metaphoric linkage between sword and speech will also recur frequently in Christian texts, from the New Testament (Heb 4:12; Rev 1:16; 19:15) to Luther ("*Das Wort ist das Schwert Gottes* . . .") and Blake ("Nor shall my sword sleep in my hand . . .").

For the seer of 48:1–6, these weapons are still hidden; they are prepared for future use, for the day when Yahveh's glory will be manifest in the emancipation of Israel. (Compare 44:23, where the glorification of Yahveh is tied in with the redemption of Israel.) This is *political* language, a political manifesto which declares, in effect, that the task of bringing about the will of Israel's God in the political sphere that Cyrus was unwilling to perform will now be undertaken by Israel itself by means of its prophetic representative.

The expression of a sense of discouragement and failure is a common topos in liturgical hymns and biographical narrative (e.g. Moses, Elijah, and Jeremiah). In this instance (vv 4, 5b) it would be natural to find an explanation in the hints of opposition to the seer's message in 40–48 that seem to become stronger and more overt with the passing of time. Hence the abundance of rhetorical questions ("Do you not know? Have you not heard?" 40:21, 28), the complaint that Israel's God is disregarding his people's just cause (*mišpāṭ*, 40:27 cf. 49:4b), the frequent reproaches (43:22–24; 45:9–13; 48:18–19) and accusations of spiritual dullness (42:18–20), stubbornness (46:12; 48:4), disingenuous worship (48:1), and a general tendency to transgress (46:8). This is a prophet who is having serious trouble persuading his public.

Now, however, the situation has changed, and the servant's mission on behalf of his people is described in general terms without reference to Cyrus and *his* mission. The four expressions with which the seer's mission is described show considerable overlap. He is to bring Israel back to Yahveh (*šûb* Pilpel), which includes the idea of reintegration and return to the land (cf. Jer 50:19; Ezek 39:27), physical restoration (cf. Isa 58:12; Ps 23:3; 60:3), and moral regeneration. The usage is similar to *šûb* Hiphil at the end of the Latter Prophets (Mal 3:24[4:6]). There we learn that, on his return, Elijah will cause children to return to parents and parents to children, a mission rightly understood by Sirach as the restoration and reintegration of dispersed Israel (Sir 48:10).

The physical return to Judah from diasporic locations is more directly expressed in the gathering in of Israel (*ʾsp* Niphal cf. 11:12 with *qbṣ*, "collect") and the return of those who had survived the catastrophe of 586 (*šûb* Hiphil), though the idea of moral reformation, "turning," is often present where this verb appears. The reestablishment or restoration (*qûm* Hiphil) of the tribes of Jacob is a more inclusive formulation. It is also of interest in view of the indications of a certain retribalization going on at that time, reflected in frequent references to "Judah and Benjamin" in Chronicles and Ezra–Nehemiah, in the prevalence of duodecimal symbolism in these books and elsewhere (e.g. 1 Chr 25:9–21; Ezra 2:2; 6:17) and, eventually, in personal names drawn from tribal traditions then known: for example, Judah (Ezra 10:23; Neh 11:9), Benjamin (Neh 3:23); Manasseh (Ezra 10:33); and Joseph (Ezra 10:42; Neh 12:14).

After the assurance of ultimate vindication, repeated more firmly and emphatically later (50:7–9), the prophet is given a further mission of even broader scope. Strange, indeed, it must seem by normal standards, this responding to the complaint of inadequacy and failure by adding a further and heavier burden of responsibility. The terms in which this additional task is stated provide the clearest indication that the prophet is taking over a mission originally confided to Cyrus, if with some significant differences, for it was Cyrus who was designated "a light to the nations" in the first place (42:6). What the metaphor entails is clarified somewhat by the statement later on that Yahveh's *tôrâ* and *mišpāṭ* will serve as a light for the peoples (*ʾôr ʿammîm* 51:4), which implies the establishment of a just order based on law.

As we learn from the comment on the present passage, the servant is to replicate the other charge to Cyrus, that of serving as a covenant for the people (49:8 cf. 42:6). This also involves obligation and the rule of law (see the Comments on 42:6). The goal of this double commission, in favor of Israel and the Gentile world, will be achieved when Yahveh's salvation is available throughout the world. "Salvation" (*yĕšûʿâ*) is one of those slippery terms that have different connotations to different people and in different situations. In chs. 49–66 it appears several times twinned with *ṣĕdāqâ* (51:6, 8; 56:1; 59:17; 62:1), the latter meaning not "righteousness," as elsewhere, but "triumph," "victory." Salvation is proclaimed when God's kingdom (52:7) is finally established, and the essence of the kingdom is the imposition of a just order based on law and therefore, necessarily, involving coercion (cf. 45:22 and the metaphor of Yahveh's arm, 52:10).

How the prophet was to discharge this task we are not told, though we may be sure it involved projecting into the political sphere the power of the spoken and perhaps also the written word. This apostrophe opens up one of the great issues in the history of the Jewish people, leading up to and during the Second Commonwealth—that of relations with the Gentile world.

The traditional Christian explanation, illustrated (for example) by the annotations of the Scottish minister John Smith to the translation of Bishop Robert Lowth published in 1794, was that, after the failure of his mission to the Jews, the Messiah here turns to the Gentiles. But apart from the fact that the prophet's commission vis-à-vis his own people is not rescinded, we shall see that the issue was one with which Jewish communities struggled throughout the entire period of the Second Commonwealth and that the struggle between a more integrationist and a more expansive attitude has left its mark on the book at several points.

TWO COMMENTS ABOUT THE SERVANT (49:7–13)

(McConville 1986; Merendino 1982a; Patrick 1984; Rendsburg 1983; Thomas 1968; Werlitz 1997)

TRANSLATION

i

49 [7]These are words of Yahveh, Israel's Redeemer, Israel's Holy One, to one despised,[a] to one abhorred[b] by the nations, enslaved to foreign rulers:[c]

"When they see you, kings will rise to their feet;
princes will pay you homage
for the sake of Yahveh, who is faithful,
the Holy One of Israel who chose you."

ii

[8]These are words of Yahveh:
"At the time of my good pleasure I answer you;

on the day of salvation I assist you;
I preserve[d] you and present you
as a covenant to the people,
to establish the land,[e]
to apportion the devastated holdings,
[9]to tell those in prison to come out,
those in darkness to emerge.[f]
They will feed by all the waysides,[g]
with pasture on all the bare heights;
[10]they will suffer neither hunger nor thirst;
neither scorching wind nor sun will afflict them.
For the One who pities them will guide them,
lead them to springs of water.
[11]I will make all my mountains into pathways,
my highways[g] will be built up.
[12]Look, these are coming from afar;
look, these others from the north and the west
and yet others from the land of Syene."[h]

iii

[13]Sky, shout for joy; earth, rejoice!
Mountains break out[i] into joyful song!
For Yahveh has comforted his people;
he has pitied his afflicted ones.

NOTES

[a] MT *libězoh*, preposition + Infinitive Construct = "to despise," "a despising"; a Cairo Geniza fragment reads *lěbōzēh*, "to one despising," as in LXX *hagiasate ton phaulizonta tēn psuchēn autou*, "sanctify him that lightly esteems his soul," a meaning accepted by G. R. Driver (1935, 401) with reference to 49:4, though *nepeš* should probably be read as an intensitive cf. 2 Sam 5:8; 1QIsa[a] supported by 4QIsa[d] reads *libzûy* Qal passive, "to one despised," cf. Aqu., Symm., Theod., and Syr.; Tg. also but in pl. (*ldbsyryn*); [b] reading passive participle *mětōʿab* for MT *mětāʿēb* with LXX *ton bdelussomenon hupo tōn ethnōn*, "the one abhorred by the nations"; Vulg. *ad abominatam gentem*, "to an abominated people," may represent Jerome's own distortion of the meaning; [c] literally, "a slave of rulers"; [d] LXX[A] *eboēthēsa soi*, "I helped you," and LXX[B] *eplasa se*, "I formed you," and Tg. also derives *vě'eṣṣārěkâ* from *yṣr*, "form," "fashion," cf. 44:12, but a derivation from *nṣr* is correct and is supported by Vulg. *servavi te*; [e] many commentators suggest adding an adjective e.g. *ṣiyyâ*, "parched," *metri causa*; Tg., "to raise up the righteous who lie in the dust," goes its own way; [f] in the Hebrew of 9a–b, "come out" and "emerge" are imperatives in direct speech; [g] 1QIsa[a] has "on all the mountains" (*ʿl kl-hrym*), but MT is acceptable and supported by LXX *en pasais tais hodois*; the verb *rʿh* is more

commonly used of animals feeding rather than of people, though Israel is also represented as a herd or flock (e.g. 40:11); but the verb can also be used transitively e.g. Isa 40:11; 61:5; [h] MT *mēʾereṣ sînîm*, not "from the land of the Chinese," as in Modern Hebrew (a suggestion made by F. Delitzsch); the ancient versions were reduced to guesswork e.g. LXX "the land of the Persians," Tg. *dĕrômâ*, "the south," cf. Vulg. *de terra australi*; 1QIsa[a] *svnyym*, a gentilic, points to Syene = Aswan cf. Ezek 29:10; 30:6; [i] following Q and 1QIsa[a] rather than K, "let them break out" (Jussive).

COMMENTS

This section follows the previous one with two sayings of unequal length (vv 7, 8–12), rounded off with a hymn stanza (13). The repeated introductory formula has misled several commentators into making unnecessary adjustments and "improvements" to this passage. For Westermann (1969, 212–14), for example, 7b was the original conclusion of the one oracle of salvation; in his translation it therefore follows 49:12; and since he believes that the second introduction (8a) was added after 7b was moved to its present position, he omits it. The hypothesis could be correct, since 7b sounds like a conclusion (cf. somewhat similar endings in 40:23 and 55:5), but unfortunately Westermann omits to explain why, on this reading, 7b was moved back several verses to its present position. The hypothesis is in any case unnecessary, since 7b does in fact conclude a saying, and the repetition of *qĕdôs yiśrāʾēl* ("the Holy One of Israel") rounds off this brief saying (v 7) with an inclusio.

The common understanding of these sayings as commentary on the autobiographical statement of the anonymous Servant immediately preceding is supported by the similar structure of 42:1–4, followed by the comment in 42:5–9, this too rounded off with a hymn stanza (42:10–13). However, the two sayings need not, and in fact do not, interpret the preceding passage in the same way. The first of the two "words of Yahveh" (49:7) takes up the key term *ʿebed*, "servant," but uses it not as an honorific title but in the sense of a menial, a slave (*ʿebed mōšĕlîm*, literally, "a slave of rulers"). The referent is clearly the Israelite people as a whole, not an individual, and the description of their present political situation, followed by the scenario of the eschatological triumph of Yahveh to be realized through his people (cf. 45:23; 60:3, 10–11; 62:2), points unmistakably in the same direction.

The second saying (49:8–12) alludes more directly to the role of the anonymous servant in 49:1–6, though with exclusive reference to the mission to Israel confided to the servant, the description of which (vv 9–12) is compatible with the less-specific terms of the commissioning in the previous statement (5–6). Since 8–12 is also connected with 1–6 by means of the catchword nexus (*yĕšûʿâ*, "salvation," vv 6 and 8), a frequent linking device in these chapters, it seems that v 7 was inserted at the stage in which the individual-prophetic understanding of the servant of 49:1–6 gave way to the collective interpretation.

The first of the two "words" introduces Yahveh as Redeemer and Holy One, attributes of frequent occurrence in these chapters (see 41:14). It is addressed to Jews under foreign rule, a condition that lasted from 604 to 141 B.C.E. (1 Macc 13:41–42) and, after a brief interlude, for centuries thereafter. If the saying dates to the early Persian period, as seems probable, we would have to assume that the language describing the attitude of the imperial power is somewhat inflated, since indications are that the Persians were in general well disposed toward the Jews in their Empire. At the same time, subjection to foreign rule remained basically unacceptable, as we see from Nehemiah's prayer, which also describes it as a form of slavery: "We are slaves this day in the land you (Yahveh) gave to our ancestors to enjoy its fruit and its good gifts; yes, we are slaves" (Neh 9:36). The attitude of the nations described in 49:7 is, at any rate, dictated by the fact that the Jews are a defeated and subject people; there is no evidence for religious or cultural anti-Judaism before the Greco-Roman period.

The rapid reversal of fortune between the first and the second part of the saying dramatizes the contrast between the attitude of the nations toward Israel and the attitude of their God, who is faithful (*ne'ĕman*, predicated of God only here and Deut 7:9)—faithful to his promises spoken through the prophets, faithful in not abandoning the people he has chosen (cf. 41:8–9; 43:10, 20; 44:1–2; 45:4). The perspective is one more commonly encountered in the final chapters of the book, where a reversal of fortune is presented not as an empirically realizable goal but as a hope for a future hidden with God, a future in which the roles will be reversed and the political powers and potentates will serve Israel (60:3, 10–11; 62:2). This theme of reversal from humiliation to triumph, from *kenōsis* to *doxa*, is a well-attested and familiar aspect of early Christian apocalyptic.

The second saying (49:8–12) is addressed to the individual whose voice we have just heard (vv 1–6). It consists in reassurance (form-critically, an oracle of salvation) about the original mission to Israel and therefore responds to the servant's expression of discouragement and dejection. The time at which the positive response and the assistance will be forthcoming is not clearly stated. Addressing Jerusalem Yahveh says, "In my anger I struck you, but in (the time of) my good pleasure I took pity on you" (60:10), which suggests a summary of Jerusalem's history of destruction in the recent past followed by present or hoped-for reconstruction. The time of God's good pleasure is whenever God elects to answer prayer and come to the assistance of the disappointed and defeated; this is a commonplace of liturgical piety:

Yahveh, my prayer is to you.
My God, in the time of your good pleasure,
in the abundance of your love, answer me;
with your faithful will to save, rescue me. (Ps 69:14)

Early Christian writers who used this Isaian text (Luke 2:14; 2 Cor 6:2) perceived correctly that, though the work of salvation had not yet taken effect, it was now assured, a matter already decided in principle. This is made quite clear in that the prophet is already destined to be a covenant to the people. The designation used here (v 8b) repeats verbatim the mission confided to Cyrus with respect to the people of Israel, while omitting the additional predicate of a light to the nations (42:6b). We have seen that Cyrus's mission was essentially and in the first place to be undertaken on behalf of Israel (45:4), and to consist in the restoration of Jerusalem and Judah.

The implication seems to be that the prophetic individual whom we heard speaking in 49:1–6 is convinced that the mission originally confided to Cyrus has now passed by default to him. This is not as strange as it may sound. Throughout the history of the kingdoms and on into the time of Babylonian and Persian hegemony, prophets were involved in political life, often playing a decisive role and not infrequently losing their lives in the process.

The more detailed account of the mission that follows (8b–12) is essentially the same as Cyrus's mission (42:7; 44:26–28; 45:13) and restates in more specific terms the task placed on the servant in 49:5–6. The task of "establishing the land" corresponds to establishing the tribes of Jacob (49:6 with the same verb, *hēqîm*). That is, as the continuation of the verse makes clear, the task is to make a new allotment of land holdings (*naḥălôt*), to repeat the distribution of land carried out by Joshua after the conquest (Josh 13–19) in obedience to the charge laid on him by Moses (Deut 3:28; 19:3; 31:7). I take this to be one more indication of close ideological links between this prophetic author and the Deuteronomists active at about the same time, for whom the reoccupation of the land and reestablishment of a commonwealth on the basis of a schematic and fictive twelve-tribal union formed a crucial part of the agenda. The successive deportations and the expropriation of the real estate of the deportees (2 Kgs 25:12; Jer 39:10; 52:16), for which justification could easily be contrived (Ezek 11:14–17; 33:23–24), would have made title to land a crucial issue in the event of a return of the original titleholders or their heirs.

The account of the mission and its predicted outcome is described in terms familiar from the mission originally confided to Cyrus, the principal factor being release from the constraints of involuntary exile in a foreign country represented as prison and darkness (cf. 42:7, 13, 16, 18–19, 22; 45:13). The themes and even the language of chs. 40–48 are simply repeated and juxtaposed: Yahveh is the shepherd, Israel the flock (40:11); the bare hills are transformed into pastureland (41:18); hunger and thirst are satisfied (48:21); abundant sources of water are provided (41:18; 43:20; 44:3; 48:21); and mountains no longer constitute obstacles on the way back to the land (40:4; 42:16).

All of this leads up to the return from the diaspora, not just from Babylon but from all points of the compass (cf. 43:5–6). The only place named is one far to the south. Syene (Aswan), the military and commercial center at the southern boundary of Egypt, on the east bank of the Nile opposite the island of Jeb (Elephantine), is mentioned often in the Aramaic papyri discovered on the island and twice in Ezekiel (29:10; 30:6). One of several centers in Egypt with a Jewish population at that time (cf. those listed in Jer 44:1 and, perhaps somewhat later, the five Egyptian cities in which Hebrew was spoken, Isa 19:18), it was no doubt the Jewish settlement furthest southwest known to the author.

The address of the servant and the addenda (vv 7 and 8–12) conclude with a hymn stanza: an invocation to the sky and the earth, therefore to all creation, to rejoice (v 13). This brief stanza has a verbal link with the second addendum (vv 8–12) through the reference to the divine pity (*mĕraḥămām*, 10; *yĕraḥēm*, 13b). The verbal stem *rḥm*, "to show pity, compassion" (vv 10, 13, 15), is a *Leitmotif* in this chapter, reminding us also of the merciful and compassionate God addressed in the Qur'an (*al-raḥmān, al-raḥeem*). The present stanza also follows the stylistic pattern of chs. 40–48, according to which announcements about Yahveh's servant Cyrus and Yahveh's servant Israel provoke the same hymnic call to celebration (42:10–13; 44:23; 45:8). The reason is that Yahveh God is the merciful, the compassionate One. The prophetic announcement of the comfort of God with which these chapters began (40:1) is therefore now being fulfilled in the events taking place and about to take place (cf. 51:3, 12; 52:9).

THE WOMAN ZION AND HER NEW FAMILY (49:14–23)

(Blythin 1966a; Darr 1994, 110–13, 174–76; Forster 1993; Gruber 1981–1982; Jeppesen 1993; Merendino 1982b; Sawyer 1989b; J. Schmitt 1985; Steck 1986)

TRANSLATION

i

49 [14]But Zion says, "Yahveh has deserted me;
my lord[a] has forgotten me."

[15]"Can a woman forget her baby
and show no love[b] for the child of her womb?
But even if women should forget,[c]
I will not forget you.
[16]See, I have inscribed you on the palms of my hands;
your walls are present to me always.
[17]Those who build you up[d] work faster
than those who tore you down.[e]
Those who laid you waste have left you alone.
[18]Lift up your eyes, look about you;
they are all assembled, to you they have come.
As I live—a pronouncement of Yahveh—
surely you shall wear them all like an ornament,[f]

you shall deck yourself with them like a bride.
[19]Surely your ruins, your desolate places,
and your devastated land—[g]
surely your land is too confined for its people,
while those who destroyed you have gone far away.
[20]The children born when you were bereaved[h]
will say once again in your hearing,
'This place is too cramped for us;
make room for us to settle.'
[21]Then you will say to yourself,
'Who has begotten these children for me
when I was bereaved and barren,
exiled, cast aside;[i]
who has brought them up?
I was left all alone;
where then have all these come from?'"

ii

[22]This is a word of Yahveh:
"Observe: I raise my hand to the nations,
I lift up a signal for the peoples;
they will carry your sons in their laps,
your daughters will be borne on their shoulders;
[23]kings will look after your children,
their queens will serve you as nurses;
with their face to the ground, they will pay you homage
and lick the dust of your feet.
Then you will acknowledge that I am Yahveh;
those who wait for me will not be disappointed."

NOTES

Some words and fragments of words are preserved in 4QIsa[b,c,d] but with no divergence from MT. [a] 1QIsaiah[a] adds *v'lvhy*, "and my God," superscript above *v'dvny*, "and my lord"; [b] MT *mēraḥēm* is supported by LXX *tou mē eleēsai*, "not to take pity . . ."; the often-suggested alternative reading *mĕraḥēm*, participle (e.g. Whybray 1975, 143–44: "a loving mother") is unlikely, since fem. *mĕraḥemet* would be expected in the context, even though not absolutely required (see GKC §122a); [c] MT, supported by 1QIsa[a] and 4QIsa[d], has an unusual construction with pl. pronoun (*gam 'ēlleh*) where we would expect sing. fem. pronoun cf. LXX *ei de kai epilathoito tauta gunē*, "even if a woman should forget these things," and Vulg.: *et si illa oblita fuerit*, "even if she should forget"; BHS suggests *hiškāḥannâ* with *nun energicum* (GKC §58l) to preserve sing.; repointing as Niphal *iššākaḥnâ*, "if these are forgotten" (Cairo Geniza fragment), is not an improvement; [d] reading *bānāyik* with 1QIsa[a], Aqu.,

Theod., Vulg. *structores tui* for MT *bānāyik*, "your sons" (also Symm.), though perhaps with intentional *lusus verborum*; [e] reading *mēhōrĕsayik*, (participle with pronominal suffix) for MT *mĕhārĕsayik*, which would require the reading "those who tore you down and those who laid you waste have left you alone"; cf. LXX "soon you will be built by those by whom you were destroyed"; [f] *kāʾādî*, "like an ornament," omitted by LXX, but MT is to be retained; [g] v 19a has no verb, but it seems more consonant with the context to assume the omission of a verb than to read, "though I laid you waste, made you desolate, and razed you to the ground," repointing MT with no consonantal change as follows: *kî hērabtîk vĕšomamtîk vĕʾereṣ hărastîk* (following Torrey 1928, 386–87 and NEB); LXX omits *ʾereṣ*, "land"; [h] cf. LXX *hous apolōlekas*, "whom you lost"; [i] MT *gôlâ vĕsûrâ*, omitted by LXX, is metrically intrusive and may be a gloss on the metaphoric *šĕkûlâ vĕgalmûdâ*; both Syr. and Vulg. (*captiva*) seem to have read *vaʾăsûrâ*, "captive, prisoner."

COMMENTS

Continuity is maintained by recalling the theme of the comfort and compassion of God with which the previous passage ended. By a natural and felicitous association of ideas and images, this motif segues into the language of maternal behavior and familial connections that follows, language in the service of the great theme of the creation of a new people, a people more numerous than the one effectively destroyed or dispersed during the Babylonian conquest. The way this theme is developed in the present passage can be compared with the book of Job read as a kind of parabolic retelling of the history of the people poised between the experience of disaster in the immediate past and present aspirations. Job, we recall, lost his entire family, his possessions, and land in the sequence of disasters visited on the mythical land of Uz, in which, as is made clear from the start, the God of Israel played a decisive role. But then, as a result of his patient if by no means silent waiting on God, Job obtained more abundant possessions and a new family as numerous as the old (Job 42:10–15), even though those who died at the beginning remained dead.

The key to this reading of the story is the simple notice that "Yahveh restored his fortunes" (Job 42:10). The Hebrew phrase *šûb šĕbût* used here plays on the association between the idea of returning or turning around (*šûb*) and that of captivity (verbal stem *šbh*), and in more explicitly theological passages is standard shorthand for return from exile and restoration (Deut 30:3; Jer 29:14; Ezek 39:25 etc.). The motifs developed in Isa 49:14–23 also frequently emerge when this key phrase appears in other places: God's pity and compassion for his people (*rḥm*, Jer 33:26; Ezek 39:25), the program of rebuilding (Jer 30:18; 33:7; Amos 9:14), and the restoration of the devastated land (Jer 33:26; Ezek 39:25).

The present passage and Job can therefore be read as two ways of envisaging a situation of disaster for which the national deity is considered accountable, a situation that gives rise to the complaint that he has forgotten his people and a situation that involves abandonment and bereavement. The structure and sequencing of the theme is fairly simple. Zion's complaint (v 14) is answered, typically, with a rhetorical question (v 15 cf. 40:27–28), and reassurance consists in the promise of the rebuilding of the city (16–17), its repopulation (18–21), and a mass return from the diaspora that will make a vast demographic expansion possible (22–23). The standard prophetic *incipit* at v 22 is occasioned by the solemn and explicit assurance that follows and is not otherwise structurally significant. More significant is the conclusion, familiar from the Priestly matter in the Pentateuch and Ezekiel, "you will know (acknowledge) that I am Yahveh" (23b) with its variant at the end of the next section (26b).

Psalms of communal and individual lament are full of expressions of misgiving about the ability and willingness of God to be present to his devotees, joined with the fear that he has abandoned (Ps 22:2) or forgotten them (e.g. Pss 10:11–12; 74:19, 23). In that respect the prayer of lament is a way of getting God's attention and activating God's memory. While the present passage is obviously not a lament psalm, it has no doubt drawn on typical liturgical language. The dependence can be tested by a cursory reading of Lamentations, written in liturgical form irrespective of whether it was ever actually recited liturgically. There we find motifs reminiscent of our passage: the need for and lack of comforting (1:9, 16, 21), the dark knowledge that Yahveh was responsible for the disaster (2:8, 17; 3:37), waiting for God (3:25–26), women who are widowed and deprived of their children (5:3), and women who neglect their children to the point of killing and eating them during the siege (2:20; 4:3, 20)—all leading up to the desperate cry near the end:

Why do you forget us forever?
Why have you deserted us for so long? (Lam 5:20)

In our passage the lament is placed in the mouth of Zion/Jerusalem, represented as a woman, and it carries undertones of marital desertion. As is well known, this kind of familial and marital figurative language seems to have originated or at least entered the biblical mainstream, including early Christian writings, with Hosea (Hos 1–3; 11:1–2 cf. Jer 31:20, 32 etc.). Far from being represented in female terms in the present passage, as is sometimes alleged, Yahveh at least fleetingly fills the role of the absentee husband, as is the case later (50:1a).

With this dialogue between Zion and Yahveh we reach a turning point in the book, and in the second main section of the book in particular. Up to this point the focus has been on Israel/Jacob, and Jerusalem/Zion has been mentioned only sporadically as city (35:10; 44:26, 28; 46:13) and as representative of Jewish communities (40:2; 41:27). From now on, this situation will be reversed, and the real and symbolic Jerusalem will emerge out of the shadows.

The assurance that Yahveh has not deserted or forgotten Jerusalem assumes a more concrete and specific form with the commitment that the city will be rebuilt. The implications of this promise can easily be obscured by the *post factum* reputation of Jerusalem as perpetually and inevitably at the center not only of aspirations but also of historical realities in Israel. This was not so obvious during the Neo-Babylonian period. The Babylonian punitive campaign aimed specifically at the destruction once and for all of the "rebellious city, hurtful to kings and provinces" (Ezra 4:15) and of the temple that provided the religious legitimation for the revolt. This is clear from the fact that the Babylonian generalissimo, Nebuzaradan, returned after a month to deliberately destroy the buildings, walls, and temple (2 Kgs 25:8–10). Subsequently, the administrative and no doubt also the religious center of the province was moved into Benjaminite territory, to Mizpah some miles north of Jerusalem, and no hint is given that this was a temporary move.

The inscription on the hands has nothing to do with phylacteries (*tefillin*), which are not worn on the hands (Exod 13:16; Deut 6:8; 11:18) or with tattoos, and it is quite different from the situation in which people write "belonging to Yahveh" on their hands (44:5). None of these would be appropriate in the present context. The LXX, "on my hands I have painted your walls," points us in the right direction. The blueprint (cf. *tabnît*, Exod 25:40; *mibnēh-ʿîr*, literally, "the structure of a city," Ezek 40:2) is already prepared, and its essential feature is the tracing out of the walls. A well-known parallel is the outline of the Sumerian city of Lagash in the lap of the statue of its ruler, King Gudea (*ANEP* #749). This also illustrates the ancient image of a capital city built according to a heavenly prototype or model, which was the genesis of the idea of a *civitas dei*.

Moreover, Jerusalem was to be rebuilt with miraculous speed, faster than the time it took Nebuzaradan to burn it down in 586 (2 Kgs 25:10). This is not quite the way in which it actually happened. As our principal source for the early Persian period records, the residents of Judah were accused of trying to fulfill this prophecy under Artaxerxes I (Ezra 4:12–16), perhaps in connection with the brief revolt of the satrap Megabysus, approximately 446. They may also have succeeded, at least in part, since the Judean delegation to Susa reported to Nehemiah a few years later that the wall had been broken down (again) and the gates burned (Neh 1:2–3; 2:17). By dint of conscripting the entire community, Nehemiah rebuilt the city wall once again in fifty-two days (Neh 6:15), in a manner and at a pace similar to the rebuilding of the wall of Athens by Themistocles thirty-five years earlier (Thucydides 1:89–93). At any rate, the defense of Jerusalem remains a major concern within this prophetic tradition (Isa 58:12; 61:4; 62:6–7) although, curiously, little attention is paid to the temple until it comes clearly into focus in the last section of the book (chs. 56–66).

Personified Jerusalem is invited to look around and see the throngs of people who have suddenly appeared and are ready to repopulate the city and province. The repetition verbatim of the same invitation in the last section of the book (60:4) is one of several indications of an ongoing, incremental process of reflection and *relecture* within the Isaian tradition. The theme of repatriation gathers strength as we trace the successive stages through which this tradition passes. A return from Babylon is certainly part of it (e.g. 48:20–21), but a broader perspective comes increasingly into view. Diaspora Jews will gather from all points of the compass (43:5–7): from Hamath to the north; northern and southern Egypt, Syene, and Ethiopia to the south; Assyria, Elam, and Shinar (Babylon) to the east; and the coastlands and islands of the Aegean to the west (Isa 11:11–12; 14:1–2; 27:12–13; 48:20–21; 49:12). In this respect, too, the reality did not measure up to this passionate vision of the future. Judaism did expand demographically in an impressive way between the Persian and the Roman periods but not, according to the (admittedly sketchy) archeological record, during the early Persian period, and it is highly unlikely that there was any mass immigration at that time.

As the prophet-poet develops his theme and is carried away by it, the figurative language loses something of its coherence and becomes difficult to follow. The "children of your bereavement" (translated literally) would be children conceived or born after the loss of earlier children—a common situation then and much later. This new family would be those who survived the disasters, were deported, and returned—themselves or their descendants—to repopulate the city and land. Their rough demand for *Lebensraum*, something like "get out of my way so I can settle," prefigures the predictable conflict between those who returned from abroad during the Persian period and the indigenous populations. The mother's musings about this superfluity of offspring continue to puzzle the exegetes. She is presumably not wondering whether she could have had them all herself and no longer recalled with whom. If we can overlook the fact that the word here translated "begotten" (*yālad*) is masculine, we might consider an allusion to the countries of origin of the children considered as surrogate or proxy wives, rather like Hagar who bore children for Sarah (Gen 16:1–3). But we do not need to salvage the good name of this mother. The language is caught between the figurative and the referential. She is simply asking, in hyperbolic fashion, how can I have given birth to so many children? The Babylonians defeated us, and they have lost their children (47:8–9, the same imagery); we were defeated by them, and the land is too small to hold all of ours.

In the final asseveration (vv 22–23) Yahveh promises that the task of repatriating diaspora Jews will be assigned to foreign peoples, a strange concept, more characteristic of a later and more polarized situation in the community, reflected in the final section of the book (chs. 56–66), than it is of chs. 40–55 (see especially 14:2 and 60:9). Not only will foreign peoples, and especially their rulers, bring the dispersed sons and daughters of Israel back to Judah, they will minister to them there as construction workers (60:10), shepherds, plowmen, and vintners (61:5) and, in this instance, child-minders, a role often filled by slaves. The reversal of fortune is intensified by kings' filling the office of *ʾōmēn*, that is, "tutor" or "child-minder" in the royal household (cf. 2 Kgs 10:1, 5 cf. Greek *paidagōgos*) and queens serving as wet nurses.

The servile obeisance and licking the dust can be explained as an element of court protocol; witness the way the ruler of Tyre addresses the Pharaoh in a letter from the early fourteenth century B.C.E.: "Thus Abimilku thy servant: seven times and seven times I fall prostrate at the feet of the king my lord; I am the dirt under the feet of the king my lord," *ANET* 484). Many commentators, and presumably many readers, have nevertheless found it offensive; Duhm (p. 376), for example, believes it cannot be from Deutero-Isaiah and asks whether Gentiles had to become the lowest, dust-licking slaves in order for Jews to recognize that they were right to trust Yahveh. This is an understandable reaction, but such articulations of what has been called "the fantasy of the oppressed" can perhaps be understood only by those who have themselves been subject to oppression, and they should, in any case, be balanced by quite different approaches to the destiny of the nations in writings from the Second Commonwealth, including Isaiah (e.g. 56:1–8; 66:18–21).

FURTHER REASSURANCE GIVEN AND OBJECTIONS ANSWERED (49:24–50:3)

(Falk 1967; Merendino 1985a; Unterman 1995)

TRANSLATION

i

49 [24]Can prey be taken from a warrior?
Or can prisoners of a tyrant[a] be rescued?
[25]This, then, is what Yahveh says:
"Prisoners will be taken from a warrior,
prey will be rescued from a tyrant;[b]
I myself shall contend with your adversary,[c]
I myself shall save your children.
[26]I shall make your oppressors eat their own flesh,
they will get drunk on their blood as on wine;
then all flesh will know that I, Yahveh, am your Savior,
your Redeemer, the Strong One of Jacob."

ii

50 [1]This is what Yahveh says:
"Where[d] is your mother's bill of divorce
by which I put her away?
Or to which of my creditors
have I sold you into slavery?
It was, rather, for your wickedness that you were sold,
for your transgressions that your mother was put away.
[2]Why was no one there when I came?
Why did no one answer when I called?

Is my reach[e] too short to rescue?[f]
Do I lack the strength to deliver?
By my rebuke I dry up the sea.
I turn rivers into barren land;
their fish stink, deprived of water,
and dying[g] on the parched ground.[h]
[3]I clothe the sky with mourning garb;[i]
I make sackcloth its covering."

NOTES

[a] Reading *ʿārîṣ* with 1QIsa[a], Syr., and Vulg. cf. 25b for MT *ṣaddîq*, "righteous," "innocent"; LXX "if one takes someone captive unlawfully, will he be saved?"—perhaps an attempt to make sense of *ṣaddîq*; [b] 1QIsa[a] reverses the order of *malqût* ("prey") and *šĕbî* ("prisoners") to align it with the order in v 24; LXX "if one takes a giant captive, he will (be able to) take spoil; taking them from a strong man he will be saved"; [c] MT has sing. *yĕrîbēk*, some MSS have pl. *yĕrîbayik*, as also in 1QIsa[a], though the yod superscript makes it uncertain; LXX *ego de tēn krisin sou krinō*, "I will judge your cause," presupposes *rîbēk* cf. a similar problem in Ps 35:1 (*yĕrîbay* or *rîbî*); [d] rather than *ʾê zeh*, "what sort of?" as in LXX (*poion*) cf. a similar ambiguity in 66:1; [e] literally, "hand"; [f] read *mippĕdôt* Infinitive Construct with pronomial suffix for *mippĕdût*, "for rescue"; [g] both parallelism and meter favor the view that a word has fallen out; Duhm (p. 379) suggests *bĕhemtām*, "their marine creatures," e.g. crocodiles; [h] "dying of thirst" (*baṣṣāmāʾ*) is possible but less appropriate; [i] *qadrût* is hapax, as is Mal 3:14 *qĕdoranît*, but cf. the verb *qdr* = "to be dark, to mourn."

COMMENTS

These two brief passages develop the same theme in different but related ways. In the first, two rhetorical questions expressing discouragement and, indirectly, skepticism about the power of the national deity are put in the mouth of the prophet's audience and answered in reverse order. In the second pronouncement, the two questions imply serious accusations directed by the children (Judeans) against their father (Yahveh): he has divorced their mother and sold them into indentured service. The first two rhetorical questions (v 24) are answered more briefly than the previous one (49:14–23) by another asseveration of Yahveh, using the same language as the complaint and giving another reassurance about the future. Here, too, we catch echoes of liturgical laments both in the complaint and in the answer: for instance, when the psalmist prays for Yahveh to "contend with those who contend with me" (Ps 35:1) and to "defend my cause against an impious people" (Ps 43:1). The question and answer immediately preceding were concerned with whether Yahveh had the intent and the will to bring about a restoration. Here the issue is, rather, power and powerlessness, which also comes to expression in the second passage (50:2–3) and is, perhaps, the fundamental issue throughout the entire book.

The sense of ruthless and overwhelming power is expressed by describing Babylon as warrior (*gibbôr*) and tyrant (*ʿārîṣ*), and those subject to Babylonian imperial rule, not confined to Jews resident in Babylonia, as prisoners and prey. The solemn pronouncement affirms that these "prisoners" can and will be set free because Yahveh himself will take up their cause. The verb *rîb*, usually translated "contend," goes beyond the common forensic connotation, as reproduced in LXX, to mean something like entering the lists on behalf of another.

That the prisoners will end up eating their own flesh and drinking their own blood cannot refer literally to cannibalism, to which people could be and have been reduced during a protracted siege (Deut 28:53–57; 2 Kgs 6:24–31; Lam 2:20; 4:10), since people in such straits would presumably not eat their own flesh and would not drink blood—their own or others'. People who are of the same flesh are kin, members of the same extended family (Gen 2:23; 29:14; Judg 9:2; 2 Sam 5:1); hence, the natural reference would be to internecine strife (Isa 9:19[20]; Zech 11:9). In other words, Babylon will self-destruct, a not unreasonable conjecture during the latter part of the reign of Nabonidus.

Reference to flesh (v 26a) (*bāśār*) leads into the acknowledgment by all humanity (v 26b, literally, "all flesh," *kol-bāśār*) of the divinity of Yahveh (for this "acknowledgment formula," see 41:23; 45:3; 49:23; 60:16; and frequently in the Priestly source and Ezekiel). To affirm divinity is to affirm and demonstrate someone's ability and willingness to be a savior (*môšîʿâ* 43:3, 11; 45:15, 21) and redeemer (*gōʾēl*, see 41:14). To these titles, and in keeping with the context of force and counterforce, the prophet adds the old title "the Strong One of Jacob" (*ʾăbîr yaʿăqob* Gen 49:24; Isa 1:24; perhaps originally "the Bull of Jacob," *ʾăbbîr yaʿăqob*).

The second passage raises again the issue of theodicy with regard to the fall of Jerusalem and attendant disasters, an issue that haunted the writer's generation. It is reflected in several of the psalms of communal lament (e.g. Ps 44: 12–25[13–26]) and occasions frequent rebuttal and exoneration on the part of Yahveh (e.g. Isa 42:18–25; 43:22–28). In this instance the response to the implied accusations goes along with the figurative language: if I divorced your mother, where is the *sēper kĕrîtût*, the documentary evidence? The point is not that the separation is only temporary because no bill of divorce was handed over (as in Whybray 1975, 148–49), but, rather, that the accusation is simply false.

Regarding the other charge—how could I sell you into indentured service if I have no creditors whom I must satisfy?—subjection to Babylonian rule, whether in Judah or elsewhere, is represented as indentured service (*ṣābāʾ*) at the beginning of the second major section of the book (40:2). The language of godforsakenness, of being forgotten by God (49:14–15), of being handed over to thieves and plunderers (42:24–25), appears elsewhere, always with the rejoinder that the real reason for the disasters was the moral failure of Israel (40:2; 42:22, 24–25; 43:27–28; 46:8). The question whether this is in every respect an adequate explanation, of particular poignancy in the aftermath of the Holocaust, is raised in the most direct and dramatic way in the book of Job.

The figure of Yahveh and the land or the people as spousal partners, perhaps suggested by the old pattern of the sacred marriage (*hieros gamos*), is developed in different and sometimes odd ways in the prophetic tradition from Hosea to Jeremiah and Ezekiel and will be taken up and developed in different directions in early Christianity. Jeremiah 3:1–5 appeals to the law governing palingamy in Deut 24:1–4 to make the point that, once the divorce between Yahveh and Israel has gone through and Israel has had relations with other gods, there can be no return to the original relationship. This bleak prospect is modified in the comment in 3:5–10 which speaks of a period of temporary sexual relationships rather than marriage, and therefore of the possibility of restoring the original relationship with Yahveh.

The fall of the Kingdom of Samaria marked, however, a final break in the relationship with that part of Israel, a divorce made definitive by the *sēper kĕrîtût* (later, *ketubba*), a document that in real time presumably made provision for the return of the marriage price (*mohar*) and care of the children. In biblical texts divorce, whether realistic or metaphorical, is always initiated by the male partner, from which it has been concluded that women could not initiate divorce proceedings in Israel of the biblical period. This may be so, but it may also mean that the precarious economic situation of most women practically ruled out divorce as an option. In the Jewish colony at Elephantine in Upper Egypt women could initiate divorce, but this may be due to Egyptian or even Persian influence.

The other metaphor, selling someone into indentured service in order to repay debt that could not otherwise be amortized, is regulated in the laws (Exod 21:1–11; Deut 15:12–18) and must have been of common occurrence in a subsistence agrarian economy both before and after the fall of Jerusalem (e.g. 2 Kgs 4:1; Neh 5:5).

The language of God coming and finding no one home, and especially calling out and receiving no answer, will be a recurring motif in the last section of the book (58:9; 65:1, 12; 66:4). Of particular interest is 65:1 in which Yahveh allows himself to be sought out and found by those who do not inquire after or seek him (*nidraštî, nimṣeʾtî* Niphal *tolerativum*, GKC §51c) which, in the context, is intended to explain why the preceding communal lament (63:7–64:12) remained unanswered. The parallels with these last eleven chapters extend to other expressions: that Yahveh's reach ("hand") is not too short to rescue (cf. 59:1 and Num 11:23) and that Jerusalem/Zion will finally be united with her spouse (*bĕʿûlâ* 62:4–5). Some commentators have concluded that the author of chs. 56–66, or one of the authors, must have edited and expanded the work of Second Isaiah, but it seems more likely that this is one of several instances of the progressive and cumulative reuse and reworking of existing material that we have had many occasions to note throughout the book.

We find a parallel to this need to be there when God comes, to answer when he calls, in the prescriptions for the post-disaster situation offered by the

Deuteronomists—to "turn" (more conventionally, "repent") and seek Yahveh (Deut 4:29–30; 30:2, 10), a spiritualization of the old language of seeking the deity by visiting a sanctuary or soliciting an oracle (e.g. Gen 25:22; 1 Sam 9:9; 2 Kgs 1:2). Here, too, the alert reader will detect links between these chapters of Isaiah and the preeminent theological "school" active at that time (e.g. Isa 51:1; 55:6–9; 58:2; 65:1, 10).

Just as positive action is expressed in terms of ecological transformation and the renewal of nature (41:17–20; 43:19–21; 44:3–4; 48:21; 49:9–11; 51:3; 55:12–13), so destructive divine power, demonstrations of power to intervene decisively in the political arena, is expressed in the language of ecological degradation throughout the book (e.g. 40:24; 42:15; 44:27) as in some of the liturgical hymns (e.g. Ps 107:33). At this point there does not seem to be any allusion to a cosmogonic conflict myth, which is usually linked with more explicit reference to the Exodus tradition (e.g. 43:16–17; 51:9–11). The poem breaks off abruptly with the remarkable image of the sky in mourning perhaps, as has been suggested (e.g. Westermann 225), on account of the insertion of the Servant's address that follows.

THE PROPHETIC SERVANT OPPOSED AND ABUSED (50:4–11)

(Begrich 1963, 54–55; Beuken 1973; Corney 1976; Dell'Acqua 1993; Elliger 1933, 34; Holter 1992; Lindsey 1982b; Melugin 1976, 71–73; Merendino 1985b; Schwarz 1973; Werlitz 1997; Yalon 1966)

TRANSLATION

i

50 [4]The Sovereign Lord Yahveh has given me
the tongue of those who are instructed,[a]
to know how to sustain[b] with a word[c] the dispirited.[d]
Morning after morning he sharpens my hearing[e]
to listen as disciples do.
[5]The Sovereign Lord Yahveh has opened my ears,[f]
and I, for my part, was not defiant,
nor did I draw back.
[6]I offered my back to those who beat me,
my cheeks to those who plucked out my beard.
I did not hide[g] my face from insults and spittle.
[7]The Sovereign Lord Yahveh is my helper;
therefore, no insult can touch me,
therefore, I set my face like flint;
I know I will not be disappointed.
[8]The one who will vindicate me is at hand;

who dares to bring an accusation against me?
Let us confront each other.
Who will pass judgment on me?
Let him draw near to me.
[9]Yes, the Sovereign Lord Yahveh is my helper;
who is the one who will condemn me?
They will all wear out like a garment,
the moth will devour them.

ii

[10]Whoever among you reveres Yahveh,
let him heed[h] the voice of his servant;
whoever is walking in the dark[i]
and has no glimmer of light,
let him trust in the name of Yahveh
and rely on his God.
[11]But all you who light your own fire
and set your own firebrands alight,[j]
walk by the light[k] of your fire
and by the firebrands you have kindled.
This is my message for you:[l]
You shall lie down in torment.

NOTES

[a] *Limmûd* = "a disciple, pupil, one under instruction," rather than abstract plural (GKC §§124d, f), as in Torrey 391; and G. R. Driver 1935, 406; [b] *ʿûr* Qal hapax has given rise to a plethora of emendations among which the least implausible is *laʿănôt*, "answer" (Duhm 1922, 379); the meaning given here is suggested by the context and has the support of Vulg. *sustentare*; LXX "The Lord gives me a tongue of wisdom to perceive *in season* (*en kairō*) when I am to speak a word," apparently reading *lāʿēt* for *lāʿût*; [c] *dābār*, adverbial accusative; in 1QIsa[a] the two letters after *db* are unintelligible due to erasure; [d] the addition of *paseq* (a vertical stroke)in MT after the first *yāʿîr* indicates uncertainty about this word; 1QIsa[a] and Vulg. appear to attach it to the next verse, reading: *yāʿîr babōqer / babōqer yāʿîr lî ʾozen*, but on the whole it seems better to simply omit it; [e] literally, "he arouses my ear"; [f] there is no reason to delete this verse as an accidental repetition of the previous verse; [g] 1QIsa[a] has *hsyrvty* (*hasîrôtî*), "turn aside," for MT *histartî*; [h] reading *yiṣmaʿ* apodosis after *mî* as indefinite pronoun (GKC §137c), with LXX (*akousatō*) and Syr. as paralleling *yibtaḥ* and *yiššāʿēn*; [i] literally, "the one who walks" (*ʾăšer hālak*); [j] reading *meʾîrê* for MT *mĕʾazzĕerê*, "girding on [firebrands]"; [k] reading *bĕʾôr* for MT *bĕʾûr* "in the fire"; [l] literally, "from my hand this is for (to) you."

COMMENTS

This passage begins with a declaration made by a prophet (vv 4–9) who is identified as a "servant of Yahveh" only in the comment appended to it (vv 10–11). He expresses confidence in the assistance of God in carrying out a mission in spite of opposition. That the mission is to his fellow-Judeans is evident from the wording ("sustaining the dispirited"), especially when taken in the context of frequent expressions of discontent and skepticism about the message in the preceding chapters and the constant need of the prophetic author to administer encouragement and rebuke (40:27–31; 42:22; 43:22; 46:12; 48:4, 8; 49:14). This is especially clear in 40:27–31, in which the preacher's public is described in the same language as here (*yāʿēp*, "weary," "dispirited"; *yēlkû vĕlōʾ yîʿāpû*, "they shall walk and not be weary"). Pointing in the same direction is the comment added to the prophet's statement, which (on the reading proposed above) distinguishes between those in the community who are receptive to the message and those who choose to ignore it (vv 10–11).

Opposition, which has now reached the point of physical abuse, has therefore arisen within the Judean community, whatever other problems the speaker may have had. There is no indication that the speaker has been imprisoned by the Babylonian authorities and is awaiting trial, a conclusion sometimes derived from v 10; darkness is an appropriate way to speak of imprisonment (42:7; 49:9), but walking in darkness is not. The peculiar form *ḥăšēkâ* ("the dark"), in addition, is generally used metaphorically (Gen 15:12; Isa 8:22; especially in Ps 82:5: "they have neither knowledge nor understanding; they walk about in the dark," *baḥăšēkâ yithallākû*). The abuse heaped on the speaker also seems more of the random and casual kind of violence rather than state-inflicted punishment.

One of the major problems facing the interpreter of 50:4–11 is the problem of locating the passage within chs. 40–55 as a whole. Duhm (1922, 379) concluded from the lack of linkage with what precedes and follows that this third of his *Ebedlieder* ("servant songs") was inserted into the book at this point. It is true that here as elsewhere clear thematic and linguistic interconnections between units are not easy to detect, but they are not entirely absent either. The three brief discourses that follow (51:1–3, 4–6, 7–8) address people who still maintain belief in redemption in the face of opposition and contempt (51:7), not unlike the people addressed by the commentator on the prophetic servant's statement (50:10). Moreover, the fate of the opposition is formulated with the same metaphor of the moth-eaten garment we noted in the servant's statement (51:8 cf. 50:9).

More importantly, 50:4–9 marks a further stage in the disclosure of a prophetic voice and therefore a prophetic presence through the very rare appearance of first-person, self-referential discourse throughout this section of the book. The voice is first heard inquiring about the message to be promulgated (40:6). Then, setting aside for the moment the enigmatic 48:16b reminiscent of the prophetic first-person voice in the last part of the book (59:21 and especially 61:1–4), we hear the voice again in the words of a "servant" who is expressing a sense of failure in a mission to his fellow-Judeans that he has undertaken (49:1–6). It is reasonable to conclude that we are hearing the same voice in 50:4–9, belonging to the same speaker, whose mission among his own people is meeting with increasingly vehement opposition. Since, moreover, these few self-referential, first-person passages fit the overall context of chs. 40–55, especially the indications of increasing disillusionment on the part of the speaker's audience and increasing opposition to the message (40:27–31; 42:22; 43:12; 46:12; 48:5, 8; 49:14; 50:1), there is good reason to identify the voice heard in 49:1–6 and 50:1–9 with the voice of the author, or at least the principal author, of section 40–55. The language and style of 50:4–9 show no significant differences and reproduce some of the characteristics of 40–55 as a whole—for example, the use of forensic terminology in vv 8–9. This reading of the section leaves open the identity of the speaker in the comment (10–11) and the complex of issues involved in interpreting statements attributed to Yahveh and a third party about a prophetic servant in 52:13–53:12. These will occupy us in due course.

The task of determining the genre of the units in 40–55 was at the center of debate during the first half of the nineteenth century (conveniently and briefly summarized in Melugin 1976, 1–7) but is not so much in evidence in recent publications, partly due to reaction against the excesses of form-critical positivism. The pronouncement of the prophet-servant has been assimilated to the psalm of individual lament (e.g. Begrich 1963; Westermann 1969, 183–84), but the similarity with a liturgical composition such as Ps 22 is limited to a brief description of undeserved contumely and the assurance of vindication. The passage is a *literary* composition in its own right that, in describing a situation likely to recur, uses familiar and traditional forms of speech without much deliberation. Kinship of vv 4–9 with the so-called "confessions" of Jeremiah looks somewhat more promising (e.g. Jer 11:18–20; 15:15–18; 18:19–23; 20:7–12) but, unlike the Isaian prophet, Jeremiah complains directly to God, and the strong call for vengeance in Jeremiah is absent from our passage. What we detect in both, however, is the emergence of a unique type of religious literature, the prophetic biography (inclusive of autobiographical elements), which will come to fuller expression in the Greco-Roman period and will influence early Christian attempts to speak about Jesus in important ways, especially in the Third Gospel.

The discourse is essentially a reaffirmation of the speaker's prophetic endowment in the face of skepticism and denial. However one construes the phrase *lĕšôn limmûdîm* ("the tongue of those who are instructed"; see Notes), it makes the point that he is qualified to speak and to be heard; he is taught of God (cf. 54:13). He has been endowed in this way to enable him to speak and by speaking to strengthen and sustain the dispirited—that is, to do what we see being done throughout these chapters (e.g. 40, 28–31, where *yʿp*, the same verbal and adjectival form, appears four times). The terms expressing receptivity to the inner word spoken by God, literally to "arouse the ear" (*yāʿîr ʾōzen*) or "open the ear" (*pātaḥ ʾōzen*), are both unusual, the more common idiom being to "uncover the ear" (verbal stem *glh* e.g. 1 Sam 9:15; 2 Sam 7:27). What they mean is that he is constantly on the alert for revelation, especially in the morning, which is, in traditional religious thinking, the time when such revelations can be expected (cf. Ps 5:4; 46:6). The idea of the absolute necessity of obeying the inner voice is characteristically prophetic: "What Yahveh says to me, that I must speak" (1 Kgs 22:14). The speaker is therefore making the point that the abuse and contumely to which he has been subjected are the direct result of his obedience to the prophetic commission.

A remarkable feature of the self-presentation of the speaker at this point is that the abuse is so simply stated; there is no protestation of innocence, no calling down vengeance on the perpetrators and, unlike the psalms of individual lament, no plea for vindication. Like Jeremiah (Jer 20:2; 37:15) he is beaten, hair is pulled out of his beard, and he is spat on. As suggested earlier, this looks more like a roughing up than officially administered punishment. Jeremiah survived several beatings; pulling out hair is painful but unlikely as a form of state-sponsored torture (Nehemiah pulled out people's hair in a fit of anger, Neh 13:25, while Ezra confined himself to pulling out his own hair, Ezra 9:3); and, while spitting does feature in some juridical proceedings (e.g. Deut 25:9 and perhaps Num 12:14), it is for the most part simply one of the grossest expressions of contempt (e.g. Job 30:10).

To repeat, the remarkable thing about this description is that the speaker offers himself as a victim of abuse and does so as the price to be paid for fulfilling his mission. In the world that the speaker and his public inhabited, insults and the resultant loss of honor, the public shaming, implied a diminution of humanity and called for immediate and drastic action of some kind to restore honor. In this instance, however, the insults have no effect (note the verbal link between *kĕlimmôt*, "insults," 6b and *lōʾ niklāmtî*, literally, "I am not shamed," 7a). Setting the face like flint (*ḥalmîš* Deut 8:15; 32:13), the hardest kind of rock, makes the same point more strongly by saying, in effect, that no hint of shame appears on the face. It is also a prophetic topos, reminiscent of Jeremiah, who confronts his opponents like iron or bronze (Jer 1:18), or Ezekiel, whose face is set as hard as diamond (*šāmîr* Ezek 3:8–9).

The reason for the speaker's confidence is the assurance of vindication, one aspect of the presentation that does match the psalms of individual lament. The point is expressed with a cluster of terms borrowed from the sphere of law and judicial proceedings:

hiṣdîq = to prove the accused innocent (*ṣaddîq*) or hand down a verdict of innocent (also 43:9, 26; 53:11)

hiršîaʿ = to prove the accused guilty or hand down a verdict of guilty (also 54:17) *rîb* = legal proceedings brought against another party, with the corresponding verb (also 41:11, 21; 49:25)

mišpāṭ = verdict; *baʿal mišpāṭ* = the one who hands down the verdict (also 41:1; 53:8)

ʿāmad (yaḥad) = to take part in legal proceedings (also 44:11; 47:13)

nāgaš approach, i.e., initiate legal proceedings (also 41:1, 21–22; 45:20–21)

The use of legal terminology does not oblige us to conclude that the speaker anticipates being brought to trial by the Babylonian authorities for sedition. The fate of other prophetic or messianic figures at the hands of the Babylonians, as reported by Jeremiah (Jer 29:21–23), shows that such an outcome was by no means unlikely and may in fact have come about subsequently. But we have seen that language borrowed from the judicial sphere is used throughout these chapters with no such implications. This last point is another indication that 49:1–6 and 50:4–9 are an integral part of chs. 40–55. The metaphor of a garment ruined by moths also occurs elsewhere in these chapters (51:6, 8 cf. Ps 39:12[11]; 102:27[26]; Job 13:28).

The concluding verses are crucial for interpreting the passage as a whole and perhaps also for the interpretation of Isa 40–55 as a whole. Unfortunately, the syntax leaves the meaning of v 10 ambiguous. One reading would be: "Whoever among you reveres Yahveh and heeds the voice of his servant, who walks in the dark and has no glimmer of light, will trust in Yahveh's name . . . ," with the relative clause referring to the servant. The syntax permits this reading, but 50:4–9 does not conjure up the image of a person walking in the dark, that is, in a state of spiritual disorientation (cf. Ps 82:5; Isa 8:22), and we have seen that it does not refer to imprisonment either.

Rather, it is those to whom the message is addressed throughout these chapters who can be described as "walking in the dark." The speaker therefore is distinguishing between those who revere Yahveh and heed the prophetic message, even though bewildered and confused, who are urged to trust that the predictions will be fulfilled, on the one hand; and those who choose to live by their own lights, on the other hand. This seems to be the point of the fire and firebrands: namely, to set up an ironic contrast between these enlightened ones, the *illuminati*, and those who remain faithful to the prophetic word, even though in the dark. The final verdict on the former anticipates the dark finale of the book (66:24). Lying down (*škb*) is a euphemism for death (e.g. 1 Kgs 2:10), as the bed (*miškāb*) is for the tomb (e.g. Isa 57:2), and there is also a hint that the fire that they themselves light is also the fire that will consume them.

Who, then, is the speaker in vv 10–11? Torrey (1928, 392–93) attributes the entire passage to the one poet, none other than the author of chs. 40–66 (actually, 34–66 with the exception of 36–39). While I do not exclude the possibility that a speaker might refer to himself in the third person, the manner in which the public is addressed makes it unlikely in this instance. It makes no essential difference to attribute v 10 to the prophetic servant and v 11 to Yahveh as a pronouncement of judgment, since this too would be spoken by a prophetic representative (Whybray 1975, 153).

The alternative would be to read vv 10–11 as a comment on the servant's statement by one who is qualified not only to speak for him but to pronounce a judgment on those who oppose him. This betokens commentary by a disciple who shares in the charisma of the master and has internalized his message. Whether the entire passage is from the hand of this commentator we do not know, but it is significant that it opens by using the language of discipleship: the prophetic servant is the disciple (*limmûd*) of Yahveh, as the commentator is of the servant. This issue of prophetic discipleship will come up again in the commentary below, on 52:13–53:12.

THREE WORDS OF COMFORT FOR THE WELL-DISPOSED (51:1–8)

(Holmgren 1969; Janzen 1986; Kuntz 1982; Reider 1935; Steck 1988; van Uchelen 1968)

TRANSLATION

i

51 [1]Listen to me, you who pursue what is right,
you who seek after Yahveh:
look to the Rock from which you were hewn,[a]
the quarry from which you were cut;[b]
[2]look to Abraham your father
and to Sarah who gave you birth.
When I called him, he was but one,
but I blessed him and made him many.[c]
[3]Yahveh comforts Zion,
he brings comfort to all her ruins;
he will make[d] her wilderness like Eden,
her deserted places like the garden of Yahveh.
Gladness and joy will be in her,
thanksgiving and the sound of music.[e]

ii

[4]Pay heed to me, my people,
my nation,[f] listen to me!
A law will go out from me,

my justice as a light for the peoples.
[5]In an instant I will bring about my victory,[g]
my deliverance goes forth like light,[h]
my arm will govern the peoples.
The islands wait for me,
they look to my arm for protection.[i]
[6]Raise your eyes to the sky,
look at the earth beneath[j]—
for the sky will be dispersed like smoke,
the earth will wear out like a garment,
its inhabitants will die like gnats;[k]
but my salvation will endure forever,
my triumph will not be eclipsed.

iii

[7]Listen to me, you who know what is right,
you people who have taken my law to heart:
do not fear any human reproach,
do not let their insults dismay you.
[8]Grubs will consume them like a garment,
worms will devour[l] them like wool,
but my triumph will endure forever,
my salvation for ages to come.

NOTES

4QIsaiah[b] has vv 1–2 and 4QIsa[c] 3 letters of v 8. [a] The verb is pointed as Pual but was probably originally Qal passive; LXX *elatomēsate* presupposes *ḥăṣabtem* active; [b] LXX *ōruchsate* presupposes *nĕqartem* active; MT *bôr*, "pit," "cistern," absent from Syr., is probably a gloss on the rare (hapax) *maqqe-bet*, "quarry"; [c] 1QIsa[a] has *v'prḥv*, "I made him fruitful"; LXX adds *kai ēgapēsa auton*, "and I loved him," perhaps on account of a traditional description of Abraham as "friend (*philos*) of God" cf. Isa 41:8; Jas 2:23; [d] read *vĕyāśîm* without vav consecutive and therefore future sense in keeping with v 3c cf. Tg. *vyšvy*, LXX *thēsō*, and Vulg. *ponet*, "he will place"; [e] 1QIsa[a] mistakenly adds "sorrow and mourning will flee" from 51:11b cf. 35:10; [f] LXX has *basileis*, "kings"; [g] MT appears to have the wrong verse division, to judge by departure from an exceptionally regular 3:3 meter; 5a should read *ʾargîaʿ ʾaqrîb ṣidqî*; *rgʿ* Hiphil, "to do something in an instant of time" (Jer 49:19 = 50:44), serves to modify an accompanying verb adverbially, which counsels emending MT *qārôb* to *ʾaqrîb* cf. LXX; [h] *kaʾôr*, "like light," added, following LXX MSS with *hōs phōs*, *metri causa*; [i] literally, "they hope for my arm"; [j] 1QIsa[a] has *mtḥth* with suffix for MT *mittaḥat;* [k] the final phrase in MT, "its inhabitants will die *kĕmô-kēn*," is usually emended, since it does not seem to make good sense to say they would die "like so" cf. LXX *hōsper tauta*, "like these things"(?); but *kēn* can be read as a collective (pl. *kinnîm*), "small insects, gnats or fleas," Exod 8:12–14; Ps 105:31; Num 13:33, *vekēn hayînû bĕ ʿênêhem* can be translated "and we were (like) gnats/fleas in their sight" cf. MH *kînâ*, "worm" or "louse," an option superior to [1] 1QIsa[b] *kmvkn* read as *kĕmôkēn*, "like a locust"; no need to emend, therefore; the second *yoʾkĕlēm* is often emended e.g. to *yĕkallēm*, "will destroy them," but the repetition appears to be part of a deliberate stylistic device involving assonance:

ki kabbeged yoʾkĕlēm ʿās
vĕkaṣṣemer yoʾkĕlēm sās.

COMMENTS

These three brief exhortations are directed to the well disposed among the prophet's audience addressed in the previous passage (50:10). Those who pursue what is right and who seek after and revere Yahveh are therefore those in the Judean community who are receptive to the prophetic message, as opposed to those who choose to follow their own lights. Drawing a line through the community in this way, a line that will be clearly visible and definitive in the final judgment, is an indication of an incipient sectarian viewpoint that we will observe gathering strength throughout subsequent chapters.

The three stanzas of roughly equal length are well integrated in style, language, and theme. The first, addressed to those who pursue what is right, corresponds quite closely to the third, addressed to those who know or recognize what is right. Repetition, beginning with the call for attention (vv 1, 4, 7) and the summons to focus the mind on certain things (*habbîṭû*, 1, 1, 2), helps to give the passage a certain cohesion. Key terms are repeated: *tôrâ* ("instruction," 4, 7), *ṣedeq*, *ṣĕdāqâ* ("right conduct, triumph,") (1, 5, 7), *yēšaʿ*, *yĕšûʿâ* ("salvation," 2, 3), sometimes in striking combinations such as, for example:

ki kabbeged yoʾkĕlēm ʿāš
vĕkaṣṣemer yoʾkĕlēm sās (v 8a)

grubs will consume them like a garment,
worms will devour them like wool

or:

višûʿātî lĕʿôlām tihyeh, vĕṣidqātî lōʾ teḥat (6b)
ṣidqātî lĕʿôlām tihyeh, yĕšûʿātî lĕdôr dôrîm (8b)

my salvation will endure forever,
my triumph will not be eclipsed

my triumph will endure forever,
my salvation for ages to come.

The first of the three addresses (vv 1–3) seeks to strengthen the resolve of the well disposed in the community by appeal to a shared historical tradition. The attitude of the people addressed is fundamentally positive but they are disheartened, and the reasons for their discouragement are apparent from the exhortation addressed to them: they are few in number, Jerusalem still lies in ruins, and they are being reproached and insulted by their fellow-Judeans. Situations of this kind tend to induce a sense of disorientation and alienation from tradition, illustrated by the lament that "Abraham does not acknowledge us, Israel does not recognize us" (63:16a). In earlier days, to seek God (verbal stem *bqš*) meant to visit a sanctuary in order to obtain an oracle (e.g. Exod 33:7; 2 Sam 12:16; 21:1), but by the time of writing it stood for a fundamentally open and receptive religious ordering of one's life (e.g. Deut 4:29; Ps 27:4, 8).

Medieval exegetes (e.g. Ibn Ezra) took the rock (*ṣûr*) and the pit or quarry (*maqqebet*) to refer to Abraham and Sarah, respectively, encouraged no doubt by the semantic link between *maqqebet* (hapax) and *nĕqēbâ*, "female," both derived from the root *nqb*, "to bore or pierce." Alternatively, both terms could stand for God, "Rock of ages," who brought Israel into existence. In the Song of Moses, "the Rock (*ṣûr*) that begot you" is in parallelism with "the God (*ʾēl*) who gave you birth" (Deut 32:18), and this entire poem hymns the God of Israel as the Rock, as do other ancient poetic compositions (2 Sam 22; Ps 18) no doubt well known to Isaian authors (cf. Isa 26:4; 30:29). But, in the context, a reference to the ancestral couple seems preferable.

The triad of Abraham, Isaac, and Jacob is attested at least as early as Deuteronomy and the associated History (e.g. Deut 1:8; 6:10; 9:5, 27; 30:20; 34:4; 1 Kgs 18:36; 2 Kgs 13:23) but, with one possible exception (Josh 24:2–3), the earliest reference to Abraham as an individual figure appears in Ezekiel (33:24). Outside of Genesis Sarah is mentioned only here (51:2). It is clear from a reading of Isa 40–48 that the eponymous ancestor of Israel is Jacob, but there are indications of an alternative tradition according to which Abraham was father of the people and Sarah the mother (Isa 29:22; 41:8; Josh 24:3).

These variant traditions were eventually schematized and reconciled in the genealogical narratives in Genesis. It seems that Abraham first came into prominence as a model for the faithful Jew in the early post-destruction period. The parallels between the stylized narratives in Gen 12–25 and what we know of the situation during the Neo-Babylonian and early Achemenid period are unmistakable. Abraham is summoned from Mesopotamia to Canaan (Judah) and receives the assurance of land and nationhood (Gen 12:1–3); he lives in close and not always friendly contact with Egyptians, the people of the Judean Negev (Edomites), and Arab tribes (12:9–20; 16:15; 20:1–18; 21:25–34; 25:1–6); he avoids contact with the local women and sends back to Mesopotamia for a wife for his son (24:1–61); he purchases a plot of land as the first step toward occupying the land (23:1–18); and he sets up the genuine worship of Yahveh and supports the Jerusalem (Salem) cult by tithing (14:17–20). All of these reflect what we know of policies and attitudes in the Judean community in the early Persian period.

The issue that occasions the reference to Abraham at this point is demography, and it is confronted in the Genesis narratives in the unfolding of the "great nation" theme: "I will make of you a great nation and I will bless you" (12:2) cf. "I blessed him and made him many" (Isa 51:2). The close parallel to our passage in Ezek 33:24 deals with the other theme, land: "Abraham was but one, yet he took possession of the land; we are many, so the land is given to us to possess." Interestingly, this is a quotation attributed to the indigenous inhabitants of the province, who elsewhere justify expropriating the real estate of the deportees on the grounds that the latter have in effect been expelled from the Yahvistic cult community and have therefore forfeited their property rights (Ezek 11:14–15). This might suggest a similar origin for the appeal to Abraham in Isa 51:2. At any rate, the figure of Abraham can be discerned behind aspirations toward nationhood and land later in Isaiah, even when the ancestor's name is not mentioned (e.g. 60:21–22).

In chs. 40–48 Jerusalem-Zion is for the most part emblematic of the people (40:9; 41:27). The historic Jerusalem, the city deliberately and systematically destroyed by the Babylonians, is not a major focus of interest except insofar as it is to be rebuilt and repopulated by Cyrus (44:26, 28; 45:13). In the following section (chs. 49–55), however, Jerusalem gradually emerges out of the shadows, and we note how dialogue between Yahveh and the city alternates with passages describing the mission and the vicissitudes of the prophetic-messianic servant (apostrophes to Zion appear in 49:14–26; 51:11–52:2; 52:7–10; and 54:1–17).

In the final section of the book (chs. 56–66) Jerusalem and its temple, "my holy mountain," are fully in focus. This progressively more central place of Jerusalem in the book corresponds to the reality attested in our sources, few and sketchy as they are. The period begins with the Babylonian authorities' relocation of the administrative center of the province to Mizpah, and it ends with Nehemiah's rebuilding of the Jerusalem city wall, his (probably not entirely voluntary) repopulation of the city (*synoikismos*), and its establishment as the capital of an autonomous province within the Persian Empire. That Yahveh has comforted Zion, even though the city is still in ruins, may be taken to be a prophetic perfect tense: the restoration of Jerusalem is decided in principle and will therefore certainly come about. The transformation of the city from a heap of ruins to a paradise restored is expressed by means of a variant of the Eden myth, most fully developed in Gen 2–3. This does not imply that the writer had read Gen 2–3, the composition of which cannot be dated with certainty. As with the Abraham tradition, we begin to hear allusions to the Garden of Eden only in the post-destruction period (Ezek 28:11–19; 31:8–9, 16, 18; 36:35; Joel 2:3), generally by way of contrast with a land or city rendered uninhabitable as a result of destructive human or nonhuman agency.

Since there is no compelling reason to read "peoples" and "nations" in v 4 (pace Westermann 1969, 235), the second stanza (vv 4–6) is also considered here to be addressed to a Judean public. We are reminded at once of what was said earlier about Cyrus, who was commissioned to establish a just order (*mišpāṭ*) internationally and whose law (*tôrâ*) the coastlands eagerly await (42:1–4 with the comment in 42:5–9). It seems that by this time it was apparent that Cyrus had not lived up to expectations and that, if a new world order favorable to Israel was to be established, it would have to be brought about by a different agency. The present stanza suggests that this will happen by direct intervention of Yahveh and that it will be associated with a catastrophe of cosmic proportions.

The arm of Yahveh signifies divine power (cf. 51:9; 52:10; 59:16; 63:12) deployed in defending the powerless (33:2), punishing the guilty (48:14), or in exercizing strong and just rule, as here (51:5 cf. 40:10). The dire predictions about the fate of the created world and its inhabitants may be understood as a way of making a strong asseveration about the reality and durability of divine saving power, as if to say, "heaven and earth will pass away before my words will pass away" (cf. Matt 24:35).

In prophetic rhetoric, critical political events are often surrounded by cosmic reverberations (e.g. the Babylon poem in Isa 13:1–22). The description of the end time assumes many forms throughout Isaiah: the darkening of sun, moon, and stars (13:10; 24:22–23); the light of the sun and moon enhanced sevenfold, which would, if anything, be worse (30:26); the sky rolled up like a scroll (34:4); destruction of the earth by fire or water (13:5; 24:1–3, 17–20); the earth depopulated (13:12; 24:1, 6); and, as the book nears its conclusion, a new heaven and new earth (65:17; 66:22). Such apocalyptic scenarios express collective anxiety at anticipated major changes in the political and social order, and the note of anxiety will be heard increasingly in the remaining chapters of the book.

The third stanza (vv 6–8) appears to be related more closely than the preceding two to the statement of the prophetic servant and the comment that follows it (50:4–11). As suggested earlier, it would be natural to identify those who know what is right and have taken Yahveh's law to heart with those who fear and trust in God addressed by the servant's disciple (50:10). The injunction for the addressees to look beyond present reproaches and insults inflicted by their fellow-Judeans also brings to mind the insults suffered by the prophetic servant (50:6), and the fate of the addresses' opponents is described in the same way: like a garment, they will be eaten up by grubs (cf. 50:9). We are not justified in regarding these God-fearers who take the law of Yahveh to heart as a specific group of prophetic disciples or a sect, or even a party. But in due course similar language will be used to describe groups of the faithful who are rejected and ostracized, who make pacts together, and who exhibit the kind of apocalyptic beliefs characteristic of the Jewish sects of the Greco-Roman period (e.g. Isa 65:13–16; 66:5; Mal 3:16–18).

An Urgent Prayer for Divine Intervention (51:9–16)

(Anderson 1962; Day 1985; Ginsberg 1958; Hermission 1998b; Ludwig 1973; Ringgren 1971; Seidl 1983)

TRANSLATION

i

51 [9]Rouse yourself, rouse yourself, put on strength,
arm of Yahveh!
Rouse yourself as in days of old,
as in ages long since.
Was it not you that hacked[a] Rahab in pieces,
that ran the Dragon through?
[10]Was it not you that dried up the Sea,
the waters of the Great Deep?
Was it not you that made[b] the depths[c] of the Sea
a route for the redeemed to traverse?
[11]Those ransomed by Yahveh will return,[d]
shouting for joy they will enter Zion
crowned with joy everlasting;
gladness and joy will be theirs,
sorrow and sighing will depart.[e]

ii

[12]I, I myself am the one who comforts you;[f]
why, then, fear[g] mortals doomed to die,
who fare no better than grass?[h]
[13]You have forgotten Yahveh who made you,
Yahveh who stretched out the sky,
who established the earth.
You are in constant fear all day long
of the fury of oppressors[i] set on destruction;
but where now is the fury of these oppressors?
[14]The one who now cowers will soon be released;[j]
he will not go down to death, to the Pit;
he will not lack for food.
[15]But I, Yahveh your God,
who stirs up[k] the sea so that its waves roar
[Yahveh of the hosts is his name],[l]
[16]who stretched out[m] the sky and established the earth,
who says to Zion, "You are my people,"

[I put my words in your mouth,
I hide you in the shadow of my hand].[n]

NOTES

[a] 1QIsaiah[a] reads *hammōḥeṣet* > *mḥṣ* "strike (down)," also 4QIsa[c] and cf. Vulg. *percussisti*, and the same verb is used with Rahab in Job 26:12; but MT is the more difficult reading and should stay; [b] MT accentuation makes *haṣṣāmâ* into a 3rd-person fem. perfect, but the original would have been a fem. participle agreeing with *zĕrôaʿ*, "arm," therefore *haśśāmâ* with *milraʿ*; [c] 1QIsa[a] reads *bmʿmqy*, "in the depths"; [d] beginning with *yĕšûbûn*, the verbs are taken to be in Jussive; for MT *pĕdûyê*, "ransomed," 1QIsa[a] has *pzvry*, "dispersed"; [e] for MT *nāsû*, "have fled," read *venāsû*, as in 35:10b and 1QIsa[a] cf. Syr. and Tg.; [f] MT has pl. suffix, LXX and Symm. masc. sing., but there is insufficient reason to emend MT; [g] MT *mî-ʾatt vatîrʾî*, literally, "who are you (fem. sing.) that you fear . . . ?" is problematic; for the interrogative *mî*, "how, why," cf. Amos 7:2, 5, *mî yāqûm yaʾăqob*? "how can Jacob stand?"; read *mî-ʾattâ vatîrāʾ*, and for the construction, consecutive clause after interrogative, see GKC §111m; [h] the construction of the phrase, literally, "and (from) human beings grass are placed," is extremely elliptical cf. GKC §155h, but the idea is clearly that of impermanence cf. 40:6; [i] MT *hammēṣîq*, sing. understood as collective; the 1QIsa[a] scribe omitted most of 13c (*kaʾăšer . . . hammēṣîq*) by haplography but fitted it in subsequently above the line; [j] the translation is speculative: the meaning of *ṣōʾeh* ("the one who cowers") is uncertain cf. Jer 2:20 and 48:12 ("lie down, overturn") but also Isa 63:1 ("stride"), as in Vulg. *cito veniet gradiens ad aperiendum*; moreover, *ptḥ* in Niphal is not used elsewhere to mean "setting free"; see further the Comments; [k] no need to emend *rgʿ* (also Jer 31:35 and Job 26:12, both with *hayyām*) to *gʿr*, "rebuke"; [l] I take this to be a scribal assertion suggested by a common finale to hymn stanzas cf. Amos 4:13; 5:8; 9:6; it also follows the identical verse in Jer 31:35; [m] read *lintôt*, "stretch out," for MT *lintōaʿ*, "plant"; [n] 16a and 16b are transposed, since 16b is awkward following on the statement to an individual prophetic figure, which is clearly out of place in the context.

COMMENTS

As we have found to be so often the case, the connecting links between these passages and the ones immediately preceding are far from obvious. The injunction not to be afraid of or discouraged by opposition (51:7–8) is repeated with different words (vv 12–13), and what has previously been said about divine intervention through the figure of the arm of Yahveh (51:5) will occasion the first of several apostrophes here (51:9–11). The clearest structural indicator in what follows, however, is the repeated imperative introducing three apostrophes, each followed by a response in *oratio recta* of Yahveh: the first (51:9–11 + 12–16) is addressed to Yahveh's arm, the second and third (51:17–20 + 21–23; 52:1–2 + 3–6) to Jerusalem/Zion.

The repeated verb (*ʿûrî, hitʿorĕrî, ʿûrî*) can signify a call to battle (addressed to Deborah, Judg 5:12); a summons to a special mission, such as when Yahveh aroused the spirit of Cyrus (41:2,25; 45:13), or to a prophetic calling (50:4); or, finally, a gathering up of spiritual and physical energies for decisive action. The repetition itself indicates a sense of urgency and conveys the impression that a critical point has been reached. The repetition further along urging departure, presumably from Babylon (*sûrû, sûrû, ṣĕʾû miššām* 52:11), connects structurally with the first passage in chs. 40–55, which also opens with a repeated imperative (*naḥămû, naḥămû* 40:1), and with the same injunction at the end of section 40–48 (*ṣĕʾû mibbābel*, "depart from Babylon," 48:20–22). These parallels must have formed an important structuring device at some stage in the editorial history of the book. In addition, both of these finales (48:20–22; 52:11–12) are followed immediately by passages that speak of a prophetic servant (49:1–6; 52:13–53:12), one and the same prophetic servant, as I shall argue. It bears repeating that the fractioning of the text required by commentary writing must not lead us to neglect these broader structural features and interconnections that are part of the total meaning.

The first repetition introduces an invocation of the arm (i.e. the power to act) of Yahveh (vv 9–11) followed by Yahveh's response (12–16). The invocation is reminiscent of the psalms of communal lament that include an attempt to motivate the deity to intervene, and the response corresponds to the positive outcome that is also a feature of this type of psalm. The motivation will at times consist in a recital of the *res gestae* of the deity. Psalm 44, for example, rehearses manifestations of divine power involving Yahveh's arm (44:4), spectacular interventions witnessed in that past by means of which Yahveh helped Israel to survive oppression, and then moves to the complaint that God has forgotten his people (vv 18, 21), ending in a direct appeal for God to rouse himself, wake up, rise up (*ʿûrâ, haqîṣâ, qûmâ*).

A similar appeal appears in Ps 74 (*qûmâ* v 22) and Ps 80 (*ʿôrĕrâ* v 3). Affinity with this type of liturgical composition can be clearly detected in Ps 74:

> God is my king of old,
> working salvation in the midst of the earth;
> by your power you stirred up the Sea;
> you shattered the heads of the Dragons on the waters.
> You crushed the heads of Leviathan;
> you made him into food for the wild creatures. . . .
> Yours is the day, yours also is the night;
> you established the luminaries and the sun.
> You fixed all the bounds of the earth;
> you formed summer and winter. (vv 12–17)

The fact that addressing an arm is strange to us is due to differences in ancient and modern uses of metaphor. The arm signified strength, protection of the weak, challenge to the proud and over-confident (e.g. 33:2; 40:10; 48:14; 51:5; 52:10; 62:8; 63:5, 12). It would also have conjured up the mighty hand and outstretched arm of the Exodus tradition (e.g. Deut 4:34). In Isa 51 the metaphor is military: the warrior pulling on a tunic and armor in preparation for battle. It is also a royal image since, as defender of his people, the king was clothed in splendor and strength (Ps 93:1). That God at times had to be roused from sleep is a familiar idea in the psalms (e.g. Ps 44:24), though we are told elsewhere that Yahveh, Israel's minder, does not sleep (Ps 121:4). God also at times forgets, and prayer of this kind is a way of activating God's memory (e.g. Isa 49:14).

Throughout these chapters Yahveh has appealed to his power as cosmic Creator to strengthen the faith of a dispirited and disoriented people. Now the author, speaking for the people, echoes back to Yahveh the same theme in terms of the old myth of the victory of the god over the forces of chaos at the beginning of time. In all versions of this myth known from the Near East and Levant, these monsters both represented and inhabited the circumfluent waters of the ocean that, according to the world view of that time and place, surrounded and threatened the narrow foothold of ordered social life. In the Mesopotamian version, *Enuma Elish*, recited in the course of the autumnal *akitu* festival, the struggle is between Marduk and Tiamat, a female personification of the primeval ocean. In due course she is killed and dismembered by the god, the visible world is created out of her body, and humanity is created with the blood of Kingu, her lieutenant, mixed with earth (*ANET* 66–67). The name Tiamat is related etymologically to Hebrew *tĕhôm*, "the Deep," here and in the Genesis creation and uncreation recitals (Gen 1:2; 7:11), but the form of the myth reproduced in this passage is Syro-Palestinian rather than Mesopotamian, a circumstance that, once again, cautions us against simply assuming a Babylonian location for these chapters.

Rahab represents perilous water, the oceanic element, associated with *yam*, "Sea," and the Sea Serpent (*nāḥāš bārîaḥ* Job 26:12–13; Ps 89:11). Like Tiamat, Rahab has his helpers (*ʿōzĕrê rāhab* Job 9:13), who may be identical with the "Rahabs" (*rĕhābîm*) of Ps 40:5. The Dragon (*tannîn*), another embodiment of the mythic monster plying the primeval ocean, is the counterpart of the Ugaritic *tunnanu*. In both the Late Bronze Age mythological texts from Ugarit and Hebrew poetry, *tannîn* is associated with *ym* ("Sea") and *ltn* ("Leviathan"). The Hebrew Dragon, created by God on the fifth day (Gen 1:21), is often associated with creation (Ps 74:13; 148:7; Job 7:12), and will be present at the final unraveling of creation according to the nightmare scenarios of Daniel (7:2–3) and Revelation (13:1). In the Ugaritic Baal and Anat cycle, *yam*, embodiment of primeval, oceanic chaos, is the opponent of Baal in a struggle repeated indefinitely (*KTU*[2] I. 2 iv; I. 3 iii; I. 5 i; *ANET* 130–31).

This kind of imagery should not be dismissed as *mere* myth or *mere* poetic metaphor, since it conveys a vivid sense of the deep anxieties that fuel much of the religious language in psalms and prophecy. Chaos, the dissolution of order that makes meaningful social and individual life possible, is never far away. The Dragon sleeps but does not die. Read with discernment, the creation account in Genesis speaks of the confining not the annihilation of chaos. And since chaos still threatens, the Creator God must still take issue with it; hence, the urgency of prayers such as are found here and in several of the psalms. Inevitably, the struggle is also transferred to the political sphere. The references to Egypt as Rahab (Isa 30:7; Ps 87:4) and the Dragon (Ezek 29:3; 32:2) bring in the Sea by association, and the Sea (*Yamm*) in its turn conjures up the miraculous crossing of the Papyrus Sea during the escape from Egypt (Exod 15:8).

The closing verse of the apostrophe (51:11) is identical with 35:10, the finale of the poem about the eschatological restoration of Judah, which several scholars (e.g. C. C. Torrey and J. D. Smart) take to be an integral part of Second Isaiah. It is therefore assumed by most commentators that v 11 has been copied into 51:9–11 from 35:1–10 where it evidently belongs, bringing to a head as it does the themes of the *via sacra* and eschatological joy. However, it is not out of place thematically in its present location, since it advances the highway motif of the previous verse and marks a transition to the more prominent treatment of Jerusalem/Zion in the chapters immediately following. What makes the hypothesis of a borrowing likely, notwithstanding, is the impression of finality and consummation that the verse conveys, appropriate at the end of the first Isaiah book (chs. 1–35), less so in the present position.

By analogy with the psalms of communal lament, recall of these great deeds demands a response. Yahveh does not agree to take on the monsters once again; rather, he reminds the petitioners of some things that *they* have forgotten. Nothing of this is new. The comfort of God and the fact of human impermanence were announced at the beginning of the prophecy (40:1, 6–8). That the God who reassures is the Creator of heaven and earth has been endlessly repeated. Here, too, as we would expect, the language of liturgical address is heard. Given what we know of ancient Israelite cosmology, the central act was the setting of the earth on its foundations (verb *ysd* cf. Pss 89:12[11]; 102:26 [25]; 104:5).

According to an ancient Mesopotamian topos, the earth was founded over the *apsu* (corresponding to the Hebrew *tĕhôm*), the watery abyss (cf. Ps 24:2). The earth is also thought of as a temple for the praise of God (cf. Ps 78:69). Job 38:4–7 pictures Yahveh as a surveyor who marks out its foundations with callipers and string, and there follows the solemn liturgy for its dedication in which the morning stars and the sons of God participate. It is only when this structure is in place that the heavens can be stretched out taut above it (verb *nṭh*: 40:22; 42:5; 44:24; 45:12).

The point is that a return to these fundamental perceptions should remove or at least mitigate fear. It is difficult if not impossible to decide whether the terms used at this point—the oppressor (*hammēṣîq*) and the one who cowers (*ṣōʿeh*)—refer to specific individuals or are collective nouns. The first of the two verbs (*ṣîq* Hiphil), "oppress, constrain, oppose," can refer to verbal as well as physical violence or the threat of violence (Judg 14:17; 16:16) and even to the experience of emotional pressure (Job 32:18). The second verb (*ṣōʿeh*) is even more obscure, and the ancient versions are not much help (LXX may be translated "in saving you he will not stand still nor will he delay," perhaps with a veiled messianic allusion). Apart from the meaning "to march" required by the context in Isa 63:1 (cf. Vulg. *gradiens*), this verb appears only twice with the meaning to lie or crouch down: once with a sexual connotation (Jer 2:20), the other time with the sense of tilting a bottle (Jer 48:12 with the corresponding substantive *ṣōʿîm*, "wine stewards").

Attempts have been made to identify the oppressor with a specific historical individual. J. D. W. Watts (1987, 212), for example, suggested Darius I during the troubled period beginning in 522, while Morgenstern (1962, 31–34) opted for Xerxes in connection with his hypothesis that Jerusalem was destroyed in 485 B.C.E. Rather than speculating *in vacuo*, it might be better for us to be guided by the context, which indicates a more general, collective sense of opposition and opposition from within the Jewish community. Those addressed have just been urged not to fear opposition in general (51:7–8,12), and if the discourses immediately preceding are related to the pronouncement of the prophetic servant and the ensuing comment (50:4–11), the opponents would be identical with those who reject the servant's message (50:11). There is a long tradition of identifying the one who crouches or cowers with diaspora Jews, generally those in the Babylonian diaspora (Ibn Ezra, Kimḥi, Calvin, and most of the moderns). But if we accept the contextual linkage proposed above, the allusion may well be to the prophetic servant of 50:4–9, thereby functioning as a thematic link with 52:13–53:12. In addition, what we know of the situation of ethnic minorities in Babylonia in the late Neo-Babylonian and early Achaemenid period, as exiguous as it is, does not suggest a chronic situation of imprisonment and near-starvation.

As so often in these chapters, the passage ends as it begins, with an affirmation of creative power and presence. Attributes of Yahveh are often couched in stereotypical liturgical form; hence, it is no surprise to find similar formulations in different contexts, such as with Yahveh, both whipping up a storm at sea (cf. Jer 31:35) and stilling its waves (Job 26:12, with an alternative meaning for the same verb, *rgʿ*). Though 1QIsa[a] and the LXX are practically identical with MT 16a, the statement is clearly addressed to an individual prophetic figure and has therefore generally been regarded as intrusive in the present context (the LXX cleverly but implausibly integrates it by reading, "I will shelter you under my right hand *with which* I set up the heaven and laid the foundations of the earth").

Putting words in an individual's mouth (v 16b) is a familiar prophetic designation and endowment formula (Num 22:38; Jer 1:9; Isa 59:21), and comparison with 49:2 and 50:4 show that the statement is addressed to the prophetic servant whose voice we have just heard (50:4–9). If v 16a is an insertion, the initial confusion in suffixes (masc. pl. 12a; fem. sing. 12b; then masc. sing.

throughout, except 14, which speaks of the servant in the third person) would suggest an editorial attempt to read the entire passage as addressed to the prophetic servant of 50:4–9.

THE CUP OF WRATH (51:17–23)

(Mayer 1995)

TRANSLATION

i

51 [17]Bestir yourself, bestir yourself, rise up, Jerusalem!
You who have drunk from Yahveh's hand
the cup of his wrath;
you have drained to the last drop
the goblet[a] that made you stagger.
[18]Among all the children she had borne,
there was none to lead her;[b]
among all the children she had raised
there was none to take her by the hand.
[19]This twofold disaster has befallen you:
devastating destruction—who will grieve for you?
famine and the sword—who will console you?[c]
[20]Your children have fainted; they are lying
at the corner of every street[d]
like antelopes caught in the net.[e]
They have felt the full force of Yahveh's wrath,
the rebuke of your God.

ii

[21]Hear, then, this, you that are afflicted,[f]
you that are drunk but not with wine:
[22]Thus says Yahveh, your sovereign Lord and your God,
he who pleads the cause of his people:
"See now, I take from your hand
the cup that makes you stagger,
the goblet[g] of my wrath;
you will never have to drink from it again.
[23]I shall put it in the hands of those who afflict you,
those who torment you,[h] saying:
'Lie down, so we can walk over you.'
You made your back like the ground under their feet,[i]
like a road for those who pass by.

NOTES

[a] Mt adds *kôs*, "cup," as explanatory gloss after *qubbaʿat*, "goblet"; [b] 1QIsa[a] has *lk* for mt *lāh*, i.e., "to lead you" (fem. sing.); [c] read *yĕnaḥămĕk* 3rd person with 1QIsa[a] for mt *ʾanaḥămĕk* 1st person; [d] presence of the same phrase, *bĕroʾš kol-ḥûsôt*, in Lam 2:19 and 4:1 does not justify eliding it here; [e] the identity of the species (*tôʾ/tʾô*), only here and Deut 14:5, is uncertain; Vulg. *oryx illaqueatus*, "an oryx (wild sheep?) caught in a trap"; lxx *hōs seutlion hēmiephthon*, "like half-boiled beetroot," is bizarre; [f] an interesting variation in Vulg., *paupercula*, "you poor little thing"; [g] see Note a above; [h] adding *vmʿnyk*, "and your oppressors," with 1QIsa[a]; [i] "under your feet" added for clarity.

COMMENTS

This is the second of the three apostrophes, each of which opens with the repeated call to activity—the first addressed to Yahveh, the second and third to Jerusalem/Zion. Each of the three is followed by a reply, the second and third introduced with the traditional prophetic *incipit* "thus says Yahveh" (51:21; 52:3). This second one is not a community lament, though Westermann ingeniously reconstructed from it part of the original lament on which he believed it was based (Westermann 1969, 245). It is an apostrophe to Jerusalem by the prophet, incorporating the language of traditional laments (as in Lamentations) and the traditional prophetic topos of the cup of wrath.

We saw that in chs. 40–48 Jerusalem either stands for the people of Israel (41:27; 46:13) or is mentioned in connection with the mission of Cyrus (44:26, 28; 45:13). In chs. 49–55 the city comes much more into view as dialogue partner with the God of Israel, beginning in 49:14, and as bride, spouse, and mother, once bereaved, but now with a large and growing family (49:19–21; 51:18; 54:1–3). In chs. 56–66, finally, the social realities of city and temple in the Neo-Babylonian and early Achaemenid period, especially the social reality of conflict and struggle for control of city and temple within the community, come more clearly into the foreground.

In both ancient and modern times the metaphor of the cup stands by synecdoche for its contents—the fermented drink, usually wine, that it contains. And, since alcohol can on the one hand rejoice both men and gods, as the psalmist says, and on the other lead to depression, isolation, insensitivity, and worse, the cup is an ambivalent symbol. The cup is therefore the overflowing cup of blessing (Ps 16:5; 23:5) and the cup of consolation offered to assuage the grief of those in mourning (Jer 16:7; Ezek 24:17, 22; Hos 9:4), but it is also the cup of wrath that must be drained to the dregs.

The image used here may be drawing on the more fully developed figure in Jer 25:15–29, in which the prophet offers the wine cup of wrath (*kôs hayyayin haḥēmâ*) first to Jerusalem, then to foreign peoples. Here and in other prophetic texts the results of draining this cup of foaming, well-mixed wine to the dregs (Ps 75:8) are described in some detail: complete inebriation (Jer 25:27; Ezek 23:33) including loss of motor control (Jer 25:16; Hab 2:16), vomiting (Jer 25:27), going crazy (Jer 25:16; 51:7), exposing oneself in public (Hab 2:15; Lam 4:21), and eventually falling down and passing out (Jer 25:27). This is therefore one more way, and easily the most vivid, of describing metaphorically what had happened to Jerusalem and what Yahveh's part in bringing it about had been.

The figure of the woman Jerusalem incapacitated by drink suggested the introduction of the theme of bereavement and new family, depopulation of the city and its hoped-for repopulation (49:19–21; 54:1–3)—which, incidentally, only happened during the governorship of Nehemiah according to our principal biblical source (Neh 11:1–21). The Ugaritic Legend of Aqhat text (*KTU* I 17–19; *ANET* 149–55) records the lament of the initially childless King Daniel (*dn'il*) that he has no son who, as he is in duty bound to do, "takes him by the hand when he's drunk / Carries him when he's sated with wine" (*ANET* 150). Mother Jerusalem is described as being equally deprived, her children either having lost their lives during the siege of the city or having been subsequently deported.

The image of bodies lying in the streets—bodies of the dead, not of the inhabitants who had fainted from hunger (cf. Lam 2:21)—is reminiscent of descriptions of the city in the aftermath of the siege in Lamentations. Since the phrase "at the corner of every street" is identical with Lam 2:19 and 4:1 and does not sit well with the following verse (as Duhm put it, trapped antelopes do not usually lie around on street corners; Duhm 1922, 388), it is often bracketed as a scribal addition. This may be so, but it is also possible that the point about the antelopes may have been added to correspond more closely to the twofold disaster of the previous verse—that is, destruction and death in the city and the imprisonment and deportation of its inhabitants.

As with the previous passage, a word of reassurance follows (vv 21–23). To a people immobilized by fear, guilt, and a sense of helplessness the word is: put the past behind you. Intoxication as a metaphor for spiritual obtuseness and hebetude (cf. Isa 29:9) provides another figurative way of construing the immediate past (cf. the idea of indentured service at the beginning of these chapters, 40:2). Now those who afflicted you will themselves suffer the same fate. In view of the parallels between this passage and Lamentations, it is interesting to note that the verb *yg'* Hiphil ("afflict") in 51:23 is used in Lamentations exclusively of Yahveh's afflicting Jerusalem (1:5, 12; 3:32). The final figure of Israel's past humiliation may have been suggested by the practice, no doubt common in the incessant warfare of the Near East, of the conqueror's placing his foot on the neck or back of a subdued enemy (Josh 10:24; Ps 110:1; cf. the Anubanini and the Behistun reliefs from the twenty-third and the sixth centuries B.C.E., respectively, *ANEP* 177 #524; 78 #249), or even tramping over the prostrate bodies of the defeated (Zech 10:5).

THE COMING OF THE KINGDOM (52:1–12)

(Fichtner. 1961; Hanson 1979; Lindars 1986; Melugin 1982; Mettinger 1986–1987; Mowinckel 1954, 139–43; Steck 1989b)

TRANSLATION

i

52 [1]Zion, awake! awake! clothe yourself with your strength;
clothe yourself with your splendid robes,[a] Jerusalem, holy city!
For the uncircumcised and the unclean
will enter you no longer.
[2]Arise, shake yourself free of the dust.
Jerusalem, ascend your throne;[b]
loose[c] the bonds from your neck,
captive daughter Zion!

ii

[3]For this is what Yahveh says: "You were sold into slavery for nothing, and you will be redeemed but not with payment." [4]This is what the Sovereign Lord[d] Yahveh says: "In the beginning my people went down to Egypt to settle there, and then the Assyrians oppressed them without cause. [5]So now, what do I find here?[e] [a pronouncement of Yahveh] My people are taken away without payment, and their leaders[f] are boasting about it[g] [a pronouncement of Yahveh] and unceasingly, all day long, my name is reviled.[h] [6]Therefore, on that day my people will acknowledge my name;[i] (they will acknowledge) that I, Yahveh, am the one who is speaking; here I am."

iii

[7]How welcome on the mountains are the footsteps of the herald
announcing well-being, bringing good tidings,[j] announcing victory,
declaring to Zion: "Your God reigns as king!"
[8]Listen! Your watchmen raise their[k] voices,
with one accord they shout out for joy,
for with their own eyes they are witnessing
the return of Yahveh to Zion.[l]
[9]With one accord break out into joyful shouts,
you ruins of Jerusalem,
for Yahveh has comforted his people;
he has redeemed Jerusalem.
[10]Yahveh has bared his holy arm
in the sight of all the nations.
All the ends of the earth shall witness
the victory of our God.

iv

[11]Away! Away! Go thence,
touch nothing unclean;
purify yourselves as you depart,
you who bear the vessels of Yahveh;
[12]for you shall not leave in haste,
nor shall you depart in flight,
for Yahveh goes on before you;
the God of Israel is your rearguard.[m]

NOTES

A few words from vv 2, 4–7, 10–12 have been preserved in 4QIsa[b,c,d]. The 4QIsa[c] scribe wrote the Tetragrammaton and *ʾĕlohîm* in the archaic script. [a] LXX reads *endusai tēn doxan sou*, "put on your glory"; [b] reading MT *šĕbî* as imperative fem. > *yšb*, "sit," as in 1QIsa[a] *všby*, LXX *kathisan*, Vulg. *sede*, and Tg. *tyby ʿl kvrsy yqrʾ*, "sit on your glorious throne," cf. 47:1; [c] reading Q *hitpatĕḥî* with LXX and other ancient versions; [d] 1QIsa[a] omits *ʾădonay*, "the Sovereign Lord"; [e] read Q with 1QIsa[a] *māh-lî poh*; the exact meaning of the idiom is unclear; [f] reading Q *mōšĕlâv* pl. for K sing.; [g] a tentative translation, adding "about it" to relate it to the context; MT *yĕhêlîlû* > *yll* Hiphil, literally "howl," does not make good sense; others derive it from *hll* II Poel, "play the fool," or, with G. R. Driver (1935, 402), "have gone mad"; or read *yĕḥullēlû*, "are profaned," with reference to the Babylonian conquest cf. 43:28; the translation offered (*yĕhallēlû*) agrees with Tg.; [h] MT *minnōʾāṣ* is probably a mixed form combining *mĕnōʾāṣ* Pual participle with *mitnōʾāṣ* Hithpoel participle; [i] omitting the second *lākēn*, "therefore," with 1QIsa[a]; [j] 1QIsa[a] reverses the order of the participles; [k] reading *qôlām*, pl. with 1QIsa[a]; [l] 1QIsa[a] adds *brḥmym*, "with compassion"; [m] 1QIsa[a] adds *ʾĕlohê kol-hāʾāreṣ yiqqārēʾ*, "he is called the God of all the earth."

COMMENTS

The series of apostrophes addressed to Jerusalem beginning in 51:17–23 is taken up again in 54:1–17 after the passage on the life and mission of the servant in 52:13–53:12. The arrangement of the material in this part of the book suggests a deliberate and purposeful alternation of Jerusalem/Zion and the prophetic servant. The lines, divisions, and connections are not always clear, not surprisingly, considering the long editorial history that the book has undergone, but the arrangement can be set out more or less as follows:

servant passage (49:1–6) followed by comment (49:7–13)

Jerusalem/Zion (49:14–26) followed by comment (50:1–3)

servant passage (50:4–9) followed by comment (50:10–51:8)

apostrophe (51:9–11) to (the arm of) Yahveh

the remnant of another reference to the servant (51:12–16)

Jerusalem/Zion (51:17–52:12)

servant passage (52:13–53:12) containing comment (53:1–11a)

Jerusalem/Zion (54:1–17a)

"the heritage of the servants of Yahveh" (54:17b) looks back to the servant of chs. 49–53 and forward to the "servants of Yahveh" in chs. 56–66.

Attempts to read 52:1–12 as a coherent passage from one hand have not been successful. The apostrophe to Zion (vv 1–2) is followed by a comment introduced with the conventional prophetic discourse formula (3), which has been expanded with a further comment (4–5) in elucidation of the phrase *ḥinnām*, "without payment," "for nothing," by means of a summary history of Israel, divided into an Egyptian, Assyrian, and Babylonian phase. This in its turn has been rounded off by a projection into a more distant future (6), introduced with the only example of the *bayyôm hahûʾ incipit* in chs. 40–66, in a manner therefore much more in line with the numerous "on that day" addenda in chs. 1–39 than with chs. 40–66. While it is true that verse and prose cannot always be clearly distinguished in this and other prophetic books, section 3–6 is notably different rhythmically from sections 1–2 and 7–12, in keeping with the more discursive character of the subject matter, and can certainly be described as prose. This series of addenda is an example of the kind of cumulative and incremental editorial process much more in evidence in Isa 1–39 than in 40–66 but does not warrant a lower theological rating or the description *Epigonenarbeit* assigned to it by Duhm (1922, 389).

Jerusalem is called on to assume its rightful place as the holy city (the title also appears in 48:2; Neh 11:1, 18; and is perpetuated in the Arabic *al quds*) and, consequently, must no longer be defiled by the presence of the foreign conquerors. Ritual defilement of city and temple was the inevitable consequence of foreign occupation (cf. Ezek 44:9; Lam 1:10; Ps 79:1), but the holiness of the city is not exclusively a matter of the absence of ritual taint. Ezekiel represents the departure of the holy God from the city prior to its occupation and destruction under the symbol of the *kābôd* ("glory, effulgence"), a way of expressing the presence of the invisible God and of combining divine transcendence with immanence (Ezek 10:4, 18; 11:22–23). The return of the "glory" to Jerusalem and the rebuilt temple, seen in vision (Ezek 43:1–5), has its parallel in the present passage in the proclamation by the herald of the return of Yahveh to his kingdom in the purified city (52:7–10). Holiness is constituted therefore by the presence of the holy God.

The initial apostrophe sets up a deliberate contrast with the fate of Babylon described in ch. 47. Jerusalem shakes off the dust, Babylon sits in it; Jerusalem leaves her captivity behind, Babylon enters into captivity; Jerusalem is clothed in splendid robes, Babylon has to remove her fine clothing; Jerusalem ascends her throne (see Note b on *šĕbî*), Babylon comes down from hers. One has the impression that at the time of writing the fall of Babylon was imminent.

The prose addenda are addressed no longer directly to the city but to the Israelite community. Perhaps taking a cue from 50:1b ("to which of my creditors have I sold you into slavery?"), the author compares subjection to Babylonian imperial rule as a form of indentured service (cf. 40:2). The sociological analogy limps—someone who is next-of-kin (*gōʾēl*, "redeemer") buying back a person who is an indentured servant as a result of insolvency—as is often the case with analogies. It limps in that the fact that one receives no advantage from selling his kin into indentured service does not imply that the situation can be reversed without payment. But the point is that neither Yahveh nor his agent (originally Cyrus, 45:13) owes Babylon anything, and the act of rescue, like all God's interventions in human affairs, is a gratuitous act, an act of grace.

The second of the prose comments (vv 4–5), in effect a comment on the preceding comment, seems to have understood *ḥinnam* ("for nothing") in v 3 to refer to Israel as the *innocent* victim of aggression. The present situation is therefore set in the context of a history of subjection, divided into three epochs. First, Israelites were under Egyptian control as *gērîm*, "resident aliens," then under Assyria, and now under Babylon. If the scribe's intent was to present a history of innocent suffering, it was directly contrary to the older prophetic view, well represented in Isa 1–39; it was even contrary to the view of the author of chs. 40–48, that Israel's sufferings were deserved but that she had now "served time" and was in the clear (40:2).

In the final addendum (v 6), a scholiast, who perhaps understood the preceding pronouncement quite differently as referring to the belittling of the name of God by Israel and its leaders looks further into the future to a time when the name of God would be revered and God would be recognized for who God is. This is the rather different ambient reflected in the last eleven chapters of the book. We note in Isa 56–66 and in other late biblical texts an increasing emphasis on the divine name (Isa 56:6; 57:15; 59:19; 60:9; 63:12, 14; 64:1, 6; cf. Mal 3:16). The final *hinnēnî* ("here I am") is particularly reminiscent of Yahveh, confronted with a people that does not invoke his name, who calls out, *hinnēnî, hinnēnî*, "here I am, here I am" (Isa 65:1).

The passage about the messenger and the message (52:7–10) would follow the attempt to energize Jerusalem (vv 1–2) naturally by providing the motivation for new hope and the prospect of a different future. At the beginning of these chapters, Jerusalem was herself both the messenger (40:9) and the recipient of the message (41:27). Here the bearer of the message is a prophetic figure, and what is announced lies in the future even though stated as a *fait accompli* in the prophetic past tense. This much is clear from an examination of the language used in these verses. It is the one endowed with the spirit who is sent to bring good news to captives and the afflicted (*lĕbaśśēr* 61:1). Throughout these chapters, announcing (*šmʿ* Hiphil, used twice in v 7) is almost invariably predictive (41:22, 26; 42:9; 43:9, 12; 44:8; 45:21; 48:3, 5–6).

As the scene unfolds, it can be grasped in a straightforwardly visual way, with lookouts posted on the city walls (it would be too literalistic to point out that there were no walls at that time) catching a glimpse of the *parousia*, the return of the king to his city, and a herald announcing the imminent resumption of his reign. But prophets are also known as lookouts or sentinels (*ṣōpîm* Jer 6:17; Ezek 3:17; 33:2, 6–7; perhaps Isa 56:10 and Hos 9:8), since they function as an antenna for the community, a kind of early warning system.

A close and instructive parallel is the account of the soliciting of a visionary experience of the fall of Babylon (Isa 21:8–9). The seer is the lookout (*mĕṣappeh*), who is told to announce what he sees and to listen very hard. He assures Yahveh that he has taken his stand on the watchtower (*miṣpeh*) and occupies his station night after night until he sees, in vision, a rider approaching with the news that Babylon has fallen (*nāpĕlâ, nāpĕlâ bābel!*).

A similar instance of the soliciting of an oracle or visionary experience by a seer, perhaps in some way connected with the Isaian text, appears in Habakkuk. The prophet says, "I will take my stand on the watchtower and station myself on the rampart; I will keep watch to see what he will say to me," at which point he is told by Yahveh to write the vision (2:1–2). Returning to our text: the fact that the watchmen witness with their own eyes, literally "eye to eye" (*ʿayin bĕʿayin*), is consistent with this reading of the prophet as the watchman since "eye to eye" is a type of expression (cf. "face to face," "mouth to mouth") denoting an especially close relationship with the deity (Num 14:14).

A close parallel to 52:7a, the approach of the herald on the mountains announcing well-being, appears in Nah 2:1a[1:15a] but without the prophetic connotations that we have noted in the Isaian context. That the Nahum text continues in a way strongly reminiscent of Isa 52:1b (*kî lōʾ yôsîp ʿôd laʿăbôr-bāk*, "for [the wicked one] shall enter you no longer") would suggest that it has drawn on the Isaian text rather than the reverse, but this type of question can rarely be decided with any assurance.

So much for the messenger; what then was the message? What the herald announces is first presented in general terms, well-being (*šālôm*) and good (*ṭôb*); then, more specifically, as victory that spells salvation (*yĕšûʿâ*) and the reign of God. What the watchmen see is the return of Yahveh to the city following the victory and leading up to the enthronement, a representation developed more fully in Ezekiel, as noted earlier, and there also witnessed in a visionary experience (Ezek 43:1–5). The acclamation "your God reigns!" (*mālak ʾĕlohāyik*) addressed to Jerusalem/Zion is a modified form of the psalmic acclamation *YHVH mālak* (Pss 93:1; 96:10 = 1 Chr 16:31; 97:1; 99:1) of the Jerusalem liturgy from the time of the Judean monarchy. The hypothesis that it featured in a liturgy of the enthronement of Yahveh was propounded by Mowinckel and others. It enjoyed a degree of popularity for a while, especially through its adoption in major commentaries on Psalms by Hans-Joachim Kraus and Artur Weiser, but failed to establish itself due to lack of evidence.

The kingship of Yahveh is nevertheless a well-attested and no doubt ancient native Israelite variation of a common way of representing deity in the Near East and Levant. The acclamation, however, signifies an *event* rather than a kind of article of faith; it means that the God of Israel is about to resume his active rule among his people with the defeat of his enemies and the restoration of his city. But the acclamation also carries with it echoes and reverberations from familiar mythic patterns: the primordial victory over the forces of Chaos and negativity (the rivers, the great waters, the sea, Ps 93:1), the placing of the earth on its foundations (Ps 96:10), the theophany in the thunder cloud and lightning (Ps 97:1). To repeat a point made earlier, it is arguable that this kind of language was intended as a deliberate counter to the ideology of imperial power expressed in the liturgical celebration of the New Year *akitu* festival in Babylon and the creation myth *Enuma Elish,* recited on the fourth day of the festival. The proclamation of the universal rule of the Babylonian imperial deity in *Enuma Elish* ("Marduk is king!" *ANET* 66) prepares for the combat with Tiamat, embodiment of Chaos (cf. Isa 51:9–10), the creation of the world, and the construction of the esagila sanctuary for the victorious deity. These are the events on which the claim of the incomparability, especially the incomparable power of Marduk, is based (see Marduk's statement, "I am, and there is none other," Isa 47:10), a claim countered in similar language at numerous points by the author of Isa 40–55.

By the time of the fall of Babylon, Jerusalem had been in ruins for half a century, and even after that time any attempt to rebuild its "ancient ruins" (Isa 58:12; 61:4) could be interpreted as sedition on the part of "that rebellious city hurtful to kings and provinces" (Ezra 4:15). Here the ruins are invited to rejoice at the prospect of comfort and redemption—namely, the restoration of the city to its former state. The centrality and mythic dimensions of Jerusalem reflected in the biblical texts can easily obscure the fact that this outcome was by no means inevitable and that, for the Babylonians, Mizpah was meant to be and to remain the administrative and probably also the religious center of the province.

The call to leave Babylon (52:11–12) parallels 48:20–22 which is also followed by a passage dealing with the prophetic servant. The command to "go (out) thence" (*ṣĕʾû miššām*) no more rules out a Babylonian location for the speaker than the Exodus theme requires it. The anticipated return from Babylon is given fuller resonance by the use of language associated with the departure from Egypt: unlike the people's ancestors leaving Egypt, they will not depart in haste (*bĕḥippāzôn,* only here and Exod 12:11; Deut 16:3), and they will not easily take to flight (*mĕnûsâ,* only here and Lev 26:36). And as on that first occasion, they will be protected both in front and behind by the numinous cloud and fire (Exod 13:21–22; 14:19–20).

Somewhat unexpected is the injunction to maintain a state of ritual purity, which is addressed to the people, presumably priests, who are charged with bringing back to the temple the sacred vessels confiscated by the Babylonians. The Historian records that the golden vessels had been cut up for bullion after the first capture of the city in 597 (2 Kgs 24:13) and that all the remaining vessels were taken to Babylon after the destruction of the temple in 586 (2 Kgs 25:14–15 = 2 Chr 36:10, 18).

The author of Ezra–Nehemiah is at pains to emphasize the return of this cultic paraphernalia to Jerusalem on the occasion of the first *aliyah,* when the vessels were confided to Sheshbazzar (Ezra 1:7–11; 5:13–15; 6:5) and, much later, when Ezra arrived in Jerusalem on a mission authorized by the Persian authorities (Ezra 7:19; 8:25– 30, 33–34). On the latter occasion Ezra reminded the priests charged with the task of conveying the vessels safely to Jerusalem that both they and the vessels were holy (*qōdeš* Ezra 8:28), which suggests that this theme of continuity between the old order and the new may have been suggested to the author of Ezra–Nehemiah by Isa 52:11.

Isaiah 52:7–10 provides one of the best illustrations of the power of a canonical text to shape the identity of the community that accepts it. From this text early Christians derived both the unique form in which to tell the story of their founder—*euaggelion*, "good tidings, gospel"—and the essence of his message—the coming of the kingdom of God. Both come together in the first statement attributed to Jesus in Mark's Gospel: "The time is fulfilled and the kingdom of God has come near; repent, and believe in the good tidings" (Mark 1:15 cf. Matt 10:7–8 with echoes of Isa 52:3, and Luke 4:16–21 referring also to Isa 61:1–2). The messenger and the message in the Isaian text provided both paradigm and warranty for Christian preachers, as we see from the tendency to refer to it wherever the preaching of the gospel is the issue (e.g. Rom 10:15; Eph 6:15). It was no doubt with Isa 52:7–10 in mind that Jerome, in the Prologue to the Vulgate translation of Isaiah, described Isaiah himself as more evangelist than prophet.

THE SERVANT: FROM HUMILIATION TO EXALTATION (52:13–53:12)

(Ahlström 1969; Allen 1971; Battenfield 1982; Begg 1986; Blenkinsopp 1997; Blythin 1966b; Brownlee 1953; Chavasse 1964; Clines 1976; Collins 1980; Coppens 1963; Dahood 1960, 1971; Day 1980; G. R. Driver 1968; Elliger 1933, 1971a, 1972; Emerton 1970; Engnell 1948; M. Fischer 1963; Fohrer 1981; Gelston 1971; Gerleman 1980; Gordon 1970; E. Haag 1977b; Hermisson 1998b; O. Kaiser O. 1959, 84–129; Kapelrud 1971, 1979; Komlosh 1974–1975; Martin-Achard 1982; Mowinckel 1921, 1931; Müller 1969; North 1955, 1965; Orlinsky 1967, 1–133; Payne 1971, 1979; Raabe 1984; Reicke 1967; Rignell 1953; Robinson 1959; Rowley 1952, 3–57; Sellin 1930, 1937; Snaith 1950; Soggin 1975; Sonne 1959; Steck 1985b; Thomas 1969; Whybray 1978; Williamson 1978b; Wolff 1962; Zimmerli 1974. *The history of interpretation*: Alobaidi 1998; Aytoun 1921–22; Bachl 1982; Bundy 1982, 1983; Carmignac 1960; S. R. Driver and Neubauer 1876–1877; Euler 1934; Fascher 1958; Ginsberg 1953; Guillaume 1957; Hegermann 1954; Hooker 1959; Janowski and Stuhlmacher 1996; Koch 1972; Lindars 1961, 75–88, 134–36; Page 1985; Rembaum 1982; Rubinstein 1954; Stuhlmacher 1996; Syrén 1989; Wolff 1984)

TRANSLATION

i

52 [13]See, my servant[a] will achieve success;[b]
he will be highly honored,[c] raised up, and greatly exalted.[d]

[14a]Just as many were once appalled at him,[e]
[15]so will he astonish[f] many nations.
Because of him kings will observe silence,[g]
for what was never told them they now see,
and what they had never heard they now understand.[h]

ii

53 [1]Who would believe what we have heard?
To whom has Yahveh's power[i] been revealed?
[2]He grew up like a sapling in Yahveh's presence,[j]
rooted in the parched ground.[k]
He had no outward beauty, no distinction,
we saw nothing in his appearance to attract us,
52 [14b]so marred[l] was his appearance beyond human semblance,[m]
his form beyond human likeness.
53 [3]He was despised, shunned by people,[n]
a man who suffered, no stranger to sickness,[o]
like one from whom people turn away their gaze.
He was despised,[p] and we held him of no account.
[4]Yet it was he who bore our affliction,
he[q] who bore the burden of our sufferings.
We reckoned him stricken,
smitten by God and afflicted;
[5]yet he was wounded[r] because of our transgressions,
crushed on account of our iniquities.
On him was laid the chastisement that made us whole;[s]
we found healing because of his wounds.
[6]We had all gone astray like sheep,
all of us going our own way,
but Yahveh laid upon him
the iniquity of us all.
[7]He was abused, yet he was submissive;
he did not open his mouth.
He was led like a lamb to the slaughter,
like a ewe that is dumb before the shearers.
He did not open his mouth.[t]
[8]By oppressive acts of judgment[u] he was led away,
and who gives a thought to his fate?[v]
He was cut off from the land of the living,
stricken to death for his people's sin.[w]
[9]His grave was located [x] with the wicked,
his sepulcher with reprobates,[y]
though he had done no violence,
and no falsehood was on his tongue.

[10]But it was Yahveh's good pleasure to crush him,[z]
[he brought sickness upon him].[aa]
If his life is laid down as a guilt offering,[bb]
he will see posterity, he will prolong his days;
through him Yahveh's purpose will prevail.
[11] After his painful life he will see light and be satisfied.[cc]

iii

By his knowledge my servant will vindicate many;[dd]
it is he who bears the burden of their iniquities.
[12]Therefore, I allot his portion with the great;
with the powerful he will share the spoil,
since he poured out his life-blood to death
and was numbered among transgressors.
Yet he bore the sin[ee] of many,
and interceded for their transgressions.[ff]

NOTES

4QIsaiah[b,c,d] have some words from 52:13 and 53:1–3, 6–12; the very few variants from MT are noted below; here as elsewhere 1QIsa[b] is close to MT. [a] Targum adds *mšyḥʾ*, "the Messiah," after *ʿabdî*, "my servant"; for *ʿabdî*, Duhm (1922, 393–94) reads *ʿebed YHVH* and seems to favor Budde's emendation of *yaśkîl* to *yiśrāʾēl*, but neither change is warranted; [b] *yaśkîl*, "prosper," "succeed" (cf. Tg. *yṣlḥ*), better than "understand," as in the Vulg. *intelliget*, and assuredly not a sobriquet, Yaskil, "the Wise One," for the servant (Torrey 1928, 415); [c] the second half of the verse seems overloaded with three more-or-less synonymous verbs, and LXX does not translate the first of these, i.e. *yārûm*, literally, "he will be high"; but all three are in 1QIsa[a] (with conjunction *vyrvm*) and Tg. (*yrʾm*), and the insertion of the first cannot be an explanatory gloss on the verb *niśśāʾ* following, which is too common to require glossing; [d] LXX has a stronger expression, "he will be greatly glorified," *doxasthēsetai sphodra*; [e] this verse appears to be defective; MT reads *ʿālêkâ*, "at you" (masc. sing.), with which 1QIsa[a], 1QIsa[b], LXX (*epi se*), Vulg. (*super te*) agree; Tg. goes its own way with a messianic interpretation, but seems to assume 3rd person: "as the house of Israel waited for him many days, for his [text: their] appearance was wretched among the nations"; 3d person is supported by 2 Hebrew MSS and Syr., and fits the context better; 14b appears to be out of place: it is unlikely that successive verses would begin with *kēn*; the word breaks into the contrast between the former humiliation and the future glorification of the servant (*kaʾăšer . . . kēn*); and 14b fits better after 53:2, especially in view of the pair *tōʾar, marʾēh*, repeated in reverse order; [f] MT *yēzzeh* could be *nzh* Hiphil "sprinkle" (cultic context) or "spatter" (2 Kgs 9:33; Isa 63:3) cf. Tg. *ybdr*, "scatter," "disperse," but this does not fit the context, and in any case the construction is wrong because the preposition *ʿal* would be required; hence, the proposal to assume > *nzh* II by analogy with Arab. *nazā*, "startle," cf. LXX *thaumasontai ethnē polla ep'autō*, "many peoples will marvel at him," less drastic than emending to *rgz*, "agitate," or *bzh*, "despise"; [g] 1QIsa[a] *vqpṣv* for MT *yiqpĕṣû* suggests that the Qumran scribe attached *ʿālâyv* to what precedes rather than to what follows; [h] LXX has both verbs in the future (*opsontai, sunēsousin*); *hitbônānû* > *bîn* Hithpalel connotes paying close attention, observing carefully, viewing, examining cf. 1 Kgs 3:21 (a child); Isa 14:16 (the Babylonian king in Sheol); Ps 37:10 (a place); Job 31:1 (a young girl); [i] *zĕrôāʿ* literally, "arm" cf. 51:5, 9; [j] *lēpānayv*, "before him" (i.e. Yahveh), rather than "straight up," as in Gordon 1970 and Allen 1971; [k] literally, "like a root (*šōreš*) from the parched ground," but roots do not generally grow out of the ground; for an alternative meaning, "stem" for *šōreš*, see Millard 1969, 127; [l] If MT *ken-mišḥat* is retained, *mišḥat* will be a hapax substantive in construct > *šḥt* = "destroy," "ruin," therefore with the meaning "disfigurement," a rare use of substantive for participle cf. *ḥădal ʾîšîm, mastēr pānîm* 53:3; alternatively, with the Babylonian text tradition, *mošḥāt* Hophal participle = "ruined," "disfigured"; the ancient versions paraphrased for the most part: LXX *adoxēsei apo anthrōpōn*, "he will be dishonored by men"; Vulg. *inglorius*; Tg. *hšvk*, "wretched"; 1QIsa[a] *msḥty*, "my disfigurement" (?) or, according to Kutscher (1974, 262) and Barthélemy (1986, 387–90), > *mšḥ*, therefore "I have anointed"; but it is more easily explained either as a simple slip or *ḥireq compaginis* (GKC §90 l), as proposed by G. R. Driver (1968, 92); [m] *mēʾîš*, "beyond human semblance," preposition *min* is Privative, "from being a man," less than human; not comparative, "more than (other) men"; [n] MT *ḥădal ʾîšîm*, with the unusual pl. only here, Ps 141:4, and Prov 8:4, is a rare case of a substantive serving as participle cf. Ps 39:5, *meh-ḥādēl ʾānî*, literally, "what a lacking thing (i.e. transient thing) am I" (GKC §128q); [o] reading with 1QIsa[a] *vyvdʿ* = *vĕyôdēʿa* active participle rather than MT passive participle, unless the latter is used with the sense of "experienced (in sickness)" cf. Deut 1:13, 15 *ʾănāšîm ḥăkāmîm ûnĕbōnîm vîdūʿîm*, "wise, understanding, and experienced men"; 1QIsa[b] is ambiguous; LXX *eidos pherein malakian*, "one who knows how to bear sickness"; Vulg. *scientem infirmitatem*, "knowing infirmity"; [p] 1QIsa[a] has *vnbvzhv*, "and we despised him," cf. Syr. *vštnyhy*, but MT is acceptable and is supported by LXX *ētimasthē* and Vulg. *despectus*; [q] some medieval MSS, as also Syr. and Vulg., repeat the pronoun, which also scans better (*ûmakʾōbēnû hûʾ sĕbālām*; [r] MT *mĕḥōlāl* Polal > *ḥll* means "killed" or "pierced through" (and therefore presumably killed) in the great majority of cases and only infrequently "wounded" (Ezek 26:15; 30:24); the meaning here can be decided only in the context of the poem as a whole, on which see the Comments; Aqu. reads *mĕḥullal* Pual participle, "profaned," cf. Ezek 36:23 and Tg. "he will rebuild the sanctuary that was polluted on account of our transgressions"; [s] *mûsar šĕlômēnû*, literally, "the chastisement of our peace" is genitive of purpose cf. 51:17; Ps 44:23 (GKC §128q); [t] this short verse is present in LXX, Vulg. (in future *aperiet*), and 1QIsa[a] and should not be elided on account of repetition, common in these chapters; [u] the phrase describing how he was taken away (*luqqaḥ*), *mē'ōṣer ûmimmišpāṭ*, is difficult; in the only other occurrence of *mē'ōṣer*, the preposition signifies instrumentality (Ps 107:39 "brought low by oppression"); in addition to "justice," *mišpāṭ* can also refer to the verdict following the judicial process; I read the two nouns as hendiadys; [v] *dôr*, usually translated "generation" (cf. LXX *geneam*, Vulg. *generationem*, perhaps both with messianic undertones), is here understood by analogy with Akk. *dūru* and Arab. *dauru*, following G. R. Driver 1935, 403; [w] MT *mippeša' 'ammî nega' lāmô*, "because of the transgression of my people a blow to them," is unintelligible; though both LXX (*tou laou mou*) and Vulg. (*populi mei*) have 1st-person pronoun, read *'ammô*, "his people," with 1QIsa[a]; the proposed emendation of *nega' lāmô* is conjectural but follows LXX (*eis thanaton*), reading *nugga' lammāvet* but not understanding the latter as "(struck) grievously" (Thomas 1968b, 84); [x] either repunctuate *vayyittēn* as Qal passive *vayyuttan* or emend to 3d-person pl. with 1QIsa[a] *vytnv*; [y] *vĕ'et-'āšîr bĕmotayv*, "and with a wealthy man in his deaths" is unintelligible; apart from being in the sing., *'āšîr* does not make a good parallel with *rĕšā'îm*, even though present in LXX (*plousious*), Syr. (*'tyr'*), Tg. (*'attîrê*), and Vulg. (*divitem*); read *'ōśê ra'*, "evildoers," requiring minimal alteration, and for *bĕmōtayv* read *bāmātô*, "his sepulcher," following Albright 1957; [z] in spite of numerous efforts to construe or emend v 10, it remains obscure and the original sense almost certainly irretrievable; any translation will be tentative; [aa] *heḥĕlî* 3d- person sing. perfect > *ḥlh* Hiphil, construed as a lamed-aleph verb with aleph quiescent omitted (GKC §74k) but perhaps a gloss; for *heḥĕlî*, 1QIsa[a] has *vyḥllhv*, "and he wounded (or pierced, or slew) him"; somewhat similar in Syr. (*vmry' sb' dnmkkyvhy vnhšyvhy*, "the Lord decided to beat him down and make him suffer"), and Vulg. *et Dominus voluit conterere eum in infirmitate*, "the Lord willed to crush him with infirmity," but going in a different direction in LXX, *kai kurios bouletai katharisai auton apo tēs plēgēs*, "the Lord desires to cleanse him from the wound"; BHS follows Begrich, *heḥĕlîm 'et-śām 'āšām napšô*, "he healed him who made of his life a guilt offering," which is ingenious but not entirely convincing; [bb] though supported by 1QIsa[a] and 4QIsa[d], MT is problematic, especially with respect to the 2d-person sing. verb, reproduced in LXX but not in Vulg. (*si posuerit pro peccato animam suam*); the least radical emendations are either to repoint *tāśîm* as *tuśam* Qal passive agreeing with *napšô* ("if his life is laid down as a guilt offering"), adopted here, or to redivide words and read *'ĕmet śām 'āšām napšô*, "truly, he has offered his life as a guilt sacrifice"; for the adverbial use of *'ĕmet*, Dahood (1960, 406) adduced Deut 13:15 and Ps 132:11 cf. Isa 42:3 *le'ĕmet*, supported by Battenfield (1982, 485) by pointing out that the *mem* in *'im* 1QIsa[a] 10a is not final *mem*; [cc] the preposition in *mē'ămal* could also signify "on account of" (GKC §119y); though absent from MT, Syr., and Vulg., *'ôr*, "light," is in 1QIsa[a], 1QIsa[b], 4QIsa[d], and LXX (*deixai autō phōs*); [dd] omitting *ṣaddîq*, which overburdens the verse and was either inserted by error on account of the similar *yaṣdîq* or by a scribe who wished to identify the *'ebed* with the *ṣaddîq* of Isa 57:1; [ee] reading pl. with all Qumran copies, LXX (*hamartias pollōn*), Syr. (*ḥṭh' dsy''*), Vulg. (*peccata multorum*); [ff] with all Qumran copies and LXX; MT has "and he interceded for transgressors" (*vĕlappōšĕ'îm*), but it is unlikely that the same word would be used in successive verses.

COMMENTS

The address of a servant of Yahveh in 49:1–6 and the present passage, in which the Servant does not speak but is spoken about, both rather abruptly follow exhortations to depart from the place of exile (48:20–22; 52:11–12). The contextual isolation of 52:13–53:12 is also emphasized by the apostrophe to Zion that precedes and follows it (52:1–2, 7–10; 54:1–17). If this arrangement is intentional, it may have had the purpose of relating the fate of the Servant to some of the major themes that permeate these chapters. The passage begins and concludes with an asseveration of Yahveh that the Servant, once humiliated and abused, will be exalted; once counted among criminals, will be in the company of the great and powerful (52:13–14a, 15; 53:11b–12). This statement encloses the body of the poem (53:1–11a), in which a co-religionist who had come to believe in the Servant's mission and message, one who in all probability was a disciple, speaks about the origin and appearance of the Servant, the sufferings he endured, and his heroic and silent submission to death—whether threatened or experienced remains to be determined.

The nexus between this quite long and in several respects obscure panegyric or threnody and the opening statement of Yahveh is the allusion to the almost incredible report (*šĕmûa'*, 53:1a), long undisclosed and now passed on, in which the arm, that is, the power of God, is revealed ("what they had never heard . . . what we have heard"). But if the passage appears to break abruptly into the context at this point of the book it also has unmistakable links with previous chapters. The presentation of the servant to the nations (*hinnēh . . . 'abdî*) is reminiscent of 42:1 (*hēn 'abdî*), the reassurance of ultimate success in the face of trials and discouragement recalls previous pronouncements about a servant (49:5–6; 50:7–9), and the transition from humiliation to exaltation, from being an object of contempt to receiving deferential treatment from kings, replicates the comment added to one of the previous servant passages ("when they see you, kings will rise to their feet, princes will pay you homage," 49:7). All of the indications therefore point to the conclusion that the three passages in question (49:1–6; 50:4–9; 52:13–53:12) represent aspects of or phases in the career of one and the same individual. The first two, in which the Servant speaks about himself, have comments attached to them (49:7–13; 50:10–11), while the third, in which the Servant is spoken about, combines discourse of Yahveh and comment internally.

The resumption of this Yahveh discourse at the conclusion of the poem is not formally indicated, but it is first clearly in evidence in 11b with the reference to "my servant." It is worth observing that the designation *'ebed* ("servant," "agent") and the description of the beneficiaries of his mission as *rabbîm* ("many") are present only in the Yahveh discourse. Since *rabbîm* is used with the article, it is tempting to interpret the term in a quasi-technical sense with reference to the Servant's disciples as *hārabbîm* ("the Many"), as in Dan 12:2–4, 10, the Qumran group, and early Christianity (cf. Mark 14:24; Rom 5:15; and see Jeremias *TDNT* 1968, 6:536–45).

The interpretation of these last verses (Isa 53:11b–12) is difficult, and any translation must be considered provisional. There is the problem in the first place of punctuation and prosody. In 53:1–9 the meter is fairly regular with twelve 3–3 verses out of eighteen, whereas in the seven lines of vv 10–12 as set out in BHS only one is regular 3–3. Since it is unclear what it would mean for the Servant to be satisfied or sated with his knowledge or (even less clear) with his humiliation, it seems advisable to read *bĕdaʿtô*, "by his knowledge," as modifying the verb *ṣdq* Hiphil, here translated "vindicate" (NRSV "make righteous").

Among the alternative meanings suggested for *daʿat*, fully documented by Emerton (1970), we mention "humiliation" (Thomas 1969; G. R. Driver 1968; Day 1980), "rest" (Williamson 1978b), "obedience" (Reicke 1967), and "sweat" (Dahood 1971, 72). The first two of these rely on the Arabic cognate *wadaʿa*, "set down," but the existence of a cognate is a useful indicator of an alternative meaning of a verb as well attested as *ydʿ* only if there are cases in which such a meaning is either required or strongly suggested. This condition is not verified with *daʿat* or the corresponding verb *ydʿ*.

The passive participle *yĕdûaʿ* (53:3) can be repointed as active or understood to mean "experienced" (see textual Note), and in Dan 12:4 (*yĕšōṭĕṭû rabbîm vĕtirbeh haddaʿat*), as obscure as it is, *daʿat*, "knowledge," makes at least as good if not better sense than *daʿat*, "humiliation." The vindication of the many by knowledge will be seen to make sense in light of the Servant's statement in 50:4–9. As God promises to vindicate him (*qārôb maṣdîqî* 50:8), so he will vindicate those who follow his guidance, and he will do this through his teaching: he has the tongue of those who are taught, and his task is to sustain the dispirited through the spoken and possibly also the written word (50:4). In this respect the situation is reminiscent of the *maśkîlîm* in Daniel (11:33; 12:3–4, 10), who will instruct and vindicate the many, and will do so by their knowledge.

That the Servant bore the burden of the community's sin is repeated several times in the body of the poem, using much the same vocabulary (*sābal, nāśāʾ*; *ʿăvôn, ḥēṭʾ*) in different combinations (53:4a, 5, 6b, 10a). It is not said, at least not clearly and explicitly, that he volunteered to do this, or even that he accepted it willingly, in spite of the reference to "intercession" at the end of the passage (see below). It was Yahveh who, exceptionally, caused the sickness, suffering, and ills to fall on him (6b). According to the dominant theory of moral causality, however, the community's transgressions should have brought on themselves these "wages of sin" instead of on him. What the body of the poem gives us is an *interpretation* by a convert to the Servant's person and teaching, offered either in his own name or that of the group to which he belonged. Whatever the sad condition of the servant, to which we shall return, the speaker and no doubt many in the community at first accepted the *inter-*

pretatio communis, amply illustrated in Psalms and Job, that his condition was the result of divine punishment for sin: he was stricken, smitten by God, and afflicted (53:4b). But then it dawned on him, as it did on the author of Job, that another explanation must be possible and that for some mysterious reason Yahveh had diverted the ills that should have fallen on the community onto this one individual. The change occurs between vv 4 and 5, and the intensity and emotional immediacy of the language derive from the impact of this insight and the experience of conversion to discipleship.

It seems that it was the vocabulary of sacrifice that provided the prophetic author with the means for expressing this discovery about the significance of the Servant's suffering. The most explicit statement is that he served a function analogous to a reparation- or trespass-offering (*ʾāšām* 53:10a). According to ritual prescription, the *ʾāšām* was an animal, either a ram without blemish, a lamb, or a goat offered for sacrifice as a means of expiating for certain kinds of voluntary or involuntary sin (Lev 5:1–26[5:1–6:7]; 7:2; 14:24). The Isaian poet does not state the analogy in formal terms or explore it at length, but it is hinted at elsewhere in the poem in the image of a sheep being led to the slaughter (53:7b) and the pouring out of the life-blood (cf. Ps 141:8, the same verb, also with *nepeš*). The statement that the Servant bore the community's sin also echoes the scapegoat ritual (Lev 16), in which one of the two animals is sacrificed as an atoning sin-offering (*ḥaṭṭāʾt*), and the other carries all the community's iniquities into a solitary, literally, "cut-off land" (*ʾereṣ gĕzērâ*), recalling the Servant's being cut off from the land of the living (*nigzar mēʾereṣ ḥayyîm* 53:8b).

The body of the poem, therefore, brings out more starkly and in greater detail the almost incredible contrast between the past humiliation and present or future glorification of the Servant that is stated in more general terms in the Yahveh discourse at the beginning and end. The result is not only coherent but is in keeping with the juxtaposition of pronouncement and comment noted in the previous two servant passages (49:1–7; 50:4–11). There is therefore no need to separate off 52:13–15 as a distinct salvation pronouncement (pace Coppens 1963; Orlinsky 1967; Whybray 1975, 169). The claim that 52:13–15 and 53:11b–12 were added in order to reinterpret what is said in 53:1–11a with reference to the people of Israel rather than an individual is arguable (and the same can be said for 49:7). These verses may be one of several indications of the very early development of what was to be the standard collective interpretation of 52:13–53:12 in evidence throughout the Jewish exegetical tradition. It is arguable but no more than that, and on the whole it seems better to retain the entire passage as basically a unity.

The empathic language of 53:1–12 also renders it unlikely that the speaker represents the nations and their rulers mentioned in the Yahveh discourse. The eulogist is an individual, almost certainly a disciple, as noted earlier, and one who speaks on behalf of those who "revere Yahveh and obey the voice of his Servant" (50:10). The form of the discourse, which spans the life of the Servant from his early years to his death and burial, may have borrowed phrases from the repertoire of lament psalms but reads more like a panegyric pronounced over the catafalque. A purely formal comparison with the panegyric of Julius Caesar as reported by the historians Appian and Dio Cassius, which included the benefits that Caesar conferred on others and his sufferings and violent death, would not be out of place.

The body of the poem begins by recording the Servant's early years and describing his appearance (vv 2–3). On the assumption that the antecedent of *lĕpānayv* is Yahveh, referred to in the previous verse, growing up in Yahveh's presence could imply either a special relationship, perhaps also a special function of a cultic nature, or simply a devout religious attitude in general. When taken together with the plant metaphor, the parched ground (*ʾereṣ ṣiyyâ* cf. 41:18) from which he sprang serves as an explanation, admittedly somewhat opaque, for the description of his appearance and his blighted career. The portrayal moves from simply denying any particular external appeal to gross disfigurement due to a disease not further specified. There are analogies to this kind of description in psalms of individual lamentation or thanksgiving for recovery from sickness (e.g. Ps 22:7, 17; 31:10; 38:3–8; 102:4–12), as also in Job (7:5; 16:8–10; 17:7; 19:20; 30:30), and even verbal parallels in the description of the bruised and battered body in Isa 1:5–6, which certainly refers to a collectivity.

These descriptions also illustrate common ideas about the religious correlatives of sickness (e.g. Ps 88:8) and the social isolation that it causes (Ps 31:12; 38:12; 88:9, 19; Job 30:10). That the servant had contracted leprosy was assumed by Jerome (Vulg. 53:4 *leprosum*) and taken up by Duhm (1922, 397–98), who referred to the similar language used in the priestly diagnostic texts (Lev 13:8) and the account of the medical condition of King Azariah (2 Kgs 15:5). This is a hypothesis that is certainly plausible but can be neither proved nor disproved.

Suffering in silence is also a topos in the lament psalms (Ps 38:14–15; 39:10 *lōʾ ʾeptaḥ-pî* cf. Isa 53:7 *lōʾ yiptaḥ pîv*). The speaker in 53:1–12 was therefore stating that he and those with whom he was associated had initially taken the conventional view of the Servant's misfortune but subsequently had been led to adopt a very different interpretation, at what point in time and under what circumstances is not stated.

The new understanding is introduced by referring to sickness and suffering in inverse order: his suffering and sickness made it possible in some way for him to bear the burden of his co-religionists' transgression and iniquity. Presupposed is the relation of moral causality between sin and physical affliction. This is a diagnostic based on experience: misfortune and sickness are symptomatic of moral failure. Following this way of thinking, the speaker was led in the first instance to conclude that the Servant was suffering the consequences of his own sin, a conviction expressed forcibly in the threefold repetition: *nagûaʿ, mukkēh ʾĕlohîm, mĕunneh,* "stricken, smitten by God, afflicted." We must suppose that the consciousness of communal guilt combined with reflection on the Servant's career made it impossible at a certain point to sustain this interpretation, and it seems probable that this took place after the Servant's death.

The conventional idea that this person's distress was inflicted by God as punishment for personal sin is therefore displaced by the new insight connecting the distress with the community's history of moral failure, a history often rehearsed in the prophetic writings. At this point the language is particularly dense. Unless otherwise clearly indicated by the context (as in Ezek 26:15; 30:24), *mĕḥolāl*, "wounded," implies *fatal* wounds (Isa 22:2; Jer 14:18; 41:9; Ezek 6:13; 9:7; 11:6–7 etc. and cf. *ḥālāl*, "cadaver," Ps 89:11). By virtue of this insight, the distress and suffering attain meaning as purposeful correction (*mûsār*) of a kind that brings reconciliation or wholeness (*šālôm* cf. Ps 38:4 [3]) and healing. The insight provided for the speaker a new perspective on the history of the community in that epoch and perhaps earlier.

The figure of straying sheep and that of turning aside from the way draw on familiar metaphoric language for moral disorientation and transgression. That the prophetic Servant's distress is more than just the *result* of this history (pace Whybray 1975, 175–76) is expressed somewhat obscurely in 53:6b, "Yahveh laid upon him the iniquity of us all." The rather rare verb *hipgîaʿ* > *pgʿ* Hiphil can mean "intercede," "entreat" (Jer 15:11; 36:25) which, however, is only one instance of the more general sense of "intervene," "interpose." Taking our cue from Job 36:32 ("lightning fills his hands; he commands it to hit the mark"), we are perhaps to think of the Servant as the target toward which the consequences of the community's guilt are redirected by God.

So far (to v 6) the speaker has alluded exclusively to some form of extremely painful and abusive disease. The mention of wounds (*ḥăbûrôt* 5b) can of course refer to wounds inflicted by others (e.g. Gen 4:23; Exod 21:25; Isa 1:6; Prov 20:30), but it is also consistent with sickness. In Ps 38 the sufferer speaks of wounds in connection with a serious illness brought on by divine anger as the result of personal sin. He, too, is crushed by disease, is shunned by relatives and acquaintances, and resolves to remain silent.

But at this point (beginning with Isa 53:7) the language points unmistakably to physical violence resulting in death. That Jeremiah survived in spite of claiming in one of his "confessions" to have been led like a lamb to be slaughtered (Jer 11:19) provides no support for the view that the prophetic servant survived his ordeal (pace Whybray 1975, 176). In fact it indicates the contrary, since it is clear that Jeremiah's enemies intended his death: "let us destroy the tree while the sap is in it; let us cut him off from the land of the living" (11:19b). Unlike Jeremiah, however, the Servant *was* cut off from the land of the living (53:8b). How this happened is related in v 8a, but the wording is notoriously obscure. Some commentators give a specific and concrete sense to the first two words (*mēʿōṣer ûmimmišpāṭ*) as referring to confinement followed by judicial process leading to the verdict, but it seems safer to take them in the more general sense of an oppressive and unjust sentence (hendiadys). Likewise, *luqqāḥ* could mean that he was led away to prison or execution (Prov 24:11 refers to people taken off to death, condemned to slaughter), or it could have the fuller sense of being "taken away," referring in a general way to the end of his life (cf. Gen 5:24 and 2 Kgs 2:10 with reference to Enoch and Elijah, respectively).

A parallel instance, not impossibly connected with our passage, is the contextually isolated mention in Isa 57:1–2 of a righteous one who has been "gathered" (verbal stem *ʾsp*). The death of this *ṣaddîq* (cf. 53:11b) also went unheeded by his contemporaries (*vĕʾên ʾîs śām ʿal-lēb*, "and there is no one who takes heed," 57:1 cf. 53:8a). That the Servant actually died and was not just left "as good as dead" (Torrey 1928, 421; Whybray 1975, 177) is stated plainly enough by his being cut off from the land of the living. Wherever this expression (*ʾereṣ ḥayyîm*) appears, it means life as opposed to death (Isa 38:11; Jer 11:19; Ps 27:13 etc.) or as opposed to the abode of the dead (Ezek 26:20; 32:23 etc.).

The second half of 8b is probably the most textually obscure bit of the passage and has been reconstructed in different ways (see textual Note). But if context counts for anything, it cannot be construed otherwise than that the Servant met his death and that in some way the death was associated with the people's transgression. The unjust denial of honorable burial (v 9) means that the Servant's ill repute (cf. 4b) continued beyond death and therefore reinforces the view that the new interpretation dawned on the speaker and his associates only some time after the death of this prophetic figure.

The textual obscurities continue in the last part of the panegyric (vv 10–11a). Returning to the crushing sufferings of the Servant (cf. 5a) after recording death and burial in the previous verse is unexpected and has suggested the possibility of an addition, an afterthought, perhaps from a later contributor. On the basis of the translation offered, the point in any case would be not that Yahveh took pleasure in his agent's sufferings but that the sufferings were intelligible only within Yahveh's overall purpose (*ḥēpeṣ*), which will be brought to a successful outcome (10b). The same point would be made if we take *heḥĕlî* as it is without emendation, though both meter and sense suggest that it may be a gloss to explain the crushing of the Servant.

The second half of 10a is the despair of the exegete, but in spite of the obscurity we are entitled to fix our attention on the term *ʾāšām*, "guilt offering," "sacrifice of reparation," as particularly significant. This type of sacrifice was the indispensable means for the removal of guilt and liability for punishment in especially serious cases of encroachment on holy objects and places. It also served to make reparation for a range of transgressions (probably not listed exhaustively in the relevant ritual text, Lev 5:14–26[5:14–6:7]), such as theft, fraud, and the swearing of false oaths. In view of the opinion, unverifiable but understandable, that the Servant was suffering from leprosy, it is worth noting that the sacrifice of a lamb as an *ʾāšām* was an essential element in the treatment of skin diseases (Lev 14:12).

The idea behind this type of reparation sacrifice is that, given the right dispositions, the transgressions and the guilt of the sacrificial adepts die with the death of the *ʾāšām* animal. The analogy with the Servant is clear, but like all analogies it walks with a limp, for the servant is not an animal, and his death cannot simply be on a par with the death of a lamb or a goat. Here the panegyrist speaks in riddles and mysteries. The Servant has died, or rather has been put to death, there is no doubt about that, yet we are now told that he will have descendants (*zeraʿ*, literally, "seed"), his life span will be extended, he will see light and attain satisfaction, and (to return to the beginning of the passage) the undertaking in which he is involved will ultimately succeed.

The most natural meaning is that the Servant's project will be continued and carried to fruition through his disciples. Thus, Isa 59:21 is addressed to an individual possessed of Yahveh's spirit and in whose mouth Yahveh's words have been placed. He is a prophetic individual, in other words, who is assured that the spirit of prophecy will remain with him and with his "seed" (*zeraʿ*) into the distant future. Biblical usage, moreover, demonstrates that "prolonging one's days" does not refer exclusively to the life of the individual (e.g. Exod 20:12 = Deut 5:16; Deut 4:26, 40; 11:9; 30:18). This particular cluster of motifs, and sometimes even the language in which they are expressed, can also be paralleled in the liturgical hymns:

> Since I am righteous, I will see your face in vision.
> When I awake I will be satisfied with (a vision of) your form. (Ps 17:15)
>
> With long life (length of days) I will satisfy him;
> I will show him (let him see) my salvation. (Ps 91:16)

To see light is to live, to be preserved from the inroads of death (Ps 36:10; 56:14; Job 3:16; 33:28, 30). But, just as death is not spoken of in these hymns merely as a punctual event but also as a presence or force that militates against and diminishes the vital impulses (e.g. by disease, depression, external pressures), the language of life and light can intimate something more than biological life, as important as that is (e.g. Ps 36:10 cf. 73:23).

While it is unlikely that the author thought of the survival of death or returning from the dead in a straightforward kind of way, it seems probable that he retained a strong sense of the Servant as an active presence among his followers. In this respect the Servant may be compared to the teacher who is present to his disciples and whose voice is heard behind them—that is, from the past, from after his death, pointing out the way they are to go: ". . . Your teacher will no longer remain hidden. Your eyes will see your teacher, and whenever you turn aside either to the right or the left your ears will hear a word spoken behind you: 'This is the way, keep to it.'" (Isa 30:20–21).

Since Christopher R. North surveyed the range of opinion on the identity of the Servant in 1948 (2d ed., 1956), no significant new options have emerged. While there was then and still is a strong critical preference for an individual rather than a collective interpretation, none of the fifteen individuals named as candidates by one commentator or another and listed by North has survived scrutiny. Nevertheless, the question posed by the Ethiopian eunuch, whether Isa 53:7–8 is to be understood as referring to the prophet himself or to someone else, has been the focus of discussion since Mowinckel's *Der Knecht Jahwäs* was published in 1921, and to some extent continues to be so. The debate precipitated by Mowinckel's monograph continued into the 1930s and beyond with the involvement of prominent German-language scholars, conspicuously Sellin and Elliger in the early stages. While the opinions expressed by these scholars were not identical and seldom remained unchanged over the course of time, there was a considerable amount of overlap, and something approaching a consensus emerged. It was that, while the author of Isa 40–55 could be speaking of himself and his prophetic mission in 49:1–6 and 50:4–9, if the fourth of the servant passages is understood to refer to him it must have been composed by a disciple. On the whole, this still seems to be the most attractive solution to the problem of the Servant's identity.

What is proposed here, then, is that the Servant eulogized in 52:13–52:12 is identical with the one who soliloquizes in 49:1–6 and 50:4–9 and is presented in deliberate contrast to Cyrus, the Servant of Yahveh in 42:1–4. The inclusion of 52:13–53:12 in this section and the links with 49:1–6 and 50:4–9 favor the view that the Servant is none other than the author of the core of these chapters, the so-called Deutero-Isaiah. That the passage 52:13–53:12 *is* an insertion is suggested by the literary structure in this part of the section. The injunction to leave Babylon immediately preceding (52:11–12) reads like a finale parallel with the similar injunction in 48:20–22, immediately preceding the first of the prophetic Servant's monologues. It is also parallel with 55:12–13, concluding the section as a whole. The servant passage also interrupts the apostrophe to Zion that begins in 52:1–2, 7–10 and is taken up again in 54:1–17, with a reference to singing for joy immediately before and after the insertion (52:9; 54:1).

One point on which the scholars mentioned above were agreed, at least for a time, was that 52:13–53:12 originated among the disciples of Second Isaiah, whose activity is reflected in chs. 56–66. In the final chapters of the book we encounter a prophetic group referred to as Yahveh's servants (*ʿăbādîm*) and those who tremble at his word (*ḥărēdîm*), who have been excommunicated by the leadership of the Jewish community, who regard themselves as the elect, and who believe that they will be vindicated and their opponents condemned in the judgment soon to come (65:8–16; 66:5). The way this term (*ʿebed*, *ʿăbādîm*) is used provides an important key for decoding identities in the second half of the book. In chs. 1–39 it appears only twice in a religiously significant sense, with reference to Isaiah himself (20:3) and to David (37:35). In the great majority of cases in chs. 40–48, Israel/Jacob, the people, is the servant, whereas in the following section 49–55, as we have seen, the servant is an individual prophetic figure. The only exception is the allusion near the end to the vindication of Yahveh's servants (54:17), which alerts the reader to a major theme in the following chapters. The usage therefore expresses a crucial duality between the people as the instrument of God's purpose and a prophetic minority (the servants of Yahveh) owing allegiance to its martyred leader (*the* Servant) and his teachings. These disciples take over from the community the responsibility and the suffering inseparable from servanthood or instrumentality and, if this view of the matter is accepted, it is to one of these that we owe the tribute in 52:13–53:12.

For the history of interpretation of this passage see the Introduction, pp. 84–87.

APOSTROPHE TO ZION (54:1–17)

(Beuken 1974b; Darr 1994, 177–82; Gunn 1975; Jeppesen 1993; Korpel 1996a; Martin-Achard 1981; Sawyer 1989b; Schwarz 1971; Sommer 1998, 100–104)

TRANSLATION

i

54 [1]Sing out, you barren woman, who has borne no child;[a]
break out in shouts of joy,[b] you who have never been in labor;
for the children of the wife that was abandoned
will outnumber those of the wife with a husband.[c]
[2]Enlarge the space of your abode,
let your tent hangings out to the full,[d]
do not stint.
Lengthen your ropes, drive the tent pegs home,
[3]for you will spread out to the right and the left;
your offspring will dispossess[e] nations
and people cities now abandoned.
[4]Do not fear, you will not be disappointed;
do not cringe, you will not be disgraced;[f]
you will forget the shame of your youth,
no longer recall the reproach of your widowhood.
[5]The One who made you is the One who will espouse you;[g]
Yahveh of the hosts is his name.
your Redeemer is the Holy One of Israel;
he is called the God of all the earth.
[6]Yahveh has summoned you back
like a wife once forsaken and sad at heart,
a wife still young,[h] though once rejected,
says[i] your God.
[7]For a brief space of time I forsook you,
but with love overflowing I will bring you back.[j]
[8]In an outburst of anger[k] I hid my face from you for awhile,
but with love[l] never failing I have pitied you,
says Yahveh, your Redeemer.

ii

[9]This is for me like the lifetime of Noah,[m]
when I swore an oath

that Noah's floodwater would never again
pour over the earth;
so now I swear an oath
no longer[n] to be angry with you or rebuke you.
[10]Mountains may depart,
hills may be shaken,
but my love will not depart from you,
nor my covenant of friendship be shaken,
says Yahveh in his pity for you.

iii

[11]City in distress,[o] battered by storms,[p]
with no one to comfort!
I will lay your stones with the finest mortar,
your foundations[q] with lapis;
[12]I will set up your shields with rubies,
your gates with beryl;
the walls that enclose you will be precious jewels.
[13]When all your children will be taught by Yahveh,
great will be the well-being of your children.[r]
[14]You will be triumphantly established;[s]
you will be far removed[t] from oppression.
You will be free from fear
and from terror, for no terror will come near you.
[15]If anyone attacks you, it will not be my doing,
and whoever attacks you will fall by your side.[u]
[16]See, I have created the smith,
blowing on the charcoal fire,
making weapons, each one for its purpose.
I have also created the Destroyer to wreak havoc;
[17]no weapon designed to be used against you will prevail;
you will silence every tongue of those who contend with you.[v]

iv

This, then, is the lot of Yahveh's servants,
their vindication from me. A word of Yahveh.

NOTES

1QIsaiah[b] has some words from vv 1–6; 4QIsa[c] 3–5, 7–17; 4QIsa[d] 1–11; 4QIsa[q] 10–13. [a] 1QIsaiah[a] and 4QIsa[d] add the conjunction *vl' yldh;* [b] *rinnâ* should not be omitted *metri causa,* since it forms one phrase with *piṣḥî* cf. 44:23; 49:13; [c] Tg. identifies the two women with Jerusalem and Rome, respectively, cf. 34:9; [d] for MT *yaṭṭû* 3d-person pl. Hiphil > *nṭh*, "spread out," read either Hophal *yuṭṭû* or 1QIsa[a] imperative *yṭy*, which is adopted in the translation; [e] MT has sing., 1QIsa[a] pl. of the verb; [f] LXX has the verbs (*katēschunthēs, ōneidisthēs* in past tense; MT is correct; [g] this verse is omitted in 1QIsa[a], perhaps deliberately; the pl. form of the suffixes in *bōʿălayik* and *ʿōśayik* may be *pluralis excellentiae* (GKC §124k) or *pluralis maiestatis* and may have been adopted by the Masoretes for the same reason that the 1QIsa[a] scribe omitted the verse; [h] LXX paraphrases "a woman hated from her youth" (*gunaika ek meotētos memisēmenēn*); on the meaning of the term *ʾēšet nĕʿûrîm*, see the Comments; [i] 1QIsa[a] adds YHVH; [j] Tg. "I will bring back your exiles" (*glvtyk*); [k] there is no need to emend *šeṣep* hapax to *šeṭep* or *šēpeṣ* (BHS); [l] 1QIsa[a] and 4QIsa[c] have *ḥsdy*, "my love," cf. Syr., but MT is correct; [m] reading *kimê* (literally, "as the days") for MT *kî-mê* ("for the waters") with 1QIsa[a] and Tg. (*kyvmy*) against LXX (*apo tou hudatos ton epi Nōe*); the scribe was probably misled by *mê-noaḥ* in the following verse; [n] 1QIsa[a] adds *ʿôd* corresponding to "no longer," implied in MT; [o] literally, "distressed one" (fem.); [p] 1QIsa[a] *shvrh* = *sĕhurâ*, perhaps with the sense of "bought and sold," "traded back and forth"; [q] it seems unnecessary to emend the verbal form *vîsadtîk*, "and I will lay your foundations," in MT to the substantive *vîsôdôtayik*, "and your foundations," with 1QIsa[a] and LXX; [r] 1QIsa[a] adds a superscript vav, which changes "your children" to "your builders" (*bônayik*); [s] on the verbal form *tikkônānî* (cf. 1QIsa[a] *titkvnny*), see GKC §54c; [t] MT has imperative *raḥăqî*; the indicative *tirḥaqî* makes better sense in the context; [u] this verse is obscure: the word corresponding to MT *ʾepes* in 1QIsa[a] (*ʾks?*) is unclear; 1QIsa[a] has future *ygr* for MT *gār*; *mʾty* (*mēʾittî*) for MT *mēʾôtî*; and, together with 4QIsa[c], pl. *ypvlv*, "they will fall," for MT sing. *yippôl*; the confusion arises from the secondary meaning of the verb *gûr*, "attack"; exploiting the primary meaning, LXX finds a reference to proselytes (*prosēlutoi proseleusontai soi di'emou kai epi se katapheusontai*, "proselytes will approach you through me and flee for refuge to you"); [v] 1QIsa[a] omits this line, leaving most of a line empty, but 4QIsa[c] has it, and it was in LXX's *Vorlage*.

COMMENTS

Personification and the assignation of gender attributes to countries, peoples, and cities are extremely common in the ancient and modern world. Examples in Isaiah are the "virgin daughter Sidon" (23:12), the female prostitute Tyre (23:15–16), and the doomed queen Babylon (47:1). Since in many languages the default gender is generally masculine, grammatically and thematically, feminine attribution can also serve as a way of individuating and emphasizing special features in a poem or narrative. Right at the beginning of Isa 40–55, prophets are urged to speak tender words to the woman Jerusalem (40:2 cf. 41:27; 51:3), unlike their predecessors, who often subjected her to verbal abuse, sometimes in the coarsest terms.

In our first major section (chs. 40–48), the woman Zion represents both the Jewish people and the physical, historical city, the rebuilding of which is laid at the charge of Cyrus (44:26, 28; 45:13). She is also set in deliberate contrast to Babylon, the young queen (the Neo-Babylonian Empire not having lasted very long) now dethroned and dishonored (47:1–15). But these allusions are subordinated in chs. 40–48 to the designation Jacob/Israel, the eponymous ancestor whose life-story, pivoting on exile and return and including his marital vicissitudes, recapitulates important aspects of historical and ethnic consciousness at the time of writing.

In the following section (chs. 49–55) the focus shifts decisively from Jacob/Israel to Jerusalem/Zion. The shift no doubt corresponds to the disappointment of the actually quite-unrealistic expectations placed by the prophet and his supporters on Cyrus and a consequent falling back on the internal dynamics of the Judean community, principally the possibility of the rebuilding and repopulation of Jerusalem. (In the third section, 56–66, the question of the political and therefore also the religious *control* of the city and its temple will come to the fore).

The theme of the present passage is anticipated in 49:14–26, in which, after Yahveh replies to the complaint of spousal abandonment, the poem moves to a consideration of the physical city with its walls, also anticipating Nehemiah's rebuilding program and his repopulation (*synoikismos*) of Jerusalem (Neh 11:1–36). Enough semantic ambiguities remain, however, to keep the feminine metaphor alive (49:17a: the play on *bônîm*, "builders," as in 1QIsa[a], with *bānîm*, "children," in MT; 49:19: "desolate places" cf. 2 Sam 13:20, "desolate woman," with the same verb *šmm*). The figure of spousal disaccord and the rupture of marital bonds continues in 50:1, in which Yahveh refutes the charge leveled at him by the children of having divorced Zion his wife. The point is somewhat obscure, but the argument seems to be that the deportations represented a temporary separation for which the children themselves were responsible, rather than a final rupture sealed with a divorce document (*sēper kĕritût*).

The potential of this metaphoric field of matrimonial vicissitudes is well illustrated in Hos 1–3, in which the familiar designation *bĕnê yiśrāʾēl*, "the children of Israel," has suggested to the poet the three children of Gomer, the wayward woman who represents the land of Israel (*ʾereṣ*, fem.). Taken in sequence, the names of these children (Jezreel, Lo-ruhamah, Lo-ammi) signify a downhill historical process leading to the annulment of the marriage—that is, the end of the covenant bond: "she is not my wife, and I am not her husband" (2:4[2]). In Hosea the husband (Yahveh) takes back the wife after she has had relations with other men (alien gods), an action that would be prohibited by the Deuteronomic law of palingamy (Deut 24:1–4). In Isa 50:1 and 54:1–8, significantly, there is a reference only to a period of forced separation, with no mention of other liaisons before the reunion of the spouses.

In BHS and 1QIsa[a], Isa 54:1–17 is laid out in two stanzas (vv 1–10, 11–17), though the latter sets off v 17b (beginning "this, then, is the lot of Yahveh's servants") with a gap almost a line long, indicating that this final statement serves as a summary of the passage as a whole. This point is reproduced in the arrangement offered here. Some commentators prefer further dividing; Muilenburg (1956, 633) and Kissane (1943, 192), for example, have six strophes (1–3, 4–5, 6–8, 9–10, 11–15, 16–17) and Koole (1998, 344–45, 376) five (1–3, 4–8, 9–10, 11–13, 14–17). The only clear markers in the text itself, however, are the references to who is speaking: "your God" (v 6), "Yahveh your redeemer" (8), and "Yahveh" (10 and 17). Since there is no change of theme between vv 6 and 8, we are left with an arrangement in three stanzas and a concluding statement. The allusion to the perpetual covenant (*bĕrît ʿôlām*) with Noah in vv 9–10, presented as a type of the bond between Yahveh and Jerusalem, constitutes the link between the apostrophes to the woman (1–8) and to the city (11–17).

Coming now to the first strophe (vv 1–8): invocations addressed to the earth, the sky, and all creation to break out into joyful shouting and singing appear throughout chs. 40–55 (42:10–13; 44:23; 49:13), and Jerusalem is here invited to join in this paean of joy and praise. The language for public and vocal rejoicing (verbs *rnn*, *psh*, and *shl*) is of frequent occurrence in Isaiah and is especially in evidence in the hymns in which the praise of God and the celebration of God's kingship are the dominant themes (Pss 33, 67, 95, 96, and 98). The call to rejoice is addressed to Jerusalem as an infertile woman (*ʿăqārâ*), which corresponds to a very basic social situation, especially in evidence in an agrarian society, one in which infant mortality was very high and children were essential to the survival and economic functioning of the household. This is also the reason for the frequent prayers in the hymns for the removal of the "reproach" of childlessness and equally frequent expressions of thanks to the God who

> makes the woman in a childless house
> a happy mother of children. (Ps 113:9 NEB)

One such psalm has been put into the mouth of Hannah, mother of Samuel, in spite of the fact that only one verse fits her situation:

> The infertile woman has borne seven children,
> but the mother of many is forlorn. (1 Sam. 2:5b)

This contrast and reversal is repeated in Isa 54:1b, perhaps with the impending fate of Babylon in mind. We could go on to note that the blessing of fertility, for which prayer and thanksgiving are offered in the psalms, is transformed into a narrative topos in the stories about the ancestors. In these stories all of the leading women—Sarah, Rebekah, Rachel—are initially childless (Gen 11:30; 25:21; 29:31). This is the beginning, or the resumption, of a train of thought that will continue throughout the passage under discussion.

The new family will call for expanded living quarters. The representation of the city as a tent with curtains, guy ropes, and tent pegs is traditional and attested elsewhere in Isaiah:

Look on Zion, city of our festivals;
let your eyes look on Jerusalem,
a secure place to live, a tent that will not be moved,
whose pegs will never be pulled out,
and none of its ropes untied. (33:20)

The principal association is with the wilderness sanctuary, enclosed in a tent and also equipped with curtains, ropes, and pegs (Exod 26:7–14; 35:18; 39:40; Num 3:26, 37; 4:32, 36). This "tent of encounter" (*ʾōhel môʿēd*) housed the holy ark, which was eventually brought to Jerusalem and deposited in the temple. But as we read on, we realize that we are also being cued to think of the stories about the ancestors of the people who lived in tents and to whom the promise of the land and numerous descendants to fill it was made and often repeated.

The form in which this assurance is addressed to Jacob/Israel as he is about to go into exile is particularly close to our passage (v 3), in which, since the basic orientation is to the east, the right would be the south and the left the north: "Your descendants [*zeraʿ*, literally, "seed"] will be like the dust of the earth, and you will spread out to the west and the east, to the north and the south" (Gen 28:14). The dispossession of peoples and takeover of cities in the territory of Judah is a Deuteronomic perspective (e.g. Deut 9:1; 11:23; 18:14; 19:1; 31:3), which is also justified by virtue of the promise to the ancestors and no doubt corresponds to the same situation in the post-destruction period that we have profiled for Isa 40–55.

The exploitation of this Deuteronomic program of conquest, expropriation, and ethnic cleansing (on this last, see Deut 7:1–5) in the service of contemporary political ideology is totally unjustified, not only for evident ethical reasons, but also on exegetical and hermeneutical grounds. No text should be read atomistically and in disregard of its larger context, which includes contrasting positions represented within the Bible and development in thinking religiously about such issues as national and ethnic loyalty and relations with foreign peoples.

The strophe continues with a word of assurance addressed to the woman v 4) and reasons why it should be accepted (5–8). The language in which the reassurance is expressed conveys redundantly the pathos of the situation in which a woman deprived of the protection of a husband, or unable to bear children, would have found herself. Women in the kind of society described in the biblical texts (e.g. Judah's daughter-in-law Tamar, and Ruth) evince a resolute desire for children not because they were politically naive but because, in that kind of society based on the patrilineal household, a woman without a husband, or childless, had few acceptable options. Whatever the cause, therefore, childlessness was an object of reproach (*ḥerpâ*). At a time of military disaster, with few male survivors, seven would will grab hold of one man and promise to support themselves if only he would take away their reproach (Isa 4:1). When she finally gets pregnant, Rachel rejoices because "God has taken away my reproach" (Gen 30:23). Jeremiah 31:16–22 is of particular interest because it appears to link infertility with moral and religious transgression. Rachel (i.e. the former Kingdom of Samaria) is addressed and told to stop weeping because her children will return, but Ephraim replies, acknowledging that "I was ashamed and disgraced, for I am bearing the punishment for the reproach of my youth" (*ḥerpat nĕʿûrāy*).

We should not expect the figurative language at this point to correspond precisely, point by point, with what relatively little we know of the social reality of marriage and marital separation in that place at that time. There is no biblical law dealing with divorce, who may initiate it, under what circumstances, and with what effects. Deuteronomy 24:1–4 stipulates what is to be done in the event that a divorce took place, but it is not a divorce law. The fact that biblical narrative provides no example of a woman initiating divorce suggests but does not prove that divorce was a male prerogative. The legal situation could, of course, have evolved, and the evidence for divorce initiated by a woman documented in the Elephantine papyri of the fifth century B.C.E., from the Jewish garrison community at the first cataract of the Nile, may indicate that it did.

In Isa 50:1, Yahveh has already stated that his spouse was not divorced but sent away for a limited period. The referent is clearly exile, with perhaps the idea of indentured service for the purpose of amortizing unpaid debt. So the prospect is for the reestablishment of a broken marital relationship (54:6a) rather than a marriage (5a). The genitival phrase *ʾēšet nĕʿûrîm*, literally, "wife of youth," is somewhat problematic (cf. *baʿal nĕʿûrêkâ*, "the husband of her youth," Joel 1:8; *ʾēšet nĕʿûrêkâ*, "the wife of your youth," Mal 2:14–15). The Targum's *ʾyttt ʿlvmyn* ("wife of youth") is noncommittal; the LXX interprets it as "a woman hated from her youth," which is certainly not what the MT wished to say; and the Vulgate renders it less drastically as *uxorem ab adulescentia abiectam*, "a wife forlorn from her youth." Since the allusion is certainly not to the youth of Yahveh, the translation offered here seems to be the best option.

Behind this extended metaphor and the language of mutual obligation, love and loyalty (*ḥesed*), breakdown of relationship, and abandonment, it is not difficult to detect the Deuteronomic theory of covenant modeled on the Assyrian vassal treaties, as is now well known. One of the standard accusations in Deuteronomic writings is that of abandoning or forsaking the covenant (the verb *ʿzb* with *bĕrît*: Deut 29:24; 31:6, 8, 16; 1 Kgs 19:10, 14; Jer 22:9), which results in god-forsakenness and political disaster. The assurance given here is that the separation will last only a short time, perhaps with reference to the canonical figure of seventy-years' exile, that the anger and its effects are momentary, and that God will not hide his face forever.

The hidden face of God is a standard figure for abandonment and distance (Deut 31:17–18; 32:20; Ps 27:9; 89:47), often combined with forgetfulness (Ps 10:11; 13:2; 44:25). There are also undertones of liturgical absence in this section of Isaiah, with the temple still in ruins, since to seek or to see the face is to experience the divine presence in the act of worship. Hence the Targum translates, "I removed the presence of my Shekinah from you for a season." With the experience of this disaster a recent memory, it is not surprising to hear these laments so often addressed to the hidden or the forgetful God (in Isaiah: 40:27; 49:14).

The well-established thematic link between covenant and marriage makes vv 9–10 an appropriate nexus between Zion as woman and Zion as city. The covenant with Noah is introduced in order to affirm the oath. Yahveh now swears to foreswear anger and to assure Jerusalem that the time of trial is at an end. In Gen 9:8–17 the oath is not explicitly stated but is implicit in the perpetual covenant (*bĕrît ʿôlām*) made with Noah, his sons, and the entire created order, just as swearing oaths would be a part of any covenant.

This intercalatory passage (Isa 54:9–10) is not necessarily drawing directly on the Priestly source to which the Noahic covenant in Gen 9:8–17 belongs. In fact, a closer examination shows that the language in 54:9–10 is quite different from Gen 9:8–17. The key term is not *bĕrît ʿôlām* (as in Isa 24:5) but *bĕrît šālôm* which, in the context of the making of treaties and agreements, implied establishing good relations or reconciliation by restoring relations of amity that had been severed—hence the translation "covenant of friendship." Moreover, other traditions about Noah, a patriarchal figure from the early days of humanity, are known (Ezek 14:12–20) that have no relation with the Genesis deluge narrative.

The introduction of events from the lifetime of Noah (*yĕmê noaḥ* Gen 9:29) may have been suggested by the literary device of representing the destruction of a city as a deluge or flood storm, as in the fifth canto of the Lament over the Destruction of Ur (*ANET* 458–59). If so, the Isaiah passage may provide a clue to reading Gen 1–11 as parabolic of the religious history of Israel repositioned in the early history of humanity and transposed into the language of myth. The story, which ends in Mesopotamia, begins with the Man placed in a fertile garden (the land of Israel), given a command (the Torah), which he disobeys, the disobedience leading to expulsion and exile from the garden. The post-expulsion period then calls for a new dispensation, which the author known to modern criticism as the Priestly Writer (P) lays out in the form of a covenant and a promise.

In the third strophe (vv 11–17a) the poet speaks more directly, if in visionary fashion, about Jerusalem destroyed by the Babylonians in a deliberately punitive act and still lying in ruins. Perhaps surprisingly, there is no mention of the temple, and indeed not much interest in the temple is in evidence in chs. 40–55. What is meant by the city's being in distress and battered by storms was spelled out in 51:17–20, which added famine to conquest, destruction, and depopulation. The description of Jerusalem as not comforted (*lōʾ nuḥāmâ*) recalls the symbolic name of Hosea's daughter (*lōʾ ruḥāmâ* (Hos 1:6), generally translated "Not Pitied," though the verb is different. The need for comfort in the post-destruction trauma is a prominent theme in these chapters (40:1; 49:13; 51:12; 52:9), and the question who will comfort Jerusalem has already been answered (51:3,19). In the final section of the book, Jerusalem herself, as the mother of her children, will do the comforting (66:13).

In the biblical texts the restoration of the city is described in more or less realistic terms only in the account of the rebuilding of the wall by Nehemiah and the repopulation of the city during his governorship, which was probably not entirely voluntary (Neh 3:1–32; 11:1–24). We must suspect an element of fantasy in the way the preparations for the building of Solomon's temple are described in 1 Chr 29:1–5, detailing the accumulation of gold, silver, bronze, and various kinds of precious metals, but in the present description reality is left completely behind. Some of the details are obscure. The stones will be laid in place with *pûk* which, etymologically, would seem to refer to a substance crushed to a powder; hence the walls will be mortared rather than dry-wall construction (cf. 1 Chr 29:2 *ʾabnê-pûk*, "mortared stones"). The same word also refers to kohl or eyeliner, a point taken up by the author of a Qumran *pešer* (4QpIsa[d] = 4Q164) who interprets 54:11–12 as referring to the council of the community composed of twelve priests and the leaders of the twelve tribes. The Isaian author did not consciously use the term *pûk* meaning "kohl" with reference to Zion as a woman. With this meaning the word appears elsewhere only in regard to Jezebel and a prostitute (2 Kgs 9:30; Jer 4:30).

According to the Isa 54:11–12 visionary projection, the city is to be completely rebuilt, its foundations laid with *ṣappîrîm* (LXX *sappheiron*)—that is, blocks of lapis stone, the same substance of which the heavenly throne seen in vision by Moses and Ezekiel was constructed (Exod 24:10; Ezek 1:26). The gates will be *ʾeqdāḥ*, probably beryl (LXX *krustallon*), a very hard stone therefore suitable for defense as well as being aesthetically pleasing. The term *šimšôt* is often rendered "battlements," "ramparts," or something of the sort. Ibn Ezra took them to be windows to let in the sunlight, with or without glass (cf. *šemeš*, "sun"), but the more likely reference is to shields (as Ps 84:12) hung over the battlements of the city wall (cf. Ezek 27:11; Cant 4:4). This description would ignite the imagination of a later seer, who witnessed Jerusalem coming down from heaven with walls of jasper, gates of pearl, streets and buildings of pure gold, and foundations adorned with twelve precious stones eight of which are identical with the stones on the high priest's breastpiece (Exod 28:15–20). This image of the new Jerusalem, "Jerusalem the golden," will prove to be extremely durable, providing inspiration to Jewish and Christian visionaries and sectarians down to the present.

Almost as an afterthought, after all this dazzling array of precious stones, the poet recalls the city's future inhabitants, whose well-being, as the Targumist paraphrases it, will rest on study of the law (*ʾôrîtâ*). This is in keeping with another projection into the future, according to which "instruction will proceed from Zion, the word of Yahveh from Jerusalem" (Isa 2:3b). However, the concluding theme in the strophe shows that not all perspectives on the future represented in the book of Isaiah are mutually compatible.

Isaiah 54:15a is the most obscure verse in the passage. Reading the verb as *gûr* I = "sojourn, dwell," rather than *gûr* II = "attack," both LXX and Vulgate find here an allusion to proselytes (*gērîm*) who, drawn by Yahveh, will come to Jerusalem; in the Targum the verse refers to a return from exile. If the translation offered above is approximately correct, however, the poet foresees that attacks on Jerusalem will continue but that they will no longer be the expression of the deity's anger. On the contrary, Yahveh will see that the city is equipped to defend itself by the production of weapons in the smithy and the intervention of the Destroyer (*hammašḥît*), the same being that cut a swath of death through Egypt at the first Passover (Exod 12:23) and a swath of death among David's subjects in punishment for the census (2 Sam 24:16).

This is a quite different scenario from the demilitarized world of the messianic poems (Isa 11:9) and the beating of swords and spears into agricultural implements (Isa 2:4). We note in passing considerable overlap between our poem and the preface to the visions of Zechariah. Here, too, Zion is to be comforted (Zech 1:17) and is invited to sing and rejoice (2:14[10]); the city is to be repopulated (2:8[4]) and defended, though now both by the intervention of smiths (2:3–4[1:20–21]) and with a wall of fire (2:9[5]). Finally, in a curious coincidence with the LXX version mentioned earlier, the prophetic author of the visions foresees that proselytes will stream into the city (2:15[11] cf. 8:22–23).

The Isaiah passage ends with a recapitulatory statement referring the promise of vindication and well-being in the poem to the "servants of Yahveh." Since this designation occurs in the plural only in chs. 56–66 (56:6; 65:8–9, 13–15), 54:17b serves to introduce a major theme in the last section and functions as an important editorial link between sections. Chapter 55 may then be read as transitional between sections (see further the Introduction p. 74). Since it is clear from the final chapters of the book that these servants (*ʿăbādîm*), also known as "those who tremble at his word" (*ḥărēdîm* 66:5), form a minority rejected by the authorities in the community and since much is said there about the respective destinies of the servants and their opponents (cf. the reference to the *naḥălâ* of the servants of Yahveh in 54:17b), it may be that the conclusion to our passage, and therefore the conclusion to 40–54 as a whole, comes from the same "servant" source. By adding this codicil, the servants are appropriating for themselves the salvation promised in the address to Jerusalem.

A CONCLUDING INVITATION TO FAITH IN THE PROPHETIC WORD (55:1–13)

(Brueggemann 1968; Caquot 1965; Clifford 1983; Couroyer 1981b; Eissfeldt 1962; Lipiński 1973; Pauritsch 1971, 31–51; Sanders 1978; Seybold 1972; Troadec 1955; Williamson 1978a; Zenger 1983)

TRANSLATION

i

55 [1]All you there who are thirsty, come to the water!
Come even if you have no money;
buy food and eat;
come, buy[a] wine and milk
without money, at no cost.
[2]Why spend your money for what is not food?
Why spend your earnings for what does not satisfy?
Listen closely to me if you want to eat well;[b]
you will be delighted with the richest fare.[c]
[3]Come to me and incline your ear;
listen, and your spirit will revive.
I shall make[d] with you a perpetual covenant,
the tokens of faithful love shown to David.
[4]As I made him a witness to peoples,[e]
a prince who ruled over nations,
[5]so you will summon nations you do not know;
nations that do not know you will come running to you[f]
for the sake of Yahveh your God,
the Holy One of Israel who made you glorious.

ii

[6]Seek Yahveh while he may be found,
invoke him while he is near.
[7]Let the wicked forsake their ways,
the sinful their devices.
Let them turn back to Yahveh
that he may take pity on them,
to our God, ever ready to pardon.
[8]For my thoughts are not your thoughts,
nor are my ways your ways. [A word of Yahveh]
[9]For as high[g] as is the sky above the earth,
so are my ways above your ways,
my thoughts above your thoughts.
[10]For as the rain and the snow fall from the sky,
nor return there without watering the ground,
causing it to bring forth vegetation,
giving seed for the sower
and bread for food,[h]
[11]so is it with my word that issues from my mouth:
it does not return to me empty
but accomplishes what I purpose
and achieves what I send it to do.

iii

[12]You will go out with joy,
you will be led out[i] in peace;
mountains and hills before you will break out in shouts of joy;
all the trees in the countryside will clap their hands.
[13]In place of the thornbush, cypresses will grow;
instead of nettles, myrtles will grow.
All this will be a memorial for Yahveh,
a perpetual sign that shall not be cut off.[j]

NOTES

4QIsaiah[c] contains some words from 55:1–7 showing only minor orthographic divergence from MT; this copy appears to have a blank line between vv 5 and 6. [a] *Ûlĕkû šibrû* is absent from 1QIsa[a] through homoioteleuton rather than added to MT through dittography; it is also absent from LXX and Syr., but MT need not be emended, in spite of the repetitions; [b] literally, "listen closely to me and eat what is good"; [c] literally, "fat" (*dešen*); [d] 1QIsa[a] has imperfect, against MT, 1QIsa[b], and 4QIsa[c] cohortative, but with no essential difference; [e] read *lĕʿammîm* for MT *lĕʾûmmîm*, since a word in parallelism is required, as elsewhere where *lĕʾûmmîm* appears (41:1; 43:9; 51:4), and *ʿēd lĕʾûmmîm* is not an acceptable genitival phrase of the type *ʿēd šeqer*, *ʿēd ḥāmās* (Exod 23:1; Deut 19:16, 18; Ps 27:12; 35:11); [f] MT and 1QIsa[b] have verbs in pl. against 1QIsa[a] in sing.; hence, *gôy* in both cases is collective (cf. LXX *ethnē*, *laoi*); [g] reading *kigĕboāh* with LXX for MT *kî-gābĕhû*, "for [the heavens] are high"; 1QIsa[a] has *kîʾ kĕgôbâ*, "for like the height . . ."; [h] 1QIsa[a] *lʾkvl* (*leʾēkol*, "to eat") cf. Vulg. *panem comedendi*; LXX *arton eis brōsin*, "bread for food"; [i] 1QIsa[a] *tlkv*, "you will go/walk"; LXX paraphrases: "you will be instructed with delight"; [j] 1QIsa[a] "they will be for Yahveh as a sign and a perpetual memorial [name]; it will not be cut off."

COMMENTS

Even a cursory reading of ch. 55 shows it to be of a literary character different from the preceding chapters: more didactic and sapiential in tone, rhetorically less pointed and specific in persuading its readers to accept the offer made to them and believe the prophetic message. It also differs from the preceding pronouncements in that those addressed are not identified. At the same time, there are indications that the author was familiar with both sections 40–54 and 56–66, in whatever state they existed at the time of writing.

The first strophe concludes with a statement strongly reminiscent of 49:7b, which reads: "on account of Yahveh, who is faithful, the Holy One of Israel who chose you," and the passage as a whole ends in practically the same way as the following pronouncement in 56:1–8, which reads: "I shall give them a perpetual name that shall not be cut off" (56:8b). This suggests the following working hypothesis: chs. 49–54 end with the vindication of Yahveh's servants (54:17b), thus preparing for the final section of the book; and ch. 55 was created as a transition between sections 40–54 and 56–66, a hinge on which these major sections of the book turn. It recapitulates in more general terms the importance of accepting the (prophetic) word, confronts the doubters with the thoughts and designs of God communicated prophetically, totally incommensurable with human thoughts and designs as they are, and emphasizes once again that the prophetic word embodying the will of God will come to fruition in spite of appearances to the contrary and in spite of the skepticism of those to whom it is addressed. This recapitulatory intent is confirmed by the inclusio with which the chapter ends (55:12–13 cf. 40:3–5).

The first strophe (vv 1–5) opens with a call for attention. The Hebrew exclamation *hôy,* usually indicating a lament ("woe," "alas"), can also be a way of hailing people (Isa 18:1; Zech 2:10[6]) and is expressed in our translation as "you there" rather than the usual "Ho" or "Hey," neither of which seems quite right. The invitation to drink and eat does not echo the cry of the water vendor, as Volz and Westermann suggested. A water vendor who refused payment would soon be out of business, and one who sold milk, wine, and edibles would be more like a walking supermarket than a water vendor. Rather, the invitation echoes the invitation of the woman Wisdom (*Ḥokmâ*) in Prov 9:1–6, who invites the simple to her banquet (cf. also Sir 24:19)—in other words, to a share in her inestimable gift of wisdom. Since *ḥokmâ* is identical with *tôrâ*, the Targumist can paraphrase the call as an invitation to study and learn. Ibn Ezra also identifies the addressed as those desirous of accepting the Law. He adds the observation that "wisdom is demanded by the soul as food is by the body" and identifies that which is not food and does not satisfy (v 2) as the profane sciences (*ḥokmôt nokriyyôt*).

In chs. 40–54 water is more often than not a requirement of the soil (41:18; 43:20; 44:3–4), but there are echoes of the provision of water in the wilderness journey (48:21; 49:10), and water is also symbolic of the spirit of God (44:3 cf. 32:15), as it is in early Christian writings (e.g. John 4:10–14; 7:37–38) and in the liturgy. The summons to buy something that is freely given, without charge, is paradoxical. The unmistakable point is that the gift of God is gratuitously bestowed (*gratia gratis data*), but perhaps there is also a more covert intent to subvert the standard view of covenant as expressed in classical form in Deuteronomy. According to this understanding of covenant, God's intervention on behalf of his people is contingent on their moral performance, as in the classical Deuteronomic formulation,"Keep the commandments . . . that you may live long in the land" (Deut 4:40; 5:33; 11:9; 25:15; 32:47). We may suppose that the questioning of this view of covenant bilaterality, in evidence in the Priestly history in the Pentateuch (P), which omits an account of the Sinai covenant, grew from a more deeply felt sense of moral incapacity and a stronger conviction of the freedom of God. We understand this to be one of the more far-reaching ways in which the experience of disaster impacted religious thinking in Israel.

This brings us to the covenant with David, the only reference to David in chs. 40–66 (54:3–5). A fresh call to approach the speaker and "incline the ear"—a somewhat archaic translation of the Hebrew *haṭṭû ʾoznĕkem*, characteristic of Proverbs (4:20; 5:1, 13; 22:17)—introduces a more specific account of what the offer comprises. While the speaker does not refer directly to the covenant with David, he clearly has in mind the promise transmitted through the prophet Nathan (2 Sam 7:8–17) and even faintly echoes some of its language: David as *nāgîd*, "prince" (2 Sam 7:8); his *šēm gādôl*, "great name" (7:9); and God's *ḥesed*, "faithful love" (7:15). Solomon also appeals to this Davidic promise (1 Kgs 8:23–26), and Ps 89:27–37 speaks of God's firm covenant (*bĕrîtî neʾemenet*) with David characterized by reliability (*ʾemûnâ*) and faithful love (*ḥesed*). Only in a late poetic addition to the story about David, his Last Words, is there a reference to a *perpetual* Davidic covenant (*bĕrît ʿôlām* 2 Sam 23:5).

This language does not, however, imply a commitment to restoring the Davidic dynasty. What is promised is that the hearers will experience the same tokens of God's faithful love (*ḥăsādîm*, the relatively rare plural of *ḥesed*) that God performed in former times on behalf of David (as Ps 89:50). The reference is therefore not to deeds performed by David himself on behalf of his people but to God's gratuitous acts of favor toward David (with Williamson, against Caquot and Bonnard 1972, 303–4).

Eissfeldt (1962, 196–207) argued that the promise to David, voided by the disasters of 586, demanded a new interpretation if it was not be completely discarded. The Isaian author therefore, so to speak, democratizes it by transferring it to the people of Israel as a whole. While this seems to be suggested by the prospect of foreign nations in subjection to Israel (v 5), it goes some way beyond what the author says. Furthermore, it is difficult to understand why this analogy would be used if the author was not persuaded of the permanence of Yahveh's commitment to David and the dynasty. The freeing or paroling of Jehoiachin by Amel-Marduk (Evil-Merodach in 2 Kgs 25:27), ca. 560 B.C.E., may have been meant as a prelude to setting Jehoiachin up as a puppet king in Judah, but Amel-Marduk was assassinated shortly afterward and the project, if it ever existed, came to nothing. We do not know when ch. 55 was written, but at the time of writing there may have been sound political reasons for not speaking out in favor of the native dynasty. Support for the restoration of the monarchy is well attested in writings from the late Neo-Babylonian and early Persian periods (Jer 23:5–8 with its later commentary in 33:14–26; 30:8–9; Ezek 34:23–24; 37:24–28; Amos 9:11–12; Hag 2:20–23; Zech 3:8; 6:12), but we have no means of knowing what the views on this subject of the Isaian prophet and his disciples were.

It is also unclear in what sense David is said to be a witness to (foreign) peoples, whether as conqueror or as imposing on them vassal status by treaty. The closest parallel is the editorial addition to the "messianic" poem in Isa 11:1–9, in which a Second Temple scribe describes the Davidic dynast of the future as a standard or rallying point for the peoples (*nēs ʿammîm* 11:10). The implication appears to be that the attributes of royalty vis-à-vis the nations are transferred to Israel; hence, the glorification of Israel at the end of the strophe (cf. 44:23; 52:1).

In Isaiah, in fact, most allusions to future relations between Israel and foreign nations mention Jerusalem/Zion rather than the Davidic dynasty as the point of reference. In this passage (55:5) it is not clear in what capacity and for what purpose foreign peoples will converge on Jerusalem, whether to seek instruction in the Jewish faith (Isa 2:2–4; 19:24–25; 56:1–8), therefore as proselytes or "God-fearers" (56:1–8), or as slaves, menials, and *Gastarbeiter*—the last of disturbingly frequent appearance in the book (14:1–2; 45:14, 23; 49:23; 60:4–7, 10–14; 61:5–7).

As suggested above, the second stanza (vv 6–11) may be read as recapitulating chs. 40–54: the prophetic word recorded here is efficacious, it will bring about what it proclaims, but it does not operate according to normal human calculations. The passage comprises an exhortation of the speaker (6–7) followed by a self-referential pronouncement of Yahveh (8–11). The tone is strongly homiletic, reminiscent of the brief sermon of Azariah ben Oded in 2 Chr 15:1–7 and similarly homiletic passages from the later period (e.g. Zech 1:3–6; 8:14–17).

The exhortation to seek God (with the verbs *drš* as here, or *bqš* Piel) can be traced back to the practice of visiting a sanctuary (Gen 25:22) or a seer (1 Sam 9:9; 1 Kgs 22:8; 2 Kgs 8:8; 22:13, 18) or a medium (Deut 18:11; 1 Sam 28:7; Isa 8:19) with the purpose of receiving a favorable oracle or obtaining information not otherwise available. In the later period it is generalized in the sense of a positive and open religious attitude expressed in prayer, conversion to a better way of life (*tĕšûbâ*, "turning"), and penitential practice. Seeking God in this sense is a theme of Deuteronomic rhetoric (Deut 4:29; Jer 29:13; perhaps Amos 5:4–7,14–15). It is taken further in the language of Chronicles (2 Chr 7:14; 11:16; 15:1–7; 20:4) and is one of several indications in texts from the post-destruction period of the growing importance of prayer detached from sacrifice. The language of invocation and response will be particularly in evidence in the last section of the book, the so-called Third Isaiah (58:9 cf. Zech 7:13; Isa 65:1–2, 12; 66:4).

The lack of an obvious link between 6–7 and 8–11 has misled some commentators to strike v 7—conspicuously Duhm (1922, 416) and Westermann (1969, 288). However, the hiatus disappears if the passage is read as a summary of and theological reflection on the prophetic message of the preceding chapters. From time to time in these chapters the Judean community is taken to task for spiritual obtuseness, not unconnected with moral imperfection. The theme of divine-human incommensurability has also been expressed more than once.

The word *maḥšĕbôt*, here translated "thoughts," contains the idea of calculations, devices, or plans. Human *maḥšĕbôt* are characterized more often than not by sinful deviance (Gen 6:5; Isa 59:7; Ezek 38:10; Ps 56:6), stubborn resistance to God (Jer 18:12; Prov 15:26) and a misguided sense of self-sufficiency (Isa 65:2). Like the *maḥšĕbâ* of Haman in the book of Esther (8:3,5; 9:25), they generally end badly. Yahveh also has his *maḥšĕbôt*, whether to punish Jerusalem (Jer 18:18), destroy Babylon (Jer 51:29), or bring his people back to their land (Jer 29:10–14, using language similar to that of our passage). There is therefore a close connection between *maḥšĕbôt* so understood and *dĕrākîm*, "ways," in the sense that one's way of living morally is dictated by the "devices and desires of the heart" (The Book of Common Prayer). If the proposal about the function of this passage in the book is correct, this would apply to Yahveh's design for Israel vis-à-vis the great powers communicated through the prophet and the difficulty many of the hearers experienced in accepting it.

The metaphor of precipitation that fertilizes the earth is in keeping with recurring images in the book (e.g. 40:6–8) and in prophetic writings in general. That it returns back to the heavens might imply that the author was familiar with the phenomena of condensation and evaporation. Whether this was the case we do not know; it would not call for very advanced thinking, and the possibility may find support in a passage in Job ("he draws up the drops of water, he distills his mist in rain," 36:27). But there is also the old idea that words have a kind of life of their own; that, for example, a greeting or a prayer that is rejected by the one to whom it is addressed returns to its source, the speaker (e.g. Ps 35:13: "my prayer turns back into my bosom"; Matt 10:13: "if [the house] is not worthy, let your greeting return to you").

The poet may also have had in mind the idea of the prophet as messenger who is sent on a mission and returns to make a report, comparable to Satan as emissary in Job 1–2 and the Spirit who volunteers to deceive Ahab in 1 Kgs 22:19–23. Whatever the conscious or unconscious origins of the figure may have been, we can agree that "the creative word of Yahveh is the central theological motif of the preaching of Second Isaiah" (Hermisson 1998b, 129–30). These two verses constitute one of the most powerful and telling expressions of prophetic agency in the Bible, and it is no wonder that they have proved so influential throughout Jewish and Christian history.

The final bicolon (vv 12–13) is linked with the preceding strophe by the initial *kî* ("for"), which could be taken to imply that the return to the land and the transformation of nature represent the final fulfillment of the prophetic message. More importantly, however, 55:12–13 is the finale to section 40–55 as a whole and serves to bind its two parts (chs. 40–48, 49–55) together. Programmatic statements about return from Babylon occur at the beginning and end of chs. 40–48 (40:3–5; 48:20–22), with the emphasis on a sense of peace, security, and joy. The theme of a joyful return home from a place of exile also appears in 35:8–10 and 52:11–12, the latter perhaps serving as a finale or *excipit* at an earlier stage in the formation of this section of the book.

The transformation of nature, a theme often repeated in these chapters (35:1–2, 6–7; 41:18–20; 43:19; 44:1–5, 23; 49:13; 51:3), would more naturally refer to the goal of the journey, the land devastated by the Babylonians, rather than the route but expressed in familiar mythic language. A clue to these associations is provided by the promise in 51:3 that Zion, standing for the land, will be transformed into Eden, meaning that the ancient curse on the soil will be reversed (cf. Gen 3:18). The perspective is not, however, confined to Israel. God's purpose for Israel concerns all humanity and indeed all creation. In these final verses creation is represented by mountains and hills (cf. 44:23; 49:13) and trees. The thornbush (*naʿăṣûṣ*, only here and 7:19) and the nettle (*sirpad* hapax) will be replaced by the cypress (*bĕrôš* cf. 41:19 and Modern Hebrew) and the myrtle (*hădas* cf. 41:19).

The final couplet seems to suggest that these will be part of a kind of nature preserve or memorial park commemorating what God has wrought through the prophetic word. But if the passage is read as recapitulating the message of this section of the book as a whole, the reference would more likely be to the final actualization and culmination of God's purposes communicated through the prophet.

INDEX OF SUBJECTS

◆

INDEX OF BIBILICAL AND OTHER ANCIENT REFERENCES

◆

Proverbs

Qoheleth

Canticles

Isaiah

Lamentations

List of Key Hebrew Terms

◆

א

ʾôr gôyîm, "a light to the nations," 42:6; 49:6; 51:5
ʾēl mistattēr, "the hidden God," 45:15, 19
ʾal-tîrāʾ, "don't be afraid," 41:10, 13, 14; 43:1, 5; 44:2; 51:7; 54:4
ʾĕmet, "truth, sincerity," 48:1
ʾănî (*ʾānōkî*) *hûʾ*, "I am He" (divine self-predication), 41:4; 43:10, 12; 46:4; 48:12; 52:6
ʾănî YHVH (*ʾēl*) *vĕʾên ʿôd*, "I am Yahveh (God), and there is no other," 45:5, 6, 14, 18, 21, 22; 46:9

ב

bāḥar, bāḥîr, "choose," "chosen, elect," 41:8, 9; 42:1, 22; 43:10, 20; 44:1, 2; 45:4; 49:7; 50:10
bārāʾ, "create," 40:26, 28; 41:20; 42:5; 43:1, 7, 15; 45:6, 8, 12, 18; 48:7; 54:16
bĕrît ʿôlām, "a perpetual covenant," 55:3
bĕrît ʿām, "a covenant for the people," 42:6; 49:8
bĕrît šālôm, "a covenant of peace, well-being," 54:10
biśśēr, mĕbaśśeret, "proclaim, herald," 40:9; 41:27; 52:7

ג

gāʾal, gōʾēl, "redeem, Redeemer," 41:14; 43:1, 14; 44:6, 22–24; 47:4; 48:17, 20; 49:7, 26; 51:10; 52:3, 9; 54:5, 8
gîl, "rejoice," 41:16; 49:13

ד

dābār, "word, prophetic utterance," 40:8; 44:26; 45:23; 50:4; 51:16; 55:11
derek, "way, way of life, way of acting," 40:3, 14, 27; 42:16, 24; 43:16, 19; 45:13; 48:15, 17; 49:9, 11; 51:10; 53:6; 55:7

ה

hāriʾšōnôt, "the former events, prophecies," 41:22; 42:9; 43:9, 18; 46:9; 48:3

ז

zeraʿ, "seed, descendants (of Abraham, Israel)," 41:8; 43:5; 44:3; 45:19, 25; 48:19; 54:3

ח

ḥădāšôt, "new things, new events," 42:9; 43:19; 48:6
ḥāṭāʾ, ḥaṭṭāʾ, "sin, sinner," 42:24; 43:24, 25, 27; 44:22; 53:12

י

YHVH ṣĕbāʾôt, "Yahveh of the (heavenly) hosts," 44:6; 45:13; 47:4; 48:2; 51:15; 54:5
yĕšûʿâ, môšîaʿ, "salvation, Savior," 43:3, 11; 44:26; 45:8, 15, 17, 20–22; 51:5, 6, 8; 52:7, 10

כ

kābôd, kĕbôd YHVH, "glory, the glory of Yahveh," 40:5; 42:7, 12; 43:7; 48:11

מ

midbār, "the desert," 40:3; 41:18–19; 42:11; 43:19, 20; 51:3
melek yiśrāʾēl (*yaʿăqob*), "king of Israel (Jacob)," 41:21; 44:6
māšîaḥ, "anointed one (Cyrus)," 45:1
mišpāṭ, "justice, judgment, vindication," 40:14, 27; 41:1; 42:1, 3, 4; 49:4; 50:8; 51:4; 54:17

נ

naḥălâ, "inheritance, usually land," 47:6, 14; 49:8; 54:17

nāḥam, "comfort," 40:1; 49:13; 51:3, 12, 19; 52:9
nāqām, "vengeance, vindication," 47:3

ע

ʿebed, *ʿebed YHVH*, "servant, servant of Yahveh," 41:8, 9; 42:1, 19; 43:10; 44:1, 2, 21, 26; 45:4; 48:20; 49:3, 5–7; 50:10; 52:13; 53:11; 54:17
ʿāvōn, "iniquity," 43:24; 50:1; 53:5, 6, 11
ʿāṣāb, *ʿōṣeb*, "cult image, idol," 46:1; 48:5

פ

pesel, *pĕsîl*, "cult image, idol," 40:19–20; 42:7, 17; 44:9, 10, 15, 17; 45:20
pešaʿ, "rebellion, transgression," 43:25, 27; 44:22; 46:8; 48:8; 50:1; 53:5, 8, 12

צ

ṣĕdāqâ, *ṣedeq*, "righteousness, victory," 41:2, 10; 42:6, 21; 45:8, 13, 19, 23–24; 46:12–13; 48:1, 18; 51:1, 5–8; 54:14, 17

ק

qādôš, *qĕdôš yiśrāʾēl*, "holy, the Holy One of Israel," 40:25; 41:14, 16, 20; 43:3, 14, 15; 45:11; 47:4; 48:17; 49:7; 54:5; 55:5

ר

riʾšôn, *riʾšôn vĕʾaḥărôn*, "the First, the First and the Last," 41:4; 44:6; 48:12
rûaḥ, "wind, breath, the Spirit of God," 40:7, 13; 42:1, 5; 44:3; 48:16
raḥămîm, "compassion," 47:6, 49:13, 15; 54:7, 8, 10–11; 55:7
rānan, *rînnâ*, "gladness, joy," 42:11; 44:23; 48:20; 49:13; 51:11; 52:8–9; 54:1; 55:12
rĕšāʿîm, "reprobates," 48:22; 53:9; 55:7

ש

šālôm, "well-being, peace," 41:3; 45:6, 8; 48:18, 22; 52:7; 53:5; 54:13; 55:12
śimḥâ, "joy," 51:3, 11; 55:12

ת

tōhû, "chaos, vacuity," 40:23; 41:28; 44:9; 45:18, 19; 49:4
tôrâ, "instruction, prophetic teaching," 42:4, 21, 24; 51:4, 7

THE ANCHOR BIBLE

Commentaries (C) and Reference Library (RL) volumes on the Old and New Testaments and Apocrypha

THE CONTRIBUTORS

Susan Ackerman, Dartmouth College. RL17

William F. Albright, Johns Hopkins University. C26

Francis I. Andersen, Professorial Fellow, Classics and Archaeology, University of Melbourne. C24, C24A, C24E

Markus Barth, University of Basel. C34, C34A, C34B

Adele Berlin, University of Maryland. C25A

Helmut Blanke, Doctor of Theology from the University of Basel. C34B

Joseph Blenkinsopp, University of Notre Dame. C19, C19A, RL5

Robert G. Boling, McCormick Theological Seminary. C6, C6A

Raymond E. Brown, S.S., Union Theological Seminary, New York (Emeritus). C29, C29A, C30, RL1, RL7, RL15

George W. Buchanan, Wesley Theological Seminary. C36

Edward F. Campbell, Jr., McCormick Theological Seminary. C7

James H. Charlesworth, Princeton Theological Seminary. RL4, RL13, RL14

Mordechai Cogan, Hebrew University, Jerusalem. C11

John J. Collins, University of Chicago. RL10

James L. Crenshaw, Duke Divinity School. C24C, RL16

Mitchell Dahood, S.J., The Pontifical Biblical Institute. C16, C17, C17A

Alexander A. Di Lella, O.F.M., Catholic University of America. C23, C39

David L. Dungan, University of Tennessee, Knoxville. RL18

Joseph A. Fitzmyer, S.J., Catholic University of America. C28, C28A, C31, C33, C34C

J. Massyngberde Ford, University of Notre Dame. C38

Michael V. Fox, University of Wisconsin, Madison. C18A

David Noel Freedman, University of Michigan (Emeritus) and University of California, San Diego. General Editor. C24, C24A, C24E

Victor P. Furnish, Perkins School of Theology, Southern Methodist University. C32A

Jonathan A. Goldstein, University of Iowa. C41, C41A

Moshe Greenberg, Hebrew University, Jerusalem. C22, C22A

Louis F. Hartman, C.SS.R., Catholic University of America. C23

Andrew E. Hill, Wheaton College. C25D

Delbert R. Hillers, Johns Hopkins University. C7A

Luke Timothy Johnson, Candler School of Theology, Emory University. C35A, C37A

Craig R. Koester, Luther Seminary. C36

Bentley Layton, Yale University. RL11

Baruch A. Levine, New York University. C4, C4A

Jack R. Lundbom, Clare Hall, Cambridge University. C21A

P. Kyle McCarter, Jr., Johns Hopkins University. C8, C9

John L. McKenzie, De Paul University. C20

Abraham J. Malherbe, Yale University (Emeritus). C32B

C. S. Mann, formerly Coppin State College. C26

Joel Marcus, Boston University. C27

J.Louis Martyn, Union Theological Seminary, New York. C33A

Amihai Mazar, Institute of Archaeology of Hebrew University, Jerusalem. RL2

John P. Meier, Catholic University of America. RL3, RL9

Carol L. Meyers, Duke University. C25B, C25C

Eric M. Meyers, Duke University. C25B, C25C

Jacob Milgrom, University of California, Berkeley (Emeritus). C3, C3A, C3B

Carey A. Moore, Gettysburg College. C7B, C40, C40A, C44

Jacob M. Myers, Lutheran Theological Seminary, Gettysburg. C12, C13, C14, C42

Jacob Neusner, University of South Florida at Tampa. RL8

Jerome H. Neyrey, University of Notre Dame. C37C

William F. Orr, Pittsburgh Theological Seminary. C32

Brian Peckham, Regis College, Toronto University. RL6

Marvin H. Pope, Yale University (Emeritus). C7C, C15

William H. C. Propp, University of California, San Diego. C2

Jerome D. Quinn, St. Paul Seminary. C35

Paul R. Raabe, Concordia Seminary, St. Louis. C24D

Bo Ivar Reicke, University of Basel. C37

Jack M. Sasson, University of North Carolina at Chapel Hill. C24B

Lawrence H. Schiffman, New York University. RL12

R. B. Y. Scott, Princeton University. C18

Choon-Leong Seow, Princeton Theological Seminary. C18C

Patrick W. Skehan, Catholic University of America. C39

Ephraim A. Speiser, University of Pennsylvania. C1

Hayim Tadmor, Hebrew University, Jerusalem. C11

James Arthur Walther, Pittsburgh Theological Seminary (Emeritus). C32

Moshe Weinfeld, Hebrew University, Jerusalem. C5

David Winston, Graduate Theological Union, Berkeley (Emeritus). C43

G. Ernest Wright, Semitic Museum, Harvard University. C6